OXFORD STUDIES IN ROMAN SOCIETY AND LAW

General Editors

PAUL DU PLESSIS   THOMAS A. J. McGINN

OXFORD STUDIES IN ROMAN SOCIETY AND LAW

The aim of this monograph series is to create an interdisciplinary forum devoted to the interaction between legal history and ancient history, in the context of the study of Roman law. Focusing on the relationship of law to society, the volumes will cover the most significant periods of Roman law (up to the death of Justinian in 565) so as to provide a balanced view of growth, decline, and resurgence. Most importantly, the series will provoke general debate over the extent to which legal rules should be examined in light of the society which produced them in order to understand their purpose and efficacy.

Law in the Roman Provinces

Edited by

KIMBERLEY CZAJKOWSKI
and
BENEDIKT ECKHARDT

in collaboration with

MERET STROTHMANN

OXFORD
UNIVERSITY PRESS

OXFORD
UNIVERSITY PRESS

Great Clarendon Street, Oxford, OX2 6DP,
United Kingdom

Oxford University Press is a department of the University of Oxford.
It furthers the University's objective of excellence in research, scholarship,
and education by publishing worldwide. Oxford is a registered trade mark of
Oxford University Press in the UK and in certain other countries

First Edition published in 2020

Published in the United States of America by Oxford University Press
198 Madison Avenue, New York, NY 10016, United States of America

British Library Cataloguing in Publication Data
Data available

Library of Congress Control Number: 2020934652

ISBN 978–0–19–884408–2

Acknowledgements

This volume began as a conference held in a very hot room in the University of Münster in June 2016. Over the course of three days, amidst the heat and the beginnings of a music festival just outside, we still managed to hear a variety of papers on the operation of law across the full sweep of the Roman empire. The scholars at the conference were an international gathering who came from a range of different backgrounds, including jurists and historians, and offered multiple perspectives on the questions we had asked them to address. By the end of the conference, a new picture of law and empire was beginning to emerge.

In the past four years, the volume has evolved considerably from its beginnings, but the core idea—to explore three key issues in a large number of regional case studies from across the empire—has remained. We are very grateful to Paul du Plessis and Thomas McGinn, editors of the Roman Society and Law Series, who have been extremely supportive throughout the publication process, and to OUP for helping to keep the publication timing on track—never an easy task with such a large work.

The original conference was very generously funded by the Thyssen foundation, and the current volume would never have come to fruition without that initial grant. We would also like to extend our thanks to the University of Edinburgh for providing help with costs associated with translation of some of the chapters. Finally, thank you to our contributors for their patience, enthusiasm, and above all for their chapters which taken together will, we hope, provide a new and wide-ranging view on law in the Roman empire.

Contents

List of Tables

List of Contributors

Professor José Luis Alonso (University of Zürich)

Professor Clifford Ando (University of Chicago)

Dr Ilias N. Arnaoutoglou (Academy of Athens)

Professor Cédric Brélaz (University of Fribourg)

Professor Tiziana J. Chiusi (University of Saarland)

Dr Kimberley Czajkowski (University of Edinburgh)

Professor Athina Dimopoulou (University of Athens)

Dr Anna Dolganov (University of Vienna)

Professor Paul du Plessis (University of Edinburgh)

Professor Werner Eck (University of Cologne)

Dr Benedikt Eckhardt (University of Edinburgh)

Dr Lina Girdvainyte (University of Bordeaux-Montaigne)

Professor Ulrich Huttner (University of Siegen)

Professor Andrea Jördens (University of Heidelberg)

Dr Georgy Kantor (University of Oxford)

Professor Giovanna D. Merola (University of Naples)

Dr Anna Plisecka (Kalaidos Law School, Zurich)

Dr Meret Strothmann (Ruhr-Universität Bochum)

Professor Ioannis E. Tzamtzis (University of Ioannina)

Dr Matthijs Wibier (University of Kent)

Professor Uri Yiftach (University of Tel Aviv)

1

Introduction

Kimberley Czajkowski and Benedikt Eckhardt

1. AN EMPIRE OF LOCAL IDENTITIES?

We start with a truism: The study of the Roman Empire is not what it used to be. Compared to a hypothetical version of this introduction written a century ago, the shift in scholarly discourse on how we should approach the empire and how we should conceptualize the lives of the people within it is remarkable indeed. No longer are the imperial elites those with the dominant voice—or at least, it is no longer thought that this should be the case—and the study of indigenous populations has been emphasized in a multitude of sub-sectors. In short, in recent years the Roman emperors and aristocrats have increasingly had to make room for their subjects.

The nature of this change is perhaps nowhere more apparent than in the fate of a once prominent scholarly concept, 'Romanization'. Up to as late as the 1980s, this could be conceived as a unitary process by which the dominant culture was imposed from above. Nowadays the term has fallen out of favour, at least in anglophone scholarship.[1] Various alternatives—creolization, cultural memory, multilingualism, globalization and more—have been proposed.[2] The purpose is almost always to re-describe the relationship between Rome and her empire's inhabitants in a way that places less emphasis on uni-directional impact, and instead encapsulates a more dynamic, two-way process—if the distinction between 'Roman' and 'other' is not altogether abandoned.[3] In short, there is a growing move to reintroduce indigenous agency and not take a purely Romano-centric perspective.

The heuristic value of these approaches cannot be doubted. By reintroducing 'local identities' into the picture of 'Roman imperialism',[4] several layers of identity construction can be correlated with each other. Not only were provincials themselves actively involved in the construction of local understandings of Roman

[1] Continental scholarship has remained more willing to engage with the term (if not with all of its earlier connotations); e.g. Alföldy (2005); Cecconi (2006); Sartre (2007); Fiches (2013).

[2] See, for example, Webster (2001); Wallace-Hadrill (2008); Häussler (2013); Versluys (2014); Galinsky and Lapatin (2016).

[3] See especially Versluys (2014). [4] Revell (2009).

Kimberley Czajkowski and Benedikt Eckhardt, *Introduction* In: *Law in the Roman Provinces.* Edited by: Kimberley Czajkowski and Benedikt Eckhardt in collaboration with Meret Strothmann, Oxford University Press (2020). © Oxford University Press. DOI: 10.1093/oso/9780198844082.003.0001

culture, selectively adapting some of its features while neglecting others,[5] but in the process, their understanding of local history and culture also changed. A 'celebration of the local' accompanied the regionally diverse constructions of 'imperial identities'.[6] Traditions were rediscovered, reinterpreted or in fact invented, as parts of individual and collective strategies to make sense of one's own position between the local past and the imperial present.[7] Any enquiry into what was local and what was Roman should be directed, on this view, to provincials.

One such provincial was Chairemon, former gymnasiarch of Oxyrhynchus in Egypt, and hence well-versed in the elite culture of this Roman province. In 186 CE, after a long, apparently unsuccessful monetary dispute with his daughter Dionysia, he changed tack and petitioned the prefect, Pomponius Faustianus, to forcibly divorce his daughter from her husband based on the right given to him 'by the law'.[8] It remains the most likely interpretation that Chairemon's appeal is to a local tradition, perhaps the so-called 'Law of the Egyptians'.[9] But it is not just this tantalizing reference to some sort of native practice so at odds with the principles of Roman views on marriage that has led this case to become infamous: Dionysia's response is an extraordinary testimony to provincial reactions to such claims. The document itself is a marvel of careful collection of evidence on Dionysia's part: she assembled not just the prior petitions and letters sent concerning the dispute, but also multiple documents (three edicts from prefects, five further extracts from proceedings and one juristic opinion) in support of her case against her father's latest attack, and these were but a 'small selection' of the available decisions.[10] Her reaction was emphatic: the supposed law, in her view, did not exist to begin with; even if it did, it would not apply to her case;[11] and anyway Roman governors had already decided on previous occasions that demands such as her father's were inhumane.

The issue is one of the most important examples for the complexities of legal administration in a Roman province: not only do we have a thorough documentation of the to-ing and fro-ing between multiple provincial personnel, but Dionysia and her father both try their hand in contesting the legal order that should apply, and the very content of the 'law' cited. But this case is also important for evaluating the shift in historical perspective outlined above. In abstract terms, Chairemon behaved exactly like the archaeologists, historians and philologians cited above might expect a provincial to behave: he came up with a local tradition,

[5] Woolf (1998). [6] Ando (2010).

[7] E.g. the contributions in Dijkstra et al. (2017) on Roman Greece.

[8] P. Oxy. II 237, col. VI, ll. 4–29; l. 17 on the reference to this right, framed in response to Dionysia's husband, Horion's apparent violence against him. The bibliography on this papyrus and the issues raised therein is extensive: Kreuzsaler (2008) provides a good, relatively recent introduction to the case.

[9] Mentioned in the decision of the *epistratēgos*, Paconius Felix, included later in the papyrus (P. Oxy II 237, col. VII, l. 33). Even if this falls under the umbrella of the 'Law of the Egyptians', this is typically thought to have a Greek origin: see, *inter alia*, Mélèze-Modrzejewski (1988) and Lewis (1982); it would of course be of additional interest if Chairemon, a Greek, decided to use precedent from Egyptian law to get his way. The 'Law of the Egyptians' is documented in only six papyri; its exact nature has long been disputed. See Yiftach (2009) on its composite nature, and that it may have been a written manual for Roman judges.

[10] P. Oxy. II 237, col. VII 1. 9; col. VIII 43; col. VII, l. 14 on the 'small selection'.

[11] P. Oxy. II 237, col. VII, ll. 12–13.

adapted it to his purpose, invested it with authority and, by involving the prefect, integrated it into his construction of an imperial identity.

However, Dionysia's argument depends on very different assumptions: one cannot simply disregard the multiple past opinions and rulings of the authorities; and moreover one cannot simply make up (as she claims) a local tradition and expect people to go along with it.[12] What matters is precedent, set by Roman judges, and opinions given by recognized legal experts. That Chairemon also apparently had such precedents could be inconvenient for her construction; she can at least claim that his were not as good, not as relevant as her own.[13] And her own precedents explicitly evoke the idea that Chairemon's arguments, his 'law', were on the 'inhumane' side of the cultural divide; by locating herself on the opposite 'humane' side, she thus directly opposed what others could present as local tradition in favour of the norms and values promulgated by the imperial centre.[14]

We do not know if Dionysia won her case, and the quarrel between two individuals hardly disproves a whole model for understanding the Roman empire. It nevertheless sits somewhat uncomfortably with some of the notions detailed above—that Romanness could largely be created at will, or even that there was no recognizable 'Roman' culture opposed to others. On this occasion at least, Dionysia would happily have subscribed to what we now regard as an old-fashioned view on 'Romanization'. The case thus invites more general questions: How does the use of law in the Roman provinces contribute to the image set out by recent scholarship on the Roman empire? Did the construction of 'imperial identities' include legal regulations, or were they the invisible barrier that archaeological studies, for instance, cannot see? And how might this have varied in different regions?

2. POINTS OF DEPARTURE

That law causes problems for the 'participatory' model of Roman imperialism is perhaps not surprising, given its obvious connection with normativity and its scholarly history. Indeed, Roman law (understood as a definite, identifiable unitary body) had been one important cornerstone of the earlier view on Romanization. Particularly after 212 CE, the supposed unity of empire, emperor and law

[12] Col. VI, ll. 8–12 on past opinions; these apparently included a ruling by the prefect that private cases should not be sent to him. As part of her argumentation, Dionysia confines Chairemon's argumentation to the 'local' sphere: see Dolganov (2019) for the view that this is a move explicitly made by Dionysia; it does not, however, follow that Chairemon was therefore appealing to Roman law in his first reference (merely that it is more ambiguous than sometimes allowed for).

[13] Chairemon had apparently appended these, though Dionysia claims they were disregarded by the prefect due to their dissimilarity to the case in hand (col. VI, ll. 27–9). If Chairemon tried to participate in the Roman imperial legal order, he—so his daughter claims—failed; she could do it better. On precedents in the papyri more generally, see Katzoff (1972) and Jolowicz (1937).

[14] See Kreuzsaler and Urbanik (2008) on the *inhumanitas/humanitas* rhetoric. See the language in the case before Paconius Felix, cited in col. VII, ll. 29–30.

left little room for local agency.[15] However, in a development that parallels the emergence of new historical and archaeological approaches, advances in scholarship in the legal historical realm have recently emphasized the complexity of the legal situation in the provinces. Of particular note is the rise in popularity of historical legal pluralism studies and the recognition that multiple legal orderings can and very often do exist in a given society, the Roman empire being no exception.[16] This extends, indeed, to the situation after 212 CE, undercutting the previously supposed unitary model to allow for the survival and even thriving of local legal orderings even in a situation of universal Roman citizenship.[17] The greater attention paid to the life of local legal orderings has in turn led to a surge in regionally specific case studies that allow detailed study of the peculiarities of specific regions. The strengths of such approaches are obvious: historical, geographical and temporal specificity and nuance are maintained, emphasized and explored.

An early advocate of a more nuanced picture was Ludwig Mitteis (1891), who not only developed a differentiated view on the impact of the *Constitutio Antoniniana*, but also advocated for full inclusion of all available data. Despite the undeniable value of regionally specific analysis, there is a worth in this older approach and its broader scope which should not be entirely abandoned: regional case studies must also be brought together in order to understand the patterns and variances that we find across the empire. In order to identify and understand what is truly specific to a region and what is (in contrast) manifest across a wide area, these regionally specific studies must start to interact with each other more fully and more explicitly. This has further implications for more general methodological issues within ancient history, most specifically the problem of Egypt, not coincidentally the starting point of this introduction. Can this well-documented province ever be thought exemplary of the wider circumstances of empire?

Another stumbling block can also be re-examined along the way: the notion, prevalent at least since Mitteis, that a categorical distinction should be drawn between Eastern and Western provinces. According to common conceptions, Roman law was imposed on what is considered to be a vacuum of prior legal culture in the West,[18] whereas the East with its longstanding pre-existing traditions provided very different conditions, leading to a much more complex situation. Again, the comparison with scholarship on 'Romanization' is of interest: Many of the main contributions driving the change in perspective have focused on the West.[19] A reappraisal of the role of law in provincial societies thus needs to go beyond the Eastern evidence, and look for possible similarities even in regions where environmental conditions have not allowed for an extensive documentation of private legal dealings to survive. That new evidence has come to light recently is certainly encouraging in this regard.[20]

[15] Tuori (2007) traces the legacy of this debate, drawing (*inter alia*) on Sohm (1908), 125: 'ein Kaiser, ein Reich, ein Recht'.

[16] See, for example, Pölönen (2006); Humfress (2013); Ando (2014).

[17] See Alonso's chapter in this volume.

[18] Roman law was thus a civilizing force: see Eck in this volume for this approach.

[19] Starting, for example, with Woolf (1998).

[20] Tomlin (2016).

To make this new approach very clear, the contributions to this book are presented in what may be perceived as a counterintuitive order. Historical studies have pointed out time and again that despite regional peculiarities, Egypt should be seen as much more representative of Roman provincial administration than the history of research would suggest.[21] We therefore start in Egypt and the Near East (Part I), and then move on, via Asia Minor and Greece (Part II), to Africa and the Western provinces (Part III). Thus, the reader travels through the provinces of the empire, and in doing so may start to see the patterns that emerge in imperial attitudes and provincial behaviours. For 'patterns' one should not read uniformity, nor do we mean to eliminate the complexities or flatten the differences that emerge from detailed, regional case studies. Rather, the contributions come together to address the following thematic issues and, when taken together, integrate both 'top-down' and 'bottom-up' approaches to arrive at a more holistic appreciation of the legal culture of the empire.

3. ROMAN AMBITIONS

One question underlying the whole thematic complex concerns not provincial, but imperial agency. To what degree did Rome see itself as promoting a particular order in which people organized their affairs according to certain legal norms, be they Roman, mixed, or local? Given the recent shift in focus on what provincials made of the empire, it may almost appear that Roman ambitions can now easily be dismissed—as either irrelevant in practice or non-existent in the first place. However, it is clear that ideological concepts like *aequum et iustum* or *humanitas* do appear in cases of imperial or proconsular jurisdiction.[22] There are thus moments where the ideology of empire directly interferes with local disputes. It is still worth asking whether this happens by accident or by default, i.e. whether or not the idea of the empire as a legal order was an important part of imperial ideology. This may be an old-fashioned question, but one that can and should be treated alongside enquiries into the practical application of legal principles.

The sources that provide relevant information will normally be of a non-legal nature. Thus, one important thing to note is the stark contrast between modern descriptions of provincial agency and the image of empire conveyed by Roman authors. While elite discourse is obviously unrepresentative and cannot easily be used to clarify what was really going on, it certainly gives us insights into how the Roman elite thought about its imperial ambitions. The image is overwhelmingly one of subjection, and even of slavery: Rome is master, the provincials serve.[23] This arguably presupposes not only a clear distribution of power, but also a legal relationship: after all, any court would confirm the all-encompassing control of a master over his slaves. The very logic of such totalitarian discourse would suggest

[21] See *inter alia* Rathbone (2013), Monson (2012), Jördens (2009) and Capponi (2005) for a range of recent contributions on this issue.

[22] The principles are elucidated by Jördens, below pp. 19–31.

[23] Lavan (2013).

that Roman authorities saw a limitation of the legal options available to provincials as a necessary consequence of the imperial project.

A more tangible feature of imperial ideology that speaks in favour of wide-ranging Roman ambitions is the way the emperor himself was increasingly depicted as personally dealing with the law. It is difficult to pin down the precise chronology of this development, not least because the sources are unevenly distributed.[24] It seems clear that this particular aspect of the imperial image underwent a development from Augustan beginnings to the Severan period, when jurists were regularly among the emperor's closest advisors,[25] but it is not quite clear how significant that development really was. If the emperor was—perhaps increasingly—seen as lawgiver and judge, an obvious implication would be that legislation and jurisdiction were empire-wide concerns. There was no apparent limit to the emperor's legislation, just as there was no significant limit to his general authority. No matter how many local versions of empire might be imagined in remote parts of the *oikoumene*, everyone worshipped the same man on the very top. While it might be possible to correlate an increasing emphasis on the emperor's legal authority with a spread of Roman citizenship particularly after 212 CE (in the sense that more and more people became able to petition the emperor and hence expected him to be a source of law),[26] the building blocks were there from the very beginning. The ideal of an 'emperor of law' transcends the boundary between citizens and peregrines; it suggests that law was indeed seen as one of the universal features that held the empire together.

Further support comes from the most extensive coherent legal documents found in the provinces, namely the municipal laws. Recent finds in the Danubian provinces have rectified a picture that was until recently centered on the Spanish provinces. We know now that the legal order in a *municipium* at the Black Sea in the 170s CE did not significantly differ from the one that was given to a Spanish *municipium* under Domitian, and that both have many things in common with the order established by Caesar for another Spanish colony in 44 BCE.[27] While the amount of continuity between places far apart in both time and space is striking, new problems have also been raised. In particular, the assumption that there was a general 'Flavian municipal law', to be applied indiscriminately to the various cities, has been called into question several times.[28] However, it cannot be denied that while the order of paragraphs and the formulations could differ, and local specifics could be accommodated, these texts basically say the same things everywhere. What the municipal laws unquestionably demonstrate is that Roman

[24] Tuori (2016) offers an extensive account, but his chronological conclusions are called into question by Dolganov (2018). On the Severans as lawgivers, see Coriat (1997); on Augustus and the early principate, see Hurlet (2016) and Coriat (2016); see also several contributions on the third century in Babusiaux and Kolb (2015).

[25] For a case-study that highlights the difficulty in distinguishing imperial application existing of law from actual innovation, see Plisecka, below pp. 65–83.

[26] Hinted at by Tuori (2016), 286–90. It is debated how many provincials had received Roman citizenship before 212; Lavan (2016) offers preliminary arguments for a relatively low estimate. On the legal implications of the *CA*, see Alonso, below pp. 44–64.

[27] The reference is of course to the *lex Troesmensis*, the *lex Irnitana* and the *lex Ursonensis*. The new evidence is incorporated into the discussion by Eck, below pp. 315–31.

[28] Cf., with the pertinent references, Mentxaka (2016), pp. 10–12.

authorities had a very clear idea about what constituted a Roman legal order, and what it should look like in the provinces. It is true that in this case, the boundary between citizens and peregrines is clearly marked; from this perspective, municipal laws do not seem to be plausible instruments of promoting an all-encompassing legal order. However, there are also, and perhaps inevitably, moments where the boundary becomes porous.[29] And if we assume, on the basis of both general plausibility and the new findings, that there were hundreds of cities throughout the empire operating on the very same legal framework,[30] this in itself becomes an argument for empire-wide legislative ambitions. Not only was the same distinction between cities of Roman law and others consistently employed, which is equivalent to the planned imposition of a coherent legal order. It could also legitimately be expected that *simulacra* of Rome, as Aulus Gellius famously calls the colonies,[31] inspired emulation.

None of this diminishes the value of approaches that focus on the practical use of law rather than its role in imperial ideology. But a full picture can only be reached when we look at the problem from all sides. There are provincial responses to Roman imperial administration that seem to directly contradict any unifying ideology, some of which are discussed below. And when we find social categories with legal implications being employed in a Roman provincial context, it is legitimate and even necessary to think of the ways in which provincials could appropriate them for their own purposes. But we should not lose sight of the fact that at the bottom of such everyday perceptions and categorizations, there may be an imperial attempt to create order from apparent chaos, and to classify Rome's slaves according to status.[32]

4. MECHANISMS OF LEGAL INTEGRATION

When trying to identify mechanisms employed by Rome to live up to these ideals, there are immediate points of departure, but also reasons for scepticism. It is undeniable that one key function of Roman administration in the provinces was the establishment and maintenance of law and order: the *leges provinciae*, originally drawn up by the conquering general and a board of ten *legati* on the province's creation, would set out the basic provisions for administering the region, including assize-districts;[33] the governor and the army prioritized 'policing' functions to maintain public order and were to a large extent involved

[29] See the remarks by Strothmann, below pp. 332–345.

[30] As pointed out by Galsterer (2006).

[31] *Noctes Atticae* 16.13.9: *Quae tamen condicio, cum sit magis obnoxia et minus libera, potior tamen et praestabilior existimatur propter amplitudinem maiestatemque populi Romani, cuius istae coloniae quasi effigies parvae simulacraque esse quaedam videntur* (This condition, although it is more servile and less free, is, however, thought preferable and more advantageous because of the grandeur and majesty of the Roman people, of which these colonies seem to be miniatures, as it were, and in a way copies).

[32] The problem of categorization and order is elucidated by Yiftach, below pp. 32–43.

[33] Tzamtzis in this volume comments on the *lex provinciae* and the *formulae* of conquering generals in the initial set up of the province; see also Ando for the role of public law in the process.

in what we might classify as law enforcement.[34] At first sight, then, law and order underpinned the system entire.

On closer examination, we begin to see the fractures. *Leges provinciae* were certainly not a necessary component of the establishment of a province; any active effort on the state's part with regard to its policing functions seems to have been rather limited; Rome relied and expected her subjects to make most of the effort. Furthermore, co-option of local individuals and institutions was a vital aspect of most aspects of administration, law and order included. Indeed, one of the characteristic features of the Roman Empire is its rudimentary administrative apparatus:[35] consequently, a sceptical perspective on the effectiveness of the long arm of the law in practice seems to be well-founded. The best way to assess the practical implications of this is therefore to approach the legal infrastructure created by Rome from two sides: the providers and the users.

The assize system is the most obvious example. It took a deliberate administrative effort on the Roman side to create a venue that could be seen as a reliable guarantor of law and order.[36] However, its shortcomings are all too obvious: as the occasions were few, provincials had to travel far and wide, pay for accommodation, and could not be guaranteed a hearing.[37] In addition, governors had limited knowledge of law and had to rely on advice.[38] It was in this context that precedence became an important legal principle;[39] as a consequence, advisors, governors and even emperors began to create a rudimentary system of cross-referencing that all sides involved had to navigate. Provincials were not only up to the task but instrumental in driving forward this process: Pliny's letters as well as other cases illustrate the amount of input generated by individuals who relied on—sometimes dubious—cases from elsewhere in the empire, thus causing Roman administrators again and again to review their procedures and develop some common standards.[40] What precisely principles like *aequum et iustum* meant in practice was repeatedly called into question. The spread of archives likely facilitated this provincial activity, as did the growing availability of a range of legal experts.[41] Around a very rudimentary and deeply flawed institution, a

[34] Most recently see Fuhrmann (2012) on 'policing' throughout the empire; see also Brélaz in this volume.

[35] This is not to deny the importance given to what is often labelled public law in the initial set-up of provinces: see Ando in this volume on its role in one region; cf. Johnston (1997) on definitions of *ius publicum*.

[36] And it does seem to have been perceived as such by some provincials at least: see the petitioners of P. Euphr. 1 (who travel a long distance to seek justice) with the comments of Ando (2000), 74–5; see also Czajkowski, below p. 124 on this.

[37] See Burton (1975); see also the succinct comments of Bryen (2013), 127 on the effort involved for provincials to have their cases heard.

[38] Brunt (1975); on advisors, see Jones (2007); Weaver (2002) on *consilia*. Fournier's (2010) emphasis on the integration of locals in the capacity of not only advisors but also judges should also not be overlooked in this context.

[39] See Jolowicz (1937) and Kantor (1972) on precedents, with the usual concentration on Roman Egypt.

[40] See Kantor (2009) and Kantor's contribution to this volume on the use of the *Letters*; see Bryen (2012) on the appropriation of this development by provincials in Egypt to their own advantage.

[41] A large-scale study of public archives across the empire remains a *desideratum*: see Cockle (1984) and Burkhalter (1990) for studies of state archives in Roman Egypt.

culture of documentation and referencing emerged that was driven by both Roman administrators and provincial litigants, for very different reasons. The importance of the assizes for the spread of Roman legal concepts thus cannot be reduced to the way Rome intended them to work, or to the number of cases successfully resolved by a Roman governor.[42]

A related, albeit less clear-cut example is the emergence of a larger number of 'legal experts', sometimes discussed as the 'professionalization' of jurisprudence.[43] The assizes and the need for expertise in Roman and local law—both in the governor's court and on the side of provincials pursuing their claims—naturally created a demand for capable advisors and advocates. This would have been true from the very beginning of the assize system, and learned personnel clearly advised the emperors early on. But the real push towards what is sometimes termed an empire-wide 'professionalization' of jurisprudence seems to have come in the later second century CE, and this is also the time when local elites started to single out legal education as a marker of status and prestige in inscriptions.[44] Yet again, what may appear as a centralized process of bureaucratization was bound up with provincial agency, in this case strategies of elite representation. It is reasonable to assume that the combination of both factors made the process much more effective than it could otherwise have been.

So far, we have focused on the few centrally managed institutions that directly relate to legal questions. However, given the limited administrative capacities of the empire, we should also consider other factors that may have contributed to the spread of Roman legal ideas. One such factor is citizenship. While the reasons for bestowing *civitas Romana* on individuals or even whole communities could vary, the spread of Roman law in provincial contexts was probably not one of them. However, a mechanism that by and large served to reward certain people for their loyalty towards Rome (and was hence selectively used until 212 CE) created points of orientation for local friends, rivals and neighbours. The right to choose whether to have their case heard by a Roman magistrate was one of the elements that defined the new citizens' place in a social landscape defined by Roman rule.[45] People were not made citizens to promote a Roman legal order, but the possible recourse to that order was part and parcel of their elevated status. Quite without provident planning, they did become carriers of the Roman legal system; by exercising their privilege of recourse to it, they therefore helped propagate the idea of Rome as the ultimate guarantor of justice.

The same is true for what was by far the largest factor in any imperial budget: the military. Soldiers are not usually deployed to spread specific ideas about how to win a trial or how to sign legal documents; this is not the purpose of an army. And yet we find soldiers doing precisely that: in many provincial contexts, their

[42] Cf. Galanter (1981) on understanding the court as a 'centrifugal institution'; Czajkowski (2017), 107–8 for an application to the Roman context.

[43] Crook (1995) remains the best study of their activities and the range of experts and services available, even if there is now new evidence to add.

[44] See the discussion by Dolganov in this volume.

[45] Choice of legal forum in the face of an accusation is prominently mentioned in early examples such as IGLS III 718, the citizenship grant to Seleucus of Rhosos; there are other instances of *privilegium fori* being granted as a privilege, sometimes to groups: see the edict of Vespasian (74 CE) granting this to doctors and teachers (FIRA I 73).

interaction with locals, as far as it is on record, revolves around legal dealings.[46] Depending on the expertise of the individual soldiers, these might be carried out in a more or less Roman fashion. But in any case for many provincials Roman soldiers would have been the most visible representatives of the imperial order, and the obvious people to turn to in order to access imperial justice. Their eventual settlement in *municipia* governed by Roman law further enhanced their potential to serve as the primary transmitters of Roman legal ideas into the provinces.

What these examples show is that an appreciation of the structural framework provided by Rome cannot reasonably be limited to declared Roman aims and methods, and that it has to go beyond the relatively few institutions whose primary function was to facilitate or enforce the use of Roman law. We have to be aware of the side-effects of certain institutions, and of the various ways in which provincial agency could be essential for the spread of Roman legal ideas. Crucially though, the latter insight does not mean that the 'bottom-up' approach is the only feasible way to study the spread of Roman law in the provinces. Central mechanisms and imperial impetus can and should be identified.[47] There is rather a case to be made for the co-existence of these approaches as two sides of the same coin. Structure and agency have been the object of complex sociological debates, and applications to Roman imperialism are not lacking.[48] Taking both perspectives into account can lead to a more differentiated picture of the entanglement between imperial infrastructure and local agency.[49]

5. INDIGENOUS REACTIONS

The concentration so far has been on ideas, structures and institutions imposed or offered (depending on one's viewpoint) by Rome. This is just part of the picture. The areas brought under Roman imperial rule had their own pre-existing local legal orderings that were not eliminated with the coming of empire. Some evidence even suggests that the Roman administration actively encouraged the preservation and public display of pre-Roman legal traditions—we can think of Hadrian's interest in Draconian and Solonian legislation, or of the preservation of the Gortynian Code.[50] Furthermore, provincials reacted to the tools offered to them, and this local agency was a key determining factor in the uptake, interpretation, integration or indeed rejected of Roman law in the provinces and indeed the construction of the various local legal cultures under Rome.[51]

[46] In this volume, see the contributions by Czajkowski on Dura, Du Plessis on Britain and Eckhardt on Dacia.

[47] This is the focus chosen by Eck in this volume.

[48] E.g. Revell (2009), drawing on Bourdieu and Giddens.

[49] See Harries (1999), 212–15 on the merits of looking at both makers and recipients of law in a late antique context; the same principle applies to the earlier period.

[50] On the former, see Swain (1996), 74–5; on the latter, see Tzamtzis below, pp. 254–5.

[51] See Kantor's formulation below, p. 204 on 'the centrifugal process of local legal authorities and identities re-asserting themselves through piecemeal change or loopholes in the system' in the early empire.

It is perhaps in the tackling of these local traditions that the aforementioned dichotomy between approaches to the East and West has most clearly emerged. The sophistication with which Eastern provincials approached their legal transactions has long been acknowledged, with recent studies perhaps pushing this further to show how, at least by the second century, provincials did not just navigate between legal orderings but used the gaps in understanding that existed within the skeletal Roman administrative structure to their own advantage: by so doing, they were able to assert their own understandings of what the law, and thus the decisions in their cases, 'should' be.[52] Local populations, on these readings, thus seized on the inherent weaknesses and ambiguities within the Roman structure to their own advantage, but the results of these dialogues in turn worked their way back into Roman behaviours and legal practice. We may think back to Chairemon, Dionysia and their precedents: provincial litigants sought out useful legal tools and used them to compel Roman authorities to adjust their own conceptions to fit their own, localized, understanding.

The evidence from the East, particularly Egypt with its vast papyrological record, has allowed for this picture to emerge, and it is one that is well-founded, well-documented in the sources. But, nevertheless, it has also led to a fundamental difference in the underlying assumptions with which we approach the evidence: Eastern provincials are assumed to operate with a certain level of sophistication in their legal matters, to be able to negotiate a range of legal orderings and capitalize upon (or try to) the situation to their own advantage. Western provincials are rarely allowed such a cleverness in their transactions as a starting assumption: the 'barren' wasteland of the West lives on in modern scholarly discourse.[53]

To an extent, this conclusion is justified: the papyri have preserved a wealth of information in whole areas of law that do not survive to us in the West; the imperial discourse on these provinces, and the centre's attitude to them, also clearly sets out to bring civilization, of which law was a part, to the un-urbanized, backward Westerners.[54] From the Roman perspective the East therefore had a rich tradition of local law; the West did not. But examined more closely, there are various problems with this picture. First, the implicit assumption of a lack of legal education in the West needed to maintain the wasteland image does not seem to hold.[55] But more fundamentally, it is perhaps rather more problematic than it first appears to take this East–West contrast in provincial sophistication as an a priori assumption. When taken together, the various contributions in this volume show clearly that the decision to see a particular use of law as centrally imposed or determined by local agency is ultimately a question of method. A 'wrong' use of Roman legal formulae,[56] for example, can be interpreted as a failed attempt to follow the norm, or as provincial appropriation and instrumentalization of imperial tools that became, to some degree, uncontrollable. The documents themselves therefore cannot determine our approach towards them.[57]

[52] Bryen (2012). [53] See Humfress's (2011), 44 characterization.

[54] Eck in this volume clearly sets out aims of the municipal laws in addressing this—from the Roman viewpoint—problematic issue.

[55] See Wibier in this volume.

[56] As demonstrated by Czajkowski for Dura, and by Eckhardt for Dacia.

[57] See Czajkowski and Eckhardt (2018) for this methodological approach to the evidence.

This methodological insight is important, as it urges scholars of Roman law to engage with the new perspective on 'Romanization', and consider the evidence for actual use of law from an additional angle. Once traditional assumptions are doubted, a new picture may emerge. This is partly dependent on our reassessing our own definitions of the nature of the 'law' we are studying, and moving away from the somewhat narrow, juristic view that has traditionally dominated the field.[58]

6. MOVING FORWARD: THE IDEA OF ROMAN LAW

We are then left with the problem of how we define law, both local and Roman. The contributions show clearly that the Roman administration provided legal tools that were available to be used; they then—to an extremely great extent—relied upon provincials to find out about, acquire and use these tools as they saw fit. Provincial uptake was in part encouraged by the imperial ideology that was propagated. But the process of interaction that then arose between the tools offered and the provincial reaction means that the 'Roman legal order' in the provinces, or even 'Roman law' itself, should be understood as a contingent idea, whose exact features vary from region to region.

Framed in this way, the ultimate result of the regional studies collected in the volume would appear to be that it was more the *idea* of 'Roman law' and the way people use this concept across the provinces that had an element of consistency: the regulations and rules themselves are very frequently constructed differently depending on regional variations. Thus, when the evidence for the various regions is brought together, there is a certain dissonance, not to be exaggerated, between the ideological construct of Roman law and actual practice. This dissonance—rather than being conceived as a problem—may be the key to understanding the dynamics, and even success, of the operation of law in the provinces. If we take seriously the idea of law as a tool that could be understood and used differently according to context, then the legal order becomes part of a dialogue between rulers and ruled that was essential to maintaining the empire's function.[59] Both sides, the centralized ideology and the localized reactions, were needed for this dialogue. As it turns out, both Chairemon and Dionysia had a point.

REFERENCES

Alföldy, G. 2005. Romanisation—Grundbegriff oder Fehlgriff? Überlegungen zum gegenwärtigen Stand der Erforschung von Integrationsprozessen im römischen Weltreich. In: Z. Visy (ed.), *Limes XIX*. Pécs, pp. 25–56.

Ando, C. 2000. *Imperial Ideology and Provincial Loyalty in the Roman Empire*. Berkeley.

Ando, C. 2010. Imperial Identities. In: T. Whitmarsh (ed.), *Local Knowledge and Micro-identities in the Imperial Greek World*. Cambridge, pp. 17–45.

[58] See du Plessis in this volume on reconceptualizing law in the West using Ehrlich's (1962) 'living law'.

[59] See Kantor in this volume on law as communication.

Ando, C. 2014. Pluralism and empire, from Rome to Robert Cover. *Critical Analysis of Law: An International & Interdisciplinary Law Review* 1, pp. 1–22.
Babusiaux, U. and Kolb, A. (eds.) 2015. *Das Recht der 'Soldatenkaiser'. Rechtliche Stabilität in Zeiten politischen Umbruchs?* Berlin.
Brunt, P. A. 1975. The Administrators of Roman Egypt. *The Journal of Roman Studies* 65, pp. 124–47.
Bryen, A. Z. 2012. Judging Empire: Courts and Culture in Rome's Eastern Provinces. *Law and History Review* 30, pp. 771–811.
Bryen, A. Z. 2013. *Violence in Roman Egypt: A Study in Legal Interpretation.* Philadelhpia.
Burkhalter, F. 1990. Archives locales et archives centrales en Égypte romaine. *Chiron* 20, pp. 191–205.
Burton, G. P. 1975. Proconsuls, Assizes and the Administration of Justice under the Empire. *The Journal of Roman Studies* 65, pp. 92–106.
Capponi, L. 2005. *Augustan Egypt: The Creation of a Roman Province,* London and New York.
Cecconi, G. A. 2006. Romanizzazione, diversità culturale, politicamente corretto. *Mélanges de l'École française de Rome. Antiquité* 118, pp. 81–94.
Cockle, W. E. H. 1984. State Archives in Graeco-Roman Egypt from 30 BC to the Reign of Septimius Severus. *The Journal of Egyptian Archaeology* 70, pp. 106–22.
Coriat, J.-P. 1997. *Le prince législateur: la technique législative des Sévères et les méthodes de création du droit impérial à la fin du Principat,* Rome,
Coriat, J.-P. 2016. L'Empereur juge et son tribunal à la fin du Principat: un essai de synthèse. In: R. Haensch (ed.) *Recht haben und Recht bekommen im Imperium Romanum. Das Gerichtswesen der Römischen Kaiserzeit und seine dokumentarische Evidenz.* Warsaw, pp. 41–61.
Crook, J. A. 1995. *Legal Advocacy in the Roman World.* London.
Czajkowski, K. L. 2017. *Localized Law. The Babatha and Salome Komaise Archives.* Oxford.
Czajkowski, K. and Eckhardt, B. 2018. Law, Status and Agency in the Roman Provinces. *Past & Present* 241, pp. 3–31.
Dijkstra, T., Kuin, I., Moser, M. and Weidgenannt, D. (eds.) 2017, *Strategies of Remembering in Greece under Rome (100 BC–100 AD).* Leiden.
Dolganov, A. 2018. Review of Tuori 2016. *Journal of Roman Studies* 108, pp. 222–4.
Dolganov, A. 2019. Reichsrecht und Volksrecht in Theory and Practice: Roman Justice in the Province of Egypt (P. Oxy II 237, P. Oxy IV 706, SB XII 10929). *Tyche* 34, pp. 27–60.
Ehrlich, E. 1962. *Fundamental Principles of the Sociology of Law.* New York.
Fiches, J.-L. 2013. La romanisation, pourquoi pas? In: Hélène Ménard (ed.), *Contacts de cultures, constructions identitaires et stéréotypes dans l'espace méditerranéen antique.* Montpellier, pp. 111–16.
Fournier, J. 2010. *Entre tutelle romaine et autonomie civique. L'administration judiciaire dans les provinces hellénophones de l'Empire romain (129 av. J.-C. –235 apr. J.-C.).* Athens.
Fuhrmann, C. 2012. *Policing the Roman Empire: Soldiers, Administration, and Public Order.* Oxford.
Galanter, M. 1981. Justice in Many Rooms. Courts, Private Ordering, and Indigenous Law. *Journal of Legal Pluralism* 19, pp. 1–47.
Galinsky, K. and Lapatin, K. (eds.) 2016. *Cultural Memories in the Roman Empire.* Los Angeles.
Galsterer, H. 2006. Die römischen Stadtgesetze. In: L. Capogrossi Colognesi, L and E. Gabba (eds.), *Gli statuti municipali.* Pavia, pp. 31–56.
Harries, J. D. 1999. *Law and Empire in Late Antiquity.* Cambridge.

Häussler, R. 2013. *Becoming Roman? Diverging Identities and Experiences in Ancient Northwest Italy*. California.

Humfress, C. 2011. Law and Custom under Rome. In: A. Rio (ed.), *Law, Custom, and Justice in Late Antiquity and the Early Middle Ages*. London, pp. 23–47.

Humfress, C. 2013. Thinking through Legal Pluralism: 'Forum shopping' in the Later Roman Empire. In: J. Duindam, J. Harries, C. Humfress, and N. Hurvitz (eds.), *Law and Empire: Ideas, Practices, Actors*. Leiden, pp. 225–50.

Hurlet, F. 2016. Les origines de la jurisdiction impériale: Imperator Caesar Augustus iudex. In: R. Haensch (ed.) *Recht haben und Recht bekommen im Imperium Romanum. Das Gerichtswesen der Römischen Kaiserzeit und seine dokumentarische Evidenz*. Warsaw, pp. 5–39.

Johnston, D. 1997. The General Influence of Roman Institutions of State and Public Law. In: D. L. Carey Miller and R. Zimmermann (eds.), *The Civilian Tradition and Scots Law. Aberdeen Quincentenary Essays*. Berlin, pp. 87–101.

Jolowicz, H. F. 1937. Case law in Roman Egypt. *The Journal of the Society of Public Teachers of Law*, pp. 1–16.

Jones, C. P. 2007. Juristes Romains dans L'Orient Grec. *Comptes-rendus des séances de l'Académie des Inscriptions et Belle-Lettres* 151:3, pp. 1331–59.

Jördens, A. 2009. *Statthalterliche Verwaltung in der römischen Kaiserzeit. Studien zum praefectus Aegypti*. Stuttgart.

Katzoff, R. 1972. Precedents in the Courts of Roman Egypt. *Zeitschrift der Savigny-Stiftung für Rechtsgeschichte* 89, pp. 256–92.

Kreuzsaler, C. 2008. Dionysia vs. Chairemon: ein Rechtstreit aus dem römischen Ägypten. In: U. Falk, M. Luminati and M. Schmoeckeleds (eds.), *Fälle aus der Rechtsgeschichte*. Munich, pp. 1–13.

Kreuzsaler, C. and Urbanik, J. 2008. Humanity and inhumanity of law: the case of Dionysia. *Journal of Juristic Papyrology* 38, pp. 119–55.

Lavan, M. 2013. *Slaves to Rome: Paradigms of Empire in Roman Culture*. Cambridge.

Lavan, M. 2016. The Spread of Roman Citizenship, 14–212 CE: Quantification in the Face of High Uncertainty. *Past & Present* 230, pp. 3–46.

Lewis, N. 1982. *Aphairesis* in Athenian law and custom, In: J. Mélèze-Modrzejewski and D. Liebs (eds.), *Symposion 1977*. Cologne, pp. 161–82.

Mélèze-Modrzejewski, J. 1988. La loi des Égyptiens. Le droit grec dans l'Égypte romaine. In: M. G. Basil, ed. *Proceedings of the XVIIIth International Congress of Papyrology, Athens 25–31 May 1986*. Athens, pp. 383–90.

Mentxaka, R. 2016. Divagaciones sobre legislación municipal romana a la luz de la *lex Troesmensium*. In: I. Piro (ed.), *Scritti per Alessandro Corbino. Vol. 5*. Tricase, pp. 5–32.

Monson, A. 2012. *From the Ptolemies to the Romans. Political and Economic Change in Egypt*. Cambridge.

Pölönen, J. 2006. The case for a sociology of Roman law. In: M. D. A. Freeman (ed.), *Law and Sociology*. Oxford, pp. 398–408.

Rathbone, D. 2013. The Romanity of Roman Egypt: A Faltering Consensus? *Journal of Juristic Papyrology* 43, pp. 73–91.

Revell, L. 2009. *Roman Imperialism and Local Identities*. Cambridge.

Sartre, M. 2007. *Romanisation en Asie Mineur? In:* G. Urso *(ed.), Tra Oriente e Occidente. Indigeni, Greci e Romani in Asia Minore*. Pisa, pp. 229–45.

Sohm, R. 1908. *Institutionen. Geschichte und System des römischen Privatrechts*. 13th edn. Leipzig.

Swain, S. 1996. *Hellenism and Empire. Language, Classicism, and Power in the Greek World, AD 50–250*. Oxford.

Tomlin, R. 2016. *Roman London's First Voices. Writing tablets from the Bloomberg excavations, 2010–14*. London.

Tuori, K. 2007. Legal Pluralism and the Roman Empires. In: J. W. Cairns and P. J. du Plessis (eds.), *Beyond Dogmatics. Law and Society in the Roman World.* Edinburgh, pp. 39–52.

Tuori, K. 2016. *The Emperor of Law. The Emergence of Roman Imperial Adjudication.* Oxford.

Versluys, M. J. 2014. Understanding Objects in Motion. An *Archaeological* Dialogue on Romanization. *Archaeological Dialogues* 21, pp. 1–20.

Wallace-Hadrill, A. 2008. *Rome's Cultural Revolution.* Cambridge.

Weaver, P. 2002. *Consilium praesidis:* Advising governors. In: McKechnie, P. ed. *Thinking Like a Lawyer: Essays on Legal History and General History for John Crook on His Eightieth Birthday.* Leiden, pp. 43–62.

Webster, J. 2001. Creolizing the Roman Provinces. *American Journal of Archaeology* 105:2, pp. 209–25.

Woolf, G. 1998. *Becoming Roman. The Origins of Provincial Civilization in Gaul.* Cambridge.

Yiftach, U. 2009. Law in Graeco-Roman Egypt: Hellenization, Fusion, Romanization. In: R. S. Bagnall, ed. *The Oxford Handbook of Papyrology.* Oxford and New York, pp. 541–60.

Part I

Egypt and the Near East

2

Aequum et iustum

On Dealing with the Law in the Province of Egypt*

Andrea Jördens

In his large overview of the legal system applied in *provincia Aegyptus*, José Luis Alonso has recently dealt extensively with the relationship of Roman judges to local laws, fundamentally revising previous interpretations.[1] That the land of the Nile stood at the center of his analysis is largely due to the huge number of texts, only preserved there, which shed light on the interaction of Roman magistrates with local legal conceptions. However, the insights thus gained are not at all limited to this province alone but can lay claim to much more general validity. For, as Alonso has been able to demonstrate convincingly, provincial jurisdiction was necessarily geared to the example provided by magistrates operating in Rome, just like the competencies of judicial institutions, particularly the prefect as highest-ranking judge in the country, emerged out of the magisterial *imperium* going back to republican times. However, Alonso justly points out that the development of law over time and, above all, the decision-making power developed out of (or ascribed to) the imperial *auctoritas* changed matters fundamentally, creating entirely new forms of both jurisdiction and legislation. In the process, the former magisterial freedom in decision-making was increasingly restricted, just as the previously practiced ways of further developing Roman law gradually stiffened. Understandably, this did not affect peregrine legal practice, so that in this case, the governor retained full discretionary powers. However, this was only the case—and here Alonso's approach is particularly fruitful—insofar as the governor accepted the binding power of tradition with regard to local laws in just the same way as in Roman law. While he generally remained a source of law or, as Cicero states, *lex loquens*,[2] he saw himself obliged to act in accordance with the principles that were invested with *auctoritas*, be it derived from the emperor and the senate or from tradition, and that could hence demand adherence and conservation.

* This chapter has been translated from the German by Benedikt Eckhardt.

[1] Alonso (2013) (published in 2015, as the reworked version of his keynote speech delivered at the 27th International Congress of Papyrology at Warsaw).

[2] See Cicero, *de legibus* 3.2 with Alonso (2013), 398.

Andrea Jördens, Aequum et iustum*: On Dealing with the Law in the Province of Egypt* In: *Law in the Roman Provinces.* Edited by: Kimberley Czajkowski and Benedikt Eckhardt in collaboration with Meret Strothmann, Oxford University Press (2020).

DOI: 10.1093/oso/9780198844082.003.0002

The remarkable readiness of Roman judicial institutions—the prefect, the *iuridicus* or other procurators—to adopt the legal principles they encountered in the province *Aegyptus* had already led to several explanatory attempts in legal historical scholarship, again discussed in detail by Alonso. With this new and much more plausible interpretation, however, the opposition between 'Rome' and 'the provinces' is overcome for the first time. Now the pronouncements by the legislative powers of empire form one side, while the other is constituted by traditional legal conceptions of both Roman citizens and the various provincial families of law. This undoubtedly constitutes an important insight, but it is hardly possible from this alone to gain satisfactory information about the principles of Roman provincial administration. It is necessary to identify further factors that determined the decision-making and the administrative acts of magistrates in the imperial period. This will be the subject of the following remarks, which will focus on the guiding principles and on possible external forces that influenced them. We do not have to ask here how they were actually implemented, let alone permanently. In addition, no strict distinction should be made between judicative, executive and legislative powers according to a contemporary understanding, as the borderlines between these were quite fluid under ancient conditions, particularly in the provinces.

Some clues regarding such principles are provided by the (few) cases where the Roman judge consciously deviated from the above-mentioned practice of following, as a rule, the conventions he encountered and, holding on to his own position even if it was contrary to the legal views held by the populace, resolutely enforced it despite significant opposition. Closer inspection reveals that here as well, it is possible to detect the point when the argument of tradition lost its force, so that even time-honoured conventions were bluntly sidelined. For this seems to have happened primarily, and in the high Empire maybe exclusively, under circumstances in which imperial mandates or deep-rooted legal convictions were violated, provided that the Roman judge would even be informed of them. The best-known example from Egypt is certainly the trial of Dionysia, who successfully resisted her father's attempts to take her out of her marriage against her will.[3]

Where this did not happen, i.e. when neither party in a legal dispute invoked a concept familiar to Roman legal thought like free will in marriage, matters were handled according to the principle that there is no need of a judge where there is no plaintiff.[4] The most glaring example is undoubtedly female circumcision, which had always been just as widespread in Egypt as male circumcision.[5] And yet we hear nothing about measures against it, whereas male circumcision became a matter of public attention, and hence came to the eyes of Roman authorities, with the great Jewish revolt of 115–17 CE at the latest. Since then, special dispensations from the ban that had immediately been issued were subject to very strict controls. Egyptian candidates for priesthood, too, now had to undergo a

[3] See recently Jördens (2016a), 243–4.

[4] Encapsulated in the German saying 'Wo kein Kläger, da kein Richter'.

[5] See Hübner (2009). The fact that it was apparently never explicitly discussed under Roman rule merely conforms to expectations, since even in our days, the (in every respect delicate) problem of female genital mutilation has come to the attention of cultures not affected by it only very recently. The skepticism of Messerer (2017), 109 n. 2 is thus hardly justified.

very elaborate procedure in front of a procurator specifically assigned to the task, until they were finally allowed to carry out the circumcision that was ritually demanded.[6]

This case is all the more interesting as traditional ideas were intimately connected with religious ones, which further underlines the violent nature of the ban.[7] But it was likely based on the Roman conviction that the operation was directed *contra naturam* and therefore constituted a grave violation of natural law, common to all humans and ultimately indispensable.[8] It is thus hardly a coincidence that this happened in the time of Hadrian of all emperors, who was known for his philosophical principles and particularly his *humanitas*. For it is certainly not wrong to assume that in his eyes, tradition and customs possessed *auctoritas* only insofar as they were consonant with precisely these natural laws. The moment they militated against every ethical conviction, they necessarily lost the *auctoritas* they had previously claimed. The emperor thus saw himself entitled, without further ado, to give up on the normal practice of restraint towards local conventions and custom, and instead bring to bear his own *auctoritas*.[9]

It is difficult to overlook the strong impact contemporary philosophical discussions had on jurisdiction and decision-making, for we encounter a very similar line of thought in Origen, particularly in his dispute with the philosopher Celsus.[10] This not only points to the intensity of debates that had apparently been going on in Alexandria for decades, but also and much more broadly to the manifold influences that Roman magistrates—emperors as well as governors—were always exposed to, although they have left such clear traces in our evidence only in the rarest of instances. To approach the processes and principles of Roman decision-making and legislation in the provinces, it should therefore be helpful to return to

[6] The relevant texts have now again been collected by Messerer (2017), 109–94 with no. 23–41. As the earliest evidence comes only from the late 140s, Messerer wants to attribute the ban on circumcision to Antoninus Pius (110–11); thus also Weikert (2016), 286–302 (especially the summary 301–2). Neither gives a reason why the emperor should have deemed such a severe measure necessary at this precise moment. For a connection with the office of *archiereus*, likely introduced for this reason around 120, see Jördens (2014), 142–5. The intense debates on the ban on circumcision and all questions related to it within the field of Jewish Studies can only be hinted at here; they are unlikely to come to an end without new evidence.

[7] A parallel, of which Rudolf Haensch has kindly made me aware, may be seen in the actions taken against the Gallic druids, which were similarly justified by the cruelty of the rites; see already Strabo 4.4.5 (p. 198): *καὶ τούτων δ᾽ ἔπαυσαν αὐτοὺς Ῥωμαῖοι καὶ τῶν κατὰ τὰς θυσίας καὶ μαντείας ὑπεναντίων τοῖς παρ᾽ ἡμῖν νομίμοις*, and especially Suetonius, *Claudius* 25.5: *Druidarum religionem apud Gallos dirae immanitatis et tantum civibus sub Augusto interdictam penitus abolevit*; generally on this Freyberger (1999), 207–9.

[8] See Mélèze Modrzejewski (2003a); (2003b); on the contemporary discussion surrounding these questions, see also Abusch (2003).

[9] This ultimately pertained to imperial administration as a whole. Hadrian's importance in this regard can hardly be overstated; cf. the programmatic introductory sentence in Pringsheim (1934), 141 [= (1961), 91]: 'The reign of Hadrian marks the beginning of a new epoch in Roman administration and in the history of Roman Law'.

[10] See Fürst (2007), and especially his yet unpublished lecture 'Nomos und Naturrecht bei Origenes', delivered at the international conference *Nomos zwischen Identität und Normativität am Beispiel Alexandrias im 1.–3. Jh. n. Chr.* (Münster, 26.–28 March 2015). On the parallel, see already Jördens (2016a), 246–7.

the basic constellations in which Roman magistrates operated in jurisdictional and administrative capacities.

This encompasses, first of all, the conditions that were not shaped by humans. Roman rule in a given province had to unfold under such conditions, the significance of which nevertheless tends to be ignored. Time and again, climatic factors as well as natural and geographical features created a need for action, while at the same time limiting the capacity to act; in addition, the exploitation of resources always required legal regulations.[11] In the case of Egypt, this was particularly complex, as it was a country of extreme opposites—here the lower-Egyptian Delta, crossed by numerous creeks and primarily used for stock farming, there the strip of fertile land of the valley of the Nile, narrow but hundreds of kilometers long and including the river oasis of the Fayum in the West; then the peripheral areas and outposts, i.e. oases and the Eastern desert including the quarries and the route to India; and finally the second largest city of the empire, Alexandria. Regarding the latter, legal questions concerned the whole area of infrastructure, for example the drinking water supply, the harbor administration and road building. However, we do not hear any more about this than we do about comparable activities in the Delta, which we must assume to have taken place not least in the context of the large-scale canalization projects of the imperial period. Leaving aside the one—or two?—links between the arms of the Nile that ran parallel to the coast,[12] this concerns above all the so-called Trajan's Canal, by which the waterway from the Red Sea, previously leading into the Middle Delta, was extended as far as the top of the Delta, more precisely the Roman camp at Babylon.[13]

We are much better informed about matters in Middle and Upper Egypt. In light of the province's significance as one of the breadbaskets of Rome, the sensitive ecosystem of these parts of the country, determined by the annual flooding of the Nile, always demanded the governor's special attention. Questions regarding the watering and cultivation of land thus figured prominently in legislation; suffice it to mention the repeated reintegration edicts, which demanded the resumption and orderly execution of agricultural activities,[14] or the numerous internal administrative regulations designed to guarantee the smooth functioning of the necessary operational procedures.[15] Climatic factors became particularly relevant with regard to the monsoon rain in the African highlands, starting in May; for if the flood of the Nile, which depended on it, was too high or too low, this could lead to crop failure and serious shortfalls in supply in Egypt. As the tax moratorium granted by Hadrian in 136 demonstrates, this could even lead to an intervention

[11] Regarding water see now generally Bruun (2000), especially 553–5 on conditions in Roman Egypt and 603–4 on imperial measures, referring to SEG 32.460 = Oliver (1989), 253–73, especially 262, 264–5 no. 108 (125).

[12] On this, see recently Blouin (2008), especially 115–16; Blouin (2014), especially 31–5.

[13] See now Sheehan (2015), especially 35–53 ch. 2, as well as Cooper (2009); on the testimony of the papyri see especially Jördens (2007); on the debates about the purpose of the building project, which have intensified most recently in connection with the growing number of studies on the trade with India, see recently Aubert (2015) with the comments by Wilson (2015), especially 21 n. 31 and Lo Cascio (2015), especially 166–7.

[14] Jördens (2009), 442–58.

[15] Jördens (2009), 407–14.

by the emperor.[16] In addition, specific events and natural disasters could also create occasional, albeit rather short-lived, regulatory needs; apart from earthquakes, we may in a wider sense think of barbarian invasions as well, which, for instance, led to the upgrading of the routes through the Eastern desert and to their intensified military protection under the Flavians.[17]

However, much more relevant to our present enquiry are the conditions created by humans, and more precisely by the provincial population, particularly the pressure that could apparently be exerted on the Roman central administration by widespread petitioning. This is already indicated by the sheer quantity of requests, evidenced by the 1804 petitions that reached the governor within just two and a half days during the Arsinoitic *conventus* of, likely, 209 CE, as well as the desperate attempts at handling this flood through ever new changes in the way they were processed.[18] If certain problems thereby became apparent that called for a comprehensive regulation, this might indeed end in new legislation. A good example is the lease of state-owned land with reduced yield, the so-called *ὑπόλογος*. Here, the usual practice of granting the rights acquired in the auction only conditionally, allowing for a reversal of the purchase at any time when a higher offer came in, had provoked numerous complaints at the *conventus*, because it prevented farmers from enjoying the well-deserved fruits of their investments on a regular basis. The legitimacy of the complaint was explicitly acknowledged by the prefect M. Sempronius Liberalis, who consequently modified the tendering procedure in important respects.[19]

Lawsuits and complaints could thus prove to be adequate means to cause changes in the existing legal situation. We may therefore believe the statement Ti. Iulius Alexander made in the preamble of his great edict of 6 July 68, that he thereby reacted to continuing and apparently countrywide popular protests; in this context, his addition that the petitions came 'from smaller groups as well as from whole masses, from those who are the most affluent here (i.e. in Alexandria) as well as from peasants in the countryside'[20] seems even more significant. For according to this, provincials were able to make themselves heard in front of Roman authorities regardless of the form and number of the complaints, of origin and of social status, which in turn means that according to Roman conceptions, justice was to be granted irrespective of the person and of concrete circumstances. In most cases, this likely remained mere theory, since it was difficult enough to come anywhere near Roman magistrates in the first place, let alone put forward one's request. Still, evidence for this is time and again found in the sources. Apart from the fact that even edicts treated not only general questions, but also special cases,[21] the whole area of jurisdiction contributes to this, which after all

[16] Jördens (2009), 430–1. [17] See Cuvigny (2014a) and generally Cuvigny (2014b).

[18] See P. Yale I 61 (22 May 208–10 [209?]), and the detailed treatment by Haensch (1994).

[19] SB XXVI 16642 (8 July resp. 14 June 156), especially ll. 17–20: *κεινηθεὶς οὖν ταύτῃ αὐτῶν τῇ δικαιολογίᾳ προσῆκον ἡγησάμην καθολικήν τινα περὶ τούτου ποιήσασθαι διάταξιν*; see also Jördens (2009), 471–3.

[20] See Chalon 1964, § 2 = I. Hibis 4 (= I. Prose 57 = OGIS II 669 = IGRR I 1263 = SB V 8444), ll. 3–10 = BGU VII 1563, ll. 2–26, especially ll. 5–6 resp. 10–11: *καὶ κατ᾽ὀλίγους καὶ κατὰ πλήθη{ι}, τῶν τε ἐνθάδε εὐσχημονεστάτων καὶ τῶν γεωργούντων τὴν χώραν*; on this, see already Jördens (2006), especially 92–6.

[21] See Katzoff (1980), especially 821.

was normally concerned with individual cases. At the same time, some basic features of the system become apparent, which now merits a closer look.

It is well known that in principle, every trial could be held in front of the governor. While this is therefore attested multiple times in the papyri, it is not always clear which criteria applied in the respective cases—i.e. whether there were certain rules according to which he delegated one case but not the other, or when, how far and why possible changes occurred.[22] In trial protocols, but especially in enquiries and referrals of delegated judges we at least occasionally encounter a note that the matter in question could not properly be decided on a local level, but required a higher authority.[23] In these cases, the judge apparently saw himself incapable of reaching a verdict based on the information in front of him, i.e. the existing records and the pleas of the respective parties—be it because he was himself uncertain about the current legal situation[24] or because the preliminary examinations carried out on the spot revealed that a given issue, or even offence, went beyond his own competence.[25]

The margin of discretion accorded to the individual judge notwithstanding, there will always have been certain rules as to when a matter was to be left to other, particularly higher authorities. Definite clarity in this regard was provided under Hadrian at the latest. According to a probably imperial constitution, proceedings were henceforth to be divided into two groups, namely cases that had to be treated personally by the governor and everything else, which in contrast could also be delegated to other judges. Thus, for the whole area of serious crime, but also for a number of delicts that were particularly despicable in Roman eyes, proceedings before the *praeses provinciae* were now mandatory; apart from murder, abduction or rustling, this also concerned the falsification of documents, premature opening of a will, or insubordinate behavior of freedmen and children.[26] A common feature of all these cases may be seen in the threat to peace and order they evoked, which is why the offences listed on a papyrus almost read like a table of contents for book 47 and 48 of the Digest.

As long as the governor had to deal with individuals, this may have been manageable within the framework of criminal jurisdiction. However, things became more difficult when whole groups of people conspired, when it came to gang crime and when bands of robbers proliferated, perhaps even leading to mass phenomena culminating in social unrest. While this remained an absolute exception

[22] See already Humbert (1964), on the 'jugements qu'il prononce lui-même' especially 117–28 ch. II; also the summarizing treatment by Anagnostou-Cañas (1991), especially 178. On the system in general, see now fundamentally Bryen (2012).

[23] These reassurances would deserve a systematic study that does not seem to have been carried out yet. For the moment, see generally Montevecchi (1988), especially 429.

[24] E.g. the case of BGU XX 2863 (after 133), where the judge appointed by the prefect asks M. Petronius Mamertinus again whether the inheritance claim on the grandparents' estate, which had in the meantime been extended to Egyptian grandsons by Hadrian, should—against local legal conceptions—be applied to the children of daughters as well, including cases in which the mother had already died some time ago.

[25] E.g. the presumed case of murder by poisoning in P. Oxy. III 472 and 486 (fall 131); see recently Jördens (2016b), especially 102–4 and generally 95–6 with n. 19.

[26] See only SB XII 10929 (133–7 AD) with Jördens (2011); in detail now Jördens (2016b); on *plagium*, see especially Jördens (2016c).

in Roman imperial Egypt, the few cases—the so-called bucolic revolt, and even more so the revolt of the Jews in the late Trajanic period—were to rattle the bones of the whole province, put to an end only with additional help from outside.[27]

However, governors saw themselves in need of reassurance even on seemingly smaller occasions, as is most visible in the famous and much-discussed correspondence between Pliny and Trajan regarding the treatment of the so-called Christians.[28] Here we encounter, albeit on a higher level and with a judge with basically unlimited discretionary power, the same behavior that we have already observed with regard to the *iudices pedanei* and the *stratēgoi* in the Egyptian Chora. It was apparently triggered by insecurity about whether or not the existing legal situation was sufficient. Because comparable cases were patently lacking, neither the traditional norms nor earlier judgments and proclamations offered support in decision-making. In a moment like this, no matter what had caused it, one turned to the superordinate authority requesting advice and instructions, with the aim of receiving either an explanation and confirmation of old laws or the granting of new ones. Due to the loss of the archives—those of the institutions themselves[29] and of the persons involved—hardly anything thereof has been preserved for us, except in the case of someone like Pliny, who literarily reworked parts of his official correspondence.[30] Just how normal the procedure was is, however, also shown by the late antique collections of constitutions, since these include a large number of rescripts and legal advice of all kinds, given by the emperors not least in response to such enquiries by magistrates.

Here as well, much is already hinted at in the edict of Ti. Iulius Alexander. In his preamble, he emphasizes time and again his unrelenting efforts to do everything within his power to remedy the current grievances—but only, as he says, 'as far as it is possible for me to decide and to act; but the more significant matters that require the power and the greatness of the emperor I will explain to him in all truth', whereby the gods act as guarantors of the country's restored peace under the law.[31] In this case, we do not know anything about the emperor's reaction.

[27] Out of the rich literature on the so-called bucolic revolt, see Riess (2001), especially 55–8, and recently again, but only on the basis of the literary sources, Baldini (2009), especially 51–3 with an elaboration on the parallels to the Jewish revolt regarding the crushing of the revolt by a commander sent to the province from outside; on the Jewish revolt, Pucci Ben Zeev (2005) remains the most comprehensive treatment, see especially 167–90 on events in Egypt; briefly Harker (2012), especially 283–4; see also the recent discussion, based primarily on the literary sources, by Horbury 2014, especially 203–35 on events in Alexandria and 235–6 on the Nile valley. The precise chronology remains debated. The proclamation of a high Roman magistrate preserved in P. Mil. Vogl. II 47 = CPJ II 435, ascribed by Pucci Ben Zeev (2005), 137 to 'probably . . . the Roman prefect in office at the time, M. Rutilius Lupus' and hence dated to 14 October 115, can hardly be brought to bear on this question as it seems to stem from the Acta Alexandrinorum, which raises severe doubts about its historicity.

[28] See Pliny, *Epistulae* 10.96 and especially the introduction: *sollemne est mihi, domine, omnia de quibus dubito ad te referre*; as well as the emperor's—much shorter—response in 10.97. See the chapter by Kantor in this volume for further comments.

[29] Still fundamental is Haensch (1992).

[30] A much later parallel may be seen in Cassiodorus, except that possible queries are likely to have been brought up orally, since he himself stayed in the ruler's court.

[31] See above n. 15, especially I. Hibis 4, ll. 8–10 resp. BGU VII 1563, ll. 20–6: *προέγραψα . . . , ὅσα ἔξεστί μοι κρείνειν καὶ ποιεῖν, τὰ δὲ μείζονα καὶ δεόμενα τῆς τοῦ αὐτοκράτορος δυνάμεως καὶ μεγαλειότητος αὐτῶι δηλώσω{ι} μετὰ πάσης ἀληθείας, τῶν θεῶν ταμιευσαμένων εἰς τοῦτον τὸν ἱερώτατον καιρὸν τὴν τῆς οἰκουμένης ἀσφάλειαν.*

Regarding the above-mentioned case of the tax moratorium of 136, as well as a reform of rents carried out in 117, explicit mention is made of Hadrian's relevant *beneficia*;[32] similarly, the reintegration edict proclaimed by M. Sempronius Liberalis in 154 refers to an amnesty granted by Antoninus Pius.[33]

With these remarks, we have outlined at least the broad framework in which every provincial administration operated. On the one hand we see the *auctoritas* inherent in Roman magistrates and institutions, but also accorded to local traditions. As Alonso has shown, by negotiating the two, the magistrate determined current law, while also being able to modify it through new legislation if necessary. On the other hand, the law thus constituted was continually confronted with fresh demands and developments, the initiative undoubtedly coming for the most part, but by no means exclusively, from the population. Natural phenomena, much like the general flood of petitions and even individual complaints that highlighted grievances and required corrections, could also occasionally demand a reaction. Wherever a magistrate saw himself and his competences overstretched, he resorted to the last option available to him: turning to those who possessed higher *auctoritas* than he himself did.[34]

And yet this higher authority was itself in need of support in decision-making. The means employed, most often visible to us in rudimentary fashion only, have to be added to the basic factors described above. For the governor, the first thing to recall are the various advisory councils, primarily his staff, which was recruited from military personnel and civil magistrates close to him. In Egypt, it encompassed a number of positions that likely went back to Ptolemaic times; in the area of jurisdiction, this applies to the *εἰσαγωγεύς*, who acted as a state secretary of sorts, as well as various central functionaries responsible for the individual districts.[35] At the *conventus*, this circle was extended to include *strategoi* and royal scribes who, as the highest civil magistrates on the nome level, informed him about the situation on the ground.[36] Of higher rank and participating in jurisdiction, but less involved in daily administrative business, was the *consilium*; apart from the other procurators working in central administration, the prefect also appointed advisors known to him as *consilium* members.[37] For specific questions, particularly regarding local laws, he was also supported by specialized *iuris periti* resp. *νομικοί*.[38]

[32] On the tax moratorium of 136 see already n. 14, on the reform of rents of 117 see Jördens (2009), 473–7; Jördens (2019), 333–5.

[33] SB XX 14662 = W. Chr. 19 = BGU II 372 (29 August 154); see recently Jördens (2013); (2019), 330f.

[34] It should be noted that this concerned not only magistrates. Private individuals followed the same principles when doubts about the competences of the judge and about his decisions arose in the course of a trial; on this and on the ensuing successive appeals see now Wankerl (2009).

[35] See fundamentally Haensch (2000); (2007); and especially (2008).

[36] Haensch (1997), especially 334–42.

[37] See Jördens (2001), especially 73 in the comments on SB XXVI 16643, ll. 5–6 with bibliography, as well as Haensch (2007), 95–6; more recent attestations now in P. Oxy. LXVII 4593, l. 21 (200/1, Q. Maecius Laetus [copy of 206–11]) and PSI XV 1549, l. 6 (249/50, Aur. Appius Sabinus).

[38] See recently Jördens (2016a); for a list of evidence for such *νομικοί* see Lewis (1983), especially 123–4 (= 1995, 294–5); on (Ulpius) Dioskurides, who apparently specialized in questions of succession and is now attested in four pieces of evidence, see J. D. Thomas' comments on BGU XX 2863, l. 19 (still cited as P. Berol. 9579 by Lewis). In addition to SB XX 15147 (after 138) cited there, see now also SB XVIII 13302 (third century) and SB VI 9298 = ChLA XI 486b (15 September 249) with Aur. Aegyptus

But in addition to these official advisory councils, we always have to assume informal contacts within the governor's social environment, which could influence him considerably. For example, high-ranking personalities of the province were always and everywhere eager to maintain good relations with the Roman office-holders, be it only because they hoped to be entrusted by them with significant and possibly lucrative tasks. Thus, in Alexandria as elsewhere, there naturally existed a number of notables who took over positions of responsibility early on, also in the Chora.[39] Among them, and later among the societal elite of the whole country, were to be found the *strategoi* and royal scribes who were dispatched to the nomes, and in some cases came from the same leading families of the province for generations.[40] But men of arts and letters were no less to be found in the governor's inner circle, particularly in a cosmopolitan city like Alexandria with its range of cultural attractions of all possible sorts, where theatre and music prospered just as much as science and philosophy. We have already observed some effects of these undoubtedly stimulating discussion circles with regard to Origen; reference may also be made to the satirist and rhetorician Lucian whom we encounter in a high position at the prefect's court.[41] Finally, we have to add relationships that were ostensibly private and are reported to have cost at least one governor his office,[42] whereas Seneca praises a governor's wife for her extraordinary caution against all temptations and attempts at exercising undue influence.[43]

Apart from *leges*, *senatus consulta*, and *constitutiones*[44] on the one hand and the normative power of tradition on the other, we will also have to attribute an at least subliminal effect on the governor's decision-making to all these factors, although their position was not based on *auctoritas* and thus never comparable to law in its more narrow definition. At the same time, the references to contemporary

acting as interpreter; on this, see also Keenan, Manning and Yiftach-Firanko (2014), 222–4 no. 4.6.5. See now also J. Urbanik, '*Nomikoi* in the Roman courts', paper delivered at the 28th Congress of Papyrology in Barcelona (4 August 2016).

39 The best-known case is certainly the *archidikastes*, see Montevecchi (1988), 435–6; the same is true at least for the first 100 years of Roman rule in the case of the *exegetes*, see Hagedorn (2007), especially 198–201 as well as P. Hamb. IV 268 to 283 and the prosopography included in the appendix.

40 See Kruse (2002), 906–36, especially 908 and 924–8 on the great inscription of Apollon, son of Apollonius alias Leonidas I. Alex. Imp. 29 = IGRR I 1060 = SB V 8780 (28 October 170), in which 29 members of the family in provincial service are listed.

41 Lucian, *Apol.* 12; see Haensch (2008), 91–3.

42 Thus according to Act. Alex. VII in the case of a certain Maximus who is accused, among other things, of an affair with a ἑπτακαιδεκαετὴς παῖς from a wealthy Alexandrian family (P. Oxy. III 471, ll. 49–50; see also ll. 20, 80, 109, 125 μειράκιον), usually identified with C. Vibius Maximus who held office from 103 to 107; on this see recently Harker 2008, 73–6.

43 In the consolation letter *ad Helv.* 19.6; the woman in question is his mother's sister, according to prevalent opinion the widow of C. Galerius.

44 See already Taubenschlag (1955), 1–55 ch. 1, on *senatus consulta* and *leges* especially 32 with the note and now Keenan (2014); for an overview of the *leges* attested in connection with Roman citizens, see Cavenaile (1958), 443 in the index; an explicit attestation now also in P. Wisc. II 50 = ChLA XLVII 1439 (165). See also Bagnall (1993), on the veterans recently Sänger (2011), especially 82–91. On the legislative authority of the senate see already the prooemium to the so-called Gnomon of the Idios logos BGU V 1210, ll. 1–5, especially ll. 3–4: ὑπὸ αὐτοκρατόρων ἢ συνκλή[το]υ (read συγκλήτου); on the S.C. Orfitianum see also Anagnostou-Cañas in Keenan, Manning and Yiftach-Firanko (2014), 223 in the introduction to no. 4.6.5, on the S.C. Claudianum most recently Nowak (2018), especially 218–21.

philosophical debates discussed above urge us not to underestimate this effect, especially with regard to the creation of new laws. For while *ius* and *iustum* were fundamentally determined by statutory law, distributed by Roman magistrates and emperors, alongside it, the *aequum* always had to be taken into account. Ideally, these were congruent, but not infrequently more recent developments caused the two to drift apart from each other, so that what hitherto had been regarded as *iustum* no longer complied with the common sense of justice. In accordance with the principle *ius est ars boni et aequi*,[45] the legislating authority was in such cases obliged to enforce the *aequum* against a *iustum* that was no longer deemed appropriate, so that the *ius* might thereby need to be redefined.

This was, at least theoretically, the basic concept that determined decision-making and administrative action—and hence all law—in the provinces. In detail, this depended on many factors, not all of which had a law-creating quality, some of them perhaps not even coming close to it. Going far beyond the common conception of law, all of them nevertheless contributed to the construct that nourished the provincial administration of the imperial era; a construct that finally, cast into the form of pronouncements and decisions by Roman magistrates, took shape as provincial law. How much of this actually materialized in reality is, it should be noted, a different matter.

REFERENCES

Abusch, R. 2003. Circumcision and Castration under Roman Law in the Early Empire. In: E. W. Mark (ed.), *The Covenant of Circumcision. New Perspectives on an Ancient Jewish Rite*. Hanover - London, pp. 75–86; 220–3.

Alonso, J. L. 2013. The Status of Peregrine Law in Egypt: 'Customary Law' and Legal Pluralism in the Roman Empire. *Journal of Juristic Papyrology* 43, pp. 351–404.

Anagnostou-Cañas, B. 1991. *Juge et sentence dans l'Égypte romaine*. Paris.

Aubert, J.-J. 2015. Trajan's Canal: River Navigation from the Nile to the Red Sea?. In: F. De Romanis and M. Maiuro (ed.), *Across the Ocean. Nine Essays on Indo-Mediterranean Trade*. Leiden, pp. 33–42.

Ausfeld, C. 1905. Aequitas. *Thesaurus Linguae Latinae* I 5, pp. 1013–17.

Bagnall, R. S. 1993. Egypt and the *lex Minicia*. *Journal of Juristic Papyrology* 23, pp. 25–8 (= *Hellenistic and Roman Egypt. Sources and Approaches*. Aldershot 2006, no. XV).

Baldini, A. 2009. La rivolta dei *Boukòloi*. Riconsiderazioni tra storia e letteratura. *Mediterraneo Antico* 12, pp. 45–54.

Berger, A. 1953. Encyclopedic Dictionary of Roman Law. *Transactions of the American Philological Society* N.S. 43/2, pp. 333–808.

Blouin, K. 2008. De Mendès à Thmouis: hydrographie mobile, société mobile?. In: E. Hermon (ed.), *L'eau comme patrimoine—de la Méditerranée à l'Amérique du Nord*. Quebec, pp. 107–28.

Blouin, K. 2014. *Triangular Landscapes. Environment, Society, and the State in the Nile Delta under Roman Rule*. Oxford.

[45] Thus the famous definition by P. Iuventius Celsus, preserved by Ulpian in D.1.1.1pr; on the concept, see Wieacker (1988), 502–11 § 30, especially 506–9; Berger (1953), especially 354–5 s.v. Aequitas (aequum); on the tensions, see also Ausfeld (1905), 1013–17 s.v. aequitas, especially 1015, ll. 38–1017, l. 2 rubric IV c and the evidence given after the introduction '*saepissime* aequitas *opponitur iuri civili stricto, legibus, scripturae legum, verbis legum*' (64–5).

Bruun, C. 2000. Water Legislation in the Ancient World (*c*.2200 B.C.–*c*.A.D. 500). In: Ö. Wikander (ed.), *Handbook of Ancient Water Technology*. Leiden, pp. 537–604.

Bryen, A. Z. 2012. Judging Empire: Courts and Culture in Rome's Eastern Provinces. *Law and History Review* 30, pp. 771–811.

Cavenaile, R. 1958. *Corpus Papyrorum Latinarum*. Wiesbaden.

Chalon, G. 1964. *L'édit de Tiberius Julius Alexander. Étude historique et exégétique*. Olten.

Cooper, J. P. 2009. Egypt's Nile–Red Sea Canals: Chronology, Location, Seasonality and Function. In: L. Blue, J. P. Cooper, R. Thomas and J. Whitewright (eds.), *Connected Hinterlands. Proceedings of Red Sea Project IV*. Oxford, pp. 195–209.

Cuvigny, H. 2014a. Papyrological Evidence on 'Barbarians' in the Egyptian Eastern Desert. In: J. H. F. Dijkstra and G. Fisher (eds.), *Inside and Out. Interactions between Rome and the Peoples on the Arabian and Egyptian Frontiers in Late Antiquity*. Leuven, pp. 165–98.

Cuvigny, H. 2014b. Le système routier du désert Oriental égyptien sous le Haut-Empire à la lumière des ostraca trouvés en fouille. In: J. France and J. Nelis-Clément (eds.), *La* statio. *Archéologie d'un lieu de pouvoir dans l'empire romain*. Bordeaux, pp. 247–78.

Freyberger, B. 1999. *Südgallien im 1. Jahrhundert v. Chr. Phasen, Konsequenzen und Grenzen römischer Eroberung (125–27/22 v. Chr.)*. Stuttgart.

Fürst, A. 2007. Wahrer Gott—wahre Gerechtigkeit. Politische Implikationen des Monotheismus in der Spätantike. In: G. Palmer (ed.), *Fragen nach dem einen Gott. Die Monotheismusdebatte im Kontext*. Tübingen, pp. 251–82 (= *Von Origenes und Hieronymus zu Augustinus. Studien zur antiken Theologiegeschichte*. Berlin 2011, pp. 453–86).

Haensch, R. 1992. Das Statthalterarchiv. *Zeitschrift der Savigny-Stiftung für Rechtsgeschichte. Romanistische Abteilung* 109, 209–317.

Haensch, R. 1994. Die Bearbeitungsweisen von Petitionen in der Provinz Aegyptus. *Zeitschrift für Papyrologie und Epigraphik* 100, pp. 487–546.

Haensch, R. 1997. Zur Konventsordnung in Aegyptus und den übrigen Provinzen des römischen Reiches. In: B. Kramer, W. Luppe, H. Maehler and G. Poethke (eds.), *Akten des 21. Internationalen Papyrologenkongresses, Berlin 13.–19. 8. 1995*. Stuttgart, pp. 320–91.

Haensch, R. 2000. Le rôle des officiales de l'administration provinciale dans le processus de décision. *Cahiers du Centre Gustave-Glotz* 11, pp. 259–76.

Haensch, R. 2007. 'Dans tout le prétoire . . . '. Le personnel du préfet d'Égypte sous le Haut-Égypte. *Cahiers du Centre Gustave-Glotz* 18, pp. 93–100.

Haensch, R. 2008. Die Provinz Aegyptus: Kontinuitäten und Brüche zum ptolemäischen Ägypten. Das Beispiel des administrativen Personals. In: I. Piso (ed.), *Die römischen Provinzen. Begriff und Gründung*. Cluj-Napoca, pp. 81–105.

Hagedorn, D. 2007. The Emergence of Municipal Offices in the Nome-Capitals of Egypt. In: A. K. Bowman, R. A. Coles, N. Gonis, D. Obbink and P. J. Parsons (ed.), *Oxyrhynchus. A City and Its Texts*. London, pp. 194–204.

Harker, A. 2008. *Loyalty and Dissidence in Roman Egypt. The Case of the Acta Alexandrinorum*. Cambridge.

Harker, A. 2012. The Jews in Roman Egypt. Trials and Rebellions. In: C. Riggs (ed.), *The Oxford Handbook of Roman Egypt*. Oxford, pp. 277–87.

Horbury, W. 2014. *Jewish War under Trajan and Hadrian*. Cambridge.

Hübner, S. 2009. Female Circumcision as Rite de Passage in Egypt—Continuity through the Millennia?. *Journal of Egyptian History* 2, pp. 149–71.

Humbert, M. 1964. La juridiction du préfet d'Égypte d'Auguste à Dioclétien. In: F. Burdeau, N. Charbonnel and M. Humbert (ed.), *Aspects de l'Empire Romain*. Paris, pp. 95–147.

Jördens, A. 2001. Zwei Erlasse des Sempronius Liberalis und ein Verfahren vor Petronius Mamertinus. *Chiron* 31, pp. 37–78.

Jördens, A. 2006. Zum Regierungsstil des römischen Statthalters—das Beispiel des *praefectus Aegypti*. In: H.-U. Wiemer (ed.), *Staatlichkeit und politisches Handeln in der römischen Kaiserzeit*. Berlin, pp. 87–106.

Jördens, A. 2007. Neues zum Trajanskanal. In: J. Frösén, T. Purola and E. Salmenkivi (eds.), *Proceedings of the 24th International Congress of Papyrology, Helsinki 1–7. 8. 2004*. Helsinki, pp. 469–85.

Jördens, A. 2009. *Statthalterliche Verwaltung in der römischen Kaiserzeit. Studien zum* praefectus Aegypti. Stuttgart.

Jördens, A. 2011. Eine kaiserliche Konstitution zu den Rechtsprechungskompetenzen der Statthalter. *Chiron* 41, pp. 327–56.

Jördens, A. 2013. Amnestien im römischen Ägypten. In: K. Harter-Uibopuu and F. Mitthof (eds.), *Vergeben und Vergessen? Amnestie in der Antike*. Vienna, pp. 319–34.

Jördens, A. 2014. Priester, Prokuratoren und Präfekten: Die Tempelverwaltung im römischen Ägypten. *Chiron* 44, pp. 119–64.

Jördens, A. 2016a. Keine Konkurrenz und dennoch Recht: Zum Umgang Roms mit den lokalen Rechten. In: D. Leão and G. Thür (eds.), *Symposion 2015. Vorträge zur griechischen und hellenistischen Rechtsgeschichte* (Coimbra, 1.–4. 9. 2015). Vienna, pp. 237–50.

Jördens, A. 2016b. Die Strafgerichtsbarkeit des *praefectus Aegypti*. In: R. Haensch (ed.), *Recht haben und Recht bekommen im Imperium Romanum. Das Gerichtswesen der römischen Kaiserzeit und seine dokumentarische Evidenz*. Warsaw, pp. 89–163.

Jördens, A. 2016c. Der Menschenraub im kaiserzeitlichen Ägypten. In: D. M. Schaps, U. Yiftach and D. Dueck (eds.), *When West Met East. The Encounter of Greece and Rome with the Jews, Egyptians, and Others*. Trieste: pp. 235–53.

Jördens, A. 2019. Reflexe kaiserlichen Wirkens in ägyptischen Papyri und Ostraka. *Chiron* 49, pp. 299–342.

Katzoff, R. 1980. Sources of Law in Roman Egypt: The Role of the Prefect. *Aufstieg und Niedergang der Römischen Welt* II 13, pp. 807–44.

Keenan, J. G. 2014. Roman Law in Egyptian Documents. In: J. G. Keenan, J. G. Manning and U. Yiftach-Firanko (eds.), *Law and Legal Practice in Egypt from Alexander to the Arab Conquest. A Selection of Papyrological Sources in Translation, with Introductions and Commentary*. Cambridge, pp. 118–34.

Keenan, J. G., Manning, J. G. and Yiftach-Firanko, U. (eds.) 2014. *Law and Legal Practice in Egypt from Alexander to the Arab Conquest. A Selection of Papyrological Sources in Translation, with Introductions and Commentary*. Cambridge.

Kruse, T. 2002. *Der Königliche Schreiber und die Gauverwaltung. Untersuchungen zur Verwaltungsgeschichte Ägyptens in der Zeit von Augustus bis Philippus Arabs (30 v. Chr. - 245 n. Chr.)*. Munich.

Lewis, N. 1983. The Symbol N. In: *Festschrift zum 100-jährigen Bestehen der Papyrussammlung der Österreichischen Nationalbibliothek Papyrus Erzherzog Rainer (P. Rainer Cent.)*. Wien, pp. 121–6 (= *On Government and Law in Roman Egypt. Collected Papers of Naphtali Lewis*. Atlanta 1995, pp. 292–7).

Lo Cascio, E. 2015. Afterword. In: F. De Romanis and M. Maiuro (eds.), *Across the Ocean. Nine Essays on Indo-Mediterranean Trade*. Leiden, pp. 165–9.

Mélèze Modrzejewski, J. 2003a. 'Filios Suos Tantum'. Roman Law and Jewish Identity. In: M. Mor, A. Oppenheimer, J. Pastor and D. R. Schwartz (eds.), *Jews and Gentiles in the Holy Land in the Days of the Second Temple, the Mishnah and the Talmud*. Jerusalem, pp. 108–36.

Mélèze Modrzejewski, J. 2003b. Père ou mère? Aux origines de la matrilinéarité juive. *Clio. fr*, http://www.clio.fr/bibliotheque/pere_ou_mere__aux_origines_de_la_matrilinearite_juive.asp.

Messerer, C. 2017. Corpus des papyrus grecs sur les relations administratives entre le clergé égyptien et les autorités romaines, Vol. I. Paderborn.

Montevecchi, O. 1988. L'amministrazione dell'Egitto sotto i Giulio-Claudi. *Aufstieg und Niedergang der Römischen Welt* II 10.1, pp. 412–71.

Nowak, M. 2018. Fatherless among οἱ ἀπὸ τῆς μητροπόλεως—a Revision. *Zeitschrift für Papyrologie und Epigraphik* 208, pp. 213–26.

Oliver, J. H. 1989. *Greek Constitutions of Early Roman Emperors from Inscriptions and Papyri*. Philadelphia.

Pringsheim, F. 1934. The Legal Policy and Reforms of Hadrian. *The Journal of Roman Studies* 24, pp. 141–53 (= *Gesammelte Abhandlungen*, 2 vol. Heidelberg 1961, vol. I, pp. 91–101).

Pucci Ben Zeev, M. 2005. *Diaspora Judaism in Turmoil, 116/17* CE. *Ancient Sources and Modern Insights*. Leuven.

Riess, W. 2001. *Apuleius und die Räuber. Ein Beitrag zur historischen Kriminalitätsforschung*. Stuttgart.

Sänger, P. 2011. *Veteranen unter den Severern und frühen Soldatenkaisern: Die Dokumentensammlungen der Veteranen Aelius Sarapammon und Aelius Syrion*. Stuttgart.

Sheehan, P. 2015. *Babylon of Egypt. The Archaeology of Old Cairo and the Origins of the City*. 2nd ed. Cairo.

Taubenschlag, R. 1955. *The Law of Greco-Roman Egypt in the Light of the Papyri 332* B.C.*–640* A.D. 2nd ed. Warsaw.

Wankerl, V. 2009. *Appello ad principem. Urteilsstil und Urteilstechnik in kaiserlichen Berufungsentscheidungen (Augustus bis Caracalla)*. Munich.

Weikert, C. 2016. *Von Jerusalem zu Aelia Capitolina. Die römische Politik gegenüber den Juden von Vespasian bis Hadrian*. Göttingen.

Wieacker, F. 1988. *Römische Rechtsgeschichte. Quellenkunde, Rechtsbildung, Jurisprudenz und Rechtsliteratur I: Einleitung, Quellenkunde, Frühzeit und Republik*. Munich.

Wilson, A. 2015. Red Sea Trade and the State. In: F. De Romanis and M. Maiuro (eds.), *Across the Ocean. Nine Essays on Indo-Mediterranean Trade*. Leiden, pp. 13–32.

3

Order and Chaos in Roman Administrative Terminology

Uri Yiftach

While I was preparing this paper, I came across a billboard message that read: 'Kayaking and paddle-boarding is for everyone.' After which the author had added: *Young and old, girls and boys, men and women.* What is so nice about this message—these days quite common to see—is the emphatic use of all possible categories that comprise the 'everyone,' and the use of pairs that are intended to be exhaustive for the group in question.[1] Everyone is either young or old, boy or girl if young, and man or woman if adult. The basic idea here is 'inclusiveness', which is by no means just a fad concept. Now, you might ask 'What does kayaking have to do with law in the Roman Empire?' The answer is simple: one of the means by which the Romans made their empire manageable was the division of its constituent elements—land, persons, types of revenues, types of legal documents, and others—into distinct groups, with a clear preference for the use of all-inclusive sub-categories. There is category A, a category B, and sometimes also a category C, and all the features under consideration had to slot into one of these groups, in one way or another.

The use of all-inclusive sub-categories per se is not a Roman thing, but goes back to the very essence of the Greek city-state with its distinction between citizen and non-citizens, free man and slave.[2] Yet in the Egyptian context under study here it seems that the said method of categorization is particularly Roman, not applied, at least to the same extent, in the Ptolemaic period.[3] In terms of methodology, it would be a mistake to study the change brought about by the Romans without some prior understanding of what these all-inclusive sub-categories

[1] For a detailed account of different forms of categorization, see Nörr (1972), which is an excellent point of departure for the study of the subject in contemporary jurisprudential literature; see especially pp. 45–53. The present paper focuses on *divisio*: *divisionum autem definitio formas omnis complectitur quae sub eo genere sunt quod definitur* (But a definition by division embraces every form which comes under the entire *genus* which is defined) Cicero, *Topica* 5.28, and Nörr (1972), 20–8.

[2] Manville (1997), 11–12.

[3] See, however, famously P.Tebt. I 5.207–20 = MChr 1 (118 BCE, Tebtynis), and Mélèze-Modrzejewski (1975).

Uri Yiftach, *Order and Chaos in Roman Administrative Terminology* In: *Law in the Roman Provinces.* Edited by: Kimberley Czajkowski and Benedikt Eckhardt in collaboration with Meret Strothmann, Oxford University Press (2020).

DOI: 10.1093/oso/9780198844082.003.0003

meant in practical terms as applied in the Roman context. This is what I intend to explore here and explain accordingly.

I decided to study this phenomenon by focusing on one particular target of its application, namely the inhabitants of the province. To do so I start out by clarifying the legally relevant distinction between Romans, *astoi*/Alexandrians, and Egyptians. From there I move on to areas not usually dealt with by legal historians, specifically the collection of taxes and registration of the population. I am aware that much of the discussion relates to administrative custom and not to themes traditionally discussed by historians of law, but the proliferation and rise in the spheres of application of the 'either/or' system seems to me critically important to understanding how Roman rule was organized, and how the Roman state became manageable and enduring for a period and in dimensions that have rarely been matched either earlier or later anywhere in the European experience. For this reason, it seems useful to provide the reader with some sense of the sheer extent of this exquisitely Roman application of the 'all-embracing' categories to its various branches of the administration in the province.

My focus begins outside Egypt. Well known is the dichotomy—current in epigraphic sources from Hellenistic and Roman Greece, Asia Minor, and Cyrene—of *Ἕλληνες* and *Ῥωμαῖοι* as two population groups that in their entirety comprise the 'everyone' under discussion here.[4] In Egypt, the closest that we get to a synoptic view of the population of the province is in the census declarations contained in the Oxyrhynchite *nome*, whereby the declaring party—after giving an account of the members of his family and other residents of his household—delivers an oath that he 'does not conceal any undeclared resident', no one whomsoever is unaccounted for! The current formula runs thus: *μήτε ἐπίξενον μήτε Ῥωμαῖον μήτε Ἀλεξανδρέα μήτε ἀπελεύθερον μήτε Αἰγύπτιον μηδ' ἄλλον μηδένα οἰκεῖν* ('Neither a foreigner nor a Roman, nor an Alexandrian, nor an Egyptian, nor a freedman, nor anyone else lives in my house'). In formal terms, except for the last, all the adjectives used here are as essential as the three pairs used in the kayaking advertisement I mention at the start of this essay. Their function is simply emphatic, to stress that everyone—of any rank, race, or type whatsoever—is taken into consideration.[5] Beyond everything, the text reveals what the author conceives as the key to how he views his society as the sum total of all its discrete elements: there is no potentially undeclared resident that would not slot into one of these sub-groups. Much as the modern billboard kayaking advert cites the categories of age and gender, in non-Egyptian inscriptions the classification involves a similar all-inclusive system, in this case ethnic groups. In the case of the Oxyrhynchite census declarations, while the above mentioned categories seem to comprise the population of the province in its entirety as well, the rationale underlying this list is only partially clear: *ἐπίξενος* (foreigner) means simply anyone who does not possess an *idia* (registered permanent domicile) in the said community,[6] or, in the context of the census declaration, possibly a person not registered as resident of the domicile under

[4] E.g., IG V,1 1208 = SEG 37, 323 ll. 19–30 (42 CE, Gytheion) and Ferrari (2001), 31–2.

[5] Cf., e.g., P.Oxy. III 480 (132 CE, Oxyrhynchos) and Hombert and Préaux (1952), 126–7.

[6] See Jördens (2009), 308 n. 17 with further literature.

scrutiny. The use of the remaining four adjectives is at first sight surprising, especially when considering the regional context in which the documents were composed, namely the Oxyrhynchite *nome* (territorial division). Texts stemming from the local administration of this particular *nome*—and for that matter the *chora* in its entirety—quite frequently record the term ἀπελεύθερος; by contrast the terms Ῥωμαῖος, Ἀλεξανδρεύς, and Αἰγύπτιος are rare. The source of the formula should be sought elsewhere.

The *idios logos* (literally, private account) was an office headed by a Roman knight in charge among other things of the *bona vacantia*, i.e. property without legal heirs.[7] In many cases, the owners would enter into possession of the parental estate through succession, which would only be recognized by the State in the instance of lawful marriage. Following 'the Periclean prototype', a marriage was sanctioned only among members of the same status group, and would duly accord their children the status of their parents, and hence also the right to acquire the parental estate after the parents' death. By contrast, marriage bonds between members of different groups would entail the same rights only in the case of a *conumbium* or an *epigamia* (right of intermarriage).[8] If there was no *epigamia*, things became more complicated: the state had to determine which marriage was legitimate and which was not lawful, and hence what would be the material and personal consequences in each case. As the *idios logos* governed the collection of property without legitimate heirs, its particular interest in these questions is self-evident.

Yet what were these groups? In one case, that of article no. 18 of the *gnomon* (ll. 56–58), the text relates to *fideicomissa* bestowed by Greeks onto Romans, or by Romans to Greeks. Here we find exactly the same method of pigeon-holing as used in the non-Egyptian inscriptions noted above. Since the provision in question records a decision of the Emperor Vespasian, its non-Egyptian origin is plausible.[9] Other texts relate to the context of restrictive status units: *poleis* or *polis*-like frameworks. In this case, the *polis* members are set in opposition to 'outsiders' (ξένοι, ἀλλόφυλοι), as in the regulations relating to marriages of Paraitonian men and Krean women.[10] Yet, most other regulations relate to three status groups of Romans, Egyptians and Alexandrians. The only outstanding variant in the *gnomon* with respect to the Oxyrhynchite formula is the use (in some provisions) of the term ἀστός (townsman, citizen, LSJ p. 262, s.v.), which could signify citizens of any Greek *polis* in Egypt, or could pinpoint Alexandrian citizens only, identifying them as tantamount to Ἀλεξανδρεύς.[11] Both in the case of the Oxyrhynchite formula and the regulations of the *gnomon*, we are abruptly faced with an all-embracing division of the population, whereby two key groups alone

[7] Swarney (1965), 96–104.

[8] As is notably the case in marriages between citizens of Antinoopolis and those defined as 'Egyptians'. See, for example, WChr 27.17–24 (145 CE, Antinoopolis).

[9] BGU V 1210 §18 (56–8) and commentary, p. 26–8; Mélèze-Modrzejewski (1989), 252; 255.

[10] BGU V 1210 §12 (ll. 45–6); §13 (ll. 47–8); §57 (ll. 148–9).

[11] Unless the term *astos* refers to Alexandrians only, as has sometimes been argued. See, in general, Delia (1991: 13–21), who maintains that *astoi* signifies a citizen of any Greek *polis* in Egypt: viz. Alexandria, Naukratis, Ptoelamis Hermeiou, and Antinoopolis. Assuming that the regulation in the Oxyrhynchite census declarations aims at comprehensiveness, I cannot explain why the term Ἀλεξανδρεύς and not ἀστός is used.

possess full civic status: Roman or Alexandrian citizens. In contrast, the third category, *le tiers état*, included anyone not belonging to these groups. The author of the *gnomon* could naturally have used a different formulation: instead of labelling those lacking citizen status as 'Egyptians', he might have stated 'all others' (*οἱ ἄλλοι*). Instead he chose to apply a new and unique label.[12]

As already stated, one of the purposes of the law in question was to circumscribe the type of full marriage that would automatically accord privileges to partners and children in light of their marital status, benefits that would naturally ensue if the partners belonged to the same status group. But what if they were not? As many as fourteen of the extant provisions of the *gnomon* detail the degrees of legitimacy of marriage of members of different status groups, along with the succession rights of their offspring.[13] As if this were not enough, the *gnomon* goes further. The Romans introduced different restrictions on the freedom of hereditary disposition: even in the case of same-status unions, some forms of hereditary disposition were proscribed. In the case of the Egyptians in particular, these regulations had far-reaching consequences: the categories of Romans and Alexandrians naturally predate the *gnomon*, and the Roman occupation of Egypt. Not so for the new entity *Αἰγύπτιος* created by the Roman administration of Egypt: If you were not Roman or Alexandrian, you would automatically be subject to the rules made for this category.

The resulting standardization is evident not only in the *gnomon*. In a case presented in the court proceedings BGU I 19 = MChr 85 (135 CE, Arsinoitês) the emperor Hadrian is reported to have conceded to children of a predeceased father the right to succeed to the estate of his mother, their paternal grandmother, once she has died as well. In the case of the present court proceedings the litigant aims at having the same rule be applied in her case as well. For this purpose she applies the terminological settings of the *gnomon*. When Hadrian had originally issued his ruling (presumably in connection with a litigation as well) the parties were not *Aigyptioi*, and the present litigant aims at convincing the judge that it was the emperor's intention that the rule be applicable in the case of Egyptians as well.[14] Only this would allow her to benefit from the beneficium herself. In the case of BGU I 19 = MChr 85 the rules are external. They derive from the emperor, and one uses the terms of the *gnomon* simply to establish the extent of their applicability: who can benefit from these rules, and who cannot. Yet once the category was there, it was assumed that norms of local origin would be applicable for all members of the new group. These rules were assembled, and applied whenever the case involved 'Egyptians': quite naturally, the collection of rules relating 'Egyptians' was called 'the law of the Egyptians'.[15] How was the collection created? We may assume that litigants of non-Roman or Alexandrian affiliations came to court, citing local norms to base their claims. The judge then accepted their

[12] See, for example, Mélèze-Modrzejewski (1980) 64–7.

[13] BGU V 1210 §12 (45–6), §13 (47–8), §38 (82–3), §39 (84–6), §45 (123–7), §46 (128–9), §47 (130–1), §48 (132), §49 (133), §50 (134–5), §51 (136), §52 (137), §53 (138–9), §57 (148–9).

[14] BGU I 19.5–7 = *MChr* 85 (135 CE, Arsinoitês): *ὑπερεθέμην τὸ νῦν π[ρᾶγ]μα, ἐπὶ καθολικὸν ἦν, ἄχρι οὗ γράψω* | 6 *τῷ κρατίστῳ ἡγεμόνι ε̣ἰ [κ]α̣ὶ {α̣ι̣} Αἰγυπτίων υἱωνοῖς καὶ υἱδ[αῖ]ς δέδοται* | 7 *τὰ μαμμῷα [δι]ὰ τῆς τοῦ κυρίου Ἀδριανοῦ Καίσαρος χάριτος* with Katzoff (1970).

[15] See now, in general, Yiftach (forthcoming), Section 4, 'the laws'.

view, and since they were regarded as 'Egyptians' he made the rules applicable to all members of the same category. By the second century at the latest, the collection of these local norms assumed some written form, and was subject to interpretation by local legal experts.

The importance of the new collective term can hardly be overstated. Through the introduction of this new term, in one fell swoop all the inhabitants of the province—Romans and Alexandrians apart—were made subject to the same package of rules and legislation, whether of external or of internal origin. Nonetheless, the consequences of the change were to some extent limited. In the case of the *gnomon*, regulations relating to the key status groups are confined to the law of personal rank, marriage, and succession. One could assume that this restriction resulted from the very nature of the text involving the interest of the *gnomon* in this concrete sphere only. Yet other texts recording the terms Ῥωμαῖος, Ἀλεξανδρεύς, and Αἰγύπτιος also seem to focus on these same subjects. In addition—and this is perhaps more pivotal in the present context—the said terms are only used by the emperor and the central, procuratorial office-holders in Alexandria.[16] The further we move out of the capital of Egypt and down the Nile, the occurrence of the three terms becomes extremely rare.[17] In the analysis of documentary texts stemming from the *chora* we focus on three genres in particular: reports on the collection of revenues in kind issued by village *sitologoi*, reports issued by the *praktores argyrikôn* related to the collection of revenues in cash, and contracts.

The papyrological source material from the Roman period most commonly records two types of revenue collection: grain and cash. The former was collected by the *sitologoi*, the latter, from the Flavian period onwards, primarily by the *praktores argyrikôn*.[18] The activity of these tax collectors was closely monitored, and hence also meticulously registered. Tax collectors recorded their activity on a daily basis: the data, originally recorded in daybooks, was then transformed into a wide variety of reports, some prepared for internal use, others for informing their superiors—in particular the administration of the *nome* headed by the

[16] Ῥωμαῖοι: for example, BGU IV 1086 (160/183/215 CE, provenance unknown) [governor: letter to the *epistratêgoi*, very damaged]. Ἀλεξανδρεῖς: e.g., BGU XI 2058 (166 CE, Oxyrhynchitês) [governor: letter to the Oxyrhynchite *stratêgos*]. Αἰγύπτιοι: e.g., P.Mil.Vogl. I 25.4.18–5.15 (127 CE, Tebtynis) [*archidikastês*: court proceedings]. For a complete list see Yiftach (2018), nn.14, 15.

[17] BGU III 747.7–10 = WChr 35 (139 CE, Koptos), a letter by the *stratêgos* of the Coptitenome to the governor. The term Ῥωμαῖος is most commonly attested on documentary papyri in connection of legal institutions particular to Roman citizens (*ius trium liberorum, patria potestas, testamentum per aes et libram* and others), or when privileges the entitlement to which depended on the possession of the citizenship (e.g., the corn dole in late third-century Oxyrhynchos) were at stake. The term Ῥωμαῖος was also occasionally used in connection with other terms, such as Ἀντινοεύς and ἱππεύς, and, in one case, the petition SB XXIV 16252.28–32 (163 CE, Karanis) to denote the petitioner's quality as Roman, against that of the offender who is pejoratively designated Αἰγύπτιος. But otherwise the term is very irregularly used, frequently without any apparent reason for its application [cf., e.g., the tax list BGU IX 1897.16 (166 CE, Theadelphia)]. The term Ἀλεξανδρεύς is relatively frequently in texts focusing on personal privileges directly deriving from that status, such as the right to benefit from the core dole in late third-century Oxyrhynchos already mentioned in connection with the term Ῥωμαῖος. It is not in common, and seems inconsistent, in other types of documents. In the Roman period, the terms Αἰγύπτιος and ἀστός are never regularly applied outside the terminology of the procuratorial offices.

[18] Wallace (1938), 36–8; 290–2; 306–7.

stratêgos—of their activity.[19] Over and above all other tax collectors, the *sitologos* and the *praktôr argyrikôn* were entrusted with the collection of wide variety of taxes, from different population categories, that is from 'everyone', and in different localities that were under their jurisdiction, that is 'everywhere'. In addition, in Alexandria, there was not a single office in charge of all revenues, but many, each appointed to its own sphere of competence, yet the *sitologoi* and *praktores argyrikôn* were required to undertake the collection 'for everyone'. Consequently, the reports issued by the tax collectors on a monthly basis had to record the entire complex of population groups, locations and Alexandrian offices for which the revenues were collected. In all these respects the account needed to be exhaustive.

Let us first address the *sitologoi*. We are in possession of ninety-eight reports sent by the *sitologoi* to the *stratêgos*. Following the terminology applied in the documents themselves, some are κατ' ἄνδρα: reporting the identity of each and every tax payer, while others are ἐν κεφαλαίῳ: reporting only the population groups from which the tax was collected. A nice sample of the latter type is P.Berl.Leihg. I 1 = P.Berl.Thun. 1 = SB III 7193.[20] The text records the collection of revenues in kind, by the *sitologoi* of Theadelphia, in the month of Thoth of the fifth year of Antoninus Pius and Lucius Verus (164/5 CE). Following the opening address and introductory clauses, the text provides the totals of the various revenues collected. Within the text itself, the author applies no less than four categorization methods: one is by the office for which the revenue is collected: the *ousiakos logos*, in charge of the domain land, and the *dioikêsis*, in charge of everything else.[21] Another is by location: the *sitologia* is located in Theadelphia, and this is where most of its revenues are collected. But it is also in charge of the collection, or at least supervision of the collection of revenues for some neighbouring villages; the dichotomy used is similar: one chapter for Theadelphia, another (ὑπὲρ ἄλλων κωμῶν) for 'the remaining villages', where each village is recorded in a different section:[22] one label for a particular category, another for everything else. The third element is the nature of the payer's connection with the land from which the revenues are collected. Here we find the dichotomy: public farmers (*dêmosioi geôgroi*), and then the label *klêrouchoi*, which in the present context means, again, everyone else.[23] Finally, there is one dichotomy, this time actual rather than merely formal: this particular text records the collection of grain revenues: wheat and barley. The said sets of dichotomies are placed into a rigid scheme: main chapters by organs; within each main chapter, sections by villages; within each section an account by population category. Within each one is an account of the qualities of wheat and barley, with a designation of the specific taxes.[24]

[19] In general, see Yiftach (2015).

[20] On the terminology, see Kruse (1998), 330, n. 843, with further secondary literature.

[21] For a brief overview, see Sharp (1999), 224–5.

[22] See in particular P.Tebt. II 339^{r}.14 where a specific reference is made to the *meris* of the remaining villages: ὑπὲρ ἄλλων κωμ[ῶ]ν Πολέμωνος. Usually the geographic sphere of competence can only be inferred from the list that follows the formula. E.g., P.Giss.Univ. VI 49^{r}.2.14–19 (221 CE, Tebtynis) (ὑπὲρ ἄλλων κωμῶν).

[23] T. Kalén, P.Berl.Leihg. I, 58–9.

[24] P.Berl.Leihg. I 1, e.g., 1.7–2.4 (165 CE, Theadelphia).

P.Berl.Leigh. I 1 is an excellent test-case, but its format and categorization method are by no means unique. The accountants did not necessarily apply everywhere the same terminology, or even the same items: in the Herakleides meris (expectedly well documented, particularly in the case of Karanis), the term used to label everyone else is not *klêrouchoi*, but *katoikoi*.[25] But the categorization method using an array of dichotomies is the same. Also identical throughout Egypt as far as we can tell, is the format using the Alexandrian organ as the main heading, which is then followed by location, population group, and, within each entry, types of agricultural products.[26] The world of the *sitologoi* is completely different, then, from that of the procuratorial offices in Alexandria: in the case of Theadelphia, the number of Alexandrians and Romans was negligible, as was the implication of their status on the question at hand, making the terms inapplicable and consequently not applied. On the other hand, the question of whether the payer was primarily a public farmer or not was very pertinent, as this affected the subject's right to his land, and clearly had bearing on the amount of tax he or she was obliged to pay.[27] So was his *origo*, relevant in particular with regard to the identity of the officials who were to assess the tax quota, and eventually also to collect the revenues: as far as the identity of the tax payers is concerned, this is the most relevant piece of information.[28] At the same time, in terms of the categorization principles we note much similarity with the system discussed in the foregoing section: one category specifying one group is followed by a second, which is a formal label for everyone or everything else—Egyptians—meaning all subjects who are neither Greek nor Roman; *klerhouchoi*: everyone who is not a *dêmosios geôrgos*, all the villagers apart from those residing in Theadelphia; a specific organ for the domain land, then the *dioikêsis*, dealing with everything else.[29]

[25] Revenues related documentation from the Herakleides meris, in as much as it reflects a similar dichotomy, records not *klêrouchoi*, but *katoikoi*: cf., in particular, the tax receipt BGU III 716.4–15 (224 CE, Karanis).

[26] Best recorded is the Arsinoite *nome*, but the use of the same system in other regions by P.Oxy. XLIV 3170. Frag. C (III CE, Sinary, Oxyrhynchites): by procuratorial offices in Alexandria: *dioikêsis* (ll. 249, 253, 256), *usiaca*: (ll. 250, 258), *idios logos* (l. 155). P.Giss. I 82.9 (117 CE, Apollonopolitês Heptakomias): between main and remaining villages: *Ὑψηλῆς κ̣[α]ὶ ἄλλων κωμῶν*. The dichotomy *klêrouchoi* viz. *dêmosioi geôrgoi* is well recorded in P.Oxy. XLIX 3473.33–4 (161–169 CE, Oxyrhynchos): *παρὰ τῶν τῆς κώμης γεωργῶν καὶ κληρούχ(ων)*.

[27] Bowman, (2013), 225 and, in detail, Rowlandson (2005).

[28] Hence the frequent used of locality as a key criterion in regional reports: BGU II 657 (II CE, Arsinoitês); 659 (229 CE, Soknopaiou Nêsos); IX 1893 (149 CE, Theadelphia); P.Harr. I 164 (I–II CE, Philadelphia); P.Hib. II 218 (late I–early II CE, Hêrakleopolitês); P.Lips. I 93 (II–III CE, Hermopolis); P.Turner 32 = P.Lond. III 860a verso (Descr.) (*c.*201–11 CE, Soknopaiou Nêsos); PSI VIII 945 (III CE, Oxyrhynchitês); SB XIV 12170 (31/2 CE (?), Oxyrhynchitês); 12181 (III CE, Oxyrhynchitês); XVI 12624 (211/2 CE (?), Theadelphia); 12632 = P.Princ. I 11 (ll. 1–30) (after 30.8.35 CE, Philadelphia); XVIII 13236 = P.Haw. 244 (p.33) R (12 CE, Aueris); XX 14468 (IV CE, Prektis, Hermopolitês); 14576 = P. Princ. I 13 (after 46/7 CE, Philadelphia); 14710 = SPP XX 40 and 48 (*c.*266 CE, Hermopolis); XXII 15311 = SB XIV 11972 (367/8 or 382/3 CE, Hermopoliês); 15815 (II–III CE, Karanis); SPP XXII 169 (216 CE, Soknopaiou Nêsos); 180 (208 CE, Soknopaiou Nêsos). The importance of the origo is also stressed through the registration of the origo whenever a resident of one village pays his taxes in another. Cf., e.g., P.Mich. VI 397.11–17 (204 CE, Karanis).

[29] Note an identical interpretation of the dichotomy Greeks/Romans elsewhere in the Greek east: Ferrari (2001).

With these recognitions in mind, let us move to the accounts of the *praktores argyrikôn*. The *praktôr argyrikôn* was a tax collector, a role created in the second half of the first century for the collection of revenues in cash. This position is well documented, primarily for its role in the collection of capitation taxes, in particular the *laographia* (poll tax).[30] The introduction of the poll tax was one of the causes for the creation of the distinction between the *Aigyptioi*, on the one hand, who were liable to its payment, and on the other the Romans and Alexandrians, who were exempt. There was another privileged group, the *metropolites*, who were subject to a reduced tax rate.[31] Furthermore, special registers are known to have existed for the registration of members of these groups.[32] A priori, then, a clear account of the poll-tax liability status could be expected, in reports issued by the *praktores argyrikôn* regarding its collection. This is not the case, however. Monthly reports issued by the *praktores argyrikôn* rarely contain any reference to sub-groups, or any other hint of the tax status of the person in question; nor do they routinely include topographical data. In the case of the ἐν κεφαλαίῳ reports, they simply record the type of taxes collected,[33] while in that of κατ ' ἄνδρα they simply list the payers, frequently not even with an account of the collected revenues.[34] Nor is the situation in related sources different.

It is generally agreed that capitation taxes were collected on the basis of census returns and lists deriving thereof.[35] For this reason they also employ some means of personal identification typical of that documentary genre. Census declarations contain a variety of terms that are unique to this particular genre, just as was the case with the documentation of the procuratorial offices, or the *sitologoi* reports. In describing a tax subject, the text always records the person's age, and sometimes his occupation, registration status, and liability status. The application of this is somewhat erratic, however: even in the context of a single census declaration, the said terminology is included in the designation of some subjects but is absent from others without an apparent cause.[36] I also know of no source where the different categorization methods appear together, in a framework which

[30] For example, Rathbone (1993), 86–99. [31] Mélèze-Modrzejewski (1989), 259–80.

[32] See, for example, SB XX 14433 (II^{m} CE, Diospolis Magna); SPP IV pp. 58–83 (*c*.73 CE, Ptolemais Euergetis) ll. 331–69.

[33] BGU I 25 = WChr 270 (200 CE, Arsinoites); 41 (199 CE, Arsinoites); II 652 (207 CE, Karanis); 653; P.Aberd. 154 (195/6 CE, Soknopaiou Nêsos); P.Fay. 41 col. 1 and col. 2 (186 CE, Bacchias); 42; P.Heid. IV 312 (*synairemata*) (222 CE, Unknown Provenance); P.Köln II 83 (167 CE, provenance unknown); P. Oxy. XLIV 3174r (229 CE, Ibiôn Chysis); SB X 10566 (199 CE, Soknopaiou Nêsos).

[34] BGU I 42 (225 CE, Soknopaiou Nêsos); 199^{r} (195 CE, Sonkopaiou Nêsos) [priests]; II 392 (208 CE, Soknopaiou Nêsos); 639 (208 CE, Soknopaiou Nêsos) [occasional reference to occupations, but not consequent]; IX 1891 (133 CE, Theadelphia); 1892 (133 CE, Theadelphia); P.Hamb. IV 275 (198 CE, Theadelphia (?)) [Occasional reference to privileged status groups]; P.Lond. II 474 (p. 107) (199 CE, Soknopaiou Nêsos) (p. 107); P.Oxy. X 1283 (219 CE, Oxyrhynchos); XII 1433 col. 1; 2 (238 CE, Ksemouchis, Oxyrhynchitês); 1517 (272 CE, Oxyrhynchitês) [occasional reference to occupation]; XXIV 2413 (168/9 CE, Oxyrhynchitês); P.Stras. IX 850 (168 CE, Euhêmeria) [one record of *laographia*]; *P.Turner* 31 (201–11 CE, Soknopaiou Nêsos); PSI V 461 (290 CE, Oxyrhynchos); SB XXII 15570 (217–19 CE, Soknopaiou Nêsos) [damaged]; SPP XXII 6 (204/5 CE, Karanis) [occasional reference to occupation].

[35] Hombert and Préaux (1952), 135–44; Bagnall and Frier (1994), 26–30.

[36] For example, BGU I 115.20–2 = WChr 203 (189 CE, Ptolemais Euergetis) reporting three siblings all with designation of occupation, but only two of these siblings are designated as λαογραφούμενοι. Cf. Hombert and Préaux (1952), 104–5, 114–23.

would point towards a conceptualization of the 'everyone', in the sense discussed so far in this paper, namely as components of a total, which—from the point of view of the official in charge—would comprise the population in its entirety.

Let us summarize our discussion so far. The author of the advertisement 'Kayaking and paddle-boarding is for everyone' aimed to emphasize that 'everyone' by listing the elements of the society that would make up the total: 'Young and old, girls and boys, men and women.' In the context of Roman Egypt we found some parallels that differed according to the context in which this 'everyone' is conceived: 'Romans, *astoi*/Alexandrians and Egyptians' in the context of the procuratorial offices in Alexandria; and '*klêrouchoi* and *dêmosioi geôrgoi*' in that of the *sitologoi*-offices in the western Fayum. For the census declarations, population surveys and the collection of capitation taxes, we pinpointed certain items unique to this genre scattered through our sources, while we did not find any ancient source that comprises all of them so as to create the 'everyone'.

This is time now to come to the last source: the legal document. BGU XIV 2367 (late third century BCE, Alexandria) records sections of an early Ptolemaic *diagramma*, probably the *Justizdiagramma* of Ptolemy II Philadelphos of *c.*275 BCE.[37] The text introduces rules regarding the form of identification of parties to contracts, and is recorded in the format of a double document. The document considers not one population group but four: Alexandrian citizens, soldiers, Alexandrian citizens who are soldiers, and those who are neither Alexandrian citizens nor soldiers. In dealing with the obligatory designation for each group, the text does not provide a closed list of obligatory terms—namely, the 'everyone'—but instead indicates what *types* of terms should be applied. Thus for example, in the case of civilians who are not Alexandrians, the designation consists of personal and father's name, *patris*—city or region of origin in the Greek world—and *genos*, which denotes the person's occupational status. We may also assume that no term could be arbitrarily supplied as *patris* or *genos*: there had to be some *numerus clausus*. At the same time, it is obvious that the law would not and could not contain a list of all possible indications of origin throughout the Greek world that would serve as a *patris*. Accordingly, in terms of our kayaking advertisement, the motto of BGU XIV 2367 would be: 'Kayaking and paddle-boarding is for everyone: all those who have a recognized *patris* and a recognized *genos*.' But is this really 'everyone'? Hardly. Egyptians, the vast majority of the population, did not have *patris*. But nor are they supposed to be kayaking—that is, in our case not parties to contracts recorded in a Greek double document.

At any event, the said contractual segregation was soon to disappear, much earlier than the beginning of the Roman period, and with it all the designation methods that were introduced or regulated by means of BGU XIV 2367. Legal documents from the early Roman period no longer systematically apply unit designations. There are no components of a theoretical 'everyone': a person's identification is instead based primarily on genealogical identifiers, that is, the name of the father, mother, and paternal grandfather; in addition, in the case of some scribal offices, an account is given of visible physical defects.[38] Some impulse towards forming an alternative population unit whose total could comprise

[37] Yiftach (2014), 103–4.

[38] See, in general, Yiftach (2019), pp. 82–4.

'everyone' comes from a different quarter: already in the Ptolemaic period one can witness the application in non-contractual documentary settings—in particular in petitions—of a designation by domicile, routinely introduced by the preposition ἀπό + place of residence. In the course of the early Roman period, the domicile is included in legal documents as well. However, including the person's residence in this sphere never became obligatory in Roman Egypt, and seems to have depended on varying scribal practices, much like the other details recorded in legal documents.[39] That said, indication of formal residence turns up regularly in documents underlying the system of tax collection and recruitment of manpower: an intricate system of population registration is evident in census declarations and other types of instrument concerning personal status, as well in the monthly tax reports. This system is just one manifestation of the increasing effort—evident in edicts and petitions alike—to create a clear *idia* for all subjects, and to secure their connection with it.[40] In terms of the administration of justice, it is in this area—qualification and exemption from liturgies, covrées, forced assignment of land and taxation, and not in that of private contracts, or documents recording transactions among private persons in general—that the factor of *idia* plays an especially critical role during the Roman period.

The division and categorization of provincial populations and resources was, in Roman Egypt, a prerequisite for imperial exploitation by its rulers. Obviously, every state organ used unique categorization methods aiming to serve its particular needs. Accordingly, an *individuum* would be labelled differently depending on the organ in question and its key interests: *Egyptian* in the eyes of the procuratorial offices in Alexandria, and in regard to the law of marriage, inheritance and personal status; *dêmosios geôrgos* in the eyes of the *sitologoi*, and anyone in charge of collection revenues in kind; while an entirely different set of terms was used for the census and related lists. To organize the data, the Roman administration of Egypt frequently applied all-embracing categories: those discussed above all related to population groups: one or two categories relating to a specific population group, and another comprising 'everyone else'. One could cite a similar strategy in the case of land registry, legal documents and others, and discuss the extent to which this method finds parallels in Ptolemaic documentation in the Roman period outside Egypt; we might also ask why the said all-embracing system or any other clear organization of the data is applied in some spheres of state administration, but not in others. All this must be left for future investigation.

I would like now to offer one final observation. For the creation of an all-embracing categorization system, it would have been possible to create all the requisite categories from scratch. This never happened in any of the instances discussed above. In each and every one of the above-mentioned cases, at least some of the categories pre-existed the system as a whole: Roman and Alexandrian citizenship, or the status of *dêmosioi geôrgoi* already existed before they were integrated into the all-embracing categorization system. Within that system, in order to create comprehensiveness, one could simply state 'and all others'. This was

[39] Thus, the *apo*-formula is already relatively widespread in legal documents from first-century-CE Oxyrhynchos. In the Arsinoite source material it becomes common only in the following century.

[40] Jördens (2009), 73–5.

the case in the *sitologoi* reports when one wished to record the region in which the taxes were levied: in P.Berl.Leihg. I 1 a comprehensive coverage was achieved by distinguishing between Theadelphia, on the one hand, and 'all other villages', on the other. But in three cases the creator of the system went beyond that: for those outside the pre-existing groups he created a new label: in the epigraphical sources from outside Egypt there were Ῥωμαῖοι, Roman citizens, while the term Ἕλληνες was used for labelling all those who did not possess that status; in the *sitologoi* reports from Theadelphia there were the *dêmosios geôrgos*, while the term *klêrouchos* was used to label those not belonging to that status group; in documentation stemming from the procuratorial offices in Alexandria, there were the Romans and Alexandrians, and 'Egyptians' was a category created to label all those outside the two privileged groups. This final example is especially important, for in this particular case the introduction of the designation brought about changes much beyond the administrative habit. The use of the new label for the vast majority of the province resulted in the introduction of a unified set of rules, applicable in all cases involving 'Egyptians': the implication of the creation of the new group for the formation of the legal landscape in Roman Egypt has yet to be studied.

REFERENCES

Bagnall, R. S. and Frier, B. 1994. *Demography of Roman Egypt*. Cambridge.

Bowman, A. K. 2013. Agricultural Production in Egypt. In: A. K. Bowman and A. Wilson (eds.), *The Roman Agricultural Economy*. Oxford, pp. 219–53.

Delia, D. 1991. *Alexandrian Citizenship During the Roman Principate*. Atlanta.

Ferrari, J.-L. 2001. Rome et la géographie de l`hellénisme: réflexions sur 'hellènes' et 'panhellènes' dans les inscriptions d'époque romaine, In: O. Salomies (ed.), *The Greek East in the Roman Context. Proceedings of a Colloquium organised by the Finnish Institute at Athens May 21 and 22, 1999*. Helsinki, pp. 19–35.

Hombert, M. and Préaux, Cl. 1952. *Recherches sur le recensement dans l'Égypte romaine (P. Bruxelles Inv. E. 7616). (Papyrologica Lugduno-Batava. V.)* Leiden.

Jördens, A. 2009. *Statthalterliche Verwaltung in der römischen Kaiserzeit. Studien zum praefectus Aegypti*. Stuttgart.

Katzoff, R. 1970. BGU 19 and the Law Representation in Succession. In: D. Samuel, *Proceedings of the Twelfth International Congress of Papyrology*. Toronto, pp. 239–42.

Kruse, Th. 1998. *Der königliche Schreiber und die Gauverwaltung. Untersuchungen zur Verwaltungsgeschichte Ägyptens in der Zeit von Augustus bis Philippus Arabs (20 v. Chr. - 245 n. Chr.)*. Munich and Leipzig.

Manville, Ph. B. 1997. *The Origin of Citizenship in Classical Athens*. Princeton.

Mélèze-Modrzejewski, J. 1975. Chrématistes et Laocrites. In: J. Bingen, G. Cambier, and G. Nachtergael (eds.), *Le Monde grec: pensée, littérature, histoire, documents: hommages à Claire Préaux*. Brussels, pp. 699–708.

Mélèze-Modrzejewski, J. 1980. Un aspect du 'couple interdit'. In: *Le couple interdit, entretiens sur le racisme, le dialectique de l'altérité socio-culturelle et la sexualité, actes du colloque tenu en mai 1977 au centre culturel internatioal de Cerisy-la-Salle*. Paris and New York, pp. 53–73.

Mélèze-Modrzejewski, J. 1989. Entre la cité et le fisc: les statut grec dans l' Égypte romaine. In: F. Javier and F. Nieto, eds. *Symposion 1982. Vorträge zur griechischen und hellenistischen Rechtsgeschichte (Santander, 1–4 September 1982)* Cologne and Vienna, pp. 241–80 [= *Droit impérial et traditions locales dans l'Égypte romaine*. Aldershot, Chapter 1].

Nörr, D. 1972. *Divisio und Partitio. Bemerkungen zur römischen Rechtsquellenlehre und zur antiken Wissenschaftstheorie*. Berlin.

Rathbone, D. 1993. Egypt, Augustus and Roman taxation. *Cahiers du Centre Gustave-Glotz* 4, pp. 81–112.

Rowlandson, J. 2005. The Organization of Public Land in Roman Egypt. In: J. C. Moreno Garcia (ed.), *L'Agriculture institutionelle in Égypt ancienne: État de la question et perspectives interdisciplinaires*. Lille, pp. 173–94.

Sharp, M. 1999. Shearing Sheep: Roman and the Collection of Taxes in Egypt, 30 BC–AD 200. In: W. Eck, ed. *Lokale Autonomie und römische Ordnungsmacht in den kaiserzeitlichen Provinzen vom 1. bis 3. Jahrhundert*. Munich, pp. 213–41.

Swarney, P. R. 1965. *The Ptolemaic and Roman idios logos*. Yale.

Wallace, S. L. 1938. *Taxation in Egypt, from Augustus to Diocletian*. Princeton.

Yiftach, U. Forthcoming. Law in Ptolemaic and Roman Egypt. In: M. Canevaro and E. M. Harris (eds.), *Oxford Handbook of Ancient Greek Law*. Oxford.

Yiftach, U. 2014. Did BGU XIV 2367 Work? In: M. Depauw and S. Coussement (eds.), *Legal Documents in Ancient Societies III: Identifiers and Identification Methods in the Ancient World*. Leuven, pp. 103–18.

Yiftach, U. 2015. From Arsinoe to Alexandria and beyond: Taxation and information in early Roman Egypt: A discussion of P. Bagnall 70. *Journal of Juristic Papyrology* 45, pp. 291–312.

Yiftach, U. 2018. The Gnomon in Context: Status Designations and Bureaucratic Compartmentalization in Roman Egypt. In: K. Harter-Uibopuu (ed.), *Studien zum 'Gnomon des Idios Logos': Beiträge zum Dritten Wiener Kolloquium zur Antiken Rechtsgeschichte (Wiener Kolloquien zur Antiken Rechtsgeschichte)*. Vienna.

Yiftach, U. 2019. The rise of the flexible template: patterns of change in identification methods between the Ptolemaic and the Roman Period. In: R. Guicharrousse, P. Ismard, M. Vallet, and A.-E. Veïsse (eds.), *L'identification des personnes dans les mondes grecs*. Paris, pp. 77–89.

4

The *Constitutio Antoniniana* and Private Legal Practice in the Eastern Empire*

José Luis Alonso

1. THE PROBLEM: PEREGRINE LAW WITHOUT PEREGRINES

Ludwig Mitteis once memorably wrote that the papyri may in general allow us to see sharper but hardly ever further.[1] The gloomy aphorism is all the more unexpected considering how deeply the papyri had changed ancient legal history in Mitteis' lifetime, largely through his own contributions. Without the papyri, in particular, we would have never imagined the extent to which Eastern legal traditions survived the incorporation to the Roman Empire and even Caracalla's universal grant of citizenship. This 'second survival' of the *iura peregrinorum* especially took the generation of Gradenwitz and Mitteis entirely by surprise. Mitteis made it into the main theme of his foundational *Reichsrecht und Volksrecht*.[2]

From a social and political point of view, the phenomenon is remarkable, but easily understandable. Long-held traditions are not easy to displace, and Rome had never shown a special interest in forcing its own law on the provincial population: a policy of minimal intervention that was unlikely to change in the turbulent third century.[3] And yet this inertia poses a puzzling legal problem. In the tradition of political thought that Rome inherits from Greece, law is tied to citizenship in at least two interrelated senses: becoming a citizen entails

* Thanks are due to Kimberley Czajkowski and Benedikt Eckhardt for their kind invitation and their patience throughout the editing process. This final version has greatly benefitted from the discussion at the 2016 Münster Conference organized by the editors, as well as at the Barcelona Congress of Papyrology and the seventh 'Ancient Law in Context' Workshop at Edinburgh in that same year. The research was financed by the I+D Project DER2015-67052-P of the Spanish Government and concluded within Polish National Centre of Research project, Opus 14 (2017/27/B/HS3/01350).

[1] Mitteis (1898), 199: 'Hier wie überall bewährt sich der Satz, dass in aller Regel die Urkunde uns zwar schärfer, aber nicht sogleich auch weiter sehn lässt.'

[2] Mitteis (1891).

[3] For a reevaluation of this period, particularly regarding its position in Roman legal history, see Babusiaux & Kolb (2015). An overview of the period and a reassessment of the scholarly dispute around the idea of a crisis of the third century may be found in Ando (2012).

José Luis Alonso, *The* Constitutio Antoniniana *and Private Legal Practice in the Eastern Empire* In: *Law in the Roman Provinces.* Edited by: Kimberley Czajkowski and Benedikt Eckhardt in collaboration with Meret Strothmann, Oxford University Press (2020).
DOI: 10.1093/oso/9780198844082.003.0004

submitting to the laws of the civic body;[4] and without such a civic body—*politeuma*, in Hellenistic parlance—no 'own laws' (*idioi nomoi*)—are conceivable.[5] The latter is true of legislation but also of the ancestral laws of the community, the *nomoi patrioi*, or simply *τὰ πάτρια*.[6] Without *civitas*, there is no civil law, indeed no law proper,[7] but merely the submission to the arbitrariness of a sovereign.

From this point of view, in truth, in the case of Egypt already the 'first' survival—upon the Roman annexation—of the local legal traditions becomes a problem, since most of the inhabitants of the new province were *peregrini nullius civitatis, apolides*: everyone, in fact, except the (relatively scarce) Romans and the citizens of Naukratis, Alexandria and Ptolemais. The Roman sources leave little doubt that the legal construction that denied to such *apolides* any *ius proprium* was very much alive well into the Severan period, at least in the jurisprudential discourse, in blatant contradiction to the subsistence of local laws in Egypt, where they were endorsed by the Roman administration itself.[8] Here, I will not address

[4] This is most apparent in the preserved oaths of obedience to the laws, even if these are formulated as part of a wider allegiance to the political system as a whole. See for instance—Herzog (1942), 5–8 (§2), Segre (1952), 9–10 (§12), Schmitt (1969), 285–7 (§545)—the oath of submission to the laws of Kos imposed on the citizens of Kalymna upon the re-annexation of the latter at the end of the third century BCE: *ἐμμενῶ τᾶι καθεστακυίαι δαμοκρατίαι καὶ τᾶι ἀποκαταστάσει τᾶς ὁμοπολιτείας καὶ τοῖς νόμοις τοῖς ἐγ Κῶι πατρίοις ὑπάρχουσι καὶ τοῖς δόγμασι τᾶς ἐκκλησίας καὶ ταῖς διαγραφαῖς ταῖς ὑπὲρ ṭᾶς ὁμοπολιτείας* (ll. 14–18): 'I will abide by the established democracy, the restoration of the *homopoliteia*, the ancestral laws of Cos, the resolutions of the assembly and the provisions of the *homopoliteia*' (translation from Austin). On the inscription and its context, see Sherwin-White (1978), 125–30, and Krob (1997), 436–45. See also the 242 BCE *sympoliteia* between the *demos* of Smyrna and the troops at Magnesia, in I. Smyrna 573 II + II 2 = OGIS 229 II = Schmitt (1969), 163–72 (§492), ll. 64–5: *καὶ πολιτεύσομαι μεθ' ὁμονοίας ἀστασιάστως κατὰ τοὺς Σμυρναίων νόμους καὶ τὰ ψηφίσματα τοῦ δ[ή]μου* ('and I shall be a citizen, with concord and without faction, according to the laws of the Smyrnaeans and the decrees of the *demos*').

[5] In the Greek and Roman tradition, the right to live according to one's own laws is conceivable only regarding the citizens of a *polis*. It is, indeed, one of the main aspects of civic status: characteristic, in this sense, is the concession by Eumenes II of Pergamon to the inhabitants of Tyriaion in the first half of the second century BCE. See SEG 47, 1745, ll. 26–8: *συγχωρῶ καὶ ὑμῖν καὶ τοῖς μεθ' ὑμῶν συνοικοῦσιν ἐνχωρίοις εἰς ἓν πολίτευμα συνταχ[θ]ῆναι καὶ νόμοις τε χρῆσθαι ἰδίοις* ('I grant both you and the native people living with you to organize yourselves into one citizen body and to use your own laws'). See also the commentary in Jonnes & Rici (1997), Schuler (1999), and Boffo (2001).

[6] Cf. the reference to these *patrioi nomoi* in Herzog (1942): 5–8 (§2), see above n. 4.

[7] The idea finds an echo in Tacitus' famous characterization of Egypt in *Historiae* 1.11: *insciam legum, ignaram magistratuum* (ignorant of laws, unaware of magistracies).

[8] Particularly impressive is *Tituli ex corpore Ulpiani* 20.14: *Latinus Iunianus, item is, qui dediticiorum numero est, testamentum facere non potest: Latinus quidem, quoniam nominatim lege Iunia prohibitum est; is autem, qui dediticiorum numero est, quoniam nec quasi civis Romanus testari potest, cum sit peregrinus, nec quasi peregrinus, quoniam nullius certae civitatis civis est, ut secundum leges civitatis suae testetur* ('A Junian Latin, as well as someone who counts among the *dediticii*, cannot make testament; the (Junian) Latin, because it is explicitly forbidden by the *lex Iunia;* he who counts among the *dediticii*, because he cannot make testament as a Roman citizen, being a foreigner, nor as a foreigner, not being citizen of any specific city following the laws of which he may give testament'). That the *dediticii*, and those assimilated to them *(dediticiorum numero)*, for instance by the *lex Aelia Sentia*, could not make any kind of testament is certain (cf. Gaius, *Inst.* 3.75 for the *dediticii Aliani*, even if written from the point of view of the right to make a Roman testament), but the argumentation in *Tituli ex corpore Ulpiani* implies that this was also the case of all *peregrini nullius civitatis* (cf. also, even if possibly written after 212, Ulpian, *Trusts* 1 (D. 32.1.2)), against everything the papyrological evidence tells us. The papyri have brought to us an enormous amount of testaments made in the Egyptian chora by those who had no citizenship, both in the properly testamentary form of Greek *diatheke* and in the

this problem, which I have discussed elsewhere,[9] but will confine my attention to the situation after the *C(onstitutio) A(ntoniniana)*:[10] how could peregrine law survive the virtual disappearance of peregrines? And how did it continue to be applied now that everyone was Roman and therefore, one would expect, subjected to Roman law?

2. THE ROMANIZATION OF LEGAL LIFE IN THE EAST BEFORE AND AFTER THE *CA*

In the last few decades, there has been a tendency to minimize this problem or at least reassess its magnitude, emphasizing Romanization not only from 212 CE, but right from the birth of the Roman province of Egypt. This doctrinal shift regarding Egyptian legal history can be seen as part of a more general movement regarding the Romanity of the province of Egypt, famously spearheaded by Naphtali Lewis in Ann Arbor 1968 with his celebrated paper 'Greco-Roman Egypt: Fact or Fiction?',[11] and again, fifteen years later, as well-established doctrine, with the significant title: 'The Romanity of Roman Egypt: A Growing Consensus'.[12] This shift comes with important consequences for legal historians: it encourages the search for traces of Roman law in the rich Egyptian materials, and makes the papyrological evidence less easy for Roman law scholars to neglect.

In the same vein, when we arrive at the time of the *CA*, many important studies have tended to emphasize the many aspects in which local practice did in fact change in the decades after 212 CE. The studies of Antti Arjava on family law are

para-testamentary form of the Egyptian *divisio parentis inter liberos* (*dosis, meriteia, synchorema, diairesis*). These testaments were recognized as fully valid by the Roman administration: cf. only *Gnomon of the Idios Logos* §7, which requires only notarization (for all peregrines, as the documentary evidence confirms); among the numerous court decisions that presuppose the validity of such testamentary acts, CPR I.18 = SPP XX. 4 = MChr. 84 (124 CE Ptolemais Evergetis) and BGU XX. 2863 (after 133 CE Arsinoites), both adjudged by delegation of the prefect; and most notably P. Oxy. XLII 3015 (after 117 CE Oxyrhynchos), a collection of decisions of the prefect Sulpicius Similis on the conditions of the testamentary freedom of the *peregrini nullius civitatis* of the *chora* under their own laws (notice *πρὸς τοὺς Αἰγυπτίων νόμους* in l. 3, and *Αἰγύπτιος*, in l. 11–12: in the language of the second-century Roman administration—most conspicuously in the *Gnomon of the Idios Logos*—these are the *apolides* of the *chora*, as opposed to the *romaioi* and to the *astoi* of the *poleis*). The text in *Tituli ex corpore Ulpiani*, whoever its author, cannot be understood if not as a manifestation of the insularity that occasionally marks the jurisprudential work, disconnecting it (more or less consciously) from the provincial experience. An alternative explanation, that the text in *Tituli ex corpore Ulpiani* may have been written after 212, when the main examples of *apolides* are those in *opus publicum dati* and the *deportati* (Ulpian, *Trusts* 1 (D. 32.1.2), Marcian, *Institutes* 1 (D. 48.19.17.1)), is unlikely: cf. Avenarius (2005), 76–155, and Mattioli (2012), for a discussion of the problematic composition history of the *Tituli*.

[9] Alonso (2013).

[10] For a useful overview of the enormous literature on the *Constitutio Antoniniana* in the first decades of the twentieth century, see Sasse (1962) and (1965). Since then, see Sherwin-White (1973), Rubin (1975), Greco (1977), Wolff (1976), Mastino (1984), Pinna Parpaglia (1995), Ruggieri (1999), Buraselis (2007), Mastino (2013), Ando (2016), Imrie (2018). For the dating problem, see the summary in Mélèze Modrzejewski (2014), 299–300.

[11] Lewis (1970). [12] Lewis (1984).

representative of this tendency.[13] Yet Arjava's confinement to family law, yields, I fear, a rather partial picture. Family, inheritance and status are—for reasons that we shall come back to (infra §7)—areas where a real attempt to adjust to Roman law is clearly perceivable after 212 CE. If we move away from these areas, to the field of contracts, credit and securities, the problem that puzzled Mitteis, Arangio-Ruiz and Schönbauer is impossible to ignore. It is striking how many practices that challenged the most basic principles of Roman law continued to be common and accepted after 212 CE.

Here, a qualitative rather than merely quantitative approach is, I believe, necessary: it is striking not just how in these fields the peregrine elements prevail over the few adjustments, but even more how deeply incompatible with Roman law some of the local practices are. To mention only a few among the most obvious examples:

a) Direct agency is attested in the papyri in forms and contexts that would have been radically excluded under Roman law. The examples, studied already by Leopold Wenger, go well into the sixth century both for legal transactions and court representation.[14]
b) Credit assignment (excluded as such in Roman law, which only knew novation and court representation as surrogates)[15] through a simple deed of cession (*parachoresis*) between the assignor and the assignee was common practice in the Hellenistic world, treated as valid in the edict of Tiberius Iulius Alexander,[16] and attested in Egypt well beyond the *CA*.[17]
c) Both before and after the *CA*, loans—and in truth any money debt contracted as a fictitious loan—could be enforced in Egypt without a declaratory trial: direct execution was always possible (on specific items, through *enechyrasia* and *embadeia*,[18] not through auction of the debtor's entire estate, as in the Roman *iurisdictio ordinaria*), as long as the loan was documented in a notarial deed. Not only the direct enforcement is remarkable, but also the requirement of a written document that thus becomes a deed with 'executive force'.

[13] Arjava (1996), (1998), (1999a), (1999b). An overview, in Arjava (2014). In a nutshell, his position, as formulated in Arjava (1999b), 204 is 'daß seit der Mitte des dritten Jahrhunderts Ägypten an der römischen Rechtsgeschichte teilgenommen hat. Das heißt: die Bewohner des Niltales haben ihre neue Rechtsordnung beachtet und haben versucht, die alten Begriffe den veränderten Verhältnissen anzupassen.'

[14] Wenger (1906). Cf. Mitteis (1912), 260–4.

[15] Kaser (1971), 652–5.

[16] OGIS II 669, l. 15: . . . *ἐπειδὴι ἔνιοι προφάσει τῶν δημοσίων καὶ ἀλλότρια δάνεια παραχωρούμενοι εἴς τε τὸ πρακτόρειόν τινας παρέδοσαν καὶ εἰς ἄλλας φυλακάς* . . . (' . . . Whereas some [officials] have also had loans of others assigned to themselves under pretence of public obligations . . . '). Translation from Lewis. The fact that the edict aimed at preventing a specific case of such cession (that of private debts in favour of public officials) confirms that cession as such was deemed fully valid. Cf. Chalon (1964), 110–22.

[17] See CPR I 10 = MChr. 145 (322–3 CE Hermopolis), where an Adelphios, gymnasiarch and *bouleutes* of Hermopolis, buys seven *arourae* of land, acquiring through the same sale document the right to exact the *ἐκφόρια καὶ φόρους* (l. 8) owed by the lessees from the beginning of the year.

[18] On this complex execution procedure in detail, see Jörs (1915), (1918), (1919). An overview may be found in Rupprecht (1997) and (2014).

The wide contractual freedom that Roman law granted to the parties in a legal transaction does not cover any of these phenomena: no private agreement could under Roman law (c) make a document enforceable without a trial, or (b) operate the transfer of a claim to a new creditor; and only in very specific cases, through the concession of an *actio utilis*, could stipulations or consensual contracts concluded for third parties (a) directly bestow rights or obligations on them.

But even if we go back to family law, things are much messier than one would expect. *Patria potestas* is here a good example and potentially a rather traumatic one, since it deprives everyone whose father still lives from legal capacity and therefore from all property:

a) On the one hand, immediately after the *CA* we see both old citizens and Aurelii referring to their children as 'under their power according to the Roman laws' (*ὑπὸ τῇ χειρὶ κατὰ τοὺς Ῥωμαίων νόμους*, in short, *ὑποχείριοι*).[19] We even have instances of emancipation among the Aurelii. In one of these (CPR VI 78, 265 CE), the emancipation was made so that a daughter could acquire her maternal inheritance, without it devolving into the property of the father: in fact, the mother herself had appointed the daughter as heir under the condition of her emancipation.[20] By doing this, the mother followed a legal strategy that we find in Modestinus, in Scaevola and in a rescript of Caracalla:[21] A strategy to which only someone aware of the lack of legal capacity of *liberi in potestate* would resort.

[19] In chronological order: BGU VII 1578 (second–third century, Philadelphia), P. Diog. 18 = P. Lond. inv. 2540 + P. Harr. I 68 (225 CE, Philadelphia [?]), P. Gen. I 44 = MChr. 215 (259 CE, Arsinoites), P. Oxy XIV 1703 (261 CE, Oxyrhynchos), P. Oxy XLI 2951 (267 CE, Oxyrhynchos); SB XX 14681 (after 276 CE, Oxyrhynchos), P. Oxy XIV 1642 (289 CE, Oxyrhynchos), P. Oxy IX 1208 (291 CE, Oxyrhynchos), P. Oxy X 1268 (third century, Oxyrhynchos), SB I 5692 (third century, Oxyrhynchos), SB XVIII 13322 (third century, Oxyrhynchos), SB X 10728 (318 CE, Oxyrhynchos), P. Oxy. LIV 3758 (325 CE, Oxyrhynchos), P. Panop. 28 = SB XII 11221 (329 CE, Panopolis), SB XXIV 15913 (fourth century, Arsinoites). The Greek term, intriguingly evocative of the archaic Roman *manus*, appears so suddenly and without concurrence of others, that it seems clear it must have been introduced by some official source.

[20] CPR VI 78 = SB XXVI 16717 (265 CE, Hermopolis), ll. 3–8: . . . *ἐπεὶ ἡ μήτηρ μο[υ Αὐρηλία Διοσκοροῦς ἀπελευθέρα Δημητρίου - c.10 -] [..]... αὐτῆς ὑπεστήσατο ἐμέ τε καὶ ἕτερόν μου ὁμομήτριον ἀδελφ[ὸν Αὐρήλιον Νεῖλον κληρονόμους αὐτῆς - c.18 -] [..]..σης τῆς πατρικῆς ἐξουσίας ἢ εἰ μὴ τοῦτο γείνοιτο, τὸ μέρος μου τ[ῆς κληρονομίας εἰς τὸν προκείμενον ἀδελφόν μου καταντῆσαι - c.3 -] [με]νης μου κατὰ δὲ τὸ βούλημα ἐντὸς τῆς προθεσμία[ς] ἀπολυθῆν[αι τῆς πατρικῆς ἐξουσίας ὑπὸ τοῦ πατρός μου διὰ τῶν γραμμάτων, ὧν] [τ]ὸ ἀντίγραφον ὑποτάξασα ἐπιδίδωμί σοι ἀξιοῦσα ἐπισταλῆν[αι - c.50 -] μον καὶ προκείμενον Αὐρήλιον Νεῖλον ἀπελεύθερον, ἵν' εἰδ[ῇ - c.50 -]* ('. . . My mother [Aurelia Dioskorous, freedwoman of Demetrios . . .] instituted me and my other, maternal half-brother [Aurelius Neilos her heirs in equal shares on the condition that I shall be freed] from paternal power or, if this does not happen, she decreed that my share [of the inheritance should devolve on my above-mentioned brother]. As I have been freed [from paternal power by my father] in accordance with the will within the prescribed time [through a document whose] copy I attach below, I request you to let [. . .] the above-mentioned freedman Aurelius Neilos be informed of it, so that he knows [. . .]'). On the document, see Arjava (1999a).

[21] Scaevola, *Digest* 3 (D. 5.3.58): *Filius a patre emancipatus secundum condicionem testamenti matris adiit hereditatem, quam pater, antequam filium emanciparet, possedit fructusque ex ea possedit* . . . (A son who was emancipated by his father in compliance with a condition of his mother's will, entered upon the inheritance, which the father had possession of before he emancipated his son, and of which he had also obtained the profits . . .). Modestinus, *Excuses* 1. (D. 26.5.21.1): *Ἐὰν μήτηρ ἐπὶ ταύτῃ τῇ αἱρέσει γράψῃ υἱοὺς κληρονόμους ἐὰν ἀπολυθῶσι τῆς τοῦ πατρὸς ἐξουσίας, ἀπολυθέντων τούτων καὶ διὰ τοῦτο κληρονομησάντων αὐτὸς ὁ πατὴρ κουράτωρ χειροτονηθῆναι οὐ δύναται, κἂν βούληται, ἵνα μὴ ἄλλῃ*

b) And yet this lack of legal capacity is ignored, more or less consciously, in all the rest of our material. Children in power appear in the documents as owners; more decisively, they are recognized as such by public institutions, like the *agoranomeion*, the *katalogeion* in Alexandria and the property record offices.[22] *Patria potestas* appears in general reduced, as Taubenschlag has shown, to a sort of guardianship over minor children, with the father in fact frequently labelled as guardian.[23]

3. SCHÖNBAUER AGAINST ARANGIO-RUIZ

There is therefore no getting around the problem that puzzled Mitteis: how did peregrine law—that is, institutions and practices like direct agency, credit *parachoresis*, executive credit deeds, legal capacity of those whose father still lives—survive the virtual disappearance of *peregrini*? How could these locals, having become Romans, so blatantly defy Roman law?

Mitteis held,[24] as later did Arangio-Ruiz,[25] that local law had survived '*contra ius*', because of lack of interest or a certain tolerance on the part of the Roman authorities. In a bitter controversy with Arangio-Ruiz, Ernst Schönbauer argued that the Roman tolerance was conscious and official, and thus that the *iura*

ὁδῷ τοῦτο ὅπερ οὐκ ἠβουλήθη ἡ διαθεμένη γένηται. καὶ τοῦτο οὕτως ὑπὸ τοῦ θείου Σεβέρου νενομοθέτηται ('If a mother should appoint as heirs her children under the condition that they shall be free from paternal power, and they become free and heirs for this reason, their father cannot be appointed their curator, even if he wishes, in order to prevent what the testatrix was unwilling to take place from being done. This rule was established by the Divine Severus.'). Antoninus, C. 6.25.3: *Idem A. (Antoninus) Maxentio et aliis. Si mater vos sub condicione emancipationis heredes instituit et, priusquam voluntati defunctae pareretur, sententiam pater meruit vel aliter defunctus est, morte eius vel alio modo patria potestate liberati ius adeundae hereditatis cum sua causa quaesistis. S. prid. k. Mai. Sabino et Anullio conss.* (The same Emperor [Antoninus] to Maxentius and others. If your mother appointed you as heirs under the condition of your emancipation, and, before the will of the deceased was complied with, your father were condemned or died, and you were freed from his power by his death or in any other way, you have acquired the right to enter upon his estate.)

[22] P. Oxy. X 1268 (249 CE Oxyrhynchos): *apographe* for the registration in the *bibliotheke enkteseon* of a house acquired by means of *synchoresis* through the *katalogeion* in Alexandria; Aurelius Petosiris sold the share belonging to his daughter 'under his power according to the Roman laws' (*. . . ἀπογράφομαι ἣν κατεγράφην κατὰ συγχώρη [σιν τελειωθεῖσαν διὰ τοῦ καταλογ]είου . . . παρὰ Αὐρηλίων Πετο[σίριος] . . . [. . . τὴν ὑπάρχουσαν τῇ] τοῦ Ṗẹṭọσ̣ί̣ριος θυγατρὶ Αὐρηλίᾳ Τασεῦτι . . . [. . . τοῦ πατρὸς ἔχοντος α]ὐτὴ ὑπὸ τῇ χειρὶ κατὰ τοὺς Ῥωμαίων νόμους . . . . . . οἰκίαν καὶ αἴθριον κτλ*, ll.4–11). P. Oxy. XIV 1703 (261 CE Oxyrhynchos): Aurelius Geminos, *agoranomos, bouleutēs,* re-transfers to Aurelius Apion, *kosmetes, bouleutēs*, a share of a house that the children *in potestate* of Geminos had bought through him from Apion (*ὁ[μ]ο[λογῶ] καταγεγραφέναι σοι ἀπ[ὸ] το[ῦ] | νῦν εἰς τὸν ἀεὶ χρόνον ὃ ἐώ[νη]ντε παρὰ σοῦ δι' ἐμοῦ ọ[ἱ ὑπο]|χẹ[ίρι]ọί μου υἱοί*, ll. 5–7). P. Oxy. XIV 1642 (289 CE Oxyrhynchos): Aurelius Demetrianus appoints Didymus to represent him at the nomination made by him of Aurelius Agathinus as his succesor in the office of agoranomos 'upon the security of his property and that of the children in his power' (*ἐπὶ πόρῳ ἑαυτοῦ καὶ τῶν ὑποχειρίων τέκνων*, l. 5). SB I 5692 (third century, Oxyrhynchos): *hypomnema* to the *archidikastes* for the *demosiosis* of a *cheirographon* whereby a father sells property belonging to his minor son *in potestate* (*ὁμολογῶ πεπρακέναι σοι [ἀπὸ τοῦ νῦ]ν εἰς τ[ὸ]ν ἀẹị χρόνον τὴν ὑπάρχουσαν τῷ ἀφήλικι μου υἱῷ καὶ [. . . . . . . ὑποχειρ]ίῳ κ̣ạ[τὰ τ]ọὺς νόμọụς Αὐρηλίῳ Λουκίῳ [τῷ] καὶ Σαραπίων[ι]*, ll. 11–13).

[23] Taubenschlag (1916).

[24] Mitteis (1891) 8, 160, and *passim*.

[25] Arangio-Ruiz (1941), (1947a), (1947b), (1948a), (1948b), (1950).

peregrinorum was accepted by the imperial authority as fully in force.[26] These two positions have for a long time dominated the discussion.

Many of the examples that I have already mentioned disprove Arangio-Ruiz's notion of a mere *de facto* tolerance. Children in power are recognized as owners by the *agoranomoi*, the Alexandrian *katalogeion*, the property record offices.[27] And, if we go back to the phenomena enumerated in Section 2 (above), direct agency (a) seems also to have been accepted in trial. Furthermore, the procedure (c) that secured the execution of credit deeds, inherited from the Ptolemies, was of course official: it involved the *archidikastes* in Alexandria, the *strategoi* in the *nomoi*, and was formally presided over by the prefect. Not only this: all the other institutions and practices of peregrine law that continue appearing in the papyri after the *Constitutio Antoniniana* would not have survived for decades if they had been challenged in court. Considering all this, it is difficult not to side with Schönbauer and conclude that the Roman tolerance was official, at least (we will come back to this soon) at the level of the local administration.

The question is then how such a survival *de iure* of the *iura peregrinorum* could have been articulated. Schönbauer turned to the notion of double citizenship,[28] making this notion into one of the most disputed in our discipline. This poses especial problems in Egypt because until 200 CE most inhabitants of the province were *peregrini nullius civitatis*, lacking any citizenship[29], and it is by no means clear that Severus' concession of a *boule* to the *metropoleis* in that year[30] changed the *status civitatis* of the inhabitants of the Egyptian *chora*.[31]

4. THE *ΜΕΝΟΝΤΟΣ*-CLAUSE IN P. GISS. 40

A new door opened for Schönbauer's theory in the late fifties, with the discovery of the *tabula Banasitana* (ILMaroc 94).[32] The tabula records two grants of citizenship in favour of two generations of a prominent Mauretanian family: father and son, with their respective families, received—from Marcus Aurelius, first with Verus and then with Commodus—the Roman citizenship '*salvo iure gentis*'. These words, '*salvo iure gentis*', led William Seston to a new reconstruction of the notorious μένοντος clause in P. Giss. 40.[33]

The clause had been the object of innumerable integrations.[34] In Mitteis,[35] as in Meyer,[36] we find μ̣ένοντος | [παντὸς γένους πολιτευμ]άτων̣, i.e. in Latin '*manente quocumque genere rerum publicarum*', referring to the subsistence of the pre-existent *civitates*, even as their members are in theory subjected to the private

[26] Schönbauer (1931), (1934), (1937). [27] See above n. 22.

[28] Schönbauer (1949), (1952), (1960); cf. Arangio-Ruiz (1950).

[29] The argument is rightly emphasized by Wolff (2002), 127 and n. 78, also against Segrè's unfounded assumption of a *politeuma* of these *peregrini nullius civitatis* of the *chora*.

[30] Jouguet (1911), 344–50; Jones (1937), 329–38.

[31] Arangio-Ruiz (1948a), 97 = Arangio-Ruiz (1974), 268–9.

[32] Seston & Euzennat (1971); Gascou & de Kisch (1982), 76–91 (§94).

[33] Seston & Euzennat (1961), cf. also Seston (1966), 878–9.

[34] Cf. Sasse (1958), 13–14, further references in Wolff (2002), 124 n. 58.

[35] Mitteis (1912), 426 (§377). [36] Meyer (1920), 2 with n. to l. 8.

law of the Romans. Seston proposed instead *μένοντος* | *[παντὸς δικαίου τῶν πολιτευμ]άτων*—i.e. *salvo omnis iure gentium*—and the widely followed reconstruction of Oliver goes in the same direction: *μένοντος [τοῦ νόμου* (or, better, *δικαίου) τῶν πολιτευμ]άτων*.[37] In an interpretation of the clause that Hans Julius Wolff had already proposed before the discovery of the *tabula Banasitana*,[38] Caracalla's concession, according to Seston, would have explicitly safeguarded the former legal traditions of the new citizens.

We will soon return to this possible safeguard clause. For the moment, leaving aside the uncertainty of Seston's restitution, it is enough to keep in mind that, as often observed,[39] '*salvo iure gentis*' may well have referred in the *Tabula Banasitana* to the liturgical and fiscal duties (and privileges) of the newly enfranchised towards their *gens* of origin (that of the Zegrenses), rather than to their own legal tradition.[40] Where in the two imperial *epistulae* we read simply '*salvo iure gentis*' (ll. 12, 20), the official recording in the *commentarius civitate romana donatorum* adds (l. 37) '*sine diminutione tributorum et vectigalium populi et fisci*' (without a decrease in the tributes and taxes of the people and the treasury). This suggests, in fact, a fiscal context where neither the duties towards the community of origin (the *ius gentis*) nor those towards Rome (*tributa et vectigalia*) are to be affected by the status acquired by the newly enfranchised: citizenship is granted without *immunitas* (*ἀνεισφορία*) before the Roman *aerarium* and *fiscus*[41] and without detriment to the duties and privileges of the beneficiaries within their community of origin. A similar caveat seems likely in Caracalla's constitution: in fact, as far as the position of the Aurelii

[37] Oliver (1989), 504, cf. also Oliver (1972), 340, and Oliver (1978), 405.

[38] Wolff (1956), 367–71. Already Schönbauer (1931), 313 had integrated the clause as safeguard of the local law, under the unwarranted assumption of the existence of *politeumata* of the peregrines.

[39] D'Ors (1953), 179–93. Wolff (1976), 87–99. Mélèze Modrzejewski (2014), 322–3. A detailed discussion may be found in Sherwin-White (1973), 91–2.

[40] Together with what follows here, an argument in Sherwin-White (1973), 94 carries a certain weight against the idea that *salvo iure gentis* allows the enfranchised in the *tabula Banasitana* to keep their personal peregrine laws. The second request (approved in the *epistula* at ll. 14–21) refers solely to the wife and children of Iulianus, *princeps Zegrensium*: clearly, because he himself already had Roman citizenship—he is likely the Iulianus mentioned in the first place among the children who, together with their parents, received Roman citizenship in the first *epistula* (l. 11). It is difficult not to link this petition with the catastrophic impact of a divergent status of father and children on the inheritance rights of the latter under Roman law. Under Roman law, peregrines—such as, initially, Iulianus' children—were completely excluded from the inheritance of citizens, since they lacked the so-called *testamenti factio*: not only as heirs but also as beneficiaries of any bequest in the form of *legatum* (Gaius, *Inst.* 2. 110) or (since Hadrian: see Gaius, *Inst.* 2.285) of *fideicommissum*. The problem would not arise if Iulianus' succession did not fall under Roman law, if the clause *salvo iure gentis* under which he had been enfranchised years before (l. 12) had meant that he could continue living under the *ius* of the Zegrenses.

[41] Fiscal immunity, i.e. the full equation of the enfranchised with the *cives optimo iure*, is made explicit when granted: so, for instance, in the case of Seleucus' enfranchisement by Octavian (IGLSyr. 3, 1, 718 = FIRA I. 55): *πολειτείαν καὶ ἀνεισφορίαν τῶν ὑπαρχόν[των πάντων ? δίδ]ομεν οὕτω[ς ὡς οἵτινες τῶ]ι ἀρίστωι νόμωι ἀρίστωι δὲ δικαίωι πολεῖται [Ῥωμαῖοι ἀνείσ]φο[ρ]οί εἰσιν, α[ὐτοῖς τε στρατείας λει]τουργ[ία]ς τε δημοσίας ἁπάσης πάρε[σις ἔστω]* (ll. 20–3, ed. Raggi (2004)) (We grant citizenship and tax exemption on all (?) property like to those who are Roman citizens exempt of taxes by the best law and the best right, and let them be released from military and all public service).

before the *fiscus* goes, there is evidence that they kept paying the same *capitatio* (*laographia*) of the *peregrini*.[42]

5. ADJUSTMENTS IN LEGAL PRACTICE AFTER 212 CE

Beyond these doubts, there is a more decisive reason why the proposals of Schönbauer and Seston seem untenable: it does not seem possible to make them compatible with the immediate adjustments to Roman law that we see everywhere in the papyri, together with the continuities.

In fact, no safeguard clause or double citizenship construction spared the Aurelii from adjusting to their new situation, particularly in the areas of status, family and inheritance, traditionally dominated by the so-called personality principle (see Section 7, below). We have already discussed (see Section 2, above) how emphatically the subjection of the children to the *patria potestas* is underlined in the documents. Women no longer appear as guardians (*epitropoi*) but as assisting a male guardian (*epakolouthētriai*).[43] Although some siblings still present themselves as married a few years after the *CA*, sibling marriage then vanishes from our sources.[44] Even in contractual law, which continued virtually untouched, one needs to consider the new omnipresence of the stipulatory clause, to which we shall return soon (Section 8, below).

Probably the most revealing example of immediate adjustment is the testament. The adoption of Latin, the mention of the *mancipatio familiae* (although it is obviously unlikely that the actual ritual was performed), the consular dating, all this is already in place in the two earliest wills after the *CA*: P. Bagnall 5 (213 CE, Oxyrhynchos), P. Oxy. XXII 2348 (224 CE, Oxyrhynchos).[45] The adherence to Roman forms relaxed only when Alexander Severus allowed the use of Greek, as

[42] SB VI 9128 (= P. Mich. inv. 5503c) (213 CE Karanis), cf. Pearl (1951): notice the onomastic change, from Liberalis son of Ptolemaios in l. 4 to (ὁ α(ὐτὸς)) Aurelius Liberalis in l. 7. The case of P. Lugd. Bat. XIX 14 (248 CE Exo Pseur, Arsinoites) is different, where the *laographoumenos* does not present himself as Aurelius but still under a Greek name, Artemidoros son of Diodoros. The question of the extension of Roman citizenship in Egypt after 212, raised by documents like this one—and more pressingly by the reference to the *Aigyptioi* in the 215 CE Antonine constitution in P. Giss. 40 II, ll. 16–29, and also by the distinction between *Romaioi* and *Aigyptioi* almost three centuries later in SEG 9 356—cannot be discussed here. On this matter, see Marotta (2014); an English version is available in Marotta (2017).

[43] The last attestation of a woman *epitropos* may be found in P. Oxy. III 495 (182–9 CE, Oxyrhynchos). In SB XVI 12288 (195 CE, Ptolemais Evergetis), despite Gagliardi (2012), 425 n. 9, 446 n. 65, the *epitropos* is not the mother (who is deceased: the document concerns her inheritance) but Ploution, a brother: see Bagnall & Worp (1994). *Epakolouthētriai* are attested from 132 CE (PSI X 1159, Ptolemais Evergetis): I shall leave aside here the question whether they are an early adaptation to the Roman legal conceptions or an autonomous development.

[44] Mélèze Modrzejewski (1964). Theognostos appears as married to his sister Aurelia Dioscorous in a 217 CE census-return (P. Lond. III. 936, p. 30, Hermopolis), and still in a 234–5 CE receipt for wet-nursing wages (P. Pintaudi 42, Hermopolis, l. 5). Local institutions less incompatible with Roman law could survive: 'unwritten marriages' are still attested in the fourth century (P. Oxy. VI 903).

[45] Both papyri contain Greek versions of clearly Roman testaments: leaving aside other aspects, see the *mancipatio familiae* (P. Bagnall 5, ll. 7–9, P. Oxy. XXII 2348, ll. 41–4) and the consular date (P. Bagnall 5, ll. 10–12, P. Oxy. XXII 2348, ll. 44–8).

we know through SPP XX 35 (235 CE):[46] here, we not only have a testament made directly in Greek and in papyrus without *tabulae*, but one that also fails to mention *mancipatio familiae* and has only six witnesses.[47]

These initial, hurried adaptations in every field of the law would not have happened if Caracalla's edict had included a safeguard clause for local law, if the *μένοντος*-clause had meant '*salvo iure gentis*' in the sense understood by Seston. The same is true about Schönbauer's argument concerning double citizenship: if the survival of local law had been the result of this construction, then no adaptation at all would have been necessary.

6. *MOS REGIONIS*

A much wider consensus exists today that the doctrine of customary law that emerges in the Roman legal sources in the mid-second century may have helped Roman tolerance, making it possible to treat peregrine institutions and practices as *mos regionis*.[48] The idea was indefatigably championed by the late Joseph Mélèze Modrzejewski,[49] and more recently from a different point of view by Caroline Humfress.[50] It has found wide echo among Romanists too, including

[46] SPP XX 35 = PER 1702 = SB I 5294 (235 CE, Hermopolites), ll. 12–14: . . . [. . . *τὴν διαθήκην ἐποίησα γράμμασιν] Ἑλ̣λ̣ηνικοῖς ἀκο[λού]θως τῇ θείᾳ κ̣[ελε]ύ̣σ̣[ει τοῦ κυρίου ἡμῶν Αὐτοκράτορος Μάρκου Αὐρηλίου] Σεουήρου Ἀλεξάνδρ[ο]υ Εὐσεβοῦς Εὐτ̣υχ[οῦς Σεβαστοῦ . . .*] (. . . [. . . I have made this testament in] Greek in accordance with the divine [decree of our Lord Emperor Marcus Aurelius] Severus Alexander Pius Felix Augustus . . .).

[47] With the Greek language, the old local traditions came back so that testaments soon became, from a Roman point of view, as unorthodox as that of Aurelia Eustorgis (P. Lips. I 29 = MChr. 318, 295 CE, Hermopolis): (a) the testament is given as a codicil in epistolary form, and with the assistance of a third party (!), even though the testatrix is free from guardianship ([*Αὐρηλία Εὐστόργις*] . . . *μετὰ συνεστῶτος [ἐμαυτῇ Αὐρηλίου] Τ̣ριαδέλφου . . . τῇ ἐμαυτῆς θυγατρὶ Αὐρηλίᾳ [Ὑ]π̣ε̣ρ̣εχίῳ τῇ καὶ Ἀμμων̣ᾳ̣[ρίῳ χαίρειν]*, ll. 1–4: 'Aurelia Eustorgis . . . with the assistance of Aurelius Triadelphos . . . to my own daughter, Aurelia Hyperechion also called Ammonarion, greetings'); (b) the heir is instituted 'according to all the laws', a vague expression that seems designed for paying lip service the otherwise ignored Roman rules (*κληρονόμον σε μ[ό]ν[η]ν κατὰ πάντας τοὺς ν[ό]μους καθίστημι*, l. 5); (c) the validity of the testament is equated to that of one given before a public notary (to one, that is, of the type that the peregrines used to make before the *CA*), and the whole document is covered (unnecessarily in a testament, where no obligations are incurred) by a stipulatory clause (*τὸ ἑλληνικὸν [[βούλημα κύρι]ον ὃ̣ καὶ δισσόν σοι π[ροηκ]άμην, ὡς ἐν δημοσίῳ ἀρχείῳ κατακείμενον, καὶ ἐπε[ρωτ]ηθ(εῖσα) νοοῦσα καὶ φρονοῦσα ὡμολό(γησα)*, l. 16–17: 'this Greek testament, which I have issued to you in double copy, is valid as if deposited in a public archive, and having been asked the formal question, of sound intention and mind, I have agreed').

[48] The same construction must be rejected as an explanation of the survival of peregrine law in Egypt and the East in general after the Roman annexation: the annexation, in fact, predates by more than a century the emergence of the idea of customary law in the Roman legal tradition. On this matter in detail, see Alonso (2013). The idea of customary law, that is, the notion that customs become law through sustained usage, was also alien to the Greek legal tradition: see the careful review of the question by Wolff (1968), 118: 'Wir haben gesehen, wie dem griechischen Rechtsbewußtsein die Vorstellung, daß der bloße Brauch als solcher bindendes Recht schaffen könne, zu allen Zeiten fremd geblieben ist.'

[49] Mélèze Modrzejewski (1970), 353–7, again in Mélèze Modrzejewski (2014), 7–16, 235–40, 311–18.

[50] Humfress (2012).

Max Kaser.[51] Indeed, it has been suggested that the development of the doctrine of customary law in the second century may have been fostered by the legal diversity in the provinces.[52]

In my opinion, however, two circumstances make a certain skepticism advisable:

a) In the imperial constitutions of late antiquity, as also before in the texts of the classical jurists, *consuetudo* is usually (as Jean Gaudemet underlined)[53] the administrative practice, and very rarely refers to the legal practice of the population.[54] The evidence is so overwhelming that Gaudemet concluded: 'if custom has an important role in the Later Roman Empire, it is essentially outside the realm of private law'.
b) The second reason concerns the attitude of the third-century Imperial chancellery towards local legal traditions, such as it can be reconstructed from the rescripts preserved in Justinian's Code. Occasionally, some rules are relaxed (for instance, those regarding the stipulatory form),[55] but, in general, the chancellery implacably applied Roman law when confronted with non-Roman institutions and practices, often compromising the goals that the parties had wanted to secure, and quite likely the general trust in the law itself. Peregrine institutions and practices that could not be translated into Roman categories or did not fulfil the requirements of their Roman correlative were simply rejected.

Two examples will be enough here:

i) Every student of Roman law knows Alexander Severus' rescript denying effect to any penalty stipulated for the case of divorce: *libera matrimonia esse antiquitus placuit* (Alexander, C. 8.38.2, 223 CE).[56] An admirable text,

[51] Kaser (1971), 220 and n. 32.

[52] Nörr (1969), 359–60. The foundational Julian, *Digest* 84 (D. 1.3.32), like other key jurisprudential texts on *mos* and *consuetudo*, refers to local customs: on the text, see Alonso (2013), 379–86. On custom in the Roman legal tradition before Julian, see Alonso (2013), 365–79.

[53] Gaudemet (1956), 149–50.

[54] This prevalence of administrative practice in the use of the term *consuetudo* is constant since the late Republic: see Cicero, *In Verrem* II 3.6.15, 3.15.38, 3.57.131, 3.62.142, 3.98.227, where *consuetudo* (*superiorum, a maioribus tradita*) refers to the constant practice of Verres' predecessors in the government of Sicily in keeping the collection of the *decuma* in line with the regulations of the *lex Hieronica*. See also *In Verrem* II 5.22.57 (number of *laudationes pro reo*), *pro Quinctio* 6.28 (*missio in possessionem*), *pro Balbo* 7.17 (concession of citizenship), *pro Caecina* 8.23 (interdict). Most jurisprudential texts on local customs refer also to administrative practice: Ulpian, *On the Duties of the Proconsul* 1 (D.1.16.4.5) (*ingressus in provinciam* of the governor); Paul, *On the Edict* 6 (D. 3.4.6 pr.) (local *honores*); Paul, *On the Edict* 52 (D. 39.4.4.2) (*vectigalia*); Callistratus, *Judicial Inquiries* 1 (D. 50.2.11) (decurionate); Callistratus, *Judicial Inquiries* 4 (D. 22.5.3.6) (witness summons). Pliny, *Epistulae* 10.114–15 also concerns a question of public law. Further examples and discussion may be found in Kaser (1939), 76–81.

[55] See Section 8, below, and n. 78.

[56] Alexander, C. 8.38.2: *Imp. Alexander A. Menophilo. Libera matrimonia esse antiquitus placuit. ideoque pacta, ne liceret divertere, non valere et stipulationes, quibus poenae inrogarentur ei qui divortium fecisset, ratas non haberi constat. PP. iii non. Febr. Maximo ii et Aeliano conss.*: 'The Emperor Alexander A. to Menophilus. From ancient times it has been established that marriages must be free: therefore agreements providing that it shall not be lawful to divorce are invalid, and it is certain that

but also one that wrecks a long tradition of penalties protecting the wife against unjustified repudiation in Greek marriage contracts.[57]

ii) As Pringsheim has shown,[58] the Greek law of sale is based on the principle that buyers acquire by paying the price, regardless of *traditio*. Greek sale deeds are built on this principle in the whole East, throughout the entire Hellenistic and Roman eras: they document the sale and the payment, not the *traditio*. Under this principle, if I do not receive the price, I am entitled to recover the property and, if the property happens to be a female slave, also the offspring she may have had in the meantime. This pretension, and with it the whole Greek law of sale, is labelled by Diocletian's chancellery 'unlawful and unheard of' (*incivile atque inusitatum*: Diocletian and Maximian, C. 3.32.12, 293 CE)[59] because it ignores the effect of the *traditio*.

If these peregrine traditions were to be respected as *mos regionis*, that is a doctrine that the jurists of the chancellery, and the Emperor himself, seem to ignore. The practice of the provincial jurisdiction and administration, at least in Egypt, was more accommodating, but certainly not because from the prefect to the lowest official they all adhered to a doctrine that Emperor and chancellery ignored: they were more flexible simply because, unlike the jurists of the chancellery, they were on the ground, and because this had been the policy in the province for two centuries; after all, it was imperial law that provincial governors should not depart from well-established jurisdictional and administrative usage.[60]

stipulations whereby penalties are imposed on those who divorce are not to be considered valid.' Cf. Kaser (1977), 91–2. On the rule and its limits in Roman law, Knütel (2014).

[57] See, for example, the *hemiolion* in BGU IV 1050 (12–11 BCE, Alexandria) and the early first-century-CE petition P. Oxy II. 281 = MChr. 66 (20–50 CE Oxyrhynchos); after the *CA*, the ten gold coins of P. Ross. Georg III 28 (343 or 358 CE, Arsinoites). Notice the Greek name of the addressee in Alexander's rescript.

[58] Pringsheim (1950).

[59] Diocletian and Maximian, C. 3.32.12: *Idem AA et CC [Impp. Diocletianus et Maximianus] Alexandro. Incivile atque inusitatum est quod postulas, ut mancipium, quod tradidisti et hoc modo dominium eius transtulisti, invito eo ex nostro rescripto tibi adsignetur. unde intellegis semel ancilla emptoris facta filios etiam postea natos eius dominium sequi, cuius mater eorum eo tempore fuit. sane de pretio, si non te hoc probatum fuerit recepisse, conveni adversarium tuum. D. vi id. April. AA conss.* ('The same Augusti and Caesars [Diocletian and Maximian] to Alexander. What you demand is unlawful and unheard of, namely, that a slave, whom you handed over and thereby transferred ownership of, should be assigned to you without his [the purchaser's] consent by Our rescript. Hence you understand that once a female slave has become the purchaser's property, the children subsequently born to her fall under the ownership of the person to whom the mother then belonged. You can of course sue your adversary for the price, if it should be proven that you have not received it.') The Diocletianic chancellery was often confronted with this question, and tirelessly reminded the petitioners that the *traditio*, not the payment of the price, makes buyers acquire: C. 4.38.8, C. 4.49.6, C. 4.38.9, C. 4.38.12.

[60] Alexander, C. 8.52(53).1: *Imp. Alexander A. Apro <evocato>. 'Praeses provinciae probatis his, quae in oppido frequenter in eodem genere controversiarum servata sunt, causa cognita statuet. nam et consuetudo praecedens et ratio quae consuetudinem suasit custodienda est, et ne quid contra longa consuetudinem fiat, ad sollicitudinem suam revocabit praeses provinciae.' PP. vi k. April. Iuliano et Crispino conss.* (224 CE) (= C.8.10.3, iunge C. 8.1.1) : 'The Emperor Alexander to Aper, veteran. The provincial governor shall decide upon hearing the case, having examined what has usually been observed in the town in controversies of the same kind. For the existing custom and the reasons that gave rise to it should be upheld, and the provincial governor must take care that nothing be done

7. THE LEGAL PRACTICE OF ROMAN CITIZENS BEFORE THE *CA*

All the approaches we have reviewed share one basic assumption: that in the absence of an a*d hoc* legal dispositive or construction—a safeguard clause, double citizenship, *mos regionis*—the new situation would have required the population to submit in every aspect of their legal life to the rules of Roman law.

This assumption, if we reflect on it, turns out to be much less natural than it may seem at first sight. Let us, in fact, consider how those in Egypt who had Roman citizenship behaved before the *CA*.[61] The main lines are easily recognizable: these 'Romans' adhered to Roman law in the fields of inheritance, family and status, and seem to have felt free to follow the peregrine practice in everything else (property, contracts, credit, securities, . . .).

Inheritance, family and status are the fields that in general in antiquity come closer to what we might anachronistically call the personality principle.[62] A cursory look at the *Gnomon of the Idios logos* is enough to see how self-evident the personality principle was in these fields. The principle works in both directions, for the peregrines as well as for the Romans. Peregrines are to be judged in these matters in accordance with their own laws, as we read in the collection of court decisions of the prefect Sulpicius Similis in P. Oxy XLII 3015.[63] Those who have Roman citizenship, instead, leave more or less impeccable Roman testaments, no matter how cumbersome the Roman formalities must have appeared to people who were Greek by culture. So, for instance, to mention just one among the Roman testaments that have survived in Egypt, the freedman Tiberius Claudius Alexander, in P. Oxy XXXVIII 2857 (134 CE). His testament was originally written in Greek, with the subscription 'I, Tiberius Claudius Alexander, have read my will, according to which I wished my Roman will to be written.'[64] And, in fact, at the left of this Greek text, traces are left of the Latin

against long-standing custom.' As Humfress (2012), 31 has shown, it is again (see n. 54, above) to administrative usage that *consuetudo* refers here: the case concerns a ruined house turned into a garden, probably without the consent of magistrates and neighbours.

[61] The rather scarce Romans present in the province were mostly freedmen, soldiers, veterans, and members of the Greek elite: Taubenschlag (1959) I, 181–93. An overview of the patterns of their legal practice may be found in Taubenschlag (1959) I, 194–228; Wolff (2002), 149–72.

[62] Wolff (2002), 149–50.

[63] P. Oxy. XLII 3015 (early second century CE) ll. 1–5: [ca?]..[..] . . . [..] . . . .[*ca?*] [. . .]..*μọṿọ.κ*[*ca?*].[*ca?*]*υσι κάλλιστόν ἐστιν αὐτοὺς* [*δικ*]*αιοδοτεῖν π*[*ρὸ*]*ς τọὺς Αἰγυπτίων νόμους* [*ἐ*]*φ᾽ οἷς ἔξεστι κ*[*α*]*ὶ μεταδιατίθεσθαι. καλῶς δι*[*έθε*]*το ὁ τελευτής*[*α*]*ς*.: '. . . It is best that they judge in accordance with the laws of the Egyptians, under which it is also possible to modify the testament. The deceased made testament correctly.' The case seems to have concerned the possibility of changing a testament through its mere modification (*μεταδιατίθεσθαι*), which contrasted sharply with the entirely new testament that Roman law would have required (see, among many other texts, Ulpian on Sabinus [D. 28.1.21.1]: this explains the popularity of codicils, and of their confirmation *ex ante*). The emphatic 'it is better to judge them according to their own laws' suggests that one of the parties may have invoked the Roman rule. If so, the prefect's rejection would be even more remarkable: peregrines are to be judged in these matters not according to Roman law but *suis legibus*.

[64] P. Oxy. XXXVIII 2857, ll. 34–7 = ChLA XLVII 1413 (134 CE, Oxyrhynchos): (. . .) *Τιβέριος Κλαύδιος Ἀλέξανδρος ἀνέγνων μου τὴν διạθήκην πρὸς* [*ἣν*] *ἠθέλησα τὴν Ṛωμạϊκήν μοṿ γ*[*ρ*]*ạφῆναι.* [*συμ*]*φ̣ῳνῖ μοι* [*γ*]*ὰρ π̣ά̣ντα ὥ*[*ς πρ*]*ό̣κ*[*ιτ*]*αι.*

translation of the same testament. We therefore have here someone whose Latin was not good enough to have his testament made directly in that language, but who leaves, being a Roman citizen, a perfectly correct Roman testament.

In all other areas of the law, property and contracts in particular, Roman citizenship seems wholly irrelevant in our documents—those who have it act along the exact same lines as the peregrines. Only in the very few instances when Latin is used do we see Roman law being followed: most of these cases take place in a military milieu,[65] probably due to the availability of Latin notarial models in the army. Most of the Greek contracts made by Romans in Egypt contain nothing specifically Roman[66] They stick to the peregrine documentary forms, including those, like *synchoreseis*, *hypomnemata*, and bank-*diagraphai*, that have no equivalent in the Roman tradition.[67] Also regarding the content, they follow the local practice even when it is unheard of or aberrant from a Roman point of view: and thus we find also among Romans *parachōrēsis* of credits, direct agency, executive credit instruments, and many other peregrine practices that would have remained without effect if judged according to Roman law.[68] *Stipulatio*, instead, that most Roman of all contractual forms, is conspicuously absent among Romans, even in cases where Roman law would have required it, for instance for loan interests: in the whole of our evidence for Egypt and the Near East, there are only six instances of *stipulatio* among Romans before the *CA*.[69]

This phenomenon is not difficult to understand: it results, it seems to me, from notarization. Rome found in Egypt a tight network of notarial offices that had developed and refined the local legal practice into standard documentary models. The documents issued by these notaries enjoyed a special status that the Roman administration further fostered: so, for instance, no execution was possible on the basis of a credit document that had not been notarized;[70] and no property could be registered in the record office without a notarial deed of acquisition.[71] In Egypt, these restrictions applied to everyone, peregrines and Romans alike, and the natural consequence is that Roman citizens used the Hellenistic models provided by the local notaries as much as anyone else. Of course, all this would have been unthinkable if the Roman jurisdiction had had

[65] That is the case of the so-called soldiers' chirographs: Arangio-Ruiz (1948b), to which SB XVI 12609, and P. Duk. inv. 528 must be added. Most of the preserved Latin sale contracts also come from a military milieu (cf. CPL 120, PSI VI 729, and SB XVI 12609, and the thoroughly Roman P. Col. VIII 221).

[66] Most attempts to find Roman traits in these Greek contracts have been in vain: the cases of *acceptilatio*, stipulatory loan, and *receptum nautarum* enumerated by Taubenschlag (1959) I, 222, do not resist scrutiny. Only a small group of sale contracts, from Egypt and the Near East (P. Hamb. I 63, P. Turner 22, BGU III 887, P. Mich. IX 546, P. Dura 26), present convincing Roman elements.

[67] Sources in Wolff (2002), 164.

[68] Taubenschlag (1959) I, 224–5. Taubenschlag (1955), 310–12 (direct agency), 418–19 (*parachoresis* of credits). For distraint without trial involving Roman citizens, see in P. Berl. Leih. 10, BGU III 888.

[69] Four of them in Egypt (P. Mich. XV 707, P. Hamb. I 63, and the Latin contracts PSI VI 729, and P. Mich. VII 438), and two in the Near East (P. Turner 22, and BGU III 887). Even in the Latin loans SB XVI 12609, and P. Fouad. I 45, no stipulation covers the interest rate.

[70] *Gnomon* §105. Wolff (2002), 189–90.

[71] Wolff (1978), 174–5, 227–8.

any qualms in applying non-Roman law to the Roman citizens who followed it in their legal transactions.[72]

8. THE BEHAVIOUR OF THE AURELII: THE STIPULATORY CLAUSE

If now we ask ourselves to what extent the Aurelii may have felt compelled to adapt to their new civic status, it seems reasonable to assume that they would tend to follow in the footsteps of the old Romans, accommodating to Roman law in the sphere of inheritance, family and status, but feeling free to continue their previous peregrine practices in everything else, particularly in their contractual practice. This is almost an exact picture of what we find in our sources.[73] Almost, because the continuity that one would have expected in contractual practice is abruptly disrupted *c.*220 CE by the sudden ubiquity of the stipulatory clause.[74]

From *c.*220 CE, in fact, practically no document lacks the clause 'καὶ ἐπερωτηθεὶς ὡμολόγησα' (-σεν).[75] Although ὡμολόγησεν goes back to the Hellenistic *homologia* form, the emphasis on the question, ἐπερωτηθεὶς, leaves little doubt that this wants to be a Roman stipulation with formal question and answer. This is even more evident when the term *pistei* is added: then we have the Roman *fide promittis, fide promitto.*

Since *stipulatio* is rare in the papyri before the *CA* even among Romans,[76] its sudden omnipresence as the stipulatory clause in Egypt and the whole East after *c.*220 CE can hardly be a coincidence. It shows, *pace* Schönbauer, that even in the field of contracts a new anxiety arose among the local population, and certainly among the notaries, who rushed to include the clause in practically every single document they produced: the anxiety that things had changed, that peregrine law was no longer presentable in court without a Roman dress.

Yet the adaptation was carried out in the most perfunctory way: a thorough rethinking of the form and clauses of each contract was avoided[77] by appending to the whole document just three words, typically as a corollary of the *kyria*-clause.

[72] The incorrect assumption that provincial jurisdictional practice adhered mechanically in all areas of the law to the personality principle is not uncommon, even in highly regarded reference handbooks: Wieacker (2006), 160–1; Talamanca (1989), 513. For more nuanced views, see Wieacker (1988), 516–17, and Kaser (1971), 216–17, with references to further literature.

[73] For the adaptation regarding family and inheritance, see above Sections 2 (*patria potestas*) and 5 (maternal guardianship, sibling marriage, testaments). For the survival of contractual peregrine practice, also in forms that would have lacked any effect if judged according to Roman law, see above Section 2.

[74] Mitteis 1891: 485–91; Pringsheim 1961; Simon 1964.

[75] The clause is attested from the mid-second century: among peregrines, in SB XIV 12023 (2nd cent), l. 16, P. Oxy. VI 905 (170 CE), ll. 19–20, P. Eirene I 4 (178 CE) ll. 30–1, P. Dura 31 (204 CE) ll. 43–4; cf. also P. Yadin 20, 21, and 22; among Romans, in SB XIV 11705 (213 CE), l. 17, and SB XX 14628 (214–15 CE) ll. 11–12. What is new after *c.*220 is that we practically find no document without it.

[76] See above, n. 69 for the extant examples.

[77] So, rightly, Yiftach-Firanko (2009), 554: 'It certainly spared them the need of engaging the subtleties of the Roman contractual system. From this perspective, the appearance of the stipulatio clause may have checked, rather than promoted the Romanization of Greek contracts in Egypt.'

It is important to underline that this was in most cases unnecessary under Roman law, despite much modern speculation to the contrary:[78] not just because in legal acts from which no debt arises, like manumissions, testaments, petitions or tax returns, a stipulation is a legal absurdity; not merely because a sale, a lease, an interest-free deposit or loan are not *nuda pacta*, but perfectly enforceable under Roman law without the entire transaction being brought to a stipulation; but chiefly because since a rescript by Severus and Caracalla of 200 CE, seemingly issued during their time in Egypt, any promissory document drawn up in the presence of both parties was equivalent to a *stipulatio*, even if the document itself failed to mention that one had been concluded: a *promissio inter praesentes* is enough for the stipulatory question to be presumed.[79]

This imperial decision makes it unlikely that the practice of the stipulatory clause was caused, as it has been generally assumed, by a single traumatic event—a judicial decision (Hans Julius Wolff), an edict of the prefect (Dieter Simon), an imperial constitution (Arangio-Ruiz)—that would have forced the notaries to include it.[80] There is no trace in our sources of an imperial constitution abrogating that of Severus and Caracalla; a prefectural edict squarely ignoring an imperial constitution may be not impossible, but is certainly unlikely; and the same goes for a judicial decision, which would have been either wrong or thoroughly misunderstood.

9. CENTRE AND PERIPHERY

The general picture after 212 CE is untidy and contradictory: immediate adjustments are visible (Section 5, above), and at the same time numerous practices survive despite being blatantly *contra ius* (Section 2, above). This state of affairs lasted for a surprisingly long time, well into the fourth century.

[78] The erroneous assumption that without stipulatory clause most peregrine contracts would not be effective under Roman law has become widespread among papyrologists: thus, Wolff (2002), 130–3 includes the phenomenon, under the heading 'mandatory Romanization', among the 'cases of necessary and therefore unconditional adaptation to the imperatives of the Roman *ius civile*' (at 137). See also Mélèze Modrzejewski (2014), 330–2.

[79] C. 8.37.1. *Impp. Severus et Antoninus AA. Secundo. Licet epistulae, quam libello inseruisti, additum non sit stipulatum esse eum cui cavebatur, tamen si res inter praesentes gesta est, credendum est praecedente stipulatione vocem spondentis secutam. Accepta xvii k. Mai. Severo iii et Victorino conss.*: 'The Emperors Severus and Antoninus, Augusti, to Secundus. Although the letter that you inserted in your petition does not mention that the recipient of the promise exacted it, nevertheless, if the transaction took place in the presence of both parties, it must be assumed that the voice of the promisor followed a previous stipulatory question.' In the same sense, without mentioning the Imperial decision, Paul, *Opinions* (D. 45.1.134.1): *Idem respondit, cum Septicius litteris suis praestaturum se caverit pecuniam et usuras eius semisses, quae apud Sempronium depositae sint: si inter praesentes actum est, intellegendum etiam a parte Lucii Titii praecessisse verba stipulationis*: 'The same responded that if Septicius assured in written document, deposited with Sempronius, that he would pay the money with interest at six percent, if this was done in the presence of both parties, it should be understood that also the words of the stipulatory question were previously pronounced by Lucius Titius.'

[80] Arangio-Ruiz 1948a: 121–6; Simon 1964: 25; Wolff 2002: 132.

This cannot be explained merely by a politically motivated tolerance on the part of the Roman authorities (how do we then account for the radical, immediate adjustments?) or by an impotence caused by the third-century crisis. What seems to me to help account for the contradictions is not so much the passivity of the administration, but the conflicting directions of its activity. There was a striking contrast between centre and periphery. At a local level, the administration continued for decades to endorse the old peregrine practices. The attitude of the imperial chancellery, instead, was often (Section 6, above) the complete opposite: in the imperial rescripts, peregrine practices are either translated into Roman categories, or, as we have seen, dismissed in the name of the Roman orthodoxy.

It was of course inevitable that the Roman Emperor would give a Roman solution. This is certainly not a post-*CA* novelty, and cannot have taken anyone by surprise. What is new is the amount of petitions that arrived from new citizens unacquainted with Roman law, whose assumptions were based on their own legal traditions. Whenever the Emperor's response dismissed a well-established local tradition, it exposed its fragility with enormous disruptive force. There may have been other forces towards assimilation that escape us, but among those well attested, this one was crucial. Most of these rescripts have received scarce attention from legal historians, because they often refer to the most trivial among the Roman legal principles. Historically, though, their importance is difficult to overestimate. Their cumulative effect seems enough to lead within decades to a situation close to the one famously described in the treatise on epideictic rhetoric attributed to Menander of Laodicea.[81]

In Egypt, the critical turning point arrived in the mid-fourth century, after the *CA* and Diocletian's reforms. By then, the notarial offices, the *agoranomeia* and *grapheia* that had sustained the local traditions, vanish from our sources, and so do the *bibliotekai enkteseon*. It is also at the turn of the fourth century that the Eastern schools of Roman law are founded, including that of Alexandria. Unfortunately, the late fourth and especially the fifth century are particularly badly represented in the papyri, but this is the period that must be studied in order to reconstruct the advance of the true Romanization of legal practice in Egypt.

[81] Menander Rhetor (?), *Διαίρεσις τῶν Ἐπιδεικτικῶν* 363.4–14 (Spengel III): *Ἡ δ' αὖ δικαιοπραγία διαρεῖται εἴς τε τοὺς ἀφικνουμένους ξένους καὶ εἰς ἀλλήλους, μέρος δ' αὐτῆς καὶ τοῖς ἔθεσιν ἴσοις καὶ φιλανθρώποις καὶ τὸ νόμοις ἀκριβέσι καὶ δικαίοις χρῆσθαι. εἰ γὰρ μὴ ξένους ἀδικοῖεν μηδὲ ἀλλήλους κακουργοῖεν, τοῖς δ' ἔθεσιν ἴσοις καὶ κοινοῖς καὶ τοῖς νόμοις χρῷντο δικαίοις, οἱ πολῖται ἄριστα καὶ δικαιότατα τὰς πόλεις οἰκήσονται. ἀλλὰ τὸ τῶν νόμων ἐν τοῖς νῦν χρόνοις ἄχρηστον· κατὰ γὰρ τοὺς κοινοὺς τῶν Ῥωμαίων νόμους πολιτευόμεθα· ἔθεσι δ' ἄλλη πόλις ἄλλοις χρῆται, ἐξ ὧν προσῆκον ἐνκωμιάζειν*: 'The administration of justice is in turn divided into the one towards the visiting foreigners and the one towards each other, and a part thereof is living according to equitable and humane customs and to just and precise laws. And so if the citizens do not do injustice to the foreigners and do not wrong each other, if they live according to equitable and humane customs and to just laws, they do live in their cities in the best and most just manner. And yet in the present times (praising in an encomium of a city its) laws has become useless: we are indeed governed according to the common laws of the Romans. And yet each city has use of its customs: from these its encomium should be started.' See also the similar sentiments at 364.10–15 (Spengel III). Talamanca (1971) made these texts into a crucial source for the impact of the CA; see also (*contra*) Mélèze Modrzejewski (1982); see also now Humfress (2013). The examples chosen by Menander in the second passage may help understand his sweeping assertion: they refer primarily to family and succession, precisely the fields where the adjustment to the new personal statute as Roman citizens was inescapable.

REFERENCES

Alonso, J. L. 2013. The Status of Peregrine Law in Egypt: 'Customary Law' and Legal Pluralism in the Roman Empire. *The Journal of Juristic Papyrology* 43, pp. 351–404.

Ando, C. 2012. *Imperial Rome ad 193 to 284. The Critical Century.* Edinburgh.

Ando, C. (ed.) 2016. *Citizenship and Empire in Europe 200–1900. The Antonine Constitution after 1800 years.* Stuttgart.

Arangio-Ruiz, V. 1941. L'applicazione del diritto romano in Egitto. In: *Egitto antico e moderno. Studi e saggi I.* Milano, pp. 283–302.

Arangio-Ruiz, V. 1947a. L'application du droit romain en Égypte après la constitution Antoninienne. *Bulletin de l'Institut d'Égypte* 29, pp. 83–130.

Arangio-Ruiz, V. 1947b. L'applicazione del diritto romano in Egitto dopo la costituzione di Caracalla. *Annali del Seminario Giuridico dell'Università di Catania* 1, pp. 28–38.

Arangio-Ruiz, V. 1948a. L'application du droit romain en Égypte après la Constitution Antoninienne, *Bulletin de l'Institut d'Égypte* 29, pp. 83–130 = Arangio-Ruiz (1974), pp. 258–94.

Arangio-Ruiz, V. 1948b. Chirografi di soldati. In: *Studi in onore di Siro Solazzi*, Napoli, pp. 251–63 = *Studi Epigrafici e Papirologici.* Napoli, pp. 315–26.

Arangio-Ruiz, V. 1950. Sul problema della doppia cittadinanza nella Repubblica e nell'Impero Romano. In: *Scritti giuridici in onore di F. Carnelutti IV.* Padova.

Arangio-Ruiz, V. 1974. *Studi Epigrafici e Papirologici.* Napoli.

Arjava, A. 1996. *Women and Law in Late Antiquity.* Oxford.

Arjava, A. 1998. Paternal power in late antiquity. *The Journal of Roman Studies* 88, pp. 147–65.

Arjava, A. 1999a. Eine Freilassung aus der väterlichen Gewalt. CPR vi 78. *Tyche* 14, pp. 15–22.

Arjava, A. 1999b. Die römische Vormundschaft und das Volljährigkeitsalter in Ägypten. *Zeitschrift für Papyrologie und Epigraphik* 126, pp. 202–4.

Arjava, A. 2014. The Romanization of family law. In: J. G. Keenan, J. G. Manning and U. Yiftach-Firanko, *Law and Legal Practice in Egypt from Alexander to the Arab Conquest.* Cambridge, pp. 175–91.

Avenarius, M. 2005. *Der pseudo-ulpianische liber singularis regularum. Entstehung, Eigenart und Überlieferung einer hochklassischen Juristenschrift.* Göttingen.

Babusiaux, U. & Kolb, A. 2015. *Das Recht der 'Soldatenkaiser'. Rechtliche Stabilität in Zeiten Politischen Umbruchs?* Berlin.

Bagnall, R. S. and Worp, K. A. 1994. The Affairs of a Complex Family. *APF* 40, pp. 37–41.

Boffo, L. 2001. Lo statuto di terre, insediamenti e persone nell'Anatolia ellenistica. Documenti recenti e problemi antichi. *Dike* 4, pp. 233–55.

Buraselis, K. 2007. *Θεία δωρεά. Das göttlich-kaiserliche Geschenk. Studien zur Politik der Severer und zur Constitutio Antoniniana.* Wien.

Chalon, G. 1964. *L'Édit de Tiberius Julius Alexander.* Olten and Lausanne.

d'Ors, A. 1953. *Epigrafía jurídica de la España romana.* Madrid.

Gagliardi, L. 2012. La madre tutrice e la madre ἐπακολουθήτρια: osservazioni sul rapporto tra diritto romano e diritti delle province orientali. *Index* 40, pp. 423–46.

Gascou, J. & de Kisch, Y. 1982. *Inscriptions antiques du Maroc II. Inscriptions latines.* Paris.

Gaudemet, J. 1956. La coutume au bas-empire. Rôle pratique et notion théorique. *Labeo* 2, pp. 147–59.

Greco, M. 1977. Alcune considerazioni sulla 'constitutio Antoniniana'. *Atti dell'Accademia di Scienze, Lettere e Arti di Palermo* 35, pp.137–66.

Herzog, R. 1942. Symbolae calymniae et coe. *Rivista di Filologia e di Istruzione Classica* 20, pp. 1–20.

Humfress, C. 2012. Law and Custom under Rome. In: A. Rio (ed.), *Custom in the Middle Ages.* London, pp. 23–47.
Humfress, C. 2013. Laws' Empire: Roman Universalism and Legal Practice. In: P. du Plessis (ed.) *New Frontiers: Law and Society in the Roman World.* Edinburgh, pp. 73–101.
Imrie, A. 2018. *The Antonine Constitution. An Edict for the Caracallan Empire.* Leiden-Boston.
Jones, A. H. M. 1937. *The Cities of the Eastern Roman Provinces.* Oxford.
Jonnes, Ll. & Rici, M. 1997. A New Royal Inscription from Phrygia Paroreios: Eumenes II Grants Tyraion the Status of a Polis. *Epigraphica Anatolica* 29, pp. 1–30.
Jörs, P. 1915. Erzrichter und Chrematisten. *Zeitschrift der Savigny-Stiftung für Rechtsgeschichte: Romanistische Abteilung* 36, pp. 230–339.
Jörs, P. 1918. Erzrichter und Chrematisten. *Zeitschrift der Savigny-Stiftung für Rechtsgeschichte: Romanistische Abteilung* 39, pp. 52–118.
Jörs, P. 1919. Erzrichter und Chrematisten. *Zeitschrift der Savigny-Stiftung für Rechtsgeschichte: Romanistische Abteilung* 40, pp. 1–97.
Jouguet, P. 1911. *La vie municipale dans l'Égypte romaine.* Paris.
Kaser, M. 1939. Mores maiorum und Gewohnheitsrecht. *Zeitschrift der Savigny-Stiftung für Rechtsgeschichte: Romanistische Abteilung* 59, pp. 52–101.
Kaser, M. 1971–1975. *Das römische Privatrecht* I–II. 2nd edition. Munich.
Kaser, M. 1977. *Über Verbotsgesetze und verbotswidrige Geschäfte im römischen Recht.* Vienna.
Knütel, R. 2014. Uxores constrictae. *Fundamina* 20, pp. 467–77.
Krob, E. 1997. Serments et institutions civiques à Cos à l'époque hellénistique. *Revue des Études Grecques* 110, pp. 434–53.
Lewis, N. 1970. Graeco-Roman Egypt: fact or fiction? *Proceedings of the Twelfth International Congress of Papyrology, Ann Arbor 1968.* Toronto, pp. 3–14.
Lewis, N. 1984. The Romanity of Roman Egypt: A Growing Consensus. *Atti del XVII Congresso Internazionale di Papirologia III.* Naples, pp. 1077–84.
Marotta, V. 2014. Egizi e cittadinanza romana. *Cultura giuridica e diritto vivente* 1, pp. 1–21.
Marotta, V. 2017. Egyptians and Citizenship from the First Century AD to the Constitutio Antoniniana. In: L. Cecchet and A. Busetto, *Citizens in the Graeco-Roman World.* Leiden-Boston, pp. 172–98.
Mastino, A. 1984. Antonino Magno, la cittadinanza e l'impero universale. *La nozione di 'Romano' tra cittadinanza e universalità.* Rome, pp. 559–63.
Mastino, A. 2013. Constitutio Antoniniana: la politica della cittadinanza di un imperatore africano. *Bullettino dell'Istituto di Diritto Romano 'Vittorio Scialoja'* 107, pp. 37–56.
Mattioli, F. 2012. Un tentativo di messa a punto riguardo alla più recente dottrina sui Tituli ex corpore Ulpiani. Ipotesi e prospettive di ricerca. In: G. Purpura (ed.), *Revisione ed integrazione dei Fontes Iuris Romani Anteiustiniani. Studi preparatori II. Auctores-Negotia.* Turin, pp. 85–117.
Mélèze Modrzejewski, J. 1982. Ménandre de Laodicée et l'Édit de Caracalla. Symposion 1977. Actes du IIIème Colloque international du droit grec et hellénistique (Chantilly, juin 1977). Cologne-Vienne, pp. 335–64.
Mélèze Modrzejewski, J. 1964. Die Geschwisterehe in der hellenistische Praxis und nach romischen Recht. *Zeitschrift der Savigny-Stiftung für Rechtsgeschichte: Romanistische Abteilung* 81, pp. 69–82.
Mélèze Modrzejewski, J. 1970. La règle de droit dans l'Égypte Romaine. *Proceedings of the Twelfth International Congress of Papyrology.* Toronto, pp. 317–77.
Mélèze Modrzejewski, J. 2014. Loi et coutume dans l'Égypte grecque et romaine: les facteurs de formation du droit en Égypte d'Alexandre le Grand à la conquête arabe. *Journal of Juristic Papyrology supplements* 21. Warsaw.

Meyer, P. 1920. *Juristische Papyri. Erkärung von Urkunden zur Einführung in die juristische Papyruskunde*. Berlin.

Mitteis, L. 1891. *Reichsrecht und Volksrecht in den östlichen Provinzen des römischen Kaiserreichs*. Leipzig.

Mitteis, L. 1898. Trapezitika. *Zeitschrift der Savigny-Stiftung für Rechtsgeschichte: Romanistische Abteilung* 19, pp. 198–260.

Mitteis, L. 1912. *Grundzüge und Chrestomathie der Papyruskunde* II 1. *Juristischer Teil: Grundzüge*. Leipzig.

Nörr, D. 1969. Zur Entstehung der gewohnheitsrechtlichen Theorie. In: M. Kaser et al. (eds.), *Festschrift für Wilhelm Felgentraeger zum 70. Geburtstag*. Göttingen, pp. 353–66.

Oliver, J. H. 1972. Text of the Tabula Banasitana, A. D. 177. *The American Journal of Philology* 93, pp. 336–40.

Oliver, J. H. 1978. Review of H. Wolff, Die Constitutio Antoniniana und Papyrus Gissensis 40 I, *The American Journal of Philology* 99: 403–8.

Oliver, J. H. 1989. *Greek Constitutions of Early Roman Emperors from Inscriptions and Papyri*. Philadelphia.

Pearl, O. M. 1951. A Late Receipt for Syntaximon. *Transactions and Proceedings of the American Philological Association* 82, pp. 193–5.

Pinna Parpaglia, P. 1995. *Sacra peregina, civitas Romanorum, dediticii nel Papiro Giessen n. 40*. Sassari.

Pringsheim, F. 1950. *The Greek Law of Sale*. Weimar.

Pringsheim, F. 1961. Stipulations-Klausel. *Gesammelte Abhandlungen* II. Heidelberg, pp. 194–256.

Raggi, A. 2004. The Epigraphic Dossier of Seleucus of Rhosus: A Revised Edition. *Zeitschrift für Papyrologie und Epigraphik* 147, pp. 123–38.

Rubin, Z. 1975. Further to the dating of the constitutio Antoniniana. *Latomus* 34, pp. 430–6.

Ruggieri, P. 1999. La doppia cittadinanza prima e dopo la Constitutio Antoniniana de civitate. In: Ruggieri, P. *Africa ipsa parens illa Sardiniae. Studi di storia antica e di epigrafia*. Sassari, pp. 45–60.

Rupprecht, H.-A. 1997. Zwangsvollstreckung und dingliche Sicherheiten in den Papyri der ptolemäischen und römischen Zeit. In: G. Thür and J. Vélissaropoulos-Karakostas (eds). *Symposion 1995: Vorträge zur griechischen und hellenistischen Rechtsgeschichte (Korfu 1.–5. September 1997)*. Cologne, pp. 291–302.

Rupprecht, H.-A. 2014. Real Security. In: J. G. Keenan, J. G. Manning and U. Yiftach-Firanko, *Law and Legal Practice in Egypt from Alexander to the Arab Conquest*. Cambridge, pp. 249–65.

Sasse, C. 1958. *Die Constitutio Antoniniana: eine Untersuchung über den Umfang der Bürgerrechtverleihung auf Grund des Papyrus Giss. 40 I*. Wiesbaden.

Sasse, C. 1962. Literaturüberischt zur Constitutio Antoniniana. *The Journal of Juristic Papyrology* 14, pp. 109–49.

Sasse, C. 1965. Literaturüberischt zur Constitutio Antoniniana. II Teil. *The Journal of Juristic Papyrology* 15, pp. 329–66.

Schmitt, H. H. 1969. *Die Staatsverträge des Altertums III. Die Verträge der griechisch-römischen Welt von 338 bis 200 v. Chr.* Munich.

Schönbauer, E. 1931. Reichsrecht gegen Volksrecht? Studien über die Bedeutung der Constitutio Antoniniana für die römische Rechtsentwicklung. *Zeitschrift der Savigny-Stiftung für Rechtsgeschichte: Romanistische Abteilung* 51, pp. 277–335.

Schönbauer, E. 1934. Zur Frage der Constitutio Antoniniana. *Zeitschrift der Savigny-Stiftung für Rechtsgeschichte: Romanistische Abteilung* 54, pp. 337–8.

Schönbauer, E. 1937. Reichsrecht, Volksrecht und Provinzialrecht. Studien über die Bedeutung der Constitutio Antoniniana für die römische Rechtsentwicklung.

Zeitschrift der Savigny-Stiftung für Rechtsgeschichte: Romanistische Abteilung 57, pp. 309–55.

Schönbauer, E. 1949. Die Doppel-Bürgerschaft im römischen Reiche und ihre Wirkung auf die Rechtsentwicklung. *Anzeiger der Österreichischen Akademie der Wissenschaften. Phil-Hist. Klasse* 17, pp. 343–69.

Schönbauer, E. 1952. Deditizier, Doppel-Bürgerschaft und Personalitäts-Prinzip. *Journal of Juristic Papyrology* 6, pp. 17–72.

Schönbauer, E. 1960. Personalitätsprinzip und Privatrechtsordnung im Römerreiche. *Anzeiger der Österreichischen Akademie der Wissenschaften. Phil-Hist. Klasse* 25, pp. 182–210.

Schuler, Ch. 1999. Kolonisten und Einheimische in einer attalidischen Polisgründung. *Zeitschrift für Papyrologie und Epigraphik* 128, pp. 124–32.

Segre, M. 1952. Tituli Calymnii. *Annuario della Scuola Archeologica di Atene e delle missioni italiane in Oriente* 22–3, pp. 1–248.

Seston, W. 1966. Marius Maximus et la date de la Constitutio Antoniniana. In: *Mélanges d'archéologie, d'épigraphie et d'histoire offerts à J. Carcopino.* Paris, pp. 109–17.

Seston, W. & Euzennat, M. 1961. La citoyenneté romaine au temps de Marc Aurèle et de Commode, d'après la Tabula Banasitana. *Comptes rendus des séances de l'Académie des Inscriptions et Belles-Lettres* 105, pp. 317–24.

Seston, W. & Euzennat, M. 1971. Un dossier de la chancellerie romaine: La Tabula Banasitana. Étude de diplomatique. *Comptes rendus des séances de l'Académie des Inscriptions et Belles-Lettres* 115, pp. 468–90.

Sherwin-White, A. N. 1973. The Tabula of Banasa and the Constitutio Antoniniana. *The Journal of Roman Studies* 63, pp. 86–98.

Sherwin-White, S. M. 1978. *Ancient Cos. An historical study from the Dorian settlement to the imperial period.* Göttingen.

Simon, D. 1964. *Studien zur Praxis der Stipulationsklausel.* Munich.

Talamanca, M. 1971. Su alcuni passi di Menandro di Laodicea relativi agli effetti della 'constitutio Antoniniana'. In *Studi in onore di E. Volterra* 5, pp. 433–560.

Talamanca, M. 1989. *Lineamenti di Storia del Diritto Romano.* Milan.

Taubenschlag, R. 1916. Die patria potestas im Recht der Papyri. *Zeitschrift der Savigny-Stiftung für Rechtsgeschichte: Romanistische Abteilung* 37, pp. 177–230.

Taubenschlag, R. 1955. *The Law of Greco-Roman Egypt in the Light of the Papyri.* 2nd edition. Warsaw.

Taubenschlag, R. 1959. *Opera Minora* I–II. Warsaw.

Wenger, L. 1906. *Die Stellvertretung im Rechte der Papyri.* Leipzig.

Wieacker, F. 1988–2006. *Römische Rechtsgeschichte* I–II. Munich.

Wolff, H. 1976. Die Constitutio Antoniniana und Papyrus Gissensis 40. Dissertation. Cologne.

Wolff, H.-J. 1956. Zwei Miszellen. *Eos* 48 (= Symbolae R. Taubenschlag), pp. 355–71.

Wolff, H. J. 1968. Gewohnheitsrecht und Gesetzesrecht in der griechischen Rechtsauffassung. In: H. Dölle (ed) *Deutsche Landesreferate zum VI. Internationalen Kongreß für Rechtsvergleichung in Hamburg, 1962.* Tübingen and Berlin = Berneker, E. (ed.) *Zur griechischen Rechtsgeschichte.* Darmstadt, pp. 99–120.

Wolff, H. J. 1978. *Das Recht der Griechischen Papyri Ägyptens II.* Munich.

Wolff, H. J. 2002. *Das Recht der Griechischen Papyri Ägyptens* I. Munich.

Yiftach-Firanko, U. 2009. Law in Graeco-Roman Egypt: Hellenization, Fusion, Romanization. In: R.S. Bagnall (ed) *The Oxford Handbook of Papyrology.* Oxford, pp. 541–60.

5

The Decision of Septimius Severus and Caracalla on *longi temporis praescriptio* (BGU 267 and P.Strass. 22)

Anna Plisecka

Since the publication of the groundbreaking *Reichsrecht und Volksrecht* of Mitteis,[1] ancient law has been seen from the perspective of a dichotomy that opposes two systems of law: provincial and Roman. Consequently, legal institutes are qualified as belonging to one or the other system. An interesting example of an institute whose origins have been traced back either to Roman or to provincial law is the plea of long-lasting possession. The crucial moment in the development of that institute is the decision of Septimius Severus and Caracalla in answer to a petition of a peregrine woman Juliana:[2] this is seen in the literature as the moment of implementation of the plea of long-lasting possession in Roman law. The decision survived to us in two documents: BGU 267 from Alexandria and P.Strass. 22 from Hermopolis; both documents contain the same ruling in slightly divergent versions. The existence of two copies of the same decision demonstrates the relevance of the case for provincial legal practice.[3] In the documents the plea of long-lasting possession is indicated as *μακρᾶς νομῆς παραγραφή* and described as an exception, which the possessor can use to oppose the vindication claim of an owner, if the defined period of possession (which is dependent on the residence of the parties) is ten or twenty years.

In the documents in which the decision is quoted it is not described as an *ἀπόκριμα*, yet because of its formal characteristics and its content in the literature it is unanimously counted amongst the *ἀποκρίματα*.[4] Among such formal features is the fact that the addressee is mentioned, without any salutation, with her first name in the dative; furthermore, the answer is given in the absence of the

[1] Mitteis (1891). [2] Riccobono, FIRA I, no. 84.

[3] Other *ἀποκρίματα* passed down in multiple copies are: the decline of a right to appeal copied in P. Col. 123, ll. 8–10 and P.Amh. 63, ll. 1–6; a decision regarding *cessio bonorum* copied in P.Oxy. XII 1405, ll. 1–13, P.Oxy. XLIII 3105, ll. 1–10 and P.Oxy LXIV 4437, ll. 1–10.

[4] See Williams (1974), 89; Lewis (1978), 271; Lewis (1996), 63; Papathomas (2000), 130–1; Haensch (2007), 226.

Anna Plisecka, *The Decision of Septimius Severus and Caracalla on* longi temporis praescriptio *(BGU 267 and P.Strass. 22)* In: *Law in the Roman Provinces.* Edited by: Kimberley Czajkowski and Benedikt Eckhardt in collaboration with Meret Strothmann, Oxford University Press (2020).
DOI: 10.1093/oso/9780198844082.003.0005

petitioner, a point which differentiates *ἀποκρίματα* from *decreta*. Moreover, similarly to other *ἀποκρίματα*, the emperors instruct the petitioner on the legal regulations in force, rather than formulating a decision on presented case.[5]

While BGU 267 contains only the copy of the *ἀπόκριμα* and therefore furnishes little information on the purpose and application of the imperial decision, in P.Strass. 22 the *ἀπόκριμα* is copied together with a series of other decisions on the same topic intended for processual purpose. These include a transcript from the record books of the Egyptian prefect Subatianus Aquila,[6] which contains a decision regarding *μακρᾶς νομῆς παραγραφή* (ll. 10–24); and a decision of the prefect Mettius Rufus from 20 November 90 CE on the *usucapio* of movable goods (ll. 25–33).[7]

The copy of the *ἀπόκριμα* contained in P.Strass. 22 is less precise in comparison to the one in BGU 267,[8] therefore in this paper the version preserved in the Berlin document is considered as representative for the reconstruction of the original *ἀπόκριμα*. The Berlin text opens with a relatively long, although abbreviated, imperial titulature, which is substituted with the short 'Deified Severus and Antoninus' in the Strasbourg document. The latter expression corresponds to the common practice of imperial chancelleries and can be found in multiple documents.[9] This difference demonstrates that the copy, enclosed in P.Strass. 22, was written down after the death of Caracalla in 217 CE and is therefore older than that of BGU 267. The details of the differences between the two versions will be explained further.

BGU 267

[- c.16 -]λογ[-c.?- Αὐτοκ]ρ[άτωρ] Κ̣α̣ῖ̣σ̣α̣ρ
[Λούκιος Σεπτίμιος Σεουῆρος Εὐσεβ]ὴ̣ς
Πέρ[τ]ιναξ [Σε]βαστὸς
[Ἀραβικὸς Ἀδιαβη]ν̣ι̣κὸς
[Παρθικὸς Μέγιστος] καὶ Αὐτοκρά[τωρ] Καῖσαρ
[Μάρκος Αὐρή]λιος Ἀντωνεῖνος Σεβαστὸς
Ἰουλιανῇ Σω[σθ]ενιανοῦ διὰ Σωσθένους
ἀνδρός· [μ]ακρᾶς νομῆς παραγραφῆς
τοῖς δικαία̣[ν] α̣ἰ̣τ̣[ί]αν ἐσχηκόσι καὶ ἄνευ
τινὸς ἀμφισβητήσεως ἐν τῇ νομῇ
γενομ[έν]ο̣ι̣ς̣ πρὸς μὲν τοὺς ἐν ἀλλο-
τρίᾳ πόλει διατρείβοντας ἐτῶν εἴκοσι
ἀριθμῷ βεβαιοῦται, τοὺς δὲ ἐπὶ τῆς
αὐτῆς ἐτῶν δέκα. προετέθη ἐν Ἀ-
λεξανδρείᾳ. η (ἔτους) Τῦβι γ.

P.Strass. 22, ll.1–9

θεοὶ Σεουῆρος καὶ Ἀντωνῖνος Ἰου̣[λ]ιαν̣ῇ̣
Σωσθένους διὰ Σω̣σ̣θ̣ένους ἀνδ̣ρός.
μακρᾶς νομῆς πα̣ραγραφὴ̣ τοῖς δ̣ικαί[αν]
αἰτίαν ἐσχηκόσι καὶ ἄνευ τινὸς ἀμφισβ̣[η-]
τήσεως ἐν τῇ νομῇ γενομένοις π̣ρὸς μ̣[ὲ]ν
τοὺς ἐν ἄλλῃ πόλει διατρείψαντας ἐτῶν
εἴκοσι
ἀριθμῷ β̣ο̣ηθοῦνται, πρὸς δὲ τοὺς
ἐπὶ τῆς αὐτῆς
δέκα. προετέθη ἐν Ἀλεξ̣ανδ[ρ]εία̣
η (ἔτει) Φαρμοῦθι κδ.

'To Juliana, the daughter of Sosthenianus, through her husband Sosthenes. The plea of long-lasting possession enters into force for those who have a just cause and entered in possession without any controversy, against those namely who stay in a different city after twenty years, against those however who (stay) in the same city after ten years. Posted in Alexandria on 3 December 199.'

[5] Mommsen (1895), 196.

[6] Prefect in 206–11 CE; Reinmuth (1935), 109; Stein (1950), 111–14; Bastianini (1975), 305–6; Bastianini (1980), 85.

[7] Mettius Rufus was prefect in 89–91 CE, Reinmuth, (1935), 133; Stein (1950), 44–6; Bastianini (1975), 277–8; Bastianini (1980), 79.

[8] Eich (2009), 282–3.

[9] Coriat (1997), 577–8; Eich (2009), 283; 286, n. 78.

There are small variations in the Strasbourg papyrus which can be explained as copyist's mistakes. First, Sosthenes as patronym of the petitioner, which we find in l. 2, is most probably a mistake and should be corrected to Sosthenianos, conforming to the version in BGU 267, l. 6. The name Sosthenes is, as both documents show, the name of Juliana's husband, which is reported immediately after her patronym: that could easily lead the copyist to reproduce the husband's name as patronym. Further, both texts seem to report the plea of long-lasting possession in different cases: in BGU 267, l. 7 it appears in genitive [μ]ακρᾶς νομῆς παραγραφῆς whereas in P.Strass. 22, l. 3 it is most probably in nominative μακρᾶς νομῆς παραγραφή. However, since the last letter of that expression is a reconstruction we cannot be certain whether such difference existed. Furthermore the expression ἀλλοτρίᾳ πόλει (BGU 267, l. 10) is substituted with a shorter expression ἄλλῃ πόλει (P.Strass. 22, l. 6). The meaning 'in a different city' remains the same in both texts, but the extended expression employed in BGU 267 can be found in other imperial constitutions and better matches the official style of chancellery writing.[10] The place of residence of the claimant is also described differently in each of the documents: in BGU 267, l. 11 the verb διατρείβειν is employed, whereas in the P.Strass. 22, l. 6 a less convenient future form διατρίψειν is used. Similarly we find βοηθοῦνται in P.Strass. 22, l. 7, in place of more suitable βεβαιοῦται (BGU 267, l. 12) which refers to the confirmation of the right of possession at the end of the prescribed period of time. Furthermore in the Strasbourg document the word ἐτῶν is omitted in the indication of the time limits necessary for the plea. The meaning of the text is however unaltered by the omission. The few grammatical and terminological differences between both documents are irrelevant to the reconstruction of the ἀπόκριμα's original meaning. All of them can be explained as copyist's mistakes, for the words in P.Strass. 22 that diverge from BGU 267 both graphically and semantically resemble those employed in the former document. The mistakes could have arisen while writing P.Strass. 22 or its intermediate model. For this reason the more accurate copy preserved in BGU 267 has to be considered as closer to the text of the imperial decision and will be taken as the basis for the following analysis.[11]

Both documents date the imperial decision differently, which has for long time inspired the curiosity of scholars who give divergent explanations to the problem. Mitteis and Riccobono claimed that the earlier date, 30 December 199 (provided in BGU 267), indicates the day on which the decision was posted in Rome, while the later date, 19 April 200 (of P.Strass. 22), indicates the day on which a copy of that decision was posted in Alexandria.[12] Mitteis, followed by Chevreaux, argues further that both dates were indicated in the original document, and in the Berlin document the date of the publication in Rome was reported as the date of the publication in Alexandria by mistake.[13] Against this thesis, however, stands the fact that both documents mention only Alexandria as the place of posting and there are no indications that the text had ever been published in Rome. More recently a different explanation was offered by Eich, who holds that the later date refers

[10] FIRA, II, no. 185, l. 32 (6 BCE); P. Lond. 1912 V l. 95 (41 CE).

[11] Along these lines, see also Amelotti (1958), 180.

[12] Mitteis (1912), 286; Riccobono, FIRA I p. 438.

[13] Mitteis (1912), 286; Chevreau (2006), 108, n. 26.

to the publication in a nome or a village.[14] This hypothesis is not convincing for the same reason as the previous one: there is no indication in the documents, which both read *προετέθη ἐν Ἀλεξανδρείᾳ*, that the decision was ever published in a different place. Coriat argues otherwise, that the date mentioned in BGU 267 correctly indicates the day of posting in Alexandria, whereas the date mentioned in P.Strass. 22 indicates the day in which the copy contained in that document has been written down.[15] The interpretation offered by Coriat reminds us that the versions of imperial decisions which we find in the papyri are often not official documents, but private copies made to be used in legal processes. Two arguments speak against that interpretation: first, both dates are indicated explicitly as the day of posting by the verb *προετέθη* (BGU 267, l. 13 and P.Strass. 22, l. 8); secondly, the reduced imperial titulature, as mentioned before, indicates clearly that the copy was written down after 217 CE. Since the copy in P.Strass. 22 is generally less precise and contains omissions and mistakes, we may consider the date given in the Berlin document as correct and the one of P.Strass. 22 as erroneous. Why the mistake occurred has to be left open. Next to the explanations already offered in the literature, one more can be added, namely that the *ἀπόκριμα* in P.Strass. 22 was copied from a document containing a list of decisions published on different dates and the copyist mistakenly recorded the date of another decision.[16] This explanation would indicate that the copy of the *ἀπόκριμα* transmitted in the Strasbourg document was not reproduced directly from the original posted in Alexandria, but from an intermediary copy, which probably contained a group of decisions, possibly on similar topic.

Whether the *ἀπόκριμα* was originally formulated in Greek or translated from Latin is still a matter of debate.[17] The text itself is free from Latinisms and contains no indications that it could be a translation. In particular, the differences between the two Greek versions cannot be interpreted as different translations of the same original Latin text. Moreover, a comparison between the Greek text of the *ἀπόκριμα* and another constitution of Septimius Severus and Caracalla on the plea of long-lasting possession demonstrates that the emperors employ in Latin the expression *longi temporis praescriptio*[18] and therefore, if there was a Latin version of the text, we can assume that this expression would have been used. If we consider that the official documents were translated literally, word by word,[19] the expression in Greek translation should correspond exactly to the Latin one, yet the Greek phrase *μακρᾶς νομῆς παραγραφὴ* does not correspond to *longi temporis praescriptio*, but translates to Latin as *longae possessionis praescriptio*. For these reasons, I find more convincing the view of earlier authors who claimed the text was not a translation from Latin but was originally written in Greek.[20]

[14] Eich (2009), 282–3.
[15] Coriat (1997), 619.
[16] Amelotti (1958), 179 n. 213.
[17] Lewis (1978), 262; Nörr (1969), 75; Williams (1974), 101–3.
[18] C.7.33.1.1: *Quod si prior possessor inquietatus est, etsi postea per longum tempus sine aliqua interpellatione in possessione remansit, tamen non potest uti longi temporis praescriptione.* (If, however, the right of the former possessor has been questioned, even though afterwards he remained in possession for a long time without hindrance, he will, nevertheless, not be able to avail himself of prescription based on long time.)
[19] Brock (1979), 69–71; Adams (2003), 470–1.
[20] Stein (1915), 161; Meyer (1920), 179.

The opinion that the ἀπόκριμα of Septimius Severus and Caracalla marks the moment of introduction of the plea of long-lasting possession into Roman law dominates in the scholarly literature. In that same decision the emperors would have defined the time limits necessary for the *praescriptio*. This thesis goes back to Mitteis, who, however, later changed his views,[21] and was developed by Nörr, who argued that the imperial decision in the case of Juliana introduced *longi temporis praescriptio* as a new legal institute, which relied exclusively on Hellenistic and Egyptian legal tradition.[22] He identified the Egyptian regulations on prescription, known from the Codex from Hermopolis from the third century BCE,[23] and the πραγραφὴ of Attic law, which was in use at the end of the fourth century BCE, as models for the plea of long-lasting possession. According to Nörr, although forgotten in legal practice and jurisprudence, παραγραφὴ would have survived in rhetoric until the end of the second century CE, when it was introduced into Roman law by the decision of Septimius Severus and Caracalla.

Coriat also assumes that Septimius Severus and Caracalla relied on local regulations and not on Roman law when implementing the new legal institute.[24] In his opinion, the texts that assume the implementation of *longi temporis praescriptio* through imperial constitutions testify in favour of such view. Among such texts, Coriat identifies a fragment of *libri regularum* of Modestinus[25] and a fragment of Justinian's *Institutes*,[26] which concern, however, a specific case of *praescriptio* against the *fiscus*. Modestinus argues that, on the authority of imperial constitutions (*constitutum est*) a buyer of a plot of land, which was part of *bonis vacantibus*, after 20 years is protected by the plea of long-lasting possession, but without naming the emperor who had issued the regulation. The expression *constitutum est*, however, has a broader meaning and does not necessarily indicate an imperial constitution, it can also indicate a jurisprudential *communis opinio*.[27] The *Institutes* of Justinian assign the same regulation to Antoninus Pius on the one hand and to Septimius Severus and Caracalla on the other hand. Therefore the aforementioned texts cannot be considered a proof of the thesis that the plea of long-lasting possession was implemented by a constitution of Septimius Severus and Caracalla. Coriat draws another argument for the implementation of *longi temporis praescriptio* in the decision of Juliana's case from the difference between the ἀπόκριμα and the decision of the prefect Metius Rufus,[28] taken one hundred years earlier and also reported in P.Strass 22, which still relies on the Roman *usucapio*.[29] The difference between those decisions can, however, be explained differently. The case decided by the prefect Metius Rufus pertained to movable property, and in that time *longi temporis praescriptio* was applicable only to land, since the institute was extended to movables only after 211 CE, when Caracalla was

[21] Mitteis (1985), 613–14; see his different, later argument in Mitteis (1912), 287.

[22] Nörr (1969), 16–26.

[23] Col. IX, l. 13, 25–7; edition: Mattha and Hughes (1975); on limitation of action in that code see Nörr (1969) 16–26; Seidl (1974), 360–3.

[24] Coriat (1997), 381–8. [25] Modestinus, *Rules* 5 (D.41.3.18). [26] *Inst.* 2.6.9.

[27] Giodice-Sabatelli (1981); Honoré (2002), 155, 157, 222; Tafaro (2006), 13 n. 7.

[28] See above n. 7.

[29] P.Strass. 22, ll. 29–33.

in power as the single emperor.[30] This new regulation was also confirmed by Modestinus in his *libri differentiarum*.[31] Furthermore, since the case involved two Roman citizens, the claimant Sallustius Capito and the defendant Iulia Pytharus, it was perfectly legitimate to employ *usucapio*, which was an institute of the *ius civile*. The difference between the cases can therefore be explained without necessarily assuming a legal reform under Septimius Severus. Chevreau is also of the opinion that the plea of long-lasting possession was introduced in that particular ἀπόκριμα, without any precursor in Roman law.[32] She sees as inspiration for the plea the Attic πραγραφή, Ptolemaic regulations and the statute of limitations of a suit in Egyptian law.[33] The μακρᾶς νομῆς παραγραφὴ would be, according to Chevreau, an instrument of *cognitio extra ordinem*, which was closer to its Hellenistic models than to the *praescriptio* of the formulary process.[34]

An alternative view was offered by Seidl, who argues that a generally recognized rule operated in antiquity, according to which an attestable execution of any right during a long period of time legitimized the execution.[35] This norm of general validity, which can be found both in local regulations and in the writings of Roman jurists, was employed by Septimius Severus and Caracalla and Romanized through convergence with *usucapio*. He argues that through the imperial decision the provincial idea was introduced into Roman law and became part of the latter.[36]

Other authors have similarly seen the influence of provincial law in the μακρᾶς νομῆς παραγραφή, but were more reluctant in seeing the ἀπόκριμα as the moment of the introduction of this institute into the Roman legal system. Wilcken saw in the institute the influence of Ptolemaic law;[37] Amelotti held a similar opinion that the plea of long-lasting possession was developed on the basis of Hellenistic and Ptolemaic models without any connection to the Roman *usucapio*. The latter notices that the *longi temporis praescriptio* was most probably inserted in the edict of the provincial prefect already before the decision of Septimius Severus and Caracalla was issued, but he errs in his contention that no traces of the existence of such institute in the provincial edict can be found.[38] A fragment of the commentary to the provincial edict written by Gaius shows that already in the second century CE the *longi temporis praescriptio* was known alongside *usucapio* as a separate but analogous institute.[39]

The opposite view had already been proposed by Mommsen, who believed that since the ἀπόκριμα was directed to a peregrine woman, the plea of long-lasting possession should be seen as part of *Reichsrecht*, and not as the transfer of an institution of the *ius civile*.[40] In his opinion, however, the *praescriptio* was fully developed already under Septimius Severus and the emperors employed a

[30] Marcianus, *Rules* 5 (D.44.3.9): *Rescriptis quibusdam divi Magni Antonini cavetur, ut in rebus mobilibus locus sit praescriptioni diutinae possessionis* (It is decreed by certain rescripts of the great divine Antoninus, that prescription on the ground of long-lasting possession applies to movable property.)

[31] Modestinus, *Differences* 6 (D.44.3.3).

[32] Chevreau (2006), 108.

[33] Chevreau (2006), 108–9.

[34] Chevreau (2006), 108–9.

[35] Seidl (1973), 155–6.

[36] Seidl (1973), 156.

[37] Wilcken (1922), 41–3.

[38] Amelotti (1958), 181; Nörr (1969), 31–3.

[39] Gaius, *On the Provincial Edict* 28 (D.21.2.54 *pr.*).

[40] Mommsen (1895), 196.

well-known institution.[41] This opinion was shared by Mitteis[42] and Riccobono.[43] Partsch argued that the *longi temporis praescriptio* was introduced in the imperial constitutions in the 90s of the second century, just before solving the case of Juliana. The emperors would have therefore employed a recent and yet unknown legal institute and consequently a detailed description of it would have been necessary.[44] It must be mentioned, however, that it is one of the common features of the *ἀποκρίματα* that the emperor describes the rule of law to be applied in the case, and so this does not necessarily mean that the regulation was new.[45] More recently Hamza has formulated a thesis according to which there was a Roman predecessor of *longi temporis praescriptio*, which was called *longi temporis possessio*. It occurred in Roman jurisprudence in the second century CE, but was in decline in the postclassical period and disappeared after the reform of Justinian.[46]

According to the opinion dominant in the modern Romanistic doctrine, the plea of long-lasting possession would have remained unknown to Roman jurisprudence until 199 CE. Scholars of Roman law, who have been for decades under the influence of the interpolation-method, have rejected traces of the existence of that institute in jurisprudence prior to that year and have praised the *ἀπόκριμα* as the first mention of the institute in Roman legal writings.[47] It was commonly assumed, that the texts in which that institute is mentioned were interpolated by Justinian's compilers.[48] The authors who follow this thesis relate the alteration of jurisprudential texts to the Justinianic reform, in consequence of which the *usucapio* was kept only for immobile goods and *longi temporis praescriptio* was applied to land.[49]

Only by rejecting umpteen considerations of the plea of long-lasting possession by pre-Severan jurists as Justinianic alterations is it possible to formulate the thesis according to which the aforementioned *ἀπόκριμα* marks the moment of implementation by Septimius Severus and Caracalla of a purely provincial legal institute into *Reichsrecht*.[50] This view should therefore be confronted with the tradition of jurisprudential texts on *longi temporis praescriptio* dating back to pre-Severan times, which demonstrate that the *praescriptio* was already a fully developed institute before the decision in Juliana's case. In particular the references to such an institute by jurists active in the first and second centuries CE confirm this thesis.

Javolenus Priscus brings up *longi temporis praescriptio* in the first century CE in a text in which both *usucapio* and *longi temporis praescriptio* concern a piece of land.[51] An alteration to the text caused by the Justinianic reform, which made a

[41] Mommsen (1895), 196. [42] Mitteis (1912), 287; Mitteis (1895), 613–14.

[43] FIRA I. p. 438 (Nos. 84–5).

[44] Partsch (1906), 109–17.

[45] P. Col. 123, ll. 36–40 (15 March 200 CE); P.Oxy. LX 4068, ll. 5–12 (March/April 200 CE); P.Oxy. LXIV 4437, ll. 1–10 (January/February 200 CE); P.Col. 123, ll. 19–21 (14 March 200 CE).

[46] Hamza (1999).

[47] Amelotti (1958), 181–2, n. 223; Nörr (1969), 71–3; Chevreau (2006), 107.

[48] Amelotti (1958), 181–2, n. 223. [49] Vacca, (1993–1994).

[50] Amelotti (1958), 182; Nörr (1969), 74–5; Coriat (1997), 381.

[51] Javolenus, *Epistles* 6 (D.41.3.21): *Ei, a quo fundum pro herede diutius possidendo capturus eram, locavi eum: an ullius momenti eam locationem existimes, quaero: quod si nullius momenti existimas, an durare nihilo minus usucapionem eius fundi putes. Item quaero, si eidem vendidero eum fundum, quid*

distinction between *usucapio* valid only for movable goods and *praescriptio* employable for land,[52] can hardly be suspected. The *praescriptio* was also known to Javolenus's pupil, Julian, as demonstrated by a quotation in a text from Ulpian, in which Julian claims that, after the time necessary for the *praescriptio* has passed, the possessor can be protected by an analogous claim (*actio utilis*).[53] Gaius informs us about *longi temporis praescriptio* in his commentary on the edict of the provincial prefect.[54] The jurist of the Antonine era limits the seller's responsibility for eviction, in case he sold a thing belonging to another person, until the moment in which the buyer can be protected by *usucapio* or a plea of long-lasting possession. Gaius demonstrates in his text that he knows the *longi temporis prescriptio* and its function as a parallel to *usucapio* in the *ius civile*. Even if the above-mentioned texts do not give exact indications of the time limits necessary for the prescription they demonstrate clearly that such instrument was known and practiced in Roman law already in the first and second centuries CE before it was employed by Septimius Severus and Caracalla in their ἀπόκριμα.

The two papyri BGU 267 and P.Strass. 22 contain the only known reference to μακρᾶς νομῆς παραγραφὴ in Greek texts.[55] There are two later documents which probably refer to the same institution, without however mentioning its name.[56] The term παραγραφὴ generally indicated the expiration of a claim in Greek texts, which was a processual tool recognized in Attic law.[57] From a linguistic perspective the term παραγραφὴ has two parallels in Latin: *praescriptio* and *exceptio*.[58] Since both Latin terms have similar meanings, the expressions *longae possessionis exceptio*[59] or *longi temporis exceptio*[60] are also used to indicate the plea of long-lasting possession in the texts of Roman jurists. The expression μακρᾶς νομῆς παραγραφὴ corresponds to Latin *longae possessionis praescriptio*; the latter expression was employed by Papinian,[61] a jurist active under Septimius Severus, in his *libri responsorum*, a work completed around 212 CE.[62] What is striking in

de his causis, de quibus supra quaesii, existimes. Respondit: si is, qui pro herede fundum possidebat, domino eum locavit, nullius momenti locatio est, quia dominus suam rem conduxisset: sequitur ergo, ut ne possessionem quidem locator retinuerit, ideoque longi temporis praescriptio non duravit. In venditione idem iuris est, quod in locatione, ut emptio suae rei consistere non possit. (I leased (a piece of land) to him, against whom I was about to raise a claim based on long possession of land as an heir. I ask if you consider this lease void; if you consider it void I ask whether nevertheless the *usucapio* of the land continues. I also ask if I sell the land to that person, what is your opinion in the points which I have raised above? The answer was: if he, who was in possession of the land as an heir, leased it to the owner (of that land), the lease is void, because the owner rented his own thing. Hence it follows that also the lessor did not retain possession, therefore the prescription based on long time didn't inure. The same rule of law as in the case of lease applies to the case of sale, so that the purchase of one's own thing has no standing.)

[52] Vacca (1993–1994). [53] Ulpian, *On the edict* 22 (D.12.2.13.1).

[54] Gaius, *On the provincial edict* 28 (D.21.2.54 *pr.*). [55] Mitteis (1895), 613.

[56] The time limit of twenty years is mentioned in P.Par. 69 = W.Chr. 41, col. III, l. 21 (232 CE), immediately before (l. 20) there is a reference to an imperial constitution. The defendant in PSI 1337, l.10 (250–60 CE) seems to recall long lasting possession to his advantage.

[57] Paoli (1933), 80–103 and 117–20; Harrison (1971), 106–24.

[58] On the fusion of this two notions in the postclassical legal language see: Steinwenter (1947), 98–103.

[59] Ulpian, *Disputations* 3 (D.44.3.5.1).

[60] This expression appears for the first time in the times of Justinian: C.7.33.11; C.7.39.8pr.

[61] Papinian, *Replies* 10 (D.41.3.45 *pr.*). [62] Fitting (1908), 76–7; Liebs (1990), 91.

Papinian's account of the *praescriptio* is that he calls it, in contrast to his predecessors, by a name that corresponds exactly to the Greek expression *μακρᾶς νομῆς παραγραφὴ* employed by the emperors in their answer to Juliana. That Papinian knew not only the expression, but also the ten years' time limit for the *praescriptio* is shown in another fragment of his *responsa* passed down in the *Vaticana Fragmenta*.[63] Considering the time in which the *responsa* were composed, it cannot be determined whether the jurist already knew the institute before the year 199 CE.

Furthermore, the expression *longae possessionis praescriptio* can be found in the *responsa* of Paul[64] and in the *libri differentiarum* of Modestinus.[65] It is also mentioned by the emperors Alexander Severus,[66] Gordian,[67] Diocletian and Maximian[68] and Justin[69] in their constitutions. However, in Roman jurisprudential texts and imperial constitutions the plea of long-lasting possession is most often described with the phrase *longi temporis praescriptio*.[70] The fact that both in the *Digest* and the *Codex* of Justinian different expressions are found to describe the plea of long-lasting possession is a clear argument against the thesis that the texts were manipulated by Justinian's compilers in order to adapt them to the newly introduced reform. Moreover, since we find the expression *longi temporis praescriptio* in pre-Severan jurisprudential texts and the same expression is used by Septimius Severus and Caracalla in their Latin constitution, we can assume that they knew that institute as it operated in Roman law before deciding the case of Juliana. It is striking that in Severan times the new Latin expression, *longae possessionis praescriptio*, exactly corresponding to the Greek *μακρᾶς νομῆς παραγραφὴ*, enters into usage. Nevertheless, the older expression is not eradicated, but both continue to be used in parallel to indicate that same institution. Most probably the formulations *μακρᾶς νομῆς παραγραφὴ*, (which emerges for the first time in the *ἀπόκριμα* of Septimius Severus and Caracalla) and its Latin parallel *longae possessionis praescriptio* in Papinian's text (which appeared in roughly the same period) are not a sign of a reform of the plea of long lasting possession, but rather a purely stylistic variation.

Both in the Severan *ἀπόκριμα* and in the Roman jurisprudential texts the requirements for the plea of long-lasting possession are the same. The requirements consist of undisturbed possession, initial good faith and the related just title.[71] *Μακρᾶς νομῆς παραγραφὴ* operates similarly to *praescriptio* in Roman

[63] Papinian, *Replies* 3, VF 7. [64] Paul, *Replies* 6 (D.18.1.76.1); *Replies*. 16 (D.44.3.12).

[65] Modestinus, *Differences* 6 (D.44.3.3). [66] C.7.30.1 (226 CE).

[67] C.2.19.3 (238 CE); C.3.32.4 (238 CE). [68] C.3.32.26 (294 CE). [69] C.7.39.7.3 (525 CE).

[70] Javolenus, *Epistles* 6 (D.41.3.21); Gaius, *On the edict* 28 (D.21.2.54 pr.); Paul, *On Sabinus* 10 (D.12.6.15.1); *Pauli Sententiae* 5.2.3; *Pauli Sententiae* 5.5A.8; Ulpian, *On the edict* 22 (D.12.2.13.1); Septimius Severus and Caracalla C.7.33.1.1; Caracalla C.2.18.8; Alexander Severus C.3.44.6; Gordian III C.4.51.2; C.7.36.1; Diocletianus and Maximianus C.2.51.2; C.3.31.7 *pr.*; C.4.10.7.1; C.4.10.14; C.4.24.10 *pr.*; C.4.51.5; C.5.51.8; C.5.73.4; C.6.1.1; C.6.30.8; C.7.33.2; C.7.33.6; C.7.33.7; C.7.33.10; C.7.34.2; C.7.34.3; C.7.34.4; C.7.34.5; C.7.35.2.1; C.7.35.3; C.7.35.5; C.7.71.4.1; C.8.44.19; C.8.44.21 *pr.*; Constantinus C.3.19.2.1; Valentinian II, Valens and Gratian: C.11.48.7.3; Valentinian, Theodosius and Arcadius: C.7.38.2; Theodosius, Arcadius and Honorius: C.3.39.6; Arcadius and Honorius: C.7.38.3.1; *CTh*.10.1.15; Zenon: C.11.43.9; Justinian: C.6.43.3.3A; C.7.31.1.3; C.7.33.1; C.7.33.12 pr.; C.7.40.2.2; C.11.48.20 *pr.*; *Inst*.2.9.5.

[71] Papinian, *Definitions* 2 (D.44.3.11).

cognitio procedure;[72] this is confirmed by the origin of the institution, since *longi temporis praescriptio* appears for the first time in the context of *cognitio extra ordinem* and belongs to the *praescriptiones* of that procedure. Its origin is most probably related to the imperial prescription, in particular to the fiscal prescription after twenty years.[73] Due to formal differences, the *praescriptiones* of the *cognitio* procedure cannot derive directly from the *praescriptio pro reo* of the formulary procedure.[74] They are most probably procedural tools *sui generis* introduced into imperial law, and distinguish themselves from the exceptions of the formulary procedure because they rely on circumstances impeding the process, which the defendant brings to the magistrate in order to have their opponent's claim rejected.[75]

The decision of Septimius Severus and Caracalla includes the following among the requirements for the plea of long-lasting possession on the side of the defendant: *δικαία αἰτία* and possession that has not been contested (*νομὴ ἄνευ τινὸς ἀμφισβητήσεως*). The latter requirement, mentioned in BGU 267, ll. 8–9 has been variously interpreted in the literature. Meyer believed that only the claim of the owner could interrupt the course of time,[76] whereas Amelotti argued that not only any vindication claim, but also any other situation in which the control of the land in question had been lost caused the interruption.[77] An undisturbed possession on the side of the defendant is possible only if the owner stays inactive for a very long time. Therefore the solidification of the right on the side of the possessor corresponds to the loss of right on the side of the owner, who stayed passive for too long. This interpretation is underlined by the use of the verb *διατρίβω*, which indicates a passive loss of time, referring to the claimant.[78] Chevreau justifies the punishment of the careless owner by the necessity of the stable legal standing of land.[79]

Similarly the requirement of *δικαία αἰτία*, which is to be translated as *iusta causa*, has been disputed in the Romanistic doctrine. Some authors argue that *δικαία αἰτία* embraces only the objective requirement of the *iusta causa*, which is the *titulus*, whereas the good faith of the possessor would be irrelevant for the plea. The interpretations of Meyer and Amelotti lean in this direction, who believe that in classical law *bona fides* was not required for the enforceability of the plea.[80] In contrast, other authors follow the opinion of Wenger,[81] that *δικαία αἰτία* embraces both aspects: the objective *titulus* and the subjective good faith.[82] Further arguments for the latter opinion can be derived from the decision of the prefect Subatianus Aquila on *μακρᾶς νομῆς παραγραφὴ* reported in P.Strass. 22, ll. 10–27, which will be discussed later.

A further requirement of the *μακρᾶς νομῆς παραγραφὴ* was the established minimum time limits of the possession. The distinction between the time limit of ten or twenty years depends, according to the *ἀπόκριμα*, on the place in which

[72] Amelotti (1958), 180. [73] Partsch (1906), 112–18.
[74] Partsch (1906), 72–3; Steinwenter (1947), 79–82; Kollitsch (1959), 277.
[75] Partsch (1906), 71–2; Kollitsch (1959), 284–7. [76] Meyer (1920), 180.
[77] Amelotti (1958), 187; Chevreau (2006), 109.
[78] Chevreau (2006), 109. [79] Chevreau (2006), 110 n. 31.
[80] Meyer (1920), 180; Amelotti (1958), 185. [81] Wenger (1906), 375.
[82] Frese (1909), 13–14; Taubenschlag (1919–1920), 142–3.

the parties reside.[83] The time limit of ten years is to be employed in those cases in which both parties have residence in the same πόλις, whereas the time limit of twenty years in those in which the parties live in different cities. The jurists are less precise in describing this requirement and link the difference to a *praesentia* or *absentia* of the parties.[84] How exactly this requirement was supposed to be interpreted was discussed amongst the jurists.[85] It was only in AD 531 that Justinian has defined that a residence, not any other kind of permanence, is required and in particular not in the same *civitas*, but in the same province (*provincia*).[86] Already Partsch has convincingly shown that this decision relies on the development of the judiciary system and its respective terminology. In both decisions, the one of Septimius Severus and Caracalla in the case of Juliana and the one of Justinian, the requirement concerns the residence in the smallest judiciary district, which in Severan times was the *civitas* (πόλις) and in the times of Justinian *provincia*.[87] If we follow the thesis of Partsch the term πόλις in the Severan ἀπόκριμα indicates not just the metropolis but also the nome of which it was the capital.[88]

It was questioned up until the times of Justinian whether just the parties or also the land which was the object of the suit were supposed to be situated in the same judiciary district.[89] It can be assumed that the requirement of the uncontested possession on the side of the defendant already required the residence of the latter in the same place in which the land was located. This reasoning is confirmed by a fragment of the Syro-Roman law book,[90] a compilation of Roman imperial texts from the fifth century composed for law-school teaching in an eastern province and translated in the sixth century CE into Syriac.[91] Chapter 64 of the law book is concerned with the limitation of the claim of someone who had a servitude and had lost his *ius in rem* as a result of long inactivity. The text mentions the same time limits of ten and twenty years respectively and from the context it is assumed that the defendant stays in the place where the land in question lies.[92] Justinian also confirms such a view in one of his constitutions.[93]

[83] Mommsen (1901), 143 n. 1; Partsch (1906), 49–56; Nörr (1969), 80–1.

[84] *Pauli Sententiae* 5.2.3: *Longi autem temporis praescriptio inter praesentes continui decennii spatio, inter absentes vicennii comprehenditur.* (The prescription based on long time, however, takes roots from the period of uninterrupted ten years among the present, of twenty years among the absent.)

[85] C.7.33.12 *pr. Imperator Justinianus. Cum in longi temporis praescriptione tres emergebant veteribus ambiguitates, prima propter res, ubi positae sunt, secunda propter personas, sive utriusque sive alterutrius praesentiam exigimus, et tertia, si in eadem provincia vel si in eadem civitate debent esse personae tam petentis quam possidentis et res, pro quibus certatur: omnes praesentis legis amplectimur definitione, ut nihil citra eam relinquatur.* (Because three doubts arose among the ancient (jurists) concerning prescription based on long time: the first, with reference to the properties, where they were situated; the second with reference to the persons, whether we require the presence of both or of one of them; and the third, whether the claimant and the possessor should be in the same province or in the same city as the property in dispute, We shall comprehend all (these matters) in the pronouncement of the present law, so that nothing remains (ambiguous) out off (this regulation).)

[86] C.7.33.12.1–3. [87] Partsch (1906), 44, 51–7. [88] Meyer (1920), 181.

[89] Partsch (1906), 49–51. [90] Selb and Kaufhold (2002), Vol. II, 83–5 (§ 64).

[91] On the compilation see: Ferrini and Furlani (1968); Taubenschlag (1952); Vööbus (1982–1983); Selb and Kaufhold (2002); Kaufhold (2005); Thür (2013).

[92] Selb and Kaufhold (2002) Vol. III, 132–5. [93] C.7.33.12.3a–4.

In Roman jurisprudence *longi temporis praescriptio* is commonly presented as parallel to *usucapio* and the aforementioned requirements of *longi temporis praescriptio* are parallel to the requirements of *usucapio*. In both cases the main aim of the institute was, on the one hand, to deprive the owner, who stayed passive for too long, of the right to claim back his property and on the other hand to reassure the possessor, who maintained the property over a long time, in his right. Both institutes require on the side of possessor unchallenged possession, just title and initial good faith. However, the time limits are much shorter for the *usucapio* than for the *longi temporis praescriptio*, for they require one or two years, compared to ten or twenty years required for the plea. Moreover, since the latter was initially meant only for the possession of land, the different time limits depend on the place of residence of the parties, whereas for *usucapio*, which was valid for both mobile and immobile properties the different time limits referred respectively to movables and land, but were independent of the parties' residence.

The main difference between the two institutes is the material character of *usucapio* compared with the purely procedural nature of *longi temporis praescriptio*. That is to say, whereas *usucapio* was a means of acquiring ownership, the plea of long-lasting possession was a means of processual defence, which allowed a possessor of a provincial plot of land, after defined time limits, to oppose the vindication claim of the owner. Considering the *Aktionendenken* of classical jurisprudence, this difference might not have had such relevance for ancient jurists as is assumed in modern literature. By contrast, for ancient jurists both institutes belonged to different systems that defined who was entitled to make use of them. *Usucapio* as part of the *ius civile* was available exclusively for Roman citizens. Its main purpose was to consolidate the position of ownership after an informal transfer of *res mancipi*. That is to say when a *res mancipi* is transferred simply through a handover, without maintaining the form of *mancipatio*, the *usucapio* allows the acquirer to gain the quirital ownership in a relatively short period—one or two years. The *longi temporis praescriptio* as part of *ius gentium* could also have been employed by peregrines, and was supposed to mitigate the lack of *usucapio* in the provinces.[94] Originally the plea was meant only for provincial estates to which the Roman *usucapio* could not be applied.[95]

Since *longi temporis praescriptio* has the character of processual means, for many scholars it resembles the Attic παραγραφή more than the Roman *usucapio*. This fact induced a large part of scholarship to look for oriental models for the institute. In fact the *longi temporis praescriptio* can be seen in a wider context of forfeiture of claims.[96] The examples of such forfeiture can already be found in local provincial legal praxis in the first century CE. In P.Flor. 61 (85 CE) a time limit for penal claims of five or ten years is mentioned and the case is decided in conformity with that regulation.[97] The defendant invokes a similar regulation to his advantage in P.Oxy. I 68 (131 CE), arguing that the claimant stayed inactive

[94] On the relationship between *ius civile* and *ius gentium* see: Kaser (1993); Talamanca (1993), 274–5; Talamanca (1998), 191–5.

[95] G.2.46: *Item provincialia praedia usucapionem non recipiunt.* (Also, lands located in the provinces are not subject to *usucapio*.).

[96] Frese (1909), 13. [97] P. Flor. 61, col. II, ll. 45–7.

during the 18 years that have passed since the commencement of the loan.[98] The documents show that in the provinces too, and already before the decision of Septimius Severus and Caracalla, a general rule of forfeiture of claims after a defined period of time was being employed. Such a rule could originate from the Attic *παραγραφή*.[99] The precedents of the rule can also be found in Egyptian legal praxis in the so-called process of Hermias,[100] which demonstrate that the defendants already invoked long lasting possession to their advantage in the Ptolemaic period.[101]

The requirements of *μακρᾶς νομῆς παραγραφή* are explained with more clarity in a decision of the prefect Subatianus Aquila taken just eight years after the *ἀπόκριμα* of Septimius Severus and Caracalla. The procedure in front of the prefect took place on 13 March 207 CE between the defendant Maximus and claimant Sabinus, represented by Asklepiades. The prefect bases his judgment on some constitutions of the emperors (*P.Strass.* 22, l. 18: *διατάξεις τῶν κυρίων*), which indicates that he knew the decision of Septimius Severus and Caracalla[102] on the plea of long-lasting possession.[103]

Σουβατιανοῦ Ἀκύλα ἡγεμονεύσαντος.
(ἔτους) ιε Φαμενὼθ ιζ κληθέν[τ]ω̣ν Σαβείνου
καὶ Μαξίμου Διονυσίου καὶ ὑπακο[υ]σάντων
μεθ' ἕτερα· Ἀκ̣ύλας̣ εἶπεν· τί̣ ἀποκρ̣είνῃ
πρὸς τὸν χρόνον [τ]ῆ̣ς νο[μ]ῆς, ὥς φησι[ν] με-
τὰ τὴ̣ν ὠ̣νὴν τῆς Παυ̣σοράπιος ἐ̣τῶ̣[ν] σ̣χ̣ε̣-
δὸν δέκα τεσσάρων, καὶ τὴν ἐν τούτῳ σιωπήν;
Ἀσκληπιάδης ῥήτωρ εἶπεν· γέγονεν. Ἀκύ-
λας εἶπεν· διατάξεις εἰσὶν τῶν κυρίω̣ν̣ περὶ
τῶν ἐ̣ν̣ τοῖς ἔθνεσιν οἰκούντων· ἂν ἀ̣λ̣λα-
χόσε νομὴ παρακολουθήσῃ ἔχοντός τινος
ἀφορμὴν κἂν βραχεῖαν δικαίαν κατοχῆς,
σιωπήσαντος τοῦ νομίζοντος αὐτῷ διαφέρειν
καὶ ἀνασχομένου ὑπὲρ δεκαετίαν, ἔχειν τ̣[ὸ] βέ-
βαιον τοὺς κατασχόντας.

'To the prefect Subatianus Aquila, 13 March 207. After Sabinus and Maximus, the son of Dionysius, have been summoned and have appeared before the court. After others Aquila said: what do you answer about the time of possession, as he declares (his possession) after the purchase of Pausorapios almost 14 years ago, and (what do you answer about) the silence during that time? Asklepiades the attorney said: so it happened. Aquila said: there are constitutions of the emperors for those living in the province: if the possession passes to another (person), if someone has the starting point of his detention, although for a short period, but righteous, then, because the possessor kept silence about the fact that it belongs to him as property and endured it over the period of more than ten years, the detentors have the certainty of their right.'[104]

[98] Amelotti (1958), 177–8; Nörr (1969), 44–5.

[99] Hermann and Thalheim (1895), 122–3; Partsch (1906), 118–20.

[100] P.Par. 15 = UPZ II 161 and P.Tor. 1 = M.Chr. 31= Jur. Pap. 80 = UPZ II 162.

[101] Mitteis (1912), 29 and n. 1.

[102] Kreller (1933), 268 n. 3.

[103] Another constitution of both emperors on *longi temporis praescriptio* may be found in the *Codex* of Justinian, C.7.33.1 (see n. 107).

[104] P. Strass. 22, ll. 10–27.

The case put to Subatianus Aquila can be reconstructed as follow: Sabinus, represented by the attorney (ῥήτωρ) Asklepiades, claims the ownership of a thing that unfortunately cannot be identified more closely due to the brevity of the account. Maximus the son of Dionysius is the defendant. The claimant has sold the land in question nearly 14 years earlier to an Egyptian woman, Pausorapios.[105] The latter in the meantime has sold the land to Maximus who adds the period of possession by his predecessor and in consequence estimates his time of possession at 14 years. Most probably the transfer of rights over that land had in both cases, from Sabinus to Pausorapios and from Pausorapios to Maximus, a private character, because none of the parties invokes any kind of document.[106] There is therefore no direct contractual connection between the claimant and the defendant, which could potentially have given rise to alternative claims.

There are two arguments that speak for *accessio temporis* in this case: first, the defendant starts the calculation of his period of possession from the moment of acquisition by his predecessor; secondly, the prefect refers in his decision to a situation in which an object has been transferred from one person to another (ll. 19–20). The *accessio temporis* employed in this case by Subatianus Aquila has been recognized by Septimius Severus and Caracalla for *longi temporis praescriptio* in a rescript from 202 CE.[107] Moreover a fragment of Justinian's *Institutes*, based on a fragment of the homonymous work of Marcian,[108] confirms that Septimius Severus and Caracalla have recognized *accessio temporis* between the seller and the purchaser.[109] If the latter text is read in the context of paragraph 12, which immediately precedes it, it can be deduced that the imperial rescript mentioned in the *Inst.* 2.6.13 was also concerned with *longi temporis praescriptio*.[110] The possibility

[105] It would also be grammatically possible to understand Pausorapios, a name of a slave, as the object of the transaction, however, the *longi temporis praescriptio* was extended to movables by a constitution issued by Caracalla alone, and therefore not earlier than 211 CE, the year of the death of Septimius Severus, whereas the process takes place in 207 CE. It should consequently be assumed that the object of the suit constitutes a provincial plot of land.

[106] Wolff (1978), 46–56, 222–55; Cockle (1984); Burkhalter (1990); Maresch (2002).

[107] C.7.33.1 *pr.*-2: *Cum post motam et omissam quaestionem res ad nova dominia bona fide transierint et exinde novi viginti anni intercesserint sine interpellatione, non est inquietanda quae nunc possidet persona, quae sicut accessione prioris domini non utitur, qui est inquietatus, ita nec impedienda est, quod ei mota controversia sit. 1. Quod si prior possessor inquietatus est, etsi postea per longum tempus sine aliqua interpellatione in possessione remansit, tamen non potest uti longi temporis praescriptione. 2. Quod etiam in re publica servari oportet* (If, after the question of possession has been raised and dismissed, the things will have passed on in good faith into a new ownership, and from there will have passed anew twenty years without hindrance, the right of the person which is in possession at this time should not be questioned, like the one who doesn't use the addition (of the time of possession) of the previous owner, whose right is questioned, so (the person in possession) should not be hindered, because the claim (of property) was raised against him (scil. the previous owner). 1. If, however, the right of the former possessor has been questioned, even though afterwards he remained in possession for a long time without hindrance, he will, nevertheless, not be able to avail himself of prescription based on long time. 2. This (decision) must also be observed with reference to public property.). (see also the parallel passage, *Pauli Sententiae* 5.2.5). Cf. Rützenhoff (1986), 63–5.

[108] Ferrini (1901), 152–3.

[109] *Inst.* 2.6.13: *Inter venditorem quoque et emptorem coniungi tempora, divi Severus et Antoninus rescripserunt.* (The divine Severus and Antoninus have decided in a rescript, that the periods (of possession) of the seller and of the buyer are joined.).

[110] *Inst.* 2.6.12; Longo (1901), 228, n. 2; Zanzucchi (1904), 213; Di Marzo (1905), 116; Frese (1909), 14–15; for another assumption, see Krüger (1905) 146–7.

of adding the period of possession of the seller is also mentioned in the *libri responsorum* of another Severan jurist, Paul.[111] A purchaser could invoke the *accessio temporis* to his own advantage, if after adding the time of possession by his predecessor he would reach the prescribed period of twenty or ten years.[112]

It is worth noting that while in the imperial ἀπόκριμα the possession is indicated with the term νομὴ Subatianus Aquila uses two terms: νομὴ and κατοχή. The latter appears twice in the text: the first time in the description of the requirement of just beginning of the possession (ἀφορμὴν κἂν βραχεῖαν δικαίαν κατοχῆς), and the second time as participle (κατασχόντας), indicating possessors who have fulfilled the requirements for the plea. The employment of two different terms is not a purely stylistic act, but allows us to better understand the reasoning of the prefect. While the term νομὴ refers to possession and corresponds to the Roman *possessio*, the term κατοχὴ indicates what the Romans called *possessio naturalis*, i.e. detention, the factual physical exercise of a right over a thing. The semantic equivalency between κατοχὴ and *possessio naturalis* is mentioned in the commentary of Paul to the praetor's edict.[113] The text of Paul also concerns the detention as the beginning of possession.[114] The prefect defines the prerequisite for the plea of long-lasting possession as the beginning of detention, i.e. of factual physical execution of the right, which had to be legitimate, even if only for a short time. The term κατοχὴ is employed in the text to indicate the position of the defendant towards the object of the suit, a position which will be protected by the plea. It is the defendant who exercises actual possession over that object during the process, and not his predecessor, who possessed it for more than ten years, who will be protected in his capacity as possessor. This shows that the actual possession was one of the requirements for μακρᾶς νομῆς παραγραφή.

Subatianus Aquila describes the prerequisite of δικαία αἰτία more precisely, defining it as ἀφορμὴν κἂν βραχεῖαν δικαίαν κατοχῆς (ll. 20–1). For Mitteis the limitation indicates that the requirement concerns the subjective side of the act of acquisition, i.e. the good faith.[115] He claims, with good reason, that it would be illogical to put a time limit on the objective aspect (*titulus*). Consequently he argues against the thesis of Partsch, that good faith was unknown in classical Roman law as a prerequisite for the plea of long-lasting possession.[116]

Indeed, the decision of Subatianus Aquila demonstrates that the initial good faith was a prerequisite for the plea of long-lasting possession. In this case the known rule of Roman law *mala fides superveniens non nocet* is therefore employed.[117] The δικαία αἰτία mentioned by Septimius Severus and Caracalla in their decision about *longi temporis praescriptio* should most probably also be interpreted in this sense.

Chevreau argues to the contrary that δικαία αἰτία in the μακρᾶς νομῆς παραγραφὴ should not be seen as a result of abstract reasoning like the *iusta causa* in Roman jurisprudence. Consequently the phrase ἀφορμὴν κἂν βραχεῖαν

[111] Paul. *Replies*. 6 (D.18.1.76.1). [112] Rützenhoff (1986), 61–6; Chevreau (2006), 116–17.

[113] Paul, *On the Edict* 54 (D.41.2.1 pr.); cf. Biondi (1964), 742; Carcaterra (1966), 144–5, 211; MacCormack (1967) 51–2; Falcone (1996), 102–3, n. 287; Babusiaux (2014), 54–5.

[114] MacCormack (1967), 51. [115] Mitteis (1912), 287.

[116] Partsch (1906), 49–51. [117] Mitteis (1912), 287; Amelotti (1958), 186.

δικαίαν κατοχῆς should not be seen as a synonym to the Latin *possessio ex iusta causa* in the sense of a possession which relies on a title (*titulus*), but in a more general sense of *possessio non viziata* (*nec vi nec clam nec precario*).[118] There is, however, no reason to assume that a Roman prefect would stay unaware of the basic concepts of contemporary jurisprudence, or that he would avoid employing such concepts in exercising his judiciary authority.

The behavior of the claimant is described with the words καὶ τὴν ἐν τούτῳ σιωπήν (l. 16), which underlines what has already been expressed by the emperors in their decision about the Juliana case: that the μακρᾶς νομῆς παραγραφή is the result of the long inactivity of the owner. The vindicating owner limits his right to claim by his long silence. In order to be successful, the plea of μακρᾶς νομῆς παραγραφή required on the one hand the possession of the defendant who had a just cause, and on the other hand the inactivity of the claimant over ten or twenty years respectively, depending on the domicile of both parties.

In conclusion, the Severan ἀπόκριμα is not the starting point of the development of *longi temporis praescriptio*. In light of the sources presented in this chapter, the tempting thesis of Nörr, who claims the institute was introduced by Septimius Severus and Caracalla in this precise ἀπόκριμα, must unfortunately be rejected. As the jurisprudential texts of the first and second centuries CE demonstrate, the institute was known long before the imperial ἀπόκριμα was issued.[119] Nevertheless, the *longi temporis praescriptio* is an institute which embraces both Roman and provincial traditions. Its origins can also be traced in Greek and Egyptian legal practice, which could have had an impact on pre-Severan jurisprudence, but its affinity to the Roman *usucapio* cannot be denied. It is probable that similar rules of limitation of claims developed independently in various systems already in the pre-Severan era, as Seidl has noted. The institute encloses different legal traditions and it is both difficult and unnecessary to try to tear them apart.

The *longi temporis praescriptio* was an institute that was originally employed only in the provinces, as it was meant for plots of provincial land[120] and for the peregrine population as a substitute for *usucapio*. At the time the ἀπόκριμα was issued the institute was already developed in its main shape, with some controversy remaining relating to the interpretation of the domicile of the parties, which was later defined by Justinian. The original relevance of the plea to plots of provincial land and the fact that it was mentioned by Gaius in his commentary on the edict of the provincial praetor indicate that *longi temporis praescriptio* could have already been introduced in that edict before the decision of Septimius Severus and Caracalla was issued.[121] The time limits therefore probably originate in the edict of the praetor of the province.

[118] Nörr (1969), 85–9; Vacca (1993–1994), 154–5; Chevreau (2006), 112 n. 35.

[119] Mitteis (1895), 613.

[120] Partsch (1906), 3–6, 106–9; Meyer (1920), 179; Amelotti (1958), 183–4; Cornioley (1973), 127; Albanese (1985), 122. Other authors argue that it was applicable both to mobile and immobile property: Nörr (1969), 82–5; Chevreau (2006), 109–10 and n. 29.

[121] Mitteis (1906), 220–7; Frese (1909), 12.

REFERENCES

Adams, J.N. 2003. *Bilingualism and the Latin Language*. Cambridge.

Albanese, B. 1985. *Le situazioni possessorie nel diritto privato romano*. Palermo.

Amelotti, M. 1958. *La prescrizione delle azioni in diritto romano*. Milan.

Babusiaux, U. 2014. Funktionen der Etymologie in der juristischen Literatur. *Fundamina* 20, pp. 39–60.

Bastianini, G. 1975. Lista dei prefetti d'Egitto dal 30a a 299p. *Zeitschrift für Papyrologie und Epigraphik* 17, 263–321, 323–8.

Bastianini, G. 1980. Lista dei prefetti d'Egitto dal 30a a 299p, Aggiunte e correzioni. *Zeitschrift für Papyrologie und Epigraphik* 38, 75–89.

Biondi, B. 1964. Valore delle etimologie dei giuristi romani. In: A. Guarino, A. and L. Labruna, (eds.) *Synteleia Arangio Ruiz*. Vol. II. Naples, pp. 739–42.

Brock, S. 1979. Aspects of Translation Technique in Antiquity. *Greek, Roman and Byzantine Studies* 20, pp. 69–87.

Burkhalter, F. 1990. Archives locales et archives centrales en Egypte romaine. *Chiron* 20, pp. 191–216.

Carcaterra, A. 1966. *Le definizioni dei giuristi romani. Metodo e mezzi*. Naples.

Chevreau, E. 2006. *Le temps et le droit: La réponse de Rome. L'approche du droit privé*. Paris.

Cockle, E. H. 1984. State Archives in Graeco-Roman Egypt from 30 BC to the Reign of Seprimius Severus. *Journal of Egyptian Archaeology* 70, pp. 106–22.

Coriat, J.-P. 1997. *Le prince législateur. La technique législative des Sévères et les méthodes de création du droit impérial a la fin du principat*. Rome.

Cornioley, P. 1973. De l'origine de la longi temporis praescriptio. *Tijdschrift voor Rechtsgeschiedenis* 41, pp. 119–30.

Di Marzo, S. 1905. Appunti sulla dottrina della causa lucrativa. *Bullettino dell'Istituto di diritto romano* 17, pp. 103–22.

Eich, A. 2009. Diplomatische Genauigkeit oder inhaltliche Richtigkeit? Das Verhältnis von Original und Abschrift. In: R. Haensch (ed.), *Selbstdarstellung und Kommunikation. Die Veröffentlichung staatlicher Urkunden auf Stein und Bronze in der Römischen Welt*. Munich, pp. 267–99.

Falcone, G. 1996. Ricerche sull'origine dell'inerdetto uti possidetis. *Annali del Seminario giuridic dell'Università di Palermo* 44, pp. 5–360.

Ferrini, C. 1901. *Fonti delle Istituzioni di Giustiniano*. Rome.

Ferrini, C. and Furlani, J. 1968. *Leges saeculares*. In: *FIRA* II. Florence, pp. 751–98.

Fitting, H. 1908. *Alter und Folge der Schriften römischer Juristen*. Second edition. Halle.

Frese, B. 1909. *Aus dem Gräko-Ägyptischen Rechtsleben. Eine Papyrologische Studie*. Halle.

Giodice-Sabatelli, V. 1981. Constituere: Dato semantico e valore giuridico. *Labeo* 27, pp. 338–57.

Haensch, R. 2007. Apokrimata und Authentica. Dokumente römischer Herrschaft in der Sicht der Untertanen. In: R. Haensch and J. Heinrichs (eds.), *Herrschen und Verwalten. Der Alltag der römischen Administration in der Hohen Kaiserzeit. Cologne*, pp. 213–233.

Hamza, G. 1999. Zum Verhältnis zwischen usucapio und longi temporis praescriptio im klassischen römischen Recht,. In: *Mélanges Fritz Sturm*, vol. I, Liège, pp. 189–203.

Harrison, A. R. W. 1971. *The Law of Athens. Vol. II: Procedure*. Oxford.

Hermann, K. F. and Thalheim, T. 1895. *Lehrbuch der griechischen Rechtsaltertümer*. Fourth edition. Freiburg and Leipzig.

Honoré, T. 2002. *Ulpian. Pioneer of human rights*. Second edition. Oxford.

Kaser, M. 1993. *Ius gentium*. Cologne, Weimar, Vienna.

Kaufhold, H. 2005. Die Neuedition des syrisch-römischen Rechtsbuches. In: G. Thür (ed.), *Antike Rechtsgeschichte. Einheit und Vielfalt*. Vienna, pp. 67–80.

Kollitsch, W. 1959. Praescriptio und exceptio außerhalb des Formularverfahrens. *Zeitschrift der Savigny-Stiftung für Rechtsgeschichte: Romanistische Abteilung* 76, pp. 265–305.

Kreller, H. 1933. Spuren römischer Jurisprudenz in der ägyptischen Praxis. *Aegyptus* 13, pp. 260–74.

Krüger, P. 1905. Beitrag zur accessio temporis bei der Ersitzung. *Zeitschrift der Savigny-Stiftung für Rechtsgeschichte: Romanistische Abteilung* 26, pp. 144–8.

Lewis, N. 1978. The Imperial Apokrima. *Revue Internationale des Droits de l'Antiquité* 25, pp. 261–78 [= Lewis, N. (1995) *On Government and Law in Roman Egypt. Collected Papers of Naphtali Lewis.* Atlanta, pp. 224–41]

Lewis, N. 1996. Notationes Legentis. *Bulletin of the American Society of Papyrologists* 33, pp. 61–6.

Liebs, D. 1990. Römische Rechtsgutachten und responsorum libri. In: G. Vogrt-Spira (ed.), *Strukturen der Mündlichkeit in der Römischen Literatur.* Tübingen, pp. 83–94.

Longo C. 1901. L'origine della successione particolare nelle fonti di diritto romano. *Bullettino dell'Istituto di diritto romano* 14, pp. 225–75.

MacCormack, G. 1967. Naturalis possessio. *Zeitschrift der Savigny-Stiftung für Rechtsgeschichte: Romanistische Abteilung* 84, pp. 47–69.

Maresch, K. 2002. Die Bibliotheke Enkteseon im römischen Ägypten. Überlegungen zur Funktion zentraler Besitzarchive. *Archiv für Papyrusforschung* 48, pp. 233–46.

Mattha, G. and Hughes, R. G. 1975. *The Demotic Legal Code of Hermopolis West.* Cairo.

Meyer, P. M. 1920. *Juristische Papyri. Erklärung von Urkunden zur Einführung in die juristische Papyruskunde.* Berlin.

Mitteis, L. 1891. *Reichsrecht und Volksrecht in den östlichen Provinzen des römischen Kaiserreichs: mit Beiträgen zur Kenntnis des griechischen Rechts und der spätrömischen Rechtsentwicklung.* Leipzig.

Mitteis, L. 1895. Zur Berliner Papyruspublikation. *Hermes* 30, pp. 564–618.

Mitteis, L. 1906. Ägyptischer Schuldprozess v. J. 84/86 p. Ch. *Zeitschrift der Savigny-Stiftung für Rechtsgeschichte: Romanistische Abteilung* 27, pp. 220–8.

Mitteis, L. 1912. *Grundzüge und Chrestomathie der Papyruskunde. Vol. II: Juristischer Teil, Erste Hälfte: Grundzüge.* Leipzig (reprint Hildesheim 1963).

Mommsen, Th. 1895. Aegyptische Papyri. *Zeitschrift der Savigny-Stiftung für Rechtsgeschichte: Romanistische Abteilung* 16, pp. 181–202.

Mommsen, Th. 1901. Die Heimath des Gregorianus. *Zeitschrift der Savigny-Stiftung für Rechtsgeschichte: Romanistische Abteilung* 22, pp. 139–44.

Nörr, D. 1969. *Die Entstehung der longi temporis praescriptio.* Colgne and Opladen.

Paoli, U. E. 1933. *Studi sul processo attico.* Padova.

Papathomas, A. 2000. Ein neues Reskript der Kaiser Septimius Severus und Caracalla. *Zeitschrift für Papyrologie und Epigraphik* 131, pp. 129–34.

Partsch, J. 1906. *Die longi temporis praescriptio im klassischen römischen Recht.* Leipzig.

Reinmuth, O. W. 1935. *The prefect of Egypt from Augustus to Diocletian.* Klio: Beiträge zur alten Geschichte. Beiheft 34. Leipzig.

Reinmuth, O. W. 1967. A Working List of the Prefects of Egypt 30 B.C. to 299 A.D: Their Names, Terms of Office, and references to them which have appeared since A. Stein, *Die Praefekten Von Aegypten*, 1950. *Bulletin of the American Society of Papyrologists* 4, pp. 75–128.

Rützenhoff, H. 1986. Accessio temporis. Die Besitzanrechnung im römischen Recht. (Dissertation) Cologne.

Seidl, E. 1973. *Rechtsgeschichte Ägyptens als römischer Provinz (Die Behauptung des ägyptischen Rechts neben dem römischen).* S. Augustin.

Seidl, E. 1974. Die Verjährung als sozialer Behelf im Rechtsbuch von Hermopolis. *Zeitschrift der Savigny-Stiftung für Rechtsgeschichte: Romanistische Abteilung* 91, pp. 360–3.

Selb, W. and Kaufhold, H. 2002. *Das syrisch-römische Rechtsbuch, eingeleitet, herausgegeben, deutsch übersetzt und kommentiert.* Three volumes. Vienna.

Stein, A. 1915. *Untersuchungen zur Geschichte und Verwaltung Ägyptens unter römischer Herrschaft.* Stuttgart.

Stein, A. 1950. *Die Präfekten von Ägypten in der römischen Kaiserzeit.* Bern.

Steinwenter, A. 1947. Rhetorik und römischer Zivilprozess. *Zeitschrift der Savigny-Stiftung für Rechtsgeschichte: Romanistische Abteilung* 65, pp. 69–120.

Tafaro, S. 2006. Diritto e persona: centralità dell'uomo. *Diritto@Storia* 5.

Talamanca, M. 1993. Review of: Kaser, *Ius gentium. Iura* 44, pp. 272–307.

Talamanca, M. 1998. Ius gentium da Adriano ai Severi. In: E. Dovere (ed.) *La codificazione del diritto dall'antico al moderno (Incontri di studio).* Namples, pp. 191–227.

Taubenschlag, R. 1919–1920. Das römische Privatrecht zur Zeit Diokletians, in: *Bulletin de l'Academie Polonaise des Sciences et des Lettres.* Krakow, pp. 141–281[= *Opera Minora* I, pp. 104–59].

Taubenschlag, R. 1952. Il diritto provinciale Romano nel Libro Siro-Romano. *Journal of Juristic Papyrology* 6, pp. 103–19 [= in *Opera Minora* I, pp. 291–312].

Thür, G. 2013. Syro-Roman law book. In: S. Bagnall et al. (eds.), *The Encyclopedia of Ancient History.* Chichester.

Vacca, L. 1993–1994 [published 1998]. La riforma di Giustiniano in materia di usucapio e longi temporis praescriptio fra concezzioni dommatiche classiche e prassi postclassica. *Bullettino dell'Istituto di Diritto Romano 'Vittorio Scialoja'* 35/6, pp. 147–86.

Vööbus, A. 1982–1983. *The Syro-Roman Lawbook. The Syriac text of the recently discovered manuscripts accompanied by a Facsimile edition and furnished with an introduction and translation.* Two volumes. Stockholm.

Wenger, L. 1906. Review of Partsch, Die longi temporis praescriptio. *Zeitschrift der Savigny-Stiftung für Rechtsgeschichte: Romanistische Abteilung* 27, pp. 373–7.

Wilcken, U. 1922. Urkunden der Ptolemäerzeit. (Ältere Funde), Vol. II: Papyri aus Oberägypten. Berlin.

Williams, W. 1974. The Libellus Procedure and the Severan Papyri. *Journal of Roman Studies* 64, pp. 86–103.

Wolff, H. J. 1978. *Das Recht der Griechischen Papyri Ägyptens in der Zeit der Ptolemaeer und des Prinzipats. Vol. II: Organisation und Kontrolle des Privaten Rechtsverkehrs.* Munich.

Zanzucchi, P. P. 1904. La successio e l'accessio possessionis nell'usucapione. *Archivio Giuridico « Filippo Serafini »* 72.2, pp. 177–275.

6

Law and Romanization in Judaea

Kimberley Czajkowski

1. INTRODUCTION

In 398 CE, Arcadius, emperor in the East, issued a constitution to the praetorian prefect, Eutychianus, in which he formalized the position of Jewish tribunals throughout the empire.[1] This constitution was admirable for its clarity and its pragmatism. Jews were formally subject to Roman law and courts, since they had been Roman citizens (like other free subjects in the empire) since at least 212 CE, but could choose to abide by the decisions of the Jews or patriarchs *ad similitudinem arbitrorum* ('in the manner of arbitrators'). The latter involved voluntarily submitting themselves to a different jurisdiction. This constitution therefore resolved a potential conflict by bringing the jurisdiction of the patriarch and Jewish courts—which was probably officially informal or unrecognized before this point—under the umbrella of the Roman legal system.[2] Roman judges could then uphold the decisions of these non-Roman courts.[3] The need to iron out the perceived glitches in the legal workings of the empire could be seen as typical of late antiquity: it was only the late antique state and court bureaucracy that felt the need to formalize the previous working pragmatism.[4] This constitution should also be seen in the context of a growing amount of imperial legislation on the Jews in the later period,[5] and an increasing attempt to formalize their position.

It was not just late antique Romans who were worried about the Jews: rabbinic literature exhibits various anxieties and solutions to the 'problem' (in their view)

[1] *CTh* 2.1.10 (= *CJ* 1.9.8).

[2] On the evidence for the patriarch, see Levine (1996), 1–4; cf. Levine (1979), 651–4. It is highly unlikely that the patriarch had any real influence before the third century CE, though the extent, nature and source of their authority is much disputed: see Schwartz (1999), 214–21 for an argument for greater diasporan influence; see also Goodblatt (1994), 131–75 for a somewhat exceptional view on the source of the authority of the patriarchs.

[3] On this passage see Harries (2003) and Dohrmann (2003).

[4] See Harries (2003), 63–4 discussion of this passage: 'The two [jurisdictions] had existed in parallel and the system had worked in practice for centuries without apparent need for justification or rationalisation'.

[5] See Linder (1987) for a collection and commentary.

Kimberley Czajkowski, *Law and Romanization in Judaea* In: *Law in the Roman Provinces.* Edited by: Kimberley Czajkowski and Benedikt Eckhardt in collaboration with Meret Strothmann, Oxford University Press (2020). © Oxford University Press.
DOI: 10.1093/oso/9780198844082.003.0006

of Roman courts, and Jews' use of them. Questions included whether divorce bills given by gentile courts were valid;[6] other passages forbid recourse to gentile courts, even if their law is the same as Israelite law.[7] These texts usually refer more generally to gentile rather than specifically Roman courts, something that should not be overlooked in any discussion. But rabbinic literature (redacted from 200 CE onwards) certainly exhibits an anxiety around non-Jewish courts and judgments. Their reaction is—to generalize broadly—to try to usurp jurisdiction for themselves, a power-grab that attempts to reinforce the rabbis' own authority, founded as it was on their skills in legal interpretation.[8] In order to preserve and strengthen their own position, they needed Jews to come to them and them alone: the Roman power had to be kept separate.[9]

The one side here acts from a position of power; the other attitude is a push-back from a rather marginal, irrelevant (from the Romans' perspective) group within a backwater of a vast empire. But there are rich pickings in this later period for understanding the formal position of Jewish judges from the Romans' perspective, and rabbinic reactions to courts and laws other than their own. While the situation may not always be as clear-cut as Arcadius' constitution, an impression of the interaction of these different jurisdictions, understood in both the formal and informal sense, is possible, and we may construct a rather nuanced picture of the way each viewed the other. On the rabbinic side, this might be viewed as a conscious push-back against any kind of 'Romanization': the attempt is at separation. The Romans in some ways acknowledge the separation, but therefore subsume the indigenous institutions into their own state-sponsored structure.

The earlier picture is murkier, for the most part without such clear over-arching categorizations on the Roman side or such rich discussion on the Jewish one. Nonetheless, the above position did not emerge in a vacuum, and represents the culmination of a long interaction between Jews and Roman under the empire in the legal sphere. Some of this concerned the diaspora: the granting of certain rights and privileges to Jewish communities; the imposition of the Jewish tax in 70 CE on all individual Jews throughout the empire.[10] We also have some good

[6] The most commonly discussed passage is that from the *Mekhilta de Rabbi Ishmael*, Exodus 21:1–3, *Nezikin* 1, an halakhic midrash that was redacted in the third or fourth century: R. Eleazar the son of Azariah forbids Jews from using gentile courts even when they judge according to the laws of Israel (בדיני ישראל); in cases of bills of divorce, these will also be invalid if given by a gentile court unless it simply orders, 'Do as the Israelites tell thee' (עשה מה שישראל אומרים לך), i.e. refers him back to a Jewish court. *m. Giṭ.* 9:8 gives a similar interpretation.

[7] *b. Git.* 88a. Rabello (1996), 147–8 errs in arguing that the various passages cited here prove that the Jews of Palestine had 'concurrent judicial autonomy' in the period between 70 CE and the Bar Kochba revolt (the sages to which these sayings are attributed are tannaitic, and thus date to roughly this period): the use of rabbinic literature to prove historical *realia* is notoriously difficult, even in error, and Rabello is rather too positivistic about the use of these passages for such purposes.

[8] For a nuanced approach to the rabbinic texts and what they might tell us about the concerns of these groups, see Dohrmann (2003).

[9] This is of course a representation of the rabbinic presentation of the situation: there have long been attempts to trace more subtle interactions between Rabbinic, Roman and/or law in the rabbinic corpora. In addition to numerous studies on specific aspects or topics, Cohen (1966) compares Roman legal terminology and concepts with those of the rabbis; see Lieberman (1994) for a classic treatment of the extent of the rabbis' knowledge of Greek legal terminology; Hezser (1998) on legal forms.

[10] Rajak (1984) is still most often cited; in opposition see Eckhardt (2019).

evidence of Jews having recourse to non-Jewish law in the earlier period in diaspora settings: Babatha's archive in Roman Arabia is the prime example of this.[11] But the position of Judaea itself, and Jews living there, was somewhat different, and merits further consideration in the pre-rabbinic era. Here was where there was—unlike throughout the rest of the empire—a majority Jewish population,[12] one with their own, very distinctive legal tradition that differed significantly in nature from that of the Roman imperial state which ruled them. Nonetheless, from 6 CE Judaea was subject to direct Roman rule and—we would suppose—all the trappings of state that this entailed.

This chapter will assess how far we can delineate the presence and interaction of different jurisdictions from 6 CE, when the area first came under direct Roman rule, to the foundation of Aelia Capitolina. The odd administration of the region makes this a problematic case, and the oscillation between indirect and direct rule was a key factor in assessing the level of Roman influence we find on legal forms and institutions.[13] Thus, the available legal fora in Judaea in the first couple of centuries CE will be laid out—as far as the evidence allows us to do so—with a view to assessing how 'Romanized' this was, and thus how comparable the situation of its inhabitants was to other places within the empire. The distinctive legal tradition of the Judaeans and rather atypical administration of the region for a long period had a strong effect on the inhabitants' interaction with Roman legal institutions, and meant the region differed quite markedly from many others. It will, however, be suggested that further comparison should, perhaps, be made in future to another, more traditionally acknowledged 'oddity' within the empire: Egypt.

2. PROLOGUE: ROME AND HER KINGS

The administrative set-up of the region is the vital determinant of the legal fora available to inhabitants of Judaea. This is a truism of the provinces in general:

[11] See the chapter by Chiusi in this volume. Schiffman (2001), 179 argues that the Jews attested in the Judaean desert documents (i.e. especially the community in Roman Arabia) would have seen themselves as inhabitants of the 'Land of Israel'. In jurisdictional terms, however, the boundary mattered and seems to have done so for the provincials themselves, not just the Roman governor: indeed in the documentation regarding the Roman court, Babatha always goes to assizes within Arabia, Petra or Rabbath Moab, not over the border. These documents will therefore be kept separate from the discussion in the current chapter.

[12] There were of course plenty on non-Judaeans living in or around Judaea, and the populations varied by area within the province (rather than Judaea-proper): the Decapolis cities recognized by Pompey in the reorganization in 63 BCE are perhaps the most obvious examples to point out in the wider region.

[13] Cotton (2002) painted a picture that could be seen as broadly similar, though not as clearly formalized as in the later period: Jewish tribunals were seen by Romans as arbitration. This was, however, proven in reference to documents from Roman Arabia. The administration of Judaea means it poses a slightly different problem that should be drawn out at greater length. There is also here a problem of official cognizance: I have no doubt it would have suited the Romans to view Jewish tribunals as arbitration *when these were brought to their attention*, but—for the most part—there was little reason for this to happen on a large scale.

Roman direct rule came with certain institutional frameworks, legal among them.[14] The manner in which Rome ruled an area changed which instruments were available and could thus be utilized within a region, both in institutional terms (e.g. the assizes), and in terms of the number of personnel in an area. The latter is a vital concern in attempting to identify how certain Roman legal instruments may have spread.[15]

While these are general issues, they are brought into sharp focus by the different ways in which Judaea and its various parts were ruled. Judaea oscillated between direct rule and what might be termed 'rule by proxy'—nominally independent kingdoms, with their own native rulers.[16] In strict terms, these areas fall outside the concerns of this volume: they should have been judicially independent from Rome. Formally, there is every reason to believe this was the case. Informally, the status of these kingdoms may lead us to conclude that the judicial sphere was not always quite so separate from the long reach of Rome.

Roman era authors, indeed, did not see these kingdoms as entirely outside the imperial domain: the kingdoms were part and parcel of the empire, and the kings who ruled them *instrumenta servitutis*.[17] Certain juristic opinions appear to differ, and show the rulers as outside the bounds of the *imperium Romanum*.[18] The discussion in this realm typically concerns the right of *postliminium*, in its sense of the recovery of (lost) rights by a captured *cives* upon his return to Roman territory.[19] To take Proculus' view:[20]

> *Non dubito, quin foederati et liberi nobis externi sint, nec inter nos atque eos postliminium esse. etenim quid inter nos atque eos postliminio opus est, cum et illi apud nos et libertatem suam et dominium rerum suarum aeque atque apud se retineant et eadem nobis apud eos contingant?*
>
> I have no doubt that there are free and allied nations which are external to us, and that between us and them the right of *postliminium* does not exist. For what need would

[14] See Brélaz in this volume for officials involved in policing and criminal law, and Roman–local interactions over their functions.

[15] As outlined in the Introduction to this volume.

[16] Typically called 'client kingdoms' though the term is much contested: see Badian (1958), Rich (1989), Braund (1984), 7 for a sample of the conflicts.

[17] Tacitus, *Agricola* 14.2: 'instruments of servitude'; see also *Historiae* 2.81.1, where they are subjects (Antiochus is *servientium regum ditissimus*). See also the slightly less critical language of Strabo 17.3.25 (840): καὶ βασιλεῖς δὲ καὶ δυνάσται καὶ δεκαρχίαι τῆς ἐκείνου μερίδος καὶ εἰσὶ καὶ ὑπῆρξαν ἀεί (Kings, also, and potentates and decarchies are now, and always have been, in his (Caesar's) portion); Suetonius, *Augustus* 48: *nec aliter universos quam membra partisque imperii curae habuit rectorem quoque solitus apponere aetate parvis aut mente lapsis, donec adolescerent aut resipiscerent* (and he did not treat them all with consideration as other than parts and portions of the empire, and even was accustomed to appointing a governor for those too young to rule or who whose minds were affected, until they grew up or recovered). The position is clear here, and Suetonius sees no problem with it: these regions are *membra partisque imperii*.

[18] See Kaizer and Facella (2010), 24–5 on the contrast between ancient literature and the juristic texts, with a good summary of the evidence and literature.

[19] *Postliminium* also entails either the right of recovery of a thing from an *extraneus* or the recovery. See Paul, *On Sabinus* 16 (D.49.15.19); cf. Pomponius, *On Sabinus* 3 (D.49.15.14) for definitions. The question then is whether allied kingdoms count as outside the bounds of empire, meaning the right of *postliminium* applied, to which there was not a clear cut answer, suggesting that this was still a matter of debate in the second century (to which period most of the jurists in question date).

[20] Proculus, *Epistles* 8 (D. 49.15.7 pr.).

there be for any right of *postliminium* between us and them, as they, when with us, retain their liberty, and the ownership of their property, just as they do at home; and the same happens to us when we are with them.

The argument from this runs as follows: if *foederati et liberi* are *externi*, at least in the opinion of one first-century jurist, the territories ruled by *reges amici et socii* (generally thought to have been a more favourable status) must also have been seen as external to the empire.[21] Although external, there is not, however, a right of *postliminium* upon return from these places. The latter point is sometimes underestimated in the concept of rule that it underlines. In spite of the explicit statement of the external position of—we assume—such kingdoms, they are not so external as to merit the right of *postliminium*. Indeed, Pomponius in the second century also underlines this: *ius postliminii* applied to those nations with whom the Romans had no *amicitia*, *hospitium* or *foedus amicitiae*.[22] While, then, allied nations were *externi*, a right applicable to return from certain external peoples did not apply.[23]

The corollary to this is that Rome did not necessarily see the boundaries as that clear, and thus, while often leaving these places alone, might have also felt freer to interfere whenever this seemed necessary—and this might include in legal matters. This is particularly pertinent with regard to a region with a long history of its own kings that then was divided up within its various parts between direct and indirect rule (further details below): the changes involved should be considered carefully. In principle, the kind of legal institutions that we expect to find within a province would not have been available in an independently ruled client kingdom: the assizes circuit is the main concern here. A lack of personnel in comparison with direct rule also would have had an effect in terms of informal dissemination of legal ideas and formulae. Put simply, a lesser Roman presence in an independently ruled region of course entails less knowledge and spread of Roman legal forms. Judaea was in this situation for a long time: not subject to direct Roman rule but reliant on a very close relationship with the imperial power. After Pompey's Eastern campaigns and conquest of Jerusalem in 63 BCE Hyrcanus II

[21] Cimma (1976), 225–6.

[22] Pomponius, *On Quintus Mucius 27* (D.49.15.5.2): *in pace quoque postliminium datum est: nam si cum gente aliqua neque amicitiam neque hospitium neque foedus amicitiae causa factum habemus, hi hostes quidem non sunt, quod autem ex nostro ad eos pervenit, illorum fit, et liber homo noster ab eis captus servus fit et eorum: idemque est, si ab illis ad nos aliquid perveniat. hoc quoque igitur casu postliminium datum est.*(The right of *postliminium* is also granted in time of peace; for if there is a nation between which and us there exists neither *amicitia*, hospitality, nor any treaty of *amicitia*, it indeed is not our enemy. Anything, however, which belongs to us, and passes under its control becomes its property, and any freeman of our people taken in captivity by such a nation becomes its slave. The same rule applies if anything belonging to the said nation comes into our hands, and therefore the right of *postliminium* is conceded in this instance.)

[23] There is one problematic passage for the idea that *ius postliminii* did not apply to allied nations, namely Aelius Gallus, *Verb. Sign.* Fr 1: *cum populis liberius et confoederatis et cum regibus postliminium nobis est ita, uti cum hostibus* (with free people, with allies, and with kings, *postliminium* is for us the same as with regard to enemies). This is a much clearer statement of the idea that allies, freed people and kings were truly external. This is, however, a minority opinion and might simply evidence that the problem was still a matter of juristic contention in the second century.

was reinstated as High Priest though without the title of king.[24] He received recognition as ethnarch from Julius Caesar in 47 BCE, when Antipater also became procurator.[25] After Herod was appointed king by the senate in 40 BCE, Judaea continued as a so-called 'client kingdom' until his death in 4 BCE. But Herod's situation—himself a Roman citizen, it should not be forgotten—complicates the formal picture above as we see the results of Roman–Judaean contact at a higher level in the legal sphere.

Herod, indeed, very frequently involved the Romans in his own domestic disputes, which included legal disputes. In the trials of his sons, while his right to do as he pleased is always emphasized, he consistently either defers to the judgment of the emperor himself, or involves Roman officials in trials held in his own region.[26] This is entirely and completely voluntary, not a legal requirement of the relationship, even if it were perhaps politically savvy in cases involving the heirs to his kingdom.[27] Thus autonomy in internal civil and criminal law matters did not rule out the use of very Roman judges on a high level, especially for matters which might have an impact of future interstate relations. While this had little relevance to the majority of the population, the high profile nature of these cases did, however, mean than the imperial ideology of Rome as judge had a chance to spread even before direct rule was implemented. The resultant expectations also redraw the boundaries for 'formal autonomy'—Herod's repeated involvement of the Romans, and in some ways deferral to them in these matters, created a set of precedents about how to behave, when Rome was expected to at least be consulted, and when she was also likely have a say in these cases.[28] There

[24] See Josephus, *Antiquitates Judaicae* 14.74: *καὶ τὰ μὲν Ἱεροσόλυμα ὑποτελῆ φόρου Ῥωμαίοις ἐποίησεν, ἃς δὲ πρότερον οἱ ἔνοικοι πόλεις ἐχειρώσαντο τῆς κοίλης Συρίας ἀφελόμενος ὑπὸ τῷ σφετέρῳ στρατηγῷ ἔταξεν καὶ τὸ σύμπαν ἔθνος ἐπὶ μέγα πρότερον αἰρόμενον ἐντὸς τῶν ἰδίων ὅρων συνέστειλεν* (and he (Pompey) made Jerusalem tributary to the Romans, and took away those cities of Coele Syria which the inhabitants of Judea had subdued, and put them under the government of the Roman president, and confined the whole nation, which had elevated itself so high before, within its own bounds) (cf. *Bellum Judaicum* 1.154 on Jerusalem being subject to tribute); cf. Josephus, *Antiquitates* 14.77: *τήν τε γὰρ ἐλευθερίαν ἀπεβάλομεν καὶ ὑπήκοοι Ῥωμαίοις κατέστημεν* (for we threw away our liberty and became subjects to the Romans).The implication here is, however, starkly that of subjection: the passage continues to state that they were deprived of royal authority, which became the property of private men. On Hyrcanus II's restoration to the High Priesthood, see Josephus, *Antiquitates Judaicae* 14.73; *Bellum Judaicum* 1.153.

[25] Josephus, *Bellum Judaicum* 1.199.

[26] Josephus, *Antiquitates Judaicae* 16.90 on Herod's decision to take his sons to trial before Augustus, which is then described; *Antiquitates Judaicae* 16.332, 356–8 (cf. *Bell.* 1.535–7) for Augustus' advice being sought and received on the second trial of the sons, which is then carried out before a tribunal involving the governor of Syria and his legate, among others, at the Roman colony of Berytus; *Antiquitates Judaicae* 17.91 (cf *Bellum Judaicum* 1.617–19) for Varus as judge of Antipater; *Antiquitates Judaicae* 17.144–5, 182 (cf. *Bellum Judaicum* 1.661) for Augustus being consulted and giving his opinion before the execution of the penalty.

[27] See Czajkowski (2016) for this argument at more length; see also more recently McGinn (2019) on the trials of Herod' family members.

[28] Similar dynamics can be seen later in an incident in 62 CE, where the High Priest Ananus tries to take advantage of a temporary absence of a Roman governor to execute James, the so-called brother of Jesus (*Ant.* 20.199–203) and two groups appeal to both the incoming Roman governor and the king that Ananus' actions were illegal. Whether this is true is debatable, but even much later we see a similar voluntary calling-in of the Roman authorities into the judicial sphere. See Czajkowski (2017) for an analysis of this passage at greater length; on the much debated related issue of whether the Sanhedrin

may have been no direct influence or direct rule, but Rome's presence in the legal sphere at this highest level was nonetheless very strongly felt: she excelled her clients in authority, to paraphrase Proculus, and this had certain key implications for their practical autonomy.[29]

3. THE ADMINISTRATION OF JUDAEA

Upon Herod's death, the area was not immediately annexed. At first, it was fragmented between his sons: Judaea proper then went to Archelaus, the Peraea and the Galilee to Antipas (4 BCE–39 CE), and Batanaea and the Auranitis to Philip the Tetrarch (4 BCE–34 CE). Archelaus was deposed in 6 CE by Augustus after complaints from his subjects, and Judaea proper was then taken under direct Roman rule, surrounded by these client rulers and the Decapolis cities. This broadly remained the case, though the boundaries changed, and there was a notable return to 'rule by proxy' in Judaea proper in 41–4 CE, when Agrippa I took over a kingdom that was then as large as his grandfather's (Herod) had been. After 70 CE there was a marked shift in that the military presence in Judaea was significantly increased.[30] The governor of the province was also the *legatus* of the region, an unusual arrangement that nonetheless reinforces the need for caution in separating military and civilian administration in this region.[31] Upon the foundation of Aelia Capitolina, Jerusalem became a colony: again, this significantly changed the status of this particular city.[32] The increased presence of Roman personnel, military included, has implications both for the availability of legal fora, for particular Romans who might adjudicate cases, and on a basic level for the visibility of the imperial rulers: in the later period, they were a more present and thus perhaps a more obvious option.

Yet the period from 6 CE forms our core, and the phrase 'direct Roman rule' for the transition was chosen deliberately: despite most statements to the contrary, it seems clear that Judaea did not become an independent province when it was first

had the right to inflict capital punishment, see the comments and bibliography on *CIIP* I.2 for a good, concise overview of the issues; it remains to say that even among those who argue that the *synedrion* did have capital jurisdiction, this did not encompass the *ius gladii* (see the sensible comments of Winter (1964) 494–5), which would have been an entirely separate issue.

[29] The Digest passage directly following that quoted above encapsulates this: Proculus, *Epistles* 8 (D. 49.15.7.1): *et quemadmodum clientes nostros intellegimus liberos esse, etiamsi neque auctoritate neque dignitate neque viri boni nobis praesunt, sic eos, qui maiestatem nostram comiter conservare debent, liberos esse intellegendum est* (And just as we regard our clients as free, although, while being good men, they are not superior to us in authority or dignity; so those who should zealously defend our majesty should also be understood to be free).

[30] The *legio X Fretensis* was left garrisoned in Jerusalem after its destruction (see Josephus, *Bellum Judaicum* 7.1–3, 5, 17; cf. *Vita* 422), with vexellations also stationed elsewhere in the province. Before 70, only auxiliaries were stations in Judaea. There is some debate about whether these were all recruited locally (as Schürer (1973), I. 363–5 argues); see Speidel (1982–3) for problems with this.

[31] On this arrangement see Eck (2017), 94–5; Eck (2007), 109–10.

[32] Aelia's composition was most likely of veterans from the *legio X Fretensis* a legion which had been in the region for a while (see n.30 above): Isaac (1980), 46–7; see Belayche (2001), 129 for further details on the city's initial composition.

annexed and instead was added as an appendage to the province of Syria.[33] The date at which there was a *Iudaea provincia* is disputed: we may at least state, with Eck, that it must have been an independent province in 66/67 CE, as evidenced by the appointment of Vespasian as *legatus Augusti pro praetore*.[34] But before that, this was (for most of the period at least) a small appendage to the larger province of Syria and this should be factored into any consideration of the types and range of fora available to litigants at that time. Officially, of course, the Roman governor had jurisdiction. This was not simply the *legatus* of Syria from 6 CE: Josephus is clear in stating that the *epitropos* of Judaea has the power of life and death put into his hands by Caesar.[35] This is to do with Roman citizens so has restricted relevance: the *procurator* had *ius gladii*, i.e. the power to execute Roman citizens. This is naturally to do with what we at least would classify as criminal matters, but the key point to note is that this was the ultimate power to put in the hands of a Roman official, and so we should assume *iurisdictio* in civil matters too: if the procurator had this maximum power, then slightly lesser ones should also be included.

Thus, the prefect could preside over cases. His headquarters were in Caesarea Maritima, rather to the north of the country, and not in Jerusalem. As such, even if he presided over cases there, and—following the principle of the Roman governor's court elsewhere—was accessible to all, in practical terms only a few could have taken advantage of this, since it would have been a considerable distance for others to travel: this cost not only money but time, which should not be underestimated in an agricultural economy when it would have necessitated people being away from their land for an extended period. In practical terms his availability would therefore have been restricted to those in the immediate area. It was taken up by some: Quadratus, for example, was asked to intervene in a

[33] See Josephus, *Antiquitates Judaicae* 17.355: *τῆς δ' Ἀρχελάου χώρας ὑποτελοῦς προσνεμηθείσης τῇ Σύρων* (Now the territory subject to Archelaus was added to (the province of) Syria); *Ant.* 18.2: *παρῆν δὲ καὶ Κυρίνιος εἰς τὴν Ἰουδαίαν προσθήκην τῆς Συρίας* (Moreover, Cyrenius came himself into Judea, which was an appendage of Syria). Josephus, *Bellum Judaicum* 2.117 has been thought to contradict the *Antiquitates Judaicae*: *Τῆς δὲ Ἀρχελάου χώρας εἰς ἐπαρχίαν περιγραφείσης ἐπίτροπος τῆς ἱππικῆς παρὰ Ῥωμαίοις τάξεως Κωπώνιος πέμπεται μέχρι τοῦ κτείνειν λαβὼν παρὰ Καίσαρος ἐξουσίαν* (And now Archelaus' part of Judaea was reduced into a province, and Coponius, one of the equestrian order among the Romans, was sent as *epitropos*, having the power of [life and] death put into his hands by Caesar). Not too much should be made of this: it is possible Josephus was simply inexact in the *BJ*, a shorter work in any case. From the title of the imperial officials (i.e. *praefectus)*, the role of the *legatus* of Syria, and the small amount of territory that was encompassed in Judaea (truly tiny in terms of constituting a province), it seems quite clear this was not initially an independent province. See Eck (2017) and (2007) for detailed arguments on this; also Cotton (1999); Mason (2016).

[34] Eck (2017) (most recently; see n.33 above for earlier references): Eck's argument is based on the fact that Vespasian in 66 CE needed to command an army to suppress the revolt, and could not operate in the territory of another *legatus*; hence, Judaea was then an independent province. Eck's arguments are conclusive in the sense that *Iudaea* must have been an independent province at this point, though that does not rule out the idea that this could perhaps have occurred at an earlier stage. Cotton (1999) argues for 44 CE, after the death of Agrippa I, as likely but not definite: this is based primarily on the change in our sources from *praefecti* to *procurators*—the change in designation also indicating a change in status. Cotton does not entirely deal with the problems posed for this by Tacitus, *Annales* 12.23: *Ituraei et Iudaei defunctis regibus Sohaema atque Agrippa provinciae Suriae additi* (Ituraea and Iudaea were added to the province of Syria, when the kings Sohaemus and Agrippa died).

[35] Josephus, *Bellum Judaicum* 2.117.

case between the Samaritans and Jews in 52 CE. The extent to which he dragged his feet about making a decision might exemplify why the Roman governor was not always the best first option.[36] Paul was of course also sent on to the governor in *Acts*, after his cases (and his own actions) became increasingly problematic.[37]

The normal solution to the availability problem was for the governor to hold assizes, travelling around designated centres in the province where people could approach him.[38] There is no evidence for the assizes in Judaea in this period. Josephus does give us details that the *praefecti/procuratores* travelled between 6 and 66 CE which would fit with the assizes pattern, and Cotton and Eck are right to caution against making too much of the lack of evidence to argue that this was not operational.[39] But the absence is at least of some relevance for assessing the popularity of this forum for the population of Judaea, particularly in the context mentioned above of the fluctuation between direct and indirect rule. Notable too is the fact that Judaea proper (in the sense of Archelaus' territory) was for the most part surrounded by areas ruled by 'clients'. The short reign of Agrippa I as king is also a problem: did this then necessitate the evacuation of the governors' assizes and other markers of direct rule? This is somewhat unclear: Roman troops could certainly still be stationed in client kingdoms,[40] meaning that a continued Roman presence might actually be likely in an area that had previously been annexed, despite its nominal independence. One would strongly expect an assize circuit to cease in an area that was handed back to a native ruler—the minimum administration was, after all, one of the advantages to the Romans, who minimized their economic and personnel costs by running areas in this way.[41]

A more pressing concern is what other Roman personnel would have been available to act as judges, should Jewish provincials have wished to use them. While we focus on the governor's court in justice administration—and this was indeed the ultimate arena—it is a mistake to conceive of him as the only available judge. The governor could delegate his responsibilities to other officials, and *iudices dati* certainly operated quite widely:[42] legionary legates and other senior officials were possible, though not in Judaea pre-66/7 CE, as the troops there were auxiliaries.[43] The equestrian commanders of the auxiliaries were, however, an

[36] Josephus, *Bellum Judaicum* 2.232; *Antiquitates* 20.118–33.

[37] The governor's activity in keeping the peace is fairly well attested: see, for example, *Antiquitates* 20.173–8 and Felix's actions to suppress the quarrel between Jews and Greeks at Caesarea. On Paul: he is sent on to the governor, Felix, tried and detained there until his eventual appeal to Rome (see *Acts* 23–5), but this does not really amount to the same impulse as provincials actively bringing their (civil) complaints to a Roman authority.

[38] See Marshall (1966) for an excellent overview of the assizes, though focussed on the later Republican era; also Burton (1975) for personnel; see also Haensch (1997), 320–1 for further literature.

[39] Cotton and Eck (2005), 36. P. Cotton, as yet unpublished, is reported to confirm the existence of the *conventus* though this dates to the Hadrianic era.

[40] See, for example, Speidel (1982–3), 239 for comments on the situation under Agrippa II.

[41] See Coşkun (2005), 20–2.

[42] Cotton and Eck (2005), 41–4 suggest a possible *iudex datus* in P. Yadin 14, though it still seems uncertain whether the different titles in the document on which they base this are any more than a scribal slip.

[43] See Speidel (1982–3) on the composition of the troops in Judaea; the debate over the composition of the auxiliaries goes back to Mommsen and von Harnack (1895) (and Mommsen (1884)), and Schürer (1973), who held opposing views about whether these were recruited purely locally or not.

option.[44] Elsewhere in this volume we see the role of the military in legal transactions, and even in dispensing judgements.[45] It is perfectly possible that they also performed this role in Judaea, but again we should emphasize the lack of evidence for this: Roman judgements/judicial fora simply do not seem to have been as popular as elsewhere pre-70 CE. We might add to this that the first Greek legal documentation from Judaea dates to 115 CE at the very earliest.[46] The use of this language is usually taken as an indicator of a desire to make one's documents more accessible in a Roman court, and this could and did elsewhere spread to documents that at least initially had nothing to do with that arena. Thus its absence for such a long time in Judaean legal documents plausibly indicates a general lack of concern for the Roman authorities in their legal transactions. Put simply: if the offer of justice was made to provincials in Judaea pre-70 through the normal travelling assizes, there are indications that these subjects were simply not interested.[47]

This picture all changed dramatically post-70 CE, with the increased Roman presence and then again later with the foundation of Aelia Capitolina. But it is significant that this was the point of change in this region, not direct Roman rule in and of itself. When Judaea was incorporated into the province of Syria in 6 CE, there is a strong argument for little change in day to day legal transactions for the majority of the population.[48] The area remained markedly 'un-Romanized' in the legal sphere.

4. JEWISH COURTS, AUTONOMY, AND LAW

If the Roman options were available but unpopular, are there then strong grounds for seeing a thriving, popular and even supported sphere of Judaean jurisdiction? At the highest level, the most obvious—and most debated—indigenous institution would be the so-called Great Sanhedrin. This title is taken from rabbinic literature: the Mishnaic tractate, for example, which is redacted closest to the period under discussion here (*c.*210 CE), tells of the Great Sanhedrin of 71 members, and then smaller sanhedrins of 23 members at a local level; there is also a system of referrals from local courts upwards, and the Great Sanhedrin had the power to impose capital penalties.[49] The impression we receive from this is of a highly systematized

[44] Cotton and Eck (2005), 27.

[45] See, for example, the discussion of the *sententiae* from Dura Europos in Chapter 8 of this volume; see also the chapters of Eckhardt and du Plessis on the role of the military in the West.

[46] P. Murabaat 114; see Cotton and Eck (2002) on the date *contra* Benoit in Milik, Benoit and De Vaux (1961), who places it at 171 CE.

[47] Unlike very nearby in Roman Arabia from 106 CE, where there is a quick uptake of Roman legal institutions, and an adaptation of legal paperwork in ways designed to be more accommodating to Roman judges: see Meyer (2007) and Cotton (2003).

[48] In this context, Judaea might be profitably compared with Egypt in its slow rate of Romanization in legal matters: other provinces are much quicker in their rate of change. See Czajkowski and Eckhardt (2018) for further examples.

[49] Most clearly see *m. San.* 1:1, 1:2, 1:6 (the Sanhedrin Jerusalem as a court of 71; course of 23 for cities with at least 120 inhabitants; 3 for smaller cities) but most of the tractate is relevant for the carefully apportioned jurisdictional rules it lays out.

jurisdictional structure, with the Sanhedrin sitting at the top. This image has had a powerful and lasting impact on the scholarly treatment of this period, even among those who view the exact set up with a degree of scepticism. Here is not the place to go into the protracted debate about the historical worth of the picture created in rabbinic literature: on this specific tractate and institution, it has been amply and repeatedly demonstrated that this is a construction of the rabbis, with limited—if any—application to the historical situation pre-70.[50]

There is, however, some evidence of a high level council that has in the past been equated to and described as the Sanhedrin: while we should avoid this equation, the existence of the council in itself is not implausible, so long as we do not envisage it as a single, static and identical entity across periods. In the Roman era, this was likely a council of leading men, summoned either by the High Priest or king when needed.[51] The main sources for this in the first centuries BCE and CE are Josephus and the New Testament:[52] the council's function as a court, or it pronouncing judgement is attested, but is somewhat thin as opposed to its role as a consultative body for the king or priest(s) on a variety of issues.[53] It is also likely that the council would have been relevant primarily for the elite strata of society: the idea that more mundane cases would have reached this body on a regular basis seems somewhat dubious.

[50] See Goodblatt (1994), 130 on the 'myth' of counciliar supremacy (heavily rooted in the rabbinic depiction of the Sanhedrin) in the earlier period; see also the comments by Grabbe (2008), 13–15. For older treatments of the Sanhedrin as an institution, which are often heavily reliant on the rabbinic picture, see Büchler (1902) and Mantel (1961); attempts to marry up the picture in the gospels with the Mishnah (especially concerning the conflicting information on the capacity to pronounce capital punishment) have come up with a variety of solutions, including a 'political' and 'religious' Sanhedrin, on which see Zeitlin (1945), (1946a), (1946b).

[51] Grabbe (2008), 16.

[52] The New Testament passages refer to a *gerousia* or *synedrion*: Matt. 5:22 (which does have a context of judgement); John 11:47 (calling together the *synedrion* to plot against Jesus); Mark 14:55, 15:1, Matt. 26:59, Luke 22:66 on the trial of Jesus before the *synedrion*; various apostles also account for their actions to the *synedrion*: *Acts* 4:15 mentions the *synedrion*; see also 5:21, 'when the high priest and those with him arrived, they called together the *synedrion* and the whole *gerousia* of the sons of Israel' (*Παραγενόμενος δὲ ὁ ἀρχιερεὺς καὶ οἱ σὺν αὐτῷ συνεκάλεσαν τὸ συνέδριον καὶ πᾶσαν τὴν γερουσίαν τῶν υἱῶν Ἰσραήλ*); Paul is also brought before the *synedrion*: see *Acts* 22:30, 23:6, cf. 23:20, 28.

There are also a few possible references in 1, 2 and 3 Maccabees to some sort of high level council in the pre-Roman era: *2 Macc* 4:43–7 refers to a *γερουσία*, though this is in the city founded by Jason; the Letters in 1 and 2 Macc. have also been used as evidence for such a body (see, for example, *2 Macc* 11: 27–9, when Antiochus addressed a letter to the *γερουσία*); cf Judith 14:6–8, which refers to a *γερουσία* of the whole people of Israel; also Josephus, *Antiquitates* 12.138–46 for the decree apparently by Antiochus III which mentions a *γερουσία*.

[53] Terminology poses a problem here and references to a *gerousia*, or *boule* have often been conflated with the Sanhedrin: this is not necessarily problematic in seeking evidence for a high-level council, but the 'Sanhedrin' label is somewhat misleading in this regard. For the evidence for the council in the earlier period, see n.52 above; Grabbe (2008) collects all possible references for the monarchy onwards. In the Herodian and Roman era, of particular note is the reference to a *synedrion* as famously judging the young Herod for his execution of a group of bandits at *Antiquitates* 14.163–84, though the term is not used in the parallel passage in the *Bellum Judaicum*. For a *synedrion* as a consultative body, see *Antiquitates* 20.216–17 (Agrippa II convenes the *synedrion* to decide on a Temple matter, *c.*64 CE); many of the references to the *gerousia* in the Seleucid and Hasmonean era also present it in this manner or as a ruling council (e.g. Judith).

There are, however, further references to non-Roman courts in Judaea. Josephus mentions courts of seven magistrates in a couple of passages that rework the biblical text but in this detail departs from it;[54] this has been thought to therefore evidence actual practice in his own time. Corroboration for this is sometimes found in his arrangements for Galilee when he commanded the war there:[55]

> *συνιδὼν δὲ ὅτι τοὺς μὲν δυνατοὺς οἰκειώσεται μεταδιδοὺς τῆς ἐξουσίας αὐτοῖς, τὸ δὲ πᾶν πλῆθος εἰ δι' ἐπιχωρίων καὶ συνήθων τὰ πολλὰ προστάσσοι, τῶν μὲν γηραιῶν ἑβδομήκοντα τοὺς σωφρονεστάτους ἐπιλέξας ἐκ τοῦ ἔθνους κατέστησεν ἄρχοντας ὅλης τῆς Γαλιλαίας, ἑπτὰ δὲ ἐν ἑκάστῃ πόλει δικαστὰς τῶν εὐτελεστέρων διαφόρων· τὰ γὰρ μείζω πράγματα καὶ τὰς φονικὰς δίκας ἐφ' ἑαυτὸν ἀναπέμπειν ἐκέλευσεν καὶ τοὺς ἑβδομήκοντα.*
>
> Realizing that he would win over to his side the powerful [men], for their part, by sharing authority with them, and the entire mob, for their part, if he would issue orders in general through locals and familiar [men], he selected the seventy most prudent of the elders and established them as leaders of all Galilee, and seven in each city as judges of less significant disputes. The larger matters and the murder trials he directed [them] to send up to himself and the seventy.

While this has been taken to offer support to the idea that Josephus' additions to the Pentateuchal texts are indeed insertions of contemporary practice, this is not quite so clear. The passage here, indeed, presents Josephus as setting up what he thinks is a pragmatic solution to ensure loyalty from the locals, and is not framed either as a continuation of a pre-existing local structure or of a reinstatement of the situation before war broke out.

The existence of local courts or tribunals is plausible; their exact composition and indeed competence remains hazy.[56] In view of the apparent lack of uptake of Roman justice, and the rather shoestring-nature of the administration, it is credible that such native tribunals—whether of seven or not—were likely to be rather more popular for the majority of Jews in Judaea from 6 to 66 CE at least. These could have been established for a long period, were built on indigenous power structures, and may have been rather more accessible than the governor with his occasional visit.

From the Roman viewpoint, most of these would have been seen as informal tribunals, if indeed they ever merited any attention. But for the most part, it seems likely that they never would have done: far from being automatically classified as 'arbitration', or rather as like arbitration, as was the case in the later period, such bases for dispute resolution were in all probability assumed to exist and ignored as far as possible. They were also a necessity in a region with such a strong adherence to a slightly peculiar ancestral law of its own (see below).

[54] Josephus, *Antiquitates* 4.214 and 287. See Schürer (1973–87: II, 187) for comments.

[55] Josephus, *Bellum Judaicum* 2.570–1 (Mason's translation). See also the parallel passage in *Vita* 79.

[56] It has been suggested that passages from the New Testament also attest local criminal jurisdiction in Jerusalem. Those concerning the *synedrion* and the trial of Jesus have been dealt with above; Matthew 10:17 (*παραδώσουσιν γὰρ ὑμᾶς εἰς συνέδρια*; cf. Mark 13:9: *παραδώσουσιν ὑμᾶς εἰς συνέδρια*) are also often cited for Jesus' warning that his followers would be handed over to the councils but this is followed closely by his warning that they would also be brought before governors and kings, so the application to Judaea is not necessarily proven. Other passages primarily refer to the Diaspora: see *Acts* 9:2; 22:19; 26:11, 18:12–16 and 2 *Corinthians* 11:23.

5. CONCLUSION: JUDAEA, A SPECIAL CASE?

The lack of uptake of Roman legal institutions even when the area was under direct rule (if not a province) contrasts quite starkly with many of the other regions treated in this volume: while local traditions persisted, and there may even have been local tribunals, there is commonly more of a sense of combination, and of the local traditions being brought into the Roman jurisdictional sphere. Thus, while the persistence, survival and adaptation of local practices is a common theme, Judaea is somewhat extraordinary in the lack of uptake of Roman legal practices for such a long period.

The administrative reasons for this have already been outlined, but there are of course other concerns. The most obvious is the very nature of the Torah, which differs considerably from many of the other non-Roman bodies of law treated elsewhere in this volume. In Josephus' words:[57]

> *Ὁ δ' ἡμέτερος νομοθέτης ἄμφω ταῦτα συνήρμοσεν κατὰ πολλὴν ἐπιμέλειαν· οὔτε γὰρ κωφὴν ἀπέλιπε τὴν τῶν ἠθῶν ἄσκησιν οὔτε τὸν ἐκ τοῦ νόμου λόγον ἄπρακτον εἴασεν, ἀλλ' εὐθὺς ἀπὸ τῆς πρώτης ἀρξάμενος τροφῆς καὶ τῆς κατὰ τὸν οἶκον ἑκάστων διαίτης οὐδὲν οὐδὲ τῶν βραχυτάτων αὐτεξούσιον ἐπὶ ταῖς βουλήσεσι τῶν χρησομένων κατέλιπεν, ἀλλὰ καὶ περὶ σιτίων, ὅσων ἀπέχεσθαι χρὴ καὶ τίνα προσφέρεσθαι, καὶ περὶ τῶν κοινωνησόντων τῆς διαίτης ἔργων τε συντονίας καὶ τοὔμπαλιν ἀναπαύσεως ὅρον ἔθηκεν αὐτὸς καὶ κανόνα τὸν νόμον, ἵν' ὥσπερ ὑπὸ πατρὶ τούτῳ καὶ δεσπότῃ ζῶντες μήτε βουλόμενοι μηθὲν μήθ' ὑπ' ἀγνοίας ἁμαρτάνωμεν.*
>
> But our legislator combined both forms with great care: he neither left character-training mute nor allowed the words from the law to go unpracticed. Rather, starting right from the beginning of their nurture and from the mode of life practiced by each individual in the household, he did not leave anything, even the minutest detail, free to be determined by the wishes of those who would make use of [the laws], but even in relation to food, what they should refrain from and what they should eat, the company they keep in their daily lives, as well as their intensity in work and, conversely, rest, he set the law as their boundary and rule, so that, living under this as a father and master, we might commit no sin either wilfully or from ignorance.

Josephus naturally has an agenda here, but the agenda is in part what makes this so valuable: he presents (or claims to) the Jewish law to an outside audience, and thus translates it into culturally understandable terms for them. In short: the law is more all-encompassing than others (Greek and Roman law would little care what people ate), and deliberately designed to be so. Furthermore, in Josephus' formulation, all Jews know their law, in contrast to others in whose systems even the highest magistrates are ignorant, and have to rely on advisors.[58] Coupled with an emphasis on its nature as divinely given,[59] Josephus' picture for his outside audience is of an all-encompassing legal tradition, that goes beyond that required by other antique legislation and is better known by the ordinary people to whom it applies than in other ancient legal contexts.

[57] Josephus, *Contra Apionem* 2.173–4 (Barclay's translation).

[58] Josephus, *Contra Apionem* 2.177–8.

[59] Hence Josephus' famous formulation of the Jewish constitution as a *theokratia*: *Contra Apionem* 2.165.

We might take issue with some of this, particularly in the picture Josephus paints of legal knowledge (which may, indeed, have varied) and elsewhere of unity above all, but the basic impression of the nature of the Torah is not entirely unrepresentative. This is of course different from the idea found in many other pre-Roman states;[60] but, from a Roman perspective, it is also more formalized, particularly in being written, than the pre-Roman legal traditions found in the West. Thus there is both a real difference in nature, and a point of manifestation that would have allowed a Roman mentality to acknowledge this as 'proper' law or tradition.

This is of course manifest in the Roman treatment of diasporan Jewish communities, and their safeguarding of Jewish privileges: we can see the acknowledgment there. The emphasis placed by Jews on their own *nomoi* should also not be pushed too far: across a range of periods and areas, Jews seem very willing to go to non-Jewish tribunals and use non-Jewish laws.[61] Exclusivity is not proven, and we would be unwise to assume it. But we might perhaps expect a more entrenched, less open position on this in Judaea than in the diaspora: even with non-Jewish communities around, the Jewish population was not a small minority, but the majority. And in this climate, one can perhaps see why Roman legal fora—if offered—would have been rarely used, and why Romans may not have been so concerned to change this position for a population who were more broadly acknowledged to have their own ancestral, protected traditions. This should not be taken to come back to the old position of the inevitable clash between Rome and Judaea, or a fundamental incompatibility. We may rather say that the difference existed, was recognized by Roman rulers, and led to the region being treated somewhat differently, in all likelihood in an attempt to keep it as peaceful as possible. This in turn led to a very limited uptake of Roman legal institutions or forms in the area even after the advent of direct rule, in stark contrast to the situation we find in many other provinces, both East and West.[62] Post-70, the increase in personnel would have gradually changed this.

There is, however, one other region where there was a similar tardiness in this transformation: Egypt.[63] The population there was, of course, rather different and the persistence of certain governmental structures and legal traditions is typically put down to the importance of Egypt as a province for Rome, and the highly developed infrastructure there under the Ptolemies. But like Judaea, the process of change was slower in certain spheres, at least in terms of the uptake of Roman legal tools by provincials. Thus, while the nature of Jewish law and the administration of the region were most definitely particular contributing factors to the pace of Romanization, we go too far if we see Judaea as unique: its neighbour's reaction to Roman rule—at least in pace—in the legal sphere was in some ways

[60] Despite Josephus' formulation at one point of this in terms of forms of constitution (*Contra Apionem* 2.165).

[61] Babatha in P. Yadin being the prime example.

[62] See Czajkowski and Eckhardt (2018): a stark transformation most normally occurred within about 20 years of provincialization.

[63] See the discussion in Czajkowski and Eckhardt (2018) for a discussion of the timeframe of the 'Romanization' of Egypt in legal matters in comparison to other areas; see also Alonso in this volume for 'Romanization' in legal practice in Egypt.

similar. This may, indeed, also serve to undermine further the 'exemplarity of Egypt' arguments that have been becoming weaker and weaker in recent decades. These two Eastern provinces could fruitfully bear further comparison.

REFERENCES

Badian, E. 1958. *Foreign Clientelae (264–70 BC)*. Oxford.

Beylache, N. 2001. *Iudaea-Palaestina: The Pagan Cults in Roman Palestine*. Tübingen.

Braund, D. 1984. *Rome and the Friendly King. The Character of Client Kingship*. London and New York.

Büchler, A. 1902. *Das Synedrion in Jerusalem u. d. grosse Beth-Din in der Quaderkammer d. jerusalemischen Tempels*. 9. Jahresbericht d. isr.-theol. Lehranstalt in Wien (1902), 1–252.

Burton, G. P. 1975. Proconsuls, Assizes and the Administration of Justice under the Empire. *Journal of Roman Studies* 65, pp. 92–106.

Cimma, M. R. 1976. *Reges socii et amici populi Romani*. Milan.

Cohen, B. 1966. *Jewish and Roman Law: A Comparative Study*. New York.

Coşkun, A. 2005. Freundschaft und Klientelbildung in Roms auswärtigen Beziehungen. Wege und Perspectiven der Forschung. In: A. Coşkun (ed.), *Roms auswärtige Freunde in der späten Republik und im frühen Prinzipat*. Göttingen, pp. 1–30.

Cotton, H. M. 1999. Some Aspects of the Roman Administration of Judaea/Syria-Palaestina. In: W. Eck (ed.) *Lokale Autonomie und römische Ordnungsmacht in den kaiserzeitlichen Provinzen vom 1. bis 3. Jahrhundert*. Munich, pp. 75–91.

Cotton, H. M. 2002. Jewish Jurisdiction under Roman rule: prolegomena. In: M. Labahn and J. Zangenberg (eds.), *Zwischen den Reichen: Neues Testament und Römische Herrschaft*. Tübingen, pp. 13–28.

Cotton, H. M. 2003. 'Diplomatics' or External Aspects of the Legal Documents from the Judaean Desert: Prolegomena. In: C. Hezser (ed.), *Rabbinic Law in Its Roman and Near Eastern Context*. Tübingen, pp. 49–61.

Cotton, H. M. and Eck, W. 2002. P. Murabba'at 114 und die Anwesenheit römischer Truppen in den Höhlen des Wadi Murabba'at nach dem Bar Kochba Aufstand. *Zeitschrift für Papyrologie und Epigraphik* 138, pp. 173–83.

Cotton, H. M. and Eck, W. 2005. Roman Officials in Judaea and Arabia and Civil Jurisdiction. In: R. Katzoff and D. Schaps (eds.) *Law in the Documents of the Judaean Desert*. Leiden, pp. 23–44.

Czajkowski, K. 2016. Justice in Client Kingdoms: The Many Trials of Herod's Sons. *Historia: Zeitschrift für Alte Geschichte* 65:4, pp. 473–96.

Czajkowski, K. 2017. Civil Strife, Power and Authority in the Judicial Sphere: A Case Study from Roman Palestine. *Klio* 99:2, pp. 566–85.

Czajkowski, K. and Eckhardt, B. 2018. Law, Status and Agency in the Roman Provinces. *Past & Present* 241, pp. 3–31.

Dohrmann, N. 2003. The Boundaries of the Law and the Problem of Jurisdiction in an Early Palestinian Midrash. In: C. Heszer (ed.) *Rabbinic Law in Its Roman and Near Eastern Context*. Tübingen, pp. 83–104.

Eck, W. 2007. *Rom und Judaea: Fünf Vorträge zur römischen Herrschaft in Palaestina*. Tübingen.

Eck, W. 2017. Position and Authority of the Provincial Legate and the Financial Procurator in Judaea, 70–136 AD. In: J.J. Schwartz and P. J. Tomson (eds.), *Jews and Christians in the First and Second Centuries: The Interbellum 70–132 CE*. Leiden, pp. 93–105.

Eckhardt, B. 2019. Associations Beyond the City: Jews, Actors and Empire in the Roman Period. In: Eckhardt, B. ed. *Private Associations and Jewish Communities in the Hellenistic and Roman Cities*. Leiden, pp. 115–56.

Goodblatt, D. 1994. *The Monarchic Principle. Studies in Jewish Self-Government in Antiquity*. Tübingen.

Grabbe, L. 2008. Sanhedrin, Sanhedriyyot, or Mere Invention?, *Journal for the Study of Judaism* 39, pp. 1–19.

Haensch, R. 1997. Zur Konventsordnung in Aegyptus und den übrigen Provinzen des römischen Reiches. In: B. Kramer et al. (eds.) *Akten des 21. Internationalen Papyrologenkongresses Berlin, 13.–19.8.1995*. Band I. Stuttgart und Leipzig, pp. 320–91.

Harries, J. D. 2003. Creating a Legal Space: Settling Disputes in the Roman Empire. In: C. Heszer (ed.), *Rabbinic Law in Its Roman and Near Eastern Context*. Tübingen, pp. 63–82.

Hezser, C. 1998. The Codification of Legal Knowledge in Late Antiquity: The Talmud Yerushalmi and Roman Law Codes. In: P. Schäfer (ed.) *The Talmud Yerushalmi and Graeco-Roman Culture. Vol. 1*. Tübingen, pp. 581–642.

Isaac, B. 1980. Roman Colonies in Judaea: The Foundation of Aelia Capitolina. *Talanta* 12–13, pp. 31–54.

Kaizer, T. and Facella, M. 2010. Introduction. In: T. Kaizer and M. Facella (eds.), *Kingdoms and Principalities in the Roman Near East*. Stuttgart, pp. 15–44.

Levine, L. 1979. The Jewish Patriarch (Nasi) in Third Century Palestine. In: H. Temporini and W. Haase (eds.) *Aufstieg und Niedergang der römischen Welt: geschichte und kultur Roms im spiegel der neueren forschung* II 19.2. Berlin and New York, pp. 649–88.

Levine, L. I. 1996. The Status of the Patriarch in the Third and Fourth Centuries: Sources and Methodology. *Journal of Jewish Studies* 47, pp. 1–32.

Lieberman, S. 1994. *Greek in Jewish Palestine: Hellenism in Jewish Palestine*. New York.

Linder, A. 1987. *The Jews in Roman Imperial Legislation*. Jerusalem.

Mantel, H. 1961. *Studies in the History of the Sanhedrin*. Cambridge.

Marshall, A. J. 1966. Governors on the Move. *Phoenix* 20:3, pp. 231–46.

Mason, S. 2016. *A History of the Jewish War: AD 66–74*. New York.

McGinn, T. 2019. Herod the Great and the Iudicium Domesticum: Legal Pluralism to Die For. *Journal of Legal History* 40:2, pp. 155–81.

Meyer, E. A. 2007. Diplomatics, Law and Romanisation in the Documents from the Judaean Desert. In: J. W. Cairns and P. J. Du Plessis (eds.), *Beyond dogmatics: law and society in the Roman world*. Edinburgh, pp. 53–82.

Milik, J., Benoit, P. and de Vaux, R. eds. 1961. *Les Grottes de Murabbaʿat*. Oxford.

Mommsen, T. 1884. Die Conscriptionsordnung der Römischen Kaiserzeit. *Hermes* 19, pp. 211–34. (= *Gesammelte Schriften* VI, pp. 20–117).

Mommsen, Th. and von Harnack, A. 1895. Zu Apostelgeschichte 28,16 (στρατοπεδάρχης = princeps peregrinorum). *Sitzungsberichte der Berliner Akademie* 1895, pp. 495–503. (= Mommsen, Th. 1910. *Gesammelte Schriften VI*. Berlin, pp. 546–54).

Rabello, A. 1996. Jewish and Roman Jurisdiction. In: N. S. Hecht, B.S. Jackson, S. M. Passamaneck, D. Piattelli and A. Rabello (eds.), *An Introduction to the History and Sources of Jewish Law*. Oxford, pp. 141–67.

Rajak, T. 1984. Was there a Roman Charter for the Jews? *The Journal of Roman Studies* 74, pp. 107–23.

Rich, J. 1989. Patronage and Interstate Relations in the Roman Republic. In: A. Wallace-Hadrill (ed.), *Patronage in Ancient Society*. London, pp. 117–35.

Schiffman, L. H. 2001. On the Edge of the Diaspora: Jews in the Dead Sea Region in the First Two Centuries CE In: A. M. Maier and L.H. Schiffman (eds.), *Go Out and Study the Land (Judges 18:2)*. Leiden, pp. 175–96.

Schürer, E. 1973. *The History of the Jewish People in the Age of Jesus Christ (175 BC–AD 135)*. Revised and edited by G. Vermes and F. Millar. Edinburgh.

Schwartz, S. 1999. The Patriarchs and the Diaspora. *Journal of Jewish Studies* 50:2, pp. 208–22.

Speidel, M. 1982/3. The Roman Army in Judaea Under The Procurators: The Italian and The Augustan Cohort in the Acts of the Apostles. *Ancient Society* 13/14, pp. 233–40.

Winter, P. 1964. The Trial of Jesus and the Competence of the Sanhedrin. *New Testament Studies* 10.4, pp. 494–9.

Zeitlin, S. 1945. The Political Synedrion and the Religious Sanhédrin. *Jewish Quarterly Review* 36, pp. 109–140.

Zeitlin, S. 1946a. Synedrion in the Judeo-Hellenistic Literature and Sanhédrin in the Tannaitic Literature. *Jewish Quarterly Review* 36, pp. 307–15.

Zeitlin, S. 1946b. Synedrion in Greek Literature, the Gospels and the Institution of the Sanhédrin. *Jewish Quarterly Review* 37, pp. 189–98.

7

Legal Interactions in the Archive of Babatha

P. Yadin 21 and 22

Tiziana J. Chiusi

I

Since its discovery, the Babatha archive has been examined from the perspective of the contemporary 'juridical' life of Jews. In most cases the question how much 'Jewish' Law can be found in the legal life of the Jewish population was the decisive concern. But it is also of particular interest to try to 'read' and understand the content of the papyri from the perspective of Roman Law. A correlate to this is in fact the question of the relationship between the 'Jewish' legal tradition and Roman Law since the time of the Roman conquest of the province of Arabia.

Indeed a few years ago the potential interactions between these two legal traditions received particular attention. Dieter Nörr applied this approach to P. Yadin 28–30.[1] I myself have tried to provide evidence in the case of P. Yadin 15 that Babatha's proposed solution to the Roman governor can be found in three imperial constitutions of Alexander Severus (C. 4.29.6), Diocletian/Maximian (C. 5.51.9) and Philippus Arabus (C. 5.46.2) in 228, 293 or 246 CE.[2] In P. Yadin 15, Babatha addresses the Roman governor in the hope of getting help in her dispute with the legal guardians of her son Jesus, who had been appointed by the city council of Petra, which shows that she trusts Roman legal arrangements and is willing to use them. This is supported by the observation that the formula of the *actio tutelae* was found in Greek in the archive.[3] However, there are a number of features which indicate a certain 'Romanization' of the circle in which Babatha lived: the consequent use of the stipulation formula; the procedure before the *xenokritai*, which Nörr identified as *recuperatores*;[4] the reference to (*bona) fides*, which can often be found in a number of the documents;[5] maybe in this context

[1] Nörr (1995), Nörr (1998a), Nörr (1998b), Nörr (1999).

[2] Chiusi (1994), (2004), (2005).

[3] P. Yadin 28–30, see Lewis (1989), 118–20.

[4] Cf. Nörr (1995), 89 ff. [= (2003), 2115ff.], and Nörr (1999) [= (2003)].

[5] P. Yadin 16–18, 20–2, 28–30.

Tiziana J. Chiusi, *Legal Interactions in the Archive of Babatha: P. Yadin 21 and 22* In: *Law in the Roman Provinces.* Edited by: Kimberley Czajkowski and Benedikt Eckhardt in collaboration with Meret Strothmann, Oxford University Press (2020).

DOI: 10.1093/oso/9780198844082.003.0007

the Roman way of dating and the reference to the emperor's fortune can be mentioned too.[6]

Many other papyri from the archive should also be seen from that point of view, like the documents which the editor Lewis entitled '*Deposit*' (P. Yadin 5 and 17), '*Loan on Hypothec*' (P. Yadin 11), '*Summons*' (P. Yadin 23), '*Deposition*' (P. Yadin 24), '*Summons and Countersummons*' (P. Yadin 25), '*Summons and Reply*' (P. Yadin 26), which are in connection with '*Purchase*' or '*Sale of a Date Crop*' (P. Yadin 21 and 22) and '*Registration of Land*' (P. Yadin 16). In my opinion, the documents concerning dowry and inheritance law seem to be less promising for our research question: Roman legal categories would have hardly been found. In this paper I would like to focus on two papyri from the archive from a Roman perspective, P. Yadin 21 and 22, to which I believe one can profitably apply Roman contractual law categories.

II

1. Both documents P. Yadin 21 und 22 from the Babatha Archive are dated 130 CE. They are contractual documents which are reciprocally related to one another. They concern the annual harvest of several date plantations which were the property of Babatha's deceased husband, and which she took into possession as security for her dowry and a loan given to her husband. Simon, son of Jesus, confirms in his document that he bought the whole harvest of the land from Babatha. In return he promised the supply of a clearly designated amount of dates of a certain quality, and as a substitute to pay a defined contractual penalty. Simon should have the harvest beyond the agreed amount as compensation for his services and expenses. Babatha on her side confirms that she sold the harvest to Simon and guaranteed him free access to the plantation. She also promised him that she would keep him free of any claims from third parties.

P. Yadin 21 and 22 are written by the same scribe, Germanos, on two papyri of almost equal size. No 21 is the declaration of the buyer, Simon, No 22 the one of the seller, Babatha. The contents are symmetrical. In No 21 Simon recognizes that he bought the harvest of the gardens Pherora, Nikarchos, as well as the third 'called Molchaios's', which are in the possession of Babatha (ἠγορακέναι). Simon knows that Babatha is not the owner of the gardens, but her deceased husband Judas was. Therefore he emphasizes that Babatha declares that she is managing the gardens because of the unpaid dowry or the loan of Judas that has not been paid back to her. This is the first interesting juridical element: Babatha does not dispose of the harvest based on a right of ownership, and also not due to a hypothetical property entitlement that was based on her claims against her deceased husband; instead she takes action based on a right of use that her husband assured her as a guarantee for her dowry and her claim. The dowry results from the Aramaic P. Yadin 10,[7] the claim against the husband from

[6] See Cotton (2002), who has listed and analysed all these elements.
[7] Cf. Lewis (1989), 4.

P. Yadin 17.[8] There—the papyrus is dated 24th February 128—Babatha grants her husband Judas a loan of 300 silver *denarii*, repayable at any time. As shown in P. Yadin 18 of 5th April 128, this money was probably used a few weeks later by Judas to finance the dowry, in the amount of 500 *denarii*, of his daughter from his first marriage, named Shelamzion.[9]

2. Babatha may already have had access to the gardens before Judas died. After his death she took them into her possession. The possession becomes juridically concrete at the latest when she sells the harvest to Simon. The related capacity to harvest the dates can be interpreted as a transfer of possession *brevi manu* of the dates. Moreover, in accordance with her right of possession, she only sells the harvest but not the gardens themselves. We learn from P. Yadin 23, line 6 and P. Yadin 25, line 10 f., that Besas, the legal guardian of the children of the previously deceased brother (Jesus) of the deceased husband of Babatha (Judas), challenged her legitimation to dispose over the gardens.[10] Besas' reference to a *βία*, the violence which Babatha exercised, indicates that she independently used the gardens without a permit of the officials. It would have a certain charm to suggest the hypothesis that the use of the word *βία* could be an indication that the legal guardian or the scribe—to whom, as we will see, Roman legal categories are apparently not alien—probably had the *interdictum unde vi* in mind. But in any case it seems as though the question of the legitimacy of the disposal has not been problematic in the papyri we focus on.

3. According to Roman doctrine an essential element of a purchase is the existence of the sold object. This can be assumed in our case. The document dates to 11 September 130; at that time the dates, which are situated in a maturing process, are hanging on the palm trees, since the harvest usually begins in September, reaches its peak in October and ends in November.[11] But the quantity and quality of the dates may be unsure until the end of the harvest, so that according to Roman categories there could be a lack of determination of the object.

If we were to interpret the contract between Babatha and Simon according to Roman categories, the *emptio rei speratae* and the *emptio spei* come under consideration for its classification. In the first case, the purchase of a future object, the contract takes effect when the object exists. In this case it shall be considered that the purchase is already completed with the agreement. In the case that the seller contrived that the object does not exist, he can be prosecuted by the purchaser with the *actio empti*.[12] In case of the *emptio spei*, an esperance purchase, the purchase is effective even if the object does not exist. According to the words

[8] Cf. Lewis (1989), 71. [9] Cf. Lewis (1989), 76 f.

[10] Besas apparently assumes that his wards, the nephews of the deceased proprietor Judas, are entitled—expressed in a somehow blurred terminology—with a 'better' law to these gardens than the widow Babatha.

[11] See Lewis (1989), 94.

[12] Pomponius, *On Sabinus* 9 (D. 18.1.8 pr.): *Nec emptio nec venditio sine re quae veneat potest intellegi, et tamen fructus et partus futuri recte ementur, ut, cum editus esset partus, iam tunc, cum contractum esset negotium, venditio facta intellegatur: sed si id egerit venditor, ne nascatur aut fiant, ex empto agi posse* (There can be no sale without a thing to be sold. Nevertheless, future produce and offspring are validly purchased so that when the offspring is born, the sale is regarded as having been complete from the time of agreement. But if the vendor takes steps to prevent the birth or the growing

of Pomponius this is the case when buying a future catch of fish or birds or something that someone gets from presents thrown into the crowd.[13] Suetonius gives us an example for such presents, which are partly valuable, and sometimes symbolized by tokens, when he says that on certain occasions 'thousands of birds of all kinds, diverse food, grain, clothes, gold, silver, precious stones, pearls, paintings, slaves, draught animals and also tamed wild animals, ships, apartment buildings, estates' were shared among the people.[14] As suggested by Pomponius, D. 18.1.8 pr., the *emptio rei speratae* therefore moderates the principle, that there cannot be a purchase without *res*. Furthermore the *emptio rei speratae* is said to have entailed the *emptio spei*.[15]

The purchase of future fruits in particular shows a typical example of the *emptio rei speratae;* it is mentioned in Pomponius (D. 18.1.8. pr.) as the first example. It therefore seems reasonable to first ask the question whether the purchase in P. Yadin 21 and 22 can be qualified as *emptio rei speratae.* This is also not contradicted by the fact that the dates were probably already hanging on the tree: because there is still a residual risk, for example, of destruction by an autumn storm or the possibility of further growth, they still can be qualified as *res sperata.*[16] The parties confirm that the purchase is completed: Simon says P. Yadin 21, line 7: ὁμολογῶ ἠγορακέναι; Babatha says P. Yadin 22, line 7: ὁμολ[ογῶ πεπρακέ]ναι. This expression should not be seen as contradicting Pomponius' words in D. 18.1.8 pr. because the juridical qualification of the purchase, which takes its effect when the object is existent, has to be seen in this case from an ex-post evaluation, namely that the dates reach their promised condition at the end of the harvest. With their document the parties want to design their future legal relationship. The parties' aim is to set the intended main purpose and to express themselves accordingly at the conclusion of the contract.[17] The qualification of the deal can in no way be interpreted as an *emptio spei*: The dates which mature on the tree are more than only hope.

4. Both documents can be understood as an example for an obligatory purchase, which is mentioned in the Roman legal texts but which has not yet been found in

of produce, he will not be liable to the action on purchase). All English translations of the Digest are from Watson (1998).

[13] Pomponius, *On Sabinus* 9 (D. 18.1.8.1): *Aliquando tamen et sine re venditio intellegitur, veluti cum quasi alea emitur. quod fit, cum captum piscium vel avium vel missilium emitur: emptio enim contrahitur etiam si nihil inciderit, quia spei emptio est: et quod missilium nomine eo casu captum est si evictum fuerit, nulla eo nomine ex empto obligatio contrahitur, quia id actum intellegitur* (Sometimes, indeed, there is held to be a sale even without a thing, as where what is bought is, as it were, a chance. This is the case with the purchase of a catch of birds or fish or of largesse showered down. The contract is valid even if nothing results, because it is a purchase of an expectancy and, in the case of largesse, if there is eviction from what is caught, no purchase proceedings will lie, because the parties are deemed to have contracted on that basis.)

[14] Suetonius, *Nero* 11.2:... *milia avium cuiusque generis, multiplex penus, tesserae frumentariae, vestis, aurum, argentum, gemmae, margaritae, tubulae pictae, mancipia, iumenta atque etiam mansuetae ferae, novissimae naves, insulae, agri.* Cf. Kaser, Knütel and Lohsse (2017), § 41, N 9.

[15] See Kaser, Knütel and Lohsse (2017), § 41, N 9.

[16] On the question of the 'Kauf der Ernte auf dem Halm' see Rupprecht (1994), 127 f. On the *emptio rei speratae* in the context of sales in wine see the profound work by Jakab (2009), 156 ff.

[17] This allows an 'unconditional' expression and should not be regarded as contrary to the literary view of the *emptio rei speratae* as a 'conditional purchase' in the sense that the coming into existence of the sold good is regarded as the relevant condition.

our papyrological and epigraphical material. Kunkel noted that we define the Roman purchase as an obligatory contract because we read it like this in the legal sources. If we were to consider only the available documentary material, we would not qualify the Roman purchase differently from the purchase in the Hellenistic area and in the Orient, because the existing documents only ever confirm that the buyer payed the price and the seller provided the object. Kunkel explains this with the circumstance that the documents serve as evidence of the rendered service and that a potentially previous obligatory document was probably qualified as less important and therefore was destroyed after the fulfilment of the obligation.[18] Our parties, however, promise to give the price in the form of a certain quantity of dates, as Simon says (P. Yadin 21, line 12–15): *τελέσω σοι εἰς τοὺς αὐτοὺς κήπους πατητοῦ πρώτου καὶ δευτέρου τάλαντα τεσσαράκοντα δύω καὶ ναaρου κόρους δύω σάτα πέντε*, and to provide the possession of the object, as Babatha says (P. Yadin 22, line 20–2); this takes place by her giving Simon permission to harvest the dates. She says that she guarantees to Simon the unhindered access to the garden against anyone who might prevent him from doing so (*ἐμοῦ καθαραποιοῦντός σοι τοὺς προγ εγραμμένους κήπους ἀπὸ παντὸς ἀντιποιουμένου*). If one follows the above mentioned premise, that the documents contain Roman law and are formulated in its categories, this form seems to be adequate in order to express the obligation of the seller in such a purchase to provide possession of the object. Thus, so far these documents could be one of the rare proofs of the obligatory nature of the Roman purchase. If one follows this thesis, that precisely this guarantee-clause, which also can be found in other documents from the Judean desert, was not originally Jewish,[19] these documents could be at the same time a testimony of penetration of originally non-Jewish law into the Jewish practice.

This may be linked to the fact that this *emptio venditio* is not established on one single document which contains price, subject, conditions, and contractual penalty, but written down on two documents—actually according to the Roman designation of the contract type—one for the *emptio* and another one for the *venditio*. The documents to which Kunkel refers[20] obviously certify that the buyer payed the price and the seller provided the possession of the object for reasons of proof. In P. Yadin 21 and 22, in contrast, both parties had not yet rendered their services but undertook to render them. Therefore the *emptor* declares his obligations. These comprise on the one hand that he will pay 42 talents *πατητοῦ πρώτου καὶ δευτέρου*[21] as well as 2 Kor and 5 Sat Syrian and Naaran (?) dates, on the other hand, in the case of non-payment, that he will pay compensation in the amount of

[18] Kunkel (1973), 219 ff. Additionally, also from the perspective of the Talmud it has been shown that the payment fulfils the transfer and that for this reason the contract bears testimony to a purchase (of land) that already has taken place, cf. Schiffman (2005), 195 f.

[19] So Schiffman (2005), 199 f.

[20] Kunkel (1973), 220 with reference to the documents in Bruns, *FIRA*, and Arangio-Ruiz, FIRA III[2] as well as Pringsheim (1950).

[21] Lewis (1989), 97, translating this passage with "first and second 'splits'", refers the words 'first' and 'second' more to the date of the harvest than to the quality of the fruits. Plin. *nat.* 13.45 decribes the specific nature of the *patetae* in a highly poetic language: *nimio liquore abundat rumpitque se pomi ipsius etiam in sua matre ebrietas.*

2 *denarii* per talent and 1 μέλαν for Syrian and Naaran dates.[22] All this is secured by an enforcement clause against the assets of the buyer (P. Yadin 21, line 24: ἔκ τε ἐμοῦ καὶ ἐκ τῶν ὑπαρχόντων)[23] or of the guarantor Sammouos mentioned in line 17/18. Furthermore he declares his right to keep the leftovers from the garden. On her part the seller declares her right to the agreed price, or alternatively damages like those mentioned above, and recognizes her obligation to provide Simon undisturbed access to the gardens (καθαροποιεῖν) which means the permission to harvest the dates as well as to keep the leftovers of the garden. At the same time she promises in case of failure (ἀντιποιεῖν) to pay 20 *denarii* damages for Simon's work and expenses. This is a repeat of the content of the contract in both documents. Both documents write down what in modern terms we call the primary service obligations of the parties, but each document from a different perspective: No 21 from the perspective of Simon, No 22 from the perspective of Babatha. This again fits quite well with parties who are about to take action and therefore are at the end of the negotiation phase.

5. There is no βεβαίωσις-clause for the eviction but a καθαροποίησις-clause. Babatha promises to guarantee access if someone prevents Simon from entering. Usually such clauses are only found later. Nörr demonstrated that such 'adjustment clauses' already showed up in the fourth century BCE in Palestine's territory.[24] Since the ownership structure in the present case caused a certain danger for the buyer, because Babatha was not the owner of the date gardens, it seems plausible that the buyer was interested in a punishable defensive guarantee. When interpreting the singular κυριοποιεῖν in P. Yadin 22, line 23, Nörr considers as possible models both Ptolemaic lease clauses (with reservation of the lessor) as well as the *kyrieia*-purchase, or a search for Semitic parallels. The only evidence for καθαροποιεῖν in the later documents is the inheritance division contract P. Nessana 22 (a. 566).[25]

The contractual penalty, which both parties promise each other, fits with the *stipulatio*-clause that closes both documents. Simon promises to pay a certain amount of *denarii* for each talent, if he does not pay the owed purchase price in time, i.e. to deliver a certain amount of dates in a certain condition. On the other hand Babatha promises to pay a fixed sum of *denarii*, if she is unable to keep possible troublemakers away from Simon. Consequently the stipulation clause, with which each one respectively promises and receives a promise, corresponds to the exact intention of the parties. Therefore the clause is not only

[22] Sat, σάτον and Kor, κόρος, are volume units; talent, τάλαντον, is a weight unit. Some estimate a Sat as a volume unit of 8.56 litres (so nearly identical to the Roman *modius*, 8.62 litres), still others of 13 litres (cf. Broshi (1992), 230, 235). The Nabatean talent mentioned in P. Yadin 21 and 22, is estimated by Broshi as 24 kilo. A μέλαν, 'black' is said to be inferior to one *denarius* (see Lewis (1996), 399), according to another opinion between one and two *denarii* (see Broshi, (1992), 237). Meshorer (1992), 67, 70 proposes the identification of a 'black' with a sort of Roman *denarius*. Explicitly to the contrary, see Lewis (1996), 401: the 'black' is of semitic origin; Cotton (1994), 547, 553, n. 20 regards Meshorer's proposed identification as unacceptable.

[23] In my opinion this formulation should be interpreted as hendiadys, not in the sense of a separate enforcement *in personam*.

[24] P. Samaria 1, see Nörr (2002), 538 ff. [= (2012), 162 ff.].

[25] Nörr (2002), 539 f. [= (2012), 163 f.].

an empty 'security clause' but covers the will and the resulting obligations of the parties.[26]

The (Aramaic) signature of the buyer Shim'on Bar Yeshu'a can be found in P. Yadin 21, line 28; in No 22, line 34 Yohana Bar Makhoutha signs (in Aramaic) for Babatha as legal guardian.[27] In any case the signature of the buyer in No 21 and of the seller or her legal guardian in No 22 exist next to the signatures of the witnesses, as documented in Graeco-Roman practice, but unlike Tannaitic sources or the later Jewish legal traditions. By this a further small indication of a certain mixture between Jewish and non-Jewish procedure can be found.[28]

6. The key phrase 'intention of the parties' leads to the discussions of historians and papyrologists whether both documents contain a lease rather than a purchase, as has been advocated here.

It is obvious that both parties consider the contract as purchase and sale, *emptio venditio*. Lewis' categorization of the documents as sale and purchase, as well as his notion that the division into one document concerning the purchase and another concerning the sale might somehow derive from the Roman *emptio venditio*, are convincing.[29] and can be, as shown above, affirmed with Roman legal categories. The contract does not contain one single element of lease: neither a corresponding description of the parties, nor the cultivation of the land as obligation and right of the tenant, nor the transfer of the land by the lessor for a certain amount of time for the purpose of cultivation, nor an agreed rent which Simon would have to pay. Herrmann, in his famous studies on land lease, collected expressions for the 'work of a tenant' like digging over, ploughing, weed killing, watering, etc. which cannot be found in our documents, as well as the word *μισθώσασθαι*, which usually gets used in lease contracts;[30] but instead we have the expressions which occur in purchase contracts.[31] Lewis rightly emphasizes in his response to Isaac about this question that it is stated in the documents: *ὁμολογῶ ἠγορακέναι* and *ὁμολ[ογῶ πεπρακέ]ναι*.[32] Furthermore Rupprecht had noted in 1984 that the 'Kauf der Ernte auf dem Halm' at that time was not captured by one uniform common form, but the arrangement was dependent on different factors like date of the harvest, acquisition of the order, date of the payment, etc.[33] With these two documents the hypothesis can be advanced that Germanos tried to capture the intentions of the parties, i.e. their rights and obligations, by recourse to models of documents from the Roman purchase terminology known to him.

An important objection could be that according to late classical Roman dogma, the purchase price has to be in money.[34] It is the late classical legal expert Paulus who deals in (*ad edictum* 33) D. 18.1.1 and D. 19.4.1 with the historic origin of the

[26] Nörr (2002) rightly points out that this can be looked upon as an attempt to formulate the mutual obligations in an adequate manner by making use of clauses traditionally found in the documents.

[27] With—not quite understandable—reference to Lewis, (1989), 95, Schiffman (2005), 201, erroneously states that in both documents the subscription of the purchaser is clear.

[28] So Schiffman (2005), 202.

[29] *Contra* Nörr (2002), 539 [= (2012), 163]: It seems highly implausible that the scribe here was reacting to the Roman terminology of purchase and sale (*emptio venditio*).

[30] Herrmann (1958), 125 ff.

[31] Cf. only Pringsheim (1950), 109 ff.

[32] Lewis (1994), 243, 246; Isaac (1992), 62, 75.

[33] Rupprecht (1984), 280 ff.

[34] Cf. e.g. Kaser, Knütel and Lohsse (2017), § 41, N 12: 'Der Kaufpreis (*pretium*) muß in Geld bestehen. Ein Vorstoß der Sabinianer, auch andere Gegenstände zuzulassen . . . , blieb erfolglos.'

purchase and its distinction from an exchange. There he describes the question *an sine nummis venditio dici hodieque possit*, as disputed at his time (*dubitatur*).[35] Paulus carefully makes the decision to follow the Proculianic tradition, which rejects the inclusion of the exchange in a purchase unlike the Sabinians (*sed verior est Nervae et Proculi sententia,* D. 18.1.1.1seq.); this is justified with the different service obligations—provision of the undisturbed possession on side of the seller, transfer of the ownership of the money on side of the buyer. But this point is evidence, that the legal discussion was still ongoing at the beginning of the third century. Gai 3.141 expresses even more firmly that in his time, 160/1 CE, the question was very arguable (*valde quaeritur*) and refers to Caelius Sabinus, who has from his point of view a better perspective, according to which land can be seen as sold if the seller receives as return *pretii nomine* a slave. One can therefore imagine that the parties in P. Yadin 21 and 22, which are by the way temporally close to Gaius' *Institutes*, saw their transaction as purchase and that is why they express themselves in this manner. Hence both documents can be seen as a practical example of the application of the Sabinian theory. Furthermore the juridical discussion about the inclusion of an exchange in a purchase has a procedural background: Roman law knows the *actiones empti* and *venditi* as claims of the purchase, but no claim *ex permutatione*; in this case the praetor could only guarantee legal protection in case of advance performance of one side. Exactly this problem is avoided in our papyri by including the contractual obligations in the stipulation form, because an *actio ex stipulatu* at least was possible in front of a Roman court. Therefore the usage of the (late classical) dogma of Roman purchase law does not necessarily tell against the usage of the purchase terminology in the documents.

7. The further argument, that this is about the right to cultivate the garden,[36] misjudges, as Lewis mentions,[37] that here it is not about the cultivation of the palm garden but about the shortly imminent harvest. The statement that the contract is a lease, because Babatha intends to harvest the dates through Simon, mistakes the social-economically typified purpose of the contract (*causa*)—which for example in case of a purchase is the exchange of product and price—with the personal motives which moved the parties to conclude the contract and therefore is not of use for its correct legal recognition. For the latter only the *causa* is relevant, which in this case can be seen in the exchange of the harvest as sold object and a certain quantity of exactly and qualitatively described dates as an agreed price. Only this is important for the definition, occurrence, effectiveness, and existence of the contract and the fulfilment of resulting obligations; the personal motives due to which the parties decided to conclude a contract are irrelevant for the legal destiny of the contract. The fact that, because of the sale, the harvest really is going to happen, may be a personal motive for the conclusion of the contract, but not its *causa*.

Hence Radzyner's argumentation that this is a case of 'labor-lease' ('Werkvertrag') is probably void too.[38] His idea that this is primarily about work

[35] Here the use of the present form *dubitatur* is noteworthy. This implies that in late classical time the question was still under discussion.

[36] Isaac (1992), 75.

[37] Lewis (1994), 246.

[38] Radzyner (2005), 145 ff. The author's argumentation is difficilitated by the fact that it mixes *locatio conductio rei* (lease) and *operis* (153 ff.).

by Simon for Babatha, because he harvests the dates, fails already because Simon has to pay a high contractual penalty if he does not pay the price, i.e. the agreed quantity of dates. It does not make sense that Simon would have taken a risk—one which is, however, typical for a purchase—if he would only be interested in receiving a payment in dates for his work. Furthermore, the fact that his contractual penalty is much higher than Babatha's in case of non-fulfilment accords with the usual circumstances between buyer and seller in a purchase contract and not one between tenant and lessor in a lease.[39]

As already stated at the beginning of this chapter: the parties wanted a purchase and expressed themselves accordingly. The fact that Simon has permission to keep the leftover dates due to his expenses and work, which leads a part of the literature to consider the documents a lease or a contract for work, does not contradict this.[40] The appropriate formulation of P. Yadin 21, lines 20–1 *ἀντὶ τῶν ... κόπων καὶ ἀναλωμάτων* appears twice in P. Yadin 22. Once is in Babatha's declaration in the case of non-fulfilment, or rather non-*kathairopoiesis*: *ἐάν δέ τίς σοι ἀντιποιήσῃ τοῦ ἀγοράζματος καὶ μὴ σταθῖσα κυριοποιήσω σοι καθὼς προγέγραπτε, ἔσομαί σοι ὀφίλουσα ἀντὶ τῶν σῶν κόπων καὶ ἀναλωμάτων ἀργυρίου δηνάρια εἴκο[σ]ι κατὰ μηδὲ[ν] ἀντι[λ]έγων* (lines 22–5). This is obviously a damage clause: Babatha pays 20 *denarii* in the case that Simon's harvest is challenged. The second time this formulation appears immediately afterwards, lines 25–8, parallel to P. Yadin 21, lines 18–21, Simon has permission to keep the leftovers of the gardens for his expenses and work. In addition Broshi noted that this kind of agreement was already known in Mesopotamia and usually happened one month before the harvest, whereby the harvest was not easy to handle; according to his statement 150 days of work per hectare were needed, i.e. a half a year's work effort.[41]

The statements in P. Yadin 21 and 22, that Simon has the permission to keep the leftovers of the dates of the harvest for his expenses and work, are indeed conspicuous in the context of a purchase contract. But they would also be also conspicuous in the context of a lease contract: where the tenant pays for the cultivation of the land and to use the resulting fruits, he does not receive anything for it from the lessor. Maybe this is a remnant of a different form (or part of it), which the scribe Germanos knows, with a safeguarding 'securing action just in case'. This can be compared to the routine usage of the stipulation clause in some papyri, even though it has not much to do with the context. Pringsheim had already correctly noted that Greeks have difficulties with the sale of future fruits, which are shown in certain restrictions. These restrictions induced the Greek scribes of the document to include in such sale agreements elements of lease.[42]

8. In general I would like to propose the hypothesis that in this case the scribe Germanos wanted to look over the shoulder of *tabelliones* by trying to create a form which should fulfil the requirements of a Roman *emptio venditio*. He also wanted to fit the various interests discussed above into a Roman form, which seemed to be the more suitable one for him. The division into two declarations

[39] Radzyner (2005), 151 f. is unconvincing.

[40] For a report of the proposed arguments see Oudshoorn (2007), 168 ff.

[41] Broshi (1992), 233 ff.

[42] Pringsheim (1950), 296 f.

should perhaps also be read from this perspective—as Lewis mentioned correctly.[43]

He argued the thesis that both scribes of the Babatha-archive, who designate themselves as λιβλάριος,[44] Theenas and Germanos, are local scribes who have been partly in service for the Roman army.[45] Isaac does not agree with this but states that the usage of a Roman designation like *librarius* for a Jewish scribe in a village of the province of Arabia suggests that this function is in the context of the Roman administration, and that it can therefore be assumed that both local scribes had an official function.[46] It is particularly interesting to note his remark that one of Babatha's gardens in Maoza bordered on an imperial property which was managed by *procuratores.*[47] *Librarii* are designated as *procuratores* in inscriptions of the *tractus Carthaginiensis* and near *Ampelum*, therefore within the administration of imperial possession of the region.[48] The *librarii* in the Babatha archive therefore could be subordinated employees of the local administration, perhaps in the administration of imperial property in the region. But maybe they are only official scribes who serve the owners of the region if needed. Probably there were Jews[49] who were involved in the legal rows of the imperial administration.[50] This would fit well with the opinion presented here that Germanos gives a Roman form to a traditional agreement well known to him, since he considered it more suitable for the parties' purpose and thought it would be easier to use in front of the Roman court. As already mentioned above concerning Pringsheim's statement, Greek notaries had difficulties with the purchase of future fruits and therefore rather used lease terminology.[51] The fact that our scribe Germanos does not switch to such terminology, but rather uses the purchase terminology, indicates that he was familiar with Roman categories or at least that they were not unknown to him.

9. As already demonstrated, the parties promised each other contractual penalties in *denarii.* Simon provides a guarantor in case he does not pay the agreed price in the form of dates at 'drying time'. Babatha on her side, as mentioned above, is obligated to guarantee access and promises 20 *denarii* if she fails. This leads to the discussion of the extent of and the reasons for Babatha's legitimate right of disposal. Due to her dowry and her claims against her deceased husband Judas, she took possession of three properties, Pherora, Nikarchos and that 'called Molchaios's', which Simon and Babatha named in their declarations. This was the result of the guarantee her husband gave to her, which we know from P. Yadin 17, dated 21st February 128 CE and P. Yadin 10. In P. Yadin 17 he recognizes that he received 300 *denarii* from Babatha which she can reclaim anytime; in case of non-payment he secured for her the right of enforcement on his current and future assets. In P. Yadin 10 she received a similar guarantee for

[43] Lewis (1989), 94; cf. Lewis (1994), 246. [44] Lewis (1989), 64 *nota* on l. 38.

[45] Lewis (1989), 88. [46] Isaac (1992), 73 f.

[47] The garden in mention is called Algiphiamma, see P. Yadin 16, l. 24.

[48] So Isaac (1992), 74.

[49] One may speculate on the background of the striking name Germanos. In P. Yadin 23, l. 25; 25, l. 68; 26, l. 21; 27, l. 19 he calls himself Germanos, son of Judas.

[50] See now also Czajkowski (2017), 72 ff., 79 ff.

[51] See *supra* at n. 41. On the 'mixed forms' of purchase and lease see further Herrmann (1958), 222 ff. and Rupprecht (1984), 273 ff.

her dowry.[52] As P. Yadin 18 (5 April 128 CE) suggests, Babatha's husband apparently used the money, which he received from Babatha according to P. Yadin 17, partly to pay the 500 *denarii* dowry of his daughter Shelamzion.[53] Therefore Babatha has two 'legal grounds' for taking possession of the gardens and apparently states exactly this in P. Yadin 22, line 10 with the words ἀντὶ τῆς προικός μου καὶ ὀφιλῆς. If this formulation were a hendiadys, Babatha would only have one claim due to the 'dowry money'.[54] With regard to time and content, set in the context of the information we have from P. Yadin 17 and 18 and the distance from P. Yadin 10, this assumption is neither obvious nor necessary.

Furthermore we should note again the aforementioned considerations on Babatha's taking possession, which is designated as βία, as well as the fact that Babatha is prosecuted by the legal guardian of the nephews of her deceased husband Judas (P. Yadin 23–6) with regards to these gardens.[55] This could be a further indication that Babatha enforced her guarantee by taking autonomous possession.[56]

III

All previous attempts at the interpretation of these contracts were carried out from the perspective of finding specifically Jewish law in the legal practice of the Jewish population of the second century CE. The present article, following previous papers on the documents of the Babatha archive, instead approaches both papyri from a Roman perspective. It examines to what extent the demonstrated content of the contracts can be explained with categories of classical Roman law to draw conclusions about interactions between the Roman and the provincial legal tradition.

From the perspective of Roman law the contract recorded in the documents touches upon several problems of the law of obligations. The first remarkable thing is that the parties confirm the conclusion of the contract and the related reason for the duty of performance. This obligatory effect of the purchase contract, as the Roman jurists handed it down, is not reflected in the rest of the surviving documents, which do not bear witness to the obligations of the parties but rather the rendered obligations: usually the documents only certify the mutual receipt of performance and consideration. The present documents establish a rare, important bridge between the obligatory effect of the purchase and the documented inventory of the practice, and therefore can be seen as evidence for an obligatory purchase contract in form of the *emptio rei speratae*. The fact that the

[52] The document is an Aramaic papyrus, see Lewis (2003), 189, 190, and Yadin, Greenfield and Yardeni (1994), 75 ff.

[53] See *supra* at n. 7.

[54] Cf. the hypothesis of Cotton (1997), 179, 185 with n. 26.

[55] The question whether the three gardens mentioned in our papyri are the same as those registered in Babatha's name in P. Yadin 24 may be left open in our context: it is not important for our specific point in question insofar as there, too, the registration was made for the administration, not for Babatha's property. Contrary to an equation of Lewis (1989), 107.

[56] See *supra* section II.2.

parties promise each other a contractual penalty in form of stipulation in the case of non-fulfilment fits particularly well with the Roman legal tradition. The contract's grasp of Roman legal categories especially leads to the assumption of an *emptio rei speratae.* The sold object is indeed the totality of dates hanging on the tree in the concerned gardens, therefore an unspecified amount of fruits of unspecified quality, which are still in the maturation process. Roman law only knows two exceptions to this requirement to specify the purchased object, namely the sale of future fruits (*emptio rei speratae*) and the sale of a 'chance' (*emptio spei*). The difference appears in the legal consequences. While the *emptio rei speratae* is commonly understood as the contract being subject to the condition that the fruits come into being, in the *emptio spei* the price is due even if the hope is not realized. The differentiation can be difficult as the present documents demonstrate. The examined papyri therefore would be evidence from practice for the *emptio rei speratae.* From the point of view of the Roman law of sale it is furthermore conspicuous that the consideration is not the payment of money. This question touches upon the classical dispute between the Sabinian and Proculian schools of law about how purchase and exchange differ. Paulus as representative of late classical Roman law, which is grounded in the *Digest* according to the Justinianic tradition, describes this question as still controversial at that time and prefers—with a timid choice of words—the Proculians' point of view, which allows the application of the *actiones empti et venditi* only if the price is defined in money. Gaius on the contrary describes the dispute in his *Institutes* around the year 160 CE, only thirty years after the date of our documents, as very controversial and favours Sabinus' opinion, which allows a different object as price. The documents therefore show an example of application of the Sabinian theory in practice. This can also be explained with reference to the influence of the jurist Gaius on the practice of the eastern provinces or the other way round.

This suggests that the notary who drew up the documents had a Roman example of a purchase contract in mind when he described the parties' obligations. Previously the documents were qualified as lease or work or service contract in the literature. The reason, besides the fact that no money is owed, is the special contract clause according to which the buyer can keep the leftover harvest, namely according to the explicit provision for his 'work and expenses'. Nevertheless the parties themselves have designed their contract as purchase and the mutual obligations comply with the duties of a purchase but not with the ones of a lease or service contract as partly assumed in the literature. The contract-typical obligation of the tenant to cultivate the land and the limitation of his right of use according to time and purpose is lacking for qualifying the contract as a lease. Instead the parties are interested in the harvest of a specifically designated year. An argument against a service contract is that the contractual penalty which Simon has to pay in case of non-fulfilment of the promised dates is very high. It is certainly typical for a buyer to cover such a risk but not for a work contractor and especially not for a service provider. The clause rather could be a leftover from other documents written by the scribe—who apparently plays the role of a notary—and therefore was used in the present document in order to take the safest route, by establishing a newly oriented form based on Roman categories, in order to save this surplus for the buyer, even if a judge might not know such a purchase contract (yet).

From the perspective of the judicial practice in an Eastern province in the first third of the second century CE these statements support the assumption that the scribe tries to cover a usual local deal in a Roman purchase form to make it justifiable in front of Roman courts. Therefore the documents could be an indication that Jewish scribes,[57] if they were not part of the Roman administration, possibly practiced close to administrative functions in the province of Arabia, and not only knew Roman law but also tried to apply it, thereby adjusting it to the needs and legal traditions there. Against this background the acceptance of this clause can be qualified as a regional leftover, for which there was no need according to the Roman categories, but which the notary included in the document with the intention of finding the safest way to secure the buyer.

Thus both documents are not only a proof for the application of Roman law by the Jewish population of the province of Arabia but also a testimony of its important role, and I would even say testimony for a conscious role in applying it. The hypothesis of the interactions between Roman law and provincial law is reaffirmed.

REFERENCES

Broshi, M. 1992. Agriculture and Economy in Roman Palestine: Seven Notes on the Babatha Archive. *Israel Exploration Journal* 42, pp. 230–40.

Chiusi, T. J. 1994. Zur Vormundschaft der Mutter. *Zeitschrift der Savigny-Stiftung für Rechtsgeschichte: Romanistische Abteilung* 111, pp. 155–96.

Chiusi, T. J. 2004. Zur Wechselwirkung zwischen römischem Recht und provinzialen Rechten anhand von Dokumenten aus dem Archiv der Babatha. In: T. Gergen (ed.) *Vielfalt und Einheit in der Rechtsgeschichte. Festgabe für Elmar Wadle zu seinem 65. Geburtstag.* Cologne, pp. 1–28.

Chiusi, T. J. 2005. Babatha vs. the Guardians of Her Son: A Struggle for Guardianship—Legal and Practical Aspects of P.Yadin 12–15, 27. In: R. Katzoff, and D. Schaps (eds.) *Law in the Documents of the Judaean Desert.* Leiden, pp. 105–32.

Cotton, H. M. 1994. Rent or Tax Receipt from Maoza. *Zeitschrift für Papyrologie und Epigraphik* 100, pp. 547–57.

Cotton, H. M. 1997. Deeds of Gift and the Law of Succession in the Documents from the Judaean Desert. In: B. Kramer, W. Luppe, H. Maehler, and G. Poethke (eds.) *Akten des 21. Internationalen Papyrologenkongresses Berlin, 13.–19.8.1995. Archiv für Papyrusforschung, Beiheft 3.1.* Stuttgart and Leipzig, pp. 179–86.

Cotton, H. M. 2002. Jewish Jurisdiction under Roman Rule: Prolegomena. In: M. Labahn and J. Zangenberg, (eds.) *Zwischen den Reichen: Neues Testament und römische Herrschaft.* Tübingen, pp. 13–28.

Czajkowski, K. 2017. *Localized Law: The Babatha and Salome Komaise Archives.* Oxford.

Herrmann, J. 1958. *Studien zur Bodenpacht im Recht der graco-ägyptischen Papyri.* Munich.

Isaac, B. 1992. The Babatha Archive: A Review Article. *Israel Exploration Journal* 42, pp. 62–75.

Jakab, E. 2009. *Risikomanagement beim Weinkauf.* Munich.

Kaser, M., Knütel, R. and Lohsse, S. 2017. *Römisches Privatrecht.* 21st revised and expanded edition. Munich.

[57] See *supra* n. 49.

Kunkel, W. 1973. Epigraphik und Geschichte des römischen Privatrechts. *Vestigia* 17 (*Akten des VI. Internationalen Kongresses für Griechische und Lateinische Epigraphik München 1972*). Munich, pp. 193–242.

Lewis, N. (ed.) 1989. *The Documents from the Bar Kokhba Period in the Cave of Letters. Greek Papyri.* Jerusalem.

Lewis, N. 1994. The Babatha Archive: A Response. *Israel Exploration Journal* 44, pp. 243–6.

Lewis, N. 1996. Again, the Money Called Blacks. In: R. Katzoff, Y. Petroff and D. Schaps (eds.) *Classical Studies in Honor of David Sohlberg.* Ramat Gan, pp. 399–401.

Lewis, N. 2003. The complete Babatha: More Questions than Answers. *Scripta Classica Israelica* 22, pp. 182–92.

Meshorer, Y. 1992. The 'Black Silver' Coins of the Babatha Papyri: A Re-evaluation. *Israel Museum Journal* 10, pp. 67–74.

Nörr, D. 1995. The *Xenokritai* in Babatha's Archive (Pap. Yadin 28–30). *Israel Law Review* 29, pp. 83–94. [= T. J. Chiusi, W. Kaiser, and H.-D. Spengler (eds.) 2003. *Historiae iuris antiqui. Gesammelte Schriften. Band III.* Goldbach bei Aschaffenburg, pp. 2109–20].

Nörr, D. 1998a. Prozessuales aus dem Babatha-Archiv. In: M. Humbert, and Y. Thomas (eds.) *Hommage à la mémoire de André Magdelain.* Paris, pp. 317–41. [= T. J. Chiusi, W. Kaiser, and H.-D. Spengler (eds.) 2003. *Historiae iuris antiqui. Gesammelte Schriften. Band III.* Goldbach bei Aschaffenburg, pp. 2173–97].

Nörr, D. 1998b. Römisches Zivilprozeßrecht nach Max Kaser: Prozeßrecht und Prozeßpraxis in der Provinz Arabia. *Zeitschrift der Savigny-Stiftung für Rechtsgeschichte. Romanistische Abteilung* 115, pp. 80–98. [= T. J. Chiusi, W. Kaiser, and H.-D. Spengler (eds.) 2003. *Historiae iuris antiqui. Gesammelte Schriften. Band III.* Goldbach bei Aschaffenburg, pp. 2199–217].

Nörr, D. 1999. Zu den Xenokriten (Rekuperatoren) in der römischen Provinzialgerichtsbarkeit. In: W. Eck and E. Müller-Luckner (eds.) *Lokale Autonomie und römische Ordnungsmacht in den kaiserzeitlichen Provinzen vom 1. bis 3. Jahrhundert.* Schriften des Historischen Kollegs. Kolloquien 42. Munich, pp. 257–301. [= T. J. Chiusi, W. Kaiser, and H.-D. Spengler (eds.) 2003. *Historiae iuris antiqui. Gesammelte Schriften. Band III.* Goldbach bei Aschaffenburg, pp. 2237–81.

Nörr, D. 2002. Iurisprudentia universalis von Schreiberhand: zur *katharopoiesis*-Klausel. In: M.-J. Schermaier, J. M. Rainer, L. C. Winkel (eds.) *Iurisprudentia universalis: Festschrift für Theo Mayer-Maly zum 70. Geburtstag.* Cologne, pp. 529–47. [= T. J. Chiusi and H.-D. Spengler (eds.) 2012. *Schriften 2001–2010: Anläßlich seines 80. Geburtstags.* Madrid, 151–71.

Oudshoorn, J. 2007. *The Relationship between Roman and Local Law in the Babatha and Salome Komaise Archives: General Analysis and Three Case Studies on Law Of Succession, Guardianship, and Marriage.* Leiden.

Pringsheim, F. 1950. *The Greek Law of Sale.* Weimar.

Radzyner, A. 2005. P. Yadin 21–2: Sale Or Lease? In: R. Katzoff, and D. Schaps, (eds.) *Law in the Documents of the Judaean Desert.* Leiden, pp. 145–63.

Rupprecht, H.-A. 1984. Vertragliche Mischtypen in den Papyri. In: P. Dimakis (ed.) *Μνήμη Γεωργίου Πετροπούλου* II. Athens, pp. 271–83.

Rupprecht, H.-A. 1994. *Kleine Einführung in die Papyruskunde.* Darmstadt.

Schiffman, L. H. 2005. Reflections on the Deeds of the Sale from the Judean Desert in Light of Rabbinic Literature. In: R. Katzoff, and D. Schaps (eds.) *Law in the Documents of the Judaean Desert.* Leiden, pp. 185–203.

Watson, A. (ed.) 1998. *The Digest of Justinian. English Language Translation. Volume Two.* Revised Edition. Pennsylvania.

Yadin, Y., Greenfield, J. C., and Yardeni, A. 1994. Babatha's Ketubba. *Israel Exploration Journal* 44, pp. 75–101.

8

Law and Administration at the Edges of Empire

The Case of Dura-Europos

Kimberley Czajkowski

1. INTRODUCTION

The Eastern part of the empire has provided us with something of a wealth of information about the operation of law 'on the ground'. The rich papyrological corpus from Egypt is still unrivalled in sheer volume of documentation, but there is a growing amount of complementary evidence from the Near East. While not approaching the Egyptian evidence in volume, the nature of the documents is comparable and offers a real and valuable opportunity to begin to evaluate how 'peculiar' the province of Egypt was in respect to legal practice. Indeed, the similarities in certain patterns of behaviour in both areas, at least in the way that law is approached, is rather remarkable.

This chapter will thus provide a case study of one area within the region: that of the Middle Euphrates, with a particular concentration on the city of Dura-Europos. We have a couple of relevant papyrological collections from the area that provide a welcome opportunity to delineate a nuanced picture of the legal culture of the region over quite a large time period. While it should be emphasized that these have by no means been neglected, it is notable that over and against the Judaean desert documents—another extremely valuable corpus of evidence from the region that Tiziana Chuisi has tackled in this volume—the Dura and Middle Euphrates texts have received comparatively less attention.[1] 'Comparatively' should be stressed: the texts are indeed well known, but have more often been tackled somewhat piecemeal, or in comparison to contracts from elsewhere. The texts of the *Cohors Vicessima Palmyrenorum* also constitute a major collection of military papyri, which have naturally attracted deserved attention.[2]

[1] See, however, Merola (2012) on P. Euphrates, and her comments on these papyri in her *Perspectives* at the end of this volume.

[2] See Fink (1971) on military papyri more generally; Kennedy (1994) on the *cohors*.

Kimberley Czajkowski, *Law and Administration at the Edges of Empire: The Case of Dura-Europos* In: *Law in the Roman Provinces.* Edited by: Kimberley Czajkowski and Benedikt Eckhardt in collaboration with Meret Strothmann, Oxford University Press (2020).
DOI: 10.1093/oso/9780198844082.003.0008

And yet Dura in particular has the potential to be a rich and interesting case study for the operation of law in an area at the periphery of empire, that was indeed annexed, though for a relatively short period: thus, if we are attempting to study mixtures of legal traditions, how they combine, and how people choose between them, Dura appears to be a prime target.[3] Founded in around 300 BCE by Seleucus Nicator,[4] Dura was originally a stronghold of Macedonian colonists and a Seleucid fortress city. This remained very much a garrison city throughout its history,[5] due in no small part to its strategic position for commercial and military movement between the upper and lower Mesopotamian regions.[6] In the late second century BCE it came under the control of the Parthians.[7] It did not come under Roman control until 165 CE at the earliest,[8] during Verus' Parthian campaign; there had also been a brief prior interlude of Roman occupation in around 115 CE. It was seized by the Sassanids in 253–6 CE, seemingly with a short period of Roman reoccupation in 254 CE.[9]

The city, then, was under direct Roman control for only about 100 years in its history. There is perhaps a danger in seeing the annexation as too decisive a change: Rome did not appear out of nowhere. Because of the city's strategic position we should envisage a settlement that was, in fact, highly connected to the various powers in the area: the Palmyrenes are another group whose influence has recently been emphasized, and they should indeed be factored in here.[10] The *Cohors Vicesima Palmyrenorum* was of course garrisoned there in the third century, and may have originated from a group of Palmyrene archers.[11] The point to note, then, is that even as late as the second century when—either in 165 or the 190s—the city came under direct Roman rule, it had already for a long time been accustomed to existing between various regional and imperial powers. A sharp periodization that avoids considering these factors is to be avoided.

And yet there are reasons for including Dura in a volume on law in the Roman provinces, and for considering whether there were in fact any changes that seem to have been connected with the imposition of direct Roman rule. First, this was a key century in terms of legal change within the empire: it is notable, for example,

[3] See Kaizer (2017), 4 on Dura's potential more generally as a source of day to day life in this region.

[4] It is possible that this was a later tradition that came to be included in the city's foundation 'history', since his name only appears later. It is included in the name of the city in a divorce deed, P. Dura 32, ll. 4–5 (though 'Seleucus' is, it should be noted, restored), in 254 CE, which is often taken as evidence that the Durans revered him as founder: see, for example, Edwell (2008), 97. It should be noted that this is not the only evidence for his veneration as founder: for example, the Temple of Gadde at Dura includes in one of its reliefs Seleucus Nicator: see Dirven (1999), 118–19 and Edwell (2008), 97 for comments.

[5] See Gilliam in Welles et al. (1959), 22–6.

[6] With regard to trade, note Ruffing's (2010) arguments that Dura-Europos was more important as a local trade centre than in long distance commerce.

[7] Millar (1998); see Gaslain (2012) on the exact date.

[8] Luther (2004) proposes a later date of the 190s; cf. Kaizer (2017).

[9] This is evident since, when P. Dura 32 was written in 254 CE, the city seems to have been under Roman control: consular dating is used and the city is referred to as Colonia Europaeorum.

[10] See Kaizer (2017) 66–7 on the periodization problems and 63–74 for an emphasis on Palmyra as possible power broker in the region.

[11] As mentioned above, large number of its papers survive, including the rather famous *Feriale Duranum* (P. Dura 54, 225–7 CE).

that Dura was certainly under Roman rule at the time of the *constitutio Antoniniana* (212 CE).[12] Thus, its prior history and its location at a crucial nexus of imperial powers most certainly had a lasting impact on its laws and administration. The city was also noticeably multilingual, with languages attested in papyri, inscriptions and graffiti including: Greek, Latin, Aramaic, Hebrew, Syriac, and Palmyrene among others. But its rise to the status of a Roman colony and the fact that its inhabitants would have the universal grant means it merits inclusion in any history of the legal culture of the Roman empire. In fact, its more lengthy contact with the various powers in the region—Parthian, Palmyrene and Roman (even before annexation)—make it an important case study for potential variation within the empire even at the time of the supposed unifying status-grant of the *CA*.

Furthermore, the documentary evidence from the region is not just confined to Dura (included in the P. Dura collection),[13] but another collection comes from the line of villages nearby: P. Euphrates. In some ways I am at risk of underemphasizing potential geographical differences in taking these together,[14] though the similarities in the nature of some of the documents as well as the references to some of the same villages means a comparison is still, I would suggest, worth drawing. The study here aims, in part, to try to bring out the similarities and differences we find in these documents, and thus gives us a potential window into the variations between the legal life of a city and of villages. What is perhaps surprising is the level of similarity that we find in the legal cultures of these different settlements.

It will be suggested that both Dura and the villages fit rather well with newer conceptions of how the inhabitants of the empire thought about and approached their legal transactions, and that it offers a further point of comparison with many of the patterns that emerge elsewhere in the empire. Thus, despite being at the nexus of various imperial powers, the inhabitants of this region nonetheless reacted to and adapted to the coming of Rome in remarkably similar ways to their counterparts from elsewhere: particularly the rest of the Near East and not so far away in Egypt.

2. THE NATURE OF THE EVIDENCE

The parchments and papyri from Dura Europos (or rather in the corpus since not all come from the city itself) number around 155 documents. All were found in the northern part of the city. Of these, several are literary (11, of which 6 are fragmentary), and include fragments of Herodotus (second century) and Appian, *Bellum Mithridaticum* (third century). We also have a glossary, Greek literary

[12] The city eventually received the status of a Roman colony, as recorded in P. Dura 32: see n. 9, though this seems to have been honorific: there is no information about a resettlement of Romans, the issuing of a law (on which see Eck in this volume) and so on.

[13] It should be noted that this also includes a famous slave sale from Edessa (P. Dura 28), though this did at least end up at Dura.

[14] Kaizer (2017), 79–80 sensibly cautions against this.

fragments, Tatian's *Diatessaron* and a Hebrew prayer after meals (third century). The rest of the documents are non-literary: ninety-six of these are from the files of the *Cohors Vicesima Palmyrenorum* (of which eighteen are extremely fragmentary, bringing the more useable number of documents down to 78), most of which were found in a small room in the Temple of Azzanathkona (also known as Artemis): these number 84 documents, 81 of which relate to the *cohors*.[15] Most of these date from the late first century to the mid-third century CE, though there are a smattering of much earlier texts: P. Dura 15, a copy of a sale subject to redemption, dates to the second century BCE, and P. Dura 34, a fragmentary contract, dates to 116 BCE. Otherwise, a copy of a law related to inheritance and which will be discussed in more detail later, P. Dura 12, was copied out in 225–50 CE, though the contents date back to a much earlier time in the city's history. The legal and administrative documents from Dura are varied in type: we have a couple of deeds of divorce, a marriage contract, sales, loans, and a deed of gift. From the military archives a series of *sententiae* (judgements/decisions) by the tribune are also of special interest for the current purposes.

The papyri designated P. Euphrates in contrast have no definite place of discovery, since they came to light on the antiquities market.[16] The places mentioned in the text are generally villages from the same region: Beth Phouraia is the most common village among them, though also of note is Appadana, which was an administrative centre, probably the same as that which appears in the Dura papyri and was supplied by their soldiers. This time we are dealing with only 19 documents in Greek and Syriac: petitions (P. Euphrates 1–5, 5 documents); sales and purchases (P. Euphrates 6–10, 11, 6 documents); letters (P. Euphrates 16–17) and few others of various kinds, which include a deposit contract (P. Euphrates 12) and a hypothec (P. Euphrates 13), all from roughly the mid-third century CE.

The texts from both collections are written on papyrus and parchment: there is even a fragment of a wax tablet in the Dura corpus (P. Dura 53, second/third century, a set of accounts). In general, in P. Dura, papyrus appears only in the third century, and is strongly associated with the military. Before this, parchment is used. In the P. Euphrates corpus, there is a clear divide by document type: all petitions are written on papyrus, all sales on parchment (with the one exception being the sale of a boat in P. Euphrates 11) and there is a mixture of parchment and papyrus for others. The fact that the petitions were written on papyrus would especially support a connection between the Roman administration and this material, since these were aimed at various Roman officials or army personnel. Indeed they may have been drawn up by notaries/scribes connected with the army or administration.

We thus have evidence of legal practice from both a thriving commercial and military city of eventual *colonia* status, and a scattering of villages around it from the neighbouring area. It is not the aim of this chapter to detail all these documents, or the entire history of the region, but a couple of case studies will

[15] A significant number of roster provide details of organization: see especially P. Dura 100 (219 CE) and 101 (222 CE).

[16] For the texts see: Teixidor (1990), Feissel and Gascou (1989), Feissel and Gascou (1995), Teixidor, Feissel and Gascou (1997) and Feissel and Gascou (2000); see also the revised editions in Merola (2012).

serve well to illustrate the kind of legal culture we find in the region once Rome had arrived, and indicate how this fits in with some of the patterns elsewhere in the empire that have been demonstrated in other chapters in this volume. The essential questions behind this are: what impact, if any, does Rome have on legal practice, in which areas does this occur and when does it happen? In view of the aforementioned problems in the periodization of Dura in particular and the confluence of imperial powers in the region, the latter becomes a vital consideration in our understanding of the impact of Rome on the legal sphere.

3. TRACES OF ROMANIZATION? DATING, AURELII, AND *STIPULATIO*

If we are thinking about potential changes when the city of Dura was under direct Roman rule, there are indeed some points that are highly apparent. The increase in use of papyrus, for example, was one that has already been mentioned, and is easily explicable by the increased army presence and the infrastructure brought with it.

Dating formulae are another obvious, but vital point. In short, it is only post-annexation that Roman dating forms begin to appear.[17] These are not, however, consistently applied and often combine in various ways with prior methods of dating: consular dating is the norm in documents from the East and we find that regularly,[18] but rarely in isolation. Indeed, it is only in P. Dura 26 and 30 that the dating form is solely by consuls, both of which involve veterans. P. Dura 26 is even drawn up in the winter quarters at Sacchare. This is consistent with the method of dating in the military archive—when we have the formulae—which is purely by consuls.[19] Sometimes these are combined with dating by the year of the emperor.[20] Often, however, Roman dating (usually consular) sits alongside the Seleucid era.[21] In fact, in most of the instances where we have different versions of the texts, the Seleucid year alone is used in the abbreviated version of the inner text.[22] Thus even in something highly formulaic, adopted from necessity, prior reckonings survive in legal documentation and there is also something of a retention of the city's heritage. P. Dura 25 (Deed of Sale, 180 CE) is the most interesting example of this. The document not only uses consular dating, dating by the imperial year, and the 'the former reckoning' (i.e. the Seleucid dating), but also the priests for the year are

[17] Many of the loan words in Syriac and Aramaic in fact come as part of these dating formulae: see Healey (1995).

[18] P. Dura 25, 26 (only consular), 28, 29, 30, 31 (in the lower text), 32; P. Euphrates. 6–11.

[19] See P. Dura 63 B and 64 A.

[20] See P. Dura 25, 28, 29, 31. Dating by emperor is rarer in the P. Euphrates papyri, though see P. Euphrates 15 for one example.

[21] It should be noted that documents written in the Parthian period (by the traditional periodization) use the king's style in dating, but also date in the former, i.e. Seleucid, manner. This thus seems to have remained a consistent method of dating throughout the history of the city.

[22] This occurs when we have double documents: the text is copied out twice, and the inner version sealed to be used later as a check against forgery. On such documents see Koffmahn (1968), on the changes connected with Romanization in the Judaean Desert corpus, see Meyer (2007).

listed as a method of dating: those of Zeus, Apollo, 'the ancestors', and of King Seleucus Nicator.[23] The significance of some of these elements will be discussed later, but at this point the variance should be noted.

But Roman features go far beyond dating formula. One notable feature is the sudden appearance of *stipulatio*. This was a very early form of contract but it was taken up and spread throughout the empire in the later era, especially after the *CA*.[24] The earliest examples of *stipulatio* we have from an eastern province are in the Babatha and Salome Komaise archives,[25] but we also now have a much earlier example from one of the recently published London tablets (WT 55) in the west. And Dura and its environs, indeed, are no exception to the wider enthusiasm for this form. *Stipulatio* clauses begin to be used in a variety of contracts: in sales (P. Dura 26, P. Euphr 6–9), deposit (P. Dura 29), and a divorce document (P. Dura 31). What is noteworthy is that the formulations are not entirely consistent across the empire, and, indeed, from a Roman legal perspective, people in Dura (and elsewhere) do not quite 'get it right'.

Stipulatio was in itself a unilateral, *stricti iuris* contract. And yet if we look at the formulation in, for example, P. Dura 29 (251 CE), we find certain problems. This document is an interesting example in any case, so worth reproducing here (outer text):[26]

> In the consulship of the Third and the First,[27] on the sixth day before the Nones of October: and in the year 562 of the former reckoning, the second day of the month Hyperberetaeus, in...... Aurelia Gaia, daughter of Saturnilus, of Dura, resident in that place,......... Has acknowledged to Amaththabeile (*blank space*), of Dura, also resident in that place, that she has been paid and has got from her (Amaththabeile) as a deposit, free from all risk, on this day, one hundred denarii of good legal silver, without deduction or addition, which she will keep with her and as part of her property and will return to the above Amaththabeile whenever.... She is asked to do so, without delay or postponement: if, demand having been made, she fails to

[23] P. Dura 25, inner text, 1–4 (cf. outer text, ll. 14–20): (hand 2) [*ἐπὶ ὑπάτων Βρουντίου*] *Π̣ρ̣αισ̣ε̣ντ*... *τ̣ὸ̣ δεύτερ[ον καὶ Ἰουλίου Οὐήρου] τ̣ὸ̣ δ̣ε̣ύτερον, ἔτους̣ ε̣ἰ̣κοστοῦ τῆς Αὐτοκράτορος Κ̣α̣ίσαρος Μ̣άρκου Αὐρηλίου Ἀντωνείνου, τετάρτου δὲ [ἔτους τῆς Αὐτοκράτορος Καίσ]αρος Λουκίου Αὐρη[λίου Κομμόδου, Σεβαστῶν,] ἡγεμονίας, κατὰ δὲ τὸν πρότερον ἀριθμὸν υϙα, μηνὸς* (hand 3) *Περιτίου τετάρτῃ̣*, (hand 2) *ἐν Εὐρωπῷ τῇ̣[*- ca.20 - *Ζηνο]δ̣ό̣τ̣ο̣υ̣ τ̣ο̣ῦ̣ Ἡλιοδώρου, Ἀπόλλωνος δὲ Θεοδώρου τοῦ Ἀθηνοδότου τοῦ Ἀρτεμιδώρου, τῶν δὲ προγόνων Ἡλιοδώρου τοῦ Διοκλέους τοῦ Ἡλιοδώρου, βασιλέως δὲ Σελεύ-[κου Νικάτορος Δανύμου] τοῦ Σελεύκου τοῦ Δανύμου* (In the consulship of Bruttius Praesens for the second time and of Julius Verus for the second time, in the twentieth year of the principate of Imperator Caesar Marcus Aurelius Antoninus and the fourth of his son Imperator Caesar Lucius Aurelius Commodus, Augusti, and 491 of the former reckoning, on the fourth of the month Peritius, in Europos toward Arabia. In the year when Lysanias, son of Zenodotus and grandson of Heliodorus, was priest of Zeus; Theodorus, son of Athenodotus and grandson of Artemidorus, was priest of Apollo; Heliodorus, son of Diocles and grandson of Heliodorus, was priest of the Ancestors; and Danymus, son of Seleucus and grandson of Danymus, was priest of King Seleucus Nicator). See also P. Dura 37 (fragmentary contract, late second century) for what seems to be a similar method of dating.

[24] See the discussion of Alonso in this volume; Eckhardt also discusses *stipulatio* in the West.

[25] P. Yadin 17, ll. 38–9 (128 CE), P. Yadin 18, ll. 27–8/66–7 (128 CE), P. Yadin 20, ll. 16–17/40 (130 CE), P. Yadin 21, ll. 27–8, P. Yadin 22, ll. 29–30 (130 CE) and P. Hever 65, ll. 13–14 (131 CE).

[26] All translations of the Dura papyri are from Welles et al. (1959) unless otherwise stated.

[27] Cf. P. Dura 97, which contains this formula: the consuls were the Emperor Decius and Quintus Herennius. See Welles et al. (1959), 153 on the dating: there is a slight discrepancy between this and the Seleucid year, though this can plausibly be explained as a scribal slip.

return (the money), she shall be held liable to the penalties specified for those who violate the security of deposits, and the right of exaction shall devolve upon the above Amaththabeile and anyone else who validly presents this document in her behalf both from Gaia herself and from her property, in every manner and way. [In good] faith, the above Gaia has been asked by Amaththabeile and has acknowledged that she has been paid and has got in deposit from the above Amaththabeile the designated one hundred denarii and will return them whenever she is asked, and she has sworn the Imperial oath that these things are truly thus [...and ?] given.

I, Aurelius Theodorus, son of Bernicianus, of Zeugma, resident there, on request, have written for Aurelia Gaia, who is illiterate, but acknowledges that she has got as deposit one hundred denarii which she will also return whenever she is asked.

I, Antonius Polycrates.

I, Flavius Valerius, bear witness.

I, Aurelius Oniaces, bear witness.[28]

To summarize briefly: this is a deposit contact, in which someone call Gaia Aurelia, daughter of Saturnilus, who is a *Δουρηνή* (citizen of Dura) receives from Amaththabeile the sum of 100 denarii for safe-keeping. Amaththabeile is also a *Δουρηνή*, but not an Aurelia, and a blank space has been left for her patronymic that was never in fact filled in. So one of these women, Gaia Aurelia, is definitely a Roman citizen. This contract was written firmly after the *CA*, so we would expect Amaththabeile to be one too if she were free, but if so she is certainly not advertising it in the same way as her counterpart who does adopt Aurelia. Both women, incidentally, act without a *kyrios* (guardian), as do all the women at Dura, in direct contrast to the Judaean desert papyri. Thus there is some divergence in the legal capacity of women to act across the region in Greek language contracts.[29]

To return to the papyrus at hand: the deposit is a fairly common form of contract, which was very popular in the east. It was sometimes used genuinely for safekeeping, but also sometimes for loans or even disguising dowry

[28] P. Dura 29 (outer text only): (*hand 1*) *ἐπὶ ὑπάτων τὸ γ´ καὶ τὸ ά, πρὸ ϛ̣´ Νωνῶν Ὀκτωβρ̣[ί]ω̣ν, ἔ̣τ[ου]ς̣ δ̣ὲ̣ [κ]α̣τ̣ὰ̣ τ̣ὸ̣ν̣ πρότερον ἀριθμ(ὸν) δευτέρου ξφ´, μηνὸς Ὑπερβερεταίου δ̣ε̣υ̣τ̣έ̣ρ̣α̣, ἐν [....].... Αὐ̣ρ̣ηλία Γαία Σατορνείλου, Δουρη̣νή, οἰκοῦσα ἐνταῦθα, δι[......]...[..]....α ὡμολόγησεν Ἀμαθθαβείλῃ, vac. ? Δουρη[νῇ, οἰκο]ύ̣σ̣ῃ ὁ̣μ̣ο̣ί̣ως ἐνταῦθα, ἠριθμῆσθαι καὶ ἔχειν παρ᾽ αὐτῆς ἐν παρακαταθήκῃ [ἀκίν]δ̣υ̣ν̣.. π̣α̣ντὸς κινδύνου τῇ ἐνεστώσῃ ἡ̣μ̣έ̣ρ̣α̣ ἀργυρίου καλ̣ο̣ῦ δοκ̣ίμ̣ο̣υ̣ δη̣ν̣ά̣ρ̣ι̣α ἑ̣κ̣α̣τ̣ὸν ἀδιάγραφα καὶ ἀπρόσθετα, ἃ ἀ̣ναφυλάξει παρ᾽ ἑαυ̣τῇ κ̣α̣ὶ̣ ἐ̣π̣ὶ̣ τ̣ο̣ῖ̣ς̣ ὑ̣π̣ά̣ρ̣χ̣ο̣υ̣σ̣ι α̣ὐ̣τῆς καὶ ἀποκαταστήσει τῇ Ἀμαθθαβείλῃ ὁπότε ἂν η[....]ηη̣α̣[..]α̣ ἀ̣π̣α̣ι̣τηθῇ ἄνευ ἀναβολῆς καὶ ὑπερθέσεως· ἐὰν δὲ ἀπαιτηθεῖσα μ̣ὴ̣ ἀ̣π̣ο̣δ̣ῷ, ἐνσχεθή̣σ̣εται τοῖς διηγορευμένοις ἐπιτίμοις τῶν τὰς πίστεις τῶν π̣α̣ρ̣α̣κ̣α̣τ̣α̣θηκ̣ῶ̣ν̣ π̣α̣ραβαινόντων, vac. ? καὶ ἔσται ἡ πρᾶξις τῇ Ἀμαθθ̣αβείλῃ κ̣α̣ὶ̣ ἄ̣λ̣λ̣ῳ̣ π̣α̣ν̣τ̣ὶ̣ τ̣ῷ ὑπὲρ αὐτῆς κυρίως τὴν ὁμολογ̣ε̣ί̣α̣ν ταύτην π[ρ]ο̣φερομ̣έ̣ν̣ῳ.... [ἐ]ξ [αὐτῆ]ς̣ τῆς Γαίας καὶ ἐξ ὑπαρχόντων αὐτῇ παντῇ γε παντ̣ῶ̣ς̣. [...καλῇ] π̣ίστ̣ι ἠρίθμηται καὶ ἔχει ἐν παρακαταθήκῃ ἡ Γαία̣ παρὰ τῆς Ἀ̣μ̣α̣θ̣θ̣α̣β̣ε̣ί̣λης τὰ δηλούμενα δηνάρια ἑκατὸν καὶ ἀποδώσειν ὁπότε ἂν ἀπ̣[αι]τ̣η[θῇ, καὶ ὤ]μ̣ο̣σεν τὸν Σεβάσμιον ὅρκον ταῦτα οὕτως κ̣α̣λ̣ῶς γενέσθαι.[...].[...]..τ̣α̣ῦ̣τ̣α̣ δοθῆναι, πίστι ἐπηρώτησεν Ἀμαθθαβείλη [καὶ] π̣ί̣σ̣[τει ὡμολόγησεν Γαία.]* (*hand 2*) *Αὐρήλιος Θεόδωρος Βερνικιανοῦ, Ζευγματεύ̣ς̣, ο̣ἰ̣[κ]ῶ̣ν ἐνταῦ̣θ̣[α], ἀ̣ξιωθεὶς ἔγραψ̣α̣ ὑπὲρ Αὐρηας Γαίας, ἀγραμάτου, ὁμολογούσῃ[ς ἔχει]ν ἐν παρακα̣[τ]α̣θηκην δηνάρια ἑκατόν, ἃ κὲ ἀποδ̣ῷ[σει ὅτ]α̣ν̣ ἀ̣π̣α̣[ιτ]η̣[θῇ]. vac. ?* (*hand 3*) *Ἀντόνιος Πολυκράτης.* (*hand 4*) *Φ[λαο]ύ̣ι̣ο̣ς̣ Ο̣ὐαλέριος μαρ(τυρῶ).* (*hand 5*) *Αὐρήλιος Ὀνιακῆς μαρ(τυρῶ).*

[29] See Sommer (2017), 643–5 on women in the Middle Euphrates papyri.

payments.[30] But what we find here in l.14 ff. is precisely this formulation for recording the *stipulatio*:

> [. . . *καλῇ*] *π̣ίστι̣ ἠρίθμηται καὶ ἔχει ἐν παρακαταθήκῃ ἡ Γαί̣α̣ παρὰ τῆς Ἀ̣μ̣α̣θ̣θ̣α̣β̣ε̣ί̣λης τὰ δηλούμενα δηνάρια ἑκατὸν καὶ ἀποδώσειν ὁπότε ἂν ἀπ̣[αι]τ̣η[θῇ, καὶ ὤ]μ̣ο̣σεν τὸν Σεβάσμιον ὅρκον ταῦτα οὕτως κα̣λ̣ῶς γενέσθαι*.[. . .].[. . .]. . *τ̣α̣ῦ̣τ̣α̣ δοθῆναι, πίστι ἐπηρώτησεν Ἀμαθθαβείλῃ* [*καὶ*] *π̣ί̣σ̣*[*τει ὡμολόγησεν Γαία.*]
>
> [In good] faith, the above Gaia has been asked by Amaththabeile and has acknowledged that she has been paid and has got in deposit from the above Amaththabeile the designated one hundred denarii and will return them whenever she is asked, and she has sworn the Imperial oath that these things are truly thus [. . . . . and ?] given

A couple of points should be noted: first, the *stipulatio*, a contract in itself, has been added to a different type of contract, that of deposit. Indeed, deposit was an established contract in Roman law, but of paramount importance here is that is was a different type of contract from *stipulatio*: it was bilateral, while *stipulatio* was unilateral, and was also a contract *bonae fidei* whereas *stipulatio* was *stricti iuris*. So just to emphasise this: the *stipulatio* is thoroughly legally redundant here, since the deposit works perfectly well on its own in this type of situation in the Roman legal tradition.[31] It is of course not at all a given that even Roman citizens would have had to use Roman law in Dura, but then—if we instead think in terms of the Greek deposit contract—there would also have been no need for the Roman *stipulatio* to have been included. This, indeed, looks rather similar to what was happening in the Judaean desert documents in the early second century and what happens in Egypt post 212 CE.[32]

On top of this, in P. Dura 29 we also get another flourish at the end: the imperial oath. This seems to have represented an added guarantee for the particular individuals involved in this contract, and is not found elsewhere in Dura. These particular individuals therefore seem to like piling on these nicely Roman sounding clauses in their documentation in the third century, in a way that—despite Rome's presence in the area—had not happened before.[33] So what we have in this contract, and indeed elsewhere, is a seemingly willing uptake of Roman legal forms in ways that are redundant, but are put into practice in a fashion highly influenced by local conditions. There is no real suggestion of standardization here, which the dating form shows, and this seems determined by the provincials themselves. In some ways, this mirrors what we find elsewhere in the empire—the uptake of *stipulatio*—but there are elements in which the particular combinations are distinctive.

One final point that was touched upon in the discussion of this contract should be tackled in a bit more detail: the use of Aurelia and Aurelius in this region.

[30] See the extremely famous example of BGU I 114 *recto, col.* i, ll. 5–13: a Roman prefect in 117 CE stated in his judgement, 'We know that the deposits are dowries' (*νοοῦμεν ὅτι αἱ παρακαταθῆκαι προῖκές εἰσιν*).

[31] The ensuing comments about Roman citizens and Roman law notwithstanding, it is worth considering the position in the Roman legal tradition is here precisely because we are indeed dealing with at least one Roman legal formula (i.e. *stipulatio*). See Alonso in this volume on *stipulationes*.

[32] See Yiftach Firanko (2009), 554 on *stipulatio* in Egypt; Czajkowski (2017), 32–3, 129 for brief comments on *stipulatio* in the Judaean desert documents.

[33] Note also here that *πίστις* has been added to the *stipulatio* formulation, perhaps in a further attempt to make this clause as 'Roman' as possible.

Indeed, we start finding a large number of Aurelias and Aureliuses reasonably quickly after 212 CE,[34] attesting seemingly quite widespread knowledge of the *constitutio Antoniniana* at Dura. The situation is paralleled in the wider region: we also frequently find Aurelias and Aureliuses in the Middle Euphrates papyri.[35] Thus we might be forgiven for concluding that the *CA* in the Middle Euphrates area was well known and had the notable effect and the inhabitants of this region seized on the marker of citizenship with gusto.[36]

All this was, however, far from universal and not everyone seems to have been eager to take up the Aurelius name. In P. Euphrates 6–7, for example, the seller herself—Maththabeine, daughter of Abbas—does not use 'Aurelia', even though her brother is indeed Aurelius. The Syriac slave sale from Edessa, which also ended up in Dura, P. Dura 28 (243 CE), is also a good example of this kind of mix, and indeed more generally of the meeting of tradition we find at Dura: the seller is Marcia Aurelia, the buyer is Lucius Aurelius Tiro, and the subscriptions (including that of the scribe) are all citizens with just one exception. Aureliuses abound in this papyrus. And yet patronymics are still employed along with the Romanized name (Samenbaraz and Bar Belsamen for seller and purchaser), even in the case of the two Roman *equites* mentioned at the start of the papyri: thus the local and the Roman naming forms combine. Furthermore, by no means all of the inhabitants of the village of Beth Phouraia, documented in the P. Euphrates corpus, adopt the Aurelius name, sometimes failing to use it even when petitioning the governor, which would presumably be a prime situation to exert an exulted status, if this is what it was thought to endow.[37]

In a city with a strong military or other Roman presence, one must with care assume that the possibility of using the name could be fairly broadly known; in villages, this might have been rather less obvious. But the picture in the region is of a broad but not universal uptake, and we often have a combination of the Roman form with the local: the effects are felt, but the image we have is far from systematic.[38] Locals appear to have been able to choose which elements they wish to adopted from the imperial legal order.

[34] The effects of the *CA* are much disputed, those in the short term in particular. For a small sample of recent contributions/summaries, see Ando (2012: 76–99), Hekster (2008), 45–55, Buraselis (2007); also Bryen (2016) on the Gissen papyrus, with further literature therein; van Minnen (2016) has now identified the exact date as 11th July 212 CE.

[35] For example, in P. Euphrates 6–7, a slave sale from Marcopolis in duplicate, we have an Aurelius Kozas as the brother of the seller, an Aurelia Mathaathe (daughter of Gomaimos) as the buyer, (interestingly, a *nomikos* also appears in this contract).

[36] See comments in Ando (2012), 57.

[37] Only one of the four villager petitioners in P. Euphrates 1 is an Aurelius (and only in the subscription), although there is one in P. Euphrates 3–4. One may compare the situation of wanting to present a 'Romanized' image when appearing before the governor with the observations of Gregoratti (2016), 21 that citizens in Dura felt obliged, in the Parthian era, to present themselves as Hellenized in public documents and thus used Hellenized names; see Pollard (2007) for the possibility that they used Semitic names in more private circumstances. Thus the failure to adopt the Roman marker (of Aurelius) in a document aimed at such a Roman audience—the governor in his judging capacity—is rather notable.

[38] Again, this is familiar from elsewhere: see P. Oxy XII 1458, who includes his name before he obtained Roman citizenship: see also Ando (2012) 95 for comments.

4. JUDGMENTS AND JURISDICTION

In terms of other areas in which we see distinctly Roman touches, there is also the general matter of dispute resolution and justice administration. This takes us beyond the realm of the kind of private contracts that for the most part were the focus of discussion in the previous section: both represent an interaction with the imperial power, or the tools offered by it, but while private contracts show an uptake of forms, other documentation helps us to understand the operation of jurisdiction: when—if at all—locals chose to have recourse to Roman officials, which Roman officials these were and occasionally even how they made judgments.

The most obvious starting point for this area is the series of petitions in the P. Euphrates corpus:[39] two of these are directly to the governor of Coele Syria, as we would perhaps expect, though in one case at least the petitioners travelled a great distance to submit a petition about a local village dispute to him (P. Euphrates 1).[40] The other two, however, hint at something different. One, in duplicate (P. Euphrates 3–4), is a petition to the prefect (*eparchos*) in charge of the *praetentura* by a *bouleutēs* of Neapolis who resides in the village of Beth Phouraia. He requests that he help send a (he claims) local village troublemaker to the governor of Coele Syria: this seems to attest some sort of local policing role for the army here (the accused, from his name, Philōtas son of Nisaraiabos, does not seem to have a connection that would demand army involvement). Another (P. Euphrates 5) is addressed to a centurion in charge of public order at Sphoracene and asked for certification of a testimony in preparation for a murder charge. Locals from these villages seems to have quite quickly fastened on to the possibility of enlisting Roman help to resolve disputes in a variety of ways. In particular, in this area—and in parts of it which includes villages explicitly (e.g. Beth Phouraia)—individual army officials are used by locals in the course of settling disputes, or in seeking redress. While the evidence is not comprehensive, this appears to be a decision on their part: they actively chose to get the local Roman representative involved.

Indeed the role of the military also goes beyond what might broadly be described as policing functions in this region. Found among the paperwork of the *Cohors Vicesima Palmyrenorum* were several *sententiae* (P. Dura 125–7), or records or decisions by a tribune. They are all dated to 235 CE. Of these, P. Dura 127 is extremely fragmentary and contributes little to the question of how justice was administered, but the other two are better preserved. P. Dura 125 and 126 are both written on papyrus, and record the decisions of a military tribune, Laronius Secundianus. Both also seem to have been cut off a longer roll, meaning that the

[39] On judgements and jurisdictions, including the role of the military, see also the comments on P. Euphrates in Merola's *Perspectives* chapter.

[40] Ando (2000), 74–5: *contra* Ando, I would prefer his 'weak' answer—lack of success at a local level. This does not rule out any belief in Roman justice, but for likely cash-poor villagers to take the time, money and energy to travel such a distance and submit a petition, then wait around (at cost of lodging) for a response takes, I would suggest, a particular extra motivation rather than belief alone to go beyond the village mechanism in such spectacular style.

beginning of both papyri—and hence the cases—are missing. To start with P. Dura 125, in Latin:

(1st Hand) que debere an ṇ[on]
Abedsalman autem fi-
deiussionis nomine
in ea quantitate ịṇ
quam intervenerit
ṇọṇ teneri, soluto omni
contṛạctu emptionis.
(2nd Hand) Severo ẹṭ Quintiano cos
ḍ[u]ọḍẹc̣imum Kal Maias
Larọṇius Secundiạṇ[u]s
trib [coh X]X Palmyreno[rum]
Aḷẹx̣[an]ḍrianae s[enten-]
tiae [a m]e datae sub[scripsi.]

— — to owe, or not; Abedsalman, however, (is) not to be held on account of the guarantee for the sum for which he had obligated himself, since the entire sales agreement has been satisfied. In the consulship of Severus and Quintianus, on the twelfth day before the Kalends of May, I, Laronius Secundianus, tribune of the Cohors XX Palmyrenorum Alexandriana, have signed (this) decision given by me.

Abedsalman had been a *fideiussor*, apparently in some kind of sales agreement. It is explicitly stated that the reason Abedsalman is not to be held liable is that the contract had been satisfied: it is possible it was satisfied by an action of the seller, on the editor's suggestion in a case of defects in a slave sale,[41] though other types of sales might be possible. The loss of the first part of the *sententia* prevents us from understanding the case any more fully but this seems a sensible enough reconstruction.

Despite this, a couple of significant points should be noted. We have here a military tribune adjudicating in a case that involved at least one civilian—Abedsalman. It should perhaps be noted that Abedsalman is not an Aurelius, even though the case occurred over twenty years after the universal grant of citizenship.[42] Potentially another party to the case had a military connection, but we do not know. Moreover, Laronius Secundianus actually decides for Abedsalman, possibly at the expense of someone else who was not released from their obligation, depending on how we understand the first line of the papyrus.[43] Apparently in Dura the wider population could appeal to the Roman military, and even receive a favourable hearing.

[41] Welles et al. (1959), 396.

[42] This name does not appear among the civilians or military anywhere else at Dura: see Welles et al. (1959: 395). Furthermore, military personnel are usually identified as such in the papyri with their rank, cohors or similar (the exceptions being the rosters and list of names where it is abundantly clear and the individual ranks or designations are not necessarily needed).

[43] *Fideiussio*, initially at least, had no limitation period, could be used for any obligation (cf. Gaius, *Inst.* 3.119a) and could be used to bind just one guarantor for the entire amount, releasing all others; this changed under Hadrian, when guarantors could invoke the *beneficium divisionis*.

The second case is P. Dura 126, of the same date, but this time written in Greek:

> *(1st Hand)* [...]ι[.]ω.[..]αι[...]..[....]..[........γενο-]
> [μέ]νου μ̣ε̣ρισμο[ῦ]... μ̣ε̣τ̣αξ[ὺ αὐτῶν κατὰ τὴν]
> [συνή]θ̣ε̣ι̣α̣ν̣ τῆς κώμης ἀγράφως.[.....αὐ-]
> [τ]ὸν ἔργον πεποιη[κ]έναι ἐκεῖ κεραμικ̣[ὸν μηδὲ]
> [...]σαι αὐτῷ μηδ̣ε̣ν̣α̣ ἀλλότριον ἔρ[γον, κτῆ-]
> [σιν δ]ε̣ τοῦ κερ[α]μ̣ί̣ο̣υ̣ ἐσχηκέναι αὐτὸν Σ̣.[....καὶ]
> [τὸν] μ̣ε̣ρισμὸν τὸν γενόμενον ἀγράφω[ς.....]
> [τῆ]ς̣ κώμης βέβαιον μένειν ἐξ οὗ ἀκ[ούω]
> [το]ῦ̣ μερισμοῦ πρὸ χρόνου γενομένου [......]
> [..].του μισθοῦ παύσασθαι.
> *(2nd Hand)* [Σεο]υ̣ήρου καὶ Κυντιανοῦ ὑπάτων πρὸ δεκαδύο [Καλανδῶν]
> [Μα]ΐ̣ων Λαρώνιος Σεκουνδιανὸς χειλίαρχος σπεί[ρης εἰκοστῆς]
> [Παλ]μυρηνῶν Ἀλεξανδριανῆς τῇ ἀποφάσει ὑπ' [ἐμοῦ δεδο-]
> [μέ]ν̣η̣ ὑπέγραψα.

— — (I find that) a division having taken place between them orally, according to the custom of the village, he had performed there the labour of a potter, and no one else[44] [assigned] work to him (?) but S... himself held [possession] of the potter's shop, and the division which was carried out [within ?] the village orally remains valid from the time when, the division having taken place long ago, I hear that... ceased to receive pay.

In the consulship of Severus and Quintianus, on the twelfth day before the Kalends of May, I, Laronius Secundianus, tribune of the *Cohors Vicesima Palmyrenorum Alexandriana*, have signed (this) decision given by me.

The subscription (also in Greek) here seems to be written in the same hand as the Latin subscription in P. Dura 125, and thus in all probability belonged to the tribune himself. The reason for the different languages in these two decisions is unknown (P. Dura 127, the fragmentary one, is in Greek): the majority of the paperwork of the *Cohors Vicesima Palmyrenorum* is in Latin, the civilian contracts in Greek (with some in Syriac) so perhaps this reflects the original language in which the complaint was made and the tribune simply subscribed accordingly.[45]

Once again the point at issue is not entirely clear, but there are several significant factors for us to tease out. A division had taken place between parties. This was *ἀγράφως* (not in writing), and also [*κατὰ τὴν συνή*]*θ̣ε̣ι̣α̣ν̣ τῆς κώμης*, i.e. according to the 'custom' of the village. It is notable that tribune in question appears to uphold this: [*τὸν*] *μ̣ε̣ρισμὸν τὸν γενόμενον ἀγράφω*[*ς.....*] [*τῆ*]*ς̣ κώμης βέβαιον μένειν* (the division which happened orally... of the village remains valid). This is not an unfamiliar situation in the wider context of judgments in the empire: if we look to Egypt, essentially our best-documented example, Roman judges consistently appear to have upheld and judged according to non-Roman law, even after the *constitutio Antoniniana*.[46]

[44] Alternative translations: 'No one had set him work belonging to someone else'; 'no outsider set him a task'.

[45] P. Dura 128 (*c.*245 CE) are fragments from a journal that resembles military *comentarii* which is written in Greek but all authentications are in Latin (*legi*); flexibility of language might be a point worth considering further.

[46] See Alonso (2013) for the most emphatic statement of this.

Certain features, however, are worthy of note in patterning out the general legal culture of the area. There seems to be a flexibility here in accommodating the language of the petitioners and a willingness—perhaps more than that—to recognize and endorse non-Roman law or practice, whichever term we prefer. Furthermore, non-military had contact with the military as judges;[47] in P. Euphrates they actively ask for their help, though here that is less clear. But there is a role, it seems, for this *cohors* and other military personnel in justice administration specifically in this region and at least some of the time this was voluntarily sought out by locals rather than imposed.

5. INHERITING THE PAST

While there are therefore some rather clear examples of change that we can see during the period of direct Roman annexation, the problems of adopting a very strict scheme of periodization that were mentioned at the beginning of this chapter do nevertheless remain, and deserve more extended treatment with regard to legal practice. It has been argued above that there were quite distinctive elements that do seem to have spread with the coming of direct Roman rule, which were not apparent before the area was annexed. But drawing too strict divisions between periods may be misrepresenting the picture rather too much, especially from the point of view of the inhabitants of that region. While there are distinctive changes, we should look at the other side and consider how much effect annexation really did have, or how profitable it truly is to focus on the 'Roman era' at all when the exact time of the Roman conquest is still disputed, and it is not as though Rome was a completely new presence in the region more broadly.

Indeed, legal traditions or administrative institutions that played a key role therein were certainly not built entirely anew with Roman annexation. The aforementioned record office is one important example that is attested at Dura for the Seleucid, Parthian and the Roman periods.[48] Indeed, there seems to have been some consistency in how this was used throughout the city's history in drawing up documents. In the Parthian era, this was done, 'through an act accomplished through the royal court there.'[49] A loan was also renewed through

[47] This is perhaps to be expected, considering that soldiers and their families seem to have been thoroughly integrated into the society of the region. The soldiers and their families in fact seem to have been rather thoroughly integrated into society in the region: we see regular interactions between military and non-military in legal paperwork. For example in P. Dura 26 (227 CE), a veteran of the Cohors Tertia Augusta Thracum, Julius Demetrius, buys land in Raququeta (where he lives) from a certain Otaenaeus, son of Abdabus and the transaction occurs at that camp's winter quarters in a village called Sacchare; similarly in P. Euphrates 14 (241 CE), a soldier cancels a loan agreement for a daughter of Mazabanas.

[48] Or at least an institution which seems to have played a similar role in carrying out legal transactions: in the Parthian era, this was done by the royal court and later the *χρηματιστήριον*; the term *χρεοφυλάκιον* is used in P. Dura 25 (180 CE, with Roman dating forms). Edwell (2008: 135) suggests that the building traditionally characterized as the palace of the *Dux Ripae* may have performed the function of record office.

[49] P. Dura 18, ll. 2–3/15–16 (Deed of Gift, 87 CE): *κατὰ χ̣ρ̣ηματ̣ι̣[σ]μὸν γε̣[ν]ό̣μενο̣ν̣ διὰ τοῦ αὐτόθι βασιλικ[οῦ] [δικαστηρίου]*.

the record office slightly later in this era.[50] In the Roman period, a similar circumstance occurs though the term for the registry office has changed now to *chreōphulakion*.[51] Thus, the terminology changes, but throughout the city's history the registry seems to have a similar role in certain legal acts. This apparent consistency, along with the fact that the *chreōphulakes* seem to have been local elites,[52] led the editors of this document to conclude that, 'Dura must have been relatively free at this [i.e. the Roman] period.'[53] At the very least, this local institution with a legal role does seem to have been preserved for a long time, including post-annexation.

One rather well known parchment from Dura (P. Dura 12) is also key here. The text is worth reproducing in full:

> *Περὶ κ̣[ληρονο]μ̣... [.].[.... ν]ό̣μον χ̣ρεοφυ̣[λακ]ε̣ίου̣.*
> *τῶν δὲ τελευ̣[τη]σ̣άντω[ν τ]ὰς κληρονο-*
> *μείας ἀποδίδοσ̣[θ]ε τοῖς [ἄγ]χιστα γένους,*
> *ἀγχιστεῖς δὲ οἵδε· ἐὰν μὴ [τέ]κ̣να λείπῃ*
> *ἢ υἱοποιήσητε κατὰ τὸν νόμον,*
> *πατὴρ ἢ μήτηρ, μὴ ἄλλῳ ἀνδρὶ συν-*
> *οικοῦσα· ἐὰν δὲ μηθεὶς τούτων ἦι,*
> *ἀδελφοὶ ὁμ[οπ]άτριοι· ἐὰν δὲ μηδὲ*
> *οὗτοι ὦσιν, ἀδελφὲ ὁμοπάτριοι· ἐ-*
> *ὰν δὲ μηθὶς τούτων ἦι, πατρὸς δὲ*
> *πατὴρ ἢ πατρὸς μήτηρ ἢ ἀνεψιὸς*
> *ἀπὸ πατρὸς γεγεννημένος, τού-*
> *των ἡ κληρονομία ἔστω. ἐὰν δὲ*
> *μηθὶς τούτων ὑπάρχῃ, βασιλικὴ ἡ*
> *οὐσία ἔστω. κατὰ δὲ ταῦτα ἔστωσαν καὶ*
> *αἱ ἀγχιστίαι.*

Concerning Inheritance (?). Law of the registry office

The rights of inheriting from those who have died shall be granted to the nearest relatives, and these are as follows: if (the deceased) does not leave children or has not legally adopted a son, then the father (is next in succession) or the mother, provided she has not remarried; if neither of these survives, then brothers (succeed) who are sons of the same father; if none of these exists, then sisters who are daughters of the same father; if there are none of these, but there survives the father's father or the father's mother or a male cousin on the father's side, let the inheritance be theirs. But if there be none of these, let the property be the king's. And let the degrees of kinship also be on this wise.

P. Dura 12 was written on parchment and copied out in around 225–50 CE.[54] Unlike other examples from the city, where we have registry rolls and records of

[50] P. Dura 20, l.19 (Antichretic Loan, 121 CE): *ἐτά̣ξατο δ̣[ὲ ὁ] Β̣αρλάας ἀνανεώσεσθαι τ̣ὴν συνγραφὴν ταύτην διὰ τοῦ ἐν Εὐρωπῶι χρηματιστηρίου* (and the above Barlaas has undertaken to renew this contract through the record office in Europos). See also P. Dura 21, 22, 24.

[51] P. Dura 25, l. 8/26–7, (Deed of Sale, 180 CE): *κατὰ χρηματισμὸν γεγενημένον διὰ τοῦ αὐτόθι χρεοφυλακίου* (through a legal act performed through the registry office there).

[52] Belonging to the Macedonian families in the city, judging from their names: Theomnestus, Theodotus, and Athenodorus (cf. Welles et al. 1959: 127) for comments.

[53] Welles et al. (1959), 127.

[54] Originally published: Haussoullier (1923). See Welles et al. (1959), 78 for further bibliography, including Koschaker (1926), who thought this version of the text differed from the original.

contracts or agreements that follow on from one another, this was copied out deliberately and separately. The back of the parchment is blank and it has been neatly trimmed, with a header at the top. Thus, there was a purpose for which it was intended to be used: it was not simply a registry copy kept on file.

This parchment poses a few rather interesting problems. We know it was copied out in the third century in part through handwriting comparison with P. Dura 32 and P. Dura 129, but also because of the terminology employed in the header. This is heavily restored, but the reference to the χρεοφυλάκιον, the registry office at Dura-Europos seems secure enough. This term is attested in P. Dura 25 (l.8, 26–7), a deed of sale firmly dated to 180 CE, where a division of property is said to have been performed through this office.[55]

Under the traditional periodization, this would be firmly in the era when Dura Europos was under Roman rule: even with the later date of the 190s, it seems to have been copied out during the period when the city was annexed, after the *constitutio Antoniniana*. And yet this appears to be a much older law in content.[56] The line of inheritance does not follow Roman norms, and restricts inheritance to a small, closed group, meaning that the property will not leave the immediate family. Thus the law guarantees that this does not fall into the hands of outsiders from a potentially small, original group who owned it, and seems to predate the Roman period. There has been much debate about these terms based on comparisons to the Code of Gortyn, Gnomon of the Idios-Logos, Athenian law and so on, but the most sensible, and broadly preferred, suggestion was probably that in the original publication of this papyrus by Haussoullier. He associated it with the circumstances of the founding of the city, i.e. Macedonian veterans who had received grants of *klēroi*. Bradford Welles in his re-edition and the main publication of P. Dura similarly argued that the circumstances of this law—i.e. the inalienability of land outside of the family—were tied to these origins: it prevented land getting into non-Macedonian hands and thus preserved that community.[57] In fact it is in this connection that this parchment is most often cited, as evidence for the arrangement of Seleucid settlements. While this is certainly a key issue, the focus here is on why it was copied out so much later. Possibly it was simply still the operative law, though that relies on a close group having guarded and inherited land since the foundation of the city. This is of course not entirely impossible, but might seem a little unlikely for the city in general and ignores all those who had gradually come into it over the centuries.

Rather than take this as the operative law, we might then consider the broader social and cultural ethos of the city. There has sometimes been thought to have been something of an 'antiquarian' streak at Dura Europos in the Roman period. While I would shy away from this term, a resurgence of or restatement of Greek identity is apparent. For example, as is common throughout the Near East, we find

[55] See the discussion above on this office.

[56] See also the reference in ll. 14–15: βασιλικὴ ἡ οὐσία ἔστω. The content of the law is most commonly dated to the Hellenistic era: see Uxhall-Gyllenband *BGU* 5. 2, p. 18, Haussollier (1923) and Welles et al. (1959), 76 ff.

[57] Welles et al. (1959), 76–7, *contra* Wilcken (1932) who attributed the motivation to 'royal fiscality'. Note, though, the implications of P. Dura 15 (second century BCE), a copy of a sale, in which parts of κλῆροι seem to have been able to be alienated.

the aforementioned uptake of Roman dating conventions (consular in particular, also imperial year), but we also encounter dating by eponymous priests that we did not find before:[58] for example, P. Dura 25 (Deed of Sale, 180 CE)—the example given above for its mix of dating—has that feature of listing the priests too: those of Zeus, Apollo, 'the ancestors', and of King Seleucus Nicator.[59] 'The ancestors" cult may have been that of the Seleucid kings, and indeed their worship was common.[60] However, Welles' et al. suggestion that 'the ancestors' here were rather the Macedonian ancestors of the Durans is worth seriously considering: they argue that this evidences the inhabitants, 'determination to show themselves Macedonians.'[61] This could perhaps be set alongside the name of the city in 254 CE, which then includes that of the (supposed) founder, Seleucus Nicator. There was a distinct strand in the city that inserted such references into their legal papyri, for one reason or another, thus implicitly asserting this Macedonian background/identity within a legal context. One plausible explanation for this is that it was in contrast to the Semitic population and Roman army, which became the increasingly characteristic makeup of the city after the turn of the century in particular:[62] a supposedly 'Macedonian' element, who tried to assert what they considered, or hoped to assert as, a somehow privileged status in emphasizing their Greek heritage.[63]

The inheritance law should be fitted within this more general context. One possibility is that its copying out was for no particular purpose: it was simply part of the broader cultural emphasis on Macedonian ancestry, a further point of pride for a particular group in the city that could be used to bolster their status. This in itself would have interesting implications for the wider social impact of old laws, and indeed physical copies of them in the society of this town in the third century.

However, we may be able to posit more precise circumstances for its transcription. It should be admitted that we simply do not know how widely known or used this was when it was copied out in the third century. And as mentioned, it is worth remembering that this parchment was also deliberately and individually copied, and not just part of a roll or collection: this is an individual copy.[64] The 1959 editors, in a brief comment, were entirely correct to suggest this may have been copied for evidence in a law suit, and the implications of this are worth considering and the interpretation worth highlighting anew in light of more recent work on provincials' tactics in litigation. There was an increasing tendency throughout the late first, and second century (and going on) to support any cases with paperwork, precedents and general documentation. A couple of examples from elsewhere: P. Yadin 28–30, a Roman formula (action on guardianship) was found in an archive of the peregrine Babatha: she was having a dispute with the guardians of her son in the early second century and so one would think we have a ready context for it. However, this did not fit the exact circumstances of her

[58] See P. Dura 37 (fragmentary) and 25.

[59] See n. 21 for the text and translation. See also P. Dura 37 (fragmentary contract, late second century).

[60] Rostovtzeff (1935). [61] Welles et al. (1959), 131. [62] Welles et al. (1959), 7.

[63] See Kaizer's (2017), 255 comments on the possibility of these cults as a 'reinvention of tradition . . . a deliberate form of highlighting a Greek past.'

[64] Welles et al. (1959), 76, *contra* Haussollier (1923).

case,[65] yet she still had it (in triplicate) and seems to have intended to use it in some way. General references in Egypt to the 'Law of the Egyptians', whose exact nature is somewhat uncertain,[66] was also inserted into a smattering of the papyri, and is usually considered to have been something quite antiquated and irrelevant, brought out to try to impress the authority backing one's case on a busy and pressured Roman judge.

In broad terms: old fashioned, irrelevant or even outdated documentation or rules are also dredged up elsewhere to try to help support a case. Thus, I would be cautious about thinking of this law as widespread current practice in the later, Roman era. More likely: it was copied out for a litigant who had an inheritance dispute, and (s)he was hoping this would support his or her case (potentially disputing the selling of some family land). It could indeed also have been used in informal negotiations in such a case to try to get another party to back down, presumably in favour of an impressive looking ancient claim. The added bonus of potentially playing on this general hearkening back to the past glories of the city, the context of 'Macedonian/Greek pride', and perhaps Roman recognition of this—if we recall their allowance of Seleucus Nicator to be added to the city name later—may actually have worked to his or her advantage: it would be an attempt to use a prevalent cultural feeling in the city to one's legal benefit.

6. CONCLUSION

The aim of this chapter has been to give an impression of the kind of legal culture that we find in the Middle Euphrates area in the short time when it was occupied by Rome. This short duration did not result in a lack of impact: within a couple of generations, there is a definite and marked uptake of Roman legal forms and formulae in documentation from the area. The speed at which this happens should be noted. In this respect, the area is directly comparable to many others, Roman Arabia certainly, but also areas in the West: Dacia and Britain also seem to exhibit this relatively fast uptake of forms on the part of the natives in an earlier period (with little hint of imposition).[67] This is all, indeed, in stark contrast to Egypt where the transformatory process appears to have been much slower. Similar too is the way that the inhabitants of the region seem to be using these forms: not from any legal necessity, but either as a safety net (just in case) or to project a certain status—they added or even piled on in some cases Roman legal flourishes because they thought it made their contracts look good, look Roman, or potentially made themselves look of higher status.

But this quick uptake of features that they conceived of as Roman law, or justice, is consistently combined with an emphasis on their local culture and (a mixture of) local identities and indeed legal traditions. The *CA* did not bring conformity—as we have long known—and inhabitants of this region, as is to be

[65] See Czajkowski (2017), 93–105.

[66] See Yiftach-Firanko (2009), 551 for one possibility on this collection as a mixture of laws from different ethnic backgrounds.

[67] See du Plessis and Eckhardt in this volume.

expected, found their own dynamic ways to combine the rule of their new imperial overlords with the practices that they had used for years. This was combined, perhaps, with an emphasis on embedded local custom in lawsuits, if we do take it that the P. Dura 12 was to be used in this way. Thus, we have here a tension between the particular and the general—certain aspects (Seleucid rule; the inheritance law) were specific to the region, but the general pattern of uptake and the ways in which imperial subject managed to tread the line between the (foreign) imperial and the (familiar) local fits rather well with what we see elsewhere. Roman legal forms and instruments are utilized in a variety of ways for specific, local and sometimes highly personal reasons to create a varied and dynamic picture of the legal culture across the empire.

REFERENCES

Alonso, J. L. 2013. The Status of Peregrine Law in Egypt: 'Customary Law' and Legal Pluralism in the Roman Empire. *Papyrology AD 2013. 27th International Congress of Papyrology = Journal of Juristic Papyrology* 43, pp. 351–404.

Ando, C. 2000. *Imperial Ideology and Provincial Loyalty in the Roman Empire.* Berkeley.

Ando, C. 2012. *Imperial Rome, AD 193–284: The Critical Century.* Edinburgh.

Bryen, A. 2016. Reading the Citizenship Papyrus (P.Giss. 40). In: C. Ando (ed.), *Citizenship and Empire in Europe 200–1900. The Antonine Constitution after 1800 years.* Stuttgart, pp. 29–44.

Buraselis, K. 2007. *Theia Dorea: Das Gottlich-Kaiserliche Geschenk. Studien Zur Politik Der Severer Und Zur Constitutio Antoniana.* Vienna.

Czajkowski, K. 2017. *Localized Law: The Babatha and Salome Komaise Archives.* Oxford.

Dirven, L. 1999. *The Palmyrenes of Dura-Europos: A Study of Religious Interaction in Roman Syria.* Leiden, Boston, Cologne.

Edwell, P. 2008. *Between Rome and Persia. The middle Euphrates, Mesopotamia and Palmyra under Roman control.* London and New York.

Feissel, D. and Gascou, J. 1989. Documents d'archives romains inédits du Moyen Euphrate (IIIe s. ap. J.-C.). *Comptes rendus des séances de l'Académie des Inscriptions et Belles-Lettres, 133e année*, pp. 535–61.

Feissel, D. and Gascou, J. 1995. Documents d'archives romains inédits du Moyen Euphrate (IIIe s. après J.-C.) [I. Les pétitions (T. Euphr. 1 à 5)]. *Journal des savants*, pp. 65–119.

Feissel, D. and Gascou, J. 2000. Documents d'archives romains inédits du Moyen Euphrate (IIIe s. après J.-C.) [III. Actes divers et Lettres (P. Euphr. 11 à 17)]. *Journal des savants*, pp. 157–208.

Fink, R. O. 1971. *Roman Military Records on Papyrus.* Cleveland.

Gaslain, J. 2012. Quelques remarques sur la politique impériale des Parthes Arsacides et la prise d'Europos-Doura. In: P. Leriche, G. Coqueugniot and S. De Pontbriand (eds.), *Europos-Doura. Varia I.* Bibliothèque archéologique et historique 1 198. Beyrouth, pp. 255–66.

Gregoratti, L. 2016. Dura-Europos: a Greek town of the Parthian Empire. In: Kaizer, T. ed. *Religion, Society and Culture at Dura-Europos.* Cambridge, pp. 16–29.

Haussoullier, B. 1923. Une loi grecque inédite sur les successions ab intestat, n.s. 2. *Revue historique de droit français et étranger* 47, pp. 515–53.

Healey, J. 1995. Lexical Loans in Early Syriac: a Comparison with Nabataean Aramaic. *Studi Epigrafici e Linguistici* 12, pp. 75–84.

Hekster, O. 2008. *Rome and Its Empire, AD 193–284.* Edinburgh.

Kaizer, T. 2017. Empire, community, and culture on the Middle Euphrates: Durenes, Palmyrenes, villagers, and soldiers. In: N. Purcell (ed.), *Roman History: Six Studies for Fergus Millar*. London, pp. 63–95.

Kennedy, D. L. 1994. The Cohors XX Palmyrenorum at Dura Europos. In: E. Dąbrowa, ed. *The Roman and Byzantine Army in the East*. Krakow, pp. 89–98.

Koffmahn, E. 1968. *Die Doppelurkunden aus der Wüste Juda. Recht und Praxis der jüdischen Papyri des 1. und 2. Jahrhunderts n. Chr. samt Übertragung der Texte und deutscher Übersetzung*. Leiden.

Koschaker, P. 1926. Zu den griechischen Rechtsurkunden aus Dura in Mesopotamien. *Zeitschrift der Savigny-Stiftung für Rechtsgeschichte/Romanistische Abteilung*, pp. 290–304.

Luther, A. 2004. Dura-Europos zwischen Palmyra und den Parthern: der politische Status der Region am Mittleren Euphrat im 2. Jh. n. Chr. und die Organisation des palmyrenischen Fernhandels. In: R. Rollinger and C. Ulf. (eds.), *Commerce and Monetary Systems in the Ancient World. Means of Transmission and Cultural Interaction*. Stuttgart, pp. 327–51.

Merola, G. D. 2012. *Per la storia del processo provinciale romano: i papiri del medio Eufrate*. Naples.

Meyer, E. A. 2007. Diplomatics, Law and Romanisation in the Documents from the Judaean Desert. In: J. W. Cairns, and P. J. du Plessis (eds.), *Beyond dogmatics: law and society in the Roman world*. Edinburgh, pp. 53–82.

Millar, F. 1998. Dura-Europos under Parthian rule. In: J. Wiesehöfer (ed.), *Das Partherreich und sein Zeugnisse/The Arsacid Empire: Sources and Documentation. Beiträge des Internationalen Colloquiums, Eutin (27.–30. Juni 1996)*. Stuttgart, pp. 473–93.

Pollard, N. 2007. Colonial and cultural identities in Parthian and Roman Dura-Europos. In: R. Alston and S. Lieu (eds.), *Aspects of the Roman East: Papers in Honour of Professor Fergus Millar FBA*. Vol. 1. Turnhout, pp. 81–102.

Rostovtzeff, M. 1935. *ΠΡΟΓΟΝΟΙ*. *Journal of Hellenic Studies* 55, pp. 56–66.

Ruffing, K. 2010. Dura Europos und seine Rolle im Fernhandel der Römischen Kaiserzeit. In: R. Rollinger et al. (eds.), *Interkulturalität in der Alten Welt: Vorderasien, Hellas, Ägypten und die vielfältigen Ebenen des Kontakts*. Wiesbaden, pp. 151–60.

Sommer, M. 2017. Acculturation, Hybridity, Créolité. In: Kaizer, T. ed. *Religion, Society and Culture at Dura-Europos*. Cambridge, pp. 57–67.

Teixidor, J. 1990. Deux documents syriaques du IIIe siècle ap. J.-C., provenant du Moyen Euphrate. *Comptes rendus des séances de l'Académie des Inscriptions et Belles-Lettres, 134e année*, pp. 144–66.

Teixidor, J. Feissel, D. and Gascou, J. 1997. Documents d'archives romains inédits du Moyen Euphrate (IIIe siècle après J.-C.) [II. Les actes de vente- achat (P. Euphr. 6 À 10)]. *Journal des savants*, pp. 3–57.

Van Minnen, P. 2016. Three Edicts of Caracalla? A New Reading of P.Giss. 40. *Chiron* 46, pp. 205–21.

Welles, B., Fink, R. O. and Gilliam, J. F. (eds.) 1959. *The Excavations at Dura-Europos. Final Report V. I. The Parchments and the Papyri*. New Haven.

Wilcken, U. 1932. Urkunden-Referat. *Archiv für Papyrusforschung* 10, pp. 237–79.

Yiftach-Firanko, U. 2009. Law in Graeco-Roman Egypt: Hellenization, Fusion, Romanization. In: R. S. Bagnall (ed.), *The Oxford Handbook of Papyrology*. Oxford and New York, pp. 541–60.

Part II
Asia Minor and Greece

9

Latin Law in Greek Cities

Knowledge of Law and Latin in Imperial Asia Minor*

Ulrich Huttner

1. INADEQUATE LEGAL KNOWLEDGE ON THE PART OF OFFICEHOLDERS AND THE *SACRAE LITTERAE*

From the letters that Pliny the Younger, as governor of Bithynia and Pontus, wrote to the emperor Trajan, a number of motives may be deduced which had caused him to reach for his pen. Not least of these are, of course, the demonstration of unstinting loyalty, but also a recurrent insecurity surrounding the fulfilment of his official duties, and occasionally very concrete ignorance with regard to legal fundamentals. He also confesses his *ignorantia* (against which he sought a remedy from the very outset in his famous letter to Trajan concerning the Christians) in another letter, which concerns the validity of lapsed warrants for the *cursus publicus*.[1]

In a system in which the greatest responsibility was held not by those with an absolute specialism, knowledge gaps of this kind are, of course, to be expected. Here, Pliny is representative for of practically all governors, and also for other Roman officeholders, in whom the provincial population may have entrusted legal competence, but who also required guidance or correction from the imperial centre, and thus from the highest legal authority. A particularly informative piece of evidence is provided by the *Sacrae Litterae*, of which both Latin as well as Greek versions have been preserved in a good number of locations in the Roman province of Asia. Published in 204 CE, the text referred—on the basis of imperial authority—to a senatorial decree, which exempted senatorial estates from providing official

* This chapter has been translated from the German by Julian Wagstaff, with revisions by Benedikt Eckhardt.

[1] Plin. *ep.* 10.96.1; 45. For additional information on Pliny's governor correspondence see Williams (1990), 1–18; Millar (2004/2000), 38–41; see also the discussion by Kantor in this volume on the nature and representativeness of the correspondence. For information on the warrant for the *cursus publicus* (*diploma*) see Kolb (2000), 109. In D. 26.2.26 *pr.* Papinian considers the *imperitia* as an explanation for a legal misdetermination by governors.

Ulrich Huttner, *Latin Law in Greek Cities: Knowledge of Law and Latin in Imperial Asia Minor* In: *Law in the Roman Provinces.* Edited by: Kimberley Czajkowski and Benedikt Eckhardt in collaboration with Meret Strothmann,
Oxford University Press (2020).
DOI: 10.1093/oso/9780198844082.003.0009

hospitality.[2] The translation runs as follows: 'You appear to us to be ignorant of the *senatus consultum*, according to which, if you confer with experts, you will know that a senator of the Roman people is not obliged to receive anyone as a guest against his will.'[3] To whom the edict of Septimius Severus and Caracalla was explicitly directed cannot be unambiguously determined. It is not very likely that a senatorial officeholder, for example the proconsul, would need to be informed of his privileges, so the addressee is presumably to be found among the equestrian functionaries, whether this be (with regard to the province of Asia) the patrimonial procurator or the garrison commandant.[4] The lack of legal knowledge on the part of the addressee is explicitly reprimanded in the official rebuke, and the addressee is referred to advisors (*periti*) who could offer remedy.[5]

In other words, the first hurdle that the *senatus consultum* had to overcome on its way to implementation was the ignorance of the responsible officeholders. But in order to actually anchor it broadly in the legal consciousness of the provincial population, and to ensure the corresponding degree of publicity, the interested parties from among the senatorial families grasped the initiative, and presented the text to the public in the form of inscriptions. The evidence stems from the island of Paros, from Troas, Ephesos, Satala in Lydia, Pentapolis in Phrygia, from Antiochia in Pisidia, and from one other place which can no longer be identified. In three cases, Greek versions of the text are evidenced,[6] whereby the heading *sacrae litterae* ('imperial letters') is rendered as ἱερὰ γράμματα,[7] whereas one example, which is currently held in Ankara, is introduced by the wording ἑρμ(ηνεία) θ(ειῶν) γ(ραμμάτων).[8] This form of words makes clear to the passer-by that they are in the presence of a highly official translation from the original Latin text. Those who commissioned the stonemasons responsible for the inscriptions wanted to ensure that the text would indeed be understood.

In a province with a more or less Greek-speaking population, it appeared advisable to publish Latin texts in Greek translation.[9] It goes without saying that, when producing the inscriptions, the aim was to reproduce the wording of the imperial decree—whether in the Latin original or the Greek translation—as authentically as possible,[10] even if the result was that the rebuke of juristic ignorance was no longer directed at the original addressee, but to those passers-by who read the inscription. Thus, with the publication of the *Sacrae Litterae*, the provincial population was collectively reproached for having not the faintest notion of Roman legal statutes. In general terms, a self-evident and not

[2] Most recently Mitchell (2016).

[3] I use the composite text of the Latin version as a basis here, which comprises the seven pieces of evidence that have come down to us (Jones (1984), 94; Mitchell (2016), 636): *Videris nobis senatus consultum ignorare, qui si cum peritis contuleris, scies senatori populi Romani necesse non esse invito hospitem suscipere.* Cf. also Eich (2009), 287.

[4] Cf. also Drew-Bear, Eck and Herrmann (1977), 366.

[5] The adjective *peritus* underscores the expertise of the person in question. See Badel (2004), 60f.

[6] Two of the Greek texts are presented by Oliver (1989), 488–90 no. 256 A & B.

[7] Cf. Jones (1984), 94–6. [8] Cf. Mitchell (2016), 636.

[9] Cf. Eck (2009), 24f. (specifically on the *sacrae litterae*). For general information on Latin language knowledge in Greek-speaking provinces see Rochette (1997), 165–324; also Gärtner (2005), 13–22; Rizakis (2008), 24–8; the exemplary text is Mitchell and French (2012), 27–31.

[10] Cf. on this point Haensch (2007), 218–21; Eich (2009), 207f.

inconsiderable distance between the province and the Roman legal system is in evidence, including from the point of view of the provincial population. The fact that people in the provinces were conscious of this distance is confirmed by a speech attributed to Favorinus, which was held in Corinth, and in which Rome is described as the city of the emperor and the city of laws.[11]

2. THE TRANSLATION OF LATIN LEGAL TEXTS INTO GREEK, AND LATIN LOAN WORDS

In the conveying of Roman law to the eastern Greek provinces, the language barrier had to be overcome in every case. That those responsible were generally clear on this is evidenced by a range of documentary evidence (see also below 141–143). Familiarity with succinct terms from Roman legal terminology could not be presupposed on the part of the addressee, as a letter from M. Aurelius and L. Verus to the *logistes* of the gerousia of Ephesus, Ulpius Eurycles, in the year 163 or 164 shows: A slave of the city of Ephesus by the name of Saturninus had collected money owed to the gerousia without proper authority. The emperors underscore Saturninus's liability and instruct the *logistes* to confiscate the slave's *peculium* where necessary, should he be unable to refund the sum of money by other means. The wording of the directive in the Greek language is instructive: '...the **so-called** *peculium*, this you must collect in full!'[12] We know the possible author of this text, namely the *ab epistulis Graecis* P. Aelius Apollonides, to whom a statue was erected in Side during the rule of M. Aurelius and L. Verus.[13] Even if the role of the equestrian entrusted with the office of *ab epistulis Graecis* in the wording of the imperial letter cannot be definitively determined,[14] its scrupulous formulation may originate with P. Aelius Apollonides, whose *cognomen* shows him to be of Greek birth.[15] It was clear to him that the *logistēs* of the gerousia of Ephesus, and in particular its members, would not necessarily be familiar with the Latin term *peculium*. However, the fact that private inscriptions occasionally used the term as a straightforward matter of course, even in rural parts of Asia

[11] [Dio Chrysostom] 37.34: *εἶτα τὸν ἐπὶ τῆς Ἑλλάδος ἐν πλείονι ἀδείᾳ καὶ συγγνώμῃ κοσμίως βεβιωκότα, τοῦτον ἐπὶ τῆς Ῥώμης παρ' αὐτὸν τὸν ἄρχοντα καὶ τοὺς νόμους ἡγεῖσθε μεταβεβλῆσθαι* (Then do you believe that the man who has lived a decent life in Greece, in the midst of greater licence and indulgence, has changed his course in Rome, in the presence of the Emperor himself and the laws? [adapted from the Loeb translation]); On authorship: Barigazzi (1993), 573f.

[12] I. Ephesos 25, l.36: *τὸ δὴ προσα[γορευόμενον πε]κ̣ούλιον, τοῦτο συλλέξασθαι πᾶν ὀφείλεις*. Cf. on this inscription Oliver (1989), 347–51, no. 170. Also Weiß's commentary from 2004, 65–7, and that of Bauer (2014), 162–9. On the problem of Latinisms in this and other texts see Mourgues (1995), 124 with note 49.

[13] I. Side I, no. 62. Also Eck (1992), 240f.

[14] Cf. Millar (1992^2), 224–8; also Birley (1992), 47. Also the cautious description of functions by Townend (1961), 379: 'The great increase of correspondence with the Greek-speaking provinces must have required the attendance of a responsible imperial secretary at the emperor's side;....'

[15] He corresponded with Fronto in Greek: Cf. on Fronto p.171 VdH Eck (1992), 239f; also Salomies (2005), 244.

Minor, signals that terms borrowed from Roman law did, by degrees, indeed enter the provincial vocabulary.[16]

Analogous observations may be made in relation to the term *exemplum*, *exemplar* or *exemplarium*, which in Roman diplomatics indicates the reliable copy of a master document. In the heading of the text at the Monumentum Ancyranum, the Latin text is characterised as a *Rerum gestarum divi Augusti… exemplar*, while in the Greek title, reference is made solely to the 'translation of the deeds and gifts of the deified Augustus'.[17] The documentary reliability implied by the Latin term *exemplar* is overlooked in the Greek version. It is probable that the legal terminology was not appropriate to the addressee. A century later, general knowledge of the term could still not be presupposed across Asia Minor. In Kibyra, the bilingual grave inscription for a legionary records that two transcripts of his testament are deposited in the city archive.[18] The Latin text uses the term *exemplaria*, while the Greek text uses *ἀντίγραφα*. In this case, therefore, a translation of the specialist Latin term appeared necessary.

Elsewhere, it appears that the loan word had become generally known in the meantime. Notable evidence for this is provided once again by confessional inscriptions, specifically in this case those from the temple of Apollo Lairbenos on the upper Meander River. In a whole succession of texts, the stele, erected to appease the God, is characterised as *ἔξενπλον*, *ἐξονπλάριον* or similar, and therefore as a warning against insulting the dignity of the deity.[19] The warning gains in relevance through the juristic nuance of its formulation.[20] Ignatius of Antioch uses the word *ἐξεμπλάριον* in a metaphorical sense in his epistles to the Ephesians, Trallians and Smyrnaeans, when he honours individual community members as 'exemplars' of Christian love (*ἀγάπη*) or ministry (*θεοῦ διακονία*).[21] The Latin loan word underlines the authenticity of the people thus praised in relation to the archetype. Ignatius presupposes that the term borrowed from Roman diplomatics was familiar to the addressee. In general terms, a remarkable open-mindedness is evident among the early Christians in relation to Latin legal terminology.

[16] Cf. alongside Mitchell (2012), 298–300, no. 131 (Grave inscription from the Ankyra region, useful commentary on the nuances of meaning of the term *peculium* in the context of epitaphs) and a grave inscription from the northern end of Lake Beyşehir (MAMA VIII, no. 379 = I.Sultan Dağ, no. 608); especially a Lydian confessional inscription (Petzl (1994), 23, no. 15; Kearsley (2001), 117, no. 143); also Chaniotis (1997), 360–3 and 382f. (general information on legal vocabulary in confessional inscriptions). Also Mitteis (1891), 381–4 (proceeding from the Syrian-Roman law book).

[17] *RGDA* pref.: *Rerum gestarum divi Augusti, quibus orbem terra[rum] imperio populi Rom(ani) subiecit et inpensarum quas in rem publicam populumque R[oma]num fecit incisarum in duabus aheneis pilis quae su[n]t Romae positae exemplar sub[i]ectum.—Μεθηρμηνευμέναι ὑπεγράφησαν πράξεις τε καὶ δωρεαὶ Σεβαστοῦ θεοῦ ἃς ἀπέλιπεν ἐπὶ Ῥώμης ἐνκεχαραγμένας χαλκαῖς στήλαις δυσίν* (Below is a copy of the acts of the Deified Augustus by which he placed the whole world under the sovereignty of the Roman people, and of the amounts which he expended upon the state and the Roman people, as engraved upon two bronze columns which have been set up in Rome).

[18] I.Kibyra I, no. 106. Cf. Kearsley (2001), 68f. no. 95. General discussion of archiving clauses in grave inscriptions: Harter-Uibopuu (2013), 294–302.

[19] Cf. Petzl (1994), 161 with reference to five pieces of evidence; also Versnel (1991), 75 and 91f.; also Cameron (1931), 245; Chaniotis (2004), 43; Chaniotis (2009), 124; Versnel (2009), 31.

[20] Legal process terms are also to be found elsewhere in the confessional inscriptions. Cf. Chaniotis 2004, p.29 et seq.; Kantor (2013), 161. See also n.16 above.

[21] Ign. Eph.2.1; Trall.3.2; Sm.12.1.

Otherwise it is hard to explain Mark and Matthew's use of the Latin loan word κῆνσος for the term denoting taxation in their gospels.[22]

Further examples of legally pertinent loan words can be found in two lists, one of which originates with Archibald Cameron, who in 1931 collated the Latin terms which appeared in the inscriptions of Asia Minor,[23] while the other originates with Hugh J. Mason, who in 1974 investigated Greek terminology for institutions of the Roman administration in general.[24] Words such as *acta, codicilli, manceps, verna* and a few others may be allocated to the field of law and the administration of justice. Since then, a sarcophagus inscription has come to light, which uses the Latin word *delator* (δηλάτωρ) to describe those who report a desecration of a grave.[25] Two inscriptions from Sillyon in Pamphylia are striking, in which the commitment of the highly respected priestess and functionary Menodora is praised. Among the groupings whom she favoured with donations are to be found both the ἀπελεύθεροι as well as the οὐινδικτάριοι.[26] The Roman institution of emancipation, based on the *vindicta*, had clearly become so well known in the Greek city that one could align one's terminology with it.[27] The fact that the pieces of evidence for juristic loan words in Asia Minor are not more numerous is surely also due to the narrow legal spectrum reflected by the epigraphic texts.

The Roman authorities entrusted with the administration of the provinces were well aware of the problems presented by language barriers, which in some cases impeded the reliable conveyance of Roman law, specifically in the Greek-speaking east.[28] From the second century BCE onwards, senatorial decrees, laws (*leges*) and letters from Roman officers were published in Greek in the cities of the east.[29] Bilingual texts also persisted.[30] In the year 51/50 BCE, the then governor of Asia, Q. Minucius Thermus, wrote a circular to the administrative districts of the

[22] Cf. Bauer, Aland and Aland (1988[6]), cols. 876; Balz (1981). Mt. 17.25 also uses τέλη in addition to κῆνσος.

[23] Cf. Cameron (1931), 237–62. Expanding on Aphrodisias: Chaniotis (2011), 199 and 207, n.6.

[24] Cf. Mason (1974), 19–100. Also important are his introductory considerations on the systematisation of Latin loan words pp. 3–15. Cf. also the lists in Magie (1905), 43–154.

[25] SEG 54 (2004) no. 1338. According to Ritti (2004), 594f, no. 40. From Ritti (2004), 548 it is evident that we are not talking about a single piece of evidence from Hierapolis. Less surprising is the evidence for *delator* in grave inscriptions from the Roman colony Philippi, where the word appears in both Greek as well as in Latin texts. Cf. Pilhofer (2000), 17f.

[26] IGR III 801–2, probably datable to the high imperial period. On the texts see also Brandt (1992), 151f. Cf. on Menodora: Nollé (1994), 245–7; van Bremen (1996), 108–13.

[27] Cf. also Mitteis (1891), 103, 152 and 377f.

[28] These language barriers are also noted by Kunkel and Schermaier (2001[13]), 100.

[29] Cf. Biville (2008), 44f. On the laws: examples in Crawford (1996), nos. 12, 35 and 36. On the Senatorial decrees: the notes in Eck (2017), 33. See also below p. 143.

[30] Cf. the *Lex Gabinia Calpurnia* from Delos (58 BCE): Crawford (1996), 345–7, no. 22; the letter from proconsul L. Vinicius to the authorities in Kyme (Augustinian period): I.Kyme, no. 17; the edict on the regulation of requisitioning problems by the Roman authorities in the province of Galatia (Tiberian period, location of the inscription near Sagalassos): Horsley (2007), 232–7, no. 335; the edict of proconsul T. Aurelius Fulvus Boeonius Antoninus (the later emperor Antoninus Pius) from the Daldis region: AE 1994 no. 1645. On the decrees of C. Avidius Nigrinus in Delphi (Trajanic period) see Rousset (2008), 92–107. The *Senatus Consultum de Asclepiade*, documented in Greek and Latin, originates from Rome. See also Calabi Limentani (1991[4]), 344–9, no. 116; see also Eck (2017), 33. Further examples in Brélaz (2008), 170, n. 5; see also Rochette (1997), 99ff.—A co-operation between Latin and Greek minute-taking is signalled in SEG 16 (1959) no. 754 (Phrygia).

Hellenic *koinon*.[31] Large sections of the letter are lost. Nonetheless, it is clear that the intent of the governor was to protect the provincial population from any abuses by Roman officeholders. There are two pieces of epigraphical evidence for the letter.[32] The concluding passage has been preserved at both Miletus and at Priene; however, the Priene fragment contains only the last couple of lines. The stated intention of the governor was to create uniform laws for the entire province and to declare them publicly. The direct addressees of the letter, namely the responsible parties in Miletus, Ephesus, Tralles, Alabanda, Mylasa Smyrna, Pergamon, Sardis, and Adramyttium are called upon 'in order that you might dispatch (copies of this letter) to the cities in your own assize-district and see to it that in the most conspicuous place on a pilaster of white stone there is engraved this letter, so that common for all the province justice might be established for all time, and that all the other cities and peoples might do the same thing among themselves and that they might deposit (a copy of this letter) in the archives of the *nomophylakia* and the *chrēmatistēria*.' The distribution and publication of legal principles is achieved by means of a distribution system, which utilises the *conventus* cities as a nerve centre,[33] whereby the governor published the text in Greek from the outset, in order to guard against any ambiguities. For he continues his letter as follows: 'The reason for which I wrote in Greek, do not ask, since it was my intention that nothing contrary to the (correct) interpretation of my letter could possibly be in your mind.'[34] In this declaration of intent, a standard procedure in communication by Roman officeholders with the provincial populations in the Greek east becomes apparent, according to which the original Latin text is not always accompanied by a Greek translation,[35] although the Latin text could absolutely give rise to difficulties for the addressees.

[31] Here I follow the traditional attribution and dating. Cf. Kreiler (2008), 33–7. The name of the governor is not given in the fragments that are preserved. On alternative classifications see P. Herrmann's commentary in Inscriptions of Miletus, Part 1 (1997), 155 (on I.Milet, no. 3); Delrieux (2010), 525f.; Fournier (2010), 66f.

[32] I.Milet 3; I.Priene 13.

[33] See also Meyer-Zwiffelhoffer (2002), 223–5, who proceeds from the same text.

[34] Here is the Greek text, as it emerges from the fragments in Miletus and Priene (cf. the composite text in I.Priene 13): . . . *ἵνα τε ὑμεῖς πρὸς τὰς ἐν τῆι δ[ιοικ]ήσει τῆι ἰδίαι πόλεις διαποστείλησθε ἔν τε τῶι ἐπ̣[ι]φανεστάτωι τόπωι ἐν στυλοπαραστάδι ἐπὶ λίθου λευκοῦ ἐνχαραχθῆναι φροντίσητε τ̣[αῦ]τα τὰ γράμματα, ἵνα κοινῶς πάσηι τῆι ἐπαρχεία[ι τὸ] δίκαιον ἑσταμένον ἦι εἰς τὸν αἰεὶ χρόνον, αἵ τε ἄ̣λλαι πᾶσαι πόλεις καὶ δῆμοι τὸ αὐτὸν παρ' αὐτοῖς π̣οιήσωσιν, εἴς τε τὰ δημόσια ἀποθῶνται νομο[φυ]λάκια καὶ χρηματιστήρια· τὴν δὲ αἰτίαν δι' ἣν Ἑλλη[νι]κ̣οῖς ἔγραψα, μὴ ἐπιζητήσητε· κατὰ νοῦν γὰρ ἔσχ̣ον, μή τι παρὰ τὴν ἑρμηνείαν ἔλασσον τὰ γεγραμμένα νοῆσαι δύνησθε* (. . . in order that you to the cities in your own assize-district might dispatch (copies of this letter) and see to it that in the most conspicuous place on a pilaster of white stone there is engraved this letter, so that common for all the province justice might be established for all time, and that all the other cities and peoples might do the same thing among themselves and that they might deposit (a copy of this letter) in the archives of the *nomophylakia* and the *chrēmatistēria*. The reason for which I wrote in Greek, do not ask, since it was my intention that nothing contrary to the (correct) interpretation of my letter could possibly be in your mind). English translation slightly adapted from Sherk (1984), 96–8. Brélaz (2008), 170, n. 3 also points out the relevance of the passage.

[35] Blümel and Merkelbach refer in their commentary on I.Priene 13 to a number of official documents documented by Flavius Josephus (*Antiquitates Judaicae* 14. 191, 197 and 319), according to which letters from Roman officeholders (Caesar, M. Antonius) are to be published in cities on the Levant coast in both Latin and Greek.

Nevertheless, it remains unclear who was actually responsible for the translation of the Latin originals.[36] In any case, Q. Minucius Thermus had the translation undertaken by his own chancellery, and may even have contributed to it himself.

Even if, from the second century BCE onwards, Roman officeholders repeatedly negotiated with Greeks in their mother-tongue,[37] and even if the earliest Roman law texts were published in Greek in Asia Minor (for example the letter from the praetor M. Valerius to the council and people of Teos [193 BCE][38] or the *Senatus consultum Popillianum* [132 BCE,[39] evidenced in several copies]),[40] the personal involvement of Minucius Thermus cannot be taken for granted. Valerius Maximus idealises the old days, when the Roman magistrates still possessed sufficient self-confidence to issue their directives to the Greeks of the east in Latin. Indeed, they would have forced them to always involve an interpreter in negotiations, to ensure that communication could be conducted in Latin.[41] Conscious of an inherent superiority in power-political terms, as Valerius Maximus projected it onto the past, it would have hardly have occurred to a Roman officeholder to accommodate the Greeks with a bespoke translation service.[42] Occasionally, Roman jurists also accentuated the particular relevance of Latin, for example Gaius, who refers explicitly at one point to the fact that legacies written in Greek have no validity[43]—even if, in this instance, we are only speaking of the wills and testaments of Roman citizens.[44] The fact that, by contrast, Minucius Thermus invested particular effort in the translation into Greek, signals a political

[36] W. Blümel and R. Merkelbach speak of 'official translators' in their commentary on I.Priene 13 (I.Priene I, p.37).

[37] Cf. Momigliano (1979), 29; Gruen (1984), 256–9.

[38] SIG³ 601.

[39] For further information see Wörrle (2000), 566f.

[40] Cf. Rochette (1997), 86f.

[41] Valerius Maximus 2.2.2: *Magistratus vero prisci quantopere suam populique Romani maiestatem retinentes se gesserint hinc cognosci potest, quod inter cetera obtinendae gravitatis indicia illud quoque magna cum perseverantia custodiebant, ne Graecis umquam nisi latine responsa darent. Quin etiam ipsos linguae volubilitate, qua plurimum valent, excussa per interpretem loqui cogebant non in urbe tantum nostra, sed etiam in Graecia et Asia, quo scilicet Latinae vocis honos per omnes gentes venerabilior diffunderetur* (How carefully the magistrates of old regulated their conduct to keep intact the majesty of the Roman people and their own can be seen from the fact that among other indications of their duty to preserve dignity they steadfastly kept to the rule never to make replies to Greeks except in Latin. Indeed they obliged the Greeks themselves to discard the volubility which is their greatest asset and speak through an interpreter, not only in Rome but in Greece and Asia also, intending no doubt that the dignity of Latin speech be the more widely venerated throughout all nations). English translation from the Loeb. On the historical framework of this description, which relates to the period from the third to the first century BCE, see Rochette (1997), 89–96; Wiotte-Franz (2001), 75–81. Dubuisson (1982), 194f. assumes that Valerius Maximus seeks to historically anchor the 'language policy' of Tiberius by means of the convention of *magistratus... prisci* (see following note). Engels (2014), 215f. and 220 draws on this passage to illustrate the problem of respect for other cultures in the consolidation of a cultural consciousness.

[42] A corresponding preference for Latin is confirmed by Suet. *Tib.*71 for Tiberius. Cf. in general Dubuisson (1982), especially 209f.; Ando (2010), 27 (with reference to the Latin address by L. Aemilius Paullus in Amphipolis, which was nonetheless immediately translated into Greek by a praetor: Liv. 45.29.3).

[43] Gaius, *Inst.* 2.281: *Item legata Graece scripta non valent;* See also Mitteis (1891), 185–9 (including on inconsistent practice); Amelotti (1966), 113–17 (against the background of papyri which have come down to us); Kaser (1971), 687 (on the relevance of established Latin wording; testaments written in Greek since Severus Alexander).

[44] Cf. Jones (2007), 1335.

consciousness which recognises in the unimpeded communication of legal principles the essential precondition for the construction of a unified legal space.

The fact that the law and order function of the Roman government in the Greek provinces could be better guaranteed if one availed oneself of the lingua franca was, without doubt, learned by men like Minucius Thermus from their own experience of office. Ultimately, the same experience emerges from the diplomacy of the emperor Constantine when, at the Council of Nicaea of 325, he first addressed the meeting with a pre-formulated speech in Latin, and had this address immediately translated by an interpreter, while he used Greek in the ensuing negotiations with the bishops.[45] Up until the third century, imperial constitutions were normally published in Greek in the cities of the east,[46] no matter to which local interests the specific text owed its publication in the form of an inscription.[47] Both at the imperial court and in the offices of the governor, the Greek-speaking provincial population was accommodated and Latin placed last. Thus the Roman authorities came to terms with the fact that in the east the Greek language had asserted itself as the language of diplomacy.[48] Not until the fourth century, when extensive inscriptions had in any case become a rarity, were Greeks in Asia Minor confronted with ponderous law texts, which they could read on steles inscribed in Latin.[49]

3. ROMAN LAW SPECIALISTS IN THE GREEK CITIES OF ASIA MINOR: *ΕΚΔΙΚΟΙ* AND *ΝΟΜΙΚΟΙ*

We need to examine on a case-by-case basis which path a Latin legal text took to eventually be presented in a Greek version, and in which concrete cases it was already authored in Greek by the imperial chancellery. This is not always discernible.[50] It is similarly difficult to reconstruct in detail the concrete processes

[45] Eusebius, *Vita Constantini* 3.13. Cf. Millar (1992²), 226. That this bilingualism was not a given in the fourth century is illustrated by the honouring of Praefectus Praetorio Orientis Musonius by Ammianus 15,13,1: *facundia sermonis utriusque clarus.* For the early and high imperial period see Salomies (2005), 235: In the case of a senator, one may suppose 'that he was more or less conversant with the theory and practice of oratory, and was normally more or less familiar with *utriusque linguae.*'

[46] Cf. e.g. the Corpus of Oliver (1989); additional material in Hauken (1998). On the Latin exceptions see Brélaz (2008), 172f.

[47] On these local initiatives to publish imperial laws see Haensch (2009). Bilingual texts are also documented in the context of the imperial constitutions. By way of example, an edict from Valerian to a Senator named Apellas in Smyrna: I.Smyrna, no. 604 and Feissel (2010 [2004]).

[48] Cf. Brélaz (2008), 170–2.

[49] Cf. Feissel 2010 (1995), 25f.

[50] For the republican *Lex de praetoriis provinciis* (Crawford (1996), no. 12) with Greek text versions in Delphi and Knidos, Hassall, Crawford and Reynolds (1974), 199 posit a translation of the Latin original by Roman city archive officials. Cf. also the discussion by De Visscher (1940), 36 on the dossier of Augustan laws in Cyrene: admittedly a 'color latinus' may be observed in all of the texts, but only the fifth edict including the attendant senatorial resolution can be interpreted as a translation of a Latin text, according to De Visscher. The remaining four edicts were formulated in the Greek language from the start. Feissel (2010 [2004]), 108 discusses the problem using the example of a decree by the emperor Valerian from Smyrna which has been preserved in Latin and Greek (I.Smyrna, no. 604): The

by which the text was received on the ground. However, in general terms, it may be supposed that specialists were available in the Greek cities of the east, through whom a more or less frictionless communication of the legal texts to their addressees could be guaranteed. A particular group of such specialists, who could be assigned in some cases to an individual polis, but also to specific bodies such as a *gerousia*, seem to conceal themselves behind the so-called ἔκδικοι.[51]

Characteristic here is the function of the urban ἔκδικοι in the publication of the calendar decree initiated by proconsul Paullus Fabius Maximus in 9 BCE and implemented through a decree of the *koinon* of the province of Asia. It was the declared intention of the proconsul to prefix the text of the decree of the koinon with his own edict in both Greek and Latin.[52] The publication of the text is made concrete in the koinon's decree as follows: 'The ἔκδικοι appointed for the year will see to it that the rescript of the proconsul and the decree of the province of Asia will be engraved on white marble steles in the leading cities of the districts. These steles will be placed in the Kaisareia.'[53] It cannot be assumed that these ἔκδικοι had any influence on the translation of the original Latin edict, as the various versions of the Greek texts which have come down to us agree with one another. The assignment of the task of local publication to them, however, is explained through their juristic competence, which placed them in a position where they could ensure an authentic rendering of the original decree. A competence of this type, and one which related specifically to Roman law, is also suggested by literary evidence.

Cicero turned to the aforementioned Q. Minucius Thermus, the governor of the province of Asia, with the request that he should support one of his clients, namely Cluvius of Puteoli, who was pursuing capital claims against the two Carian cities Mylasa and Alabanda. To this end, these two cities should actually have sent *ecdici* to Rome, but the Mylasans were content to send mere *legati*, while in Alabanda the matter was apparently simply left to rest. Cicero now urged that in each case *ecdici* should be sent, because otherwise nothing could be achieved.[54] Although it

translation into Greek may be attributable to the imperial chancellery or to an imperial office on site. In the governor's chancellery, the *assessor*/*συγκάθεδρος* may have assumed the role of translator. On the *assessores* see Kunkel (1967²), 331–4; Özdizbay/Şahin (2016), 102 f.

[51] For more information on the ἔκδικοι see Marchetti (1987), 334 f.; Nollé in I.Side, Vol.2 (2001), p.474 (on no. 153); Dmitriev (2005), 213–16; also Bauer (2014), 101–3 (on the ἔκδικοι of the *gerousia* of Ephesos). For further information on the Hellenistic predecessors see Robert (1963), 487f. and Fournier (2010), 215–19. – New evidence for the ἔκδικος of a Gerousia from Nicomedeia in Çokbankir Şengül (2016), 260–2. – On the differences between a ἔκδικος and a σύνδικος, who could under certain circumstances undertake similar tasks, see Fournier (2007), 25–8: Whereas the σύνδικος was appointed for a specific situation, the ἔκδικος held office for a year.

[52] Ll. 28–30: *προστάξω δὲ χαραχθὲν ἐν στήλῃ τὸ ψήφισμα ἐν τῷ ναῷ ἀνατεθῆναι, προστά[ξ]ας τὸ διάταγμα ἑκατέρως γραφέν*. Quoted according to the reading in I.Priene, Vol. 1, p.48 (on I.Priene 14).

[53] Ll. 64–7: *προνοῆσαι δὲ καὶ τοὺς καθ' ἔτος ἐκδίκους ὅπως ἐν ταῖς ἀφηγουμέναις τῶν διοικήσεων πόλεσιν ἐν στήλαις λευκολίθοις ἐνχαραχθῇ τό τε δελτογράφημα τὸ Μαξίμου καὶ τὸ τῆς Ἀσίας ψήφισμα, αὗταί τε αἱ στῆλαι τεθῶσιν ἐν τοῖς Καισαρήοις*. Quoted according to the reading in I.Priene, Vol. 1, p.50 (on I.Priene 14).

[54] Cicero, *Ad familiares* 13.56.1: ... *Μυλάσεις et Ἀλαβανδεῖς pecuniam Cluvio debent. Dixerat mihi Euthydemus, cum Ephesi essem, se curaturum, ut ecdici a Mylasinis Romam mitterentur. Id factum non est. Legatos audio missos esse, sed malo ecdicos, ut aliquid confici possit. Quare peto a te, ut et eos et Ἀλαβανδεῖς iubeas ecdicos Romam mittere* (The people of Mylasa and Alabanda owe Cluvius money.

is not clear which specific task had to be accomplished in Rome in order to satisfy Cluvius's demands,[55] in any case only the *ecdici* and not any arbitrary *legati* possessed the appropriate decision-making competence.[56] It is self-evident that this power of authority only makes sense if the *ecdicus* is competent to carry out legally secure negotiations, and possesses the requisite linguistic knowledge.

Financial claims were also at stake in a letter in which Pliny turned to the emperor Trajan, although the case was reversed in this instance, to the extent that the municipality was making claims against a private individual. Twenty years previously, a certain Julius Piso had received a generous financial gift from the city of Amisos, which the city's *ecdicus* was now claiming back for the municipality. The name of the *ecdicus* is not mentioned, though Pliny underscores the fact that he has referred to the emperor's *mandata*, which prohibited such financial gifts.[57] The fact that the *ecdicus* of Amisos was aware of the current imperial *mandata*,[58] which primarily served the gubernatorial administration as a guiding principle,[59] in any case signalled his jurisprudence and his contacts with the Roman administration. Logically, Trajan confirms the content of his decree, even if he regards the case of Julius Piso as having lapsed.[60] We may presuppose the fact that the anonymous *ecdicus* could read and understand the imperial directives in their Latin original, particularly as in the meantime an additional piece of evidence for the relevant linguistic confidence of those local lawyers has become public. Thus, we know from Naxos the fragment of a Latin inscription,[61] from which it is apparent that an *ecdicus* (whose name is lost) had a tribute (or grave) made for a person named Athenaeus from his own funds.[62] How conversant this *ecdicus* was with Roman diplomatics is demonstrated by the concluding abbreviation *S(ua) P(ecunia) F(ecit)*. Even if Latin was not his mother-tongue, he wanted to at least create the appearance that it was. The bridging function, which is invested in

Euthydemus told me, when I was at Ephesus, that he would see that *ecdici* were sent from Mylasa to Rome. That has not been done. I hear that legates have been sent; but I prefer *ecdici*, in order that some settlement may be made. Therefore I beg you to order them and the Alabandians to send *ecdici* to Rome).

[55] Presumably this related to a hearing before the senate: see Fournier (2010), 442.

[56] Dmitriev (2005), 215; Fournier (2007), 21; Delrieux (2010), 523.

[57] Pliny, *Epistulae* 10.110.1: *Ecdicus, domine, Amisenorum civitatis petebat apud me a Iulio Pisone denariorum circiter quadraginta milia donata ei publice ante viginti annos bule et ecclesia consentiente utebaturque mandatis tuis, quibus eius modi donationes vetantur* (The *ecdicus*, Lord, has brought a claim before me against Julius Pis, for the sum of about 40,000 denarii granted to the defendant twenty years previously by joint vote of the local *bule* and *ecclesia*. He based his claim on your instructions which forbid donations of this kind). English translation adapted from the Loeb. Cf. also Jones (2007), 1338. Here it should be mentioned that the manuscripts notate the passage with *medicus* in place of *ecdicus*. The reading *ecdicus* is therefore a conjecture of the Renaissance. Cf. the critical apparatus of the edited text: Schuster (1992), 361. On the basis of an italic Latin text, a mix-up between *ec-* und *me-* is entirely plausible (see for example the table in Thompson (2008²), 315).

[58] Cf. Marotta (1991), 17 with the question concerning the publication of the *mandata*.

[59] Cf. Marotta (1991), 81–7; also Williams (1990), 9; Meyer-Zwiffelhoffer (2002), 286.

[60] Pliny, *Epistulae* 10.111: *Sicut largitiones ex publico fieri mandata prohibent,...* (Though it is true my instructions forbid the grants of public money...).

[61] The exceptional character of Latin inscriptions in Greek-speaking cities is underlined by Eck (2000), 643–5 (especially the Perge example). Cf. also Millar (2006 [1995]), 226 f.

[62] AE 1998, no. 1297: *[- - -] Athenaeo/[- - -]-us ecdicus s(ua) p(ecunia) f(ecit)* (...for Athenaeus...-us *ecdicus* made (it) with his own money.

the title of an *ecdicus* and which conveyed the substance of Roman law to the Greek cities, may also be reflected in an honorific inscription from Laodicea, which lauded an incumbent governor at the beginning of the 7th decade of the second century.[63]

The inscriptions also provide information on numerous legal scholars who may not have held official office, but who nonetheless enjoyed enormous prestige in the cities. From the imperial era onwards, in Greek texts they are honoured either in general due to their juristic competence (*ἐμπειρία τῶν νόμων*)[64] or characterised specifically as *νομικοί* (occasionally also as *πραγματικοί*), as if this was an established title.[65] Although the epigraphic evidence hardly allows a more exact description of the achievements of such *νομικοί*, in particular as regards their expertise in Roman law,[66] nonetheless indications emerge that they too served as an interface for the conveyance of legal knowledge to the Greek polis.[67] A few examples should serve to illustrate this possible interpretation:

Presumably in the third century (following the *Constitutio Antoniniana*), the guild of linen weavers of Thyateira erected a tribute to their outstanding fellow citizen Annianus (possibly Aurelius Annianus), who had distinguished himself both at provincial and municipal level: at provincial level as Asiarch and in the context of the imperial cult, and at municipal level as rhetor and jurist (*ῥήτωρ καὶ νομικός*).[68] That the juncture of rhetoric and jurisprudence should have resulted in a successful practice of law,[69] which benefitted fellow citizens in general and, presumably, the guild of linen weavers in particular, requires no further explanation. Although there is no explicit reference in the text to any particular expertise on the part of Annianus in Roman law, this may be assumed in the light of the transregional interconnectedness enjoyed by the honoree.

In any case, Thyateira seems to have offered specialists in Roman law an appropriate stone slab.[70] In a succession of inscriptions in the city, M. Cnaeus

[63] I.Laodikeia 37: *Κορνήλιον Πρόκ̣λ[ον] ἀνθύπατον ἔκδι̣[κον]*. Also Marchetti 1987. On the dating of the proconsulate see the lists in Filippini (2014), 766–9.

[64] Cf. Robert (1948), 30f. and 34.

[65] See the foundational work by Kunkel (1967^{2}), 359–63; Liebs (2002), 398–406; on the prosopographical evidence see Christophilopoulos (1973), 311–16 (without Egypt); Jones (2007), 1346–58 (Inscriptions and Papyri). Cf. Kantor (2009), 262; also Kantor (2013), 150–2 (esp. on Phrygia). For further information on the *πραγματικοί* see Robert (1940), 62 f. with n.9. Also the commentary on the inscriptions referred to below. Kunkel and Schermaier (2001^{13}), 100f. assign the *νομικοί* to the governors' courts.

[66] There is multiple evidence of knowledge in Roman law of *νομικοί* documented in Egyptian papyri. Cf. Jones (2007), 1341–3; also Fournet (2009), 425–8. Amelotti (1966), 114–16 proposes the assistive function of *νομικοί* in the preparation of testaments in Latin. Occasionally the translation of legally relevant documents was sworn to by *νομικοί* in Egypt. Cf. Peremans (1983), 14.

[67] Kunkel (1967^{2}), 359 supposes that all of the *νομικοί* documented in the inscriptions tended to be experts in local law rather than Roman law.

[68] TAM V 2, no. 933:. *Ἀννιανόν, φιλοσ[έ]βαστον ἀσιάρχη<ν> δί<ς>, ἀρχιερέα τῶ<ν> Σεβαστῶ<ν>, τὸν ἄριστον τοῦ <λ>αμπροτάτου τῆς Ἀσίας ἔθνους καὶ πρῶτον τῆς πατρίδος, τὸν ῥήτορα καὶ νομικὸν ἀνείδρυσαν . . . οἱ λινουργοί . . . . .* Cf. IGR IV 1226; Dittmann-Schöne (2010^{2}), p. 180.

[69] Cf. in this context Mitteis (1891), pp. 189–92.

[70] Also pertinent alongside the inscriptions under discussion is also the honorific inscription for T. Flavius Alexandros (TAM V 2 no. 1002): He served as an advocate among other things (perhaps as *ἔκδικος*), as *curator* of the *conventus Romanorum* and as emissary to the emperor. On the Roman components in Thyateira see also Jones (2005), 268.

Licinius Rufus is honoured for his achievements.[71] Resident in Thyateira, he rose to occupy leading equestrian positions under Caracalla and his successors, finally ending up in the senatorial ranks at the end of his career.[72] Due to his legal knowledge, he became widely known. In an inscription from Thessaloniki he is celebrated as ἐντειρότατος νόμων.[73] The Digest of Justinian indicates a knowledge of his teachings bearing the title *Regulae*.[74] At the same time, his hometown also benefited from Licinius Rufinus's legal knowledge, as the honorific inscriptions from Thyateira show. Here he is honoured as regulator of all legal questions with which his city is confronted.[75] It is characteristic that the post *ab epistulis Graecis* at the imperial court is one of the stages in the rise of this jurist.

In general terms it is of course difficult to assess the influence on their old home town of those jurists born in Asia Minor who then went on to serve the administration of the empire.[76] Herennius Modestinus, who presumably came from northern Asia Minor, became one of the most celebrated authorities on Roman law and is therefore often cited in the Digest.[77] Nevertheless, he published one of his works in the Greek language.[78] The fact that jurisprudence in Asia Minor repeatedly received impetus and enrichment directly from Rome is demonstrated by the statue of remembrance for Neoptolemos from Pednelissos in Pisidia, who died young and who was remembered by his sister in his home town. In the accompanying inscription his knowledge 'of laws and letters' (ἐν λόγοις καὶ νομίμοις) is honoured. However, Neoptolemos did not die in Pednelissos but in the imperial city of Rome (ἐν τῇ βασιλίδι Ῥώμῃ), as the inscription text emphasises. This suggests that he may have expanded his legal knowledge there.[79] T. Oclatius Athenagoras from Nicomedeia may have had a similar life story to that of Neoptolemos from Pednelissos. His gravestone, found near Rome, describes him (in Latin) as *iuris studiosus*.[80]

A bilingual gravestone for the legal scholar A. Servilius Maximus (titled νομικός in Greek and *iuris prudens* in Latin), which is now lost, originates from the region

[71] TAM V2 no. 984–8 (IGR IV 1214–1218); Herrmann (1997), 114. SEG 47 (1997) no. 1656; AE 1997 no. 1425.

[72] Essential text on this career is Millar (2004 [1999]), 445–52.

[73] IG X 2 (1) 142. Cf. Robert (1948), 29–34; also Millar (2004 [1997]), 449.

[74] Cf. Christophilopoulos (1973), 319; Liebs (1997b), 205f.

[75] Herrmann (1997), 114: ... καὶ πάντα τὰ δίκαια τῆι πατρίδι κατορθώσαντα ....

[76] On M. Aurelius Papirius Dionysius, who presumably came from Pisidia, see Kunkel (1967²), 222–4 (although with doubts as to the Asia Minor origin); Liebs (1976), 294–310 (exclusively on provincial provenance, a number of indications of an origin in the Greek east); Migliorati (2011), 440. On the possible origin of Gaius in Asia Minor cf. Kunkel (1967²), 186–213. A relationship with Asia Minor is supposed by Kunkel and Schermaier (2001¹³), 100, n. 33 (modified on p.160). Cf. also Jones (2007), 1333f. However, nothing is known about Gaius's career. Chiusi (2011), 41 refers to the fact that Roman jurisprudence became ever more cosmopolitan after the second century.

[77] For further information on Herennius Modestinus see Liebs (1997a), 195–201 and Liebs (2002), 390–4. Kunkel (1967²), 259 f. with n. 552 nonetheless doubts an origin in Asia Minor.

[78] Cf. Liebs (2002), 390f.

[79] SEG 2 (1924) no. 715; Behrwald (2003), 124, no. 8 f. Cf. also Kunkel (1967²), 269, no. 41 and p. 360 and Jones (2007), 1333 and 1352, no. 41. On the institutionalisation of legal teaching in in Rome during the imperial period see Liebs (2002), 386f.

[80] ILS 7742: *D. M./T. Oclati/Athenagorae/Nicomedensis/iuris studiosi.* Cf. Liebs (2002), 401.

of Apamea on the south coast of the Propontis (Sea of Marmara).[81] The bilingualism of the succinct inscription on the gravestone, which only references the name and profession of the deceased, should not be over-interpreted, as Apamea had been elevated to the level of *colonia* even before the time of Augustus's rule, and so consequently a whole range of Latin inscriptions were to be found on the city's territory.[82] A. Servilius Maximus, presumably the descendant of a Roman colonist, perhaps of a veteran,[83] was predestined through his origins to make a name for himself as an authority on Roman law, even if it clearly cannot be verified whether he was equally at home in the Latin language as he was in Greek. In principle the transfer of Latin legal propositions to the colonies would in any case have entailed fewer complications than was the case with other cities.[84] This is shown not least by the example of Berytos, which became a centre of Roman jurisprudence in late antiquity.[85]

Smyrna may have been a further centre in Asia Minor for the communication of Roman law.[86] There existed in Smyrna a so-called mouseion, in which legal scholars were active.[87] According to the text of his honorific inscription from Temenouthyrai in Phrygia, one of these scholars, Marcus Aristonikos, was promoted to the post of director of the mouseion because of his legal expertise and served as a judge (?) on the tribunal of the governor.[88] In other words, Aristonikos, too, was among those jurists of the province who exercised an important communication function at the interface between the Roman and Greek legal spaces.

4. A TRANSLATOR FROM COLOSSAE

Even if none of the legal scholars referred to in the inscriptions are honoured specifically due to their language abilities, it is beyond doubt that their fellow citizens expected them to possess this skill. In 2005, Alan Cadwallader found a

[81] I.Apameia/Pylai 49 with the commentary by Th. Corsten. Cf. also Kunkel (1967²), 267, no. 26 and p.360f.; Liebs (2002), 403.

[82] On the founding of the colony see Th. Corsten in I.Apameia/Pylai (1987), p.13f; RPC I ²1998, p.340; Guerber (2017), 184–92.

[83] This is Th. Corsten's supposition in the commentary on the inscription: I.Apameia/Pylai (1987), 71.

[84] Cf. also Mitteis (1891), 146f.; Jones (2007), 1336f. Rochette (1997), 144 f. is cautious on this.

[85] Cf. Hall (2004), 45–59 and 195–220; also Millar (2006 [1990]), 168–82.

[86] Cf. e.g. Liebs (2002), 405f. The grave altar of a *νομικός* from Amisos, who was buried in Smyrna, could be evidence of a site of study: I.Smyrna 893. Mitchell (2000), 126 construes the person buried as a 'law student'.

[87] I.Smyrna 191 provides evidence that within this Mouseion there was also a city archive.

[88] IGR IV 618:... *Μᾶρ[κον] Ἀριστόνεικον Τε[ι]μο[κρ]άτη καὶ ἐπὶ τῆς λαμπροτάτης μητροπόλεως Σμυρναίων πόλεως ἡγησάμενον Μουσείου ἐπὶ τῶν νόμων ἐ(μ)πειρίᾳ, καὶ παρὰ τοῖς βήμασι τῶν ἡγημόνων ἐπὶ τοῦ ἔθνους πρόκριτον γενόμενον*... (Markos Aristoneikos Teimocrates who was both the director of the *mouseion* in the most magnificient metropolis of the city of Smyrna because of his legal competence, and was distinguished in the province at the governors' tribunals). Cf. Drew-Bear (1979), 295, no. 6. Cf. also Kantor (2013), 152 on this inscription. The function of a *πρόκριτος* perhaps corresponds with that of judges, as described in the first and fourth Augustinian edicts of Cyrene. See also De Visscher (1940), 60–77. Kunkel (1967²), 267f., no. 34 and Liebs (2002), 400 assume an advocate function.

pillar-shaped plinth right on the River Lycos within the municipal area of Colossae, upon which the start of an honorific inscription for a prominent person named Marcus may be deciphered: 'For Marcus, son of Marcus, chief translator and exegete in Colossae...'—*Μάρκωι Μάρκου Κολοσσηνῶν ἀρχερμηνεῖ καὶ ἐξηγητῆ[ι]*.[89] This text does not refer to law and jurisprudence. The titles that Marcus bears cannot automatically be assigned to a specific portfolio or area of responsibility. Initially the only thing that is clear is that they have to do with the ability to comprehend cryptic original texts, and to translate and/or communicate their contents. Beyond this, the title ἀρχερμηνεύς indicates that Marcus headed up an entire department of ἑρμηνεῖς, and therefore that his functions were institutionalised within the polis.[90] Because exegetes were cult personnel, particularly in Athens and Olympia, entrusted with the task of interpreting divine instructions and holy tradition,[91] and because hermeneuts, in the Jewish tradition, elucidated divinely inspired texts,[92] it appears on the face of it plausible to comprehend Marcus's titles within a religious context.[93] Nonetheless, there are a number of arguments for situating Marcus's function within the civil sector of the municipal administration,[94] and specifically in the field of jurisprudence at the interface between Roman law and the municipal legal system. The significance of ἑρμηνεία, which was indispensable for the transmission of Roman law into Greek-speaking society, has already been made clear early in this article (see above p. 138). What Marcus's translation responsibilities looked like in practice, whether he co-operated with the city archive, for example, or if he was involved in the publication of translated texts is impossible to establish. Linguistic competence in Latin was surely a precondition[95] for successfully fulfilling the function of ἀρχερμηνεύς. Within his family there was in any case a strong affinity with Roman culture, as can be read from the statement of his name ('Marcus, son of Marcus').[96] The papyri from Egypt, where the language barriers were in part somewhat different from Asia Minor due to the relevance of Demotic, put forward a whole range of evidence, according to which ἑρμηνεῖς found their central field of action in the issuing of official documents and as translators within the context of court proceedings.[97]

What role the designation as ἐξηγητής might have played in Greek jurisprudence is elucidated by Strabo in the context of his description of the legal system in the Cappadocian city of Mazaca (Kayseri): There, the laws of Charondas applied, and there was apparently a so-called *nomōdos* ('singer of laws'): 'that is, for them,

[89] Cadwallader (2007), 113; SEG 57 (2007), no. 1382; see also Cadwallader (2015), 119f.

[90] Cf. Cadwallader (2007), 117.

[91] Cf. Nilsson (1976³), 635–7; Chaniotis (1998); see also the index to SIG³ Vol. IV, p.332, s.v. ἐξηγητής.

[92] Cf. Norelli (2005), 548–59.

[93] Cf. Chaniotis (2010), 285f. no. 25: 'It is more probable that we are dealing with religious functions, possibly of an interpreter of oracles.'

[94] To this effect also Cadwallader (2007), 115–18.

[95] Cadwallader (2007), 116 by contrast emphasises the role of other language groups (e.g. Phrygian) for the interpretation of the inscription; similarly also Canavan (2012), 13 ('multiple ethnic identities in Colossae'); Canavan in Cadwallader (2015), 119 (foreign language competence of traders).

[96] On the use of the Roman *praenomen* as *nomen nudum* in the Greek east see Rizakis (1996), 21f.

[97] Cf. Peremans (1983), 13f.; Wiotte-Franz (2001), 112–15.

an interpreter of laws (*ἐξηγητὴς τῶν νόμων*), like the *nomikoi* for the Romans'.[98] Here, then, we have come full circle, for Strabo's formulation suggests that the title of Marcus of Colossae was associated with the same field of responsibility as that of the *νομικός*. This interpretation is confirmed by a papyrus from Oxyrhynchus, in which the function of the *νομικός* Artemidoros is given as the interpretation or 'exegesis' of laws relevant to the legal process.[99] In other words the proposition has some merit, that Marcus stood ready to assist his fellow citizens in matters of law, and primarily when what was at stake was the correct interpretation of a Latin text base.

5. CONCLUSION: LAW AND COMMUNICATION

Law as a social phenomenon is necessarily dependent on the medium of language.[100] Specialists on the ground, whether as *ἔκδικοι* or *νομικοί*, played a substantial part in ensuring the knowledge and validity of Roman law in the provinces of Asia Minor. Here, translation from Latin into Greek was a particularly challenging hurdle, although not the only one. To overcome it, central authorities, be they magistrates and their assistants or the imperial *ab epistulis Graecis*, carried out essential preparatory work, which ruled out translation variants specifically where region-wide publication in the form of inscriptions was planned. In general, each specialist of course had to contend with the problem of keeping their knowledge up to date, particularly as the Roman body of laws was flexible, and subject to continuous revision and extension. Even top officials of the calibre of Pliny suffered recurring moments of perplexity, which in turn gave them the impetus to update their knowledge. Only the continuous communication of legal content guaranteed the proper functioning of the Roman system of government.[101]

REFERENCES

Amelotti, M. 1966. *Il testamento romano attraverso la prassi documentale. Vol. I: Le forme classiche di testamento*. Studi e testi di papirologia 1. Florence.

Ando, C. 2010. Imperial identities. In: T. Whitmarsh (ed.), *Local knowledge and micro-identities in the Imperial Greek World*. Cambridge, pp. 17–45.

Badel, Ch. 2004. La spécialistion régionale des gouverneurs romains: le cas de l'Orient au Haut-Empire (27 av. J.-C.–235 ap. J.-C.). *Dialogues d'histoire ancienne* 30/2, pp. 57–99.

[98] Strab. 12.2.9: *χρῶνται δὲ οἱ Μαζακηνοὶ τοῖς Χαρώνδα νόμοις, αἱρούμενοι καὶ νομῳδόν, ὅς ἐστιν αὐτοῖς ἐξηγητὴς τῶν νόμων, καθάπερ οἱ παρὰ Ῥωμαίοις νομικοί* (the Mazakeni use the laws of Charondas, and elect a *nomōde*, who is for them the interpreter of their law, like the *nomikoi* for the Romans). English translation adapted from the Loeb.

[99] P. Oxy 42.3015, ll. 9–10: . . . *Ἀρτεμιδώρου τοῦ ἐξηγουμένου τọ[ὺς] ṿόμους περὶ τοῦ πράγματος* . . . (on line 16 Artemidoros is characterised as *νομικός*). Jones (2007), 1354f. (no. 52) refers to this papyrus from the Trajanic period. To be differentiated from this is the partly trans-regional, partly city-based office of the exegete in Roman Egypt, which could also appear prominently in the context of legal processes. See also Hagedorn (2007), 198–201; Parsons (2007), 55.

[100] Cf. generally von der Pfordten (2013), 12 and 31–42.

[101] Taeuber (2015), 153 f. compares this system of government based on communication with the mechanisms of modern management.

Balz, H. 1981. *Exegetisches Wörterbuch zum Neuen Testament 2*, cols. 708–10, s.v. *κῆνσος*.
Barigazzi, A. 1993. Favorino di Arelate. *Aufstieg und Niedergang der römischen Welt* II.34.1, pp. 556–81.
Bauer, E. 2014. *Gerusien in den Poleis Kleinasiens in hellenistischer Zeit und der römischen Kaiserzeit. Die Beispiele Ephesos, Pamphylien und Pisidien, Aphrodisias und Iasos*. Munich.
Bauer, W., Aland, K. and Aland, B. 1988[6]. *Wörterbuch zum Neuen Testament*. Berlin and New York.
Behrwald, R. 2003. Inscriptions from Pednelissus. *Anatolian Studies* 53, pp. 117–30.
Birley, A.R. 1992. *Locus virtutibus patefactus? Zum Beförderungssystem in der hohen Kaiserzeit*. Opladen.
Biville, F. 2008. Situations et documents bilingues dans le monde gréco-romain. In: F. Biville, J.-C. Decourt and G. Rougemont (eds.) *Bilinguisme gréco-latin et épigraphie*. Lyon, pp. 35–53.
Brandt, H. 1992. *Gesellschaft und Wirtschaft Pamphyliens und Pisidiens im Altertum*. Bonn.
Brélaz, C. 2008. Le recours au Latin dans les documents officiels émis par les cités d'Asie Mineure. In: F. Biville, J.-C. Decourt and G. Rougemont (eds.) *Bilinguisme gréco-latin et épigraphie*. Lyon, pp. 169–94.
Bremen, R. van. 1996. *The limits of participation. Women and civic life in the Greek east in the hellenistic and Roman periods*. Amsterdam 1996.
Cadwallader, A. 2015. *Fragments of Colossae. Sifting through the traces*. Hindmarsh.
Cadwallader, A.H. 2007. A new inscription, a correction and a confirmed sighting from Colossae. *Epigrpahica Anatolica* 40, pp. 109–18.
Calabi, L. I. 1991[4]. *Epigrafia Latina*. Milan.
Cameron, A. 1931. Latin words in the Greek inscriptions of Asia Minor. *American Journal of Philology* 52, pp. 232–62.
Canavan, R. 2012. *Clothing the body of Christ at Colossae*. Tübingen.
Chaniotis, A. 1997. Tempeljustiz im kaiserzeitlichen Kleinasien: Rechtliche Aspekte der Beichtinschriften. In: G. Thür and J. Vélissaropoulos-Karakostas (eds. *Symposion 1995. Vorträge zur griechischen und hellenistischen Rechtsgeschichte (Korfu, 1.–5. September 1995)*. Cologne, Weimar and Vienna, pp. 353–84.
Chaniotis, A. 1998. *Der Neue Pauly 4* (1998), col. 339–340, s.v. Exegetai.
Chaniotis, A. 2004. Under the watchful eyes of the gods: divine justice in Hellenistic and Roman Asia Minor. In: S. Colvin (ed.), *The Greco-Roman east. Politics, culture, society*. Cambridge, pp. 1–43.
Chaniotis, A. 2009. Ritual performances of divine justice: the epigraphy of confession, atonement and exaltation in Roman Asia Minor. In: H.M. Cotton, R.G. Hoyland, J. J. Price, and D.J. Wasserstein (eds.). *From Hellenism to Islam. Cultural and linguistic change in the Roman Near East*. Cambridge, pp. 115–53.
Chaniotis, A. 2010. Epigraphic Bulletin for Greek religion 2007. *Kernos* 23, pp. 271–327.
Chaniotis, A. 2011. Graffiti in Aphrodisias. Images—texts—contexts. In: J. A. Baird and C. Taylor (eds.) *Ancient graffiti in context*. New York and Abingdon, pp. 191–207.
Chiusi, T.J. 2011. Lo straniero come compartecipe dell'esperienza giuridica. A proposito dello stato giuridico dello straniero a Roma. In: A. Maffi and L. Gagliardi (eds.) *I diritti degli altri in Grecia e a Roma*. Sankt Augustin, pp. 30–44.
Christophilopoulos, A.P. 1973. *Δίκαιον καὶ ἱστορία. Μικρά μελετήματα*. Athen.
Çokbankir Şengül, N. 2016. Bithynia'dan yeni mezar yazıtları. In: B. Takmer, E.N. Akdoğu Arca and N. Gökalp Özdil (eds.). *Vir doctus anatolicus. Studies in Memory of Sencer Şahin—Sencer Şahin Anısına Yazılar*. Istanbul, pp. 259–62.
Crawford, M.H. 1996. *Roman statutes, Vol.* 1. London.
Delrieux, F. 2010. La crise financière des cités grecques d'Asie Mineure au 1er siècle a.C. et la lettre de Cicéron à Q. Minucius Thermus (*Fam.* 13.56). In: R. van Bremen, and J.-M. Carbon (eds.) *Hellenistic Karia*. Bordeaux, pp. 505–26.

De Visscher, F. 1940. *Les édits d'Auguste découverts a Cyrène*. Louvain.

Dittmann-Schöne, I. 2010². *Die Berufsvereine in den Städten des kaiserzeitlichen Kleinasiens*. Regensburg.

Dmitriev, S. 2005. *City government in the Hellenistic and Roman Asia Minor*. Oxford.

Drew-Bear, T. 1979. The city of Temenouthyrai in Phrygia. *Chiron* 9, pp. 275–302.

Drew-Bear, Th., Eck, W. and Herrmann, P. 1977. Sacrae Litterae. *Chiron* 7, pp. 355–83.

Dubuisson, M. 1982. Y a-t-il une politique linguistique romaine? *Ktema* 7, pp. 187–210.

Eck, W. 1992. P. Aelius Apollonides, ab epistulis Graecis, und ein Brief des Cornelius Fronto. *Zeitschrift für Papyrologie und Epigraphik* 91, pp. 236–42.

Eck, W. 2000. Latein als Sprache politischer Kommnikation in Städten der östlichen Provinzen. *Chiron* 30, pp. 641–60.

Eck, W. 2009. The presence, role and significance of Latin in the epigraphy and culture of the Roman Near East. In: H. M. Cotton, R. G. Hoyland, J. J. Price, D. J. Wasserstein (eds.), *From Hellenism to Islam. Cultural and linguistic change in the Roman Near East*. Cambridge, pp. 15–42.

Eck, W. 2017. *Senatus consulta* in lateinischen Inschriften aus den Provinzen. *Quaderni Lupiensi di Storia e Diritto* 7, pp. 31–55.

Eich, A. 2009. Diplomatische Genauigkeit oder inhaltliche Richtigkeit? Das Verhältnis von Original und Abschrift. In: Haensch, R. (ed.), *Selbstdarstellung und Kommunikation. Die Veröffentlichung staatlicher Urkunden auf Stein und Bronze in der Römischen Welt*. Munich, pp. 267–99.

Engels, D. 2014. *Auf dem Weg ins Imperium. Die Krise der Europäischen Union und der Untergang der römischen Republik. Historische Parallelen*. Berlin.

Feissel, D. 2010. Épigraphie et constitutions impériales: aspects de la publications du droit à Byzance. In: D. Feissel. *Documents, droit, diplomatique de l'Empire romain tardif*. Paris, pp. 17–42 [originally in: G. Cavallo and C. Mango (eds.), 1995. *Epigrafia medievale greca e latina, ideologia e funzione. Atti del seminario di Erice [12–18 settembre 1991]*. Spoleto, pp. 67–98].

Feissel, D. 2010. Le rescrit de Valérien à Apellas (I. Smyrna, 604) d'après une copie inédite de John Covel. In: D. Feissel. *Documents, droit, diplomatique de l'Empire romain tardif*. Paris, pp. 101–15 [originally in: S. Follet (ed.), 2004. *L'hellénisme d'époque romaine. Nouveaux documents, nouvelles approches (Ier s. a.-C.–IIIe s. p.-C.). Actes du Colloque international à la mémoire de Louis Robert, Paris, 7–8 juillet 2000*. Paris, pp. 341–55].

Filippini, A. 2014. Su alcuni proconsoli d'Asia all'epoca di Marco Aurelio (168–173): Kaisergeschichte e Kirchengeschichte tra fonti letterarie ed epigrafiche. In: M. L. Caldelli and G. L. Gregori (eds.) *Epigrafia e ordine senatorio, 30 anni dopo*. Rome, pp. 745–76.

Fournet, J.-L. 2009. The multilingual environment of late antique Egypt: Greek, Latin, Coptic, and Persian documents. In: R. S. Bagnall (ed.), *The Oxford Handbook of Papyrology*. Oxford, pp. 418–51.

Fournier, J. 2007. Les *syndikoi*, représentants juridiques des cités grecques sous le Haut-Empire Romain. *Cahiers du Centre Gustave Glotz* 1, pp. 7–36.

Fournier, J. 2010. *Entre tutelle romaine et autonomie civique: L'administration judiciaire dans les provinces hellénophones de l'empire romain, 129 av. J.-C.–235 ap. J.-C.* Athens.

Gärtner, U. 2005. *Quintus Smyrnaeus und die* Aeneis. *Zur Nachwirkung Vergils in der griechischen Literatur der Kaiserzeit*. Munich.

Gruen, E.S. 1984. *The Hellenistic world and the coming of Rome*. Berkeley, Los Angeles and London.

Guerber, É. 2017. La colonie d'Apamée-Myrléa: 'un îlot de romanité en pays grec'? In: C. Brélaz (ed.), *L'héritage grec des colonies romaines d'orient. Interactions culturelles dans les provinces hellénophones de l'empire romain*. Paris, pp. 175–200.

Haensch, R. 2007. Apokrimata und Authentica. Dokumente römischer Herrschaft in der Sicht der Untertanen. In: R. Haensch, and J. Heinrichs (eds.), *Herrschen und Verwalten*.

Der Alltag der römischen Administration in der Hohen Kaiserzeit. Cologne, Weimar and Wien, pp. 213–33.

Haensch, R. 2009. Die Städte des griechischen Ostens. In: R. Haensch (ed.), *Selbstdarstellung und Kommunikation. Die Veröffentlichung staatlicher Urkunden auf Stein und Bronze in der Römischen Welt*. Munich, pp. 173–87.

Hagedorn, D. 2007. The emergence of municipal offices in the nome-capitals of Egypt. In: A. K. Bowman and R.A. Coles u.a. (eds.): *Oxyrhynchus. A city and its texts*. London, pp. 194–204.

Hall, L. J. 2004. *Roman Berytus. Beirut in late antiquity*. London and New York.

Harter-Uibopuu, K. 2013. Epigraphische Quellen zum Archivwesen in den griechischen Poleis des ausgehenden Hellenismus und der Kaiserzeit. In: M. Faraguna (ed.), *Archives and archival documents in ancient societies (Trieste, 30 September–1 October 2011)*. Trieste, pp. 273–305.

Hassall, M., Crawford, M. and Reynolds, J. 1974. Rome and the eastern provinces at the end of the second century BC. *Journal of Roman Studies* 64, pp. 195–220.

Hauken, T. 1998. *Petition and response. An epigraphic study of petitions to Roman emperors 181–249*. Athens 1998.

Herrmann, P. 1997. Die Karriere eines prominenten Juristen aus Thyateira. *Tyche* 12, pp. 111–23.

Horsley, G. H. R. 2007. *The Greek and Latin inscriptions in the Burdur Archaeological Museum*. Ankara.

Jones, C. P. 1984. The Sacrae Litterae of 204: two colonial copies. *Chiron* 14, pp. 93–9.

Jones, C. P. 2005. Culture in the careers of eastern senators. In: W. Eck and M. Heil (eds.) *Senatores populi Romani. Realität und mediale Präsentation einer Führungsschicht*. Stuttgart, pp. 263–70.

Jones, C. P. 2007. Juristes romains dans l'Orient grec. *Comptes rendus des séances de l'Académie des Inscriptions et Belles-Lettres* 151:3, pp. 1331–59.

Kantor, G. 2009. Knowledge of law in Roman Asia Minor. In: R. Haensch, R. (ed.), *Selbstdarstellung und Kommunikation. Die Veröffentlichung staatlicher Urkunden auf Stein und Bronze in der Römischen Welt*. Munich, pp. 249–65.

Kantor, G. 2013. Law in Roman Phrygia: rules and jurisdictions. In: P. Thonemann (ed.), *Roman Phrygia. Culture and society*. Cambridge, pp. 143–67.

Kaser, M. 1971. *Das römische Privatrecht. Erster Abschnitt: Das altrömische, das vorklassische und klassische Recht*. Munich.

Kearsley, R. A. 2001. *Greeks and Romans in imperial Asia. Mixed language inscriptions and linguistic evidence for cultural interaction until the end of AD III*. Bonn.

Kolb, A. 2000. *Transport und Nachrichtentransfer im Römischen Reich*. Berlin.

Kreiler, B. M. 2008. Anmerkungen zu den Statthaltern der Povinz Asia am Ende der Republik (52–42 v.Chr.). *Gephyra* 5, pp. 33–51.

Kunkel, W. 1967². *Die römischen Juristen. Herkunft und soziale Stellung*. Cologne, Weimar and Vienna (Reprinted 2001).

Kunkel, W. And Schermaier, M. 2001¹³. *Römische Rechtsgeschichte*. Cologne, Weimar and Vienna.

Liebs, D. 1976. Römische Provinzialjurisprudenz. *Aufstieg und Niedergang der römischen Welt* II. 15, pp. 288–362.

Liebs, D. 1997a. Herennius Modestinus. In: K. Sallmann (ed.), *Handbuch der Lateinischen Literatur der Antike. Vol. 4: Die Literatur des Umbruchs*. Munich, pp. 195–201.

Liebs, D. 1997b. M. Cn. Licinius Rufinus. In: K. Sallmann (ed.), *Handbuch der Lateinischen Literatur der Antike. Vol. 4: Die Literatur des Umbruchs*. Munich, pp. 205–6.

Liebs, D. 2002. Rechtskunde im römischen Kaiserreich. Rom und die Provinzen. In: M.J. Schermaier, J. M. Rainer and L. C. Winkel (eds.), *Iurisprudentia universalis. Festschrift für Theo Mayer-Maly zum 70. Geburtstag*. Cologne, Weimar and Vienna, pp. 383–407.

Magie, D. 1905. *De Romanorum iuris publici sacrique vocabulis sollemnibus in Graecum sermonem conversis*. Leipzig.

Marchetti, P. 1987. Un *ekdikos* méconnu en Asie Mineure au IIe s. ap. J.-C. In: J. Servais, T. Hackens and B. Servais-Soyez (eds.) *Stemmata: Mélanges de philologie, d'histoire et d'archéologie grecques offerts à Jules Labarbe*. Liège and Louvain-la-Neuve, pp. 333–6.

Marotta, V. 1991. *Mandata principum*. Turin.

Mason, H. J. 1974. *Greek terms for Roman institutions: a lexicon and analysis*. Toronto.

Meyer-Zwiffelhoffer, E. 2002. *Πολιτικῶς ἄρχειν. Zum Regierungsstil der senatorischen Statthalter in den kaiserzeitlichen griechischen Provinzen*. Stuttgart.

Migliorati, G. 2011. *Iscrizioni per la ricostruzione storica dell' Impero Romano da Marco Aurelio a Commodo*. Milan.

Millar, F. 1992². *The emperor in the Roman world (31 BC–AD 337)*. London.

Millar, F. 2000. Trajan: Government by correspondence. In: Millar, F. *Government, society, and culture in the Roman Empire*. London 2004, pp. 23–46 [originally published in: J. Gonzalez (ed.), *Trajano Emperador de Roma*. Madrid pp. 363–88).

Millar, F. 2004. The Greek east and Roman law: the dossier of M. Cn. Licinius Rufinus. In: Millar, F. *Government, society, and culture in the Roman Empire*. London 2004, pp. 435–64 [originally in: *Journal of Roman Studies* 89 (1999), pp. 90–108].

Millar, F. 2006. The Roman *coloniae* of the Near East: a study of cultural relations. In: F. Millar. *Rome, the Greek world, and the east 3: The Greek world, the Jews, and the East*. London, pp. 164–222 [originally in H. Solin, and M. Kajava (eds.) 1990. *Roman eastern policy and other studies in Roman History*. Helsinki, pp. 7–58].

Millar, F. 2006. Latin in the epigraphy of the Roman Near East. In: F. Millar. *Rome, the Greek world, and the east 3: The Greek world, the Jews, and the East*. London, pp. 223–42. [originally in H. Solin, O. Salomies and U.-M. Liertz (eds.) 1995. *Acta Colloquii Epigraphici Latini. Helsinki 3–6 Sept. 1991*. Helsinki, pp. 403–19.]

Mitchell, St. 2000. Ethnicity, acculturation and Empire in Roman and late Roman Asia Minor. In: St. Mitchell and G. Greatrex (eds.) *Ethnicity and culture in late antiquity*. London, pp. 117–50.

Mitchell, St. 2016. *ΕΡΜΗΝΕΙΑ*. The Greek translations of the *sacrae litterae* on official hospitality (AD 204). In: B. Takmer, E.N. Akdoğu Arca and N. Gökalp Özdil (eds.) 2016. *Vir doctus anatolicus. Studies in Memory of Sencer Şahin—Sencer Şahin Anısına Yazılar*. Istanbul 2016, pp. 635–9.

Mitchell, St. and French, D. 2012. *The Greek and Latin inscriptions of Ankara (Ancyra), vol. I: From Augustus to the end of the third century AD*. Munich.

Mitteis, L. 1891. *Reichsrecht und Volksrecht in den östlichen Provinzen des römischen Kaiserreichs*. Leipzig (Reprinted: Hildesheim, Zürich and New York 1984).

Momigliano, A. 1979. *Hochkulturen im Hellenismus. Die Begegnung der Griechen mit Kelten, Römern, Juden und Persern*. Munich.

Mourgues, J.-L. 1995. Écrire en deux langues: bilinguisme et pratique de chancellerie sous le Haut-Empire romain. *Dialogues d'histoire ancienne* 21.2, pp. 105–29.

Nilsson, M. P. 1976³. *Geschichte der griechischen Religion I: Die Religion Griechenlands bis auf die griechische Weltherrschaft*. Munich.

Nollé, J. 1994. Frauen wie Omphale? Überlegungen zu 'politischen' Ämtern von Frauen im kaiserzeitlichen Kleinasien. In: M. H. Dettenhofer (ed.), *Reine Männersache? Frauen in Männerdomänen der antiken Welt*. Cologne, pp. 229–59.

Norelli, E. 2005. *Papia di Hierapolis, Esposizione degli oracoli del Signore. I frammenti*. Milan.

Oliver, J. H. 1989. *Greek constitutions of early Roman Emperors from inscriptions and papyri*. Philadelphia.

Özdizbay, A. and Şahin, H. 2016. Neue Inschriften aus Perge 1: L. Annius Annianus, Prokonsul von Pamphylia-Lycia-Isauria. *Philia* 2, pp. 98–112.

Parsons, P. 2007. *City of the sharp-nosed fish. Greek papyri beneath the Egyptian sand reveal a long-lost world.* London.

Peremans, W. 1983. Les ἑρμηνεῖς dans l'Égypte gréco-romaine. In: G. Grimm, and H. Heinen, E. Winter (eds.) *Das römische-byzantinische Ägypten. Akten des internationalen Symposions 26.–30. September in Trier.* Mainz, pp. 11–17.

Petzl, G. 1994. *Die Beichtinschriften Westkleinasiens.* Bonn.

Pfordten, D. von der. 2013. *Rechtsphilosophie. Eine Einführung.* Munich.

Pilhofer, P. 2000. *Philippi, Band II: Katalog der Inschriften von Philippi.* Tübingen.

Ritti, T. 2004. *Iura sepulcrorum* a Hierapolis di Frigia nel quadro dell' epigrafia sepolcrale microasiatica. Iscrizioni edite e inedite. In: S. Panciera (ed.), *Libitina* e dintorni. *Libitina* e i *luci* sepolcrali. Le *leges libitinariae* campane. *Iura sepulcrorum*: vecchie e nuove iscrizioni. Atti dell' XI Rencontre franco-italienne sur l'épigraphie. Roma, pp. 455–634.

Rizakis, A. D. 1996. Anthroponymie et société. Les noms romains dans les provinces hellénophones de l'empire. In: A. D. Rizakis (ed.), *Roman onomastics in the Greek east. Social and political aspects. Proceedings of the International Colloquium on Roman onomastics, Athens, 7–9 September 1993.* Athens, pp. 11–29.

Rizakis, A. D. 2008. Langue et culture ou les ambiguïtés identitaires des notables des cités grecques sous l'empire de Rome. In: F. Biville, J.-C. Decourt, G. Rougemont (eds.), *Bilinguisme gréco-latin et épigraphie.* Lyon, pp. 17–34.

Robert, L. 1940. *Hellenica I.* Paris.

Robert, L. 1948. *Hellenica V.* Paris.

Robert, L. 1963. *Noms indigènes dans l'Asie-Mineure gréco-romaine, première partie.* Paris.

Rochette, B. 1997. *Le latin dans le monde grec. Recherches sur la diffusion de la langue et des lettres latines dans les provinces hellénophones de l'Empire romain.* Brussels.

Rousset, D. 2008. Usage des langues et élaboration des décisions dans le 'monument bilingue' de Delphes. In: F. Biville, J.-C. Decourt and G. Rougemont (eds.), *Bilinguisme gréco-latin et épigraphie.* Lyon, pp. 71–108.

Salomies, O. 2005. Redner und Senatoren. Eloquenz als Standeskultur (1.–3. Jh.n.Chr.). In: W. Eck and M. Heil (eds.), *Senatores populi Romani. Realität und mediale Präsentation einer Führungsschicht.* Stuttgart, pp. 229–62.

Schuster, M. et al. (eds.) 1992. *Plinius Minor* (Teubner). Stuttgart and Leipzig.

Taeuber, H. 2015. Die Korrespondenz hellenistischer und römischer Herrscher aus der Perspektive des modernen Managements. In: St. Procházka, L. Reinfandt and S. Tost (eds.), *Official epistolography and the language(s) of power. Proceedings of the first international conference of the research network Imperium & Officium. Comparative studies in ancient bureaucracy and officialdom, University of Vienna, 10–12 November 2010.* Vienna, pp. 153–61.

Thompson, E. M. 2008. *An introduction to Greek and Latein palaeography.* Richmond.

Townend, G. B. 1961. The post *ab epistulis* in the second century. *Historia* 10, pp. 375–81.

Versnel, H. S. 1991. Beyond cursing; the appeal to justice in judicial prayers. In: Ch. A. Faraone and D. Obbink (eds.), *Magika Hiera. Ancient Greek magic and religion.* New York and Oxford, pp. 60–106.

Versnel, H. S. 2009. *Fluch und Gebet. Magische Manipulation versus religiöses Flehen.* Berlin and New York.

Weiß, A. 2004. *Sklave der Stadt. Untersuchungen zur öffentlichen Sklaverei in den Städten des Römischen Reiches.* Stuttgart.

Williams, W. 1990. *Pliny. Correspondence with Trajan from Bithynia (Epistles X, 15–121).* Oxford.

Wiotte-Franz, C. 2001. *Hermeneus und Interpres. Zum Dolmetscherwesen in der Antike.* Saarbrücken.

Wörrle, M. 2000. Pergamon um 133 v.Chr. *Chiron* 30, pp. 543–76.

10

Local Understandings of Roman Criminal Law and Procedure in Asia Minor

Cédric Brélaz

The rise of an autocratic regime in Rome during the last decades of the first century BCE alongside the restoration of Roman control in the provinces after years of civil wars and unrests caused dramatic changes in the way law enforcement and criminal law were implemented in the provinces of Asia Minor, as in the rest of the Empire. The overall and undisputed military victory of Augustus against internal as well as external enemies led to the abolition of local armies, and the defence of the provinces was now considered an exclusive duty of the Roman legions stationed on the fringes of the Empire. As the emperor's representatives in the provinces, the governors were assigned specific tasks in the field of law enforcement and public security, and their responsibility to fight criminals was explicitly stated in the instructions they were given by the emperor when taking office.[1] As for jurisdiction, the responsibilities of local communities in criminal law were limited by the higher authority of Roman provincial administration: fines could only be imposed by local courts up to a certain amount of money, cases involving serious offences (such as murders, armed violence, and of course cases involving the Roman State security) had to be brought before the provincial tribunal automatically, and capital punishment sentences against free men were reserved for the governor. Moreover, the development of an inquisitorial procedure at the beginning of the Imperial period—consistent with the preeminent power of the emperor and the security-oriented discourse of imperial ideology—allowed Roman authorities to launch investigations and arrest people even without formal charges for the sake of preserving the imperial political and social order.[2]

However, the means assigned to Roman provincial administration to carry out this mission were insufficient to ensure public security all around the provinces. Provincial territories were not systematically controlled by the military, governors

[1] Fournier (2010), 276–94; Jördens (2011). [2] Fournier (2010), 366–8.

Cédric Brélaz, *Local Understandings of Roman Criminal Law and Procedure in Asia Minor* In: *Law in the Roman Provinces.* Edited by: Kimberley Czajkowski and Benedikt Eckhardt in collaboration with Meret Strothmann, Oxford University Press (2020).
DOI: 10.1093/oso/9780198844082.003.0010

were assisted by very few officials in their administrative and judicial tasks, and only a portion of the soldiers left at their disposal focused on law enforcement activities. In these circumstances, Roman power did not have a monopoly over the use of public force to keep order within the provinces and had to rely to a large extent on the participation of local communities. In the case of Asia Minor, day-to-day law enforcement at the local level was provided by local officials who were specially appointed by the cities to deal with policing operations in their territories. Since Roman authorities could not be aware of all of the crimes committed in the different cities of the province and since the governor's court was nevertheless the only jurisdiction authorised to try the most serious crimes, an active collaboration between local officials and provincial administration was essential for governors to fulfil their duties in the field of law enforcement, for the simple reason that criminals were usually first arrested by local officials before they were brought to their tribunal. This implied a pragmatic division of tasks between Roman power and local communities: policing activities at the local level—such as the patrolling of the countryside and the fighting of ordinary criminals—were carried out by the cities and minor offences judged by local courts, whereas Roman provincial authorities served as the superior court of jurisdiction for the most serious crimes, took care of the locations and facilities which were strategic for imperial power (such as the main roads, customs offices, imperial estates, mines, quarries),[3] and were ready to intervene to support cities with military help in emergency situations where it might be critical for the safety of local populations (internal unrests, attacks by large groups of brigands, invasions of enemies from outside the Empire).

In theory, law enforcement and criminal jurisdiction in the provinces of Asia Minor would have been implemented according to this pattern. In the everyday requirements of law enforcement, however, local communities had many occasions to act outside this framework or even to challenge it. This paper will explore various potentially conflictual situations illustrating how the prerogatives of Roman power in the field of criminal law were experienced and understood by the local communities of Asia Minor. In what follows, four instances of local interpretations of Roman criminal law and procedure will be discussed: 1. Local policing officials acting beyond their powers in criminal procedure; 2. Local communities challenging the sovereignty of Roman power with regard to criminal law; 3. Local communities acting outside the ordinary criminal procedure in emergency situations; 4. Local communities invoking Roman criminal procedure to defend their own interests. This paper will argue that adopting contrasting attitudes towards the requirements of Roman power with regard to law enforcement and criminal law depending on the context was one of the strategies used by local communities to negotiate their position within the Roman Empire. More broadly, studying how Roman criminal law and procedure was perceived, understood and implemented at the local level in Asia Minor can help reassess the more general issue of the impact of Roman provincial administration on local communities.

[3] Brélaz (2005), 254–84; Fuhrmann (2012).

1. BEYOND THE LAW: OVER-ZEALOUS LOCAL OFFICIALS AND THE RESPONSE OF THE ROMAN STATE

Since Roman provincial authorities were not able to deal with law enforcement in every single local community, city officials were responsible for public order at the local level and on a daily basis within the provinces. In the case of Asia Minor, several public offices taking care of policing and ensuring public security appeared during the Imperial period. Two of them had a remarkable expansion through these provinces: the office of *paraphylax* and the office of eirenarch. *Paraphylakes* were mainly in charge of patrolling the countryside and preventing misconducts and crimes in the rural territory belonging to cities, whereas eirenarchs, who were accompanied by a small troop of lightly armed officers, were especially active in arresting criminals and suspects. Yet, these two offices never spread uniformly over all the Roman provinces of Asia Minor. Some cities knew only one of the two offices; some others apparently had neither of them.[4] Unlike in Egypt, where the numerous local offices dealing with policing were part of a more homogeneous system of public security (consistent with the centralized and hierarchical inner structure of the administration of that province),[5] the offices of *paraphylax* and of eirenarch were certainly not created and imposed by Rome in the provinces of Asia Minor.[6] Nonetheless, a degree of standardisation can be seen over time in various local institutions in Greek cities throughout Asia Minor, likely due to recurrent competition between neighbouring cities.[7] This can be seen in many other fields, often leading to the adoption of new offices through emulation of other communities, and it likely played a significant role in the dissemination of the *paraphylax* and eirenarch. This being said, Roman power might have fostered the introduction of such local offices in the cities, since they were interested in having intermediaries in the provinces who would take care of law enforcement at the local level and who would indirectly contribute to keeping the political and social order on which imperial rule relied, in accordance with the imperial ideology of peace and security.

Local communities, however, in handling public security issues in their territories, were not acting on behalf of Rome and their engagement in that field was not the outcome of an expressly acknowledged repartition of responsibilities between them and Roman power. By struggling against brigands and by arresting criminals, local communities were taking care of their own safety. With the creation of new offices which were specifically devoted to policing operations, local communities took up the remaining available space left for them under Roman rule. It was all the more important for the cities under Roman provincial administration to make use of the autonomy which was permitted to them in the field of public security given that—with the exception of free cities which in theory were not part of the Roman provinces[8]—local communities in Asia Minor had been deprived of any military power and civic armies had been abolished under the reign of Augustus in the aftermath of the pacification of the Empire.[9] In this

[4] Brélaz (2005), 90–145. [5] Sänger (2010).

[6] The opposite view was argued by Yannakopulos (2003).

[7] Dmitriev (2005). [8] Guerber (2010), 33–77. [9] Brélaz (2008).

context, local communities, thanks to the offices of *paraphylax* and of eirenarch, were able to take the initiative to fight criminals by arresting suspects or individuals caught in the act of wrongdoing. Because of the limits which were imposed on local communities by Roman power with respect to jurisdiction—and in particular criminal law—individuals who were suspected of a crime whose punishment exceeded the local courts' capabilities had to be brought before the governor's tribunal. This was the case for instance for murderers, armed robbers, brigands, individuals accused of sacrilege and any other individual suspected of having committed a criminal offence which could be punished by death penalty according to Roman law.[10]

Yet it turns out that among the local officials who were responsible for public order, over-zealous people sometimes acted in an arbitrary way making unjustified arrests and bringing individuals before the provincial authorities merely on the basis of suspicion. In doing so, those officials were going far beyond the limits of law enforcement which were imposed upon local communities by Roman power. By deciding to arrest someone without any specific reason, local officials acted as if they were themselves empowered to lead the inquisitorial procedure and, in this respect, they usurped the Roman provincial authorities' prerogatives in the field of criminal jurisdiction. This kind of excessive behaviour from local officials in the context of policing resulted in a wide scale reaction from the Roman state. Several regulations were repeatedly enacted on this issue by both imperial and provincial authorities throughout the second century, which aimed to suppress the abuses of local officials and provide a clearer legal framework for their policing activities. In particular, as proconsul of the province of Asia in 135/6 CE, Antoninus Pius issued an edict which reproduced provisions originally coming from the instructions sent to provincial governors by the emperor, detailing how eirenarchs should proceed when arresting criminals.[11] According to these instructions, eirenarchs were required to conduct a preliminary investigation as soon as the criminal was arrested, questioning him about his motivations and his potential associates. It was then required that proceedings of this questioning (*elogium*) be sent to the provincial authorities, sealed together with other documents for the following judicial inquiry by the governor. During the inquiry (*ἀνάκρισις*)[12] the governor would start the investigation anew, as if the suspect were innocent and as if a formal accusation against him had been launched (*si quis erit qui eum arguat*), and would compare the suspect's statements with the report which had been sent by the local officials, who were required to attend the hearing. This procedure had to be followed even in the cases where the apprehended person had been explicitly sought by Roman power because of suspicious activities. As a consequence, local officials who were shown to have conducted the preliminary investigation carefully and honestly would be praised by the provincial authorities, whereas those who acted negligently in collecting the proofs needed for convicting the suspects, or—even worse—those who deliberately

[10] Fournier (2010), 331–96.

[11] Marcian, *On Public Prosecutions* 2 (D. 48.3.6).

[12] Note that in this context the jurist Marcianus used the original word, written in Greek characters, which he no doubt found in Greek versions of the imperial decisions he was referring to.

(*maligne*) forged the reports in order to accuse innocent people, would be censured or even punished.

Repeated abuses by local officials during policing operations forced Roman power to legislate on the first stages of the criminal procedure before the launching of the judicial investigation. With such close monitoring of the activities of local officials dealing with law enforcement, Roman authorities tried to prevent unjustified arrests and to ensure a fairer administration of justice as well as a greater sense of humanity in the government of the Empire, in accordance with some of the core values of imperial ideology proclaiming the happiness and safety provided by Roman rule. Although the principle of presumption of innocence as such was unknown to Roman law,[13] these regulations sought to avoid people being considered to be convicted (*quasi damnati*) even before the trial. For that reason, valid proofs had to be provided by local officials to justify the arrest of a suspect. It is interesting to note that although in the context of the inquisitorial procedure the governor was allowed to launch an investigation on the simple basis of a suspicion or denunciation, an accusatorial component was still necessary for the arrest to be considered legitimate (see below § 4). Another more prosaic and administrative reason led Roman power to repress unfounded accusations. By threatening to rebuke local officials who arrested people and brought them before the governor's tribunal without sufficient evidence, Roman authorities tried to prevent local communities from using provincial justice unnecessarily and to limit access to Roman courts to the most important and explicit cases. The requirement of a thorough preliminary investigation by local officials under threat of a penalty and the disqualification of charges supported by insufficient evidence were also ways to avoid congestion in the courts, a structural problem which Roman power consistently tried to address during the Imperial period through specific regulations, in particular by limiting the cases which could be brought to Roman courts and by restricting the right of appeal to the provincial or imperial tribunals.[14]

The regulations mentioned above were intended to supervise the policing duties of local officials in the various provinces of the Empire as a whole. The focus of Roman power on eirenarchs in these regulations, however, not only by Antoninus Pius as governor of Asia, but by other emperors as well, was due to the fact that eirenarchs were the main officials in charge of suppressing crimes at the local level throughout most of the provinces of Asia Minor. Unlike in many provinces, especially in the Western part of the Empire where most local communities lacked specialized officials who would take care of law enforcement, eirenarchs were seen by the Roman power as privileged partners in the field of fighting criminals in Asia Minor, since those officials were part of the criminal procedure once they had arrested a suspect and brought him to the governor. The significance of eirenarchs for the Roman power and, furthermore, for the local communities themselves, is reflected in the fact that this was considered one of the most prestigious offices one could achieve during a political career in many cities of Asia Minor, like for instance in Ephesus.[15] Although abuses from local officials during policing operations were not unique to Asia Minor and must rather have been quite common in the rest of the Empire too, another set of evidence shows that the Roman power

[13] Bauzon (2004). [14] Fournier (2010), 573–91. [15] Kirbihler (2012).

had specific concerns about the behaviour of eirenarchs in those provinces. Indeed, the appointment of those officials in the cities of the Roman province of Asia was monitored by successive governors during the second half of the second century CE. The full process leading to the appointment of eirenarchs in Asia at that time was described in detail in the autobiographical *Sacred Tales* of the orator Aelius Aristides, who in the year 153 struggled to be relieved from the office of eirenarch (which his small home city of Hadrianoi in Mysia wanted him to hold) and was only successful after several appeals to the provincial authorities:

> In those times there was sent to the governors from each city each year the names of ten leading men. The governor had to examine these and appoint one, whomever he approved, from all of them, as keeper of the peace. From a town in Mysia, whose name I have no need to say, the names, which had been selected, reached him. As yet knowing nothing certain of my affairs, except that he had heard that I had possessions in this place, and, I suppose, that my rank was not undistinguished, he ignored and dishonored all the names which had been sent, and chose me to hold office (. . .). And he sent a letter to the officials (of the city), but did not address it to them, but to me. They came and gave it to me. The letter ordered me to take charge of the peace.[16]

A similar procedure for appointing eirenarchs in the province of Asia can be inferred from an inscription from Phrygian Acmonia which was erected in honour of a member of the local elite, named Gaios Klaudios Loukianos, who in the early 190s was said to have been 'eirenarch twice among those selected by the proconsul of Asia M. Sulpicius Crassus'.[17] The appointment procedure, which consisted in three different stages, can be reconstructed as follows:[18] 1. In each city, ten potential candidates for the position of eirenarch were selected by the local Council, which did not need the formal consent of the men whose names would be included in the list; 2. The lists, each of them containing ten names, were then sent by the cities to be examined by the proconsul of Asia, who would pick one name out of the ten for each city, judging on the basis of the reputation, wealth and integrity of the various candidates; 3. The decision of the governor was sent back to the cities, which then formally appointed those candidates chosen by the provincial authorities as eirenarchs. Such an intervention of Roman power into the civic life of local communities was uncommon in Asia Minor, since Roman authorities did not, in principle, interfere in the way local officials were appointed in cities. The intention of Roman authorities in doing so was not to undermine local autonomy nor to deprive local communities of their capacities in the field of law enforcement. Rather, the administrative monitoring of the appointment process of eirenarchs by the Roman State in the second-century province of Asia was more likely another consequence of the measures taken by Antoninus Pius in 135/6 during his proconsulship to curb the abuses committed by those officials. The nomination of candidates by the cities and selection by the governor were seen as a way to make sure that dishonest and violent people would not be appointed eirenarchs.

[16] Aristides, *Orationes* 50.72–3.

[17] AE 2006, 1424 = SEG LVI 1493, with a new reading by Blanco-Pérez (2013) (AE 2013, 1528; SEG LXIII 1223). For further possible emendations, see P. Hamon, Bull. ép. 2014, 469.

[18] Brélaz (2011).

Recurrent misconducts by eirenarchs during the first decades of the second century in Asia should not be used to argue for increased criminality or the sudden emergence of unexpected risks and threats. On the contrary, this was without doubt one of the most peaceful and safe periods experienced in the Roman provinces of Asia Minor. Still, it is usually admitted that the office of eirenarch first appeared in the Greek cities of Asia Minor at the end of the first or at the very beginning of the second century.[19] Abuses might then have been committed by the over-zealous holders of a newly established office, at a time when their duties and the conditions of their cooperation with Roman power had not yet been clearly defined. Local communities were certainly enthusiastic about the idea of having their own officials to deal with criminal repression. As suggested by the dozens of honorific inscriptions praising them for their deeds, eirenarchs, having been chosen among the local elite, were very proud to be responsible for the safety of their fellow-citizens.[20] This might have led some officials to arrest people without sufficient proof and to treat suspects as though they had already been convicted. However, the regulations enacted by Roman power which set out the procedure for arrests by local officials reminded local communities that, regardless of the century-long autonomy Greek cities had enjoyed in Asia Minor and to some extent were still benefitting from under Roman rule, local customs and rights were superseded by the sovereignty of Rome in the field of criminal law.[21] With the response of the Roman State, local communities in Asia Minor must have understood that only a few decades after they had created local offices for the purpose of ensuring public order, their prerogatives in this area, just as in many others, were clearly restricted by Roman rule.

2. ENACTING CRIMINAL LAWS AT THE LOCAL LEVEL: LOCAL COMMUNITIES' RESPONSE TO ROMAN RULE

With the exception of those matters for which the prerogatives of the provincial authorities were explicitly stated and provided by law because they fell within the overarching authority of Roman power, local communities had a large degree of autonomy in the field of law enforcement and jurisdiction. As seen above, this can be illustrated by the appearance and the development of numerous local offices and institutions in charge of policing and public security throughout Asia Minor. More generally, most Greek cities in those provinces maintained and nurtured during the Imperial period—in an age when local armies no longer existed—a military culture which resulted in the glorification of policing operations carried out by local officials or the local population. The arrest of robbers and criminals, the fight against brigands, the setting up and training of para-military troops like ephebic associations, and the contribution to the imperial war effort through extraordinary levies of men were all presented as heroic deeds proving the

[19] Brélaz (2005), 114–22. [20] Brélaz (2005), 102–8.

[21] The submission or 'enslavement' (*douleia*) of Greek cities to Roman rule was emphasized by Greek orators of the time: Plutarch, *Moralia* 813 E; 814 E-F; 824 C; 824 E; Dio Chrysostom, *Orationes* 31, 125; 165; 34, 51.

capacity of local communities to take care of their own safety, and if necessary to assist the imperial armies.[22] This was all the more true for free cities which in some cases were extremely proud to show off their theoretical independence towards Rome and their formal non-belonging to the Roman provincial system through the vestiges of their military organization, such as Rhodes, for example, which maintained some parts of its fleet and continental empire, or Termessos which sent some of its citizens as soldiers to strengthen the Roman legions—those men being called 'allies' (*symmachoi*) in compliance with the old treaty between that city and Rome, as if both parties were on an equal footing.[23] Apart from taxation, where free cities also usually enjoyed exemptions and immunities, privileges for that category of local communities were in practice primarily found in the field of jurisdiction: in principle, free cities were allowed to impose the death penalty against their own freeborn citizens.[24]

Apart from the specific case of free cities, the other local communities in Asia Minor which were under direct provincial administration were able to have their own courts and to exercise jurisdiction over their citizens within the limits imposed by Roman rule. In this context, local communities could also legislate and enact regulations, including with regard to criminal law, as long as the prerogatives of the provincial authorities in the corresponding field of law were respected. In that regard, Phrygian Hierapolis, which was never a free city, seems to have had an intense legislative activity on the issue of law enforcement and criminal repression. One can cite for instance a decree which was issued by the Council of Hierapolis at some point during the first or second century CE and was displayed in a village (Thiounta) located in the territory belonging to the city, north of Hierapolis. The decree aimed at controlling abuses which were committed by city policing officials, *paraphylakes*, during their stay in the villages when patrolling the countryside.[25] In order to avoid undue requisitions from the villagers in the future, as well as bullying by the *paraphylakes*, the city listed what could be legally requested from the villages by these officials for their livelihood (such as firewood, fodder for their horses and accommodation). Further provisions aimed to prevent extortion, which was practiced by *paraphylakes* in the villages in the form of honours voted to them by these communities under duress. These regulations were the local equivalent, within the city of Hierapolis, of the measures implemented by Roman authorities after complaints by villages to the governor or emperor, which aimed to restrict Roman officials and soldiers harassing local communities on their way through Asia Minor (see § 4 below). The ability of the city of Hierapolis to enact regulations regarding the conditions in which the law was enforced and public security was ensured in its surrounding territory is made clear by the fact that, in order to enhance the decision's scope and implementation, it was explicitly stated at the end of the document that 'the decree [was] legally authoritative and binding' and that provisions were made for fines and punishments in case of non-compliance by the *paraphylakes*.

[22] Brélaz (2008).

[23] Brélaz (2015). Rhodes: Strabo. 14.2.5; Dio Chrysostom. *Orationes*. 31; AE 1993, 1537; Brélaz (2005), 199–203. Termessos: TAM III 106; Brélaz (2005), 303–8; Vitale (2011).

[24] Fournier (2010), 469–501; Guerber (2010), 33–77.

[25] OGIS 527 (Brélaz (2005), 394–6, no. C 51).

We know of the (fragmentary) epigraphic copy of another official document regarding law enforcement which was also found in the territory of Hierapolis, close to its north-eastern fringes. In that case, from the third century CE, the regulations aimed to prevent damage to vineyards, especially by wandering flocks, and to punish the careless shepherds.[26] Attempts have been made by scholars to identify which authority issued these regulations. In the fourth volume of the *Monumenta Asiae Minoris Antiqua*, W. Buckler, W. Calder and W. Guthrie, followed then by D. Magie, argued it was an edict from the Roman governor.[27] It is very doubtful, however, that such specific regulations expressly regarding the city of Hierapolis were issued through an edict by Roman provincial authorities. The context was in fact exclusively local: the document refers to policing officials named *paraphylakes*, who operated in Hierapolis;[28] some provisions regarded other local officials, known as 'the land managers' (ἐπιμεληταὶ τῶν χωρίων),[29] who were guilty of not having taken sufficient care of the vineyards and of not having barred flocks from entering them; finally and most significantly, mention was made in this document (as in the decree seen above) of Apollo Archegetes, the tutelary god of Hierapolis, presumably because an oath had to be sworn on that deity by local officials in order to make them liable for compliance with the rules. It is therefore more likely, as L. Robert suggested,[30] that this document was actually a decree issued by the city of Hierapolis in response to recurring problems with vineyards and land property protection in the countryside. A further argument in support of this interpretation has recently been provided thanks to the discovery of another fragmentary copy of the same document at another place of the territory belonging to Hierapolis, close to Thiounta.[31] The fact that at least two copies of the same regulations were displayed in villages located in the territory of Hierapolis demonstrates that it was a civic decree—as was the case with the previous regulations aiming at curbing abuses by *paraphylakes*—and that the

[26] MAMA IV 297 (Brélaz (2005), 396–8, no. C 52). [27] Magie (1950), I. 647.

[28] Further references to *paraphylakes* in Hierapolis include Ramsay (1895–1897), I. 143–4, no. 31 from Thiounta (Brélaz (2005), 394, no. C 50: but in this case the *paraphylax* might have been just a guard within a private association rather than the homonymous city official dealing with law enforcement; for a probable similar guard in Ephesus, see I. Ephesos 20b [Brélaz (2005), 386, no. C 20]); SEG LXII 1188–91 from the sanctuary of Apollo Karios north-east of the city (in SEG LXII 1189 a *paraphylax* is praised for having fulfilled his duties ἀνεπιβαρετῶς, 'without causing any burdens', which is a reference to the potential abuses that were committed by these officials and that the city tried to curb through specific regulations). For an eirenarch, see AE 2003, 1696 = SEG LIII 1464 (Brélaz (2005), 371, no. C 80a).

[29] It is uncertain whether χωρίον should in this context be understood as 'estate' or rather as 'fortified village' or 'settlement', as was often the case in Hellenistic Asia Minor (Schuler (1998), 49–53; Chaniotis (2005), 26–9). In any case, these officials dealt with the administration of the rural territory of the city.

[30] Robert (1935), 462–3. As a consequence, another verb instead of [κελεύω] should be restored at the end of line 8 in MAMA IV 297, since the Roman governor cannot be the subject of the phrase. In this context, the verb refers to the requirement expressed by the city that the slaves serving as shepherds should be flogged. When it comes to permissions rather than prohibitions or orders, the decree uses the verb ἐξεῖναι (ἐξῖνε in ll. 11–12, also restored in lines 1 and 3).

[31] SEG LVIII 1504, corresponding to ll. 10–17 of MAMA IV 297. Side B of SEG LVIII 1504 preserves 58 mutilated lines among which only 5 have been deciphered. It is clear from the extant portion of the text that Side B—albeit some orthographical inconsistencies—originally contained additional provisions of the same regulations pertaining to vineyards and shepherds.

city of Hierapolis had been regularly enacting and implementing a consistent set of criminal laws from the first to the third century with a view to ensuring and improving public security within the geographical boundaries of its jurisdiction. In the case of the decree about the misconducts of policing officials, penalties against brutal *paraphylakes* included fines to be paid to the city's treasury and the deprivation of all honours, as well as a prohibition against making offerings to the sanctuary of Apollo. The decree regarding the vineyards, on the other hand, provided that the landlords would have the right to seize the flocks which damaged their vineyards and to take as much as they wanted from them as compensation. As for the shepherds, the punishment would depend on the legal status of each person: freeborn individuals, as well as the owners of the flocks themselves, would have to pay a fine or a bond, whereas slaves serving as shepherds (who would have been reported to *paraphylakes* for oversights in the conservation of vineyards) would be flogged.[32] How significant the city of Hierapolis considered the enactment of such a decree to be for law enforcement is reflected in the presentation of the damages caused to vineyards by careless shepherds as 'a continuous injustice'.[33] Such compliance with the Roman imperial ideology of fighting wrongdoers on behalf of public security by labelling them as criminals, as well as the punishment by flogging of offending slaves,[34] both find a close parallel in a decree issued about the same time, in the early third century, by the Carian city of Mylasa about the exchange of currency.[35] The decree aimed to curb speculation on, and illegal transactions of, money in the city within the context of a lack of small change in bronze.[36] As the invocation of the emperors Severus and his sons at the beginning of the decree makes clear, as well as the acclamations which were reportedly raised during the assembly after the decision had been voted on, the measures taken by the city to address the issue were seen as a contribution to the preservation of the Roman political and social order. The connection between the struggle at the local level against speculators who were blamed for their 'evildoing and villainy' (*ἐκ κακουργίας καὶ πανουργίας ὀλί[γων τινῶν]*) and described as 'bad guys' (*[πονη]ρευόμενοι*) on one hand, and the enforcement of Roman law on the other hand, was enhanced in this case by the implications that the dearth of liquidity in the city of Mylasa might have had for Roman taxation, as the decree itself emphasized.

There is another field in which one can notice local communities in Asia Minor increasingly taking the initiative to augment their prerogatives in the enforcement of criminal law: it has to do with the funerary fines and all the legal measures taken to protect tombs. The protection of burials and related issues (conservation of the funerary monument, status of the land on which the tomb was erected, ownership and use of the burial site, etc.) were addressed in a specific chapter of Roman

[32] The new copy of the same decree discovered in the vicinity of Thiounta included further provisions about the possible status of the offenders: SEG LVIII 1504, B, ll. 41–5 assumed that the offender might be a citizen, a foreigner, a slave, a freeborn person, a hired worker, or a freedman.

[33] SEG LVIII 1504, A, ll. 3–4: [*ἐπι*]*μόνου ἀδικί*[*ας*]. Thus, the same word, rather than *λ̣*[*ηστείας*], should be restored in MAMA IV 297, l. 11.

[34] For flogging as a punishment used by local officers dealing with law enforcement, known as *mastigophoroi*, see Brélaz (2005), 171–82; AE 2006, 1403 (flogging of competitors having breached the rules during a contest).

[35] I. Mylasa 605. [36] Katsari (2011), 137–51 with App. 1, pp. 254–5.

civil law, and public legal actions could be taken against offenders by anyone considering that the tomb was misused or defiled even without any family relationship to the deceased.[37] The respect due to the dead and to burials was considered in Rome a matter of public concern. In the Imperial period, if serious infractions were committed (such as desecration of a tomb or insult to a dead body) offences were punished by criminal law.[38] In the provinces, governors were empowered to exercise jurisdiction in this matter.[39] Since respect towards graves was motivated by religious considerations and beliefs, such infringements also had implications for sacred law and, at least in Italy, the college of pontiffs was responsible for watching over rituals pertaining to burials. For that reason, permission was required from the governor to move a burial or to transfer mortal remains to another tomb.[40] Moreover, penalty clauses and funerary fines aiming to prevent all kinds of offences—such as the opening or the moving of a tomb, the reuse of a burial site by people other than the deceased and his relatives, the erasing of the epitaph together with its legal clauses, etc.—, were frequently mentioned in the epitaphs carved on burials in Asia Minor during the Imperial period.[41] The Roman imperial treasury, or in some cases the representatives of Roman power within the provinces such as the provincial quaestor or soldiers stationed in the area, were commonly indicated as recipients of the fines in the event of a tomb being harmed.[42]

Yet, one can observe in a large number of epitaphs in Asia Minor that local communities or local institutions such as corporate bodies (for instance, the *gerousia* or the *boulê*) or even sanctuaries were also mentioned as recipients of the funerary fines alongside the imperial treasury, or even instead of it. Hence, the question arises as to which authority was able to serve as the guarantor of compliance with the legal provisions included in the epitaphs, to enact laws in this matter and, where necessary, to provide access to justice and to impose the sentences prescribed in the penalty clauses on the funerary monuments. Another major issue relates to the potential conflict of responsibilities and jurisdiction between local communities and Roman authorities in this field, since penalty clauses contained in epitaphs from Asia Minor could, depending on the case, refer either to local laws or to imperial/provincial regulations, or to both at the same time.[43] The problem is made even more complex by the fact that in some cases the fines were not payable to civic communities and political entities, but to private clubs, such as occupational or religious associations. It is conceivable, however, that in order for associations to collect penalties they had to be formally designated as beneficiaries of the fines after a trial had been held before the courts of the city. In Ephesus, rural communities located in the territory of the city were among recipients of funerary fines. In that case too, the implementation of the penalty clauses was almost certainly enabled by judicial decisions emanating from the

[37] De Visscher (1963), 138–42. [38] Ritti (2004), 527–8.

[39] Ulpian, *On the Praetorian Edict* 25 (D. 47.12.3.7); see De Visscher (1963), 150–61.

[40] Laubry (2007); Tybout (2016). [41] Ritti (2004).

[42] Ritti (2004), 545–6. For fines to be paid to soldiers, see Brélaz (2005), 262; AE 2013, 1575 = SEG LXIII 858 (Aphrodisias).

[43] Ritti (2004), 530–4.

civic courts.[44] In any event, although the amounts of fines reaching up to several thousand or even several million sesterces, mentioned in some epitaphs, were obviously overstated, one should not assume that penalty provisions had no practical purpose and relevance or that they only functioned as a deterrent in order to prevent misuses and violations of tombs. On the contrary, close examination of the legal clauses included in epitaphs reveals a large variety of potential offences against burials and litigations regarding the ownership of tombs, as well as the mention of various possible judicial prosecutions. All this implies a careful attention to legal matters and a deep knowledge of civil and criminal judicial procedures. One can infer that such detailed provisions could be invoked by the owners of the damaged burials or by the relatives of the deceased in case of a trial and that they were intended to have a legally binding purpose in obtaining reparation from the offenders. Admittedly, in theory the collection of penalties did not require a trial and a simple administrative report before local officials would have been sufficient for the injured person, and in some cases even for any citizen, to claim payment of the fine.[45] In practice, however, legal actions were probably needed to compel offenders to pay.

The division of tasks between Roman authorities and local communities with respect to jurisdiction in the case of charges involving damages to burials must have depended on how serious the offences were. The most outrageous offences which were seen as crimes and which deserved harsher punishments according to Roman criminal law—such as the desecration of a tomb, the mutilation of a dead body or other acts infringing sacred law—would certainly have been brought before the governor's court, or at least, that would have been required in compliance with the prerogatives of Roman power in the field of criminal law and death penalty.[46] By contrast, disputes involving civil law (issues regarding the purchase or transmission by inheritance of a burial site, ownership and use of the ground where a tomb was erected, etc.) could be judged by local courts, especially when the litigants did not possess Roman citizenship. Although local law was relevant in this matter, one can notice an influence coming from Roman civil law, especially in relation to the Roman law of succession, on the procedures laid down in the funerary legal clauses.[47] However, a general trend can be noted in the field of the legal protection of tombs in Asia Minor toward increasing judicial capacities for local communities. Funerary legal provisions frequently mentioned that a copy of the epitaph including the corresponding penalty clauses had been deposited in the public archives of the city.[48] Such specifications were intended, through the official acknowledgement and recording of these clauses, to assert the validity and enhance the binding value of the provisions, suggesting that the city was the

[44] Harter-Uibopuu (2014), 161, 174–5. The courts of the city of Ephesus must have been also competent in the cases where copies of the legal clauses included in the epitaphs were deposited in the local archives of the rural communities rather than in Ephesus.

[45] Harter-Uibopuu (2014), 176–7.

[46] In Thessalonica, people guilty of reusing the tomb were said to be 'subjected to the death penalty by crucifixion' (*σταυροῦ ὑποκῖστε κινδύνου*) (*IG* X 2, 1s, 1351) or 'liable before the governor in office' (*λόγον ὑφέξει τῷ κατὰ καιρὸν ἡγεμόνει*) (*IG* X 2, 1s, 1434).

[47] Ritti (2004), 506–7; Harter-Uibopuu (2010), 264–6.

[48] Ritti (2004), 483–4, 558–62.

competent authority guaranteeing their enforcement.[49] This was also a way to state that the place of jurisdiction and applicable law were those of the city itself, with its own courts and laws. One must then admit that fines payable to the imperial treasury were in most cases imposed by local courts rather than by the governor's tribunal. It is interesting to note, in this respect, that not every epitaph providing that a fine should be paid in case of violation did mention the imperial treasury as the recipient in Asia Minor and that the proportion of funerary inscriptions which did so—as compared to other recipients for the fines such as the local community—fluctuates a lot according to the city under consideration. This observation shows that there was no positively established delimitation of responsibilities in this matter and that local communities, or even individuals when laying down the penalty clauses for their burials, were free to include—or not include—the Roman imperial authorities among the recipients of the fines.

In Ephesus for instance (as in Thessalonica for the province of Macedonia), the vast majority of the epitaphs naming recipients for the fines did mention the imperial treasury, whereas in Smyrna or Miletus only some of them did so.[50] Since Ephesus was the base of the Roman provincial administration of Asia, the proximity of the governor most likely led the city to allocate a fair number of the funerary fines, or at least a part of them, to the Roman imperial treasury, in any case more than in other cities of the province, like Smyrna and Miletus, which were visited only periodically by the proconsuls during their judicial tours.[51] The same can be said for other areas of public life in Ephesus for which it appears that the city was more inclined to ask for the governor's intervention or arbitration because the governor was closer for Ephesus than for the other, more distant local communities of the province. The constant presence of the Roman provincial administration in the city could of course mean potential encroachments on local autonomy in Ephesus, but it was also an opportunity for the city—when it was deemed useful—to more easily acquire the endorsement of the governor to confirm local decisions.[52] Especially because Roman provincial administration could also in theory investigate outside the boundaries of the city, local communities (as well as the owners of the burials themselves of course) sought to evoke Roman authority by stating explicitly that part of the funerary fines should be paid to the imperial treasury. The inclusion of Roman power among the recipients was probably thought to have a larger impact, and therefore to help prevent offences against tombs. On the other hand, where references to the imperial treasury as a recipient of funerary fines were less common, local communities were presumably more eager to assert their autonomy by suggesting that they were able to deal with law enforcement and to implement criminal law by themselves without relying on Rome's preeminent authority.

The attempts of local communities to extend their capacities in the legal protection of tombs can be seen in many other ways. The simple fact that legal clauses in epitaphs provided for fines which would have been imposed by local courts not only for minor offences, but also in some cases for the most serious

[49] De Visscher (1963), 121–2.

[50] Harter-Uibopuu (2010); Harter-Uibopuu (2014), 173; Harter-Uibopuu and Wiedergut (2014), 157–8. For Thessalonica, see Nigdelis (2006), 397–8.

[51] Dalla Rosa (2012).

[52] Brélaz (2007a), 132–5.

offences (which would in principle require harsher punishments up to the death penalty according to Roman criminal law) is an illustration of this phenomenon. The criminalisation of many delicts, which was a general trend of Roman law over time during the Imperial period, was in this case countered by the efforts made by local communities to gain more control over law enforcement in their own territories. Since local communities lacked the right to put freeborn people to death, crimes such as the desecration of a tomb—or *tymbôrychia* as it was called in some penalty clauses[53]—were in these circumstances *de facto* downgraded to delicts punished by fines, accompanied in some cases with measures involving the deprivation of honours, cursing, or exclusion from the community.[54] The trend of local communities replacing Roman provincial authorities in an effort to increase their duties in this area is also documented by the testimony of Dio Chrysostom, reporting that the city of Nicomedia in Bithynia voted on a decree allowing the relocation of burials. In theory, however, this was a prerogative of the governor, since, as seen above, the process had implications for sacred law.[55] In Carian Aphrodisias, penalty clauses in epitaphs explicitly mentioned that not even 'the decision resulting from a petition before the governor' (*διὰ ἐντεύξεως ἡγεμονικῆς*)—as was the case for a decree of the people or a decision of the Council—could go against the provisions taken by owners of burials prohibiting the reuse of the tombs, emphasizing the privileges Aphrodisias had as a free city: that unlike other local communities, its rights would not be encroached upon by provincial authorities.[56] In other cities, however, very few epitaphs included funerary fines, especially in Ionia.[57] On the whole, regional variations predominated through the provinces of Asia Minor with regard to the legal formulas used in penalty clauses.[58]

These conflicting attitudes of local communities towards Roman power with regard to burial law were typical for Greek cities in Asia Minor during the Imperial period, which on the one hand were competing to display their loyalty to Rome and contending for the benefits of Roman support, and at the same time were very patriotic and tried to keep their own customs and their autonomy untouched by Roman hegemony.[59] An interesting intermediary case comes from Aphrodisias where an epitaph stated that the fine should be paid 'as a contribution to the honours (i.e. the statues) for the emperors'.[60] In linking the payment of the fine with worship of the emperor, the city asserted its ability to enact its own laws in the field of criminal law—which was all the more true for a free city—and at the same time seized the opportunity to point out its allegiance to Roman rule,

[53] Ritti (2004), 534–9; Harter-Uibopuu and Wiedergut (2014), 158–60.

[54] Fernoux (2011), 335–7. For the reference to curses against desecrators in epitaphs, see Strubbe (1997).

[55] Dio Chrysostom, *Orationes* 47.16. See Laubry (2007), 174.

[56] IAph2007 12.1107; 13.151; AE 2013, 1575 = SEG LXIII 858. A similar expression should be recognized in IAph2007 13.702 according to Robert (1966), 385. For funerary fines in Aphrodisias, see Rupp (2015).

[57] Harter-Uibopuu (2014), 157, n. 2.

[58] Harter-Uibopuu (2014), 167–9; Harter-Uibopuu and Wiedergut (2014), 150, 164.

[59] Heller (2006); Guerber (2010).

[60] AE 2012, 1545 = SEG LXII 808.

a paradox which was common in Aphrodisias.[61] Enacting criminal laws was another way for the cities of Asia Minor to negotiate their position towards Rome, as well as towards their peers.

3. ACTING OUTSIDE THE LAW ON BEHALF OF ROME: THE CONTRIBUTION OF LOCAL COMMUNITIES TO IMPERIAL PEACE

Despite the control exercised by Roman authorities within the criminal procedure over the policing officials in the cities of Asia Minor (see above § 1) and despite the restrictions imposed upon local courts because of Rome's sovereignty (see above § 2), local communities in Roman Anatolia sometimes faced emergency situations that led them to take exceptional measures to ensure their security. The sudden appearance of a threat—or of an event considered to be so—in cities was at times addressed by the use of a summary form of justice through popular intervention and collective violence. Spontaneous gatherings of the urban population played a major role in this context, and angry mobs could in some cases put pressure on the local officials to hold unlawful and speedy trials. Several examples of this kind of popular revenge exacted against murderers or robbers are staged in Apuleius's novel *The Golden Ass*, and similar instances of local people lynching wrongdoers caught in the act are known in the Roman Empire.[62] In the same way, according to martyrological literature the crowd's rage apparently was a strong incentive for the arrest of Christians in Asia Minor, even during periods when no repressive policy was specifically operated by imperial power against them: bishop Polycarp, for instance, was arrested by local officials in mid-second-century Smyrna at the pressing request of the mob and was then brought before the governor's tribunal for a trial.[63] In this case, though, the trial itself was held in accordance with the law, since the Roman governor—rather than the local population—served as the judge. In principle local populations were not supposed to take justice in their own hands, especially in the field of criminal law where capital punishment was a prerogative of Roman power. Acting outside the rule of law and usurping the Roman authorities' prerogatives in judicial matters could cause interference by Rome in the internal affairs and political institutions of a city, and depending on the seriousness of the infringement, could lead to retaliation measures, such as the governor issuing specific decisions aiming at solving the problem on the ground, the temporary ban on political assemblies or public meetings, the conviction of individuals for rioting, or even the intervention of Roman troops—all things which are attested in different contexts during the Imperial period because of political or social disturbances emerging in local communities.[64] Local elites were fully aware of the implications that a Roman reaction to riots and collective violence would have for the autonomy of their city. For that reason, after the

[61] Chaniotis (2003); Sion-Jenkins (2010).

[62] Riess (2001); Fournier (2010), 388–94.

[63] *Martyrium Polycarpi* 3 (Musurillo (1972), 2–12).

[64] For examples in Asia Minor, see Brélaz (2005), 56–64.

silversmiths rose up against the apostle Paul in Ephesus, accusing him of undermining their business because of his preaching against pagan worship, and after the crowd spontaneously gathered in the theatre to deal with this issue, the secretary of the people, the most important official of the city, urged his fellow-citizens not to hurt the apostle and not to make hasty decisions:

> 'Citizens of Ephesus, who is there that does not know that the city of Ephesus is the keeper of the temple of the great Artemis and of the statue that fell from heaven? Since these things cannot be denied, you ought to be quiet and do nothing rash. You have brought these men here who are neither temple robbers nor blasphemers of our goddess. If therefore Demetrius (i.e. the silversmiths' leader) and the artisans with him have a complaint against anyone, the courts are open, and there are proconsuls; let them bring charges there against one another. If you seek anything further, it must be settled in the regular assembly (*ἐν τῇ ἐννόμῳ ἐκκλησίᾳ*). For we are in danger of being charged with rioting (*στάσεως*) today, since there is no cause that we can give to justify this turmoil'. When he had said this, he dismissed the assembly.[65]

The chaotic popular gathering which was about to take action against Paul and his companions was clearly unlawful and the secretary did his best to prevent the crowd from doing anything which would have lacked a legal basis. In the same way, Aelius Aristides warned the Rhodians who were tearing themselves apart through opposing political factions that the situation had become so bad that Roman power would probably not tolerate such a disruption of public order any longer and that there was a danger that their status as a free city would be removed, as this already happened several times in the past:

> If things continue in this fashion, it is quite possible that you will be in danger of being deprived of this apparent liberty. And if you do not voluntarily heed this advice, another will come who will forcibly save you, since, as a rule, rulers are neither ignorant of such behaviour nor disregard it. Therefore if for no other reason, then for the sake of being free and doing what you wish, abandon this present conduct so that you may not suffer anxieties which will be as great as your present audacity, and so that you may not lose your ancient source of pride.[66]

Similar recommendations were made to the local politicians of their time by Plutarch in his 'Precepts of Statecraft' as well as by Dio through speeches he delivered in various cities of Asia Minor including his home town of Prusa, urging his audience not to claim powers which were now reserved for Roman authorities—especially in the areas of defence, law enforcement and of jurisdiction—and not to do anything that would cause the Romans to interfere.[67]

In some extreme circumstances, however, local communities had no choice but to act outside criminal procedure and to take emergency action in their own interest and by their own means. This happened mostly in cases where large groups of brigands similar to armed troops unexpectedly attacked territories of cities or towns themselves. Because of the number of criminals involved and of the nature of the wrongdoings committed, ordinary policing institutions of local communities with their few lightly armed officers were insufficient to face the problem. Since local communities in the Imperial period did not have permanent

[65] *Acts* 19.23–40. [66] Aristides, *Orationes* 24.22. See Franco (2008).
[67] Plutarch, *Moralia* 814 B–815 E; 824 E-F; Dio Chrysostom, *Orationes* 34.48; 46.14.

armed forces or civic armies any more, the only remaining option was a general call to the civilian population to take up arms and kill the brigands. Paradoxically, far from blaming local communities for taking harsh measures against people who in theory should have been sent through the regular criminal procedure, Roman authorities expressed congratulations for their commitment towards law enforcement. Emperor Commodus, for instance, extended acknowledgement to the Lycian city of Boubon for getting rid of brigands by its own means and celebrated the courage of the local population in their fight against the criminals in a letter to the city:

> I have commended you for your zeal and bravery and I have endorsed the federal decision of the Lycian league. For you set out with such great zeal to catch the brigands and you defeated them, and either killed or took them captive; and the Lycian league acted justly when, in response to those (deeds), it bestowed upon you the appropriate honour of increasing your votes by one (i.e. the number of votes Boubon commanded within the Lycian federal Council). This was bound to enhance your reputation, and it made others more eager to carry out such brave deeds.[68]

A similar reaction can be found in the letter that Emperor Severus wrote to the city of Syedra in Cilicia praising the local population for having successfully resisted the Roman soldiers who had attacked them on behalf of Pescennius Niger in the context of the civil war between the two rivals:

> I have been the first to hear about the great zeal that you displayed to withstand the assault of all those impious and sacrilegious persons who, choosing Super as their leader, overran your city, and (I have been the first) to praise you for your resistance. Unquestionably, Super has now received the punishment he deserved, having fully paid for the harm he caused to you. As for the centurions, who—according to what you say—also stood with Super, they will not get away without punishment either. That matter being now closed, you and your fellow-citizens who at that time were removed by force from their homeland, but who have now come back and live together with you, should make a sacrifice, organize a festival, and celebrate your past deeds, considering that through such behaviour you increased your own fame and confirmed your prior dedication to Rome.[69]

The resistance of Syedra undoubtedly implied the use of armed force, since the chief of the troop which overran the city, Super, apparently died, either killed during the battle or put to death after his arrest. In Syedra as in Boubon, Roman imperial authorities admitted that it had been justified, and even necessary, for the local communities to bypass criminal procedure, given that their security and conservation had been put at stake due to the massive attacks they experienced. In the cases where groups of brigands organised large-scale looting raids within the provinces, Roman power typically reconsidered the legal characterization of the offences and spoke rather in this context of the action of 'public enemies' (*hostes*) instead of 'bandits' (*latrones*). Brélaz (2005), 285–90. Labelling someone as a 'public enemy' could be very ideological in Rome, in particular in the context of political struggles or civil wars when this expression was used to undermine the claims and the legitimacy of a rival. For the same reason, the soldiers of Pescennius Niger who attacked Syedra were called 'impious' and 'sacrilegious' by Severus. From

[68] AE 1979, 624. See Kokkinia (2008), 32–4, no. 5.

[69] AE 2014, 1331 = SEG LXIV 1496.

a legal point of view, considering criminals to be declared enemies of the Roman people allowed ordinary criminal law to be ignored and the use of means usually reserved for war. The task of fighting 'public enemies' was one of the prerogatives of the Roman State which opposed external threats through imperial armies stationed in the periphery of the Empire. However, since the provinces of Asia Minor—apart from Cappadocia which corresponded to the external border of the Empire towards the East—were free of substantial military garrisons such as legionary camps, the small military troops left at the disposal of each governor were generally too scattered and too far from the places where attacks occurred to be able to intervene effectively.[70] Therefore, Roman power was forced to let local communities take initiatives in this field. In fact, in the absence of Roman military help, local communities were even encouraged to provide measures for defence through their own means. Municipal by-laws issued by Roman power for colonies included, for instance, provisions regarding the levy of the civilian population (citizens and foreign residents) in case of emergency to defend the territory of the community.[71]

The need for local communities in Asia Minor to rely on their own resources became even more urgent during the third century CE when repeated invasions of enemies from outside the Empire and recurring attacks from the Isaurian tribe in Central Anatolia, in a general context of pressure on the external borders of the Empire, made Roman military response very difficult and erratic. In Pisidian Termessos, the situation became so critical in the 270–280s because of the attacks by Isaurians that improvised troops were set up by private individuals to defend the city's territory. In the defence of Termessos, the crucial role played by a certain Hermaios—a local notable who led a troop made of young men against the bandits and for that reason was celebrated through the honorific title of 'brigand-chaser'—was praised not only by the official institutions of the city itself, but also by representatives of Roman power in the area, such as senior military officers and the provincial governor himself.[72] The use of private militias by local dignitaries to ensure security at the local/regional level became more and more frequent in Late Antiquity. As abuses such as violence and arbitrary arrest were perpetrated against local populations, a fair number of imperial regulations aimed at curbing this increasing phenomenon.[73] Roman power was not ready to abandon its sovereignty in the field of law enforcement and struggled to maintain control on the use of force in the public sphere. An exception was made for emergency situations. In acknowledging the contributions of local communities which successfully defeated bandits, both to law enforcement and to the preservation of the provinces, Roman authorities implicitly admitted that this should have been the duty of Roman provincial administration and of the Roman army. Ironically, acting outside the law and not complying with the ordinary legal procedure were, in this context, seen as ways to ensure the political order provided by Roman rule and, through the desperate attempt by local communities to

[70] Aristides, *Orationes*, 26.67; Apuleius, *Metamorphoses* 2.18.

[71] Crawford (1996), 393–454, no. 25, § CIII (*lex Ursonensis*).

[72] SEG LI 1813–14 = AE 2008, 1431–3. See Brélaz (2005), 308–19; Kuhn (2012), 308–11.

[73] Brélaz (2007b).

oppose enemies of the Roman peace, even considered an expression of loyalty towards Rome, as was emphasized by Severus in his answer to Syedra.

4. IN THE NAME OF THE LAW: LOCAL COMPLAINTS ABOUT ROMAN OFFICIALS' ABUSES

Because of their collaboration with Roman provincial authorities in the field of law enforcement, local communities were aware of the existence of Roman imperial and provincial legislation aiming to regulate police activities. This is especially true because, as seen above (§ 1), part of this legislation had been enacted with the goal of reducing misconducts by local officials in charge of police duties and was explicitly devoted to outlining the criminal procedure with which officials would have to comply during arrests. Local officials were not the only ones targeted by these regulations. Similar regulations existed for Roman officials and soldiers as well. An entire section of imperial legislation was dedicated to the problem of trying to circumscribe the actions of Roman officials and soldiers in the provinces and to prevent abuses against local populations. Roman officials and soldiers could not act with impunity and, when performing policing operations, they had to comply with the criminal procedure. In particular, they were not allowed, when travelling through the provinces, to require from local populations more benefits in kind for their livelihood and lodging than was prescribed by imperial legislation, and they were not supposed to bully provincials. Such abuses against local populations, however, were quite common.[74]

Wrongdoings from Roman officials and soldiers in the provinces of Asia Minor are mainly known to us thanks to the epigraphic copies which were made of the complaints (*petitiones*) sent by local communities to provincial or imperial authorities in connection with those wrongdoings. Successful local communities, after having received a favourable answer to their grievances, were proud to display copies of their correspondence with Roman power and of the official documents emanating from the governor or, even better, from the emperor himself, proving that they had been right to oppose the unscrupulous or violent imperial agents. The public display of their request (*libellus*) and of the decision issued by the Roman most powerful authorities as a response had a symbolic function for the local communities involved, enhancing their prestige and serving as a warning for future officials and soldiers passing by who might be oblivious to the imperial legislation regarding their behaviour—and by way of contrast, negative answers to their complaints were never displayed through epigraphic copies by local communities, in accordance with a general trend of administrative correspondence between local communities and Roman power.[75] The vast majority of the *petitiones* which have reached us were submitted by local communities from Asia Minor and date from the late second century and from the first half

[74] Brélaz (2005), 64–8.

[75] Burton (2002); Brélaz (2007a). For an example of a negative answer to a complaint emanating from a local community, known thanks to correspondence between Pliny, governor of Bithynia and Pontus, and the Emperor Trajan, see Brélaz (2002).

of the third century CE. Apart from the fact that the epigraphic habit was very strong in Western Asia Minor, this must be linked to the increasing presence of officials and soldiers throughout the provinces of Asia Minor at that time. The aggressive foreign and military policy of Roman emperors in the East from the end of the second century, as well as the Gothic, Persian and Palmyrene invasions of Asia Minor during the third century, led to many troops crossing the Anatolian peninsula to reach the Eastern front in the subsequent decades.[76] Another reason for the increasing number of Roman officials and soldiers present in the provinces of Asia Minor is the centralizing tendency in the imperial government from the Severan emperors onwards who, in the aftermath of the civil war between Septimius Severus and Pescennius Niger, started relying more and more on the use of imperial agents to deal with administrative and taxation issues.[77] Nevertheless, *petitiones* should not be considered to be a typical illustration of the so-called 'Crisis of the Third Century'. Admittedly, abuses from Roman officials and soldiers against local communities became more and more frequent during the third century, but this in fact represented a recurrent and structural phenomenon in the Roman Empire, since the earliest examples we know of complaints from local communities and of legislation on this topic date from the first century CE.[78] Whatever the circumstances were, the mere presence of Roman officials and soldiers nearby could mean a risk for local communities, even in stable periods.

Most *petitiones* were modelled after the same pattern and had a common layout.[79] They opened with an address to the emperor or governor, and with a praise of the benefits brought by the imperial government as well as of the emperor's benevolence. Then followed the presentation of the miserable condition of the local communities which were harassed by imperial agents and the narrative of the events. The complaints ended with a request from the local community for help or intervention from Roman authorities. Most of the time local communities tried to move the emperor and to seek his compassion for them, describing their weakness and poverty and using moral arguments, arguing that the violence they were experiencing was unworthy of the happiness of his reign. Other local communities used more practical and effective arguments in order to provoke a reaction from Roman power and alerted the emperor to the disastrous implications the impoverishment of provinces would have on the tax collection for Rome in the future. Yet, in some cases, local communities used rather a detailed and highly elaborate argumentation relying exclusively on legal considerations and aiming at proving the unlawfulness of the Roman officials' and soldiers' behaviour. The most explicit example in this respect is to be found in the complaint submitted to emperors by an anonymous village lying in the territory of the Lydian city of Philadelphia (today called Kemaliye), probably in the Severan era. The villagers, who might not have found sufficient support from the city they were part of, decided to write to the emperors themselves and to denounce the attacks they had suffered from Roman officials. Apparently, *kolletiônes* (imperial agents

[76] Brélaz (2005), 296–9; Speidel (2009). [77] Eich (2005).

[78] Evidence earlier than the late second century for abuses from Roman soldiers and officials include SB I 3924; AE 1976, 653; ILS 214; SEG XVII 755; PSI V 446; AE 2009, 1428; AE 2011, 1156; AE 2014, 1178.

[79] Hauken (1998), 258–89; Brélaz (2002).

sent into the provinces to deal with administrative tasks) unexpectedly entered the village during a raid and brutalized the local population. The arguments made by the villagers of Kemaliye in their complaint to denounce the misdeeds committed by *kolletiônes*, perhaps together with other imperial agents or soldiers, read as follows:

> [- - -] (those people) regarding their own decision as establishing law even if there is neither a lawful accuser (*μήτε νομίμου κατηγόρου τινὸς ἐξιστ[αμένου]*), nor even is there an established charge (*[μ]ήτε ὑποκειμένης αἰτίας*), nor a declared criminal accusation from a private person (*μηδὲ φανεροῦ τι[νος ἐγκλήμα]τος ἰδίου τινὸς ὄντος*), these—alone or with the troops indicated—overrun and shake down the village.[80]

What the villagers were complaining about here was probably the unjustified arrest of some members of their community along with extortion and damages caused by the imperial agents during their visit. Arbitrary arrests were also denounced in other *petitiones* from Asia Minor, like for instance in a complaint from peasants working on an imperial estate located in the region of Philadelphia in about the same period:

> [- - -] in order to leave an impression that such an outrage was justified, they arrested nine (villagers), put them in chains, and asserted that they were sending them under escort to your most excellent procurators, as the most excellent Aelius Aglaus is also acting as provincial governor. And after having exacted more than a thousand Attic drachmas as a price of his safety, they released one of the nine, but kept the others in chains, and we do not know for sure, most divine of emperors, whether they will escort them alive to the most excellent Aglaus or may dispose of them too as they did with the previous ones.[81]

In the case of Kemaliye, the offences committed by the imperial agents were opposed strictly from a legal point of view. The inhabitants of the village argued that the Roman officials acted in total disregard for the rule of law. In particular, the officials were said to have carried out an operation in the village—most likely arresting people on this occasion, as was the case in the imperial estate whose petition has just been mentioned—deliberately ignoring the various stages of ordinary criminal procedure. The imperial agents made arrests even though the people apprehended were not specifically sought by Roman authorities and they were not ordered to do so by the governor. Moreover, their action did not originate from any formal accusation or criminal complaint. On the contrary, the whole action of the officials against villagers had according to them remained entirely groundless and unjustified. For that reason, the villagers of Kemaliye considered that the officials' arbitrary decision to arrest people violated 'peace-giving justice' that was provided to all inhabitants of the Empire thanks to Roman rule and that in this case the brute force of the soldiers overpowered the law.[82]

[80] Hauken (1998), 58–73, ll. 1–5 with emendations in AE 2011, 1306. The exact interpretation of the wording of these lines with regard to which kind of imperial agents or soldiers were responsible for the abuses committed against the villagers is still problematic.

[81] Hauken (1998), 35–57, ll. 3–16 with emendations in AE 2011, 1305.

[82] An unpublished letter of Emperor Severus to the Lycian League refers to acts of torture employed unlawfully by Roman soldiers against civilians throughout the cities of the province. I thank Gary Reger, who will publish the inscription shortly, for providing me with this information.

The legal arguments that were used by the villagers of Kemaliye show that one could have a deep knowledge of the Roman criminal procedure even at a very local level in the countryside of Asia Minor, in this case in a remote place of Lydia. It is highly likely that the villagers hired the services of a legal expert for the purpose of writing down their complaint, as most local communities would have done in similar circumstances. Such professional jurists (*nomikoi, pragmatikoi*) were most likely to be found in the city of Philadelphia itself, in the territory of which the village of Kemaliye was located. Philadelphia was the primary centre of one of the Roman judicial districts (*conventus*) within the province of Asia, periodically hosting the judicial assizes of the governor, and for that reason it should not have lacked legal experts offering their services to individuals—or, as for the village of Kemaliye, to rural communities—wanting to lodge complaints with the Roman authorities.[83] Similar legal arguments, also denouncing the non-compliance of officials with the procedural requirements of policing operations and arrests, can be found in the Christian martyrological literature. In mid-third-century Smyrna, for instance, the priest Pionios opposed the local official who was trying to make him admit his alleged faults and offer a sacrifice for the emperor's sake, arguing that that official lacked the required judicial capacities and that only the governor would be entitled to go further with the enquiry.[84] From a procedural point of view that was entirely correct. Just as in other martyrological narratives depicting Christians challenging local or Roman authorities on the basis of legal arguments—and in particular in the passages of the *Acts of the Apostles* where the apostle Paul invoked his Roman citizenship to oppose his arrest and mistreatment at Philippi and in Jerusalem,[85] serving as an archetype for this motif in later martyrological literature—in this case one must admit that in order to fill the narrative with such details the author either had a legal education himself or, if we consider that these legal arguments were genuine, had the ability to access the minutes of court sessions where the defence strategy of the Christians was carefully recorded.[86]

To turn back to the complaint from Kemaliye, it is worth noting that it is one of the very few pieces of evidence proving explicitly that the inquisitorial criminal procedure in the Imperial period still had accusatorial features.[87] Even if a formal accusation, along with the inquisitorial procedure, was no longer needed for the Roman authorities to launch an investigation and even if a simple denunciation was now sufficient for them to arrest people,[88] the criminal procedure nevertheless had requirements including elements which could be compared to some extent to an accusation.[89] As seen above with the provincial and imperial legislation aiming at limiting the eirenarchs' tasks (§ 1), local policing officials, as well as probably imperial agents, needed to have reasonable grounds to arrest someone in cases where they were not acting expressly on behalf of the governor. In particular, before bringing the suspect to the governor's tribunal, the officials had to hold a

[83] Dalla Rosa (2012); Kantor (2009); Kantor (2013). For the *syndikoi* serving as public lawyers on behalf of local communities, see Fournier 2007.

[84] *Martyrium Pionii* 15 (Robert, Bowersock & Jones (1994)). See Brélaz (2005), 271–5.

[85] *Acts* 16.37–8; 22.24–9.

[86] Bryen (2014).

[87] For a preliminary discussion of this issue, see Brélaz (2013).

[88] Santalucia (2010); Santalucia (2011).

[89] Botta (2000); Rivière (2002), 263–305.

preliminary enquiry to support and justify why they decided to proceed to an arrest. The complaint submitted by the villagers of Kemaliye was even more explicit regarding the accusatorial nature of the policing procedure. All of the terms used by the villagers in their complaint to denounce the lack of legal bases for the arrests conducted by the soldiers (κατήγορος, αἰτία, ἔγκλημα) were typical of a procedure involving a formal accusation.[90] Thus, the villagers suggested that the only way for an arrest to be valid—given that, in this case, the soldiers were not acting on behalf of the governor[91]—would have been to proceed from an accusation made through a formal indictment or from a complaint made by a private person. These elements are consistent with what the regulations regarding the eirenarchs' policing duties teach us about the next stage of the criminal procedure: according to these regulations, the governor himself, during the judicial investigation, should conduct the hearing as 'if there was someone wanting to accuse' the arrested person (*si quis erit qui eum arguat*), even if this person was explicitly sought by Roman authorities because of a suspicion of criminal behaviour.[92] All this shows that even within the inquisitorial procedure a form of accusation was still necessary to start a criminal investigation, not only for practical reasons—because Roman authorities were not aware of all of the crimes which were committed in the provinces and therefore needed to be alerted that way—, but even to legitimize the enquiry.

In the context of the petition from Kemaliye, the legal advisers of the villagers might have overemphasized the procedural aspects regulating the policing activities led by Roman officials, in order to strengthen their defence before the emperors. Nevertheless, this example shows that local communities in the Roman provinces of Asia Minor, including smaller settlements like villages, could have in-depth knowledge of Roman criminal law and were able to take advantage of the law imposed by the ruling power as long as it served their own interests. The use of Roman law for themselves as a protection and a guarantee against arbitrary decisions coming from imperial agents is a further illustration of the integration of local communities of Asia Minor into the political order, and in this case also the legal order, provided by the Roman Empire.

5. CONCLUSION: EXPERIENCING ROMAN LAW, ASSERTING LOCAL AUTONOMY

Although there was a clear—even if not expressly stated—division of tasks between Roman authorities and local communities in the provinces of Asia Minor with regard to law enforcement and criminal jurisdiction, many situations could occur leading to non-compliance with the established criminal procedure and even, in some cases, to conflicts between the two jurisdictions. Local communities were not necessarily responsible for all breaches of ordinary rules or

[90] Laffi (2013), 29, 39–40, 54–5, 60, 90–1.

[91] Hauken (1998), 58–73, ll. 14–19 with emendations in AE 2011, 1306.

[92] Marcian, *On Public Prosecutions* 2 (D. 48.3.6).

tensions. In many instances, potential or actual undermining of the regular criminal procedure and of the theoretical allocation of duties between Roman power and local communities in the field of law enforcement arose from failures of Roman provincial administration. Among these various failures we can notice several things: 1. The lack of means at the disposal of provincial government to ensure security at the local level which led local communities to rely on themselves for their everyday safety and to take more and more initiatives in the field of law enforcement, sometimes going beyond their powers and rights; 2. The contradictory expectations of Roman provincial administration towards local communities with regard to law enforcement, urging them on the one hand to contribute to the imperial peace in fighting criminals within their territories, and on the other hand restricting their powers in criminal jurisdiction; 3. The absence of any systematic regulation regarding the duties of local officials dealing with policing activities, especially as far as their cooperation with provincial jurisdiction was concerned; 4. The abuses repeatedly committed by imperial officials and Roman soldiers against local communities, in total disregard of imperial legislation and criminal procedure. These several examples can be seen as proof of the structural dysfunctions of Roman provincial administration, which were not caused by the economic and political crisis experienced by the Roman Empire from the late second century onwards, but which for the most part were already attested during the second or even the first century CE, from the very beginning of the Imperial period.

However, we should not assume that Roman power would have conceptualized law enforcement in the provinces as though it was its own monopoly. There was no centralized, state-sponsored agency dealing with law enforcement in the Roman Empire. When taking care of public security in their territories, local communities of Asia Minor were not acting as parts of a uniform system belonging to imperial government. Cities in the provinces of Asia Minor were not administrative units ensuring security at the local level on behalf of Roman power, but political entities protecting their own population through their local policing officials. This is probably one of the unique characteristics of the provinces of Asia Minor, at least of the Western half of the Anatolian peninsula, in comparison with other regions of the Eastern Mediterranean under Roman rule: most local communities in Asia Minor were patterned after the political model of the Greek city-state, enjoying a century-long local autonomy, having well-established political institutions, and being deeply aware of their local specificities and identities. As in many other areas (such as diplomatic relations with imperial power as well as with other cities, honorific titles and precedence within the province, cults and festivals, public works, etc.), law enforcement and criminal jurisdiction became, in this context, a matter of pride and competition for local communities. In particular, local communities used law enforcement and criminal jurisdiction to assert their autonomy, to enhance their powers within the limits permitted by Roman rule, and to situate themselves in relation to imperial and provincial power as well as in relation to their peers. For that reason, local policing officials tried to increase their powers during law enforcement operations and criminal procedure at the expense of the prerogatives of Roman provincial administration; local communities enacted regulations in the field of criminal law in order to take advantage of the inability of Roman power to deal with every single issue pertaining to public security at the local level; and local communities were eager to suggest that, in defeating large groups of brigands with their own means, they were replacing the deficient Roman army and were contributing to the defence of the Empire.

These conflicting attitudes of local communities towards Roman criminal law and procedure—in some cases trying to bypass or even go beyond Roman regulations, in others deliberately contributing to the imperial political order or even acting in the name of Roman law—were typical of the variability of the relationship between cities of Asia Minor and Roman power. The interpretation and implementation of Roman criminal law were another means for these communities to express their autonomy under Roman provincial administration. Even in a field which might seem extremely formal and regulated, since it fell under the sovereignty of Rome, law enforcement and criminal jurisdiction were used by local communities of Asia Minor to negotiate their position within the Roman Empire.

REFERENCES

Bauzon, E. 2004. La présomption d'innocence et la charge de la preuve en droit romain. In: *La Présomption d'innocence. Essais de philosophie pénale et de criminologie.* Paris, pp. 25–32.

Blanco-Pérez, A. 2013. C. Claudius Lucianus: an Eirenarch from Akmoneia Selected by the Proconsul M. Sulpicius Crassus. A Note on *SEG* 56.1493. *Zeitschrift für Papyrologie und Epigraphik* 186, pp. 190–4.

Botta, F. 2000. L'iniziativa processualcriminale delle *personae publicae* nelle fonti giuridiche d'età giustinianea. In: S. Puliatti and A. Sanguinetti (eds.), *Legislazione, cultura giuridica, prassi dell'Impero d'Oriente in età giustinianea tra passato e futuro.* Milan, pp. 285–378.

Brélaz, C. 2002. Pline le Jeune interprète des revendications locales: l'*epistula* 10, 77 et le *libellus* des Juliopolitains. *Appunti Romani di Filologia* 4, pp. 81–95.

Brélaz, C. 2005. *La sécurité publique en Asie Mineure sous le Principat (Ier–IIIe s. ap. J.-C.). Institutions municipales et institutions impériales dans l'Orient romain.* Basel.

Brélaz, C. 2007a. Motifs et circonstances de l'ingérence des autorités romaines dans les cités grecques sous le Principat. In: A. Baroni (ed.), *Amministrare un impero. Roma e le sue province.* Trento, pp. 109–43.

Brélaz, C. 2007b. Lutter contre la violence à Rome: attributions étatiques et tâches privées. In: C. Wolff (ed.), *Les Exclus dans l'Antiquité. Actes du colloque organisé à Lyon les 23–24 septembre 2004.* Lyons–Paris, pp. 219–39.

Brélaz, C. 2008. L'adieu aux armes: la défense de la cité grecque dans l'empire romain pacifié. In: C. Brélaz and P. Ducrey (eds.), *Sécurité collective et ordre public dans les sociétés anciennes.* Geneva, pp. 155–204.

Brélaz, C. 2011. Aelius Aristide (*Or.* 50.72–93) et le choix des irénarques par le gouverneur: à propos d'une inscription d'Acmonia. In: N. Badoud (ed.), Philologos Dionysios. *Mélanges offerts au professeur Denis Knoepfler.* Geneva, pp. 603–37.

Brélaz, C. 2013. L'apport des *petitiones* anatoliennes à la connaissance de la procédure pénale romaine: le dossier de Kemaliye (Philadelphie, Lydie). *Cahiers du Centre Gustave Glotz* 24, p. 297.

Brélaz, C. 2015. Cultura militare e identità collettive nelle città greche sotto l'Impero romano. In: E. Franchi and G. Proietti (eds.), *Guerra e memoria nel mondo antico.* Trento, pp. 259–86.

Bryen, A. Z. 2014. Martyrdom, Rhetoric, and the Politics of Procedure. *Classical Antiquity* 33, pp. 243–80.

Burton, G. P. 2002. The Roman Imperial State (AD 14–235): Evidence and Reality. *Chiron* 32, pp. 249–80.

Chaniotis, A. 2003. The Perception of Imperial Power in Aphrodisias: The Epigraphic Evidence. In: by L. de Blois et al. (ed.), *The Representation and Perception of Roman Imperial Power. Proceedings of the Third Workshop of the International Network Impact of Empire (Roman Empire, 200 BC–AD 476)*. Amsterdam, pp. 250–60.

Chaniotis, A. 2005. *War in the Hellenistic World: A Social and Cultural History*. Oxford.

Crawford M. H. et al. 1996. *Roman Statutes*, I. London.

Dalla Rosa, A. 2012. Praktische Lösungen für praktische Probleme: Die Gruppierung von *conventus* in der Provinz *Asia* und die Bewegungen des Prokonsuls C. Iulius Severus (*procos.* 152/53). *Zeitschrift für Papyrologie und Epigraphik* 183, pp. 259–76.

De Visscher, F. 1963. *Le droit des tombeaux romains*. Milan.

Dmitriev, S. 2005. *City Government in Hellenistic and Roman Asia Minor*. Oxford.

Eich, P. 2005. *Zur Metamorphose des politischen Systems in der römischen Kaiserzeit. Die Entstehung einer 'personalen Bürokratie' im langen dritten Jahrhundert*. Berlin.

Fernoux, H. 2011. *Le* Demos *et la Cité. Communautés et assemblées populaires en Asie Mineure à l'époque impériale*. Rennes.

Fournier, J. 2007. Les *syndikoi*, représentants juridiques des cités grecques sous le Haut-Empire romain. *Cahiers du Centre Gustave Glotz* 18, pp. 7–36.

Fournier, J. 2010. *Entre tutelle romaine et autonomie civique. L'administration judiciaire dans les provinces hellénophones de l'empire romain (129 av. J.-C.–235 apr. J.-C.)*. Athens.

Franco, C. 2008. Aristides and Rhodes: Concord and Consolation. In: W. V. Harris and B. Homes (eds.), *Aelius Aristides between Greece, Rome, and the Gods*. Leiden, pp. 217–49.

Fuhrmann, J. 2012. *Policing the Roman Empire: Soldiers, Administration, and Public Order*. Oxford.

Guerber, E. 2010. *Les cités grecques dans l'Empire romain. Les privilèges et les titres des cités de l'Orient hellénophone d'Octave Auguste à Dioclétien*. Second revised edition. Rennes.

Harter-Uibopuu, K. 2010. Erwerb und Veräusserung von Grabstätten im griechisch-römischen Kleinasien am Beispiel der Grabinschriften von Smyrna. In: G. Thür (ed.), *Symposion 2009. Vorträge zur griechischen und hellenistischen Rechtsgeschichte*. Vienna, pp. 247–70.

Harter-Uibopuu, K. 2014. Tote soll man ruhen lassen . . . Verbote und Strafen zur Sicherung von Gräbern am Beispiel der Inschriften von Ephesos. In: J. Fischer (ed.), *Der Beitrag Kleinasiens zur Kultur- und Geistesgeschichte der griechisch-römischen Antike*. Vienna, pp. 157–80.

Harter-Uibopuu, K. and Wiedergut, K. 2014. Niemand anderer soll hier bestattet werden . . . Grabschutz im kaiserzeitlichen Milet. In: G. Thür (ed.), *Grabrituale. Tod und Jenseits in Frühgeschichte und Altertum*. Vienna, pp. 147–71.

Hauken, T. 1998. *Petition and Response, An Epigraphic Study of Petitions to Roman Emperors 181–249*. Bergen.

Heller, A., 2006. *'Les bêtises des Grecs'. Conflits et rivalités entre cités d'Asie et de Bithynie à l'époque romaine (129 a.C.–235 p.C.)*. Bordeaux.

Jördens, A. 2011. Eine kaiserliche Konstitution zu den Rechtsprechungskompetenzen der Statthalter. *Chiron* 41, pp. 327–56.

Kantor, G. 2009. Knowledge of Law in Roman Asia Minor. In: R. Haensch (ed.), *Selbstdarstellung und Kommunikation. Die Veröffentlichung staatlicher Urkunden auf Stein und Bronze in der Römischen Welt*. Munich, pp. 249–65.

Kantor, G., 2013. Law in Roman Phrygia: Rules and Jurisdictions. In: P. Thonemann (ed.), *Roman Phrygia: Culture and Society*. Cambridge, pp. 143–67.

Katsari, C. 2011. *The Roman Monetary System. The Eastern Provinces from the First to the Third Century AD*. Cambridge.

Kirbihler, F. 2012. Un *cursus honorum* à Éphèse? Quelques réflexions sur la succession des magistratures de la cité à l'époque romaine. In: P. Goukowsky and C. Feyel (eds.), *Folia Graeca in honorem Edouard Will, Historica*. Nancy, pp. 67–107.

Kokkinia, C. (ed.), 2008. *Boubon. The Inscriptions and Archaeological Remains. A Survey 2004–2006*. Athens.

Kuhn, C. T. 2012. Emotionality in the Political Culture of the Graeco-Roman East: The Role of Acclamations. In: A. Chaniotis (ed.), *Unveiling Emotions. Sources and Methods for the Study of Emotions in the Greek World*. Stuttgart, pp. 295–316.

Laffi, U. 2013. *In greco per i Greci. Ricerche sul lessico greco del processo civile e criminale romano nelle attestazioni di fonti documentarie romane*. Pavia.

Laubry, N. 2007. Le transfert des corps dans l'Empire romain: problèmes d'épigraphie, de religion et de droit romain. *Mélanges de l'École française de Rome Antiquité* 119, pp. 149–88.

Magie, D. 1950. *Roman Rule: Roman Rule in Asia Minor to the End of the Third Century after Christ*. Two volumes. Princeton.

Musurillo, H. 1972. *Acts of the Christian Martyrs*. Oxford.

Nigdelis, P. M. 2006. *Επιγραφικά Θεσσαλονίκεια. Συμβολή στην πολιτική και κοινωνική ιστορία της αρχαίας Θεσσαλονίκης*. Thessalonica.

Ramsay, W. M. 1895–1897. *Phrygia: The Cities and Bishoprics of Phrygia*. Two volumes. Oxford.

Riess, W. 2001. *Apuleius und die Räuber. Ein Beitrag zur historischen Kriminalitätsforschung*. Stuttgart.

Ritti, T. 2004. *Iura sepulcrorum* a Hierapolis di Frigia nel quadro dell'epigrafia sepolcrale microasiatica. Iscrizioni edite ed inedite. In: Libitina *e dintorni. Atti dell'XI Rencontre franco-italienne sur l'épigraphie*. Rome, pp. 455–634.

Rivière, Y. 2002. *Les délateurs sous l'Empire romain*. Rome.

Robert, L. 1935. Épigraphie grecque d'Asie Mineure. *L'Antiquité Classique* 4, pp. 459–66.

Robert, L. 1966. Inscriptions d'Aphrodisias. Première partie. *L'Antiquité Classique* 35, pp. 377–432.

Robert, L., Bowersock, G. W. and Jones, C. P. 1994. *Le martyre de Pionios, prêtre de Smyrne*. Dumbarton Oaks.

Rupp, A. 2015. Verbote und Strafzahlungen auf Grabinschriften am Beispiel von Aphrodisias. *Zeitschrift für Altorientalische und Biblische Rechtsgeschichte* 21, pp. 143–58.

Sänger, P. 2010. Zur Organisation des Sicherheitswesens im kaiserzeitlichen Kleinasien und Ägypten. Rezension eines neuen Buches und komparative Studie zur Eirenarchie. *Tyche* 25, pp. 99–122.

Santalucia, B. 2010. Praeses provideat. Il governatore provinciale fra *iudicia publica* e *cognitiones extra ordinem*. In: D. Mantovani and L. Pellecchi (eds.), Eparcheia, autonomia e civitas Romana. *Studi sulla giurisdizione criminale dei governatori di provincia (II sec. a. C.–II d.C.)*. Pavia, pp. 69–88.

Santalucia, B. 2011. 'Accusatio' e 'inquisitio' nel processo penale romano di età imperiale. In: *Atti del Convegno 'Processo civile e processo penale nell'esperienza giuridica del mondo antico. In memoria di Arnaldo Biscardi'*. Milan, pp. 249–57.

Schuler, C. 1998. *Ländliche Siedlungen und Gemeinden im hellenistischen und römischen Kleinasien*. Munich.

Sion-Jenkins, K. 2010. La perception du pouvoir impérial en Asie Mineure à l'époque julio-claudienne: l'exemple d'Aphrodisias. In: L. Callegarin and F. Réchin (eds.), *Espaces et Sociétés à l'époque romaine: entre Garonne et Èbre*. Pau, pp. 69–95.

Speidel, M. A. 2009. Les longues marches des armées romaines. Reflets épigraphiques de la circulation des militaires dans la province d'Asie au IIIe siècle apr. J.-C. *Cahiers du Centre Gustave Glotz* 20, pp. 199–210.

Strubbe, J. 1997. *ΑΡΑΙ ΕΠΙΤΥΜΒΙΟΙ. Imprecations against Desecrators of the Grave in the Greek Epitaphs of Asia Minor. A Catalogue*. Bonn.

Tybout, R. A. 2016. Dead Men Walking: The Repatriation of Mortal Remains. In: L. de Ligt and L. E. Tacoma (eds.), *Migration and Mobility in the Early Roman Empire*. Leiden, pp. 390–437.

Vitale, M. 2011. Die *insulae* im Stadtterritorium der 'Bergpolis' Termessos: Eine neue Münzprägung mit der Abbildung eines *Aphlaston*. In E. Schwertheim (ed.), *Studien zum antiken Kleinasien VII*. Bonn, pp. 133–46.

Yannakopulos, N. 2003. Preserving the *Pax Romana*: the Peace Functionaries in Roman East. *Mediterraneo antico* 6, pp. 825–905.

11

Navigating Roman Law and Local Privileges in Pontus-Bithynia*

Georgy Kantor

The province of Pontus-Bithynia[1] has had a place in discussions of law in Roman provinces ever since the Renaissance. It was already the *De antiquo iure provinciarum* of Carlo Sigonio, the earliest attempt at a systematic survey of Roman provincial institutions, that, despite its general bias towards the Republican period, stressed the significance of Pliny the Younger's correspondence as a governor of the province with the emperor Trajan as a source for the provincial legal situation.[2] Some of Pliny's evidence, notably on the *lex Pompeia*, has been central to generalizations on Roman provincial law ever since. It will nonetheless be argued here that important aspects both of Pliny's correspondence and of the underlying legal situation in his province have been relatively neglected. Behind the deceptively straightforward presentation of legal issues in Pliny's letters to the emperor there can be discovered a much more complex interaction between the interests of individuals, communities, their legal representatives and the governor himself.

In the first and second parts of this chapter, I shall explore some salient features of Pliny's and Trajan's official letters (Pliny, *Epistulae* 10.15–121), which form by far the largest part of our evidence for Pontus-Bithynia, and then try to work out a methodology for using them as a source for Roman provincial legal practice. In the third part I shall then attempt to offer, on the basis both of Pliny's letters and of the scattered (and sadly insufficient) evidence of legal and documentary sources, a new interpretation of the Bithynian legal situation in the High Empire, looking especially at similarities and differences with other eastern Roman provinces. Particular attention will be paid to the continuing (and arguably diminishing) role of the *lex Pompeia*, an uncharacteristically extensive set of

* This chapter could not have been written without stimulating discussions with Neil McLynn; I am grateful also to the participants of the Oxford Ancient History sub-faculty seminar in Trinity Term 2017 for perceptive questions and comments on an earlier version of this paper. The responsibility for remaining misconceptions obviously remains mine.

[1] For the form of the province's name (never 'Bithynia et Pontus', by far the most common form in the secondary literature, before the third century CE), see Wesch-Klein (2001) (summary in *SEG* LI 1717).

[2] See Sigonius (1568), 78.

Georgy Kantor, *Navigating Roman Law and Local Privileges in Pontus-Bithynia* In: *Law in the Roman Provinces*. Edited by: Kimberley Czajkowski and Benedikt Eckhardt in collaboration with Meret Strothmann, Oxford University Press (2020).

DOI: 10.1093/oso/9780198844082.003.0011

Roman regulations for the province. In conclusion, I shall return to one of the overriding themes of this volume: can an increase in the role of Roman law and jurisdiction be posited before the *Constitutio Antoniniana*? It will be argued that Pontus-Bithynia offers material for a different model, where the initial radical impact of Roman annexation was to an extent dissolved by later legal developments, some of them initiated by provincial actors.

1. TRAJAN'S APPOINTEE

Before discussing how the interplay between various actors on the provincial legal scene can be seen through the prism of the Pliny–Trajan correspondence, we need to deal with three basic problems of interpreting Pliny's Bithynian appointment and the possibility of using the surviving correspondence as a record of it, which will have significant implications for what follows. Two of them are familiar chestnuts, namely the typicality of Pliny's role as a governor and the frequency of his correspondence with Trajan; the third, the extent to which Pliny's correspondence was edited for literary purposes *post eventum*, has come to the forefront of scholarly discussion only recently.

Let us begin with the last of these issues. The near universal consensus of earlier scholarship, taking Pliny's letters as an authentic and largely complete record of his two years in the province, has been challenged recently by Greg Woolf, who has argued for a heavy degree of literary revision by Pliny himself, who was 'contributing to a long running discourse on the virtues and role of a governor' and asks, relevantly, 'if they were really not intended for publication, why are they so readily comprehensible'?[3] As Woolf points out, Pliny largely ignores the cultural peculiarities of Pontus-Bithynia, paying relatively little attention to its Greekness, creates opportunities for displaying a range of senatorial and imperial virtues in himself and Trajan, and shows a relatively frictionless provincial administration (which Woolf contrasts in this respect with Cilicia of Cicero's correspondence). Abuse and conflict are the thing of the past, now being conscientiously rooted out by the governor. Furthermore, as he rightly stresses, 'Pliny's main concern remains with the Romans in his province', rather than with the peregrine provincials.[4]

While Woolf raises some crucial questions concerning the image of Bithynia as a province and the nature of its governor's concerns, emerging from the Pliny–Trajan correspondence, which will be important for us later on, his provocative argument cannot be accepted in its entirety. The traditional view that the abrupt end of the collection and the absence of any reference to Pliny's actual or even impending departure from the province imply his death in office

[3] Woolf (2006), (quotations from pp. 103 and 97 respectively), developed further in Woolf (2015); argued independently by Stadter (2006), who makes some important observations on the editorial processes in Book 10. A similar view has been more cautiously advanced by Noreña (2007), 268–71, as part of his seminal discussion of the 'social economy' of Book 10.

[4] Woolf (2006), 101. I shall attempt to qualify this statement below.

remains persuasive.[5] It is less than clear, furthermore (and the answer is not necessarily made easier by the existence of Fronto's correspondence, which is private and based on a much more intimate relationship with the imperial house), that it would have been deemed permissible for Pliny or for his literary executors to edit to any considerable degree the official replies of a reigning emperor to fit a literary purpose, taking into account in particular their possible legal validity. As is well known, Trajan's reply to Pliny concerning Christians (*Ep.* 10.97) could at the very least be used rhetorically as an authentic presentation of the Roman criminal procedure over eighty years later (Tert. *Apol.* 2.6–9); *a fortiori*, one would expect the emperor's words to be taken seriously while he or his immediate successor were in power.[6] Pliny's letters themselves are an important piece of evidence for the collection and circulation of imperial replies by provincial lawyers (*nomikoi*).[7]

It will be contended here that it is more fruitful to explore these questions in relation to the distinguishing features of Pliny's province and, above all, to the rhetorical strategies used in addressing the emperor. As has been convincingly demonstrated by Myles Lavan in his recent seminal article, Pliny's letters exhibit a striking degree of similarity with Roman official correspondence as attested in the surviving documentary record and can be productively explored as an example of the genre.[8] The (often extremely deceptive) clarity of Pliny's missives finds an easy explanation in this context: not only did he need to impress his distant emperor, but his letters could be accessible to other elite Romans at the emperor's end of the correspondence, and to the parties to a dispute at the provincial, to say nothing of the *nomikoi* accessing official copies in the archive of their *conuentus* centre.[9] The

[5] The view goes back to Mommsen (1869), 430–3 and Wilcken (1914); for Pliny's health in office, see Talbert (1980), 421; a concise restatement of earlier views in Williams (1990), 13. See also below on the circumstances of Pliny's arrival. For the debate on the governorship's date see Sherwin-White (1966), 80–1, and Millar (2004), 38 (arguing for 109–11 CE), and Eck (1982), 349–50 (arguing for 110–12 CE). I hope to argue for the former date in more detail elsewhere.

[6] A view re-asserted recently by Eck (2016), 107. For an argument that the Pliny–Trajan exchange lacked broader legal significance (not entirely conclusive in the absence of Book VII of Ulpian's *De officio proconsulis*), see the important recent contribution of James Corke-Webster (2017b); cf. also Corke-Webster (2017a) on ancient reactions to this particular Pliny–Trajan exchange. While I accept that it was certainly an example of the emperor in a 'reactive mode', very much in the fashion envisaged by Fergus Millar (1977), what is important for me at this point in the discussion is not whether Trajan intended a broad legal statement, but whether his reply could be plausibly represented as such. For the most recent assessment of Fronto's correspondence, compare Griffin (2014). For the need to secure imperial approval for publication, Stadter (2006), 63–4.

[7] Pliny, *Epistulae* 10.56–7; 10.65.3; 10.72–3, with Kantor (2009), 258–62. Compare Jones (2009) (*SEG* LVIII 1536), a community petition from 129 CE to copy an *apophasis* of the emperor Hadrian, issued while on his provincial tour.

[8] Lavan (2018). His work has been adumbrated by the important study of bureaucratic language in Book 10 of Pliny's correspondence in Coleman (2012) (with whose assessment of Book 10 I do not, however, fully agree, as will become clear below). For a useful comparison with collections of jurists' letters, cf. also Harries (2018), 275–8, and for an introductory study of imperial letters in Latin, Millar (2016). Compare also Stephen Mitchell's observations on Trajan's letter to Smyrna (*A&R* 14 = *IAph2007*, no. 8.33): "Both the crisp, businesslike tone of this short communication, and the principle underlying the decision, that no one from the free cities be compelled to perform a liturgy connected with the Asian *koinon*, are strongly reminiscent of Trajan's replies to Pliny in the Bithynian correspondence, notably ep. 10. 48, 55 and 109" (Mitchell (1984a), 296).

[9] Note a telling small detail, observed already by Wilcken (1914), 128: an addition of *Pontici* to *Bithyni* in the letters sent from the assize tour of Pontus, no doubt reflecting local sensibilities.

need to frame and effectively present the governor's case was present already at the stage of writing the original letter, as was the need to create a *persona* of the emperor's trusted adviser. Instead of viewing that as a function of later editing, meant for the reading public at Rome, it may be more productive to use this as a starting point of exploration of agency in the legal process from the point of view of a Roman magistrate rather than of provincial litigants.[10] Posterity need not be privileged among his audiences, and the governor was a party with a case to make in the legal proceedings that reached the emperor, just as the litigants were.[11]

Nor is the Romano-centric nature of the correspondence necessarily surprising, even if it is undoubtedly telling of the nature of Roman elite concerns. It has been observed already by Tyrrell and Purser in their commentary on our only comparable literary dossier of Roman governor's letters, those of Cicero from Cilicia in 51/50 BCE, that 'his correspondence, copious and unreserved as it is, tells us about the history, the geography, the manners and customs of his province—nothing.'[12] Bithynia, while it belonged to the Greek cultural area and was part of international performance circuits (both athletic and intellectual), which occasionally impacted on Pliny's activity and, as we shall see, formed an important exception to the general principle formulated by Woolf,[13] was not invested with ancestral cultural significance such as postulated by Pliny himself in his advisory letter to Maximus for 'this true and pure Greece', the province of Achaia (Plin. *Ep.* 8.24.1: *illam ueram et meram Graeciam*).[14] Local institutions were hardly 'ancestral', that significant word in Roman provincial ideology and legal framework. Pontus-Bithynia was not even particularly notable for ancient *mirabilia* of the kind that would attract a Mucianus, and in earlier Roman history it figured mainly in connexion with the invasion of Mithridates VI, if not with Caesar's time at the court of Nicomedes. There is no reason to think that Trajan or Pliny would have seen more intrinsic interest in Bithynia than Cicero had seen in Cilicia, and the bias of their correspondence can be taken as representative of that (Trajan is certainly dismissive even when inclined to be generous, and Pliny is more excited by a lake than by local buildings): this

[10] For approaches to agency in Roman provincial legal process (both starting from local perspectives), see above all Bryen (2012) and Czajkowski (2017), 17–21. This is not, of course, to deny that a degree of literary care must have gone into eventual publication (certainly the inclusion of his private correspondence with the emperor alongside the official was an important and not self-evident decision) or that Pliny while in the province could have envisaged publication of his letters as a collection, but to emphasize some limitations of that approach.

[11] For general observations encouraging the approach to Pliny's official correspondence as exercises in persuading the emperor, see now Griffin (2018), 293–5 (a previously unpublished lecture of 2007).

[12] Tyrrell and Purser (1914), xi.

[13] Pliny, *Epistulae* 10.58–60 (Flavius Archippus); 10.81–2 (Archippus and Dio Chrysostom); 10.118–19 (prizes at iselastic games).

[14] Note the disdainful comparison with Bithynia itself in 8.24.8–9, contrasting provincial service *inter seruientes* and *liberos* respectively. The contrast would be emphasized even more strongly if (as seems plausible) Maximus belonged to a family from Alexandria Troas himself; see on this the perceptive discussion of Kuhn (2012), 428–30, with further references. Her discussion of Arrian, *Epicteti dissertationes* 3.7.30–1, on the qualifications of Maximus for acting as a judge (κρίνειν), or lack thereof, is not irrelevant to Pliny's situation.

dismissive attitude could no doubt have consequences in the legal sphere, to which we shall come in the third part of this chapter.[15]

Even insofar as we take Pliny's letters as a product of his official, rather than literary, activity, it is of course still necessary to assess the typicality of governor's attitudes and activities as shown in them. As mentioned above, this has been questioned on the grounds both of the 'special' nature of Pliny's appointment as the first imperial appointee to Pontus-Bithynia and as the *legatus pro praetore consulari* (or more likely *proconsulari*) *potestate*,[16] and of the Pliny's supposed excessive frequency of contacts with the emperor and excessive hesitancy in reaching the decision himself, due either to incompetency or to the specially difficult circumstances of his province. In other words, if we treat Pliny's correspondence as our test case for agency in provincial legal process, just how much agency lies with him and quite how typical is he in that regard? And if he is typical, does that mean that the provincial governor mattered relatively little in major litigation, as for the more complicated (or, simply, more valuable) disputes he would simply serve as an intermediary with the emperor? Trajan's responses to Pliny are sometimes viewed as if the emperor was about to erupt into something like (in the words of a mediaeval king of Sicily to his official) 'now you have stupidly written to consult me'.[17] Even Coleman's brilliant study of Pliny's language, despite recognizing for the first time hesitation as a bureaucratic trope and a part of his bureaucratic strategy,[18] overplays Pliny's perceived helplessness, at least as his self-presentation strategy: '[i]n Book 10 . . . Pliny controls neither administrative affairs, nor the discourse, nor the stylistic register: much of the time he is writing because he does not know what to do, nearly half the letters are from Trajan, and the language is the bureaucratic tool of officials whose job it was to put problems and their solutions in writing'.[19]

A different perspective (not, of course, an entirely new one) may be more fruitful. Over the two years of his governorship, Pliny sent to Trajan 61 letters

[15] Trajan dismissive: Pliny, *Epistulae* 10.40.2; Pliny and the lake: 10.41–2; 10.61–2. For ancient attempts to connect Bithynia with the Greek past, Mitchell (1984b), 131.

[16] For the most recent overview of senior Roman officials in Pontus-Bithynia, see Loriot (2011). For the opposing views on Pliny's official title, see Cotton (2000), 233–4, and Vervaet (2007), 129–32. It is, at any rate, clear that the number of the governor's lictors, "the most visible signs" of his authority (Noreña (2007), 243 n. 14), was a crucial aspect of Pliny's unique title; see already Mommsen (1869), 432 n. 3. For classic discussions of the nature of and reasons for Pliny's appointment, making earlier treatments obsolete, see Levick (1979) and Talbert (1980), emphasizing typical aspects of his role; compare also Millar (1977), 325–8. There does not seem to be any strong reason to view Pliny, with Haensch (1997), 282, as 'möglicherweise in ungewöhnlich großem Maße ein "reisender Statthalter"'; on the contrary, his proconsular predecessors must have visited Pontus more frequently, having only one year to spend in the province.

[17] Dunbabin (1998), 23: *nunc Maiestatem nostram inaniter consulasti* (her translation). Compare Syme (1958), i.37: "The letters that passed between Trajan and the governor of Bithynia disclose the best side of the Emperor and the worst of the senator. Trajan is firm and sagacious, his mandatory timid and pedantic." In the view of Talbert (1980), 422, commenting on Pliny, *Epistulae* 10.45, "it is hard to imagine that many other consular legates would need to consult the emperor on such a basic regulation" (contrast, however, Talbert (1980), 430–5, on Pliny's "forcefulness"). Most recently, Corke-Webster (2017a), 249, views *Epistulae* 10.96 as "an inexperienced and overexposed governor's effort".

[18] For *haesito* and *haesitatio* as examples of bureaucratic language, see Coleman (2012), 193.

[19] Coleman (2012), 233.

(though note a possible lacuna before 10.86B).[20] This number includes three letters on the circumstances of his arrival (10.15, 10.17A, 10.17B), one short note on the arrival of his legate (10.25), five 'Christmas cards', informing the emperor of the vows taken at the beginning of the year, his birthday, and his *dies imperii* (10.35, 10.52, 10.88, 10.100, 10.102), and six letters of essentially private character (10.26, 10.51, 10.75, 10.94, 10.104, 10.120). Two letters refer to matters related to foreign policy (10.67 and 10.74). This leaves us with only 44 letters proceeding from Pliny's provincial administration, some of which may be viewed as simply forwarding petitions to the emperor (though this is arguably a gross simplification), some do not require any decision, and some concern the military.[21] The number of those letters that proceed from Pliny's exercise of his jurisdiction is smaller still, though some cases are difficult to determine, and an exact number might be misleading. (Is it, for instance, impending litigation or Pliny's own desire for neatness that provoked *Epistulae* 10.112 on the *summae honorariae*? The former seems inherently much more likely, but can hardly be proved.)

Our most famous and frequently invoked comparandum, the register of the Severan prefect of Egypt Subatianus Aquila at the assize session at Arsinoe, with its 1,804 petitions entered in three days (*P.Yale* 61), may not be a very reliable guide to the amount of judicial business before the governor of Pontus-Bithynia. It is hardly to be doubted, however, that in two years, conducting at least three sessions each year in Bithynia (in Nicaea, Nicomedia, and Prusa), and probably two during his visit to Pontus, Pliny's count of law cases ran at least into thousands, not counting petitions received *in transitu*.[22] Far from obsessively referring his problems to the emperor or displaying studied incompetence, Pliny in fact kept consultation of Trajan in legal cases to the bare minimum, and we

[20] Cf. on the possible missing letters Sherwin-White (1966), 533–5, who convincingly argues for the essential completeness of the collection. For convenient checklists, Wilcken (1914), 134–6; Millar (2004), 42–6. With about two letters a month this was perhaps the necessary minimum to keep Rome assured that the governor was neither dead nor up to something nefarious. It is of course equally true that any considerably larger number would have made the situation of the 'emperor at work' unbearable; cf. Millar (1977), 325, for the frequency of Pliny's letters likely being typical on these grounds.

[21] Sherwin-White (1966), 547, counted only 39 letters where "Pliny submitted problems for solution or actions for approval" (cf. also Harris (1980), 887): the exact count is a matter of perception. Cf. also Fournier (2010), 371, tabulating the parties with whom the initiative lay in the correspondence.

[22] Cf. Corke-Webster (2017b), 377: "This unmanageable administrative mountain is how we should imagine Pliny's judicial inbox" (with a misprint in the number of petitions at Arsinoe). For the *conuentus* system and city statuses in Pontus-Bithynia, the most comprehensive treatment is still Haensch (1997), 282–90 and 598–609 (esp. at p. 287); see more recently Loriot (2011). Sinope and Amisus stand out among places from which Pliny's letters were sent; other possibilities include Prusias ad Hypium and Amastris; Amaseia by that point would serve as the centre of the separate procuratorial province of Pontus Galaticus/Mediterraneus, cf. Marek (1993), 73–82; Marek (2003), 45. Guerber (2009), 319, confuses Apamea-Celaenae in Phrygia with Bithynian Apamea, which may still deserve consideration; Haensch (1997), 287 n. 143 is almost certainly right to argue that Byzantium was not a *conuentus* centre. It may be significant that, with one exception, an inscription for a law student dying abroad, all commemorations of *nomikoi* in Pontus-Bithynia—in its old Pompeian boundaries—come from cities on this list (one each from Apamea, Nicomedia, and Amisus, two each from Amaseia and Amastris, three from Nicaea): see Jones (2007), 1347–8 no. 8 and 1350–2 nos. 27–37, counting Euchaita, which did not receive *polis* status until late antiquity, as part of the territory of Amaseia.

know only one case through his entire governorship (and that concerning capital punishment of Roman citizens in a situation of considerable legal uncertainty) where the litigants themselves were referred to Rome. Both Trajan himself and elite Roman readers of the published Book 10 would have realized that instantly. The contrast between the number of Pliny's letters and the amount of judicial business that can be assumed to come his way shows that mechanisms by which the emperor was 'screened from needless routine' were clearly working, as far as Bithynian jurisdiction under Pliny was concerned.[23]

Could it be, however, that it was, contrary to the usual assumption, precisely Pliny's enhanced status as emperor's personal appointee that allowed him to consult the emperor more rarely? This seems unlikely. Two important comparanda relevant for Bithynia are, first, the scant remains of Fronto's speech *On testaments from Asia*, possibly dealing with a case involving Bithynian litigants (*ad M. Caesarem* I.6.2–9, pp. 10–13 van den Hout), and, secondly, for the somewhat later period, a rescript of Severus Alexander to the Bithynian *koinon* concerning appeals, preserved both in the Digest by way of Paul's *Responsa* and in two copies on papyrus (D. 49.1.25; P.Oxy. XVII 2104; XLIII 3106).[24] The former involves issues of private law only; the latter extends to those of capital jurisdiction.

In 143 CE, Fronto found it appropriate to argue before Antoninus Pius against bringing the case under consideration to the emperor's court at all, despite both parties evidently being Roman citizens (since a testament under Roman law was disputed). Fronto draws a picture of the state of things that would emerge in provincial litigation if such a decision would be taken as precedent (incidentally, this is an important piece of evidence for the court decisions of the emperors having the force of precedent) and of delays that would arise out of the reluctance of the party with the weaker legal position to leave the province and go to Rome: 'for he is not stupid enough to go to Rome and lose instead of staying in Asia and remaining in possession'.[25] It is clear that the case had already been reviewed by the proconsul and *possessio* granted to one of the parties while the appeal to the emperor was pending.[26] A long list of possible seasonal excuses for delay is ironically reviewed, and it is evident from Fronto's openly sarcastic attitude that encouragement of such appeals to Rome was not supposed to be common practice in his time.

[23] Lewis (1976), 163, for this phrase. By way of comparison, of 568 surviving legal petitions in Egypt only one was addressed to the emperor (P.Coll.Youtie II 66, with Kelly (2012), 79; note also P.Harr. I 67, a *subscriptio* of Pius, and now possibly Benaissa (2018), 61–72 no. 2). A classic statement of the case for the necessity of most of Pliny's consultations is Sherwin-White (1966), 546–55, whose arguments I attempt to amplify here. This need not imply any attempt to idealize Pliny, as I shall try to show further below: a Roman governor exercising jurisdiction effectively within his own terms of reference is hardly a universally admirable figure and we need not be deceived by the aura of benevolence.

[24] Cf. van den Hout (1999), 27, and 423–4, on the possible identity of the speeches *de Asianis testamentis* and *pro Bithynis* (as assumed in a marginal manuscript note to *ad amicos* 1.14.2, p. 180 van den Hout). For the text of the rescript of Severus Alexander, see also Oliver 1989, no. 276A–B and App. 12; cf. on it Kantor (2009), 256–8, with earlier bibliography.

[25] Fronto, *ad M. Caesarem* 1.6.4 (p. 11 van den Hout): *non ille ita stultus est ut malit uenire ad Caesarem et uinci quam remanere in Asia et possidere*. On the value of the emperor's decision as a precedent, stressed by Fronto, see now Tuori (2016), 215 and 220.

[26] So, rightly, van den Hout (1999), 27–9.

The rescript of Severus Alexander, on the contrary, is concerned precisely with improper attempts by the governors to prevent appeals by intimidating the litigants or arresting them, and reasserts the principle of the emperor's personal care for 'the liberty of the governed' (τῆς τῶν ἀρχομένων ἐλευθερίας); the tantalizingly fragmentary sentence preserved only in the papyrus version shows, however, that governors were supposed to perform some kind of verification over appeals in capital cases (P.Oxy. XVII 2104, ll. 15–18; XLIII 3106, ll. 9–11). The situations envisaged by Fronto and in the Severan rescript are obviously different, but it is clear from both texts that Bithynian governors exercised a very considerable measure of control over the process of contacting the emperor and were hardly encouraged to involve him frivolously.

This constitutes a strong reason to think that Pliny was not to any significant degree different in that respect from other governors of the province and the picture of the emperor's relative lack of involvement in his jurisdiction was fairly typical. Nor, despite Trajan's own connexion of Pliny's mission with the need for reforms in the province, is there a need to assume either that Pliny's *mandata* contained much that was new specifically in the sphere of jurisdiction (which does not figure in his references to *mandata*), or that *repetundae* trials of recent governors implied closer supervision of that sphere by the emperor.[27] The recent publication of a honorific inscription dated to the governorship of Varenus (*SEG* LXII 978 = *An. Ép.* 2012, no. 1419), besides demonstrating the correct form of his name, Rufius Varenus, firmly put his governorship in 102/3 CE, rather than in 105/6 CE, as had been widely assumed.[28] Pliny's appointment, at least five years after Varenus' trial on this new chronology, could not have been a direct reaction to the case itself or to the alleged excessive number of Bithynian *repetundae* cases: the seven known trials were spread over a century from 15 CE, and Trajan did not have Brunt's chronology of extortion trials in front of him.[29] If an immediate explanation for Pliny's appointment is needed, it is probably to be sought in the untimely death of his proconsular predecessor providing a need for an *extra sortem* appointment, and imperial concerns as revealed by the correspondence have more to do with finance and civic administration.[30]

[27] Pliny, *Epistulae* 10.32: *Meminerimus idcirco te in istam prouinciam missum, quoniam multa in ea emendanda adparauerint.* For references to Trajan's *mandata*, 10.56, 10.96, and 10.110, with Fournier (2010), 285–7.

[28] Full discussion of the new evidence in an online paper by C. P. Jones, https://www.academia.edu/22452301/Rufius_Varenus_and_Pliny_Ep._5.20.1_online. See now also Mitchell (2017), 808.

[29] Explanation of Pliny's appointment by Bithynian *repetundae* cases offered already by Hardy (1889), 48. Most recently in Corke-Webster (2017b), 378–9, who is not yet aware of the Rufius Varenus inscription; note also Griffin (2018), 294 (more cautiously). There is no reason to assume, as Corke-Webster does, that P. Servilius Calvus (*PIR*[2] S579), known only from Pliny, *Epistulae* 10.56–7, was Pliny's immediate predecessor. Though Calvus was probably indeed 'responsible for some ambiguous sentencing', Trajan's reply, promising to ask him personally for the reasons behind his amnesty edict, clearly implies that he was neither under prosecution nor in disgrace with the emperor. For *repetundae* cases by province, Brunt (1990), 90–5. As noted by Levick (1979), 125, 'Asia was not far behind with five'; the same number for Africa, Baetica, and Crete-Cyrenaica—if we had Tacitus' narrative for the Flavian period the totals could easily change.

[30] Cf. Sherwin-White (1966), 582. As he points out, it is notable that the detailed correspondence concerning Pliny's arrival (*Epistulae* 10.15–18) makes no reference to the absence of his predecessor, legally obliged to wait for him in the province (*D.* 1.16.10 pr), and that Pliny's arrival on 17 September

2. THE IMPORTANCE OF BEING EARNEST

Important conclusions for our theme follow from the argument above. While on the one hand it implies that Pliny's correspondence can indeed be taken as representative of two relatively typical years of Pontic-Bithynian jurisdiction, on the other we need to admit that it gives only a top slice of what even the governor's jurisdiction was and cannot provide us with a genuine insight into a Bithynian assize session, let alone with a broader picture of the judicial scene in the province. This imposes limitations on our uses of his evidence, but it also provides opportunities. What we can find out from it is what kind of cases deserved this kind of special treatment, and to what extent what we might consider as difficulties of law (rather than status of the parties or needs of publicity) were involved either in their selection or in their handling by Pliny. Insofar as only an extremely small percentage of the cases was dealt with this way, any decision to kick a problem upstairs and in which particular way to do so should have been a very deliberate one for him. It will not come as a revolutionary conclusion that both aspects were involved; more nuance, however, seems to be possible.

I shall begin with a well-known case which illustrates neatly the problems inherent in high profile litigation: that of the accusation advanced against Dio Chrysostom by Eumolpus, the advocate of his political opponent Flavius Archippus, during Pliny's *conuentus* session at Prusa.

> 'While I was attending to official business, sire, in my lodgings (*intra hospitium*) at Prusa by Olympus, on the same day that I was intending to leave, the magistrate Asclepiades reported that an appeal had been made to me by Claudius Eumolpus. When Cocceianus Dio at a session of the council (*in bule*) requested that a building, the supervision of which he had undertaken, should be handed over to the city, at that moment Eumolpus, acting as counsel for Flavius Archippus, said that the accounts of the building should be demanded from Dio before it was transferred to the community, because he behaved otherwise than he ought to have done (*quod aliter fecisset ac debuisset*). He further added that your statue had been placed in the same building as well as the bodies of persons who had been buried, the wife and the son of Dion, and he requested that I should take a formal enquiry into the case (*postulauitque ut cognoscerem pro tribunali*). When I had said that I will do so at once and that I would postpone my departure, he asked me to give him a longer period to put his case together, and to hold the hearing in another city. I answered that I would hear the case in Nicaea. When I had taken my place on the bench there in order to hold the hearing (*ubi cum consedissem cogniturus*), this same Eumolpus began to apply for an adjournment on the grounds that he was not fully prepared, while Dio in response demanded that the case should be heard. Many things were said on either side, also about the case (*etiam de causa*).'[31]

implies a departure from Rome considerably later than required by the standard proconsular calendar (on which see Barnes (1971), 260–1; Bérenger-Badel (2003), 77–9).

[31] Pliny, *Epistulae* 10.81.1–4. Transl. here and elsewhere Williams (1990), with minor adjustments, particularly in legal terminology. The fullest treatment remains Sautel (1956), with good discussion of the connexion of the charges to Roman law on *pollicitatio*, and to the prohibition of burial within city boundaries (*Pauli Sententiae* 1.33.2 Liebs); contrast Jones (1978), 192 note 87, for the tradition of intra-urban burial of Greek civic elites; see on it now more broadly Schörner 2014. I cannot quite accept Sherwin-White's view (1966), 678 that Pliny 'is not satyrical'.

Pliny goes on to stress that Eumolpus and Archippus have not provided the *libelli* he requested, while Dio supplied his as requested, which Pliny forwards. It would initially seem that the governor duly receives the reply from the emperor reasserting the stance he has taken:

> 'You could have been in no uncertainty, my dearest Secundus, about that matter on which you decided that I should be consulted, since you were very well aware of my determination not to obtain respect for my name through inspiring men with fear or terror or through charges of treason. Accordingly that charge which I should not allow even if it were supported by the precedents (*etiam si exemplis adiuuaretur*) should be dropped; rather let the accounts of the building carried out under the supervision of Cocceianus Dio be examined, since the interest of the city requires it and Dio does not object, nor ought he to object' (Pliny, *Epistulae* 10.82).

While legitimate doubts about Dio's legal position have been raised in modern scholarship, the way Pliny frames the whole situation has not yet received enough attention.

It has been widely accepted that the central element of the case for Pliny and Trajan was the *maiestas* charge, with its Tiberian undertones and a possibility of creating precedent: 'Pliny's major worry is not the public accounts, but the potentially treasonable act of having placed the emperor's statue near a grave'.[32] No doubt this is where Pliny would like to focus the emperor's (and our) attention, but we need not follow him. That far into Trajan's principate the emperor's standing policy on this kind of *maiestas* cases would have been well known to the imperial elite. Even though Pliny very probably aims at providing the emperor with a 'photo opportunity', this does not fully explain the amount of attention he gives to the charge, or indeed the reasons why Archippus and Eumolpus pressed the charge in the first place when their chances of success were slim.[33] The answer, I would suggest, hides in plain sight: Pliny was concluding his assize session and departing from Nicaea (it could hardly be a coincidence that Dio only presented his accounts as the governor was packing his bags). A civil lawsuit concerning the building accounts would not get an urgent hearing, and perhaps even more importantly, would have been delegated by the governor, possibly to one of the judges enrolled at the Prusa *conuentus*, which seems to be something the city authorities and Archippus were keen to avoid (the earlier objection to Archippus being enrolled acquires extra significance in this context).[34] A criminal charge against a Roman citizen, even if dismissed later, guaranteed that the governor will intervene in the case.

[32] Swain (1996), 237; cf. Sautel (1956), 439–40 (with a cringeworthy description of Pliny, "plongé dans une ambience orientale favorable à la divinisation du souverain"); Sherwin-White (1966), 678–9; Williams (1990), 130.

[33] "From a purely legalistic perspective, the behaviour of the main characters may seem inexplicable" (Bekker-Nielsen (2008), 134). The role of Eumolpus, who went out of his way to stress that he was acting on instructions, is important for the Roman context of the trial, and his emphasis on his particular role need not imply that he had cold feet; compare Czajkowski (2017), 88–106, on the agency of legal advisers.

[34] For the conflict between Archippus and Dio, see Desideri (1978), 401–6; Jones (1978), 114; Bekker-Nielsen (2008), 133–6; and above all, Kokkinia (2004). The suggestion of Sautel (1956), 442, that Dio could be one of Archippus' anonymous accusers in *Epistulae* 10.58, is plausible, if inevitably unprovable.

The tactic backfired, at least partly, whether because Pliny did not appreciate being corralled into an ongoing local feud, or because Dio's lobbying with him had already been successful. It is notable that his adjournment to the next *conuentus* was distinctly favourable to Dio: in order not to lose their case by default, Archippus and Eumolpus had to go to Nicaea straightaway to catch up with the governor's movements, and while Dio already had his accounts ready, they were not given any time to prepare the counter-case. Their inability to present the *libelli* immediately does not expose them as vexatious but blundering litigants, the impression Pliny strives to create; it was an inevitable consequence of the time-table imposed on them by the governor.[35] As regards the accounts, where the meat of the accusation case must have been, Pliny zooms in on the incidentals: his own visit to Dio's portico, while resolving the relative position of Trajan's statue and the graves, resolves neither the in-town burial issue nor the allegations of financial misconduct. When the case was framed this way, the decision to dismiss it could be viewed as natural. So it is significant, once we understood Pliny's tactics, that Trajan did not in fact fully go along with them: he ordered Dio's accounts to be produced and examined, and pointedly noted that Dio had not objected to them being produced, something Pliny had not addressed at all.

How much of this is about 'law' at all? On one hand, it is notable that Pliny, who for the most part spares the emperor names of local actors, provides four in this letter, including that of the Prusan archon—the only local magistrate mentioned by name in the whole of Book 10.[36] The reasons, while we certainly need not revive the Philostratean image of Dio as an intimate friend of Trajan, are clearly to do with the 'name recognition' and imperial contacts: the prestige of these particular litigants was sufficient for the imperial involvement to become desirable, and for precision and literary skill in describing the individuals involved.[37] Questions of legality seem sidelined, and it is indeed hardly clear under what substantive law the financial aspect of the trial was to be considered. While Archippus, Dio, and Eumolpus were all three of them Roman citizens, Prusa was a peregrine community, and the initial notice of the trial was served to Pliny by Asclepiades (not a Roman citizen himself), as an appeal, presumably from some kind of a local process. The question does not seem to concern either Pliny

[35] On vexatious litigants, compare Kelly (2012), 287–326.

[36] Contrast e.g. 10.47.1 (official response from Apamea introduced by the anonymised *responsum mihi est*); 10.56.2 ('a man has come to me and informed me that his opponents . . . are still residing in the province'); 10.65 ("there is an important dispute, and one which affects the whole province", but the parties are not named); 10.72 ("certain persons are requesting"); 10.79.4 ("asked what my opinion was by the censors-elect"); 10.83 ("having been requested . . . by the people of Nicaea as a community"); 10.92 (memorandum of the Amiseni); 10.110.1 ("the *ecdicus* of the city of the Amiseni").

[37] Lendon (1997), 201–22, focussing in particular on the slightly later case of Aelius Aristides in the province of Asia, is fundamental on the issue. In Egypt, an imperial reply to a petition was published because of 'the eminence of the petitioner' (P.Harr. I 67, col. II, l. 15). As mentioned above, this forms an important exception to the general disinterest of Pliny in Bithynian culture, noted by Woolf (2006), and so at least to some extent supports the view of the significance of Greek 'intellectuals' going back to Bowersock (1969). It seems clear, at any rate, that the significance of Dio (and, even more so, of Archippus) in Pliny's correspondence is not primarily due to their local role or material resources. On what little is known of Dio's links with Trajan, Jones (1978), 52–4; Swain (1996), 237; few will accept with Desideri (1978), 273, the historicity of Dio's participation in Trajan's triumph as related by Philostratus.

or Trajan very much. Even in the *maiestas* aspect, the discussion seems to focus on the *exempla* (presumably from the proconsular court, as the term is used by Pliny elsewhere), rather than on Roman statute law, and that only to be dismissed in favour of a direct expression of the emperor's will.[38] The palpable power play is about the case being considered at all, and assertion of the emperor's, governor's, and litigant's authority, not about competing rules of substantive law (compare similar pressure applied on behalf of Aelius Aristides, who eventually makes a token appearance in court accompanied by organized cheerleaders: Arist. *Or.* 50.89–92).[39]

On the other hand, the process is hardly a free for all, and the approach is distinctly legalistic in other respects. At least on this high-up level, not only is the conflict played out in the courts, and in a Roman court at that, rather than being resolved politically, but also the tactics used by the parties (including the governor himself) were predicated on the procedural rules of the Roman *conuentus* and appeal system, and involved reframing the legal nature of the case by focussing on its public law aspects. Even though, as argued above, substantive (as opposed to procedural) rules get sidelined in this letter exchange, at least until the last moment, when Trajan resolved that the examination of Dio's accounts should still take place—which is unfortunately precisely the moment at which we lose the sight of the case—we should not lose sight of the fact that the whole argument remains legalistic at its core. Law as shown here is played and renegotiated by the actors in the case as it unfolds, and yet it is about applying (or not applying) rules, and the negotiation happens within a rule-bound framework. As stressed by Jose-Luis Alonso, 'to a discretionary jurisdiction, the law does not appear—cannot appear—as a system of binding rules. No rule is strictly binding, and yet it is law, and applied as such: applied, that is, until some pressing reason of *aequitas* or *utilitas* advises otherwise'.[40] This seems to describe the legal dispute in Prusa perfectly. Notably, general considerations of justice also seem to be the grounds on which the appeal to proconsuls from city council decisions was allowed in an (unfortunately very fragmentary) letter of Hadrian or Antoninus Pius to Nicomedia, perhaps not entirely irrelevantly for Dio's situation.[41]

[38] For *exempla proconsulum* compare Pliny, *Epistulae* 10.68; 10.72.

[39] Kantor (2012) and Alonso (2013) argue the case for hierarchy of authority rather than of rules in Roman provincial jurisdiction from two different ends. See also Benton (2002), 4, on the legal orders of early modern empires as 'patterns of structuring legal authorities'. This chapter treats Pliny's case as an example of that, with important limitations that will be discussed below. For the opposing paradigm of the 'conflict of laws', see above all Cotton (2007). Compare Meyer (2004), 296: 'The empire was the opposite of a constitutional monarchy: rather than the monarch taking its legitimacy from the laws, late-antique law borrowed its legitimacy in society at large from an acceptance of the authority of the emperor.' While the variety of sources of authority in Pliny's Pontus-Bithynia was clearly greater, and not everything here comes back to the emperor, a question to which I shall return in the next section, the similarities in approach will be obvious.

[40] Alonso (2013), 399. Compare the perceptive observations of Davis (2012), 107–8, on institutions (rather than just rules) of recognition in Hindu law.

[41] F. Dörner, *TAM* IV.1 3 = Oliver (1989), no. 94, where *ἡ βουλὴ μὴ δικαίως*, 'if the council unjustly', in l. 5 is followed after a lacuna by [- - - *ἐπὶ τοὺς*] *ἀνθυπάτους ἐκκαλῆσθαι* (= *ἐκκαλεῖσθαι*, Dörner), 'appeal to the proconsuls'; the omission of *ἐπὶ τοὺς* by Oliver is unnecessarily cautious. See on this inscription Fernoux (2004), 261; Fournier (2010), 521; Ando (2014), 14–15 (cf. *SEG* LXIV 1267; adherence to principles of Roman law is not, however, an issue here); for correspondences between

Similar patterns of agency and negotiation are in evidence elsewhere in Book 10. Thus, for instance, in forwarding to Trajan the petition of Apamea (*Epistulae* 10.47), which asked for reconfirmation of their 'privilege and long-established custom of running their community according to their own judgement (*priuilegium et uetustissimum morem arbitrio suo rem publicam administrare*)', Pliny puts his stress on its irrelevance to the disputed issue (*ad id, de quo quaeritur, non pertinere*) and on the universal welcome given to his inspection. Trajan takes his cue in the reply (*Epistulae* 10.48). He refrains from addressing the (in fact perfectly obvious) reasons for which Apamea wanted to re-confirm earlier precedents, limiting himself to stating that Pliny's inspection will take place 'without prejudice to the privileges which they now possess (*saluis, quae habent, priuilegiis*)', leaving the door open for future changes to the privileges.[42] Trajan may or may not have read the whole petition of the Apamaeans; what is significant is that Pliny frames the request in such a way as to guide the emperor to what should have now appeared as the easiest decision.[43]

In a similar fashion, Pliny's letter asking Trajan to transfer to the city of Prusa an apparently abandoned piece of imperial property for building a bath-house and bypass legal covenants put on it (a consecration of a part of the courtyard to divine Claudius and conditions made in the will of Claudius Polyaenus, its last private owner), he evades some of the significant legal issues while directing the emperor's gaze elsewhere (*Epistulae* 10.70). It is not clear from his report of the situation why the income from the property accrued to the city rather than to the *fiscus*, a somewhat unusual arrangement, but the stress on its unprofitability for the treasury should have encouraged the emperor in the right direction; it is equally unclear (as Trajan points out in his reply) whether the consecration took place, but Pliny does stress that the existing copy of the will is faulty and that the movables mentioned in the will have disappeared—clearly it is not something that the emperor should take too seriously. He is not as successful on this

the Greek and the Latin terminology, Laffi (2010), 68–9. The suggestion that this might be a proconsular rather than an imperial letter, raised by Fernoux and Fournier, seems improbable to me: a proconsul would be extremely unlikely to bind his successors by a general reference to 'the proconsuls', and would tell the petitioners to 'appeal to me'. Given that the document deals with people who unjustly raise prices, it was probably issued in the aftermath of a famine or another crisis (the earthquake under Antoninus Pius, mentioned in Cassius Dio 70.4.1, may be too late for Pontus-Bithynia still being a proconsular province, see now Jones 2018 for the date; for an earthquake under Hadrian, see Fernoux (2004), 258). The appeal procedure may not, however, be standard, and could be reserved for a specific class of cases.

42 For the motivations of the Apameans, we may compare the care taken at Aphrodisias to not set a precedent when inviting proconsuls to the city (*A&R* nos. 16 and 48), on which cf. Kokkinia (2008), 52–3; on the *ius Italicum* of Apamea, see Ulpian in D.50.15.1.10, and note 67 below. Apamea's status is now discussed more broadly by Blanco-Pérez (2015) and Guerber (2017); the former is more persuasive on the Greek dimension of Apamean polity, perhaps deliberately ignored by Pliny. For Pliny 'constantly coping with attachments', cf. Coleman (2012), 212.

43 Sherwin-White (1966), 631, for the view that Trajan may not have read the *libellus*; Williams (1990), 107, stresses the possibility of future disputes. I am not as convinced as he is that this is clear evidence for the response not being prepared by a 'civil servant': imperial advisers may well have been just as prepared to kick the can down the road as the emperor himself. For reframing the scope of a similar request, compare I.Eph. II 217, a striking third-century response to a petition of Ephesus for re-confirmation of its privileges, addressing the city for older privileges to what is included in the *De officio* treatises by Ulpian (a new and considerably modified text is being prepared by Denis Feissel).

occasion: Trajan's reply (*Epistulae* 10.71) is not only vague as to the actual request, but importantly takes a stance on the consecration of the plot to Claudius at odds with a general principle earlier enunciated by himself (and agreeing with dogmatic claims of Roman jurists and land-surveyors) that 'land in a peregrine community is incapable of being consecrated in accordance with our law'.[44]

Similar considerations govern the rhetorical strategies in Pliny's famous missive on the question of capital jurisdiction concerning Christians (*Epistulae* 10.96), as it has long been recognized, and has recently been brought into focus anew in Corke-Webster's seminal contribution to the debate. Ultimately he is not negotiating the question as one which needs to be analyzed in terms of rules, but rather as one to be governed by consideration of prudence, general justice, and support for the governor's authority. Pliny frames the presentation of the situation in such a way as to make unquestionable his execution of anonymously reported practicing Christians on what could only be legally dubious grounds, and at the same time to lead the emperor to consider the release of those who apostasize the logical solution (there could well be a legal argument that the release of the apostates was as illogical as Tertullian later made it be). As stressed by Barnes in one of the most important discussions of the legal aspect of the problem, Pliny's 'letter is designed both to elicit an answer and to persuade Trajan to sanction their release'.[45] Elsewhere, Barnes observes that 'it is unfortunate that Pliny's elegant and decorous language combined with his eloquent plea for Trajan to show clemency <. . .> have blinded many modern exegetes on the precise nature of the legal question on which he sought the emperor's clarification'.[46] I would argue that, whether unfortunate or not, this is precisely the result that Pliny was trying to achieve.

Corke-Webster has argued that 'Pliny, fearing a backlash, writes because he wants formal, physical proof of imperial support that will guarantee his reputation and bolster his authority in future interactions with provincials'.[47] We cannot fully know quite how troublesome the situation was for Pliny (though allowing appeals to Rome against a capital sentence, another issue on which he spends much less time than he might have done, is no doubt indicative of potential problems), but we need not be looking for career-defining trouble, and this captures Pliny's mode of operation more often than just in the Christian case. The need both to reassert the governor's authority and to allow the emperor to show his solicitude for the province remains central, and is connected, as I have tried to show above, with the hierarchy of authority and the rules of jurisdiction (rather than interpretation of substantive law) being at the heart of what both Pliny and Trajan understand by legality.

[44] Pliny, *Epistulae* 10.50; compare Gaius, *Inst.* 2.6–7a; Agennius Urbicus, *De controversiis agrorum*, p. 20.1–20 Campbell. I make my own attempt to unravel the legal issues involved in Kantor (2017). I cannot agree with Williams (1990), 122, that the implication of Trajan agreeing to use the land for the bathhouse, insofar as a consecration to Claudius was not in the way, is that the property will be transferred to the city: if anything, 'we can use . . . for the building of the bathhouse (*possumus . . . ad exstructionem balinei uti*)' is more likely to imply the opposite.

[45] Barnes (1971), 153 n. 2. See now Corke-Webster (2017b). As he stresses, 'Pliny was encouraging Trajan to read back the Christians' later refusal to sacrifice into his initial interactions with them" (Corke-Webster (2017b), 385), thus framing their behaviour as deserving of punishment. I have tried to address the question of governor's judicial discretion in these letters in Kantor (2012).

[46] Barnes (2010), 11. [47] Corke-Webster (2017b), 375.

3. THE *LEX POMPEIA* AND 'THE LAWS OF EACH CITY'

The argument developed above has important and obvious limitations, and I am not arguing here for a world in which the governor's and the emperor's discretion was all that there was to provincial legality, much as some of the exchanges we have discussed may leave precisely that impression. Insofar as we recognize that authority in this scheme could rest not only with individuals but with rules and customs, substantive law would of course continue to play an important role.[48] In particular, as we deal with Pontus-Bithynia, we need to think of the role of the *lex Pompeia*, promulgated by Pompey when the Roman province was first set up, one of the two best attested and arguably also the most comprehensive examples of a so-called *lex prouinciae*, a set of Roman regulations for a particular territorial province, binding beyond and above an individual governor's edict.[49]

The *lex Pompeia*, as revised by Augustus in 20 BCE, remained in force—and, what is more, continued to matter—in Pliny's day and beyond, since we know that some of its provisions provided the basis both for Pliny's consultations with Trajan, and for juristic interpretations.[50] This shows us the governor and the *princeps* in a somewhat different mode from the one we discussed in the previous section, concerned primarily about the interpretation of substantive law. These considerations, however, are more complex than a simple interpretation of the norms of the statute, and involve appellation to other sources of authority. Significant similarities between the two modes can be discovered, and it will be argued here that both of them indeed represent different facets of the same attitude to legality. Before we can address the ways in which the *lex Pompeia* was used in the High Empire, however, we need to concern ourselves with its scope (a somewhat artificial subject division as our knowledge is based on the imperial period interpretations, but still useful for clarity's sake).

As is well known, Pompey was in a position to institute wide-ranging change when establishing the new double province, particularly in its Pontic part, where he set up eleven *poleis* from earlier territorial divisions of the royal period.[51] Evidence of Pliny and the jurists shows that the *lex Pompeia* regulated such matters as citizenship (including a ban on double citizenships within the province), age requirements for council membership, and rules of enrolment in city councils.[52] As Walter

[48] See n. 40 above for the methodological stance taken here. It is not impossible to argue for higher relative authority of statutory law in Italy as opposed to the provinces (contrast the stance taken by Pliny himself in *Paneg.* 65), but this is outside the scope of my argument here.

[49] The best brief introduction is still Crawford (1990), 113–15, but see now Wörrle (1988), 77–100, for Lycia, and Wörrle (2000), 567–73, and Coudry and Kirbihler (2010), for Asia (with important general discussion at pp. 133–8). The other well-attested example of the genre is of course the Sicilian *lex Rupilia*.

[50] Modifications by Augustus: Cassius Dio 54.7.4, with Ameling (1984), 19–20 note 6; Syme (1995), 354; Fernoux (2004), 184.

[51] For historical context, see Jones (1971), 156–62; Mitchell (1984); Marek (1993), 26–41; Kallet-Marx (1995), 323–31; Morrell (2017), 79–80. On the important evidence of Strabo 12.3.1.541C, Mitchell (1993), i.41, is authoritative. For the latest attempt to reconstruct the lists of Pontic cities under Pompey and Augustus, Loriot (2011).

[52] Citizenship: Pliny, *Epistulae* 10.114 (ban on double citizenships); Celsus and Ulpian in *D.* 50.1.1.2 (a child of a Pontic mother having the status of a *Ponticus* 'based on a grant of Pompey the Great'); age

Ameling has demonstrated in an important study, the structure of civic offices in Bithynia in the Roman period was unusually homogenous for a Roman province.[53] The *lex Pompeia* has thus often been seen as a more radical step than taken by the Roman power elsewhere, 'a drastic and premature remodelling'.[54] This, in turn, has been used to explain the legal activities of Pliny (and therefore to counter an explanation of them by any increase in imperial interference in local affairs from Trajan onwards). The legal regime of Pontus-Bithynia could be seen as based primarily on the *lex Pompeia* and on the *exempla* (precedents) of Roman proconsuls, rather than on law inherited from the royal period of other local origin. 'By definition the resolution of consequent disputes or the modification of these rulings could only be legitimately implemented in the provinces by the provincial governor, whether acting autonomously or after consultation of the emperor'.[55]

This broad interpretation, however, has not remained undisputed. Starting from A.J. Marshall's important article of 1968, much of the emphasis in recent scholarship has been on narrowing down the scope of the *lex Pompeia*. Marshall suggested that the famous passage in the second-century *Institutes* of Gaius, telling us as part of his discussion of the *tutela mulierum* that 'a law of the Bithynians, for instance (*ut ecce lex Bithynorum*), ordains that if a woman enters into any transaction, it must be authorized by her husband or full-grown son' is more likely to have referred to some statute of a Bithynian city than to the *lex Pompeia*.[56] Furthermore, Julien Fournier has argued recently that the *lex Pompeia* probably did not cover judicial competences.[57] Particularly if that latter view is correct, then the significance of Pompeian and Augustan provincial regulations in the grand scheme of things would be relatively limited.

Not all arguments would carry equal conviction, however. It is notable that (as Sherwin-White had already argued plausibly in his commentary) Pontus-Bithynia, along with Asia and possibly Achaia, was one of the provinces where provincial *quaestiones* likely existed in the early imperial period, perhaps on a model similar to that known from the Augustan edicts in Cyrene, which would

requirements: Pliny, *Epistulae* 10.79; rules of enrolment: Pliny, *Epistulae* 10.112; 114–15. The fullest recent discussion is Fernoux (2004), 129–46 (whose comparison with the *tabula Heracleensis*, a heterogenous municipal legal collection, somewhat obscures the issues). Contrast Cicero, *In Verrem* II.2.121–5 on the *leges datae* issued by various Roman magistrates in Sicily to regulate civic offices and election to city councils in some cities, and evidently different from the *lex Rupilia*. On the broader question of the Roman role in the change of the institutional model of the Greek city councils, Ferrary (2017), 21–34, seems to me to get the emphasis right.

[53] Ameling (1984), note esp. 30: 'die Verfassungen aller bithynisher Städte sind einander sehr ähnlich; es dürfte schwerfallen eine Gruppe von Städten ausserhalb Bithyniens zu finden, deren Einrichtungen so nah miteinander verwandt sind'. Later regulations for enrolment in city councils in a rescript of Marcus Aurelius and Lucius Verus to Lollianus Avitus (D. 50.2.3.2), briefly discussed by Millar (2016), 70.

[54] Syme (1995), 116.

[55] Burton (1998), 17, discussing the example of Pliny, *Epistulae* 10.78–9.

[56] Gaius 1.193 (tr. F. de Zulueta), with Marshall (1968), 104–7; his view is endorsed by Crawford (1990), 114; Kaser (1971), i. 220 note 36 leaves the question open. On the *kyrieia* of Greek women in the post-classical period, Velissaropoulos-Karakostas (2011), i. 231–8, with further references.

[57] Fournier (2010), 272.

imply jurisdictional arrangements being part at least of the updates of 20 BCE.[58] More conclusively, the undoubted concern of the *lex Pompeia* with citizenships and personal statuses, including the ban on double citizenships (however inefficient it became in the long run) and possible establishment of subordinate statuses of *Bithyni* and *Pontici* for rural populations without *polis* citizenships, could hardly be entirely unconnected from the crucial question of the cities' rights over non-citizen residents and thus jurisdiction.[59] The position of any permanent non-citizen population in the countryside would have particularly required immediate regulation; while the question of non-citizens seems to have been left to the governor's discretion in the Sicilian *lex Rupilia* (Cic. *Verr.* II.2.32), one would expect greater clarity where the statuses were instituted by Roman authority in the first place. These issues may have needed regulating again in the second century CE, as a fragmentary constitution of Hadrian from Nicomedia suggests.[60]

On the other hand, a few pieces of evidence in Pliny may further support Marshall's view that private law was left out of the purview of the *lex Pompeia*. The rights of Nicaea to intestate property, conceded by Augustus (Pliny, *Epistulae* 10.83–4), may have gone back to the family inheritance law (*ἀγχιστικὸς νόμος*) of Mithridates VI, as we know from the confirmation of similar privileges in a rescript of the Bosporan king Aspourgos to the city of Gorgippia in 15/16 CE.[61]

[58] Pontus-Bithynia: Pliny, *Epistulae* 10.58.1 (Pliny enlisting judges) and Dio Chrysostom, *Orationes* 40.10 (assize status meaning the right to 'judge ourselves' for Prusa), with Sherwin-White (1966), 639–40. A reference to 'cities subject to the court of the Nicomedians' in Dio Chrysostom, *Orationes* 38.26 (*τὰς πόλεις τὰς συντελούσας τὸ παρ' ἐκείνοις δικαστήριον*) may also be relevant, though it may refer just to the assize session. Asia: ILS 6286, ll. 7–8; 7789, ll. 6–8; I.Didyma 272, l. 19; IGRR IV 618, l. 14; Phil. VS 1.22.524. Achaia: IG V.i 541, ll. 17–19; and now SEG LVIII 330, a crucial piece of evidence. For a possible imitation of these arrangements at Chersonesus in Tauris under Trajan (which was in my view likely to have been taken over from the provincial rather than Italian practice), see SEG LXI 607.

[59] Double citizenships: Fernoux (2012) and Jones (2012). An argument for a special subordinate status of the *Bithyni* has been advanced by Jones (1971), 160–1, on the basis of a reference in I.Prusias 17, ll. 13–14 and 19–21, to a dichotomy between 'those on the register' (*τοῖς ἐνκεκριμένοις*) and the 'inhabitants of the countryside' (*τοῖς τὴν ἀγροικίαν κατοικοῦσιν*), and a mention in Dio Chrys. *Or.* 38.26 of the 'tithes of the Bithynians'; cf. also W. Ameling, I.Prusias, pp. 78–9. This was a tax clearly distinct from the Roman *tributum* mentioned earlier in the same section (cf. Heller (2006), 154), which would support Jones's interpretation. For the view that the *Pontici* of D.50.1.1.2 are a parallel lower status rather than citizens of Pontic cities, Marshall (1968), 107–9; contrast, however, Greg. Thaum. *Can.* 7 (*PG* 10.1040), where the term *Ποντικοί* clearly designates any inhabitants of the province. It is interesting in this context that it might have been worthwhile to note one's citizen status within your own city's territory: cf. SEG LXIII 1026, a dedication to Zeus Kersoullos, made on account of Trajan's victory by Asclepiades and Papas, sons of Papas, citizens of Prusa (*πολῖτε Προυσα<έ>ων*), with the comments of the *edd. pr.* (Battistoni and Rottenhöfer (2013), 103–4) on the vexed question of borders in that area. Note, however, that this is clearly not the way in which the terms *Bithyni* and *Pontici* were ever used by Pliny.

[60] TAM IV.1 5 (=Oliver (1989), no. 93), arguably concerning resident foreigners (l. 11: *ὅτι ξέ[ν - - -]*), with Fernoux (2004), 260–1. Contrast the emperor's concern with *ευανδρεί[α]* (l. 6) with the *ὀλιγανδρία* at Chersonesus in the same period (SEG LV 838 = LXI 607, l. 2).

[61] SEG XLVI 940, bl. A, ll. 9–10: *δοκιμάζω ε̣ἰς τὸ λοιπὸν τὰς κ[λ]ηρονομία[ς] | μένειν αὐτοῖς βεβαίως κατὰ τὸν Εὐπάτορος ἀνχισ̣τ̣ευτικὸν νόμον*, with Saprykin (1991) (in Russian, summary in SEG XLI 614), who does not make a connection with Pliny's evidence. On the rules governing *ἀγχιστεία* in Hellenistic royal legislation, see Velissaropoulos-Karakostas (2011), i. 324–30; ii. 482–3, with further references; see also Robert (1963), 472–3, on the rights of the city of Hanisa in the kingdom of Cappadocia in an intestacy case. For differing views on the involvement of the imperial *fiscus*, Sherwin-White (1966), 680–1; Millar (1977), 159–60 and 397.

Nor was there any rule Pliny could discover dealing with the rights of the so-called θρεπτοί, 'foundlings' (Pliny, *Epistulae* 10.65), and the documentation adduced by him in the letter to Trajan consisted largely of a dossier of imperial letters to governors of and communities in the province of Achaia, the relevance of which to the situation in Bithynia becomes an important question.[62] A particularly illuminating piece of evidence is, however, Pliny's letter to Trajan concerning the rights of cities in enforcing debts, clearly not covered by the *lex Pompeia* or the Augustan regulations either.

> 'I ask, sire, that you write back about what rights you wish the cities both of Bithynia and of Pontus (*et Bithynicas et Ponticas*) to have in recovering sums of money which are owed to them from leases or from sales or for other reasons. I have discovered that the right of prior claim was granted to them (*concessam iis protopraxian*) by very many of the proconsuls, and that this has come to have the force of law. I think, however, that by your forethought some rule ought to be decided upon and laid down through which their interests may be safeguarded forever (*in perpetuum*). For the practices which have been introduced by them, even though they may not have been wisely conceded, are nevertheless short-lived and precarious (*breuia tamen et infirma sunt*), if your authority does not uphold them'.[63]

All of this brings us back to the problem of dealing with multiple legal authorities, and to the role of the emperor in their hierarchy: the stress on precariousness of proconsular decisions is particularly significant. Trajan's reply is even more important for our purpose. Rather than introducing or endorsing specific rules, the emperor rules that the rights of the community 'should be determined in accordance with the law of each city (*ex lege cuiusque animaduertendum est*)', which is interestingly different from the proconsular concessions emphasized by Pliny. The application of statutory law and the weighing of authority that we addressed in the previous section come together here. And while here we are dealing with a range of individual proconsular and local decisions, Pliny's mode of action in cases involving the *lex Pompeia* itself was in crucial respects similar, as his attempt to come to grips with the double citizenship problem and membership of the city councils demonstrates.

> 'Under the Pompeian law, sire, the Bithynian cities are allowed to enrol any persons they choose as citizens (*adscribere sibi quos uellent ciues*), provided that none of them come from those cities that are in Bithynia. In the same it is laid down (*sancitur*) for what reasons men may be expelled from a senate by censors. And so some of the censors decided that they should consult me about whether they ought to expel a man who came from another city. I myself, because the law, although it forbade a foreigner to be enrolled as a citizen, yet did not order a man to be expelled from a senate for that reason, and because, moreover, I was assured that in every city there were many councilors from other cities and that the result would be that many men and many cities would be thrown into confusion by that part of the law which had long since become a dead letter by a kind of general agreement (*consensu quodam*), thought it

[62] Kantor (2009), 260–1, with references to earlier literature.

[63] Pliny, *Epistulae* 10.108. The rights appear to be rights more considerable than in other provinces: see Sherwin-White 1966, 717, for a discussion of legal evidence; cf. Kaser (1971), i. 185 n. 1, for further bibliography.

necessary to consult you about what course you think should be followed. I have appended the chapters of the law to this letter (*capita legis his litteris subieci*)'.[64]

While on the one hand, Pliny ends the letter with a reference to particular chapters of the law, the question does not ultimately rest just on their interpretation, but, once more, on weighing of relative authorities, in this case of long-standing practice as against the potentially obsolete statute. This is, as is well known, a question that seriously concerned Roman jurists, from the classical period to the mediaeval glossators. Pliny, however, does not assume that there is any firm 'secondary rule' (in H.L.A. Hart's terms) such as in the classic passage of Salvius Julianus, only marginally later in date than his correspondence, establishing a hierarchy of 'written statutes' (clearly local in the original context), 'customs and usage' (similarly local), and 'law used in the city of Rome' in default of both.[65]

This raises a further question. The difference between Pliny and Salvius Julianus can certainly be taken to show that Pliny belonged to the period before any such hierarchical relationship became firmly settled and the imperial state was thus fully able to 'produce a monopoly on legal authority or on the assignments of political and legal identity'.[66] Should we, however, take a further step? Even without any significant coverage of private law beyond the law of personal status, the scope of the *lex Pompeia* (particularly if, as argued above, it did cover the matters of jurisdiction) was very considerable and its initial impact on the provincial legal landscape could only have been profound. In the almost two centuries between Pompey's departure and Pliny's arrival, however, many developments complicated the picture. Some communities were merged with Roman colonies, as Apamea, Heraclea and Sinope, in the case of Apamea and Sinope followed by a grant of the *ius Italicum*, placing them in some important private law respects outside the province.[67] Others were granted a new treaty with Rome, as Amisus, gaining in the process at least some reassertion of the right to develop their own legislation, even if for Pliny it seems to depend on Trajan's benevolence.[68] Trajan

[64] Pliny, *Epistulae* 10.114. Compare Callistratus, in D.50.2.11, on Severus and Caracalla allowing the Nicomedians to transgress age requirements for the city council because of a 'long-established custom' (*longa consuetudo*). It is unclear to me quite how much significance we should attach to Pliny's preference for sending a copy rather than just a reference to the chapters in question. Does he assume that the *lex Pompeia* is not easily available in Rome, or simply behave as modern email correspondents attaching documents to their message instead of inserting hyperlinks do?

[65] D.1.3.32 pr., arguably dealing only with the cases involving civic office-holding. For late antique developments in the status of custom, see now Humfress (2012).

[66] Benton (2002), 259. Cf. also the important observations of Dresch (2012), 15, on 'the arbitrary assertion of state supremacy' in much of the analysis proceeding from modern law.

[67] Guerber (2017), 191, rightly raises the question of whether the *lex Pompeia* still applied at Apamea. The *ius Italicum* of Apamea and Sinope: D.50.15.1.10. For recent literature on its legal effects, see SEG LXIV 2157. For the status of the colonists, Fernoux (2004), 188–93; Blanco-Pérez (2015), esp. 146–9. The colony at Heraclea probably did not survive into the imperial period: Brunt (1971) 600.

[68] The characterization of Amisus in an inscription of 132 CE as 'free, autonomous, and sharing a treaty with the Romans' (OGIS 530, ll. 2–4: *Αμισοῦ ἐλευθέρας καὶ αὐτο|νόμου καὶ ὁμοσπόνδου Ῥω|μαίοις*) is better explained by the view of Jones (1940), 324 note 67, that a full treaty was concluded under Augustus, than by the suggestion of a less formal status made by Sherwin-White (1966), 688. Situation under Trajan: 'The free and allied city of the Amiseni uses its own laws through the benefit of your generosity (*beneficio indulgentiae tuae legibus suis utitur*)' (Pliny, *Epistulae* 10.92).

himself, when considering the question of permitting associations (*eranoi*), strongly emphasizes the difference:

> 'If the Amiseni, whose memorandum you had attached to your epistle, are permitted by their own laws, which they employ through the benefit of a treaty (*quibus beneficio foederis utuntur*), to have an *eranus*, we cannot stand in the way of their having one, all the more readily if they use contributions of this kind not on crowds and unlawful assemblies, but to support the poverty of the humbler people. In the other cities, which are bound by our law (*qui nostro iure obstrictae sunt*), anything of this kind is forbidden'.[69]

Further complications would have been introduced by the Augustan reforms of 20 BCE, new city (re-)foundations such as Iuliopolis, Caesarea Germanice, Claudiopolis, or Flaviopolis, decisions of individual proconsuls, local custom or (less likely) legislation.[70] Spread of Roman citizenship in the province could bring in new situations never envisaged by Pompey or even by Augustus.[71]

This ought to mean that the Pompeian scheme was turning from a definitive foundational document to just one competing authority among many. And if this suggestion is correct, then, at least up to a point, what we are dealing with in the early Empire is not yet a process of imperial legal consolidation, but rather a centrifugal process of local legal authorities and identities re-asserting themselves through piecemeal change or loopholes in the system, and accepted by Rome (as in the case of double citizens on city councils, or underage councilors at Nicomedia, or of associations at Amisus) for considerations of prudence.

There were, without doubt, other tendencies at play: the most visible manifestation of them in Pontus-Bithynia is the appearance of weights inscribed with the name of the governor from late in the reign of Trajan (it is tempting to connect this precisely with the activities of Pliny and his successor Tertullus, but the series starts later).[72] While this epigraphic practice is paralleled only in three examples from Egypt, and can hardly be taken as representative of a concerted empire-wide centralization drive, it ought to go beyond mere documentary habit.[73] They did not, however, prevail straightaway, and traces of the centrifugal tendency can still be seen considerably later than Pliny, as the passage of Callistratus on recognizing the local custom at Nicomedia demonstrates (D.50.2.11).

[69] Pliny, *Epistulae* 10.93. As Sherwin-White (1966), 688, points out, 'at Amisus, since the city was not originally 'free', the local rules would derive from the *Lex Pompeia*'. This militates against the view (e.g. Jones (1940), 132) that the privileges of Amisus could be limited to the laws enjoyed at the time when the treaty was granted.

[70] Fernoux (2012), 279: in his responses to Pliny Trajan does not cite any new legislation. Fournier (2010), 287, on Trajan re-asserting custom. For possible changes to civic offices in Pontus-Bithynia in this period, Dmitriev (2005), 201–3.

[71] Fernoux (2004), 208–14 on the exercise of Roman citizenship rights (largely general considerations); he traces its spread in Fernoux (2004), 166–7; 174–80; 201–8.

[72] SEG LV 1369–88; LXIV 1269–71 (cf. edd. pr., Haensch and Weiss (2005), (2007), and (2014), for important discussions, and add now Öztürk (2018)), starting in the 18th year of Trajan (SEG XX 786 = LV 1369, more likely of 114/5 CE than 113/4 CE).

[73] Haensch and Weiss (2005), 445, for Egyptian parallels.

4. CONCLUSION: PONTUS-BITHYNIA AND THE TREND TOWARDS LEGAL CENTRALIZATION

The pattern that emerges is, then, a messy one. The legal landscape of Pontus-Bithynia does change in the High Empire, and it would not be believable that this is to do only with patterns of evidence survival (not as dependent on environmental change in Asia Minor as in Egypt) or with changes in documentary culture, important as they no doubt were. What we see, however, is not simply a unidirectional movement towards greater legal uniformity and broader application of specifically Roman law. In parallel with the process of imperial legal consolidation and subordination of local sources of authority to an imperial hierarchy, proceeding from 'politics of legal ordering' at the provincial level, such as studied by Lauren Benton for early modern empires, we can observe a countervailing tendency.[74] Competition of authorities (both rules and institutions) could for a time create not only possibilities for 'inflation of procedures' towards Roman tribunals, but also for greater assertion of local peculiarities.[75] For a time, perhaps precisely up to the point at which we get the evidence of Pliny, this countervailing tendency appears to be prevalent and to go beyond mere respect for ancestral institutions, a consideration which must in fact have played a lesser role in Pontus-Bithynia than elsewhere. Letters of Pliny allow us (though admittedly only for a top slice of very high profile cases) to see both processes at work. They show that, just as recent studies have been putting emphasis on studying 'Roman religion as communication', the most profitable way to study provincial law in action is to see it as communication.[76] And communication, of course, went both ways and should not be viewed primarily through an imperial lens.

REFERENCES

Alonso, J. L. 2013. The status of peregrine law in Egypt: 'customary law' and legal pluralism in the Roman empire. *Journal of Juristic Papyrology* 43, pp. 351–404.

Ameling, W. 1984. Das Archontat in Bithynien und die *lex provinciae* des Pompeius. *Epigraphica Anatolica* 3, pp. 19–31.

Ando, C. 2014. Pluralisme juridique et intégration de l'empire. In: G. de Kleijn, S. Benoist (eds.), *Integration in Rome and the Roman World.* Leiden and Boston, pp. 5–19.

Barnes, T. D. 1971. *Tertullian: A Historical and Literary Study.* Oxford.

Barnes, T. D. 2010. *Early Christian Hagiography and Roman History.* Tübingen.

Battistoni, F., and Rottenhöfer, P. 2013. Inschriften aus dem Raum Keles und Orhaneli (Provinz Bursa, Türkei). *Epigraphica Anatolica* 46, pp. 101–65.

Bekker-Nielsen, T. 2008. *Urban Life and Local Politics in Roman Bithynia: The Small World of Dion Chrysostomos.* Aarhus.

Benaissa, A. 2018. Two Petitions Concerning Civic Magistracies by a Gymnasiarch and Son of a Veteran. *Chiron* 48, pp. 53–76.

[74] Benton (2002), 253, for the phrase.

[75] 'Inflation of the procedures': Fournier (2010), 503–91.

[76] Religion as communication: Rüpke (1997) is fundamental. Compare the observations of Czajkowski (2017), 204–5, on the 'ground-up' approach.

Benton, L. 2002. *Law and Colonial Cultures: Legal Regimes in World History, 1400–1900*. New York.

Bérenger-Badel, A. 2003. Le voyage des gouverneurs à l'époque impériale. In: H. Duchêne (ed.), *Voyageurs et antiquité classique*. Dijon, pp. 73–86.

Blanco-Pérez, A. 2015. Apamea and the Integration of a Roman Colony in Western Asia Minor. In: S. Roselaar (ed.), *Processes of Cultural Change and Integration in the Roman World*. Leiden, pp. 136–53.

Bowersock, G. W. 1969. *Greek Sophists in the Roman Empire*. Oxford.

Brunt, P. A. 1971. *Italian Manpower, 225 B.C.–A.D. 14*. Oxford.

Brunt, P. A. 1990. *Roman Imperial Themes*. Oxford.

Bryen, A. Z. 2012. Judging Empire: Courts and Culture in Rome's Eastern Provinces. *Law and History Review* 30, pp. 771–811.

Burton, G. P. 1998. Was There a Long-Term Trend to the Centralisation of Authority in the Roman Empire? *Revue de philologie* 72, pp. 7–24.

Coleman, K. M. 2012. Bureaucratic Language in the Correspondence between Pliny and Trajan. *Transactions of the American Philological Association* 142.2, pp. 189–238.

Corke-Webster, J. 2017a. The early reception of Pliny the Younger in Tertullian of Carthage and Eusebius of Caesarea. *Classical Quarterly* 67:1, pp. 247–62.

Corke-Webster, J. 2017b. Trouble in Pontus: the Pliny–Trajan correspondence on the Christians reconsidered. *Transactions of the American Philological Association* 147:2, pp. 371–411.

Cotton, H. M. 2000. Cassius Dio, Mommsen and the *quinquefascales*. *Chiron* 30, pp. 217–34.

Cotton, H. M. 2007. Private international law or conflict of laws: Reflections on Roman provincial jurisdiction. In: R. Haensch and J. Haenrichs (eds.), *Herrschen und Verwalten: Der Alltag der römischen Administration in der hohen Kaiserzeit*. Cologne, pp. 234–55.

Coudry, M., and Kirbihler, F. 2010. La *lex Cornelia*, une *lex prouinciae* de Sylla pour l'Asie. In: N. Barrandon and F. Kirbihler (eds.), *Administrer les provinces de la République romaine*. Rennes, pp. 133–69.

Crawford, M. H. 1990. Origini e sviluppi del sistema provinciale romano. In: A. Schiavone (ed.), *Storia di Roma*, vol. 2.1. Torino, pp. 91–121.

Czajkowski, K. 2017. *Localized Law: The Babatha and Salome Komaise Archives*. Oxford.

Davis, D. R. 2012. Centres of Law: Duties, Rights, and Jurisdictional Pluralism in Medieval India. In: P. Dresch and H. Skoda (eds.), *Legalism: Anthropology and History*. Oxford, 85–113.

Desideri, P. 1978. *Dione di Prusa: un intelletuale greco nell'impero romano*. Florence.

Dmitriev, S. 2005. *City Government in Hellenistic and Roman Asia Minor*. New York.

Dresch, P. 2012. Legalism, Anthropology and History: a View from Part of Anthropology. In: P. Dresch and H. Skoda (eds.), *Legalism: Anthropology and History*. Oxford, pp. 1–37.

Dunbabin, J. 1998. *Charles I of Anjou: Power, Kingship and State-Making in Thirteenth-Century Europe*. London.

Eck, W. 1982. Jahres- und Provinzialfasten der senatorischen Statthalter von 69/70 bis 138/139. *Chiron* 12, pp. 281–362.

Eck, W. 2016. The Emperor, the Law and Imperial Administration. In: P.J. Du Plessis, C. Ando and K. Tuori (eds.), *The Oxford Handbook of Roman Law and Society*. Oxford, pp. 98–110.

Fernoux, H.-L. 2004. *Notables et élites des cités de Bithynie aux époques hellénistique et romaine (IIIe siècle av. J.-C.–IIIe siècle ap. J.-C.). Essai d'histoire sociale*. Lyon.

Fernoux, H.-L. 2012. À propos de Pline le Jeune, *Lettres*, 10.114–15: la gestion politique de la double citoyenneté dans les cités bithyniennes. In: A. Heller and A.-V. Pont (eds.), *Patrie d'origine et patries électives: les citoyennetés multiples dans le monde grec d'époque romaine*. Bordeaux, pp. 267–83.

Ferrary, J.-L. 2017. *Rome et le monde grec.* Paris.

Fournier, J. 2010. *Entre tutelle romaine et autonomie civique: L'administration judiciaire dans les provinces hellénophones de l'Empire romain (129 av. J.-C.–235 apr. J.-C.).* Athens.

Griffin, M. T. 2014. The Prince and his Tutor: Candour and Affection. *Scripta Classica Israelica* 33: 67–85 [repr. in M.T. Griffin, 2018. *Politics and Philosophy at Rome: Collected Papers.* Oxford, 707–21].

Griffin, M. T. 2018. Pliny's Letters: Between History and E-mail. In: M.T. Griffin, *Politics and Philosophy at Rome: Collected Papers.* Oxford, pp. 287–95.

Guerber, E. 2009. *Les cités grecques dans l'Empire romain: Les privileges et les titres des cités de l'Orient hellénophone d'Octave Augutste à Dioclétien.* Rennes.

Guerber, E. 2017. La colonie d'Apamée-Myrlea: 'un îlot de romanité en pays grec'? In: C. Brélaz (ed.), *L'Héritage grec des colonies romaines d'Orient.* Paris, pp. 175–200.

Haensch, R. 1997. *Capita provinciarum: Statthaltersitze und Provinzialverwaltung in der römischen Kaiserzeit.* Mainz am Rhein.

Haensch, R., and Weiss, P. 2005. Gewichte mit Nennung von Statthaltern von Pontus et Bithynia. *Chiron* 35, pp. 443–98.

Haensch, R., and Weiss, P. 2007. Statthaltergewichte aus Pontus et Bithynia. Neue Exemplare und neue Erkentnisse. *Chiron* 37, pp. 183–218.

Haensch, R., and Weiss, P. 2014. Weitere 'Statthaltergewichte' von Nikomedeia. Neue Ergebnisse zur Stadt- und Reichsgeschichte. *Chiron* 44, pp. 514–49.

Hardy, E. G. 1889. *C. Plinii Caecilii Secundi epistulae ad Traianum imperatorem cum eiusdem responsis.* London.

Harries, J. 2018. 'Saturninus the Helmsman, Pliny and Friends: Legal and Literary Letter Collections. In: A. König and C. Whitton (eds.), *Roman Literature under Nerva, Trajan and Hadrian: Literary Interactions, AD 96–138.* Cambridge, pp. 260–79.

Harris, B. F. 1980. Bithynia: Roman Sovereignty and the Survival of Hellenism. *Aufstieg und Niedergang der römischen Welt* II.7.2, pp. 857–901.

Heller, A. 2006. *'Les Bêtises des Grecs.' Conflits et rivalités entre cités d'Asie et de Bithynie à l'époque romaine.* Bordeaux.

Humfress, C. 2012. Law and Custom under Rome. In: A. Rio (ed.), *Custom in the Middle Ages.* London, pp. 23–47.

Jones, A. H. M. 1940. *The Greek City from Alexander to Justinian.* Oxford.

Jones, A. H. M. 1971. *The Cities of the Eastern Roman Provinces.* Second edition. Oxford.

Jones, C. P. 1978. *The Roman World of Dio Chrysostom.* Cambridge.

Jones, C. P. 2007. Juristes romains dans l'Orient grec. *Comptes rendus des séances de l'Académie des Inscriptions et Belles-Lettres,* pp. 1331–59.

Jones, C. P. 2009. A Petition to Hadrian of 129 CE. *Chiron* 39, pp. 445–61.

Jones, C. P. 2012. Joys and Sorrows of Multiple Citizenship: the Case of Dio Chrysostom. In: A. Heller and A.-V. Pont (eds.), *Patrie d'origine et patries électives: les citoyennetés multiples dans le monde grec d'époque romaine.* Bordeaux, pp. 213–19.

Jones, C. P. 2018. A Letter of Antoninus Pius and an Antonine Rescript concerning Christians. *Greek, Roman and Byzantine Studies* 58, pp. 67–76.

Kallet-Marx, R. M. 1995. *Hegemony to Empire. The Development of the Roman* Imperium *in the East from 148 to 62 B.C.* Berkeley.

Kantor, G. 2009. Knowledge of law in Roman Asia Minor. In: R. Haensch (ed.), *Kommunikation und Selbstdarstellung: Die Veröffentlichung staatlicher Urkunden auf Stein und Bronze in der römischen Welt.* Munich, pp. 249–65.

Kantor, G. 2012. Ideas of law in Hellenistic and Roman legal practice. In: P. Dresch and H. Skoda (eds.), *Legalism: Anthropology and History.* Oxford, pp. 55–83.

Kantor, G. 2017. Property in land in Roman provinces. In: G. Kantor, T. Lambert and H. Skoda (eds.), *Legalism: Property and Ownership.* Oxford, pp. 55–74.

Kaser, M. 1971. *Das römische Privatrecht.* Second Edition. 2 vols. Munich.

Kelly, B. 2012. *Petitions, Litigation, and Social Control in Roman Egypt*. Oxford.
Kokkinia, C. 2004. The philosopher and the emperor's words: Trajan, Flavius Archippus and Dio Chrysostom. *Historia* 53, pp. 490–500.
Kokkinia, C. 2008. Aphrodisias' 'rights of liberty': diplomatic strategies and the Roman governor. In: C. Ratté and R.R.R. Smith (eds.), *Aphrodisias Papers 4: New research on the city and its monuments*. Portsmouth, RI, pp. 51–60.
Kuhn, A. B. 2012. Herodes Atticus and the Quintilii of Alexandria Troas: Elite Competition and Status Relations in the Graeco-Roman East. *Chiron* 42, pp. 421–58.
Laffi, U. 2010. *In greco per i Greci: Richerche sul lessico greco del processo civile e criminale romano nelle attestazioni di fonti documentarie romane*. Pavia.
Lavan, M. 2018. Pliny, *Epistles* 10 and Imperial Correspondence: The Empire of Letters. In: A. König and C. Whitton (eds.), *Roman Literature under Nerva, Trajan and Hadrian: Literary Interactions, AD 96–138*. Cambridge, pp. 280–301.
Lendon, J. E. 1997. *Empire of Honour: The Art of Government in the Roman World*. Oxford.
Levick, B. M. 1979. Pliny in Bithynia—and what followed. *Greece & Rome* 26, pp. 119–31.
Lewis, N. 1976. Notationes legentis. *Bulletin of the American Society of Papyrologists* 13, pp. 257–70.
Loriot, X. 2011. La province de Pont-Bithynie sous le Haut-Empire: assise territoriale et administration. In: S. Benoist, A. Daguet-Gagey, and C. Hoët-van Cauwenberghe (eds.), *Figures d'empire, fragments de mémoire: Pouvoirs et identités dand le monde romain imperial*. Villeneuve d'Ascq, pp. 257–86.
Marek, C. 1993. *Stadt, Ära und Territorium in Pontus-Bithynia und Nord-Galatia*. Tübingen.
Marek, C. 2003. *Pontus et Bithynia: Die römischen Provinzen in Norden Kleinasiens*. Mainz am Rhein.
Marshall, A. J. 1968. Pompey's organisation of Bithynia-Pontus: Two neglected texts. *Journal of Roman Studies* 58, pp. 103–9.
Meyer, E. A. 2004. *Legitimacy and Law in the Roman World:* Tabulae *in Roman Belief and Practice*. Cambridge.
Millar, F. 1977. *The Emperor in the Roman World*. London.
Millar, F. 2004. *Government, Society and Culture in the Roman Empire*. Chapel Hill, NC.
Millar, F. 2016. Imperial letters in Latin: Pliny and Trajan, Egnatius Taurinus and Hadrian. *Scripta Classica Israelica* 35, pp. 65–83.
Mitchell, S. 1984a. Aphrodisias and Rome. *Classical Review* 34, pp. 291–7.
Mitchell, S. 1984b. The Greek City in the Roman World—The case of Pontus and Bithynia. In: *Acts of the Eighth Epigraphic Congress*, vol. 1. Athens, pp. 120–33.
Mitchell, S. 1993. *Anatolia: Land, Men, and Gods in Asia Minor*. Two volumes. Oxford.
Mitchell, S. 2017. Ruler worship and provincial organisation in the Roman East and the oath of loyalty sworn to Augustus. *Journal of Roman Archaeology* 30.2, pp. 805–10.
Mommsen, T. 1869. Zur Lebensgeschichte des jüngeren Plinius. Repr. in T. Mommsen, 1906. *Gesammelte Schriften*, vol. 1, pp. 366–468.
Morrell, K. 2017. *Pompey, Cato, and the Governance of the Roman Empire*. Oxford.
Noreña, C. F. 2007. The Social Economy of Pliny's Correspondence with Trajan. *American Journal of Philology* 128, pp. 239–77.
Oliver, J. H. 1989. *Greek Constitutions of Early Roman Emperors from Inscriptions and Papyri*. Philadelphia.
Öztürk, H. S. 2018. A New Date for L. Egnatius Victor Lollianus' Governorship in the Province of Pontus et Bithynia. *Acta Classica Mediterranea* 1, pp. 43–51.
Robert, L. 1963. *Noms indigènes dans l'Asie-Mineure gréco-romaine*. Pt. 1. Paris.
Rüpke, J. 1997. Römische Religion und 'Reichsreligion': Begriffsgeschichte und methodische Bemerkungen. In: H. Cancik and J. Rüpke (eds.), *Römische Reichsreligion und Provinzialreligion*. Tübingen, pp. 3–24.

Saprykin, S. Yu. 1991. Evpatorov zakon o nasledovanii i ego znachenie v istorii Pontijskogo tsarstva [Eupator's law of inheritance and its significance in the history of the Pontic kingdom]. *VDI* 197, pp. 181–97.

Sautel, G. 1956. Aspects juridiques d'une querelle de philosophes au IIe siècle de notre ère: Plin., *ad Traian.*, ep. 81–2. *Revue Internationale des droits de l'antiquité* 3, pp. 423–43.

Schörner, H. 2014. Revival of the Intraurban Burial in Greek *Poleis* during the Roman Imperium as a Creation of Identity. In: B. Alroth and C. Scheffer (eds.), *Attitudes Towards the Past in Antiquity. Creating Identities.* Stockholm, pp. 151–62.

Sherwin-White, A. N. 1966. *The Letters of Pliny: A Historical and Social Commentary.* Oxford.

Sigonius, C. 1568. *De antiquo iure prouinciarum libri duo.* Venetiis: Ex officina Iordani Ziletti.

Stadter, P. A. 2006. Pliny and the ideology of empire: the correspondence with Trajan. *Prometheus* 32:1, pp. 61–76.

Swain, S. 1996. *Hellenism and Empire: Language, Classicism, and Power in the Greek World, AD 50–250.* Oxford.

Syme, R. 1958. *Tacitus.* Oxford.

Syme, R. 1995. *Anatolica: Studies in Strabo.* Ed. by A.R. Birley. Oxford.

Talbert, R. J. A. 1980. Pliny the Younger as governor of Bithynia-Pontus. In: C. Deroux (ed.), *Studies in Latin Literature and Roman History.* Vol. 2. Brussels, pp. 412–35.

Tyrrell, R. Y., and Purcer, L. C. 1914. *The Correspondence of M. Tullius Cicero.* Vol. 3. Second edition. Dublin and London.

van den Hout, M. P. J. 1999. *A Commentary on the Letters of M. Cornelius Fronto.* Leiden.

Velissaropoulos-Karakostas, J. 2011. *Droit grec d'Alexandre à Auguste (323 av. J.-C.–14 ap. J.-C.* 2 vols. Athens.

Vervaet, F. J. The reappearance of the supra-provincial commands in the late second and early third centuries A.D. In: O. Hekster et al. (eds.), *Crises and the Roman Empire.* Leiden, pp. 125–140.

Wesch-Klein, G. 2001. Bithynia, Pontus et Bithynia, Bithynia et Pontus: Ein Provinzname im Wandel der Zeit. *Zeitschrift für Papyrologie und Epigraphik* 136, pp. 251–6.

Wilcken, U. 1914. Plinius' Reisen in Bithynien und Pontus. *Hermes* 49, pp. 120–36.

Williams, W. 1990. *Pliny: Correspondence with Trajan from Bithynia (Epistles X 15–121).* Warminster.

Woolf, G. 2006. Pliny's Province. In: T. Bekker-Nielsen (ed.), *Rome and the Black Sea Region.* Aarhus, pp. 93–108.

Woolf, G. 2015. Pliny/Trajan and the Poetics of Empire. *Classical Philology* 110, pp. 132–51.

Wörrle, M. 1988. *Stadt und Fest im kaiserzeitlichen Kleinasien: Studien zu einer agonistischer Stiftung aus Oenoanda.* Munich.

Wörrle, M. 2000. Pergamon um 133 v. Chr. *Chiron* 30, pp. 543–76.

12

Law and Citizenship in Roman Achaia

Continuity and Change

Lina Girdvainyte

1. INTRODUCTION: BETWEEN *GRAECIA VETUS* AND *PROVINCIA ACHAIA*

While the history of independent Greece came to an end in 146 BCE with the destruction of Corinth, and there is some evidence for Roman procedural presence in Greece from that date onwards, it was not until Caesar that *Graecia* was organized as a separate administrative unit with a governor of its own.[1] After Caesar's death, the region was briefly coupled with Macedonia and Illyricum, then detached again in 27 BCE and, together with Thessaly and part of Epirus, organized into an independent public province under the name of *Achaia*.[2] The following history of the province is rather convoluted too: it was governed by an imperial procurator jointly with Moesia and Macedonia from 15 CE, returned back to the proconsuls by Claudius in 44 CE, declared free by Nero in *c.*67 CE, until finally subjected again by Vespasian on the grounds that 'the Greeks had forgotten how to be free'.[3]

It takes little effort to see that the 'old Greece' occupied a rather special place in the Roman thought.[4] Declarations of admiration and respect for the region's

[1] Macedonian governor's judicial activity in Greece: *Syll.*³ 684, discussed below; praetor's tribunal in Athens in the 80s BCE: Poseid. *FGrH* 87 F 36, with Färber (2014), 226; presence of legates prior to Caesar's organization: Cicero, *Pro Flacco* 63. For the proconsular appointment of 46 BCE, see Broughton (1952), 299.

[2] *Graecia* with Macedonia and Illyricum: Cic. *Phil.* 10.26; *RRC* 502.2 (42 BCE); organization of *provincia Achaia*: Strabo 17.3.25; Dio 53.12.4. Although the official name of the new province was *Achaia*, the terms *Achaia* and *Graecia* or *Hellas* continued to be used interchangeably: Suetonius, *Claudius* 16.2; Pliny, *Epistulae* 8.24. For discussion of literary and epigraphic sources in this regard, see Corsten (1997), whence *SEG* 47.461.

[3] Nero's grant: *IG* VII 2713, ll. 12–15 (=*SIG*³ 814; *ILS* 8794) from Boiotia; Vespasian's revocation of the grant: Paus. 7.17.4; Philostratus, *Vita Apollonii* 5.41.

[4] See Cicero's *Flacc.* 62–3 for a juxtaposition of the Greeks from the 'old Greece' (*ex vera atque integra Graecia*) and those from the Asian provinces; cf. *Pro Flacco* 60; 100; *ad Quintum fratrem* 1.1.6, 27. For the summary of Cicero's views on the Greek culture, see Zetzel (2003). For Roman attitudes toward the Greeks in general, see Balsdon (1979, 31–9), Gruen (1992, 237–71), Spawforth (2012), *passim*.

Lina Girdvainyte, *Law and Citizenship in Roman Achaia: Continuity and Change* In: *Law in the Roman Provinces.* Edited by: Kimberley Czajkowski and Benedikt Eckhardt in collaboration with Meret Strothmann, Oxford University Press (2020).

DOI: 10.1093/oso/9780198844082.003.0012

history and culture often resulted in preferential treatment of some of the *poleis* under Rome, manifesting in grants of autonomy, liberty, and immunity, regardless of their former enmity toward Rome. A nice illustration is Appian's account of Caesar accepting the Athenians' plea after Pharsalos, yet reproaching them for the numerous concessions they had already received: 'How often will the glory of your ancestors save you from self-destruction?', he asks.[5] Another classic example is Pliny's letter to Maximus upon the latter's appointment to Achaia, *illa vera et mera Graecia*, as Pliny calls it, reminding his friend of its 'freedom' and numerous achievements that make it worthy of special treatment.[6]

To what extent, if at all, did this idea of *vera et mera Graecia* as unique in its freedom and privileged status translate to the judicial administration of *provincia Achaia*? And did stories such as that of the law of the Twelve Tables as derived from the Greeks have any bearing on Roman attitudes toward local laws on the ground?[7] Indeed, dispite numerous proclamations of freedom and autonomy of individual *poleis* and territorial leagues, evidence from Roman Achaia reveals both the continuity of pre-existing institutional and legal mechanisms, and considerable innovation and change brought about by the advent of Rome.

This chapter will explore the extent of legal contact between the 'Roman' and the 'local' in the province of Achaia. I will start by expounding the main changes undergone by local judicial institutions, in relation to the introduction of governor's court and the rise of imperial jurisdiction. A closer look into the accessibility and functionality of local and Roman judiciaries will work to establish the options available to litigants of different juridical statuses, and enable a further discussion of the developments in substantive law. I will then turn to the complexity of legal statuses, and why this matters for any discussion of provincial legal development, particularly in the region consisting of separate more or less autonomous city-states. Finally, I will discuss the matters of substantive law, such as the nature and implications of Roman legislative activities in Achaia, in relation to the extent of and the conditions for the survival of local legislation and legal institutions under Rome.

With this chapter, I hope to demonstrate how not only geographical and administrative features of a region, but also its culture and history could influence provincial legal development, and promote the continuity of local judicial and legal institutions. At the same time, certain developments characteristic of most provinces of the Roman Empire could not escape even the 'old Greece'.

2. JURISDICTIONAL DEVELOPMENTS

Rome's treatment of Greece after the Achaian war presents several important jurisdictional problems. We read of the general settlement of Greece enacted by

[5] Appian, *Bella civilia* 2.88. Cf. Plutarch, *Sulla* 14.5.

[6] Pliny *Epistulae* 8.24.

[7] On the Twelve Tables as partially derived from the Greek laws: Livy 3.31; Pliny, *Naturalis historia* 34.11; Pliny, *Epistulae* 8.24. For the Greek influence on particular Roman laws: Cicero, *De legibus* 2.23, 25, 59, 64; Gaius in D.10.1.13; D.47.22.4.

L. Mummius and the Ten Commissioners who, in Pausanias' words, 'put down democracies' by introducing governments based on property qualification, dissolved territorial leagues, and imposed tribute on communities hostile to Rome in the preceding wars.[8] These measures aside, Mummius followed the earlier examples set by T. Quinctius Flamininus and L. Aemilius Paullus, and declared the Greek *poleis* free.[9] The imposition of tribute onto some communities and confirmation of the freedom and autonomy of others resulted in divergent fiscal and, by extension, juridical statuses throughout Greece.[10]

Though the extent of this 'freedom' is debatable, it is clear that at least some Greek communities saw the events of 140s BCE as an opportunity to establish closer diplomatic ties with Rome. Toward the end of the second century BCE, for example, Rome concluded a treaty (*φιλία καὶ συμμαχία*) with Epidauros, upon the city's request through an embassy.[11] Around the same time, an honorary decree from Troizen in Peloponnese celebrates a benefactor who led an embassy to Rome for the purpose of securing a treaty.[12] Further agreements were concluded with the island of Astypalaia in 105 BCE and with Thyrreion in Akarnania in 94 BCE.[13] Unlike the treaties of the third and the early second centuries BCE, these later ones involve places of minimal strategic or otherwise importance, and have little to do with Roman military action or imminent danger from a nearby aggressor. The fact that nominally free Greek *poleis* continued to request treaty relationships with Rome after 146 BCE, suggests that such status was now perceived as more advantageous than that of a *civitas libera*, particularly for those city-states which had lost the security of local federal structures. Rather than being purely symbolic, a treaty relationship would provide a city with certain tangible benefits, such as protection of territorial rights and possibility to petition the Roman Senate directly and, one might suspect, more effectively.[14] For Rome, such agreements provided a considerable degree of foreign policy control through clauses such as an obligation to maintain the same enemies and provide aid in case of an attack.[15] This secured the pro-Roman stance of local political elites

[8] Pausanias 7.16.9–10. A few years later, 'out of pity', the leagues were restored, fines remitted, and some other restrictive measures waived.

[9] Flamininus: Polybius 18.46.5; Plutarch, *Flamininus* 10; Paullus: Livy 45.18.2–3; Mummius: Dio 21.72 ('declared them all to be free and independent except the Corinthians'), cf. *Syll.*[3] 684 (=*RDGE* 43), ll. 15–16. Compare a dedication to Mummius from Elis, *c.*146 BCE: *I.Olympia* 319 (=*Syll.*[3] 676). On Rome's adoption of the Greek 'slogan of freedom', previously employed by the Hellenistic kings, see Dmitriev (2011), chs. 5–7.

[10] For the territory of Corinth as *vectigalis* and Roman *ager publicus*: Cicero, *Leg. agr.* 1.5; for exemptions in the otherwise taxable Boiotia: *IG* VII 2413/2414 (=*RDGE* 44), end of the second c. BCE; *IG* VII 413 (=*RDGE* 23), 73 BCE; Cicero, *De natura deorum* 3.49; for Euboia: *RDGE* 22, 78 BCE.

[11] *IG* IV^2 1.63, *c.*111 BCE.

[12] *IG* IV 791, ll. 4–5: *εἰς Ῥώμαν ὑπὲρ φ[ιλίας καὶ] συμμαχίας*. On the dating of the decree: Gruen (1984), 738; cf. *SEG* 55.420.

[13] *IG* XII 3.173 (=*RDGE* 16); *IG* IX 1^2 242 with Freitag (2007). For treaty terms in Latin, see *IScM* III 1 (=*CIL* I^2 2.2676, 106–101 BCE) from Kallatis in Thrace, with Avram (1996). For a checklist of all epigraphically attested Roman treaties, see Schuler (2007), 67–74.

[14] Cf. *lex de provinciis praetoriis*: *RS* 12 *Cnidos* IV, ll. 22–4 (100 BCE).

[15] For the best preserved treaties of the sort, see *SEG* 35.823 (=*I.Aeg.Thrace* 168, cf. *SEG* 53.658) from Maroneia in Thrace, and *OGIS* 762 from Kibyra in Phrygia, both dated to *c.*167 BCE. Later dates have been argued for the Maroneian treaty: Gruen (1984), 739 for the mid-140s BCE, and *SEG* 47.1067 for 85 BCE.

responsible for making foreign policy decisions. Although the practice of establishing new treaties disappears from the evidence after Augustus, requests to renew treaty conditions remain characteristic of the diplomatic language under the empire.[16]

The growing network of 'friendship' and treaty relationships between Rome and the Greek city-states in the second and the first centuries BCE resulted in Rome's growing role as an arbitrator in the disputes involving the allied *poleis*.[17] Indeed, one of the most conspicuous jurisdictional changes in the region at this time is the decline of Greek interstate arbitration, practiced since the eighth century BCE.[18] Ever since Rome's increased influence in the region, the Roman Senate was invited, by means of embassies and petitions, to get involved in settling Greek interstate affairs, replacing in this regard the authority of Hellenistic kings and territorial leagues.[19] When delegating such cases to legates or other Greek communities for arbitration, the Senate would sometimes include an instructive formula spelling out the criteria or principles according to which a dispute should be resolved. One of such principles was precisely the entry into friendly relations with Rome, though the extent to which this acted as a sort of temporal terminus or 'limit of legal memory' has been overstated in modern scholarship.[20] Though certainly a departure from traditional practice, the Senate's behaviour was not entirely unprecedented: a close parallel can be found in royal arbitrations, wherein kings' subordinates or representatives acted as arbitrators between the Greek city-states in accordance with the general outlines provided in the royal *diagrammata*.[21]

Nonetheless, the legal implications of the emphasis on friendly relations with Rome found in epigraphic sources of this period resonate closely with what we have just discussed. While the cities or legates appointed by the Senate had the power to establish the matter of law in question upon hearing the testimonies and consulting the evidence, it is clear that being a 'friend and ally' of Rome had become increasingly more advantageous in interstate conflicts, particularly if the opposing party could not brag of the same status.[22] By entering the world of Hellenistic diplomacy and assuming the role of a powerful protector, Rome gradually took over the fundamentally Greek institution of interstate arbitration, and did so chiefly by local initiative. Crucially, then, the disruption of local

[16] Cf. *SEG* 53.659 (=*I.Thrac.Aeg.* 180) from Maroneia, 45/6 CE, with Clinton (2003) and Wörrle (2004).

[17] On *amicitia* relationship in the Greek East, see Badian (1984), Snowdon (2015). Cf. bibliography in http://www.altaycoskun.com/apr/.

[18] For collections of documents: Ager (1996), Camia (2009).

[19] Cf. Marshall (1980), 640; Doukellis & Zoumbaki (1995), 209. The practice itself was not unfamiliar to the Romans, as Bispham (2014), 236–7 makes a compelling case for Rome's participation in a kind of third party arbitration in territorial disputes and internal conflicts within Italy since the fourth century BCE.

[20] See e.g. *Syll.*³ 683 (=*IvO* 52), ll. 52–5, 63–6 (*c.*138 BCE): a territorial dispute between Messene and Sparta, delegated by the Senate to Miletos for arbitration. For recent discussion of Roman instructive formulas, see Snowdon (2014), 429, with a useful summary of earlier literature in n. 27.

[21] Cf. *Gonnoi* II 93 (=Ager (1996) No. 54), ll. 7–10: a territorial dispute between Gonnoi and Herakleion. Cf. Arrian 7.15.4–5; Diodorus 17.113.3.

[22] Cf. Kallet-Marx (1995a), 173; Freitag (2007), 347.

jurisdictional patterns preceded the establishment of the provincial administration by at least a century.

A similar development can be observed in the judicial capacities of territorial leagues, whose councils were often involved in handling quarrels between their member states. The only attestation of such a council (*synedrion*) adjudicating a dispute in the Roman period comes from Thessaly, and records close communication between the league officials and the provincial governor.[23] Though the exact circumstances remain unclear, the most likely scenario is that the governor was approached by the disputing parties and chose to delegate the case to the *synedrion* of the Thessalian league to which the two communities belonged. The league's officials then sought to secure the governor's approval by discussing some matters with him in person (l. 10) and communicating to him the final verdict. Whether the governor's sanction was truly necessary for the validity of the *synedrion*'s decision is a separate question. The eventual publication of the entire correspondence with the governor seems to support this conclusion, though it could equally have been a deliberate decision of the winning party to advertise the governor's involvement in the dispute, thus preventing any follow-up litigation. Richard Bouchon and Bruno Helly, discussing the present case alongside an imperial rescript of Hadrian advising the Thessalian *koinon* of the hierarchy in which cases involving the use of violence and theft ought to be treated, suggested that the judicial powers of the Thessalian league would have been 'fairly wide-ranging' in the imperial period.[24] However, Hadrian's rescript, though addressed to the Thessalians, clearly concerns the court of the governor rather than the 'federal' court of the *koinon*, and thus says nothing of the latter's judicial capacities.[25] Territorial leagues certainly retained a number of regulatory functions, such as control over exploitation of economic resources and taxation, but their role in arbitration gradually became redundant.[26]

Indeed, it appears that, by the early first century CE, most inter-community disputes in Achaia fell entirely under the jurisdiction of Roman authorities. The role of the Senate declined with the Principate, but the petitions for Roman arbitration continued to flow, now directed to the governor as the highest provincial judicial authority, or the emperor, depending on the disputing parties' status and the nature of their quarrel. Interestingly, the occasional imposition of a temporal terminus corresponding to the parties' first contact with Rome is no longer observed in the imperial period, and the disputes are commonly settled by confirming an earlier decision or on the basis of the oldest available evidence.[27]

[23] *IG* IX 2.261 (=*I.Thess.* 1.13), r. Tiberius, with Decourt (1995) No. 13. Cf. *SEG* 45.610. The governor involved was C. Poppaeus Sabinus, the imperial legate of Moesia, Macedonia, and Achaia in 15–35 CE.

[24] Bouchon & Helly (2015), 243. The rescript: D. 5.1.37.

[25] Compare, in this respect, Severus Alexander to the Bithynian *koinon*: *P.Oxy.* XVII 2104 & XLIII 3106, and Septimius Severus' letter to the Lykians (as yet unpublished; the text presented by Gary Reger).

[26] An excellent example of the continuous importance of federal organization under Rome is Hadrian's letter to Naryka (*SEG* 51.641, 138 CE), which mentions the community's participation in the territorial *koinon* of Boiotia as one of the defining features of a *polis*.

[27] Note e.g. Tacitus, *Annales* 4.43.1–3, and the arguments presented to Tiberius in 25 CE by the delegations from Sparta and Messene regarding their ongoing territorial dispute.

As for internal jurisdiction, most cities retained their own judiciaries—civic tribunals, political institutions, and office-holders with varying jurisdictions—which were to act as the first point of contact in disputes between members of their own community. The availability of courts and officials able to exercise jurisdiction could vary between the *poleis*, depending on the status of a community in question, namely, whether or not it had retained or been granted autonomy.[28] That is, of course, not to say that the nature of these institutions remained unchanged and the scope of their jurisdiction was not impaired.

In his recent article, Marcel Piérart linked the prominence of *synedria* as a new type of civic council in the Peloponnese in the second half of the second century BCE to L. Mummius' settlement.[29] A Similar development is attested for Boiotia and other regions which later came to form the province of Achaia.[30] By the first century BCE, chief office-holders and city councils seemingly took charge of the most important decision-making process, as well as legislation and judicial activity. That said, epigraphic evidence of the imperial period attests to the continuous relevance of the popular assemblies in local administration of justice both before and, indeed, after the Antonine Constitution.[31]

James H. Oliver, in his discussion of Roman Athens, maintained that the old courts no longer continued upon the advent of Rome due to dramatic changes brought about by the provincial government.[32] However, some *poleis* such as Delphi, whose constitutions were not meddled with by Rome, display similar restriction of popular participation in the administration of justice too, which suggests that this development took roots already in the pre-Roman period. Other pre-provincial developments such as an increased use of foreign judicial commissions (see below) were no less important.[33] In any case, though epigraphic attestations of the δικαστήρια in the sense of popular jury courts significantly diminish from the first century BCE onward, they do not completely disappear from the record.[34]

Indeed, the well-known letter of Marcus Aurelius to Athens regarding a complicated series of appeals demonstrates a variety of functional courts and office-holders with separate jurisdictions, thus providing some insight into the complexity of judicial landscape of at least some of the Greek *poleis*.[35] The letter also reveals that the prominence of the Areopagos in the imperial period had to do

[28] Cf. Pliny *Epistulae* 10.93 on charitable organizations: *in ceteris civitatibus, quae nostro iure obstrictae sunt, res huius modi prohibenda est.* On the varying levels of autonomy, see Fournier (2010), 397–501, Guerber (2009), *passim*.

[29] Piérart (2013), revisiting an old hypothesis of Guarducci (1932).

[30] Müller (2005), cf. Müller (2014). Cf. *SIG*³ 646, ll. 22–4: *senatus consultum de Thisbensibus* of 170 BCE, explicitly stating that the civic offices of Thisbe could only be held by pro-Roman individuals for the next ten years. Compare Knoepfler (1990) on Chalkis and Eretria.

[31] See e.g. *IG* V.1 1208 (Gytheion, 42 CE), ll. 26–8; *IG* II² 1100 (Athens, *c*.124/5 CE), ll. 46–56; *IG* XII.9 906 (Chalkis, after 212 CE), l. 28, and *Syll.*³ 884 = *IG* VII.2226/2227 (Thisbe, early third c. CE), ll. 6, 8.

[32] Oliver (1983), 57.

[33] For a similar conclusion, see Fournier (2010), 112–37, noting on the continuous functionality of popular courts on Rhodes well into the imperial period.

[34] For Athens, see e.g. *IG* II² 1732–3 (r. Augustus), mentioning ἐπιμεληταὶ δικαστηρίων, and *SEG* 29.127 (*c*.174/5 CE), ll. 7–9.

[35] *SEG* 29.127, *c*.174/5 CE, with Oliver (1970a), Jones (1971), and Oliver (1989) No. 184.

with the Roman sentiment toward and an archaicizing treatment of this age-old institution, no less than with any practical concerns.[36] Outside Athens, considerable penal jurisdiction of local communities is attested for a number of *poleis* too, both in locally issued legal enactments (e.g. manumissions, endowments) and in proconsular regulations.[37] This, together with the prevalent practice of delegation cases to lower courts on both proconsular and the imperial levels suggest considerable clarity in the perception of jurisdictional separation between various judicial organs.[38]

Apart from local judiciaries, the institution of 'foreign judges' (*τὰ ξενικὰ δικαστήρια*) was widely employed in the Hellenistic period for the purpose of internal jurisdiction. Commissions of one or more judges from one *polis* would be invited by another to decide in local cases according to the laws of the inviting city.[39] The cases remitted to them mostly had to do with complaints over delicts, commercial and debt litigation, contracts, and obligations.[40] Sometimes, the state itself was involved, especially in cases over public finance or obligations, which demonstrates a conspicuously wide scope of jurisdiction and authority of these judicial tribunals.[41] Continuous activity of foreign judicial commissions is attested in a number of documents following the Achaean war too.[42]

However, a degree of conformity of the institution of foreign judges to Roman authority is revealed by two decrees from Demetrias broadly dated to the mid-second century BCE, recording that the invited judges from Messene adjudicated the cases in accordance with the decrees and judgements of the Romans and with the laws.[43] The *νόμοι* here must mean the local laws of the inviting *polis* (in this case, Demetrias), while the *δόγματα* and *ἀποκρίσεις* of the Romans may in fact refer to the legal enactments pronounced during the Roman settlements of the region, and any decisions taken by the commanders and the senatorial commissioners in the aftermath of the Macedonian and the Achaean wars.[44] Crucially, again, the inclusion of Roman positive legislation and verdicts in the judicial

[36] Cf. Cicero: *De natura deorum* 2.29.74; *ad Atticum* 1.14.5; *ad Atticum* 5.11.6; *ad familiares* 13.1; Tacitus: *Annales* 2.55 for a forgery case; *Acts* 17:19: Apostle Paul before the Areopagus, etc. Cf. Oliver (1989) No. 173, 165 CE: M. Aurelius on the Areopagos as 'the most respected court'. For discussion, see Geagan (1967), 32–61, Lanni (2006), 78–82.

[37] Local: *IG* V.1 1390 (Messene, 24 CE), *IG* V.1 1208 (Gytheion, 42 CE); proconsular: *Syll.*[3] 884 = *IG* VII.2226/2227 (Thisbe, early third c. CE).

[38] On proconsular delegation, see e.g. Ulpian in *D.*1.16.4–6; *D.*1.16.11–13.

[39] Cf. *IG* VII 21, decree of Orchomenos to the judges of Megara (early second c. BCE), ll. 10–12: *ἐποιήσαντο δ[ὲ] | τὰς κρίσεις κατὰ τοὺς νόμους τᾶς πόλιος Ὀρχομενίων καὶ | κατὰ τὸ διάγραμμα ἀξίως τᾶς ἐνχειρισθείσας αὐτοῖς πίστιο[ς]*.

[40] Robert (1973), 773. [41] Robert (1973), 773.

[42] Béquignon (1935) No. 3 (Athens, end of the second century BCE); *SEG* 50.453 (Tegeia in Arkadia, *c.*100 BCE), etc. For more examples and discussion: Robert (1973), Crowther (2006), Cassayre (2010), and Scafuro (2015). Regardless of the popularity of the institution in the Hellenistic period, Robert's thesis that foreign judicial commissions had largely replaced local civic tribunals prior to the advent of Rome is an exaggeration. Cf. Fournier (2010), 103–4.

[43] Bardani (2013) No. 7, ll. 54–5: *ἐν τῆι δικαστείαι καὶ κεκρικέναι τάς τε δίκας καὶ εὐθύνας δικαίως καὶ κατὰ τὰ δόγματα | τὰ Ῥωμαίων καὶ κατὰ τοὺς νόμους*; ll. 69–70: <. . .> *τοῖς δὲ διαδικήσασιν ἴ|σως καὶ δικαίως κατὰ τὰς Ῥωμαίων ἀποκρίσεις καὶ τοὺς νόμους*.

[44] Cf. *IG* VII 20 (Tanagra) and *IG* VII 21 (Orchomenos), dating to the mid-second c. BCE, which may also be viewed as referring to Roman measures. See discussion in Cassayre (2010), 88–9.

process of foreign tribunals from Messene implies joint application of the local and the Roman rules as early as the mid-second century BCE.

The key question, of course, is whether the institution of foreign judges survived the provincial organization of Caesar and Augustus. While foreign judges continue to be attested into the Antonine period, it is not entirely clear whether the few epigraphic references that we have, indeed, prove an actual continuation of the institution or, rather, reflect the re-emergence in the epigraphic tradition of a by-now honorary title.[45] That said, the disappearance of honorific decrees to foreign judges may well be a result of the reduced importance of inter-*polis* relations and, consequently, less need to advertise them, and not the decline of the institution itself.[46] The lack of conclusive evidence aside, it is not difficult to imagine how retention of this institution would be perceived as beneficial in the eyes of Roman provincial administration. The overarching idea of impartiality of foreign judicial commissions would have reduced the looming potential of civic disturbances and complaints regarding judicial corruption, thus reducing the volume of appeals addressed to the provincial governor.

As for the latter, since Greece did not have a governor of its own until Caesar's organization, some scholars have argued that it fell under the jurisdiction of the Macedonian governor from 146 BCE onward.[47] This view of formal subjection should nonetheless be rejected as unsupported by any direct evidence. Nonethless the activity of legates from Rome in the region in this interim period is well-attested, while the Macedonian governors could and did intervene in the affairs of southern Greeks when requested.[48]

The so-called Dyme affair, dating to a few years after L. Mummius' settlement, is particularly revealing of the situation which followed the Achaian war.[49] The leaders of a civic strife at Dyme enacted 'laws contrary to the type of government (*πολιτεία*) granted to the Achaians by the Romans', and caused a revolutionary movement, burning down the town hall together with all public and private records.[50] The members of the city council (*σύνεδροι*) of Dyme sent a report to the governor of Macedonia, Q. Fabius Maximus, complaining of the disturbances, and asking for his resolution in the matter. The governor, together with his advisory board, passed judgement on the rebels, and his decision was published

[45] *SEG* 11.491 (Sparta, *c*.115–50 CE), ll. 4–5: *δικασταγωγὸς ἀπὸ Σάμου, ξενοκρίτης | εἰς Ἀλάβαντα*; *IG* V 1.39 (Sparta, mid-second century CE), ll. 25–7: *δικ̣[α]|σταγωγὸς ἀ|πὸ Ἀσίας*, cf. *SEG* 11.493, 496, 869. See Fournier (2005) on imperial Sparta. See now Kantor (2016) on dedications to foreign judges at Mylasa, re-emerging at 93/4 CE for several decades.

[46] For inter-*polis* relations in the imperial period, see Mack (2015), ch. 5.

[47] Larsen (1938), 307–11; Sherk (1969), 244; Gruen (1976), 46. See also Accame (1946), 1–14 for the view that a part of Greece was annexed to Macedonia after 146 BCE, while a part remained independent. Cf. Ferrary (1988), 206.

[48] *Syll.*[3] 705 (=*FD* III 2.70), 118 BCE: C. Cornelius Sisenna and the Dionysiac artists. Cf. Cicero, *in Pisonem* 37: Cicero criticizing a statute which allowed L. Calpurnius Piso, the governor of Macedonia in 57–56 BCE, exercise some form of jurisdiction in 'Achaia, Thessaly, Athens, and the whole of Greece'; also, Cicero, *In Verrem* 2.1.44 on Verres' transgressions in Achaia, while in the capacity of a legate. Compare Cicero, *Pro Flacco* 63 for a positive picture of Valerius Flaccus' activity in Achaia.

[49] *Syll.*[3] 684, 144/3 BCE. On alternative dating to 115 BCE, see Crawford (1977). For a full discussion of the inscription, see Kallet-Marx (1995b).

[50] Lines 9–10: *τοὺς νόμους γράψας ὑπεναντίους τῆι ἀποδοθείσηι τοῖς | [Ἀ]χαιοῖς ὑπὸ Ῥωμαίων πολιτ[εία]ι.*

as part of the city's decree.[51] The inscription from Dyme finely illustrates the immediacy of local cities' re-orientation toward Rome, and the growing tendency to approach Roman authorities at hand regarding not only inter-community but also domestic affairs. Needless to say, the jurisdictional restrictions mentioned by Cicero could certainly be ignored when the Roman order (*ἀποδοθείσῃ τοῖς Ἀχαιοῖς ὑπὸ Ῥωμαίων πολιτεία*) was at stake.

This rather *ad hoc* nature of Roman supervision of the Greek affairs in the late second and the early first centuries is curiously reminiscent of the situation of the early second century BCE, when numerous Roman commanders and legates on the ground are found handling not only administrative but also legal matters, making decisions over property, and meddling with local jurisdictions.[52] In this sense, the establishment of governor's court in Achaia in the late first century BCE did not mark a major change in the legal landscape of the newly organized province. It did, nonetheless, facilitate access to Roman jurisdiction for the numerous Roman citizens resident in the region since the early second century BCE (see below). At the same time, the position of the governor as the highest provincial judicial authority prompted recourse to Roman jurisdiction by the locals who wished to bypass indigenous courts.[53]

Julien Fournier has recently attempted to reconstruct a judicial assize system in Achaia, the existence of which is often assumed on the basis of parallels with the better-documented Eastern provinces.[54] However, there are no straightforward attestations of a judicial *conventus* (*διοίκησις, ἀγορὰ δικῶν*) for the province of Achaia.[55] Cicero's correspondence with Sulpicius Rufus, the first governor appointed by Caesar, alludes to the governor's travel from Athens to Boiotia due to judicial obligations, though it is perhaps best explained by Boiotia's taxable status, as some disputes would inevitably arise from fiscal obligations.[56] Nonetheless, this and similar pieces of evidence that we gather of the governors' travels make it clear that they moved around the province, and could be approached with requests to administer justice in more than one locale. Whether or not Achaia constitutes an exception to most other Eastern provinces—perhaps due to the numerous *civitates liberae*, which were, strictly speaking, outside the governor's jurisdiction—remains an open question, but one which does not modify the

[51] Note that one of the conspirators was ordered by Maximus to appear before the peregrine praetor in Rome (ll. 23–7). It is noteworthy, too, that the governor did not travel to Dyme, but heard the case and passed judgement at Patrai (l. 11), which shows the governor's presence south of the perceived bounds of *provincia Macedonia*.

[52] Decisions over property: *IG* IX 2.338 (Chyretiai, 196–194 BCE); Bouchon (2014): L. Aemilius Paullus' letters to Gonnoi in Thessaly regarding a dispute over confiscated land, where Paullus asks the *polis* to refer any similar cases to him, thus assuming jurisdiction over disputes stemming from his land confiscations (ll. 17–19; 20–9). Compare M'. Acilius Glabrio in *c.*190 BCE, deciding over property and the extent of local jurisdiction at Delphi: *RDGE* 37, ll. 4–5. Cf. *RDGE* 38 (189–188 BCE), ll. 17–20.

[53] Plutarch, *Moralia* 814e–815c; Dio Chrysostom 38.33–48 on Greeks' recourse to the governor in the first instance as detrimental to their autonomy.

[54] Fournier (2010), 88–98.

[55] See the mention of proconsul Gallio at Corinth (*Acts* 18:12), cf. Libanius, *Or.* 1.19. Cf. Suetonius, *Nero* 28, mentioning Nero and Sporus visiting *conventus mercatusque* in Greece. However, none of these allusions proves the existence of a *conventus iuridicus*.

[56] *Ad Familiares* 4.12 (45 BCE): *cum . . . digressus essem . . . , ut ab Athenis in Boeotiam irem reliquamque iuris dictionem ab solverem.* Cf. Fournier (2010), 89.

general picture of the governor's court as the highest judicial instance province-wide, approachable by the provincials, albeit at a considerable cost.[57]

Roman administrative staff in Achaia could not have been very numerous and, as such, was heavily reliant on local office-holders, many of whom were granted Roman citizenship. The lack of personnel contributed to the increasing use of delegate jurisdiction at both proconsular and imperial levels, as well as the extension of judicial powers of some of the other administrative officials.[58] Provincial juries, drawn from both Greeks and Roman citizens, handled some civil and criminal cases too, either as aid to the governor or on their own, by delegation.[59] The governor's *consilium*, drawn from his entourage and enfranchised locals learned in law, was expected to assist in judicial functions as well. Philostratus' *Life of Apollonius* contains an anecdote about a proconsul of Achaia at the end of the first century CE, who was so ignorant of the Greek language and customs that members of his council could easily profit from tampering with justice.[60] On a more serious note, epigraphic evidence carries a number of attestations of these *consilia* (*in consilio adfuerunt*; ἐν συμβουλίῳ ἐγένοντο) used not only by the governors but also by appointed judges and imperial legates sent to handle cases outside proconsular jurisdiction.[61]

In the imperial period, emperors themselves adjudicated certain cases, including but not limited to those involving interprovincial boundaries, territorial rights and privileges of the *civitates liberae*, and Roman colonies. The popularity of the emperor's jurisdiction as a means of securing an ultimate *res iudicata* resulted in the overflow of requests for imperial adjudication, both in the first instance and on appeal. Compare, for instance, the lingering dispute between Koroneia and Thisbe in Boiotia under Hadrian and Antoninus Pius, and Marcus Aurelius' response to numerous appeals from Athens.[62] Unsurprisingly, then, we find a letter of an unknown Roman authority—either a governor or an emperor—inscribed at Sparta in the second century CE, which regulates the process of appeal from civic to Roman tribunals, imposing a monetary limit on regular cases, as well as the need for a previous judgement or pre-judicial ruling in capital cases or those concerning status.[63] The key feature of imperial jurisdiction and, one might guess,

[57] Aelius Aristides (*Orationes* 50) calculated the cost of his request at the assizes of Ephesos at 500 drachmas. Cf. Corbier (1992, 239). See also Cicero, *de provinciis consularibus* 6–7 on the prohibition for provincial governors to exercise jurisdiction *in civitates liberos*: that is, in cases where a *civitas libera* was party to a dispute.

[58] Cf. Burton (1993) on imperial procurators. See e.g. *SEG* 11.778 (Sparta, 102–14 CE), celebrating an imperial procurator for his δικαιοσύνη.

[59] See Fournier (2010), 25–34. A fragmentary inscription from Troizen, dated by the editor to the reign of Caracalla and Geta, refers to a trial by a jury of 100 men, selected by census: *SEG* 58.330, ll. 4–5.

[60] Philostratus, *Vita Apollonii* 5.36.5. For a different side of the same coin, see Valerius Maximus 8.7.6 on P. Licinius Crassus learning the different Greek dialects of Asia in order to give rulings in the same dialect as the petitioners'.

[61] Appointed judge: *IG* IX 1.61 (Daulis in Phokis, 118 CE); imperial legate: *FD* III.4 290–5 (Delphi, 114–17 CE).

[62] *SEG* 42.411 (161 CE); *SEG* 29.127 (*c.*174/5 CE). On the rise and nature of imperial jurisdiction, in general: Tuori (2016).

[63] *IG* V 1.21 II, ll. 5–9. The decree was ascribed to Hadrian by Oliver (1970b; 1979), doubted by Millar (1977), 453. Cf. Fournier (2005) for this letter as originating from a provincial governor rather than an emperor.

the main reason behind its popularity, was that petitions and appeals to the emperor could be made irrespectively of the civic or personal status of the claimant, thus creating an illusion of accessibility and impartiality.[64]

3. COMPLEXITY OF LEGAL STATUSES

Indeed, one of the defining features of pre-provincial Greece and, later, the province of Achaia was its juridical heterogeneity, not only between but also within local communities. The three main catalysts for this development were numerous Italians and Romans resident in or around the Greek communities since the early second century BCE, the foundation of Roman citizen colonies after the civil wars, and the increasing Roman citizenship extension from the first century BCE onward. The notion of people of differing legal statuses forming single political entities is significant for our understanding of jurisdictional matters, as well as those of substantive law.

Coexistence of Greek and resident Roman communities is attested prior to the conquest and, increasingly so, over the second and the first centuries BCE. Though often referred to as *negotiatores* (συν-/πραγματευόμενοι), members of the imperial diaspora within the Greek *poleis* are also found collectively identified as simply residing in town (παρ-/ἐπιδημοῦντες; παρ-/κατ-οικοῦντες) or, more specifically, as owning or having the right to own land (ἐνγαιοῦντες; ἐνκεκτημένοι).[65] These Romans and Italians were involved in numerous activities within the Greek communities, such as buying and selling goods, trading, money-lending, and agriculture, all of which necessitated transactions which had to be performed in a mutually acceptable legal framework.[66] From the late second—early first centuries BCE, resident Romans as a collective body start to appear as active participants in local civic life, conferring honours, sending envoys, and acting as authors or co-authors of civic decrees, alongside the cities and their political institutions.[67]

The variety of identifiers used for these communities of Ῥωμαῖοι, and their distinction in the epigraphic sources from the remainder of the non-citizen population poses a curious problem of juridical status.[68] Indeed, the evidence

[64] See, for instance, *FD* III.4 287–8 (98–9 CE): Trajan's letter to Delphi, promising to personally adjudicate a case of a certain Pythodoros (ll. 5–9). Cf. Aelius Aristides, *Orationes* 26.32–3 on the frequency with which governors consulted emperors regarding legal suits and claims of the provincials.

[65] For πραγματευόμενοι: *IThesp* 373 (Thespiai), *IG* IV 604 (Argos), *IG* V 2.515B (Megalopolis); 'resident': *IG* VII 190 (Pagai), *Achaïe* III 19 (Pellene); 'owning land': *SEG* 17.197 (Elis), *IG* V 1.143 (Messene), etc. See Eberle (2017, 324–31) on the word *negotiatores* changing meaning in the first century BCE: while widely understood as traders or businessmen under the Principate, in the late Republic the term designated the entire Italian diaspora. Cf. Zoumbaki (2013) on the various occupations of Italian immigrants in Achaia. It is noteworthy, too, that the term Ῥωμαῖος/-οι was normally used to refer to resident Romans, Italians, and Italiote Greeks alike, regardless of their possession of the Roman *civitas*.

[66] For discussions of the Roman (Italian) diaspora, see Hatzfeld (1919), Purcell (2005), Zoumbaki (2008), Eberle (2016), Eberle & Le Quéré (2017).

[67] Joint dedications: *SEG* 17.197 (Elis, early first century BCE); *IG* VII 1862 (Thespiai, first century BCE); *IG* V 2.268 (Mantineia, 10 BCE–10 CE), etc.

[68] Separation from other non-citizen residents: *IG* VII 190, ll. 15–16 (Pagai, mid-first century BCE); cf. *SEG* 58.367 (Messene, first century CE).

for integration of some of these resident Roman communities into the civic and legal framework of the Greek *poleis* reveals both a considerable disruption of local legal structures, and the absence of a uniform model for their juridical position throughout Greece. It seems, then, that individual Greek communities retained the right to establish different forms of status for and relationships with their non-citizen populations, including the Romans. The fact that resident Ῥωμαῖοι could evidently belong to different juridical and fiscal categories within the same community only reinforces this point.[69]

On an individual level, the legal rights and privileges within a Greek *polis*, much like at Rome, were closely linked to possession of local citizenship.[70] Greek civic affiliations continued to define local property rights, guarantee protection of law, and confer various economic benefits. It is, therefore, not surprising that, from the early second century BCE, some individual settlers from Italy—surely, the wealthier ones—are attested receiving grants of legal and economic rights in their host communities, e.g. the right to acquire land and real estate (γῆς καὶ οἰκίας ἔνκτησις), immunity from local taxation (ἀτέλεια), access to local courts (προδικία), and even the right to intermarry (ἐπιγαμία).[71] While undoubtedly part of the Hellenistic framework of honour or proxeny, the conferral of these rights was not merely symbolic. Instead, upon proper implementation, they carried real practical value in facilitating the recipients' socio-economic and juridical integration in their host communities.

Around the same time, we find several Romans taking up local citizenships, when the so-called principle of incompatibility of the Roman *civitas* would have still been in force.[72] In addition to πολιτεία grants, people with Roman-type names are attested on ephebic lists, dedications, and funerary monuments, as well as taking up offices confined to local citizenry, all of which point to permanent residence and, not infrequently, citizen status.[73] If successfully implemented—by means of registration and enrolment in the relevant civic bodies—local citizenship offered full access to local courts and legal institutions and, in theory, would have

[69] *IG* V 1.1433 (Messene, *c.*39 BCE), ll. 8, 14. On the date of the inscription, see Migeotte (1997) and Rizakis (2001, 82 n. 100). On procedural matters, see Migeotte (2008). Cf. *IG* XII.4 2.1142 (=*PH* 344, Kos, r. Augustus), ll. 4–8.

[70] For the most recent attempt to compare the nature and qualities of the Greek *politeia* and the Roman *civitas*, see 'Introduction' in Cecchet and Busetto (2017).

[71] Among the earliest examples from the second century BCE: *Gonnoi* II 42 (Gonnoi in Thessaly), *SEG* 52.543 (Amphissa in Phokis), and *IG* IX 12 208 (Akarnanian league), specifying that the privileges to individual Ῥωμαῖοι were conferred κατὰ τὸν νόμον (ll. 8–9). Note also *IG* II^2 907 (Athens, *c.*170 BCE), recording the conferral of landownership rights upon a certain L. Hortensius at his own request (ll. 1–8): [δοκεῖ τῆι] | [βουλῆι . . . δεδό[σθαι] | [δὲ αὐτῶι κ]αὶ [πρ]οξε[ν]ία[ν] καὶ γῆς καὶ ο[ἰ]|[κίας ἔγκτησιν] αἰτησαμ[έ]νωι κατὰ τὸ[ν] | [νόμον.

[72] *Gonnoi* II 20 (Gonnoi, early second c. BCE)); *IG* IX 2.1 (Herakleia Trachinia in central Greece, second century BCE). For incompatibility of the Roman *civitas* as a matter of legal controversy by the first century BCE, see Cicero, *pro Balbo* 28–30; *pro Caecina* 100; Nepos, *Atticus* 3.1.

[73] For attestations of Romans on ephebic catalogues from Messene, see the index in Rizakis et al. (2004); cf. *SEG* 58.367. Romans as office-holders: *IG* VII 2727 (Akraiphia, early first century BCE); *IG* VII 1777 (Thespiai, the first century CE), etc. For Athens, see Errington (1988, 155) and the prosopography of Byrne (2003), who concludes that from the time of their first appearance in the mid-second century BCE to the mid-first century CE, Roman citizens attested in Athens were mainly immigrants, rather than enfranchised locals. On the problems of onomastics in the epigraphical material, see Ferrary (2008) and (2014), 39–70.

subjected its beneficiaries to local laws and obligations. There is no way of knowing whether Roman citizens who took up local civic affiliations considered themselves renouncing their Roman *civitas*, or whether they were simply unaware or neglectful of such legal implications. Either way, it is not difficult to imagine these people, particularly in the pre-provincial period, making full use of the courts of their adoptive communities, as well as the private law rights inherent in local citizenships.

The legal framework within which the resident Romans who retained their *civitas* functioned within the Greek communities is somewhat less clear. Access to local courts, albeit limited to certain types of actions, can be assumed in parallel with other non-citizen residents, as well as their capacity to enter contracts of lease, loan agreements, transactions of commercial nature, and so on.[74] A well-known decree from Gytheion, dating to 71/70 BCE, offers some insight into how this relationship could have functioned. The inscription honours two Romans, Numerius and Marcus Cloatii, identified as holders of proxenic status and benefactors of the *polis* (l. 2), for aiding the city and its individual citizens financially, thus relieving them of various exactions imposed.[75] The brothers, resident in or around Gytheion, had contracted several loans to the *polis* throughout the years, all of which the latter had struggled to pay back.[76] As an earlier loan was remitted by the brothers (l. 8)—presumably, due to the city's insolvency—Gytheion tried to get out of repaying the next one, too (ll. 10–11). This time, however, the negotiation between the *polis*' authorities and the creditors escalated into a dispute and, prompted by a certain Marcilius, went to the Athenian arbitration (ll. 12–13: *λαβόντες ἐπὶ Μαρκιλίου κριτὰν Ἀθηναίων δᾶ|μον*), finally resulting in the brothers' concession to a lower sum.[77]

This particular bit, often overlooked by commentators, is important for our purposes here. Since Gytheion was one of the parties to the dispute, it is not surprising to find the resort to third-party arbitration. L. Marcilius, mentioned in the context of the said arbitration, was most likely one of the legates of M. Antonius Creticus (l. 33), and was responsible for requisitions from the Greek *poleis* in relation to the latter's war against the pirates.[78] Leopold Migeotte suggested that Marcilius exercised some sort of judicial powers alongside those of requisition, and was agreed upon as an arbiter by both parties.[79] While the idea of

[74] Cf. Whitehead (1977), 89–90 on metics in the courts of Classical Athens, and Brock (forthcoming), noting on the status of foreign residents from Archaic to Hellenistic periods.

[75] *IG* V 1.1146, ll. 32–40 (=*Syll.*³ 748, *SEG* 50.386), with discussions in Baladie (1980), Migeotte (1984), 90–6, Errington (1988), 152, Fezzi (1998), and Santangelo (2009). Gytheion, though a *civitas libera*, was subject to various demands for contributions payable to Roman magistrates operating in the area.

[76] Romans resident in Lakonia in the Augustan period: *SEG* 11.924 (*Ῥωμαῖοι | οἱ ἐν ταῖς πόλεσιν τῆς | Λακωνικῆς πραγματευό|μενοι*), and specifically in Gytheion: *IG* V 1.1208 (42 CE).

[77] Only a couple of years later, the Cloatii extended a new loan to the city, at an interest rate as high as 48% p.a.—the same rate that was claimed by Scaptius and Brutus at Salamis in *c.*56 BCE, much to the horror of Cicero who fixed the maximum interest rate at 12% in his provincial edict (*ad Atticum* 5.21.11–12). Yet again, Gytheion managed to renegotiate the terms, as the surviving decree praises the brothers for reducing the interest rate by a half.

[78] Note ll. 18–19 which mention soldiers and other burdens, and l. 26, referring to exactions of grain and clothing by Roman legates. Compare *IG* V 1.1433 from Messene, *c.*39 BCE.

[79] Migeotte (1984, 95).

Creticus' legates exercising actual judicial functions in the region is perhaps too much of a stretch, the disputants' resort to a Roman official and the latter's suggestion of a third party tribunal would be perfectly in line with what we have already observed in the first section.

Indeed, the mention of Marcilius in this context suggests that Roman magistrates and commanders operating in the area could be approached regarding the disputes of, broadly speaking, interstate nature. It is equally important that the case between the Cloatii and Gytheion appeared before the Athenian tribunal and not, for instance, that of the Macedonian governor. The outcome of the case, namely, the creditors' concession to a lower sum payable by the *polis*, did not exactly favour the brothers either. The relationship between Gytheion and the Cloatii was thus primarily one of business: the two parties entered into several loan agreements (συναλλάγματα) upon interest (τόκος) and could resort to arbitration in case of a breach of terms.

So, in the period leading up to the provincial organization of Achaia, we find resident Romans negotiating their status in the legal framework of the Greek *poleis* through collective participation in local political institutions on the one hand, and individual exchange of rights and services on the other. Among the most valuable rights a *polis* could confer was that of ἔνκτησις, a prerequisite in most city-states for investment of capital in land, providing sureties, or entering public leases and other transactions necessitating real security. By retaining juridical control over their legal and economic rights, the Greek *poleis* sought to ensure compliance with local legal regulations. It is noteworthy, too, that the presence of resident Roman communities in Achaia continue into the imperial period, contrary to what has been suggested by some.[80]

Admittedly, the establishment of governor's court in the second half of the first century BCE would have increased resort to Roman jurisdiction, thus considerably reshaping the dynamics between resident Romans and their adoptive communities.[81] Around the same time, creation of Roman citizen colonies further disrupted local legal structures and redefined juridical relations within and between the communities directly or indirectly affected by colonization. That said, colonial structures in Achaia, much like elsewhere in the Greek East, reveal a considerable degree of adaptability to local context.[82] The case of Patrai, in particular, demonstrates the existence of a much more complex socio-juridical structure than the traditional dichotomy of *coloni* as the privileged members of the colonial body and *incolae* as those deprived of all civic rights would allow.[83]

With an increasing Roman citizen presence in the region, instalment of provincial administration, and creation of colonies, Roman citizenship extension picked up speed too. The main source of traffic for its transmission seem to have been ties with imperial families and members of Roman provincial

[80] *IG* V 2.515B (Megalopolis); *Achaïe* III 19 (Pellene); *IG* IV.606 (Argos); *IG* IX 1.283 (Opous). For the disappearance of resident Roman communities by the imperial period: Wilson (1966, 150–1), Loukopoulou (1996), cf. Kremydi-Sicilianou (2005), 104 for Macedonia.

[81] Cf. Cicero's letters to provincial governors with requests to protect the interests of individual *negotiatores*: *ad Familiares* 13.17; 13.19; 13.22; 13.26; 13.50.

[82] Rizakis (2004a); Brélaz (2016).

[83] For discussion of Patrai, see Rizakis (1996), 310; Rizakis (2004), 80.

administration (proconsuls, legates, etc.). Further dissemination surely followed through practices of manumission and intermarriage. However, the evidence for advancement of these enfranchised individuals to prominent positions in Rome is confined to only a few examples.[84] More often so, we observe them retaining close ties with their native communities, and using their newly acquired status to exercise positions of power and prestige locally.[85]

Nicholas Purcell stressed that the Romans engaging in economic enterprises and having useful connections in the East could have acquired 'particular interpretative and advisory skills', especially in terms of private law, and demarcation between what is Roman and peregrine.[86] Equally so, members of this new elite of enfranchised locals with continuous interest in their native communities can be seen as the carriers of legal knowledge too, negotiating between the 'local' and the 'Roman'. See, for instance, the dossier of a certain Cn. Cornelius Pulcher from Epidauros, known as an expert of Greek law, who served under Hadrian as procurator of Epirus and *iuridicus* of Egypt and Alexandria, both positions involving some high-calibre judicial functions.[87]

Enfranchised locals are also found serving as judges (*iudices dati*) appointed by governors or emperors to handle disputes in or around their native communities: a certain T. Flavius Euboulos, a native of Chaironeia, was prompted by the governor of Achaia to pronounce a verdict in a dispute between a nearby city of Daulis and a Roman landowner, while one Mestrius Aristonymos of Boiotian origin was appointed by Hadrian and, subsequently, by Antoninus Pius, to settle an ongoing controversy between Koroneia and Thisbe.[88] The choice of these judges by the provincial and imperial government could not have been accidental. Instead, they must have been perceived by the Roman authorities as the most capable to reconcile the disputing parties, perhaps by appealing to their common origin, no less than familiarity with local legal norms.

4. LEGAL CONTACT: LEGISLATION AND APPLICATION OF LAW

We have so far observed the main changes undergone by local judicial institutions in terms of functionality and extent of jurisdiction, and established the complexity

[84] The first senators to come from Athens and Sparta are found in the reigns of Trajan and Hadrian, respectively. For a full account on Roman senators from the 'old Greece', see Oliver (1983), 115–32, cf. Zoumbaki (2008).

[85] Cf. *IG* IX 1.282, r. Augustus: a certain Cn. Calpurnius Helix, the priest of imperial cult, archon, *agoranomos*, and *agonothetes*, dedicating a water fountain to the *δῆμος Ῥωμαίων*, Augustus, and the *δῆμος Ὀπουντίων*.

[86] Purcell (2005), 100.

[87] *Corinth* VIII.1, No. 80 (r. Hadrian), ll. 1–5. Cf. *Corinth* VIII.1, Nos. 81–3; VIII.3, Nos. 138–41; and *SEG* 26.253 (Athens).

[88] Euboulos: *IG* IX 1.61, 118 CE (discussed below); Aristonymos: *IG* VII 2870 (=*SEG* 32.468). C. Avidius Nigrinus, sent by Trajan to settle disputes between Delphi and neighbouring communities (*FD* III.4 290–5), was not entirely unfamiliar with Delphi either, as both his father and uncle had served as proconsuls of Achaia. See Stadter (2014), 78.

of legal statuses not only between but also within the Greek *poleis*. While an increasing influence of Roman jurisdiction is undeniable, particularly in interstate matters, Roman citizens residing in the province are found complying with local legal structures both individually and as a collective body too. In what follows, I will explore the legal contact in Achaia by looking at Roman legislative activities on the one hand, and the evidence for the survival and continuity of local legislation and legal institutions on the other.

Indeed, both literary and documentary evidence points to Rome's positive legislation in the region long before the establishment of provincial administration. L. Mummius and the Ten Commissioners are attested to have handed down 'laws' to the Greek *poleis*, formerly members of the Achaian league, as part of the settlement which followed the Achaian war.[89] Polybius himself claims to have stayed in Greece to visit towns and decide all questions arising from the settlement. Soon, he made the inhabitants 'content with the *πολιτεία* given to them... and left no difficulty connected with the laws on any point, private or public, unsettled'.[90] The *πολιτεία* here refers to the constitutional restructuring of the *poleis*, such as reorganization of the civic councils and introduction of property qualification necessary to enter political functions. The *νόμοι*, then, must have primarily dealt with ensuring the observation and effectiveness of this new establishment. Polybius' phrasing (*μήτε κατ' ἰδίαν μήτε κατὰ κοινὸν ἐκ τῶν νόμων*) nonetheless reveals that Mummius' regulations pertained not only to public but also to private law matters. Indeed, Pausanias mentions Mummius' temporary prohibition of property acquisition and intermarriage across the civic boundaries.[91]

The legislative activity of Mummius reminds us of two earlier instances, namely, the legislation of T. Quinctius Flamininus in Thessaly after the Second Macedonian war, and that of L. Aemilius Paullus in Macedonia after the Third one.[92] Certain regulations (*νόμοι*, *leges*) were thus imposed by all three generals alike during their post-war settlements, and were mainly aimed at controlling local political structures and interstate affairs. Some private law matters were regulated too, including property rights, marriage, and, possibly, manumission (see below). It appears, then, that the 'laws' laid down by the Roman commanders upon senatorial instruction were not perceived by Rome as contradicting or cancelling out the *αὐτονομία* of the Greek *poleis* granted to them at the same

[89] *SEG* 23.180, ll. 9–13 from Nemeia, *c.*145 BCE.

[90] Polybius 39.5.2–3: *ἐποίησε πρὸς λόγον τοὺς ἀνθρώπους στέρξαι τὴν δεδομένην πολιτείαν καὶ μηδὲν ἀπόρημα μήτε κατ' ἰδίαν μήτε κατὰ κοινὸν ἐκ τῶν νόμων γενέσθαι περὶ μηδενός*. The extent of Mummius' legislation, according to Pausanias (8.30.9), was confined to former member states of the Achaian league, thus leaving the constitutions and legal autonomy of the rest of the Greek *poleis* intact.

[91] Pausanias 7.16.9–10.

[92] Flamininus: Polybius 18.46.5; Livy 34.48–51; Plutarch, *Flamininus* 10.1–6; cf. *IG* IX 2.89 *B*, ll. 15–19: the Senate's adjudication of a dispute between two Thessalian communities in *c.*140 BCE, upholding an earlier verdict reached 'in accordance with the laws of the Thessalians... which the consul Titus Quinctius [*sc.* Flamininus] had granted them on the advice of the ten *legati*, approved by a decree of the Senate'; Paullus: Livy 45.32.7 (*leges Macedoniae dedit*); cf. Just. 33.2.7 on Macedonians still using the laws 'accepted' from Paullus in the first century CE.

time.[93] That said, the right to use their own laws never meant the right to alter those imposed by Rome. The aforementioned example of Dyme where a local *nomographos* was sentenced to death for attempting to pass laws 'contrary to the πολιτεία prescribed to the Achaians by the Romans', makes the latter point abundantly clear.[94]

Nonetheless, this rhetoric of granting and accepting the laws suggests that Roman positive legislation of the pre-provincial period was to be perceived as part of the local laws. The second-century-BCE paradigm of Roman general as a lawgiver reappears in Appian's narrative of the Mithridatic war, as he reports how Sulla 'forgave the others and gave to all of them [i.e. the Greeks] laws in all respects similar to those previously decided by the Romans'.[95] By contrast, the decrees for foreign judges from Messene discussed above are explicit in demonstrating that the δόγματα and ἀποκρίσεις of the Romans have entered the domain of applicable law *alongside* local laws.[96]

Roman legislative intervention, in the sense of providing a territorial unit or a community with a set of laws, appears to have decreased over time. The only attested example of similar behaviour in the High Empire is Hadrian's revision of the Athenian laws upon the city's request.[97] Even then, from the epigraphical attestations of this activity, we see that Hadrian's legislation primarily focused on local economic and financial matters, such as regulations on produce, prices, export, and taxation.[98] Some of the provisions also specified which jurisdiction the future suits stemming from these regulations should fall under. Most importantly, these laws were drafted to fit *local* rather than provincial or imperial conditions and concerns, and were thus inherently local rather than Roman in nature and inspiration.

Apart from Athens, Hadrian was also celebrated as a lawgiver (νομοθέτης) at Megara and Thespiai, though nothing of his legislation for these *poleis* survives.[99] Unlike the practice of legislating through edicts or rescripts, the assumption of the role of a νομοθέτης suggests a more profound involvement in local legislation. Overall, imperial legislative activity in this period was more localized, mostly

[93] The grants of legal autonomy are, of course, no less significant in demonstrating that αὐτονομία was within Rome's power to confer. See, for instance, *SEG* 41.545(1), ll. 3–10: Rome 'granting' to Pharos its city, lands, and laws, shortly after 219 BCE. For proclamations of political and legal autonomy as a Hellenistic tradition, see Ma (1999), 151–74, drawing on Bickerman (1939); cf. Dmitriev (2011), *passim*, Eckstein (2011), 636–42. Requests for confirmation of these privileges continue well into the imperial period: e.g. *SEG* 32.469 (Koroneia, 161 CE).

[94] *Syll.*^{3} 684 (=*RDGE* 43), 144/3 BCE.

[95] Appian, *Mithr.* 6.39: νόμους ἔθηκεν ἅπασιν ἀγχοῦ τῶν πρόσθεν αὐτοῖς ὑπὸ Ῥωμαίων ὁρισθέντων. While Geagan (1967), 375 took this to mean a new 'constitution' for Athens, Santangelo (2007), 44 suggested it merely refers to restoration of conditions preceding the war.

[96] Bardani (2013) No. 7, mid-second century BCE.

[97] Jerome, *Ab Abraham* 2138: *Hadrianus Atheniensibus leges petentibus ex Draconis et Solonis reliquorumque libris iura composuit.* Cf. Dio 69.16.1–2.

[98] *IG* II^2 1100, *c.*124/5 CE (=Oliver (1989) No. 92): the 'Oil law', regulating the production and export of olive oil; *IG* II^2 1103 (=Oliver (1989) No. 77): law exempting fishermen of Eleusis from the Athenian two-obol tax; *IG* II^2 1104: law concerning defaulting debtors. On the 'Solonian' inspiration of these laws, see Graindor (1934), 30–2, Follet (1976), 117. For Hadrian's legislation outside Athens, see *FD* III.4 302 from Delphi, *c.*125 CE, on local rights to a harbour and pasturage.

[99] Megara: *IG* VII 70–2; *IG* VII 3491; Thespiai: *IThesp* 437.

applicable to single city-states or communities only.[100] Furthermore, most of the regulations attested were laid down by request rather than blatant imposition. At the same time, unlike the one-off interventions by the Republican commanders and the Senate, this kind of *ad hoc* legislation became increasingly frequent and ever more pervasive, affecting various fields of local legal and economic life, including land distribution and use, taxation, trade, building and agricultural activities, and so on.

A considerable part of imperial regulations had to do with questions of status, such as determining or confirming civic privileges or, indeed, local citizenship policies. For instance, Cassius Dio mentions Augustus' prohibition of citizenship 'sale' in Athens, while an epigraphically attested letter of Claudius to Delphi encourages the city to extend their *πολιτεία* to outsiders in order to avoid depopulation.[101] Compare also the letter of M. Aurelius to Athens on the *trigonia* rule determining the admission to local political and judicial functions.[102] Furthermore, some imperial regulations are found establishing a working legal relationship between the cities and their non-citizen residents, thus proving that juridical heterogeneity of local communities continued to be a pressing issue.[103]

The general provincial edict of the governor would have provided further regulations on matters related to civic finances, debt, interest, perhaps also transactions in property, and so on.[104] The case of Cloatii in Gytheion discussed above is a good example of what the lack of provincial regulation on interest rates could result in, particularly in light of the complexity of juridical statuses within the provincial communities. This aside, a number of *ad hoc* proconsular edicts originated on the locals' request and initiative too, thus applicable to particular cities or communities only (see the discussion of a proconsular edict from Thisbe below).

As regards strictly local legislation, surviving civic decrees suggest a more or less uninterrupted continuity under Rome: the Greek *poleis* continue to confer civic honours and local citizenships, and pass decrees regarding religious matters, local taxation, trade, management of public lands, and so on.[105] As seen in the preceding section, the process of passing these decrees, particularly, the honorific ones, could involve resident Roman communities alongside the usual *polis*' institutions.[106] With the rise and establishment of emperor worship, some *poleis* are

[100] Cf. *SEG* 32.460–71, 125–61 CE: imperial letters to Koroneia, regulating various matters.

[101] Augustus: Cassius Dio 54.7.2; Claudius: *FD* III.4 286, 52 CE.

[102] *SEG* 29.127, *c.*174/5 CE.

[103] *IG* X.2 2.52: Hadrian's letter to Koroneia in Boiotia advising local authorities on civic contributions expected of their non-citizen landowners; cf. *SEG* 32.463: Hadrian to Herakleia Lynkestis, and *IGBulg* IV 2263: Antoninus Pius to Parthikopolis in Macedonia, determining the extent of jurisdiction that the *polis* could exercise over its non-citizen landholders. Cf. Pomponius in *D.*50.16.239.2 on resident foreigners in the Greek *poleis.*

[104] Cf. Cic. *ad Atticum* 6.1.15.

[105] Note, however, *FD* III.4 98, *c.*118–20 CE: the grant of Delphian citizenship to C. Iulius Pudens is enacted by the board of *damiourgoi* (*ἐν ἐννόμῳ | δαμιουργίῳ· ἔδοξεν τοῖς | δαμιουργοῖς*) without the involvement of either the *boule* or *demos*. For the management of public lands, see *SEG* 48.592 (Delphi, second c. CE) with Rousset, Tirologos, & Fadin (2006).

[106] Cf. *IG* V 2.515B (Megalopolis in Arkadia, early imperial period): *ἔδοξε τοῖς συνέδροις καὶ τ[ῷ δά]||[μ]ῳ [κ]αὶ Ῥωμαίοις τοῖς πραγματευομένοις ἐ[ν Με]||[γάλ]ᾳ πόλει.*

found passing the so-called *leges sacrae* containing regulations on imperial cult, which may have required imperial sanction.[107]

Due to the nature of the surviving evidence, mainly consisting of public inscriptions, little is known of private law in Roman Achaia, compared to the other Eastern provinces. As Georgy Kantor points out in his overview of the Greek law under Rome, extant evidence for private law in the Greek cities is largely limited to manumissions, wills, trust foundations, and matters of land ownership, leaving other fields, such as that of obligations, considerably more obscure.[108] Nonetheless, legal norms and institutions in most of the Greek *poleis* were fully developed long before the arrival of Rome, and no particular need for change was envisaged, so long as their functionality was preserved and raised no threat to provincial government.[109]

A good example is provided by manumissions which continue to be performed in accordance with local legal regulations in a number of individual *poleis* in Achaia. In Delphi, for instance, acts of manumission are continuously presented as fictitious sales to Apollo, recording the price and receipt of payment, presence of warrantors, guarantee of inviolability of the freed persons, and immunity to anyone who defends them from seizure.[110] A number of manumission acts from Delphi and elsewhere in Achaia also prescribe *paramone*, or continuous service of the slave to their master, before the slave's freedom can take effect—normally, until the master's death.[111]

Some federal legislation of territorial leagues retained their force throughout the provincial period too. The Thessalian manumission inscriptions, for instance, refer to a *νόμος* regulating the manumission procedure which involved payment to the *polis* (either for the act or for its registration and/or publication) and to the manumittors.[112] The sum of fifteen staters or, after 27 BCE, twenty-two and a half *denarii* payable to a city's treasury by the slave appears to be uniform in all places throughout Thessaly.[113] It is possible that these regulations regarding manumission and, specifically, the payment originate with Flamininus' reorganization of the Thessalian *koinon*.[114] Comparably, Claire Grenet observed that certain changes in the manumission acts from Chaironeia and Orchomenos in Boiotia, such as the involvement of *synedria* and disappearance of private witnesses, had to do with the dissolution of the Boiotian league by Rome in 171 BCE.[115] On another

[107] *SEG* 58.343 (Gytheion, r. Tiberius). [108] Kantor (forthcoming).

[109] Cf. *SEG* 51.641, *c.*138 CE: Hadrian's letter to Naryka, mentioning their use of 'the laws of the Opountians'. For an outline of Greek legal norms and practices between Alexander and Augustus, see Velissaropoulou-Karakostas (2011).

[110] Cf. *SEG* 33.436, late first century CE (l. 13: *κατὰ τὸν νόμον τᾶς πόλιος*).

[111] For examples and discussion of the clause, see Sosin (2015), *contra* Zelnick-Ambramovitz (2005), 134–7; 208–12.

[112] *IG* IX 2.109a (Phthiotic Thebes, 47/6 BCE), ll. 4–9: *ἐκ τοῦ νόμου*; *IG* IX 2.415 (Pherai, *c.*27 BCE), ll. 10–14, and *IG* IX 2.13 (Hypata, 47 CE), ll. 3–5: *κατὰ τὸν νόμον*.

[113] For a full treatment of Thessalian manumission inscriptions, see Zelnick-Ambramovitz (2013). Outside Thessaly, see *IG* V 2.345 from Orchomenos in Arkadia, recording a payment to the council for public inscription, and a separate payment to the manumittors (l. 2: *κατὰ τὸν νόμον*; l. 16: *ἐκ τοῦ νόμου*).

[114] Zelnick-Ambramovitz (2013), 55–69, cf. Vlassopoulos (2014) on the possible connection between this provision and the Roman *vicesima libertatis*.

[115] Grenet (2014).

occasion, we find 'the laws of the Magnesians' governing the local manumission procedure, although the dating of this inscription remains uncertain.[116]

Unlike the provisions of Roman private law, manumission of a slave under Greek laws did not provide for his or her enfranchisement. The fact that manumission—though, in essence, a private act—was closely regulated by the city's or federal laws, reveals a continuous concern of the Greek *poleis* with keeping track of their non-citizen population and preventing the illegal usurpation of full citizen rights.[117] Nonetheless, limited epigraphic evidence suggests that, at least in some places, manumission acts could provide the freed persons with landownership rights or even with full citizenship.[118] Curiously, the choice of whether or not the freed men and women should be granted these privileges may have lain with the manumittor, as a peculiar case from the mid-second century BCE Lilaia in Phokis records a slave-owner specifically *denying* his manumitted slave the right to reside and take up citizenship outside the bounds of Lilaia without his consent.[119]

With this considerable mix of local and Roman laws and regulations at work, the crucial question, as ever, becomes that of application of law. For this, we need to start with the few examples in our sources where applicable law is clearly defined. An inscription from second-century-BCE Thestia in Aitolia specified that regulations regarding building activity were to adhere to 'the civic law of the Thestians'.[120] Similarly, various legal acts which specify that they had taken place according to the law/s of the *polis* would suggest that any litigation stemming from them would also be handled in accordance with local regulations—think again of manumission acts or citizenship conferrals. The institution of foreign judges is another example of a clear definition of applicable law: epigraphically attested decrees specifically state that the cases were settled according to the laws of inviting *polis*.[121] The addition of Roman 'decrees' and 'judgements' in mid-second century BCE Demetrias was an innovation and, indeed, is spelled out as such. The two sets of applicable rules nonetheless presented as complementary rather than competing.

Some documents display a counter-position between local laws or legal customs and the so-called 'common' laws, whether used in the sense of federal legislation or, more generally, to denote the entirety of laws and regulations applicable to the parties involved.[122] A good example from the imperial period can be found in Hadrian's

[116] *IG* IX 2.1100b from Demetrias.

[117] Note, however, Vlassopoulos (2014), for the important observation that manumission inscriptions are confined to central and northern Greece, with very few examples stemming from Peloponnese, which raises questions of the exact function of these documents.

[118] *IG* IX 2.1290 (Pythion in Thessaly, late second century BCE); *IG* IX 1.34 (Stiris in Phokis, second century BCE).

[119] *SGDI* II 1718, ll. 10–11: *μὴ οἰκησάτω δὲ Ἀσία ἔξω | Λιλαίας μηδὲ πολιτευσάτω ἄνευ τᾶς Ἐπιχαρίδα γνώμας.*

[120] *SEG* 23.398, ll. 14–16: *καθὼς ὁ πο|[λι]τικὸς νόμος τᾶς πόλιος τῶν Θεστιέων | [κελεύει].* Cf. Klaffenbach (1936, 380–5); Pleket (1964) No. 47. Note an identical expression in a *sympoliteia* treaty from Stiris in Phokis, 175 or 135 BCE: *IG* IX 1.32, ll. 22, 46–7.

[121] Cf. *SEG* 26.677, l. 27 from Larissa, second century BCE.

[122] *IG* IV^2 1.59 (Epidauros, 250–200 BCE), ll. 7–9: *ἃ κὰτ] | τοὺς τᾶς πόλιος νόμο[υς γίνεται, καὶ τῶν ἄλλων] | συναλλαγμάτων, ἃ κὰτ τ[οὺς κοινοὺς νόμους*; cf. *FD* III 2.70 (Delphi, 112/11 BCE): *παρὰ τοὺ[ς κοινοὺ]ς νόμους τῶν τεχνι[τῶν.*

letter to Delphi regarding the representation in the Amphiktyonic council. Among other things, the emperor appoints a certain Claudius Timokrates to collect and send to him those decrees of the member states which are in conflict with one another or with the 'common laws', so that an investigation can be made, thus demonstrating a clear understanding on his part of possibly conflicting local legislation.[123]

The establishment of the governor's court as the highest judicial authority province-wide provided a new venue for the provincials—Greeks and Romans alike—to voice their complaints. Indeed, in Achaia, as anywhere else, claims based on indigenous laws and legal practices were admitted in Roman provincial courts. In his letter to Sulpicius Rufus, Cicero commends a certain Lyson of Patrai, whose son had been adopted by Cicero's client C. Maenius Gemellus.[124] The latter, Cicero says, had become a citizen of Patrai when exiled from Rome, and thus adopted Lyson's son according to the Patraian laws (*Patrensium legibus*). Nonetheless, Cicero asks Rufus to support Lyson's son's legal claim to the inheritance—presumably, after Gemellus returned to Rome and regained his *civitas*—thus making sure that the transfer of property is overseen by the governor rather than by local authorities.[125] In her discussion of Cicero's recommendation letters, Hannah Cotton rightly stressed that the purpose of the majority of these requests was to prevent or speed up rather than influence litigation.[126] Furthermore, Cicero is more frequently found asking the governors to exercise their *auctoritas* rather than actual judicial functions.[127] This, in fact, is paradigmatic of Roman provincial administration of justice: the governor was perceived as an authority and a potential arbitrator even in cases where he had, strictly speaking, no jurisdiction.[128]

In theory, Roman citizens residing in the province should have resorted to Roman courts and Roman law in their personal dealings, but, in reality, things were considerably more complex and dependent on circumstance. This becomes particularly clear with the increasing Roman citizenship extension, which resulted in more and more people juggling two (or more) sets of socio-juridical relations.[129]

In early imperial Gytheion, a Roman citizen named Phaenia Aromation made a gift of 8,000 *denarii* to the *polis*, to be used for provision of oil 'for the citizens of

[123] *FD* III 4.302 (125 CE), ll. 38–9: *τῶν Ἀμφικ[τυονικ]ῶν δογμάτων | ὅσα ἢ ἐνά[ντι]α ἀλλήλοις ἐστὶν [ἢ νόμοις τοῖ]ς κοινο[ῖς]*. Oliver (1989), 190 and Birley (1997), 187 take the 'common laws' here to mean the Roman *ius gentium*, despite the distinction made by Dionysios of Halikarnassos (*Antiquitates Romanae* 4.25.3) between the laws of each city and the 'common', i.e. Amphiktyonic, laws. Compare *D.*14.2.9, with Aubert (2007): rescript of Antoninus Pius regarding piracy, acknowledging a potential conflict between Roman law and the customary sea law of the Rhodians.

[124] *ad Familiares* 13.19 (46 BCE).

[125] Cf. *ad Familiares* 13.30: Cicero's letter to Manius Acilius Glabrio in Sicily, asking that a certain L. Manlius Sosis, an enfranchised Italian, obtains his inheritance and property in Sicily.

[126] Cotton (1986), 452; cf. Cotton (2014).

[127] *ad Familiares* 13.26, *ad Familiares* 5.5, cf. *ad Atticum* 11.1.12.

[128] Cf. *ad Familiares* 5.5 (62 BCE), with *ad Atticum* 1.13 (61 BCE): Cicero asks the governor of Macedonia to assist Atticus in recovering a debt from the free city of Sikyon, which was outside the Macedonian governor's direct jurisdiction.

[129] On the *civitas* extension in relation to dual (multiple) citizenships: Sherwin-White (1973), 291–336, Thomas (1996), Ferrary (2005), Heller & Pont (2012), and Fournier (2012).

Gytheion and the foreigners', and to be managed by the city.[130] In order to validate her transfer of funds in the eyes of Roman law, Phaenia acted in the presence of her legal guardian P. Ophellius Crispus who, somewhat overzealously, signed the document as *ὁ φροντιστὴς καὶ κύριος* (ll. 62–3).[131] In addition to the lengthy terms of her donation, Phaenia entrusted her freedmen and *threptoi* to the *polis* and its *synedroi*, who were to ensure their protection from seizure and harassment (ll. 49–56). In so doing, Phaenia referred to the Greek institution of *parakatathēkē*, attested in financial transactions, manumissions, and entrustment of persons to guardians.[132]

It appears, then, that Phaenia deliberately sought for her freedmen the protection of local law, thus demonstrating how compliance to Roman procedural requirements, such as the need for a legal guardian, could be divorced from resort to local jurisdiction and legal institutions in the provincials' transactions. In the case of mismanagement of funds, the inscription reads, 'it shall be possible for anyone who wants—of the Greeks or the Romans—to prosecute the *polis* for neglect before the assembly of the Gytheatai'.[133] This once again brings out the coexistence of Greeks and Romans in Achaia, and points to the latter's share in the civic and legal life of the *polis*. One of the questions that this volume asks is whether a differentiation between Roman and local law could be made according to context. Indeed, Phaenia's resort to a local legal institution in order to protect her freedmen at a nominally free and autonomous Greek *polis* is driven by largely the same underlying concerns as Babatha's resort to the Roman *actio tutelae* to protect the interests of her son in the newly acquired province of Arabia.[134]

That is, of course, not to deny a gradual shift toward the protection of Roman authorities at a communal level, sought by the free and the tributary cities alike. An inscription from the same Gytheion, some hundred years later, records the governor's expression of support for the civic endowment of Tiberius Claudius Atticus, a Roman senator of Athenian origin.[135] It appears that, upon being offered a donation from Atticus, the *polis*' authorities sent an embassy to Hadrian to request that the funds be protected by Rome in the form of a special declaration. The emperor communicated his positive response to the governor of Achaia, who then issued an edict (*διάταγμα*, l. 15) declaring protection and inviolability of the terms of Atticus' endowment.[136] The so-called Eleusinian endowment of *c.*135–40 CE contains a similar declaration of protection regarding the donation to the Eleusinian sanctuary by a Roman senator from Crete.[137]

[130] *IG* V 1.1208 (42 CE), with Harter-Uibopuu (2004). Cf. *SEG* 13.258. For the most recent discussion of Phaenia and her family, see Rizakis (2013).

[131] Note Taeuber (1994) on the fact that the Greek women, unlike the Roman, did not need a legal guardian to make such donations. Cf. Harter-Uibopuu (2004), 3.

[132] For a discussion of the institution with examples, see Harter-Uibopuu (2004), 13–14.

[133] Lines 26–8: *ἐξέστω] τῷ βουλομένῳ καὶ Ἑλλήνων καὶ Ῥωμαίων [κα]||[τηγορῆσαι ὀλι]γωρίας τῆς πόλεως ἐπὶ τοῦ δήμου [τῶν Γυθε]||[ατῶν*. Other examples of the voluntary prosecution clause: *SEG* 11.923 (Gytheion, 15 CE), ll. 17–18, 32–3; *SEG* 37.356 (Neapolis, second century CE), l. 26.

[134] *P.Yadin* 28–30, 125 CE.

[135] *IG* V 1.1147, r. Hadrian.

[136] For a full discussion of this and similar documents regarding civic endowments, see Oliver (1953), 963–81.

[137] *IG* II^2 1092, with Oliver (1952).

While the nature of the evidence available for Achaia deprives us of any direct insights into dispute resolution between private individuals of differing legal status, semi-private disputes shed some light on the practices at hand. One such example is provided by an inscription recording a territorial controversy between a city of Daulis in Phokis, represented by two ἔγδικοι, and an individual named Memmius Antiochos.[138] The controversy, which lasted for several years, was investigated and settled by one T. Flavius Euboulos, an appointed judge and boundary delineator (ὁ δοθεὶς κριτὴς καὶ ὁριστής, A, ll. 11–12) upon proconsular delegation.

Memmius Antiochos, himself a Roman citizen, had acquired a considerable amount of land over four different locations in the territory of Daulis.[139] It is not entirely clear whether the *polis* contested the extent of Antiochos' estate or his claim to the land altogether, but the case was resolved by ascribing certain portions of land in each of the locales to Memmius Antiochos, and giving 'the remainder' to the *polis* (A, ll. 20–30). Further provisions were made for land measurements in order to determine and set up boundaries between the property of Antiochos and that of Daulis.

Another document inscribed on the same stele postdates Euboulos' verdict, and regards the same dispute. It appears that Antiochos had not received the full amount of land prescribed to him by Euboulos' decision in one of the four locales, and his heiress laid a claim to recover the missing part. This time, no proconsular involvement is recorded. Instead, a locally constituted commission of twelve, comprising five citizens of Daulis, four members of the neighbouring communities of Antikyra and Tithoreia, and three Roman citizens of Greek origin, delivered a new verdict which allowed Antiochos' heiress, Serapias, to make action against the city, in case the outstanding part of the land was not recovered (B, ll. 12–28).[140]

We know that at least one of the parcels of the disputed land—precisely, the bone of contention in the follow-up dispute—was purchased by Antiochos 'from the heirs of Klea' (A, ll. 20–4), who herself was most likely a Roman citizen too.[141] What we find here, then, is a Greek *polis* contesting (the extent of) the property within its territory that was acquired by means of a private sale transaction between Roman citizens with local ἔγκτησις rights. Furthermore, two rather different judicial procedures are applied in the course of the same controversy. While the Roman-ness of Euboulos' procedure has been stressed by every

[138] *IG* IX 1.61 (118 CE), with Grenet (2011). For an English translation and a new discussion of the document, see now Girdvainyte (2019). On ἔγδικοι as legal representatives of the *poleis*, see Dmitriev (2005), 213–16, Magie (1950), 1517–18, and Fournier (2007), 25–8.

[139] Based on his *nomen*, Antiochos' family had most likely received their *civitas* through P. Memmius Regulus, *legatus Augusti pro praetore* between the years 35–44 CE, responsible for numerous enfranchisements in the region, particularly around Delphi.

[140] While Luzzatto (1965), 51; 55 saw this panel as a 'modified version of foreign judges', Grenet (2011), 137 suggested it was either mutually agreed upon by the parties, or designed by the proconsul, leaning towards the latter option. However, local constitution of this panel seems to be the most convincing: see Girdvainyte (2019), 165–7.

[141] Note Kapetanopoulos' (1966) suggestion of identifying this Klea with the famous friend of Plutarch. Cf. Jannoray (1946), 254–9 on Plutarch's Klea as *Φλαουΐα Κλέα ἡ ἀρχηΐς* in *SEG* 1.159 (r. Antoninus Pius). The aforementioned Phaenia Aromation is a good example of a wealthy and influential Roman woman of Greek origin too; see also *IG* VII 3418 (Chaironeia, 73 CE): a dedication to Vespasian by one Caecilia Lampris, made 'on behalf of the city'.

commentator, the governor's choice of Euboulos as *iudex datus* was hardly a coincidence.[142] As an enfranchised member of the Chaironeian elite, Euboulos would have been seen by the disputing parties as someone invested with provincial authority but nonetheless familiar with the local legal culture. With this in mind, the question of applicable law is of particular interest. As the document itself contains no clues and no allusions to Roman law, Claire Grenet assumed that both the ἀπόφασις of Euboulos and a κρίσις of the judicial commission were reached in accordance with local legal norms.[143] However, the notion of a sale transaction between Roman citizens, as well as Antiochos' daughter's capacity to inherit, provide some nuance to this picture.[144]

Similarly to Phaenia's case above, the distinction between the 'Roman' and the 'local' here seems rather murky. The inscription reads that Serapias' claim to Antiochos' property was confirmed on the basis of written evidence (B, ll. 13–15: κατὰ τὴν προκομισθ[εῖ]|σαν χεῖρα) without any reference to the law applied. Indeed, it may be of some importance that the records of dispute resolution in the imperial period often lack the specification of applicable law.[145] It is interesting, in this context, that the aforementioned regulation from Sparta, enforcing restrictions on appeals to Roman jurisdiction, explains this measure as follows: 'people should neither be completely deprived from the right of appeal, nor fall victim to the abusers of the system who do so in order to avoid their public and private matters being judged in accordance with the laws' (ll. 4–5: ὡς τά τε δημόσια καὶ ἰδιωτικὰ | μὴ τελεῖσθαι κατὰ τοὺς νόμους).[146] The phrasing makes it clear that Roman jurisdiction operated in a manner quite different from the local courts.[147] As judicial discretion and *ad hoc* nature of rulings at the proconsular and imperial levels became more prominent, similar tendencies may have ensued at a local level too, in cases where more than one set of rules was involved. At the same time, the fact that individual decisions regarding appropriate jurisdiction continue to be made at this time points to the lack of a uniform model throughout the empire or even a single province in dealing with the 'conflict of laws' situations.[148]

A related question to that of applicable law, and one of no smaller importance, concerns the basis upon which a norm was perceived as either Roman or

[142] Cf. Grenet (2011), 130: 'l'affaire était jugée selon une procédure juridique romaine'. On the Roman procedure in territorial dispute resolution, see Ulpian in *D.* 10.1.8.1. Note, however, that a very similar process, involving the hearing of testimonies, autopsy of lands, and consultation of documents was employed by the Greeks in the pre-provincial period too: Ager (1996), Rousset (1994), 104–9, and Chaniotis (2004) for examples.

[143] Grenet (2011), 142.

[144] We know that only the children of *iustum matrimonium* could inherit property from their Roman citizen parents in the provinces up until Antoninus Pius (Pausanias 8.43.5). That said, the right of ἔγκτησις in the Greek *poleis* was normally subject to hereditary transmission.

[145] Thus, in contrast to some of the Republican evidence, cf. *IG* IX 2.89 B (*c.*140 BCE), ll. 15–19: the Senate upholding a verdict reached 'in accordance with the laws of the Thessalians'.

[146] *IG* V 1.21 II, ll. 2–5.

[147] Cf. Fronto, *Epistulae ad M. Caesarem* 1.6.2–3: Marcus Aurelius' attempt to warn Antoninus Pius that his rulings would set precedents for the magistrates in all provinces.

[148] See Hadrian's rescript mentioned in *D.* 50.1.37 pr. Cf. *SEG* 50.1096: Hadrian's letter to Aphrodisias in Karia, providing that financial cases between citizens be tried locally, while those involving citizens of other Greek communities were to go to the provincial court.

indigenous. We have already seen in our discussion of legislation that this need not have depended on its provenance: the *nomoi* granted to the Greeks by the Roman commanders and the Senate in the second century BCE were styled as local ('the laws of the Thessalians . . . granted to them') rather than Roman, while the imperial legislation such as that of Hadrian for Athens and Delphi was specifically tailored to fit the local needs and conditions, and was largely driven by local initiative. Proconsular edicts, especially when enacted upon locals' request, are equally difficult to place.

An example from Thisbe in Boiotia, dating to the first quarter of the third century CE, is a case in point.[149] The inscription consists of two documents: a proconsular edict drawn by Marcus Ulpius (ll. 1–54), and a letter of his successor Geminius Modestus, addressed to the Thisbeans, only the beginning of which has survived (ll. 55–8). The edict of Ulpius prescribes the so-called emphyteutic land lease contracts, encouraging the inhabitants of Thisbe to take up and cultivate public lands that were in neglect. On the face of it, the present decree is a straightforward intervention of the Roman proconsul who prescribes a measure practiced in Roman law to a community in Boiotia, thus encroaching upon the administration of its public lands.[150]

However, the execution and management of the proposed scheme, including the jurisdiction over any future disputes stemming from non-compliance, are entrusted entirely to the city's office-holders and political institutions (ll. 18–22). Equally telling is the stipulation that an heir to the lease must be a citizen of Thisbe, so that the land stays strictly in the hands of the civic community (ll. 35–54). In case the tenant died intestate or left the land to an illegitimate heir, e.g. 'a foreign relative or friend', the full property and tenure rights returned back to the city. Similarly, if the land acquired through the concession scheme was mortgaged to a foreign creditor, the city had the right to invalidate the transaction and recover the land. These conditions clearly demonstrate the city's intention to maintain and secure full property rights over its public land by restricting its lease to citizens only.[151] These provisions make it fairly likely that, instead of demonstrating a proconsular imposition, the document records an outcome of cooperation between the proconsul and the city in finding an agreeable solution to an agricultural issue.[152]

Regardless of the similarity of Ulpius' edict to the provisions set out in the Roman laws regulating the cultivation of imperial estates in North Africa, similar land lease schemes are found throughout the Greek world of the

[149] *Syll.*³ 884 (=*IG* VII 2226/2227), with Pernin (2014).

[150] For a discussion of *emphyteusis* in the Greek *poleis* under Rome, see Rizakis (2004b).

[151] Cf. *SEG* 30.568 (*c*.193 CE): a decree from Battyna in Macedonia, recording a plea presented to the Roman governor by local ambassadors, and insisting on restricting the possessions of non-citizen landholders (ἐπαρχικοί), who had illegally occupied their lands (ll. 10–15). Publication of the decree shows that the embassy's request had been granted, and the city's plea thus overruled the regulation laid down by the previous governor.

[152] Cf. Pernin (2014), 449. Compare *SEG* 55.678 from Beroia in Macedonia, early second century CE: a proconsular edict providing a solution to the financial struggles of the gymnasium by setting up a deposited endowment (ἐνθήκη), and recording cooperation between the proconsul, the *boule*, and the *protoi* (ll. 9–11).

pre-Roman period too.[153] Furthermore, a locally issued decree from Gazoros in Macedonia prescribes a very similar scheme without any traces of Roman involvement.[154] Given this and, indeed, the Greek name by which it eventually enters the Roman legal sources in the fourth century CE, the development of emphyteutic land lease in Roman law bears witness to a Greek legal norm influencing the provisions of a Roman one, rather than the other way around. It is similar, in this regard, to the development of *hypotheca* in Roman law, identical in many respects to the Greek form of real security known by the same name, gradually adopted into the Roman practice.[155]

With this in mind, the question of whether the land lease contracts proposed by the proconsul would have been perceived by the Thisbeans as Roman or local in nature is beside the point. The emphasis on the city's retention of jurisdiction over its public lands, and the restriction of concession schemes to citizens only demonstrate a continuous functionality of local property regimes and political institutions beyond the Antonine Constitution. Proconsular edicts of this sort were meant to legitimize and protect the measures which could have well been driven entirely by local initiative.

5. CONCLUSION

Needless to say, mainland Greece underwent significant changes under Rome, including but not limited to altered constitutions of a number of local communities, curtailed powers of local judiciaries, and a near-complete takeover of interstate jurisdiction by the Roman authorities. Furthermore, positive legislation was introduced by Rome as early as the second century BCE, and Roman legal enactments and judicial decisions are found entering the domain of locally applicable law around this time too. In this sense, Achaia provides an excellent example of how Roman intervention in the legal and the judicial spheres was not necessarily congruent with the actual organization of the province.

That said, while Roman authorities assumed an arbitrating role in inter-community disputes, acted as appellate courts, and handled cases of higher importance, the majority of Greek *poleis* retained a considerable degree of legal and judicial autonomy. Furthermore, the epigraphic evidence reveals an uninterrupted importance of local civic affiliations in terms of defining and protecting the rights of their citizens, conferring legal and economic benefits, and providing access to legal remedies. The Greeks under Rome continued to make use of local

[153] For examples and discussion: Pernin (2014). For the *lex Manciana* and *lex Hadriana*: *CIL* VIII 25902 (116 CE), 25943, and 26416 (198–209 CE): a republication of provisions under Septimius Severus. On the potential outreach of these laws beyond Africa, see Tate (1997), 60. Compare also Herodian 2.4.6.

[154] *SEG* 24.614, 158/9 CE.

[155] For a thorough discussion of the relationship between the Greek ὑποθήκη and the Roman *hypotheca*: Harris (2012).

courts and their own private law institutions. Grants and confirmations of legal autonomy, attested well into the imperial period, further demonstrate the acknowledgement on Rome's part of indigenous legal systems in their own right.

The above enquiry into the legal life of Achaia reveals a curious intersection between an increasing popularity of Roman jurisdiction on the one hand, and continuation of local legal traditions on the other. The evidence for dispute resolution, for instance, displays a considerable inclusion of local elites into the framework of Roman provincial judicial administration: governors and imperial legates alike are attested making use of *consilia* comprised of people versed in indigenous laws, while judges appointed at both proconsular and imperial levels often display familiarity, if not common origin, with the communities whose disputes they were asked to adjudicate.

One of the defining features of Achaia was its juridical heterogeneity—a combined result of the presence of Romans resident in the region from the early second century BCE, foundation of Roman citizen colonies in the latter half of the first century BCE, and increasing Roman citizenship extension. It is noteworthy, however, that some *Ῥωμαῖοι* resident in Greece of the pre-provincial period are found complying with local legal structures and norms both individually and as collective bodies, while the evidence for legal activity of enfranchised Greeks of the imperial period often displays resort to local legal institutions alongside the requirements of Roman procedural law.

Although disputes between people of differing legal statuses were far more likely to appear before the provincial rather than local courts, this had more to do with perception of authority than with application of law. Indeed, the law applied in the provincial courts was anything but purely Roman, as the governors and appointed judges were free to admit claims based on indigenous legal practices. To an extent, the governor's court and that of the emperor were seen as guarantors of impartiality, replacing, in this respect, the pre-existing extra-civic jurisdictions: namely, the royal or territorial league jurisdictions, as well as the institution of foreign judges. Roman procedure thus came to play an increasingly more important role—not least due to the opportunistic behaviour of the provincials—yet Roman legal norms did not supersede the local ones completely, neither before nor immediately after the Antonine Constitution.

Finally, it is interesting to observe that Roman positive legislation for the Greeks in the second century BCE was styled as 'local', while later imperial and proconsular legislative or regulatory activities were often tailored to fit the needs and conditions of the Greek communities, and were thus driven by local rather than imperial or provincial concerns. Ultimately, the question of whether a legal norm or regulation was perceived as 'Roman' or 'local' becomes trivial, as we observe in our sources the *making* of law, more often than dissemination or influence of one legal system onto another. It is equally clear that neither the principle of personality nor that of territoriality sufficiently explains the applicability of jurisdiction and law in Roman Achaia. The lack of a uniform model in dealing with the 'conflict of laws' situations resulted in the preponderance of *ad hoc* decisions—particularly, at the proconsular and the imperial levels—and a resort towards other criteria, such as monetary, in establishing the working legal relationship between juridically heterogeneous components of the provincial society.

REFERENCES

Accame, S. 1946. *Il dominio romano in Grecia dalla guerra Acaica ad Augusto*. Rome.

Ager, S. L. 1996. *Interstate arbitration in the Greek world, 337–90 B.C. Hellenistic Culture and Society* 18. Berkeley and Los Angeles.

Aubert, J.-J. 2007. Dealing with the abyss: the nature and purpose of the Rhodian sea-law on jettison (Lex Rhodia de iactu, D. 14.2) and the making of Justinian's Digest. In: J.W. Cairns and P. du Plessis (eds.), *Beyond Dogmatics. Law and Society in the Roman World*. Edinburgh, pp. 157–72.

Avram, A. 1996. Der Vertrag zwischen Rom und Kallatis: *CIL* I^2 2, 2676. In: B. Funck (ed.), *Hellenismus: Beiträge zur Erforschung von Akkulturation und politischer Ordnung in den Staaten des hellenistischen Zeitalters*. Tübingen, pp. 491–511.

Badian, E. 1984. *Foreign Clientelae (264–70 B.C.)*. Oxford.

Baladie, R. 1980. *Le Péloponnèse de Strabon: étude de géographie historique*. Paris.

Balsdon, J. P. V. D. 1979. *Romans and aliens*. London.

Bardani, V. 2013. *Τιμὲς Μεσσηνίων δικαστῶν. Ἐπιγραφικὲς συμβολὲς στὴν ἐξέταση τοῦ θεσμοῦ τῶν ξενικῶν δικαστηρίων*. Volos.

Béquignon, Y. 1935. Études Thessaliennes: VII. Inscriptions de Thessalie. *Bulletin de Correspondance Hellénique* 59, pp. 36–77.

Bickerman, E. 1939. La cité grecque dans les monarchies hellénistiques. *Revue philologique* 13, pp. 335–49.

Birley, A. R. 1997. *Hadrian: The restless emperor*. London.

Bispham, E. 2014. Roma iudex. Interstate arbitration and Rome's Mediterranean hegemony. In: J. Dubouloz, S. Pittia, & G. Sabatini (eds.), *L'Imperium Romanum en perspective. Les savoirs d'empire dans la République romaine et leur héritage dans l'Europe médiévale et moderne, Actes du colloque de Paris*. Paris, 26–8 November 2012, pp. 231–42.

Bouchon, R. 2014. Démophilos de Doliché, Paul-Émile et les conséquences de la troisième guerre de Macédoine à Gonnoi. *Topoi* 19:2, pp. 484–513.

Bouchon, R. & Helly, B. 2015. The Thessalian league. In: H. Beck & P. Funke (eds.), *Federalism in Greek antiquity*. Cambridge, pp. 231–49.

Brélaz, C. 2016. Des communautés de citoyens romains sur le territoire des cités grecques: statut politico-administratif et régime des terres, in F. Lerouxel & A.-V. Pont (eds.) *Propriétaires et citoyens dans l'Orient romain*. Bordeaux, pp. 69–85.

Brock, R. forthcoming. Law and citizenship in the Greek poleis. In: E. Harris & M. Canevaro (eds.), *The Oxford handbook of ancient Greek law*. Oxford.

Broughton, T. Robert S. 1952. *The magistrates of the Roman Republic*, Vol. 2. New York.

Burton, G. P. 1993. Provincial procurators and the public provinces. *Chiron* 23, pp. 13–28.

Byrne, S. G. 2003. *Roman citizens of Athens*. Leuven.

Camia, F. 2009. *Roma e le poleis. L'intervento di Roma nelle controversie territoriali tra le comunità greche di Grecia e d'Asia Minore nel secondo secolo a.C.: le testimonianze epigrafiche. Tripodes* 10. Athens.

Cassayre, A. 2010. *La justice dans les cités grecques. De la formation des royaumes hellénistiques au legs d'Attale*. Rennes.

Cecchet, L. & Busetto, A. (eds.). 2017. *Citizens in the Graeco-Roman world: Aspects of citizenship from the Archaic period to 212 AD*. Leiden.

Chaniotis, A. 2004. Justifying territorial claims in Classical and Hellenistic Greece. The beginnings of international law. In: E.M. Harris & L. Rubinstein, L. (eds.), *The law and the courts in ancient Greece*. London, pp. 185–213.

Clinton, K. 2003. Maroneia and Rome: Two decrees of Maroneia from Samothrace. *Chiron* 33, pp. 379–417.

Corbier, M. 1992. City, territory and taxation. In: J. Rich & A. Wallace-Hadrill (eds.), *City and country in the ancient world*. London, pp. 211–39.

Cotton, H. 1986. The role of Cicero's letters of recommendation: *iustitia versus gratia*? *Hermes* 114:4, pp. 443–60.

Cotton, H. 2014. The evolution of the so-called provincial law, or: Cicero's letters of recommendation and private international law in the Roman world. In: G. De Kleijn & S. Benoist (eds.), *Integration in Rome and in the Roman world: Proceedings of the tenth workshop of the International Network Impact of Empire, Lille, June 23–25, 2011*. Leiden, pp. 43–56.

Crawford, M. 1977. Rome and the Greek world: Economic relationships. *The Economic History Review* 30:1, pp. 42–52.

Crowther, C. 2006. Foreign judges in Thessaly in the Hellenistic period: A second century phenomenon? In: G. A. Pikoulas (ed.), *Inscriptions and history of Thessaly. New evidence: Proceedings of the international symposium in honour of Professor Christian Habicht, Volos, April 7–8, 2006*. Volos, pp. 31–48.

Decourt, J. C. 1995. *Inscriptions de Thessalie. I: Les cités de la vallée de l'Enipeus*. Paris.

Dmitriev, S. 2005. *City government in Hellenistic and Roman Asia Minor*. Oxford.

Dmitriev, S. 2011. *The Greek slogan of freedom and early Roman politics in Greece*. Oxford.

Doukellis, P. N. & Zoumbaki, S. 1995. De Flamininus aux Antonins: Conquête et aménagements de l'espace extra-urbain en Achaïe et Macédoine. *Dialogues d'Histoire Ancienne* 21:2, pp. 205–28.

Eberle, L. P. 2016. Law, empire, and the making of Roman estates in the provinces during the late Republic. *Critical Analysis of Law* 3:1, pp. 50–69.

Eberle, L. P. 2017. Making Roman subjects: Citizenship and empire before and after Augustus. *Transactions of the American Philological Association* 147:2, pp. 321–70.

Eberle, L. P. & Le Quéré, E. 2017. Landed traders, trading agriculturalists? Land in the economy of the Italian diaspora in the Greek East. *Journal of Roman Studies* 107, pp. 27–59.

Eckstein, A. M. 2011. Review of S. Dmitriev *The Greek slogan of freedom and early Roman politics in Greece* (2011, Oxford). *International Journal of the Classical Tradition* 18:4, pp. 636–42.

Errington, R. M. 1988. Aspects of Roman acculturation in the east under the Republic. In: P. Kneissl & V. Losemann (eds.), *Alte Geschichte und Wissenschaftsgeschichte. Festschrift fur Karl Christ zum 65. Geburtstag*. Darmstadt, pp. 140–57.

Färber, R. 2014. *Römische Gerichtsorte: räumliche Dynamiken von Jurisdiktion im Imperium Romanum*. Munich.

Ferrary, J.-L. 1988. *Philhellénisme et impérialisme: aspects idéologiques de la conquête romaine du monde hellénistique*. Rome.

Ferrary, J.-L. 2005. Les Grecs des cités et l'obtention de la *ciuitas Romana*. In: P. Fröhlich and C. Müller (eds.), *Citoyenneté et participation à la basse époque hellénistique*. Geneva, pp. 51–75.

Ferrary, J.-L. 2008. L'onomastique dans les provinces orientales de l'empire à la lumière du dossier des mémoriaux de délégations de Claros. *Cahiers du centre de Gustave Glotz* 19, pp. 247–78.

Ferrary, J.-L. 2014. *Les mémoriaux de délégations du sanctuaire oraculaire de Claros, d'après la documentation conservée dans le Fonds Louis Robert*. Paris.

Fezzi, L. 1998. Osservazioni sul decreto di Gytheion in onore dei Cloazii (IG, V, 1, n. 1146). *Annali della Scuola Normale Superiore di Pisa* 3, pp. 327–38.

Follet, S. 1976. *Athènes au IIe et au IIIe siècle: études chronologiques et prosopographiques*. Paris.

Fournier, J. 2005. Sparte et la justice romaine sous le Haut-Empire. À propos de IG V 1,21. *Revue des études grecques* 118, pp. 117–37.

Fournier, J. 2007. Les syndikoi, représentants juridiques des cités grecques sous le Haut-Empire romain. *Cahiers du Centre Gustave Glotz* 18, pp. 7–36.

Fournier, J. 2010. *Entre tutelle romaine et autonomie civique: L'administration judiciaire dans les provinces hellénophones de l'Empire romain (129 av. J.-C.–235 apr. J.-C.)*. Athens.

Fournier, J. 2012. L'essor de la multi-citoynneté dans l'Orient romain: problèmes juridiques et judiciaires. In A. Heller & A.-V. Pont (eds.), *Patrie d'origine et patries électives: les citoyennetés multiples dans le monde grec d'époque romaine*. Bordeaux, pp. 79–98.

Freitag, K. 2007. Der Symmachievertrag zwischen Rom und Thyrrheion aus dem Jahre 94 v. Chr. Ein Neues Fragment zu IG, IX 1, 1^2 242. In: G. Cresci Marrone and A. Pistellato (eds.), *Studi in ricordo di Fulviomario Broilo. Atti delle giornate di studi epigrafici, Venice, October 14–15, 2005*. Padova, pp. 341–52.

Geagan, D. J. 1967. *The Athenian constitution after Sulla*. Princeton.

Girdvainyte, L. 2019. Memmius Antiochos and Daulis (*IG* IX.1.61): Between Roman procedure and local law? *Zeitschrift für Papyrologie und Epigraphik* 209, pp. 159–74.

Graindor, P. 1934. *Athènes sous Hadrien*. Cairo.

Grenet, C. 2011. Un litige foncier à Daulis au IIe ap. J.-C. (*IG* IX, 1, 61). In: N. Badoud (ed.), *Philologos Dionysios: mélanges offerts au professeur Denis Knoepfler. Recueil de travaux publiés par la Faculté des Lettres et sciences humaines de l'Université de Neuchâtel* 56. Geneva, pp. 103–48.

Grenet, C. 2014. Manumission in Hellenistic Boeotia: new considerations on the chronology of the inscriptions. In: N. Papazarkadas (ed.), *The epigraphy and history of Boeotia: New finds, new prospects*. Leiden, pp. 395–442.

Gruen, E. S. 1976. The origins of the Achaean War. *Journal of Hellenic Studies* 96, pp. 46–69.

Gruen, E. S. 1984. *The Hellenistic world and the coming of Rome*. Berkeley.

Gruen, E. S. 1992. *Culture and national identity in Republican Rome*. Ithaca.

Guarducci, M. 1932. Nota di epigrafia Spartana. *Rivista di Filologia e Istruzione Classica* 60, pp. 84–6.

Guerber, E. 2009. *Les cités grecques dans l'Empire romain. Les privilèges et les titres des cités de l'Orient hellénophone d'Octave Auguste à Dioclétien*. Rennes.

Harris, E. M. 2012. Hypotheca in Roman law and *ὑποθήκη* in Greek law. In: B. Legras (ed.), *Transferts culturels et droits dans le mond grec et hellénistique*. Paris, pp. 433–41.

Harter-Uibopuu, K. 2004. The trust fund of Phaenia Aromation (IG V.1 1208) and imperial Gytheion. In: *Studia Humaniora Tartuensia* 5, available from: <http://www.ut.ee/klassik/sht/2004/harter-uibopuu1.pdf>.

Hatzfeld, J. 1919. *Les trafiquants Italiens dans l'Orient Hellénique*. Paris.

Heller, A. & Pont, A.-V. (eds.), 2012. *Patrie d'origine et patries électives: les citoyennetés multiples dans le monde grec d'époque romaine*. Bordeaux.

Jannoray, J. 1946. Inscriptions delphiques d'époque tardive. Inscriptions de Lébadée. *Bulletin de Correspondance Hellénique* 70, pp. 247–62.

Jones, C. P. 1971. A new letter of Marcus Aurelius to the Athenians. *Zeitschrift für Papyrologie und Epigraphik* 8, pp.161–83.

Kallet-Marx, R. M. 1995a. *Hegemony to Empire. The development of the Roman imperium in the East from 148 to 62 BCE*. Berkeley.

Kallet-Marx, R. M. 1995b. Quintus Fabius Maximus and the Dyme affair (Syll.[3] 684). *The Classical Quarterly* 45:1, pp. 129–53.

Kantor, G. 2016. Towards the dating of the inscriptions of foreign judges at Mylasa. *Epigraphica Anatolica* 49, pp. 131–5.

Kantor, G. Forthcoming. Greek law under the Romans. In: E. Harris & M. Canevaro (eds.), *The Oxford handbook of ancient Greek law*. Oxford.

Kapetanopoulos, E. A. 1966. Klea and Leontis: two ladies from Delphi. *Bulletin de Correspondance Hellénique* 90, pp. 119–30.

Klaffenbach, G. 1936. Neue Inschriften aus Aetolien. *Sitzungsberichte der Preussischen Akademie der Wissenschaften zu Berlin, philologisch-historische Klasse* 27, pp. 358–88.

Knoepfler, D. 1990. Contribution à l'épigraphie de Chalcis. *Bulletin de Correspondance Hellénique* 114, pp. 473–98.

Kremydi-Sicilianou, S. 2005. Belonging to Rome, remaining Greek: Coinage and identity in Roman Macedonia. In: C. Howgego, V. Heuchert and A. Burnett (eds.), *Coinage and identity in the Roman provinces*. Oxford, pp. 95–106.

Lanni, A. 2006. *Law and justice in the courts of Classical Athens*. Cambridge.

Larsen, J. A. O. 1938. Roman Greece. In: T. Frank (ed.), *An Economic Survey of Ancient Rome*, Vol. 4. Baltimore, pp. 259–498.

Loukopoulou, L. D. 1996. The fortunes of the Roman *conventus* of Chalcidice. In: A.D. Rizakis (ed.), *Roman onomastics in the Greek East: Social and political aspects (Meletemata 21)*. Athens, pp. 143–8.

Luzzatto, G. I. 1965. Processo provinciale e autonomie cittadine. *Journal of Juristic Papyrology* 15, pp. 49–64.

Ma, J. 1999. *Antiochos III and the cities of Western Asia Minor*. Oxford.

Mack, W. 2015. *Proxeny and polis: Institutional networks in the ancient Greek world*. Oxford.

Magie, D. 1950. *Roman rule in Asia Minor: to the end of the third century after Christ*. Princeton.

Marshall, A. J. 1980. The survival and development of international jurisdiction in the Greek world under Roman rule. *Aufstieg und Niedergang der römischen Welt* II.13, pp. 626–61.

Migeotte, L. 1984. *L'emprunt public dans les cités grecques: recueil des documents et analyse critique*. Québec.

Migeotte, L. 1997. La date de l'oktôbolos eisphora de Messène. *Topoi* 7, pp. 51–61.

Migeotte, L. 2008. L'organisation de l'oktobolos eisphora de Messène. In: C. Grandjean (ed.), *Le Péloponnèse d'Epaminondas à Hadrien*. Pessac, pp. 229–43.

Millar, F. 1977. *The Emperor in the Roman World*. London.

Müller, C. 2005. La procédure d'adoption des décrets en Béotie de la fin du IIIe s. av. J.-C. au Ier s. apr. J.-C. In: P. Fröhlich & C. Müller (eds.), *Citoyenneté et participation à la basse époque hellénistique*. Geneva, pp. 95–119.

Müller, C. 2014. A *koinon* after 146? Reflections on the political and institutional situation of Boeotia in the second half of the second century BC. In: N. Papazarkadas (ed.), *The epigraphy and history of Boeotia: New finds, new prospects*. Leiden, pp. 119–46.

Oliver, J. H. 1952. The Eleusinian endowment. *Hesperia* 21:4, pp. 381–99.

Oliver, J. H. 1953. *The ruling power: A study of the Roman Empire in the second century after Christ through the Roman Oration of Aelius Aristides*. Philadelphia.

Oliver, J. H. 1970a. *Marcus Aurelius: Aspects of Civic and Cultural Policy in the East*. Princeton.

Oliver, J. H. 1970b. Hadrian's reform of the appeal procedure in Greece. *Hesperia* 39, pp. 332–6.

Oliver, J. H. 1979. Greek applicants for Roman trials. *American Journal of Philology* 100, pp. 543–58.

Oliver, J. H. 1983. *The civic tradition and Roman Athens*. Baltimore.

Oliver, J. H. 1989. *Greek constitutions of early Roman emperors from inscriptions and papyri*. Philadelphia.

Pernin, I. 2014. Land Administration and Property Law in the Proconsular Edict from Thisbe (Syll.[3] 884). In: N. Papazarkadas (ed.), *The epigraphy and history of Boeotia: New finds, new prospects*. Leiden, pp. 443–59.

Piérart, M. 2013. Une nouvelle proxénie argienne de la basse époque hellénistique et les synèdres d'Argos. In: A.I. Ivantchik (ed.), *Monumentum Gregorianum. Tribute to Gregory Bongard-Levin*. Moscow, pp. 275–89.

Pleket, H. W. 1964. *Epigraphica* I. *Texts on the Economic History of the Greek World*. Leiden.

Purcell, N. 2005. Romans in the Roman world. In: K. Galinsky (ed.), *The Cambridge companion to the age of Augustus*. Cambridge, pp. 85–105.

Rizakis, A. D. 1996. Les colonies romaines des côtes occidentales grecques. Populations et territoires. *Dialogues d'Histoire Ancienne* 22:1, pp. 255–324.

Rizakis, A. D. 2001. La constitution des élites municipales dans les colonies romaines de la province d'Achaïe. In: O. Salomies (ed.), *The Greek East in the Roman context. Proceedings of a colloquium organised by the Finnish institute at Athens, May 21–22, 1999.* Helsinki, pp. 37–49.

Rizakis, A. D. 2004a. La littérature gromatique et la colonisation romaine en Orient. In: G. Salmeri, A. Raggi & A. Baroni (eds.), *Colonie romane nel mondo greco.* Rome, pp. 69–94.

Rizakis, A. D. 2004b. L'Emphytéose sous l'Empire en pays Grec. In: S. Follet (ed.), *L'Hellénisme d'époque romaine. Nouveaux documents, nou-velles approches (Ier s. a.C.–IIIe s. p.C.). Actes du Colloque international à la mémoire de Louis Robert. Paris, 7–8 July 2000.* Paris, pp. 55–76.

Rizakis, A. D. 2013. Commerce de parfums et evérgétisme civique en Laconie (Gytheion) sous l'Empire. *Mediterraneo Antico* 16:2, pp. 549–62.

Rizakis, A. D., Zoumbaki, S. & Lepenioti, C. E. (eds.), 2004. *Roman Peloponnese II. Roman personal names in their social context (Meletemata 36).* Athens.

Robert, L. 1973. Les juges étrangers dans la cité grecque. In : E. von Caemmerer (ed.), *Xenion, Festschrift für Pan. I. Zepos anlässlich seines 65. Geburtstages am 1. Dezember 1973,* Vol. 1. Athens, pp. 765–82.

Rousset, D. 1994. Les frontières des cités grecques. Premières réflexions à partir du recueil des documents épigraphiques. *Cahiers du Centre Gustave Glotz* 5, pp. 97–126.

Rousset, D., Tirologos, G. & Fadin, L. 2006. Le lotissement de terres à Delphes au IIe s. ap. J.-C. Du texte au terrain. *Bulletin de Correspondance Hellénique* 130, pp. 639–63.

Santangelo, F. 2007. *Sulla, the elites and the empire. A study of Roman policies in Italy and the Greek East.* Leiden and Boston.

Santangelo, F. 2009. What did the Cloatii do for Gytheum? A note on Syll.[3] 748. *Historia* 58:3, pp. 361–6.

Scafuro, A. C. 2015. Decrees for foreign judges: Judging conventions or epigraphic habits? In: M. Gagarin and A. Lanni (eds.), *Symposion 2013: Vorträge zur griechischen und hellenistischen Rechtsgeschichte. Akten der Gesellschaft für Griechische und Hellenistische Rechtsgeschichte. Cambridge, MA, 26–9 August 2013.* Vienna, pp. 365–95.

Schuler, C. 2007. Ein Vertrag zwischen Rom und den Lykiern aus Tyberissos. In: C. Schuler (ed.), *Griechische Epigraphik in Lykien: eine Zwischenbilanz: Akten des Int. Kolloquiums München. 24–6 February 2005.* Munich, pp. 51–79.

Sherk, R. K. 1969. *Roman documents from the Greek East.* Baltimore.

Sherwin-White, A. N. 1973. *The Roman citizenship.* Second edition. Oxford.

Snowdon, M. 2014. 'In the friendship of the Romans': Melitaia, Narthakion and Greco-Roman interstate friendship in the second century BCE. *Historia* 63, pp. 422–44.

Snowdon, M., 2015. Beyond clientela: The instrumentality of amicitia in the Greek East. In: M. Jehne & F. Pina Polo (eds.) *Foreign clientelae in the Roman Empire: a reconsideration.* Stuttgart, pp. 209–24.

Sosin, J. D. 2015. Manumission with paramone: Conditional freedom? *Transactions of the American Philological Association* 145, pp. 325–81.

Spawforth, A. 2012. *Greece and the Augustan cultural revolution.* Cambridge.

Stadter, P. A. 2014. *Plutarch and his Roman readers.* Oxford.

Taeuber, H. 1994. Stifterinnen im griechischen Osten. In: E. Specht (ed.), *Frauenreichtum: Die Frau als Wirtschaftsfaktor im Altertum.* Vienna, pp. 199–219.

Tate, G. 1997. The Syrian countryside during the Roman era. In: S.E. Alcock (ed.), *The early Roman empire in the East.* Oxford, pp. 55–71.

Thomas, Y. 1996. *Origine et 'commune patrie.' Étude de droit public romain (89 av. J.-C.–212 ap. J.C.).* Rome.

Tuori, K. 2016. *The emperor of law: The emergence of Roman imperial adjudication*. Oxford.

Velissaropoulou-Karakōstas, J. 2011. *Droit grec d'Alexandre à Auguste (323 av. J.-C—14 ap. J.-C.): personnes, biens, justice*. Kentron Hellēnikēs kai Rōmaikēs Archaiotētos. Athens.

Vlassopoulos, K. 2014. Review of Taxing Freedom in Thessalian Manumission Inscriptions by R. Zelnick-Abramovitz. *Bryn Mawr Classical Review* (2014.08.35), available from: <http://bmcr.brynmawr.edu/2014/2014-08-35.html>

Whitehead, D. 1977. *The ideology of the Athenian metic*. Cambridge.

Wilson, A. J. N. 1966. *Emigration from Italy in the Republican age of Rome*. Manchester.

Wörrle, M. 2004. Maroneia im Umbruch. Von der hellenistischen zur kaiserzeitlichen Polis. *Chiron* 34, pp. 149–67.

Zelnick-Ambramovitz, R. 2005. *Not wholly free: The concept of manumission and the status of manumitted slaves in the ancient Greek world*. Leiden.

Zelnick-Ambramovitz, R. 2013. *Taxing freedom in Thessalian manumission inscriptions*. Leiden.

Zetzel, J. 2003. Plato with pillows. Cicero on the uses of the Greek culture. In: D. Braund & C. Gill (eds.) *Myth, history and culture in Republican Rome. Studies in honour of T. P. Wiseman*. Exeter, pp. 119–38.

Zoumbaki, S. B. 2008. The composition of Peloponnesian elites in the Roman period and the evolution of their resistance and approach to the Roman rulers. *Tekmeria* 9, pp. 25–52.

Zoumbaki, S. B. 2013. In search of the horn of plenty: Roman entrepreneurs in the agricultural economy of the province of Achaia. In: A.D. Rizakis and I.P. Touratsoglou (eds.), *Villae rusticae: Family and market-oriented farms in Greece under Roman rule. Proceedings of an international congress held at Patrai. 23–4 April 2010*. Athens, pp. 52–73.

13

The Integration and Perception of the Rule of Law in Roman Crete

From the Roman Conquest to the End of the Principate (67 BCE–235 CE)*

Ioannis E. Tzamtzis

'If the Cretan constitution seemed to me worthy of description, it is owing to its peculiar character and its fame; but there no longer remains much of these *nomima*, and the administration of the Cretans takes place, in great part, through the decrees of the Romans, as is the case in the other provinces'.[1] Is the image which Strabo gives of Roman Crete in this passage of his *Geography* valid for both the Republican period and the Principate? A calm and silent island under the wing of the Roman *regula*?

Most modern scholars are still surprised by the contrast between the bloody wars which the Romans had to wage until they managed to vanquish the Cretans and what is usually interpreted as a total submission of those which Cicero persisted in qualifying, still in 44/43, as *dura natio*.[2] Wildcats, therefore, tamed? Other scholars, less numerous, do not even accept Strabo's indications, given in other passages of his work, that certain *nomima* from ancient times (Lacedaemonian in origin) still lived on in certain Cretan cities, or that the *syssitia* had maintained the appellation of *andreia*:[3] according to these scholars, the Romans would have undermined the institutions that they deemed menacing to their authority. Is it possible to accept this vision of things? Would the Cretans then

* This chapter has been translated from the French by Raphaëla Dubreuil, with revisions by Benedikt Eckhardt.

[1] Strabo 10.4.22: *Ἀξίαν δ' ἀναγραφῆς τὴν τῶν Κρητῶν πολιτείαν ὑπέλαβον διά τε τὴν ἰδιότητα καὶ τὴν δόξαν· οὐ πολλὰ δὲ διαμένει τούτων τῶν νομίμων, ἀλλὰ τοῖς Ῥωμαίων διατάγμασι τὰ πλεῖστα διοικεῖται, καθάπερ καὶ ἐν ταῖς ἄλλαις ἐπαρχίαις συμβαίνει.*

[2] Cicero, *Orationes Philippicae* 5.13.

[3] Strabo 10.4.17: *μεῖναι δὲ τῶν νομίμων παρὰ Λυττίοις καὶ Γορτυνίοις καὶ ἄλλοις τισὶ πολιχνίοις μᾶλλον ἢ παρ' ἐκείνοις· καὶ δὴ καὶ τὰ Λυττίων νόμιμα ποιεῖσθαι μαρτύρια τοὺς τὰ Λακωνικὰ πρεσβύτερα ἀποφαίνοντας* . . . and 18: *τὰ δὲ συσσίτια ἀνδρεῖα παρὰ μὲν τοῖς Κρησὶν καὶ νῦν ἔτι καλεῖσθαι.*

Ioannis E. Tzamtzis, *The Integration and Perception of the Rule of Law in Roman Crete: From the Roman Conquest to the End of the Principate (67 BCE–235 CE)* In: *Law in the Roman Provinces.* Edited by: Kimberley Czajkowski and Benedikt Eckhardt in collaboration with Meret Strothmann, Oxford University Press (2020). © Oxford University Press.
DOI: 10.1093/oso/9780198844082.003.0013

have been deprived of structural elements of their civic life, just as they found themselves forbidden to have a fleet?[4]

On the other hand, it must be noted that Strabo remains silent concerning the island's history during the whole of the Roman period before Augustus. Luckily, we have various sources, literary or other, that enable us to reconstruct the events that took place between the conquest and the battle of Actium; a task which has proved difficult for scholars and which has led many of them to sometimes questionable conclusions.

We shall start with a close examination of the political and military dimension as well as the juridical and administrative structures that were in place before Rome's decision to incorporate Crete into its empire (1.). This will provide the necessary background for evaluating, with a view to its development over time, the interaction between the juridical superstructure imposed by Rome and the pre-existing infrastructure of this insular microcosm, both with regard to the private dealings of its inhabitants and to the institutional organization of the Cretan cities (2.).

1. CRETE'S ENTRY INTO THE EMPIRE AND THE ASSEMBLING OF ROME'S BASIC ADMINISTRATIVE FRAMEWORK

The Cretans experienced repeated contact with Rome from the second century BCE onwards, when Roman envoys were active on the island and the Cretan cities appealed to the senate to resolve their territorial conflicts.[5] A characteristic decision is the Roman senate's referral of the dispute between Itanos and Hierapytna to the judges of Magnesia on Maeander on two occasions, separated by thirty years: the pronouncements of the Magnesians, both in favour of Itanos, date respectively from 140 and from 112/11 BCE.[6] The last of these two cases marks a qualitative differentiation of Rome's role in Cretan affairs, for the parties' acceptance—especially Hierapytna—of the application of the same procedure signifies a subscription on their part to the law established by Roman rule and makes it difficult to discern the line which separates arbitration and recourse to a superior authority.[7]

[4] Strabo 10.4.17: *καὶ γὰρ ναυκρατεῖν πρότερον τοὺς Κρῆτας . . . νῦν δ' ἀποβεβληκέναι τὸ ναυτικόν*; cf. 10.4.9.

[5] On the requirement, formulated by Flamininus, to stop the military collaboration between Nabis of Sparta and the Cretans (195 BCE): Livy 34.27 and 35; the intervention of Q. Fabius Labeo in Crete in order to obtain the cessation of the conflict between Kydonia and the occasional Cnosso-Gortynian alliance and the liberation of many Roman *captivi* (189 BCE): Liv. 37.60.3–6; MRR 1.361, 366; Ager (1996), 262–3; the embassy of Appius Claudius [Pulcher ?] settling the differences between Gortyn and Cnossos at war (184 BCE): Ager (1996), 297–8 no. 110; Polybius 22.15.1–6; Gruen (1984), 106, 233; the mediation of a Quintus [Fabius ?] concerning the Creto-Rhodian conflict (153 BCE): Polybius 33.15.3–4; Van Effenterre (1948), 267–9; Ager (1996), 394 no. 144.

[6] IC III 4.9–10, p. 91 and 106–11, 394–5. Ager (1996), 437–46 no. 158; cf. Cary (1926), 194–200; Spyridakis (1970), 49–66; Sanders (1982), 3; Kallet-Marx (1995), 177–83; Guizzi (1997), 38–46; (2001), 373–82.

[7] Tzamtzis (2013), 37–45.

However, the first military strike against Crete happened forty years later. While it fitted within Rome's expansive efforts to eradicate piracy in the eastern Mediterranean, it also answered a need to efficiently cover the rear of Lucullus' army that was fighting Mithridates VI in Asia.[8] The campaign was entrusted to the praetor of 74 BCE, Marcus Antonius, who, after he had faced the pirates in the eastern Mediterranean, turned against Crete. There he died after he had concluded a 'peace' (*eirene*), according to Diodorus Siculus, between the summer of 72 and the winter of 71/70. Despite the widespread opinion in modern scholarship, which is needlessly entrenched, that Antonius' army experienced disaster on Cretan soil, the *cognomen* 'Creticus' was not given to the general by his contemporaries in mockery: it belongs to a period of the Republic when the senate easily conceded the victory titles (*cognomina ex virtute*) to magistrates without major victories (or even to those who had not engaged in battle).[9] The death of Antonius sealed a military campaign with limited success where the adversary of Rome not only had not been crushed but had also landed significant blows on the invader in a spirit of cruelty similar to that which often animated the Romans. The term '*eirene*' suggests more than a provisional cessation of hostilities, which is also suggested by the *senatus consultum*, mentioned again by Diodorus, which recognized the Cretans as *amici et socii* in 70–69, on the occasion of their embassy to the senate.[10] In turn, this qualification bestowed by the Romans upon past opponents places their relationship in the context of the *fides* conceded by an '*hegemonia*'/empire, a concept that Proculus later assimilated to the bond between patron and client.[11] Before dying, Antonius must have at least laid the foundations for the conclusion of a treaty (*foedus*), unequal of course (*iniquum*), probably by integrating certain results of the contacts which Lucullus had made on the island in 85. Nevertheless, the aforementioned *senatus consultum* came into conflict with the *veto* by the tribune of the plebs P. Cornelius Lentulus Spinther.[12]

Following these events, the second campaign against Crete was entrusted to the consul of 69 BCE, Caecilius Metellus.[13] During the hostilities, however, the Cretans

[8] For Cretan piracy from the middle of the second century to the conquest of the island see Brulé (1978); Ormerod (1924) 127–8 and 138–50; De Souza (1999), 43–4, in particular 80–4. For Rome's eastern politics during that period see Sherwin-White (1984), 175–85; cf. Keaveney (1992), 75–98.

[9] Livy, *Periochae* 97: *M. Antonius praetor bellum adversus Cretenses parum prospere susceptum morte sua finiit*; cf. Appian, *Sic.* 6.1; Cassius Dio 111.1; Plutarch, *Antonius* 1.1; Florus 1.42; Pseudo-Asclepius 202, 259 St.; *Scholia Bobiensia* 96 St. Since Orelli & Baiter (1838), 47–8, there has been a tendency to depreciate heavily M. Antonius while considering his *cognomen* 'Creticus' as a mockery, e.g. Klebs (1894), 2594; Foucart (1906), 574–5; Ormerod (1924), 224–7; Van Ooteghem (1954), 163–4; *id.* (1967), 231–2; Will (1982), 488; Traina (2003), 4–5. Against this erroneous thesis: Linderski (1990), 157–64; Tzamtzis (2013), 53–5; Tzamtzis (2018), 13–45, especially 17–29, 30–1, 34, cf. (for a position in the middle) Kallet-Marx (1995), 309–11, 319–20; De Souza (1999), 141–8.

[10] Diodorus Siculus 40.1.1–2: φίλους καὶ συμμάχους τῆς ἡγεμονίας; cf. Tzamtzis (2013), 56–8.

[11] Concerning this expression which belongs to the technical terminology of Roman diplomatic language: Cursi (2014), 186–94; cf. Gruen (1984), 25–6, 54–95. For the Romans, to elevate an opponent who had vanquished them to *amicus et socius* would constitute a major paradox, contrary both to their practices, well established by this later date, and to their mentality: Linderski (1990), 162, has clearly understood that the Romans imposed conditions; *contra*, most recently, Viviers (2004), 17–24. On the *fides* between Rome and other *civitates liberae*: D. 49.15.7.1 (on the definition of *liber populus*); cf. Burton (2003), 333–69.

[12] Diodorus Siculus 40.1.2.

[13] Diodorus Siculus 40.1.3; Appian, *Sic.* 6.1–2; Florus 1.42.4.

surrendered to Pompey, interpreting the *imperium* that the latter had obtained for all the Mediterranean basin (in virtue of the *lex Gabinia de piratis persequendis*) as superior to that which Metellus possessed: thus they provoked a political conflict between the two generals, which mutated into a military clash on Cretan territory.[14] Crete fell under Roman rule in 67. Metellus also received the *cognomen* 'Creticus', but he had to wait almost four years in order to celebrate his triumph as *ex insula Creta*, for the friends of Pompey in the senate prevented the triumph from taking place.[15]

It could be assumed that Crete was the object of a provincial law that laid down the Roman legal framework in which the conquered population now had to operate. It has, however, been proven that in the majority of cases the victorious general issued one or more *formulae* in order to specify, in the first instance, the fiscal status of cities. Sometimes we notice an accumulation or a succession of diverse elements: initial *formula*, the sending of the senatorial committee of ten *legati* and the subsequent vote of *leges* in Rome in order to resolve the problems that arose.[16] This should have been the case for Illyricum and for Macedonia in 167, where 'the *formula* for Macedonia was issued' (*Macedoniae formula dicta*);[17] yet Aemilius Paullus' delivery of the constitutional texts in the different cities of the four Macedonian regions is designated by the phrase 'he gave laws to Macedonia' (*Leges Macedoniae dedit*).[18] Livy's *Periocha* 100 contains a similar sentence designating Crete's crucial submission to Rome's legal system: 'After the Cretans had been subdued, Q. Metellus gave laws (*leges dedit*) to the island that had been free up to this time'. *Lex provinciae*, therefore, or Metellus' *formulae*? Doubt is caused less by the silence of our sources concerning a *lex Caecilia* (*Metella*), but rather by the fact that Crete was later unified with Cyrenaica into one province.

Once Crete was conquered it was the senate, probably in 66, that decided on the abovementioned administrative plan and, in this case, it is perhaps possible to speak of a *lex provinciae*.[19] The official designation of the new province was *Creta et Cyrenaica* as appears on the series of coins carrying *KPHT/KYPA* which, according to E.S.G. Robinson, belong to this period.[20] Rome's choice to place two locations that are separated by hundreds of miles of high seas under a unique proconsular administration should not be surprising. Besides the strong probability that Pompey's friends in the senate wanted to stop Metellus' potential influence in Crete, it is important to consider that a single proconsul's governance allowed

[14] Cassius Dio 36.1a, 36.18–19; Velleius Paterculus 2.34.1; Livy, *Periochae* 98; Appian, *Sic.* 6.2; Florus 1.42.4–5; Phlegon of Tralles, *FGrH* 257 F 12.12; Valerius Maximus 7.6.1; Orosius 6.4.2; Cicero, *de imperio Cn. Pompeii* 35 and 46; Plutarch, *Pompeius* 29.3–4; cf. Piatkowski (1973), 215–20; Sanders (1982), 3–4; De Souza (1999), 160–1; Guizzi (2001), 407–8; Tzamtzis (2013), 64–7, Tzamtzis (2018), 36–42.

[15] Florus 1.42.6; 2.13.9; Cassius Dio 36.19.3; Cicero, *In Pisonem* 58; Velleius Paterculus 2.34.2 and 40.4–5; Eutropius 6.11, 16; cf. Van Ooteghem (1954), 270–1, 283; Van Ooteghem (1967), 236–7.

[16] Lintott (1993), 28–9, 30–1.

[17] Livy 45.26.15 and 31.1: L. Anicius and L. Aemilius Paulus respectively; the technical word in Greek for the formula was *τύπος*, as the epigraphical evidence from Aphrodisias demonstrates: Reynolds (1982a), no.15, l. 13–14; cf. no. 14, l. 3.

[18] Livy, *Periochae* 100; cf. Appian, *Sic.* 6.2: [Metellus] *ὑπηγάγετο αὐτὴν* (= Crete) and: . . . *τὴν νῆσον ἐξεργασάμενος*; in any case no trace of a *lex Caecilia* (*Metella*) has been found in our sources.

[19] Tzamtzis (2013), 68–9.

[20] BMC, Cyrenaica, CCII; Romanelli (1943), 50; the opposing view situates the coins between 40 and 34: Perl (1970), 329; Laronde (1988), 1013.

for the control of the waterways in the south of the Mediterranean (along the north-east coast of the African continent) and of the first part of the route that wheat shipments followed when leaving Cyrenaica for the Peloponnese.[21] Between 66 and 44, the initial status of the administrative unity created by Crete and Cyrenaica successively swung between abolitions and restorations:[22] we know that in the aftermath of the Ides of March, the two territories were separated.[23] The reunification took place under Augustus and, after another statuary fluctuation during the Severan period, the separation was considered final under Diocletian.[24]

Laws, *senatus consulta*, imperial constitutions, decrees of the praetor, custom (especially in integrative dimension with regard to local rules) and jurisprudence are the sources from which flow the rules of Roman law applied in Crete for centuries: one finds its traces in legal texts like the *Digest* but also in literary sources and epigraphy.[25] This echoes, evidently, the passage from Strabo cited above.

This image of lawfulness is supported by the examination of the way in which the Roman government structured this province. The proconsul of Crete-Cyrenaica[26] exercised *iurisdictio* and *coercitio*, principal components of his *imperium*, the limitations of which, set up during the Republican period, faded after the establishment of the Principate. It also initiated the development of the

[21] Kallet-Marx (1995), 308; Harrison (1988), 144–8, particularly 145–6; also noteworthy is Sartre (1991), 22, who asserts that Creta-Cyrenaica was a 'bicephalous province' with two capital cities, Gortyn and Cyrene, at least from the time of Augustus.

[22] The status of unified administration was kept until 63 BCE when Mithridates VI disappeared and Pompey found himself in Palestine: Plutarch, *Pompeius* 41; Josephus, *Antiquitates Judaicae* 14,53–4; Appian, *Bellum Mithridaticum* 113; and Cassius Dio 37.12–13; Livy, *Periochae* 102; cf. Van Ooteghem (1954), 242–3. Depending on the interpretation of the presence in 62–61 of the questor M. Iuventius Laterensis in Cyrenaica, the status of this unity was perhaps prolonged; the uncertainty increases with the Ciceronian mention of M. Nonius Sufenas and Cn. Tremellius Scrofa, who may have governed Creta-Cyrenaica or part of it: Cicero, *ad Atticum* 6.1.13; Münzer (1936), 900–1; Münzer (1937), 2287–9; MRR 2.243; MRR 3.116; Jashemsky (1950), 84–5, 131, 153–4; Perl (1970), 331–3; Perl (1971), 371–3; Laronde (1988), 1013; Kallet-Marx (1995), 319 n. 119; Tzamtzis (2013), 73–82.

[23] Through the *senatus consultum* Crete was entrusted to M. Iunius Brutus and Cyrenaica to C. Cassius Longinus, instead of Macedonia and Syria that were originally destined for them, the government of which was finally entrusted to the consuls of 44 P. Cornelius Dolabella and Mark Antony—the son of Creticus: Appian, *Bella civilia* 3.8, 12, 16, 36; also Cicero, *Orationes Philippicae* 2.97; Cassius Dio 45.32.4; 46.23.3; cf. Syme (1939), 118–19; Perl (1970), 332–4; Fröhlich (1899), 1727–36, especially 1729, 1731; Romanelli (1943), 58; Laronde (1988), 1013.

[24] On the evolution of the administrative status of Crete and Cyrenaica from the time of Septimius Severus to Diocletian (AE 1969/1970, 636–7: start of the third century) cf. Lepelley (1998), 304; Laronde (1988), 1014, 1060; Sanders (1982), 133.

[25] For general studies on the sources of Roman law, 'ancient' (the Republic) and 'new' (the Empire), applied successively in Crete given the date of its conquest: Gaudemet (1967), 380–95, 570–605; Johnston (1999), 1–11; a good example of sources of law at the start of the Principate are the four Augustan decrees (7–6 BCE) that concern the African part of the province and the *senatus consultum Calvisianum* (4 BCE), of general relevance, discovered at Cyrene: SEG 9.8 = Oliver (1989), 40–55 (commentary: 50–5); cf. De Visscher (1940); *id.* (1964), 321–33; also illustrative is the imperial *mandatum* addressed to the proconsul, in 64–63 BCE, attested in the inscription of Pyranthos: IC I, XXVI, no. 2; cf. Tzamtzis (2013), 96–7; A *lex rogata* focusing exclusively on Crete is that of 44/43: Cic. *Phil.* 2.97; cf. Cassius Dio 45.32.4; on the qualification of this *lex de insula Creta* as *Iulia* or *Antonia*, as well as on the doubts pertaining to its taking effect, see esp. Rotondi (1912), 430; Yavetz (1990), 113.

[26] For a review of the proconsuls that served in Crete and that subsequently followed professional paths leading to very high senatorial magistracies: Tzamtzis (2013), 101–4; cf. Baldwin Bowsky (1983), *passim*.

cognitio extra ordinem and of the *ius gladii*.[27] It is worth mentioning the area of proconsular jurisdiction that touched upon the surveillance of deportees, since Crete seems to have served as a place of deportation (Cassius Severus, in 24 BCE).[28] The—admittedly late—trial and execution of the *Ten Christian Martyrs* (*Agioi Deka*) at Gortyn in 251 is a notorious example of a combined application of jurisdictional and coercive proconsular power.[29] Concerning the proconsular *conventus*,[30] the host cities in Cyrenaica were Cyrene and Ptolemais (Berenice tried, without success, to be added to the list under Hadrian),[31] whereas in Crete, Cnossos, although a Roman colony,[32] is the most probable stop for the proconsul's assizes in light of the high volume of transactions between colonists and indigenous people.[33] There was possibly another stop in the eastern part of the island—why not Hierapytna[34]?

From a *stricto sensu* administrative point of view, the proconsul was responsible, in Crete as elsewhere, for the organisation and the operation of public archives both in his headquarters and also in the most important cities of his province: the diligence of the governor largely effected the conservation, the publication and the diffusion of official documents coming from Rome or edited by himself.[35] An inscription from Hierapytna dating to the second century CE mentions the *grammatophylakia* of this city, whereas several *chreophylakia* are already attested from the second century BCE in other cities, including Gortyn.[36]

[27] Concerning the proconsular *imperium* and its operation, the combination of the finds from Strachan-Davidson (1912), 1.100–1, Magdelain (1967), 51–57, and Sherwin-White (1963), 1–23, produces a complete picture. On the system of provincial trials in general as well as on the *quaestiones provinciae*: Wlassak (1919); Santalucia (1998), 183–8. On the relationship between the application of proconsular justice to the criminal and the permanent tribunals in Rome: Mommsen (1893), 3.302–3, 308–9; 2.166–9; Garnsey (1966), 167–89; *id.* (1968), 52–9, who presents an intelligible summary of Mommsen's theory on the evolution of the *provocatio* and the—relative—guaranty that this institution gave to the Roman citizen: escape from abusive punishment by the proconsul (the *leges Porciae* and, later, the *appellatio* to the emperor played a pivotal role here); cf. Lintott (1972), 226–67; Jones (1960), 51–65; *id.* (1972), 22–5, 32–3, 105–6. Cf. for the working of the *cognitio* and the *arbitrium iudicandis* and for the link with the *ius gladii*, after having noted Ulpian's passage in the Digest, 1.18.6.8 (taken, characteristically, from *De officio proconsulis*: *Qui universas provincias regunt, ius gladii habent et in metallum dandi potestas eis permissa est*), see esp. Sherwin-White (1963), 3–5, 17, 20–2; Garnsey (1968), 52–9; Liebs (1981), 217–23; Manfredini (1991), 103–26; also Tzamtzis (2009), 543–63; Tzamtzis (2013), 106–12.

[28] Tacitus, *Annales* 4.21; cf. 1.72.

[29] *Patr.C.C.* 565–73; cf. Franchi De Cavalieri (1946), 27–40; Sanders (1982), 7, 45; Haensch (1997), 512. In addition, a case that relating to the proconsular *coercitio* of Crete-Cyrenaica (P. Sextius Scaeva: De Visscher (1940), 78–80) is the object of the fourth decree of Cyrene: SEG 9.8 (II), l. 40–55 = Oliver (1989), 9, 42–3.

[30] On the tour of provincial governors in order to hold court in the principal cities of their provinces, see in particular: Burton (1975), 92–106; Meyer-Zwiffelhoffer (2002), 173–4; Porena (2005), 13–92, esp. 28–9.

[31] Reynolds 1978, 111–21; Oliver 1989, 281–2.

[32] See *infra*, p. 257.

[33] Tzamtzis (2013), 123–4.

[34] Tzamtzis (2013), 123.

[35] Noteworthy is the rule that imposed a written correspondence for the diffusion of documents in the affairs where a hearing by the governor was not required: D. 1.16.9.1; for the expertise and the activities of the proconsul in Crete see in detail Tzamtzis (2013), 123–4; cf. Pautasso (1994–5), 75–108.

[36] Gortyn: IC IV 232; Cnossos: IC I.X.4A; Lato et Olous: IC I.X.5; Polyrrhenia: IC II.XXIII.6A; cf. Willetts (1955), 200–3; Velissaropoulos-Karakostas (2011), 2.263–7.

There the presence of a *tabularius* at the start of the third century CE also demonstrates the keeping of archives, economic by nature, in the capital of the province.[37] Moreover, the proconsul was also responsible for public finances, and broader economic matters, for he had the power to introduce new taxes in the name of public interest.[38] The proconsul was, of course, responsible for the construction, preservation, reparation and amelioration of the infrastructure available to the social collective.[39] The proconsuls who 'restored' many constructions are mentioned on numerous Gortynian inscriptions.[40] It is within this context that Gortyn's odeon was restored in the year 100.[41] One of the proconsul's important political tasks was to supervise, or even to control, the elections of local dignitaries to ensure that *idonei* suitable to Rome were chosen.[42]

In his annual government of a province, the proconsul was assisted, according to the law, by a *quaestor* and a *legatus*, named also for a year. Amongst his other financial responsibilities, the *quaestor* had to issue provincial money: doubtless the money that was circulated by various proconsuls of Crete-Cyrenaica was the result of their quaestors' activities.[43] Nothing indicates that the *legatus* was a *iuridicus* whose tasks was confined to Cyrenaica.[44] The activity of the *procuratores*—without a *subprocurator*—is attested in Crete,[45] as well as the presence of an *advocatus fisci*,[46] and even of a *curator civitatis*, '*logistes*', for Gortyn, in late antiquity.[47] While not numerous, the clues that prove the existence of a cohort that followed and supported the proconsul exist, since the sources give

[37] IC III 3, 30; ILS 1496.

[38] On the Roman system of imposition, see also *infra*, p. 252.

[39] On the collaboration of the proconsul and local dignitaries for the construction or distribution of the facilities: Meyer-Zwiffelhoffer (2002), 172–3; 186–222.

[40] IC IV 326 and 327: *Vestalis procos. Res|tituit—Οὐεσ|τάλις ἀνθύπα[τος] | ἀποκατέστη[σεν]*; for the maintenance and improvement of the road networks of Crete, and more generally, of the infrastructure under Tiberius, Claudius and Vespasian: Charlesworth (1924), 212; Harrison (1988), 153; Van Effenterre (1990), 767–78.

[41] IC IV 331: *Imp. Caesar Divi Nervae f. | Traianus Aug. Germ. p. m. t. pot. | IIII p. p. cos. III civitati Gortyniorum | Odeum ruina conlapsum restituit | curante L. Elufrio Severo pro cos.*

[42] D. 50.4.11.1:... *Epistula Divi Pii ad Titianum exprimitur. Etsi lege municipali caveatur, ut praeferrentur in honoribus certae conditionis homines, attamen sciendum est, hoc esse observandum, si idonei sint*...; oddly, this passage escapes the notice of Burton (1975), but not that of Sanders (1982), 7 n. 51.

[43] Cf. Nicolet (1978), 914–15; Jacques & Scheid (1999), 169–70; Kunkel & Wittmann (1995), 510–33. The *quaestor* of Crete-Cyrenaica was *pro praetore* and sat, like the proconsul, in Gortyn: Haensch (1997), 206–7.

[44] *Pro magistratu legatus*: CIL I 24; D. 1.16.13 (Pomponius): *Legati proconsulis nihil proprium habent, nisi a proconsule eis mandata fuerit iurisdictio*; also 1.16.5 and 1.16.11–12; cf. Arnold (1914), 67–8; Thomasson (1991), 54–72. No *legatus proconsulis* is attested as *iuridicus* strictly confined to Cyrenaica—even if it is conceivable that a circumstantial allocation took place according to geographical areas of competence: Haensch (1997), 206–7; Tzamtzis (2013), 138–40.

[45] Activities of *procuratores* in Crete: IC I.VIII.48; Baldwin Bowsky (1987), 218–29; Baldwin Bowsky (2004), 95-150, especially 116-7; Ducrey (1969), 846–52; Frend (1962), inscription on p. 235; IC IV 333; CIL III 7130; cf. Pflaum (1950), no. 75, 170. The *procuratura* in Crete was a post of *centenarius*: Demougin (2001), 24–34. On the jurisdictional activities of *procuratores*, it is always useful to consult Millar (1964), 180–7, 165, 362–7.

[46] *Advocatus fisci*: IC I.XVII.27; a *tabularius* also in ILS 1496; a *praefectus rei frumentariae* (in 331): IC IV 285.

[47] IC IV 336 a–b; see the commentary of Guarducci on p. 358.

us the names of some *comites* and *amici*.[48] The *officium* of the proconsul would have certainly also included *lictores*, *viatores*, and *praecones*, as well as the necessary staff, such as priests and auxiliaries, for religious and cultic activities.[49]

The Roman dignitaries that served in Crete were subject to the *repetundarum* legislation that, since the *leges Cornelia* of 81 and *Iulia* of 59 BCE, had continued to expand the number of people at risk of being accused of this crime.[50] It seems logical to assume that Gortyn and Cyrene were the two cities where the proconsul of Cyrenaican Crete filed the *rationes confectae collataeque* before his departure to Rome at the end of his service.[51] The trials for *crimen repetundarum* could be combined with other accusations such as that of *crimen maiestatis*. Caesius Cordus was confronted with this type of double accusation in 21 BCE. From then on starts a period marked by the trials of a series of pro-magistrates from Crete-Cyrenaica who were judged for misconduct during their service in the province.[52] It was the Cretans who accused Cestius Proculus of *repetundae* although he was acquitted in 56.[53] The proconsul of the same year, Pedius Blaesus, was condemned in 59 after an accusation issued by the Cyreneans.[54] During the same period, the *procurator* Acilius Strabo was also accused; he had been in charge of sorting out *ad hoc* the problems concerning the exploitation of imperial land in Cyrenaica.[55] Finally, the proconsul of 70, M. Antonius Flamma, was exiled after a *repetundarum* condemnation.[56]

[48] For those of Occius Flamma, for example: Seneca, *Controversiarum excerpta* 9.4.19–20; cf. Orth (1973), 255–63.

[49] Person (1878), 264; Jones (1960), 151–75; the mention of the *officium* in the Digest dates the introduction of the term in legal texts to Marcus Aurelius' time: D. 48.14.1.27. An example of the way in which the *officium* was constituted is given in an *epistula* by Fronto to Antoninus Pius (*Ad Pium* 8:...*propinquos et amicos meos, quorum fidem et integritatem cognoveram, domo accivi*...); cf. Jacques & Scheid (1999), 177; Seeck (1901), 622–79, especially 622–5; Arnold (1914), 68–9; Nicolet (1978), 915.

[50] Ponteney de Fontette (1954); Brunt (1961), 189–228; Eder (1969); Santalucia (1998), 104–5, 141–2, 157–8; 258–9. The circle of people targeted by the *repetundarum* did not cease to expand since the first constitution of the *quaestio* in 149 BCE until the Principate: Marcian, *Institutes* 14 (D.48.11.1). Although the penal qualification covered a diversity of action that was always expanding, the procedure was also growing; the dispositions of the *s.c. Calvisianum* of 4 BCE are typical: Oliver (1989), no. 12, 43–5, l. 80–2, 106–7, 121–2, 134. The prohibition of the *laudationes* and other gestures of congratulation on the part of the provincial *concilia/koina* towards the pro-magistrates during their service and for a length of time after their departure is telling: Paul, *frg Leyd.* 2; Cassius Dio 56.25.6; Tacitus, *Annales* 13.31 (in particular concerning the declarations of the Cretan Claudius Timarchus); cf. Brunt (1961), 198, 216.

[51] The proconsul's obligation to surrender his post, to file his final report of his administration and of his management in the two principal cities of his province was certainly planned by the *lex Iulia de repetumdis* in 59 BCE: Cicero, *Ad familiares* 2.17.2: *Quoniam lege Iulia relinquere rationes in provincia necesse erat eosdemque totidem verbis referre ad aerarium*, and 5.20.2: *quod lex iubebat, ut apud duos civitates*...*rationes confectas collatasque deponeremus*; cf. *ad Atticum* 6.7.2; *In Pisonem* 61. Logic would suggest that in the case of the proconsul of Crete-Cyrenaica, the two cities were Gortyn and Cyrene: Tzamtzis (2013), 152.

[52] *Repetundae* in combination with *maiestas*: Tacitus, *Annales* 3.38; cf. Brunt (1961), 224, no. 5; Köstermann (1955), 72–106, especially 98–9.

[53] Tacitus, *Annales* 13.30: *Absolutus Cestius Proculus repetundarum, Cretensibus accusantibus.*

[54] Tacitus, *Annales* 14.18; cf. Brunt (1961), 226, no. 28.

[55] Tacitus, *Annales* 14.18; cf. Brunt (1961), 226, no. 33; Laronde (1988), 1017. *Procurator in loco proconsulis*: Pflaum (1962), 1232–42.

[56] Tacitus, *Historiae* 4.45.2.

2. THE EVOLVING INTERACTION BETWEEN THE ROMAN LEGAL SUPERSTRUCTURE AND THE CRETAN INSTITUTIONAL REALITY

There is much to learn from a study of the composition of the population from the perspective of their personal status. Based on viritane rather than communal awards (the extended use of which appears to be limited to exceptional cases), the diffusion of the *civitas Romana* among the indigenous population did not result in few large groups holding the same *nomen gentilicium*, but in a remarkable variety of *nomina* that go back to the Republican as well as the imperial period.[57] Kydas the Gortynian's grant of citizenship presents a difficult case to diagnose: Cicero confirms his inscription into the *album iudicum* of the *tertia decuria* that the Antonii composed in 44, following less demanding census criteria, in order to take control of Rome's judiciary.[58] One should not be surprised that the sons of Antonius *Creticus* should favour a Cretan: it is certain that the Antonii family had much support from their clients on the island.[59] The epigraphical evidence suggests a sporadic presence of Romans, non-Cretan in origin, before Metellus' conquest as well as a slow but continuous flux of *negotiatores* until the Julio-Claudian period.[60] The first senators that came to this corner of the empire appear much later, during the second century, and are the descendants of Italian traders as well as members of prominent Cretan families.[61] The distinction between *honestiores* and *humiliores* goes without saying.[62]

There exist two important examples concerning the existence of social and civic structures. An important Greek inscription, from Lyttos, dating from the second century or the end of the third,[63] provides evidence for the retention of the *syssitia/andreia* after Crete's integration into the Roman *imperium*.[64] This concerns a monetary distribution to the *startoi* of *phylai* (tribes) under terms that, however, conform to the practice of euergetism, which was already well developed

[57] Romanelli (1956), 661; Baldwin Bowsky (2002), 25–65, especially 34–6.

[58] Cicero, *Orationes Philippicae* 5.13; 7.27; cf. Orelli and Baiter (1838), 207, 370; Nicolet (1974), 2.1091; Tzamtzis (1998), 539–56.; Paluchowski (2005b), 54–80, esp. 75–6; Ferriès (2007), 104–5, 311, 383, 385–6; Ferriès (2012), 55–72, esp. 65–6.

[59] Three generations of Antonii included Crete in their political and military acts: Marcus Antonius 'the orator' undertook a campaign against the pirates in Cilicia in 103 or 102 (Livy, *Periochae* 68; Obsequ., *Prodig.* 44); his son operated against the Cretans in 72–70 (see *supra*, p. 245); his grandson was the consul of 44 and later the *triumvir*; cf. Tzamtzis (2013), 55, 169 n. 12.

[60] On the pre-Roman period of the island: Hatzfeld (1919), 158; after the conquest: Romanelli (1936), 661–2; in particular: Baldwin Bowsky (2001), 97–119, especially 99–105.

[61] Reynolds (1982b), 671–9; see Aurelius Victor's statement that makes Nerva an Italian of Cretan origin, *De Caesaribus* 12.1: *Quid enim Nerva Cretensi prudentius maximeque moderatum*; on the truth of this cf. Sanders (1982), 179; Sonnabend (2004), 25–8, esp. 27.

[62] Cardascia (1950), 305–37, 461–85. On the proof of this distinction in Crete see Tzamtzis (2013), 177–8.

[63] IC I.XVIII.11; cf. also Guarducci (1933), 488–91.

[64] On the immediate abolition of the *syssitia* after Metellus' conquest: Chaniotis (1988), 62–89, especially 79–80; it is clear that this theory must be discarded: Paluchowski (2005 c), 421–44, especially 439–40; cf. Sanders (1982), 33, who chooses a middle way and argues for a decline of the *syssitia* already in the Hellenistic period, with Rome only delivering the coup de grâce.

across the empire.[65] Another inscription, in Latin this time and dating from 195/196 CE,[66] gives proof of the existence in Gortyn of an organized structure for the Roman part of the population. Despite the hesitations of certain scholars, the initials 'c. R. q. G. c.' mark the presence of an important *conventus civium Romanorum* (with *decuriae* and *curator*), composed, it seems, of *negotiatores* of Roman or Italic origin and of Greeks who held *civitas Romana*.[67]

The status of land in Roman Crete is intriguing since, aside from the similarities of our finds compared to those we know from other provinces, our approach to land ownership in Rome Crete must contain other elements particular to this insular society.

Noticing that in the Roman period, Cretan estates of arable land could belong to cities or temples but also to individuals, I. F. Sanders placed the development of private landownership at the end of the Hellenistic period. He considered it a consequence of the decline of public estates belonging to the cities, itself caused in turn by the cessation of the *syssitia*, 'until the Roman conquest brought new pressures in the form of imperial taxation'.[68] Indeed, the political stance adopted by the Romans in the management and the exploitation of provincial soil consisted in giving the status of *ager publicus* to a section of the land and, for the rest, in tolerating the pre-existing modes of property management by imposing either the *stipendium/tributum* or a *vectigal*.[69]

It is true that the discovery at Araces of *horoi* with a Latin inscription *Fines pub(lici) rest(ituti)*,[70] and of *deiktes*-miliaria at Hierapytna, with Augustus' initials engraved upon them,[71] allows us to conjecture the existence of public lands that adjoined private ones, crossed by a road network. On the other hand the inscriptions of Pyranthos prove the attempt, eventually abandoned in 63 CE, by individuals to occupy lands that belonged to the city of Gortyn: 'Based on the authority of Nero . . . , the proconsul L. Turpilius Dexter restituted and established the boundaries of all the public estates of Gortyn that had been occupied by private persons'.[72] The aforementioned proconsular *restitutio* and *terminatio* calls to mind the action undertaken by a procurator for the restitution, still under Nero, of five *iugera* of Aesculapius from the colony of Cnossos.[73] The fact that in 120, the *hieron* of Skyllios Zeus at Rhytion faced a similar problem, as well as a catalogue of 6 CE from Diktynnaion that includes different types of income

[65] On the *startoi*, a subdivision of the *phyle*, but also on the euergetic aspect of the regulation reported on the inscription in question: Latte (1946–7), 54–75; Paluchowski (2005c), 430–4.

[66] IC IV 278; cf. Mommsen's commentaries in CIL III Suppl. 12038 and of Guarducci *in loco*.

[67] Tzamtzis (2013), 183–7; cf. Kornemann (1900), 1185; Hatzfeld (1919), 158, 282, 286.

[68] Sanders (1982), 33.

[69] The payment of 10% of the crops or of a fixed sum is qualified as *stipendium* but also as *tributum*; the *vectigal* is a fixed sum but is linked to the size of the exploited land and not to its yield; cf. Bove (1960); Grelle (1963); Nicolet (1988), 195–205; Lintott (1993), 81–2.

[70] IC I.V.II.44 and 45 (63 CE).

[71] *Imp. Caes. D. f. Aug D C C E*: IC III 3, 62 and 63.

[72] IC I.XXVI.2: *Ex auctoritate Neronis . . . L. Turpilius Dexter procos. praedia publica Gortyniorum pleraque a privatis occupata restituit terminavitque.*

[73] IC I.VIII.48: . . . *Aesculapio iugera quinque data a divo Aug. confirmata a divo Claudio restituit C(oloniae) I(uliae) N(obili) C(nosso) per P. Licinium Secundum proc.*

derived from agricultural and animal rearing activities, both confirm (directly or indirectly) that Cretan sanctuaries possessed exploitable land as well.[74]

It is indicative that the qualification of a piece of land as *sacer* or *religiosus* prompts Gaius, at the beginning of the second book of his *Institutes*, to present the theory that ownership of provincial soil belongs to the emperor and the Roman people, allowing only for possession and usufruct by the inhabitants.[75] Besides the fact that this theory justifies the *vectigalia* and the *stipendia*, it is crucial to note its connection with (but not its derivation from) a particular understanding of land ownership which seems to have been established in Crete during the Archaic and Classical periods and which was preserved in the Gortyn Code: as H. Van Effenterre has suggested by proposing a different interpretation of the sentence ἐνεῖ αἶς κα μὲ Ϝοικεὺς ἐν Ϝοικεῖ/ἐπὶ κόραι Ϝοικίον, the farmers of the *klaroi* of Messara must not be considered either as cultivating public lands nor as having a direct enjoyment, without intermediaries, of their lots.[76] This was an ownership regime *sui generis* where the beneficiaries, Ϝοικεῖς, managed the *klaroi* and derived property revenues from them, but where the city was the recipient and redistributor of the yield.[77] If this thesis is accepted, then we can suppose that the application of Roman practices after the conquest did not lead the Cretans to face a completely unknown reality: the reminiscence of the old logic of 'semi-ownership' still lingered in 100 CE above the *cavea* of Gortyn's odeon.

But this picture—where we see that there is room for smaller and larger properties, such as temples and cities, as well as for an *ager publicus* and probably domains that also held *latifundium* pretentions[78]—remains incomplete if we do not mention the introduction of the 'Campanian factor'. The presence of this Italian element in a fertile corridor of central Crete originated in Octavian's promise in 37 BCE to the *Capuani* of the income of the Cnossian *chora*, as compensation for having deprived them of their fertile lands in Italy after the redistribution of lots to veterans.[79] The works of G. Perl, I. F. Sander and K. J. Rigsby have proven that Octavian's gesture was not linked to the creation of the *colonia* at Cnossos—despite the persistence of some erroneous opinions that still see a direct link—[80]and there was no *en masse* installation of Campanians in Crete: nothing but the presence of an *arcarius Cretae* at Capua, attested by the epigraphical evidence, allows us to assert that the *ager* conceded to the Capuani was cultivated, for the most part, by Cretans, who paid the owed *vectigal*.[81]

[74] IC I.XI.3.

[75] *Inst.* 2.7: *Sed in provinciali solo placet plerisque locum religiosum non fieri, quia in eo solo dominium populi romani est vel Caesaris, nos autem possessionem tantum vel usufructum habere videmur*...

[76] Gortyn Code (= C.Gort.): IC IV 72: IV, l. 34–5; Van Effenterre (1998), 191–5.

[77] Van Effenterre (1998), 195, with a reference to Aristotle, *Politica* 2.1271b and to Dosiadas *apud* Athenaeus 4.143b.

[78] Contracts for property purchase are mentioned in IC IV 337–40. A great concentration of land, as much in Crete as in Cyrenaica, in the hands of Flavius Ursus: Statius, *Silvae* 2.6.60–8; see the analysis of the archaeological finds of Sanders (1982), 30–1, 33, who only assumed *latifundia*.

[79] Cassius Dio 49.14.6–49, 15.1; Velleius Paterculus 2.81.2.

[80] See *infra*, p. 257 and n. 105.

[81] ILS 6317; Cnossos was not a colony of Capua: Perl (1970), 343–4; 14; Rigsby (1976), 313–30; Tzamtzis (2013), 192–4; the fact that it is not possible to deduce 36 BCE as the date for the creation of the Roman colony at Cnossos from the texts of Dio and Velleius has been underlined by Sanders (1982), 5.

What of the legal reality of everyday life? Crete has yielded many examples, varied but not abundant, of commercial activities, manufacturing of tiles, amphoras and lamps, of the exploitation of forests and quarries (activities that necessitated an important number of legal transactions and acts),[82] *venditiones* of products from the land and rearing,[83] *locationes* of slaves and animals,[84] *manumissiones*,[85] foundations of *collegia* and of *sodalitates*,[86] but also, to our delight, a *rescriptum* of Hadrian addressed to Salvius Carus 'the proconsul of Crete', contained in the *Digest*, that answers a procedural question in the context of a case where the *tutor* declared himself *accusator* on behalf of the *pupillis*.[87]

With regard to legal activity specifically concerning affairs where the parties are Greek, we inevitably have to discuss, in the context of this article, the subject of the effective application of the clauses of the Great Inscription of Gortyn at the turn of the first and second century. Much discussed in the past, it has to a certain extent been put aside during the last few decades in favour of an in-depth analysis that aims to determine the different layouts and give a global evaluation of this text's impact, since it marked the birth of written law in this area of Dorian Crete.[88] The question, in effect, is this: what are the reasons for which the Roman administration chose to give the order or to allow the permanent display, at the Gortyn odeon, of the 'Grand Code' accompanied by the 'Little Code', as well as for an arrangement of the pieces carrying the inscription that allowed a successive reading of the layouts?[89] A.W. Lintott provided a common sense answer: 'Against this background it seems unlikely that the engraving of the laws of Gortyn in a portico at the rear of the *cavea* of the *odeion* was simply an historical memento or

[82] A fragmentary inscription dating to 82–4 CE and found in Cnossos, a list either of tariffs or of sums owed, is a certain clue of commercial activity: IC I.VIII.59. An inscription from Phoenix proves that maritime trade was allowed to shipowners with Roman citizenship: CIL III 1, 3 = IC III XX, 7 (102–14 CE). Production of whetstones and imperial regulation: D.39.4.15; Pliny, *Naturalis historia* 36.164. Exploitation of forests and production of wood to build boats and housing: Pliny, *Naturalis historia* 16.197; Vitruvius, *De architectura* 2.9.4–5 and 13. Intensive production of tiles: IC I.XVII.58–9; XXXI. 10; XVII.58–9; IC IV 526–7, 531. Manufacturing of lamps: IC I.II, 27, 28; IC I.XIV, 6; II.XXX, 13; and III IX, 9; cf. Wardle (1972), 274–84; Sanders (1982), 34; Harrison (1988), 151–2; Baldwin Bowsky (2004), 115–25.

[83] See the inscription from Dyktynnaeum: IC II.XI, 3, *passim*; apiculture and exportation of honey; IC II.XI, 3, l. 39–41; CIL IV 5526; 6299; 6448–9; cf. Sanders (1982), 32; Chaniotis (1988), 62–89; *id.* (1999), 181–220; De Caro (1992–3), 307–12; Harrison (1993), 66–7; Francis (2016), 83–100.

[84] IC II.XI (Diktynna), 3, l. 9–15.

[85] Act of *manumissio* from Pyloros: IC I.XXV,4: IC.I.XXV, 4 (first century CE).

[86] *Sodalitas* at Hierapytna: IC III, 3, 7, p. 53–6 (125 CE), cf. Paluchowski (2005c), 438. *Thiasoi* and *negotiatores* in Gortyn: IC IV 266 (first century CE); IC IV 267 (first century CE); IC IV, 290, 291. List of members of a *collegium* at Lyttos: IC I.XVIII, 62.

[87] D. 48.16.14 (Ulpian): *Divus Hadrianus Salvio Caro proconsuli Cretae rescripsit tutorem, qui pupilli causa instituerat accusationem, defuncto pupillo, cuius causa accusare coeperat, non esse cogendum accusationem implore.* Cf. Hurlet (2006), 268, Tzamtzis (2013), 206–8.

[88] On this topic, the argument of Youni (2011), 9–55, is masterful and the conclusions are definitive.

[89] Some theories, based on the assumption that the law inscribed on the walls had long been abandoned, argue that the preservation of these texts was a Roman homage to the glory of ancient Gortyn, displaying it as a cultural monument, or that the carved stones that carried the inscription were simply recycled in order to be used as constructing material for the building of the odeon. The opposing theories have considered the text as belonging to the local laws that were still in application (whether in their entirety or not) in the mid-imperial period.

tourist attraction, but the affirmation that these local Cretan rules of private law had still some validity, even though Gortyn was the residence of the Roman governor of Crete'.[90]

And no doubt a Roman official would easily have noticed similarities, in nature and in spirit, between the rules displayed in the Great Inscription and Roman law—Archaic or later—that he knew.[91] Concerning adoption, for instance, the requirement that the act of adoption (*anpansis*) take place before the citizens gathered in the agora[92] could only remind a Roman of the *adrogatio* before the *comitia curiata*, even if the *anpansis* was not imbued with the religiosity imposed by the *adrogatio* in the presence and under the supervision of the *pontifex maximus*.[93] In the same manner, how could a Roman, who was used to the *iudex unus*, be taken aback by the principle of there being a single judge that permeates the Code?[94] Thus, as J. W. Headlam has lucidly remarked at the end of the nineteenth century, the Cretan legislator established a bipartite procedure similar to that of the Romans, where the phases *in iure* and *apud iudicem* follow one another, with the difference that this procedure did not ascribe the first part of the trial to the magistrate and the second to the *iudex*: the Gortynian judge is responsible for the whole of the procedure and presides over the trial alone.[95]

In light of these observations, the re-display of these rules of local law on a key building of the social life of Roman Gortyn makes complete sense. This is emphasised when we factor in the well-founded supposition that the Romans had from the start conceded to the Cretans the ability to maintain their private rights and their legal institutions (for the most part) through the *lex provinciae* or the *formulae*. It should be pointed out that M. S. Youni has recently highlighted the widespread practice in Cretan cities beyond Gortyn to have legislative texts engraved on the walls of their temples and public buildings.[96] The retaining of these laws written on the walls of public buildings and temples betray Rome's tolerance of the rules of local law that had survived for so long.[97]

There is no doubt that an elaborate system of judicial structures was already in place when the Romans conquered Crete. At least the important cities, such as Gortyn, Cnossos or Lyttos, could boast a corps of *dikastai* and a good organization of the judicial institutions, with a distinction and classification of different types of legal dealings, and archival and scribal functions such as the *mnamones* or the

[90] Lintott (1993), 158.

[91] It is practically inconceivable for the *proconsul*, the *legatus* and the *quaestor* of a province to have been ignorant or have little knowledge of Roman law and of the Greek language. The Roman aristocracy, from which these officials originated, considered these two elements as basic qualifications for its members. Members of the *cohors*, an *accensus* or an officer of the detached legion at the seat of the proconsul, also had to hold a general idea of the context and mentality of the *ius civile*, an elementary knowledge of the decemviral code as well as of the procedural rules in broad terms (*actiones* and *cognitio extra ordinem* procedures).

[92] C.Gort. X, l. 34–9.

[93] Aulus Gellius, *Noctes Atticae* 5.19.4.

[94] Youni (2011), 133–4, especially 135–54.

[95] Headlam (1892–3), 48–69; in the same vein: Willetts (1955), 204–13, especially 210–13.

[96] Youni (2011), 19–20, especially 49–92.

[97] Tzamtzis (2013), 208; 213–15.

grammateis.[98] It is also indisputable that the *kosmoi* continued to have judicial competences.[99]

It is around this *substratum* that the Roman system of distributing justice was articulated. Bearing in mind that, according to F. Jacques and J. Scheid, the rules of operation for the jury in the provinces of the empire '. . . devraient être identiques ou comparables à ceux organisés par Auguste pour la Cyrénaïque',[100] the absence of sources for Crete must be underlined, which forces us to reason through analogy. Let us be reminded, however, that between Crete and Roman Cyrenaica there is a basic, original, difference that resides in the *constitutio* of Lucullus which the Cyreneans themselves had asked of him in 76[101] and which goes hand in hand with the fact that, during the Hellenistic period, the cities of the African coast were completely subjected to the centralized administration of the Ptolemies and to the corresponding law, whereas the Egyptian influence in Crete was limited to the religious sphere.[102] As a natural consequence the *formulae* of Metellus in 67/66 took into account the state of complete autonomy in which each Cretan city found itself.

Augustus' decrees for Cyrenaica, combined with what we know of the *lex Rupilia* in Sicily and the decree of Scaevola for Asia, can certainly give us an idea of the system which the Romans must have applied in Crete, with a distribution of judicial power that allowed the *dikasteria* of cities to administer affairs among Greeks, albeit under high proconsular surveillance.[103]

It is after Antony's defeat at Actium that the status of cities displays the diversity that we also habitually find in the other provinces of the empire. In 31,

[98] The long tradition of systemisation in the exposition of the rule of law resulted in the constitution of a group of men specialised in the attribution of justice: IC I.XIX, 3A (honorary *psephisma* of Hellenistic Malla for the *dikastai* of Cnossos and Lyttos); cf. Willetts (1955), 147–8; 185. Specialisation of the *kosmoi* at Eltynia and at Gortyn: κόσμος ὁ ἐπὶ τῆς πόλεως (IC I.X, l. 2); ξένιος κόσμος and ξένιαι δίκαι (IC IV, 14, g–p; 30, l. 4; 78, l. 4; 79, l. 15; C.Gort. XI, l. 16–17); cf. Youni (2011), 104–5, 107–11; 113. The principal skill of the *kosmoi* seems to have progressively become judicial, and the coexistence of the κόσμος and of the δικαστής in the Gortyn Code already betrays the evolution towards a graded structure: Gagarin (2001), 41–52; Youni (2011), 142, 144. To limit ourselves to this single document, μνάμονες are mentioned in IX, l. 32; XI, l. 16, 53.

[99] Cicero's fear (*Orationes Philippicae* 5.13) concerning the harshness of Kydas the Gortynian when he was to judge the *quaestiones* of Rome suffices to prove the continuation of judicial activity in the cities of Crete.

[100] Jacques & Scheid (1999), 182.

[101] Plutarch, *Lucullus* 2–3: κατεστήσατο τὴν πολιτείαν . . .

[102] The dissemination of Egyptian cults on the island and the corresponding erection of temples were not linked to any long lasting political influence of the Lagids on Crete's cities: Spyridakis (1970), 98–105.

[103] The *lex Rupilia* of Sicily provides the basic rules: Cicero, *In Verrem* 2.2.32: *quod civis cum cive agat, domi certet suis legibus*. Scaevola's decree for Asia: Cicero, *ad Atticum* 6.1.15 (. . . *multaque sum secutus Scaevolae, in iis illud, in quo sibi libertatem censent Graeci datam, ut Graeci inter se disceptent suis legibus* [. . .] *Tamen se αὐτονομίαν adeptos putant*). An interpretation of the system that was established by the decrees of Cyrene for the Greeks in that part of the province, through analogies with the *lex Rupilia*, is given by De Visscher (1964), 324–6, 330–1. On the complexity—and its limit—of this system that must also cover the recourse, or appeal, by one city to the judges of another (the ξενοδίκαι), and the trials of Greeks belonging to the city before the court of another (the ξενοκρίται), see Larsen (1948), 187–90, Mellano (1977) and Marshall (1980), 628–61. The decrees of Cyrene do not concern Crete; in order to have an idea of the rules applicable on the island, one must synthesize our evidence with what we know of the provinces of Sicily and Asia: Tzamtzis (2013), 221–5.

Octavian left the cities of Lappa and of Kydonia free, for having supported him in his struggle against Antony,[104] and it was he who created the *Colonia Iulia Nobilis Cnos(s)os*, very probably in 27, and not his opponent in 36, as modern scholars have often wrongly believed.[105] Inscriptions and coins do not show any divergence in the layout of magistracies and of priesthoods at Cnossos that depart from the usual make-up of a colony, and more generally from that of the typical Roman city: there is clear evidence for *duumviri*, *aediles*, *augur* and *sacerdos* of the imperial cult as well as probably for a *flamen*.[106] A natural consequence of the city of Cnossos' Roman status was its Latinization in all the official texts preserved by the epigraphic evidence, which nevertheless belong to the first century CE.[107] In contrast, the cultural reality of everyday life presents a different picture: private inscriptions, even from people of Italian origin and more generally the vast majority of inhabitants with a Roman status, are in Greek.[108]

Apart from Lappa and Kydonia, the *civitates* of Crete were reduced to the status of *stipendiariae*, a status that, perhaps, these two free cities found themselves in during the first half of the first century CE.[109] The weight of the Gortynian tradition as a leader amongst the Cretan cities, combined with its status as the seat of the proconsul during the whole time of the Roman administration, is expressed in its public infrastructure: the theatres, an odeon and a *circus*, to cite only these few, adorned the city in the middle of the second century CE, not to mention the praetorium of substantial dimensions.[110]

The traditional political institutions of the Cretan cities, *archontes*, *gerousia* (*boule*) and *demos*, continued to exist, as was the case elsewhere in the immense empire. *Kosmoi*—though in diminishing numbers—but also *agoranomoi*, *pregistoi*

[104] Cassius Dio 51.2.3; see also *infra*, n. 109.

[105] For a dating of the colony to 36 BCE as a creation of Mark Antony, on behalf of whom Licinius Crassus would have acted: Grant (1946), 55, 169, 261–3; Keppie (1983), 143–4, 329; Bicknel (1977), 325–42, especially 340–2; cf. in favour of the hypothesis that the colony was a creation of Caesar: De Caro (1992–3), 307–12, especially 310. Since Burnett, Amandry & Ripollès (1992), 234, have shown that C. Iulius Antonius does not belong to the corpus of the *duumviri* in the monetary emissions of Cnossos, the idea of a creation of Antony has no support anymore; cf. already Chapman (1968), 16, n. 2, *in fine*; furthermore, it is impossible to deduce the dating to 36 from Cassius Dio 49.14.4–6 and Velleius Paterculus 2.81.2, as Sanders (1982), 5, 14 has shown. Cf. Perl (1970), 343–4, who does not draw the necessary conclusion. Rigsby (1976), 313–30, especially 322–5, considers that the foundation of the colony came later when the Campanian lands of Cnossos were already being exploited. For neutral positions: Harrison (1988), 145; Harrison (1993), 55–7; Baldwin Bowsky (2002), 27–8. The creation of the colony can only be dated to after 31: Tzamtzis (2006), 255–75, especially 359–62; Tzamtzis (2013), 229–33.

[106] A certain M. Sonteius Casina had, for example, exercised all his magistracies and priesthoods, except that of *flamen*, as proven by an inscription of 18 CE: IC IV 295. Especially on the case of the *flamen*, there is a debate: *flamen* of the *colonia Cnosos* or *flamen provinciae*? Cf. IC I.VIII.54: *aeditu[o] . . . flamin[i] . . . d[iui] V[espasiani] IIviro . . . patro[no Coloniae . . .]*; Nicols (1990), 81–100 appendix *A* n. 1; Rouanet-Liesenfelt (1994), 7–25, especially 19.

[107] Baldwin-Bowsky (2004), passim, but especially 96–101, 134–42.

[108] See for example: IC I.VIII.22 (first century BCE): *Λ]ουκίου Καμπανίου [Σ]υμφόρου Εὐκάρπου folium τ*[- -]; IC I.VIII.21 (first/second century CE): *Νωνία Ἀνχαρία Πρόοδος Κόρης*; IC I.VIII.30 (second century CE): *Π. Σέργιος | Ἐπαφρόδιτος | κατασκευάσας αὐτῷ | Αὔγουρεῖναν τὴν | σύμβιον ἔθηκεν | μνήμης χάριν*; IC.I.VIII.20 (second/third century CE): *Κλαυδία Πρ[- - - - ὑπέρ τῶ]ν τέκνων χαριστήριον ἔδωκεν*; total absence of bilingual inscriptions that name Romans, Baldwin Bowsky (2004), 137.

[109] Tzamtzis (2013), 237–43; on the *komai*: 238; cf. Rouanet-Liesenfelt (1994), 12–13.

[110] Di Vita (1984); Di Vita (1986–7), 327–52; Di Vita (2000); Harrison (1993), 137–8, 145–6.

of the *boulai*, *mnamones* and *grammateis*, and other local dignitaries ruled their cities without clashes and obstacles over the centuries, as they generally did not encroach on the limits imposed by Rome.[111] This absence of serious tension in the Cretans' relationship with the Roman authorities during the Principate (which often makes an impression on modern scholars, as was stated at the beginning) is especially notorious considering that the cities of the island had not been swallowed up by the Hellenistic kingdoms, and had preserved the status and spirit of independent *poleis*.[112]

This situation does not betray, on the political and social front, a psychological state where proud and hardened men would have collapsed after a bitter military defeat, and, traumatized, would have then behaved themselves for several centuries. There is another explanation: the conditions for the running of civic life stayed oligarchic in nature, provided that the limited democratization of the political system in Cretan cities during the Hellenistic period did not have an adverse effect on the populations' attitude towards the ruling plutocracy;[113] this was an attitude that was perfectly adapted to the Roman administrative model. In effect, the victors of 66 BCE were faced with constitutions that had evolved, certainly, but that had not lost their Dorian soul.[114] A significant example of this is the procedure of the voting of laws in the Cretan cities where, according to Aristotle, the assembly was limited to 'confirm' (or deny) what appeared good to the *kosmoi* and the *gerontes*:[115] this is extremely similar to the logic found in the Roman *lex rogata* which implies the *iussum populi*.[116]

Thus, the hypothesis that Rome's intervention in the functioning of this institutional equilibrium was very measured is not unfounded: similar views regarding the spirit of a civic system of government found expression in a reluctance to impose radical changes to the pre-existing status. It is also not difficult to understand more generally the behaviour of the Cretans when faced with such a minimal intervention on the part of the Romans: the continuation of the traditional rhythm of urban public life must have produced a feeling of security which, no doubt, helped remove any potential tendency towards conflict with the local Roman authorities.[117] Besides, almost a quarter of a century after the Roman conquest, the island experienced a political and institutional calm that tempered the negative repercussions of its initial submission to the Roman *regula*.

[111] *Κόσμος ἱεροργός*: IC IV 409, 416; *κόσμων μνάμων*: IC IV 260 (second/first century BCE). For a list of the *πρωτόκοσμος* during the Principate see Paluchowski (2005a). A cumulation (?) of offices seems to be attested at Arcades where we find a *πρωτόκοσμος/κόσμων μνάμων*: Ducrey & Van Effenterre (1973), 281–90. Sanders (1982), 10 finds *κόσμοι* in fifteen (or sixteen) of the cities of the Roman period. Reiteration of this annual magistracy at Chersonessos: IC I.VII.5; at Gortyn: IC IV 293; cf. Oehler (1922), 1495–8; Paluchowski (2005c), 421–44. *ἀγορανόμος*: IC IV 250, 251, 254. *ἀγορανόμοι/οἰκονόμοι*: Ducrey & Van Effenterre (1973) *ἀγορανόμος-γυναικονόμος*: IC IV 25. *πρήγιστος*: IC III.III.7 and 52; IV 294. *γραμματεὺς τῆς βουλῆς*: IC IV 257, *βουλὴ καὶ δῆμος*: IC IV 297, 298, 300. *κοινόν*, *βουλή*, and *δῆμος*: IC IV 297; cf. Paluchowski (2005c), *passim*; Tzamtzis (2013), 243–57.

[112] Willetts (1955), *passim*, but in particular: 234–41.

[113] Chaniotis (1992), 287–322; cf. Paluchowski (2005c), 423–7.

[114] Polybius 6.46: the democratic element resides in the annual nature of Cretan magistrates (*δημοκρατικὴν ἔχει διάθεσιν*); cf. Tzamtzis (2013), 245–6.

[115] Aristotle, *Politica* 1272a: *Ἐκκλησίας δὲ μετέχουσι πάντες, κύρια δ᾽ οὐδενὸς ἐστὶν ἀλλ᾽ ἢ συνεπιψηφισίσαι τὰ δόξαντα τοῖς γέρουσι καὶ τοῖς κόσμοις.*

[116] Tzamtzis (2013), 253–4, 256.

[117] Tzamtzis (2013), 243–4, 255–6, 288–9.

One must take it for granted that Crete was *libera* during a short period after the assassination of Julius Caesar until the victory of Octavian at Actium.[118] The combination of epigraphic, numismatic and literary evidence that mentions a great Cretan personality of the first century BCE, Kydas the Gortynian, *Kretarchas* and *Archos* (who was almost a judge in Rome), throws light on a rather nebulous period of the island's history;[119] at the same time, this delineates a very interesting legal truth, singular in the sense that we see the rather unusual emergence of a pan-Cretan institutional structure. This is situated on the fringes of the usual laws laid out by the Romans: this is the only known case of a *koinon* that would have served in the context of the establishment and operation of a real state entity *immunis et libera*,[120] even if it was in a position of *cliens* with regards to Rome, represented by Antony.

This 'confederal' client-state that had at its head the *Kretarchas* was amputated between 36 and 34 in the region of Itanos and the Island of Leuke, where the Lagids possessed naval bases during the time of Ptolemy Philometor: Antony conceded these 'few parts of Crete' (Dio Cassius' expression, 49.32.4–5) to Cleopatra VII.[121] The idea that *Creta Libera* should share boarders with Ptolemaic

[118] Offering two successive variants which are misinformed, Grant (1946), 55–8, 262 (initial thesis) and *id.* (1972), 165–6, 203 (modified thesis) supports the idea that Antony had placed the whole island under Egyptian control either between 37 and 34 BCE—apart from the Roman colony of Cnossos that he dated to 36 (see also *supra* n. 103)—or between 34 and 31, with the exception of a few cities which stayed free. Notwithstanding criticism, this thesis was initially, and curiously, adopted in its broad lines by Chapman (1968), 13–14, 22; a combination of the Grant's opinions is accepted by Bicknell (1977), 340–2.

[119] A Gortynian inscription of the first century BCE mentions a Kydas, son of Kydas, *Κρητάρχας καὶ Αρχὸς*: IC IV 250; see the commentary of Guarducci, p. 307–8, and perhaps also the inscription n. 251; cf. Rouanet-Liesenfelt (1984), 343–52; Paluchowski (2005b), 56. A silver cistophorus tetradrachma showing on the reverse *Κύδας Κρηταιέων Κρητάρχας*, dated between 44 and 33: Svoronos (1890), 334 n. 1; Robinson (1927), CCIX n.2; Burnett, Amandry & Rippolès (1992), 222 and 224—n. 926; Raven (1938), 133–58; cf. Rouanet-Liesenfelt (1984), 344, 357–350; Ferriès (2007), 105. Two exemplars of an important series of bronze coins from Cnossos, belonging to the decade of 39–30 BCE and produced sequentially by Greek magistrates that counted amongst their number also a Kydas, are struck over *dupondii* already minted by a Crassus: Svoronos (1890), 83–8, ns. 138–73; Robinson (1927), CCXI–CCXXIII; Chapman (1968), 13–26, especially 17–20 and 23–6; Burnett, Amandry & Rippolès (1992), 222–5—ns. 929–37. The monetary emissions, with Greek captions for Cyrenaica and with Latin ones for Crete, of a Lollius and of the aforementioned Crassus, are usually dated between 39/38 and 34: Robinson (1927), CCIII–CCVII, nos. 2 bis – 23 bis a; CCXIII–CCXVI and 114–15, 117; Perl (1970), 319–54 and in particular 338–40 with extensive bibliography; Buttrey (1983), 23–46, especially 24–5. On the chronological correlation between the Cnossian emission and those of Lollius and Crassus: Chapman (1968), 18, 21–3; but also: Burnett, Amandry & Rippolès (1992), 222–3; Carrier & Chevrollier (2016), 70–1, 73–7, 89. The two passages of the Philippics where Cicero mentions a Kydas, originally from Gortyn, amongst Antony's friends that were held as *iudices* for the *tertia decuria*, the creation of which was planned by the *rogatio* de L. Antonius in 44 BCE: see above p. 251 and n. 58.

[120] Tzamtzis (2013), 260, 263–4, 274, 289. The *kretarchia*'s dating to the Republican period and the political nature of the post distinguishes this Cretan structure from the other *koina* of the Roman period: cf. Deininger (1965) 43, 85; Rouanet-Liesenfelt (1984), 349–50; Paluchowski (2005b), 58, 75–6. As an example of a mistaken approach to the *kretarchia* during the imperial period: Van der Munsbrugge (1931), 71–2.

[121] Concessions of Antony during his meeting of Cleopatra VII at Antioch, in the winter of 37/36: Cassius Dio 49.32.4–5 (*Κρήτης τέ τινὰ*). Spyridakis (1970), 87–8, followed by Sanders (1982), 5, only thought of the region of Itanos; the island of Leuke must also be added, mentioned in the inscription of Itanos/Magnesia (111 BCE): Ager (1996), n. 158, IIA, l. 109, 114; also l. 100. Cf. Tzamtzis (2006), 264–5; Tzamtzis (2013), 270–1.

possessions was not a felicitous one. Less sympathetic towards the queen than Antony, the confederation did not avoid frictions with the former: the proof is to be found in the Cnossian coins of this period where, besides the successive issues of the *koinon*, we also find the *dupondii* of Roman-Egyptian provenance, which had been overstruck.[122] Antony corrected his error in 34: the confederal territory was restored to its state dating from 37/36.[123] In any case, the experience of 'Free Crete' was ended with the victory of Octavian at Actium.

Under the Principate, the *koinon* continued to exist according to the same logic that ruled the rest of the *koina* of the empire. Without doubt its mission did not change from the Augustan period, whatever we make of the change from *ΚΡΗΤΑΙ[Ε]ΩΝ* to *ΚΡΗΤΩΝ* under Tiberius. The Latin designation of this superstructure stayed the same: *Commune Cretensium*.[124] The number of the city-members and of their representatives is not known and only a hypothesis can be put forward.[125] Just like the other provincial *koina*, the *koinon* of the Cretans was involved in activities that took place on a higher level than that of the cities, like support for the imperial cult. Other activities were linked to the administrative conduct of the successive pro-magistrates and to their attitude towards the Cretans, leading to resolutions that were, for the most part (but not without rare exceptions) gratulatory or honorific.[126]

The supreme magistracy, held by the *archiereus*, an eponymous archon, for the length of a year with a possibility of a reiteration, demonstrates the responsibility

[122] Tzamtzis (2006), 365–8; Tzamtzis (2013), 270–3; cf. Rouanet-Liesenfelt (1984), 352. It is usually thought that the striking of the head of Zeus and the eagle of Kydas over the crocodile and the prow of Crassus' *dupondius* betrays a succession of governments, implying the establishment of a new authority over the previous one: Chapman (1968), 16–20, 21, 23–6; cf. Buttrey (1983), 24–5; Buttrey (1987), 171–2; Burnett, Amandry and Ripollès (1992), 222–5, nos. 929–37; Paluchowski (2005b), 68–1. In fact, whatever date and scope of functions scholars assign to Crassus (and whatever chronological relationship they postulate between him and L. Lollius), they feel entirely obligated to have him precede the Kydas of the Cnossian coins because of the overstrikes: Perl (1970), 339–40, 346, and, even in his modified thesis, Grant (1972), 207, 274 n. 20. For Lollius' coins, the most likely hypothesis is that of Alföldy (1966), 25–43, who sees them as a production for the use of the fleet; cf. Carrier & Chevrollier (2016), 76.

[123] There is no mention of Crete in the list of territories which Antony promised to give to Ptolemy Philadelphos, Alexandros Helios and Cleopatra Selene in 34, in the donations of Alexandria: Cass. Dio 49.41.3; cf. Tzamtzis (2006), 364–9; Tzamtzis (2013), 268–9, 271–4.

[124] Rouanet-Liesenfelt (1994), 11–17. M. Nonio m. f.] *Balbo pro cos* | [*Commune*] *Cretensium Patrono*: CIL X 1430–2; Baldwin (1983), 83–8. *Cretenses*: Tacitus, *Annales* 3.60–3; 4.14; 13.30; also Cicero, *De imperio Cn. Pompeii* 35: *Cretensibus* . . . ; 46: *Commune Cretensium*.

[125] The number of *poleis* of the *koinon* could oscillate between 14 and 25 according to the count that we adopt, taking into account the numismatic and epigraphical finds that mention the *kosmoi* or more generally that betray the importance of a city at different periods of the Roman period. The number of representatives is unknown: Rouanet-Liesenfelt (1994), 12, 17–18, admits this difficulty and calculates between 45 and 48 men; Guizzi (2001), 407 and n. 199 points to the correspondence between the number of Cretan ambassadors sent to Rome in 70/69 and that of the cities that had signed the treaty with Eumenes II, although he notes that the 300 hostages that the Romans demanded just before the Metellian attack is the multiplication of the number by ten. On these uncertainties and the risks of a reasoning through analogies on the basis of what we know from other *koina*: Tzamtzis (2013), 273–8.

[126] See for example, Gortyn: IC IV 298, 306 (honours to Q. Roscius Murena and to C. Papirius); at Lyttos, also a member of the *Panhellenion*: IC I.XVIII.55–6. It was, however, also the *koinon* who accused *repetundarum* the proconsul Gestius Proculus, in 56 BCE: . . . *Cretensibus accusantibus* . . .

of the *koinon*.[127] Under the aegis of the *koinon*, a great agonistic event took place every five years: the 'five-year sacred agon of the Cretans' *koinon*' at Gortyn (isolympic at the time of the *koinon* of the *Kretaieon*, isopythic afterwards).[128] The organization of the athletic part reveals the importance of these games, as it had its own separate magistracy, the xystarchy—for the event included a part formed of theatrical and musical competitions.[129]

* * *

The history of Crete during the Roman period presents, in the end, a series of particularities which one cannot gleam simply from reading Strabo's description. It is not so much the preservation of the *syssitia* and the few other *nomima* which distinguishes Crete from the rest of the territories that formed the *Pars Orientalis* of the Empire; it is more the rather long process of political and economic fermentation until the island was placed under the stable laws of the Roman *imperium*: Crete underwent half a century of repeated changes and adaptations of the status of its cities, of its *koinon* in relation to Rome and its territory with regards to Cyrenaica, in the sense that it was faced with varied solutions with regard to the layout of provincial administration.

Crete's meanderings on the Roman road give the impression that it was conditioned by a *modus vivendi* between the Romans and the Cretans where each party enjoyed the invaluable benefits of tranquility. The coexistence of the two elements, the mentalities of which were relatively similar on a number of points, was completely peaceful and devoid of the tensions that we observed in Cyrenaica, a fact that indicates acculturation on both sides. Through an extremely complex and multidimensional process of evolution, the Cretans smoothly transitioned into the Roman order. This Roman order appears more as a frame and not a cage: an envelope that was rather transparent, and not at all hermetic, in which not only the Dorian elements of civil society were preserved, but also a more general perception of life, particular and specific to the population of the island.

REFERENCES

Ager, S.L. 1996. *Interstate Arbitrations in the Greek World, 337–90 B.C.* Berkeley.

Alföldy, A. 1966. Commandants de la flotte romaine stationnée à Cyrène sous Pompée, César et Octavien. In: J. Heurgon, W. Seston & G. Charles-Picard (eds.), *Mélanges d'archéologie, d'épigraphie et d'histoire offerts à Jérome Carcopino*. Paris, pp. 25–43.

[127] Five men carrying the title of *archiereus* are attested: IC III.IX.10; IV 275, 305, 306, 330. We can also add another, even if the title is not explicitly mentioned: AE 1965, 326; 1967, 522; cf. Rouanet-Liesenfelt (1994), 19, 21. The case of Claudius Timarchus is dubious: Tacitus, *Annales*. 13.28 and 31; 15.22; cf. Sanders (1982), 8; Rouanet-Liesenfelt (1994), 22; Tzamtzis (2013), 282. The *maximum magistratum* was also offered to a non-Cretan, Asilius Sabinus: Seneca, *Controversiae* 9.4.19; cf. Sanders (1982), 9; Tzamtzis (2013), 279–80. Orth (1973), 257–9 and Sonnabend (2004), 27 wrongly think of the *Kretarchia*.

[128] Winner in the underage category: IG VII 1859 (Thespies); IG XII.1, 77 = IGR IV 1128 (Rhodes). Rouanet-Liesenfelt (1994), 22–3, is right in linking the downgrading of the isolympics into isopythics with the change of appellation of the *koinon* from '*Kretaieon*' to '*Kretôn*'.

[129] *Xystarche*: IC I.XVIII.55; cf. Sanders (1982), 8; winner in tragedy: Rouanet-Liesenfelt (1994), 23 n. 103; winner in flute competition: CIG 1719.

Arnold, W. T. 1914. *The Roman System of Provincial Administration to the Accession of Constantine the Great*. 3rd ed. Oxford.

Baldwin, M. A. W. 1983. Fasti Cretae et Cyrenarum. *Imperial Magistrates of Crete and Cyrenaica during the Julio-Claudian period*. Diss. University of Michigan.

Baldwin Bowsky, M. A. W. 1987. Roman Arbitration in Central Crete: An Augustan Proconsul and a Neronian Procurator. *Classical Journal* 82, pp. 218–29.

Baldwin Bowsky, M. A. W. 2001. Gortynians and Others: the Case of the Antonii. *Eulimene* 2, pp. 97–119.

Baldwin Bowsky, M. A. W. 2002. Reasons to Reorganize: Antony, Augustus, and Central Crete. *Electrum* 6, pp. 25–65.

Baldwin Bowsky, M. W. 2004. Of Two Tongues: Acculturation at Roman Knossos, In: G. Salmeri, A. Raggi, A. Baroni (eds.), *Colonie romane nel mondo Greco*. Rome, pp. 95–150.

Bicknell, P. J. 1977. Caesar, Antony, Cleopatra and Cyprus. *Latomus* 36, pp. 325–42.

Bove, L. 1960. *Richerche sugli 'agri vectigales,'* Naples.

Brulé, P. 1978. *La piraterie crétoise hellénistique*. Paris.

Brunt, P. A. 1961. Charges of Provincial Maladministration under the Early Principate. *Historia* 10, pp. 189–228.

Burnett, A., M. Amandry & P. Ripollès 1992. *Roman Provincial Coinage, I: From the Death of Caesar to the Death of Vitellius (44 BC—AD 69)*. London.

Burton, G. P. 1975. Proconsuls, Assizes and the Administration of Justice under the Empire. *Journal of Roman Studies* 65, pp. 92–106.

Burton, P. J. 2003. *Clientela* or *Amicitia*? Modeling Roman International Behavior in the Middle Republic (264–146 B.C.). *Klio* 35, pp. 333–69.

Buttrey, T. V. 1983. The Roman Coinage of the Cyrenaica, first Century BC to first Century AD. In: C. N. L. Brooke, B. H. I. H. Stewart, J. G. Pollard & T. R. Volk (eds.), *Studies in Numismatic Method presented to Philip Grierson*. Cambridge, pp. 23–46.

Buttrey, T. V. 1987. Crete and Cyrenaica. In: A. Burnett & M. H. Crawford (eds.), *The Coinage of the Roman World in the Late Republic*. Oxford, pp. 165–74.

Cary, M. 1926. A Roman Arbitration of the Second Century B.C. *Journal of Roman Studies* 16, pp. 194–200.

Carrier, C. & Chevrollier, Fr. 2016. Définitions chronologiques et gèographiques des frontières de la province de Crète - Cyrénaïque au Ier s. a.C. : l'apport des sources textuelles et numismatiques. In: H. Berthelot, A. Boiché, P.-A. Caltot, M. Diarra, F. Réveilhac & É. Romieux-Brun (eds.), *Vivre et penser les frontières dans le monde méditerranéen antique*. Bordeaux, pp. 67–80.

Chaniotis, A. 1988. *Vinum Creticum excellens*. Zum Weinhandel Kretas. *Münstersche Beiträge zur antiken Handelsgeschichte* 7, pp. 62–89.

Chaniotis, A. 1992. Die Inschriften von Amnisos. In: J. Schäfer (ed.), *Amnisos nach den archäologischen, historischen und epigraphischen Zeugnissen des Altertums und der Neuzeit*. Berlin, pp. 287–322.

Chaniotis, A. 1999. Milking the Mountains. Economic Activities on the Cretan Uplands in the Classical and Hellenistic Period. In: A. Chaniotis (ed.), *From Minoan Farmers to Roman Traders. Sidelights on the Economy of Ancient Crete*. Stuttgart, pp. 181–220.

Chapman, A. E. 1968. Some First Century B.C. Bronze Coins of Knossos. *Numismatic Chronicle* 8, pp. 13–26.

Charlesworth, M. P. 1924. *Trade Routes and Commerce of the Roman Empire*. Cambridge.

Cursi, M. F. 2014. International Relations in the Ancient World. *Fundamina* 20, pp. 186–95.

De Caro, S. (1992–3). Vino di Cnosso dei Campani: un nuovo document epigrafico per la storia di vino cretese in età romana. *Annuario della Scuola archeologica italiana di Atene* 70–1, pp. 307–12.

Deininger, J. 1965. *Die Provinziallandtage der römischen Kaiserzeit von Augustus bis zum Ende des dritten Jahrhunderts*. Munich.

Demougin, S. 2001. Considérations sur l'avancement dans les carièrres procuratoriennes équestres. In: L. de Blois (ed.), *Administration, Prosopography and Appointment Policies in the Roman Empire*. Amsterdam, pp. 24–34.

De Souza, P. 1999. *Piracy in the Graeco-Roman World*. Cambridge.

De Visscher, F. 1940. *Les édits d'Auguste découverts à Cyrène*. Louvain [repr. 1965].

De Visscher, F. 1964. La justice romaine en Cyrénaïque. *Revue Internationale des Droits de l'Antiquité* 11, pp. 321–33.

Di Vita, A. 1984. Gortina. In: *Creta antica: Cento anni di archeologia italiana (1884–1984)*. Rome, pp. 69–116.

Di Vita, A. 2000. Il Pretorio tra il I sec. a.C. e l'VIII d.C. In: A. Di Vita (ed.), *Gortina V.1. Lo scavo del Pretorio (1989–1995)*. Padova, pp. XXXV–LXXIV.

Ducrey, P. & Van Effenterre, H. 1973. Un règlement d'époque romaine sur les bains d'Arcadès. *Kretika Chronika* 25, pp. 281–90.

Eder, W. 1969. *Das Vorsullanische Repetundenverfahren*. Bonn.

Ferriès, M.-C. 2007. *Les partisans d'Antoine (des orphelins de César aux complices de Cléopâtre)*. Bordeaux.

Ferriès, M.-C. 2012. L'ombre de César dans la politique d'Antoine. In: O. Devilliers and K. Sion-Jenkis (eds.), *César sous Auguste*. Bordeaux, pp. 55–72.

Foucart, P. 1906. Les campagnes de M. Antonius Creticus contre les pirates. *Journal des Savants* 4, pp. 569–81.

Franchi De Cavalieri, P. 1946. I dieci martiri di Creta. In: *Miscellanea Giovanni Mercati*, Vol. V. Vatican, pp. 27–40.

Francis, J. E. 2016. Apiculture in Roman Crete. In: J. E. Francis and A. Kouremenos (eds.), *Roman Crete: New Perspectives*. Oxford, pp. 83–100.

Garnsey, P. 1966. The *Lex Iulia* and Appeal under the Empire. *Journal of Roman Studies* 56, pp. 167–89.

Garnsey, P. 1968. The Criminal Jurisdiction of the Governors. *Journal of Roman Studies* 58, pp. 52–9.

Gaudemet, J. 1967. *Institutions de l'Antiquité*, Paris, 1967.

Grant, M. 1946. *From Imperium to Auctoritas. A Historical Study of Aes Coinage in the Roman Empire. 49 B.C.–A.D. 14*. Cambridge (repr. 1969).

Grant, M. 1972. *Cleopatra*. London.

Grelle, F. 1963. *Stipendium vel tributum. L'imposizione fondiaria nell dottrine giuridiche del II e III secolo*. Naples.

Gruen, E. S. 1984. *The Hellenistic World and the Coming of Rome*. Berkeley.

Guarducci, M. 1933. Intorno alla decima dei Cretesi. *Rivista di Filologia e d'Istruzione Classica* 11, pp. 488–91.

Guizzi, F. 1997. Conquista, occupazione del suolo et titoli che danno diritto alla proprietà: l'esempio di una controversia interstatale cretese. *Athenaeum* n.s. 85, pp. 35–52.

Guizzi, F. 2001. *Hierapytna. Storia di una* polis *cretese dalla fondazione alla conquista romana*. Rome.

Haensch, R. 1997. *Capita provinciarum. Statthatersitze und Provinzialverwaltung in der römischen Kaiserzeit*. Mainz.

Harrison, G. W. M. 1988. Background to the First Century of Roman Rule in Crete. *Cretan Studies* 1, pp. 125–55.

Harrison, G. W. M. 1993. *The Romans and Crete*, Amsterdam.

Hatzfeld, J. 1919. *Les trafiquants italiens dans l'Orient Hellénique*. Paris (repr. 1975).

Headlam, J. W. 1892–3. The Procedure of the Gortynian Inscription. *Journal of Hellenic Studies* 13, pp. 48–69.

Hurlet, F. 2006. *Le proconsul et le prince d'Auguste à Dioclétien*. Bordeaux.

Jacques, F. & Scheid, J. 1999. *Rome et l'intégration de l'empire. 44 av. J.C.-260 ap. J.-C. Tome 1: Les structures de l'empire romain.* Fifth edition Paris.

Jashemsky, W. 1950. *The Origins and History of the Proconsular and the Propraetorian* Imperium *to 27 B.C.* Chicago.

Johnston, D. 1999. *Roman Law in Context.* Cambridge.

Jones, A. H. M. 1972. *The Criminal Courts of the Roman Republic and Principate.* Oxford.

Kallet-Marx, R. M. 1995. *Hegemony to Empire. The Development of the Roman Imperium in the East from 148 to 62 B.C.* Berkeley.

Keaveney, A. 1992. *Lucullus. A Life.* London.

Keppie, L. 1983. *Colonization and Veteran Settlement in Italy, 47–14 B.C.* London.

Klebs, E. 1894. Antonius [29]. *Pauly's Realencyclopädie* 1, col. 2594.

Kornemann, E. 1900. Conventus. *Pauly's Realencyclopädie* 4.1, col. 1173–1200.

Köstermann, E. 1955. Die Majestätsprozesse unter Tiberius. *Historia* 4, pp. 72–106.

Kunkel, W. & Wittmann, R. 1995. *Staatsordung und Staatspraxis der römischen Republik,* 2: *Die Magistratur.* Munich.

Laronde, A. 1988. La Cyrénaique romaine, des origines à la fin des Sévères (96 av. J.-C.–235 ap. J.-C.). *Aufstieg und Niedergang der Römischen Welt* II.10.1, pp. 1006–64.

Larsen, J. A. O. 1948. Foreign Judges in *Ad Att.*, vi. 1. 15. *Classical Philology* 43, pp. 187–90.

Latte, K. 1946–7. Kollektivbesitz und Staatsschatz in Griechenland, *Nachrichten der Akademie der Wissenschaften zu Göttingen, Philologisch-Historische Klasse*, pp. 64–75.

Lepelley, C. 1998 (ed.). *Rome et l'intégration de l'Empire. 44 av. J.-C.–260 ap. J.-C. Tome 2: Approches régionales du Haut-Empire romain.* Paris.

Liebs, D. 1981. Das *ius gladii* der römischen Provinzgouverneure in der Kaiserzeit. *Zeitschrift für Papyrologie und Epigraphik* 43, pp. 217–23.

Linderski, J. 1990. The Surname of M.Antonius Creticus and the *Cognomina ex victis gentibus. Zeitschrift für Papyrologie und Epigraphik* 80, pp. 157–64.

Lintott, A. W. 1972. *Provocatio.* From the Struggle of the Orders to the Early Principate. *Aufstieg und Niedergang der Römischen Welt* I.2, pp. 226–67.

Lintott, A. W. 1993. *Imperium Romanum. Politics and Administration.* London.

Magdelain, A. 1967. *Recherches sur l' 'imperium.' La loi curiate et les auspices d'investiture.* Paris.

Manfredini, A. 1991. Ius gladii. *Annali dell'università degli Studi di Ferrara* 5, pp. 103–26.

Marshall, A. J. 1980. The Survival and Development of International Jurisdiction in the Greek World under Roman Rule. *Aufstieg und Niedergang der Römischen Welt* II.13, pp. 628–61.

Mellano, L. D. 1977. *Sui rapporti tra governatore provinciale e giudici locali alla luce delle Verrine.* Milan.

Meyer-Zwiffelhoffer, E. 2002. *Πολιτικῶς ἄρχειν. Zum Regierungsstil der senatorischen Statthalter in den kaiserzeitlichen griechischen Provinzen.* Stuttgart.

Millar, F. 1964. Some Evidence on the Meaning of Tacitus *Annals* XII, 60. *Historia* 13, pp. 180–7.

Mommsen, T. 1893. *Le droit public romain.* 6 vols. Paris.

Nicolet, C. 1974. *L'ordre équestre à l' époque républicaine (312–43 av. J.-C.).* Paris.

Nicolet, C. 1978 (ed.). *Rome et la conquête du monde méditerranéen. 264–27 avant J.-C. Tome 2: Genèse d'un empire.* Paris.

Nicolet, C. 1988. *Rendre à César. Economie et société dans la Rome antique.* Paris.

Nicols, J. 1990. Patrons of Greek Cities in the Early Principate. *Zeitschrift für Papyrologie und Epigraphik* 80, pp. 81–100.

Oehler, J. 1922. Kosmoi. *Pauly's Realencyclopädie* 22, col. 1495–8.

Oliver, J. H. 1989. *Greek Constitutions of the Early Roman Emperors from Inscriptions and Papyri.* Philadelphia.

Orelli, I. C. & Baiter, I. G. 1838. *Onomasticon Tullianum.* Vol. 2. Turicum.

Ormerod, H. A. 1924. *Piracy in the Ancient World. An Essay in Mediterranean History*. London.

Orth, W. 1973. Ein vernachlässigtes Zeugnis zur Geschichte der römischen Provinz *Creta et Cyrenae*. *Chiron* 3, pp. 255–63.

Paluchowski, A. 2005a. *Fastes des protocosmes des cités crétoises sous le Haut Empire*. Wroclaw.

Paluchowski, A. 2005b. Le *koinon* crétois au temps du gouvernement de Marc Antoine à l'Est. *Eos* 92, pp. 54–80.

Paluchowski, A. 2005c. Le régime des cités crétoises sous le Haut Empire. *Klio* 87, pp. 421–444.

Paluchowski, A. 2012. La progression de la citoyenneté romaine parmi les notables crétois. *Eos* 99, pp. 91–151.

Pautasso, A. 1994–5. *Aνθύπατος Κρήτης και Κυρήνης*. Osservazioni sull'attività dei proconsuli nella provincia nei primi secoli dell'impero. *Annuario della Scuola Archeologica di Atene a delle Missioni Italiane in Oriente* 72–3, pp. 75–108.

Perl, G. 1970. Die römischen Provinzbeamten in Cyrenae und Creta zur Zeit der Republik. *Klio* 52, pp. 319–54.

Perl, G. 1971. Nachträge. *Klio* 53, pp. 369–79.

Person, E. 1878. *Essai sur l'administration des provinces romaines sous la République*. Paris (repr. 1970).

Pflaum, H.-G. 1950. *Les procurateurs équestres sous le Haut-Empire romain*. Paris.

Pflaum, H.-G. 1962. Légats impériaux à l'intérieur des provinces sénatoriales. In: M. Renard (ed.), *Hommages à Albert Grenier*. Brussels, pp. 1232–42.

Piatkowski, A. 1973. La résistance crétoise contre la conquête romaine commentée par Dion Cassius. In: *Πεπραγμένα του Γ' Διεθνούς* Κρητολογικού *Συνεδρίου*. Vol. 1: *Προϊστορικοί και αρχαίοι χρόνοι*. Athens, pp. 215–20.

Ponteney de Fontette, F. 1954. *Leges repetundarum. Essai sur la repression des actes illicites commis par les magistrats au détriment de leurs administrés*. Paris.

Porena, P. 2005. Forme di partecipazione politica cittadina e contatti con il potere imperiale. In: F. Amarelli (ed.), *Politica e partecipazione nella cità dell'impero romano*. Rome, pp. 13–92.

Raven, E. J. P. 1938. The Hierapytna Hoard of Greek and Roman Coins. *Numismatic Chronicle* 18, pp. 133–58.

Reynolds, J. M. 1982a. *Aphrodisias and Rome. Documents from the Excavations of the Theater of Aphrodisias conducted by K.T. Erim*. London.

Reynolds, J. M. 1982b. Senators originating in the Provinces of Egypt and of Crete and Cyrene. *Tituli* 5, pp. 671–83.

Rigsby, K. J. 1976. Cnossus and Capua. *Transactions of the American Philological Association* 106, pp. 313–30.

Robinson, E. G. S. 1927. *Catalogue of the Greek Coins of Cyrenaica*. London: British Museum.

Romanelli, P. 1936. The Province of Crete and Cyrenaica. In: S. A. Cook, F. E. Adcock & M. P. Charlesworth (eds.), *The Cambridge Ancient History. Vol. XI: The Imperial Peace, A.D. 70–192*. Cambridge, pp. 659–75.

Romanelli, P. 1943. *La Cyrenaica romana (96 a.C.–642 d.C.)*. Verbania: Airoldi (repr. 1971).

Rotondi, G. 1912. *Leges Publicae Populi Romani. Elenco cronologico con una introduzione sull'attivita legislativa dei comizi romani*. Milan (repr. 1966).

Rouanet-Liesenfelt, A.-M. 1984. Le Crétarque Kydas. In: *Aux origines de l'Hellénisme. La Crète et Grèce. Hommage à H. Van Effenterre*. Paris, pp. 343–52.

Rouanet-Liesenfelt, A.-M. 1994. Remarques sur l'assemblée provinciale crétoise et son grand-prêtre à l'époque du Haut-Empire. *Ktéma* 19, pp. 7–25.

Sanders, I. F. 1982. *Roman Crete. An Archeological Survey and Gazetteer of Late Hellenistic, Roman and Early Byzantine Crete.* Warminster.

Santalucia, B. 1998. *Diritto e processo penale nell'antica Roma.* 2nd ed. Milan.

Seeck, O. 1901. Comites. *Pauly's Realencyclopädie* 4.1, col. 622–79.

Sherwin White, A. N. 1963. *Roman Society and Roman Law in the New Testament.* Oxford (repr. 2000).

Sherwin White, A. N. 1984. *Roman Foreign Policy in the East, 168 B.C. to A.D. 1.* London.

Sonnabend, H. 2004. Roman Rule and Cretan Identity. The Impact on Society and Culture. In: M. Livadiotti and I. Simiakaki (eds.), *Creta romana e protobyzantina.* Vol. 1. Padova, pp. 25–8.

Spyridakis, S. 1970. *Ptolemaic Itanos and Hellenistic Crete.* Berkeley.

Strachan-Davidson, J. L. 1912. *Problems of the Roman Criminal Law.* 2 vols. Oxford.

Svoronos, J. N. 1890. *Numismatique de la Crète ancienne, accompagnée de l'histoire, la géographie et la mythologie de l'île.* Macon (repr. 1972).

Syme, R. 1939. *The Roman Revolution.* Oxford (corr. repr. 1952).

Thomasson, B. E. 1991. *Legatus. Beiträge zur römische Verwaltungsgeschichte.* Stockholm.

Traina, G. 2003. *Marco Antonio.* Rome.

Tzamtzis, I. E. 1998. Les Grecs qui faillirent juger à Rome. *Revue historique de droit français et étranger* 76, pp. 539–56.

Tzamtzis, I. E. 2006. Antoine, Cléopâtre et la Crète. A propos de Dion Cassius, 49, 32, 4–5. In: G. Traina (ed.), *Studi sull'età di Marco Antonio.* Lecce, pp. 353–75.

Tzamtzis, I. E. 2009. Cognitio, ius gladii *και θανατώσεις Χριστιανών κατά την περίοδο της Ηγεμονίας.* In: *Αλεξανδρινός Αμητός. Αφιέρωμα στη μνήμη του I. M. Χατζηφώτη.* Vol. 2. Alexandria, pp. 543–63.

Tzamtzis, I. E. 2013. *Creta Romana. Πηγές δικαίου, πολιτικοί και κοινωνικοί θεσμοί στην Κρήτη κατά τη ρωμαϊκή περίοδο (67 π.Χ.–235 μ.Χ.).* Chania: Instituto Krētikou Dikaiou.

Tzamtzis, I. E. 2018. Un cas de *foedus* avorté: Rome et les Crétois en 70–69 av. J.-C. *Quaderni Lupiensi di storia e diritto* 8, pp. 13–45.

Van der Munsbrugge, M. 1931. *The Cretan Koinon*, New York.

Van Effenterre, H. 1990. *Cretica selecta.* Amsterdam.

Van Ooteghem, J. 1954. *Pompée le Grand, bâtisseur d'empire.* Brussels.

Van Ooteghem, J. 1967. *Les Caecilii Metelli de la République.* Brussels.

Velissaropoulos-Karakostas, J. 2011. *Droit grec d'Alexandre à Auguste (323 av. J.-C.–14 ap. J.-C.). Personnes, biens, justice.* 2 vols. Athens.

Viviers, D. 2004. Rome face aux cités crétoises: trafics insulaires et organisation de la province. In: M. Livadiotti & I. Simiakaki (eds.), *Creta romana e protobyzantina.* Vol. 1. Padova, pp. 17–24.

Wardle, K. 1972. Two Notes from Knossos. *Annual of the British School at Athens* 67, pp. 274–84.

Will, E. 1982. *Histoire politique du monde hellénistique. Tome II (323–30 av. J.-C.).* 2nd ed. Nancy.

Willetts, R. F. 1955. *Aristocratic Society in Ancient Crete.* London.

Wlassak, M. 1919. *Zum römischen Provinzialprozess.* Vienna.

Yavetz, Z. 1990. *César et son image. Des limites du charisme en politique.* Paris.

Youni, M. S. 2011. *Η γένεση του γραπτού νόμου στη Δωρική Κρήτη.* Thessaloniki.

14

Lesbos in the Roman Empire

Treaties, Legal Institutions, and Local Sentiment towards Roman Rule

Athina Dimopoulou

The process of integration of Lesbos in the Roman Empire relied both on war and diplomacy. The history of the cities of the biggest island of the northern Aegean, during the events that led to the consolidation of Roman dominion from the time of Sulla to that of Augustus, makes them typical examples of the exercise of Roman policy in the East.[1] The city of Antissa was destroyed in 167 BCE by the Romans for having given shelter to Perseus' fleet, and its territory was integrated into that of its neighbouring city, Methymna.[2] The three remaining cities of Lesbos—Mytilene, Methymna, and Eresos—cultivated independent diplomatic relations with Rome, initially enjoying the status of free and autonomous cities. Several epigraphic testimonies of late Republican and early Imperial times from Lesbos give us some insight into the interaction of the local population with their Roman rulers on the confirmation of certain rights and privileges, on the rapports cultivated among members of the local elite with Roman patrons and on the process of integration and acceptance of Roman rule. Within this corpus, evidence available on law and justice in Roman Lesbos is quite limited and, in order to follow continuity or change regarding its legal systems, we must rely on the bigger picture, try to understand the process of integration of local societies into the empire and follow the overall operation of civic institutions.

Methymna and Mytilene, aided by their geographical importance in controlling the commercial routes to the Black Sea and the hinterland of Asia Minor, had concluded *foedera amicitiae* with Rome, the texts of two of which have been preserved on inscriptions found in Lesbos. Methymna, after assisting Rome in the

[1] Sherk (1969), 26. On the history of the institutions and law in the cities of Lesbos in Roman times, see Labarre (1996). On the discussion and extended bibliography of inscriptions from Lesbos dating from the Roman period, cited in this article, see Dimopoulou (2015), 455–674.

[2] See Buchholz (1975), 153, Mason (1995).

Athina Dimopoulou, *Lesbos in the Roman Empire: Treaties, Legal Institutions, and Local Sentiment towards Roman Rule* In: *Law in the Roman Provinces.* Edited by: Kimberley Czajkowski and Benedikt Eckhardt in collaboration with Meret Strothmann, Oxford University Press (2020). © Oxford University Press.
DOI: 10.1093/oso/9780198844082.003.0014

war against King Prusias II of Bithynia and obtaining war reparations for raids it had suffered,[3] in 129 BCE concluded a *foedus amicitiae*[4] with Rome, acquiring the status of a *civitas foederata ex jurejurando*.[5] Although such treaties were generally considered part of the *ius gentium*, their terms were drafted by Rome and reflected the Roman legal practice, as also attested in the Lesbos inscriptions. The terms of the early treaty of Methymna[6] are typical of Roman *foedera aequa*, such as those of Maroneia, Ainos, or Astypalaia, including the standard terms of mutual military assistance.[7] Eresos also developed contacts with Rome in the second century BCE, as attested by a small number of honorary decrees, one of which is honouring an unknown citizen *inter alia* for participating in embassies to Rome and contributing to avert 'major risks' for the city.[8] Mytilene's relations with Rome were at first also those of a friend and ally,[9] although no formal conclusion of a *foedus amicitiae* between them is known for the earlier period. A tombstone inscription[10] from Mytilene, referring to fallen soldiers as having fought 'like lions', 'as allies with their spears on the side of the Roman rulers,[11] for their homeland, for the rule of law,' may be connected to military assistance provided by Mytilene to Rome in one of its campaigns in the East,[12] which granted the city the *de facto* status of Rome's ally.

Mytilene, however, lost the status of *civitas libera* after siding with Mithridates and delivering to him Manius Aquilius, the former consul and friend of Marius sent by Rome to subdue the revolt. The so-called *Mytilenaeorum perfidia*, the treason of the Roman interests that led to Aquilius' torture and execution, shocked public opinion in Rome, leading to severe reprisals.[13] Following Mithridates' treaty with Rome, Mytilene was the only city that continued to resist Rome, suffering a four-year siege by Lucullus, during which the young Julius Caesar obtained his first military palms, the distinction of the *corona civica*.[14] Mytilene was finally conquered, sacked, and looted by the Roman army.[15] Being, according to Cicero, submitted to Roman rule *belli lege ac victoriae iure*,[16] its lands became

[3] Plb. 33.13.8. See Magie (1939), 180, Magie (1950), 116–17. [4] IG XII 2, 510.

[5] Chicorius (1889), 440–7, Donati (1965), 18–20, Täubler (1913), 54, Jones (1940), 118, Ferrary (1990), Sanchéz (2009), 246, suggests that this treaty was a reward for Methymna for the military help it gave to Rome during the war with Aristonicus. Gruen (1984), I. 49, dates the Methymna–Rome treaty after 129 BCE or even later, in the 90s BCE.

[6] Characteristic of the Roman legal terminology is the reference (l.5) to δόλος πονηρός, *dolus malus*.

[7] SEG 3:310. [8] IG XII Suppl. 692, Dimopoulou (2015), 470–2.

[9] In 190 BCE Mytilene offered two triremes to C. Livius Salinatore, during his war against Antiochus III of Syria. It also offered its harbour to the Roman fleet, incurring the occupation of its περαία on the coast of Asia Minor by the enemy.

[10] IG XII 2, 285, Dimopoulou (2015), 473–4.

[11] The name of the Romans as the rulers mentioned allies of the Mytilenians in the missing word of the inscription is restituted.

[12] Livy, *Ab urbe condita* 37.12.5; 37.21.4. [13] Velleius Paterculus 2.18.3.

[14] Suetonius, *Divus Iulius* 2. [15] Plutarch, *Lucullus* 4.2–4, Livy, *Periochae* 89.

[16] Cicero, *De lege agraria* 2.16.40: 'by the law or war and right of victory.'

part of the *ager publicus populi Romani,* were integrated in the Province of Asia, and Mytilene became a *civitas stipendaria.*

The fortune of Mytilene would change eighteen years later, at the end of the third Mithridatic war, thanks to the friendship of Theophanes, one of its most distinguished citizens, with Pompey.[17] Theophanes acted as the *praefectus fabrum*[18] of Pompey and would become the historian of his deeds and his liaison with the Greeks. He became the most well-known Greek of his time in Rome, through whom even Cicero or Caesar would have access to Pompey.[19] He is the first Greek of the East known to have acquired Roman citizenship,[20] named Gnaeus Pompeius Theophanes after his patron. As a Roman citizen, Theophanes continued to act in the best interest of his native city.[21] A major accomplishment—given the city's treason and conquest by the Roman army—was the restitution of Mytilene's status as *civitas libera* by Pompey[22] during his visit to the city in 62 BCE.[23] This act, which exceeded Pompey's legal authority in the context of the campaign against Mithridates under the *lex Manilia,* was later ratified by the *lex Iulia de actis Cn. Pompei.*[24] Mytilene submitted itself to Pompey's patronage, in gratitude to whom eighteen dedications as *σωτήρ, εὐεργέτης, αὐτοκράτωρ, ἰμπεράτορ,* and *κτίστης*[25] were found in Lesbos, a greater number than in any other part of the empire (except Delos). As for Theophanes, for rendering the city its liberty he had the exceptional fortune of being the only simple citizen of a Greek city who was worshiped by his fellow-citizens as a god, reflecting a practice previously attested only for Hellenistic kings.[26] This *adulatio Graeca,* as stated by Tacitus,[27] would, however, later cause the disgrace of Theophanes' descendants in Rome under Tiberius.

The bonds of friendship between Pompey and Theophanes and the unexpected restoration of Mytilene's freedom did not spare all of the city's dominions from

[17] For the relations between the two men, see Plutarch, *Pompeius* 42, Velleius Paterculus 2.18, Pliny, *Naturalis historia* 5.139. Gold (1985), describes Theophanes as a 'foreign client' of Pompey and their relationship as 'patronage'. For the history of the relations between eminent Mytilenians and Romans, see Rowe (2002), 124.

[18] For this office, see Welch (1995), for Theophanes se especially 140–2.

[19] Cicero occasionally approached Pompey via Theophanes, whom he sometimes called simply *Graecus* (Cicero, *ad Atticum* 5.11.3) and other times *Mytilenaeus* (Cicero, *ad Atticum* 7.7.6), considering him an individual with influence over him (Cicero, *ad Atticum* 2.17.3, 5.11.3).

[20] The award was made by Pompey during the campaign (*in contione militum*), see Ferrary (2005), 55–6, Sherwin White (1980), 308. The acquisition by a foreigner of the status of Roman citizen did not entail the loss of citizenship in the city of his origin: see Gaudemet (1982), 532–4. Theophanes therefore remained a citizen of Mytilene too.

[21] Spawforth (2012), 42.

[22] This view, which has been reproduced by most scholars, has been subjected to criticism by Anastasiades (1995).

[23] Plutarch, *Pompeius* 42.8, Velleius Paterculus 2.18.3.

[24] The *lex* was voted by the *comitia centuriata* in 59 BCE, thanks to a successful manipulation by Caesar, who introduced as consul a proposal to that effect, without the previous consent of the Senate, which had thitherto been a usual, though not legally necessary, precondition. see Cassius Dio 38.7.5, Appian, *Bella civilia* 2.9, 2.13, Suetonius, *Divus Iulius* 19.2, Plutarch, *Pompeius* 48.3.

[25] Kantiréa (2007), 21–3.

[26] IG XII 2, 163 (= Syll^3 753). For the publication of the inscription and commentary, see Kantiréa (2009), 161–9.

[27] See Robert (1980), 7.

the requests of the *publicani*. To this end, Pompey, as the city's patron, introduced in 55 BCE at the Roman Senate the *senatus consultum de agris Mytilenaeorum*. This *senatus consultum* (which is preserved in poor condition in an inscription found in Mytilene),[28] confirmed certain rights of the city regarding the enjoyment of its possessions, probably in some geographical areas delineated in the lost part. The grant included the right of the Mytilenians of ἔχω[σιν κατέχωσιν καρπίζων-ται] immobile properties of all sorts, translating the terms *habere, possidere, frui*, which refer to the Roman legal concept of the *iure peregrino* right of possession and exploitation of land. Similar terms are attested in the *lex Antonia de Termessibus*, which had accorded equivalent rights to Termessos of Pisidia.[29] The lands in question belonging to Mytilene were probably located on the mainland of Asia Minor, an area surrounded by and included within the territory of the Province of Asia, and thus subject to contestations on behalf of the publicans. The censors (mentioned in l. 12 of the inscription) were probably instructed to exclude these lands from the catalogue of tax farming areas.

After Pompey's defeat,[30] another local aristocrat from Mytilene, Potamon, would take the lead as spokesman of local interests before the Roman authorities, from his first encounter with Caesar[31] on the shores of Asia Minor in the 40s BCE, to his death, when he was over the age of 90. Potamon became a famed philosopher and orator.[32] His intellectual prestige radiated far beyond Lesbos and he was one of the three candidates for the position of tutor to Tiberius.[33] The Mytilenians later dedicated to this scholar the *Ποταμώνειον* a monument at the acropolis of Mytilene (latter destroyed by an earthquake), on the walls of which were transcribed[34] copies of the official documents related to his public career and deeds.[35] Among the inscriptions identified as part of the *Potamoneion* are three letters by Julius Caesar,[36] and two *senatus consulta* dating from Augustus' rule, confirming or granting privileges to the citizens of Mytilene, and honorary decrees for Potamon by the city. The lacunar text that has been identified as a first letter[37] is probably Caesars' reply to an embassy lead by Potamon, whereby the author is expressing his goodwill towards the Mytilenians right after Pompey's flight from the island of Lesbos. The words τῆς φιλίας ἀσφάλειαν preserved in a second letter, referring to the *terminus technicus* of *amicitia*, imply that a treaty of alliance—the text of which is not known—between Mytilene and Rome was at the time considered valid.[38] Potamon could have succeeded in having an alliance with Rome *de facto* renewed under Caesar by offering the city's military assistance to

[28] IG XII Suppl. 11 (= Sherk 25), frg b.col II.1. See Dimopoulou (2012).

[29] For a detailed commentary on this *lex*, see Ferrary (1985) and Crawford (1996), 331–40.

[30] Plutarch, *Pompeius* 74–5.

[31] For Potamon and his contacts with Caesar, see Sherk (1963).

[32] He was a famous rhetorician and author of books on history and rhetoric, none of which have survived. See Bowie (2011), 51–3.

[33] According to the Suda (s.v. '*Θεόδωρος Γαδαρεύς*'), three candidates competed for the position of Tiberius' tutor, Potamon, Antipater and Theodorus of Gadara, and the latter was chosen.

[34] IG XII 2, 23 to 57, IG XII Suppl. 6 to 12 and 112, Charitonides (1968), 6–15, 26, 60, Evangelides (1924/5) 45–6.

[35] See the recording of the texts, and the related bibliography in Mommsen (1895), 887–901, Ehrengerb and Jones (1976), no. 307, Hodot (1982).

[36] Dimopoulou (2010).

[37] IG XII 2, 35, Sherk 26.

[38] IG XII 2, 35 col b.1 (= Labarre 20 B, Sherk 26).

the Roman army, perhaps in the form of provisions brought by Potamon himself to Caesar's army for the battle of Zela, the famous *veni, vidi, vici* campaign in Cappadocia against king Pharnakes. This hypothesis is supported by the isolated words 'provisions' and 'Cappadocia', preserved in a fragmentary honorary inscription of Mytilene for Potamon himself, which also stood in the *Potamoneion*.[39] The Mytilenians latter dispatched an embassy to Rome in order to have their status of *amici et socii* of Rome *de iure* also ratified by the Senate.[40] The Senate's decision, as well as an *ad hoc* edict issued by Caesar, granting a special request of the Mytilenian ambassadors, were sent to Mytilene with a third letter by Caesar, drafted in 46/45 BCE during his third dictatorship.[41] These were inscribed on the *Potamoneion*. The main objective of this embassy, to renew the earlier treaty of 'amity and friendship' between the Mytilenians and the Romans, was accomplished, though no new specific obligations on either side are recorded in the *senatus consultum*. The ambassadors appearing before the Senate were offered the *hospitia publica*, their requests were granted, the terms of the treaty were inscribed on a bronze table, and sacrifices were offered to Jupiter Capitolinus. The ambassadors also asked for previous grants of privileges (τὰ φιλάνθρωπα), probably concerning the exemptions of certain lands from taxation granted under Pompey with the *senatus consultum de agris Mytilenaeorum*, to be republished on the same occasion.[42] Apparently the preservation of local revenue was a subject of great local concern, since Caesar in his letter is mentioning similar—insisting—previous demands by the ambassadors of Mytilene, in response to which he issued an edict confirming that no exemption from taxation was to be recognized in Mytilene and acknowledged the city's right to exploit in peace any income, civic or rural (τῆς πόλεως καὶ τῆς χώρας προσόδοις καθ' ἡ[συχίαν]). This measure by Caesar was probably aimed at members of the local aristocracy who had obtained tax exemptions in the past, being one of the first actions of the Romans in the direction of restricting such privileges,[43] as Augustus would also later do by imposing similar restrictions upon Cyrene.[44] The Mytilenians, who in Caesar found a new patron, honoured him by celebrating his birthday with the Καισάρεια in Mytilene[45] and in Eresos,[46] while the name Ἰούλιος became very popular among

[39] IG XII 2, 30 (= IG XII Suppl. 9), see Dimopoulou (2015), 512–15.

[40] For these events, see Magie (1950), 417–18.

[41] IG XII 2, 35, Col b.

[42] We do not know though, if these privileges also included the city's right to judge in its own courts and by its own laws any case related to its lands and taxes, even if one of the parties was a Roman subject, as it seems that had been the case in Termessos through the privileges accorded by the *lex Antonia* of 68 BCE.

[43] Josephus (*Antiquitates Judaicae* 14.190–98) has preserved the text of a similar decision of Caesar's concerning Judea. Rostovtzeff (1917), 33, notes that the text of the decision conveyed by Josephus has similarities with the respective one for Mytilene, including the same reference to φιλάνθρωπα measures, and that the same procedure was observed, i.e. a first decision by Caesar that then had to be ratified by a decree of the Senate, following the dispatch of an embassy to Rome by the interested parties.

[44] An edict issued by August (SEG 9:8) regarding Cyrene ordered that the provincials who had received Roman citizenship should not be exempted from their tax obligations towards their cities, except if such ἀνεισφορία (tax immunity) had been expressly awarded to them upon the grant of Roman citizenship. See Ehrenber and Jones (1976), 139 ff., no. 311; Ferrary (2005), 72–3.

[45] IG XII 2, 26.

[46] IG XII Suppl. 129.

the inhabitants of the island.[47] On an altar in Mytilene, Caesar is also honoured as *pontifex maximus,* a title that he himself considered important as signifying his close connection to the divine, εὐεργέτης, and σωτήρ.[48]

The status of Mytilene as an ally of Rome would once more be confirmed under Augustus. This is attested by the *senatus consulta Silaniana,* and is also included on the *Potamoneion* monument.[49] This was named after M. Iunius Silanus, the consul who introduced them before the Roman Senate while sharing the office with Augustus during his ninth consulate. Augustus, who at the time was in Tarragona, probably received an embassy from Mytilene headed by Potamon and the poet Krinagoras, who undertook the long voyage to Iberia in order to meet the emperor in person. Following an exchange of correspondence between Silanus and Augustus, Silanus brought to a vote in the Senate two *senatus consulta* which validated the preexisting *foedera* with Mytilene and concluded a new treaty of alliance under oath (*foedus ex iure iurando*). The terms of this treaty, although badly preserved, probably recognized the *maiestas* of Rome and, in exchange, confirmed several privileges regarding the possession of land and judicial prerogatives of local citizens.

In the lacunar inscription of the Greek translation of the *foedus* sent to Mytilene (*IG* XII 2, 35), the end of the first line is missing, but according to the most probable reconstruction it contained the *maiestas* clause: the recognition of the majesty of the Roman people in exchange of some privileges granted.[50] At the end of the treaty some recognition was provided of the territories where the rights granted to Mytilene applied, both on the island of Lesbos itself ([καὶ ὅσα ... Μυτιλη]ναίων ἐγένοντο ἐν νήσωι [Λέσβωι]), and perhaps also on the city's περαία on Asia Minor.[51] Privileges regarding the administration of justice were included in the most damaged part of the *foedus* inscription, only some words of which survive. Although the *civitates liberae* were geographically incorporated into Roman provinces, they were not subject to the jurisdiction of the Roman governors, and reserved the right to apply their own laws and to refer their citizens to their own courts. The right to maintain their own jurisdiction appears to have been established by the *lex Iulia de repetundis* passed in Rome in 59 BCE at the proposal of Julius Caesar. According to Cicero, this law made free people 'fully and truly free.'[52] The citizens of the allies of the Romans were thus protected against arbitrary indictment and sentencing on behalf of Roman governors, on whose authority the force of the treaty rested. Despite the introduction of this *lex,* Rome also concluded bilateral treaties with free cities and regions, such as the Lycian League, specifying detailed jurisdictional issues and recognizing privileges for local citizens. The specification of these terms had been dictated from the experience of the co-existence of Romans and peregrines, citizens of the free cities,

[47] In Mytilene the name Ιούλιος (Julius) appears 21 times in inscriptions.

[48] IG XII 2, 151, 165, 166.

[49] See Arangio-Ruiz (1942/43), Sherk (1984), no. 97. On the commentary of these see Dimopoulou (2017).

[50] Ferrary (1990). For different proposals regarding the restoration of the term *maiestas,* see Famerie (2009), 274–5.

[51] See Robert (1937), 114, n. 1, Fournier (2010b), 455. For the mainland possessions of Lesvos, see Carusi (2003), 85–6.

[52] Cicero, *In Pisonem* 37.

and the jurisdiction-related disputes that had arisen in practice, as for example in Colophon.[53] Similar privileges may have been granted by Augustus to Mytilene in the context of the renewal of the *foedus*, concerning the jurisdiction of specific categories[54] of disputes[55] or transactions.[56] This is indicated by the words (l. 12–13) [ἄρχωιν ἢ ἀν]τάρχων (*magistratus* or *promagistratus*), which must be those of the Province of Asia, who are instructed to to grant something (l. 14, ἀποδιδότω). Mainly, the term (l. 8) προκριματ[. . .] refers to πρόκριμα κεφαλῆς, translated into Greek the procedure of *praeiudicium capitis*, the juridical process that allowed the person accused of a crime that incurred capital punishment to appeal to the Roman authorities. The related accusations against Roman citizens could on principle only be tried by the *quaestiones perpetuae* in Rome.[57] The Mytilene inscription is unfortunately too damaged to provide more information on this point and on the manner of application of this privilege. Finally, if the reconstitution in the last line of [αὐτο]/νόμου δήμ[ου] is correct, this adjective could emphasize the right of Mytilene as a *civitas libera*[58] to apply, its own laws unless otherwise specified in the its own laws, *foedus*, and to be exempt from the *imperium* and *iurisdictio* of the Roman governor[59] of the province of Asia.[60] The terms of this treaty, one of the last known under Augustus, confirmed the coveted status of free city for Mytilene, although the city for all intents and purposes was *de facto* brought under the orbit of Roman power.

This *foedus* being the last major treaty attested in Lesbos, the island thereafter accelerates the process of its peaceful integration in the empire. Telling of the

[53] See Fournier (2010b), 455.

[54] Aranzio-Ruiz (1942/43), 130, had suggested that it concerned specifically the protection of private law in Mytilene against the Roman authorities. See also Fournier (2010b), 458.

[55] Sanchez (2007), 380–1, interprets l. 9–12 as a 'convention judiciaire'.

[56] The distinction of the jurisdiction depending on the nationality of the accused had been the object of other treaties of Rome with its allies, as for example with Lycia, see Fournier (2010b), 452–6. The privilege of *praeiudicium capitis* had also been granted to the admiral Seleucus of Rhosus in Syria, for providing important military assistance to the Romans, see Sherk (1984), 106–9 no. 86, esp. p. 109 n. 13. According to the inscription preserving a letter and an edict by Octavian, if Seleucus or his relatives were accused for an offense drawing capital punishment, they could send a message to the Senate in Rome or the Roman ἄρχοντες or ἀντάρχοντες. What would happen in this case is not mentioned in the letter, but probably the accused would have the option to bypass the local jurisdiction and be subject to the Roman jurisdiction, see Garnsey, 1968, 56. In the honorary inscription for Menippos from Colophon (SEG 39:1244), another *civitas libera*, this citizen is honored for managing through embassies in Rome to end the practice of Roman authorities of subjecting to their own jurisdiction citizens and submitting them to the payment of guarantees, see Ferrary (1991). During another embassy, he managed to secure the authority of local laws applied even in accusations against Roman citizens, who would be judged in Colophon, as well as in the case of local citizens accused of capital crimes and for killing a Roman. The occasion had risen when the consuls considered a sentence passed in Colophon inadmissible and summoned a local citizen to Rome to reply to the charge of killing a Roman. Menippos probably managed to have the pre-eminence of local jurisdiction confirmed even in capital crimes.

[57] *Contra* Ferrary (1991), 566–77, who suggests that in Claros the related jurisdiction was also applied against Roman citizens by the city itself, based on a special privilege recognized by Rome.

[58] Pliny, *Naturalis historia* 5.139.

[59] By analogy, in a letter sent by the proconsul of Asia to Chios under Augustus, repeating the terms of a *senatus consultum* of 80 BCE, following the harsh treatment of the city by Mithridates, the city's laws, customs, and privileges are confirmed, it is forbidden to all magistrates and promagistrates to send an order in writing, and all Roman residents must comply to the city's laws.

[60] Fournier (2010b), 444.

endorsement of Roman rule is the fact that the greatest number of honorific inscriptions for the Julio-Claudian dynasty among all the regions of the Roman Empire has been found in Lesbos. The Mytilenians named Augustus honorary *eponymous archon* of their city.[61] Divine honors and lavish celebrations were instituted for the *Sebastoi*, including theatrical games, sacrifices, and public feasts, described in a partially preserved decree of Mytilene.[62] One noteworthy feature of this decree is the application by analogy of penalties prescribed in a law named *Diakos nomos*,[63] which regulated matters pertaining to the prizes of religious games as part of the cult of Zeus.[64] From now on probably local judges would be swearing oaths not only to Lesbos' ancestral divinities, but also to the *Sebastoi*, a *de facto* recognition before the local courts (about which very little is known during this period)[65] of both the divine status of the Emperor and of Roman supremacy. On the same stele another decree by Mytilene is preserved,[66] celebrating with most complicated eloquence the deification of Augustus. The author of this elaborate text—which also seems to contain excuses for the deification of Theophanes in Lesbos—may be no other than Potamon himself,[67] following his personal encounter with the emperor. A copy of this decree was dispatched to Rome to be exposed at the Capitol. The ambassadors, bearing the gift of a golden crown for the emperor, were instructed to thank the Senate, the Vestal Virgins, Livia, the emperor's sister, and the rest of his family and friends.[68] The Mytilenian ambassadors had evidently come into personal contact with Augustus' intimate circle during their stay in Rome, which possibly lasted several months, and the significance of such personal contact is underlined in their thanksgiving.

Another fragment of a badly preserved decree[69] of Mytilene implies that the regulations regarding the imperial cult of Augustus and Livia were considered of the utmost importance for the city. Any transgression of the rules regulating this cult is considered a crime against the imperial house and an attempt against 'liberty, democracy, and the Lesbian confederacy'. The term democracy (l. 12, *δαμοκρατία*), making one of its last appearances in Greek inscriptions, is hereby considered synonymous with the city's privileged status of a *civitas libera*, a status that, according to local sentiment, could be jeopardized by failure to express due respect to the Roman authorities.[70] Transgression entailed strict penalties, of which only a partial reference to the right for immediate seizure and imprisonment of the transgressor has been preserved (l. 13, *κατ' αὔτων καὶ ἐνδείξιος καττὰ διατετάγμενα*), constituting a rare indication on the local procedural law applied at the time in Mytilene. The importance attached to the imperial cult demonstrates that the attitude towards Roman authorities was one of reverence mixed with fear, a fear rooted in the past experience of the city, and that strict legal

[61] IG XII 2, 152–7. [62] IG XII 2, 58 a.1.

[63] Perhaps this law was proposed by Dies, son of Matroclus, Potamon's grandfather, from whom it took the name '*Διακός*', in line with the Roman practice of giving the proposing magistrate's name to the laws.

[64] See David (1913), 7, no. 1.

[65] For court practice in the Greek-speaking provinces of the Empire, see Fournier (2010a).

[66] IG XII 2, 58 b. [67] Price (1984), 54–7. [68] IG XII 2, 152–7. [69] IG XII 2, 59.

[70] As would later be the case with the neighboring city of Cyzikos under Tiberius, who lost its status after being accused of failing to finish a *heroon* dedicated to Augustus, Cassius Dio 57.24.6.1–7.1.

measures against any offense to the Roman authority were aimed at safeguarding local liberties.

The imperial cult, organized by the local elite, would from now on flourish in Lesbos, including all its ideological aspects. The high priests are often designated directly by the emperor himself or under his supervision,[71] working as agents of Roman interests. In the first-, second-, and early third-century-CE inscriptions, twenty-one priests[72] are honoured in Mytilene. Their names reveal that some of them are Roman citizens, while others are locals. In some cases, the names testify the fusion of Greek with Roman families, or the progressive Romanization of Greek families. A testimony of the devotion to the imperial cult in Lesbos comes form an honorific inscription from Eresos.[73] This was for a citizen who, among many offerings of wine and other delicacies to locals and Romans residing in the city, imperial family during celebrations at the occasion of the good news of an imperial victory, personally financed the building or renovation of no less than five temples and altars dedicated to the imperial family. A reference in the last line of this decree to the 'rest of the province', according to Louis Robert[74] is not an indication of the integration of Lesbos to the province of Asia, but rather that one of the temples had been erected by the anonymous benefactor in Pergamon, a city in which Augustus had allowed the erection of temples in his honour.

Lesbos' natural beauty, its vicinity to the shores of Asia Minor and its stimulating intellectual life attracted early on several members of the Roman *nobilitas*, some of whom had established themselves on the island in voluntary exile or on paid extended visits.[75] In 12 BCE, Augustus, in order to limit the luxurious life of the exiled members of the Roman elite, forbade those condemned to the *interdictio aquae et ignis* to live on the mainland or on islands at a distance shorter than 400 stadia from the shore, excluding though from this prohibition the islands of Kos, Samos, Rhodes and Lesbos.[76] Dio states that he does not know the reason for the exclusion of these islands, since they did indeed offer a beautiful and comfortable stay to exiles. Lesbos remained thus a favorite Roman destination, offering a high quality of life to the members of the Roman elite, even considered excessively comfortable by some:[77] when Junius Gallio was stripped of his senatorial rank and sent into exile by Tiberius, 'as men complained that he would endure his exile with equanimity, since he had chosen the famous and lovely island of Lesbos, he was dragged back to Rome, and confined in the houses of different officials'.

[71] Dmitriev (2005), 312–13.

[72] For the name list of the priests of Mytilene and Eresos and for the recording and a detailed analysis of the related inscriptions, see Frija (2012).

[73] IG XII Suppl. 124.

[74] Robert (1980), 7.

[75] Among them, C. Memmius, a candidate for the consulship in 54 BCE, who had been accused of corruption, Marcus Claudius Marcellus, a consul who had opposed Caesar, Brutus, Sextus Pompeius, the son of Pompey; see D.C. 49.17–18, App. *BC*, 4.113–14. DeRose Evans (1987) suggests that during his stay on the island Sextus Pompeius had minted coins. Agrippa also spent a long time in Mytilene, a stay interpreted either as a form of auto-exile, or as being on a special mission by Augustus. See Josephus, *Antiquitates Judaicae* 15.350. According to Magie (1908), he stayed in Lesbos in order to negotiate with the Parthian king the return of the *Aquilae* of the Roman legions captured by the Parthians, a diplomatic victory later celebrated by Augustus with a triumph in Rome.

[76] Cassius Dio 66.27.

[77] Tacitus, *Annales* 6.3.

Under the *pax Romana*, the island would enjoy a period of prosperity attested by a series of elaborate and rich villas dating from this period and lavish public buildings, including a major aqueduct.[78] Lesbos became, according to Louis Robert, a 'milieu très romanisé'.[79] Other than members of the elite, Roman *negotiatores* set themselves up on the island. In 32 BCE, the *Cives Romani qui Mityleneis negotiantur*, according to a Latin inscription found near Ancona, erected a statue *honoris causa* to their patron M. Titius,[80] proconsul of the province of Asia.[81] The locals also cultivated close links with Roman patrons, such as Lucius Calpurnius Piso the Augur, proconsul of Asia under Augustus, who was honoured by Mytilene as benefactor of the city.[82] Through interaction and intermarriage of Romans with the locals, a progressive fusion and Romanization of the population took place. In several inscriptions from Mytilene,[83] Methymna,[84] and Eresos,[85] the 'Romans'—as an ethnic group—proceeded to make dedications, with or without the participation of locals. Overall, in early imperial inscriptions 378 Roman names have been identified[86], among which there are *ingenui* bearing the *tria nomina*, and 164 Lesbians who had acquired the *civitas romana*, including 34 *Pompeii*, 21 *Julii*, 14 *Claudii*.[87] A great number of Latin *nomina* and *praenomina* is attested among the members of the local gymnasium, confirming the fusion and participation of Romans alongside the Greeks in local educational and athletic institutions.[88] The symbiosis and interaction of Romans and Lesbians certainly must have entailed many transactions and contracts ending in legal disputes, for which, however, almost no traces survive in the sources. Funerary inscriptions contain a few references to Roman institutions familiar to the Lesbians. Among funerary monuments instituting fines for grave violations, in one instance the fine is to be paid both to the local *boule* and to the Roman *fiscus*.[89] References to private institutions include the associations or *decurions*, who at the time were the heads of *collegia* of *familiae* of slaves serving Roman families, as well as to *familiae* of gladiators, whose spectacles in the theatre of Mytilene became very popular under the early Empire, as several reliefs of gladiatorial games integrated in the city's castle and other structures attest.

Members of the local elite took advantage of the privileged relations they cultivated with Roman authorities in order to advance their career. In Rome, the Romanized descendants of Theophanes followed the *cursus honorum*, serving in various public posts.[90] Theophanes' grandson, Q. Pompeius Macer, in 15 CE would serve as the first Praetor of Greek origin in Rome. He would advise Tiberius on the creation of some new *iudicia maeistatis* in Rome, not foreseeing that some

[78] Kourtzellis, Pappa, Kakes (2018). [79] Robert (1960), 279–80.

[80] Ehrenberg and Jones (1976), no 189. M. Titius, who in addition to proconsul had served as head of Anthony's fleet as of 35 BCE, was also the patron of the Samians, who dedicated to him an honorary inscription, and he was honoured by Clarus and Athens—see Canali De Rossi (2001), 93, n. 7, Eilers (2002), 140–1, 219.

[81] They probably made his acquaintance when he was sent in 35 BCE to Lesbos, to chase Pompey's son, Sextus Pompeius, who had taken refuge in Mytilene.

[82] IG XII 2, 219. Eilers (2002), 249. He is the same person who later would become disgusted at the judicial corruption of Rome.

[83] IG XII 2, 111. [84] IG XII 2, 517, 518. [85] IG XII Suppl. 124.

[86] Sarikakis (1993–4). [87] Hatzfeld (1975), 90–5. [88] Chankowski (2010), 278.

[89] IG XII 2, 407. [90] Spawforth (2012), 45–6.

years later, in 33 CE, he would face similar charges himself and be forced to commit suicide,[91] following the exile of his sister also accused for the crime of *maiestas* and the suicide of their father. Tiberius' wrath, according to Tacitus, was connected to the divine worship[92] offered in Mytilene to their ancestor Theophanes.[93] When members of this family originating from Lesbos became prominent power-brokers in Rome, what must have been a local cult of minor importance became a matter of lèse-majesté in the very heart of the empire. The family was not though exterminated, since to another descendant of Theophanes, M. Pompeius Macrinus, are dedicated no less than seven inscriptions[94] enumerating the steps of his impressive *cursus honorum* in various posts of the Roman administration, including the offices of *quatuorvir, quaestor, propraetor* of Pontus and Bithynia, *tribunis plebis, praetor* in Rome, *curator viae Latinae, imperator* of the *sexta Victrix legio, legatus* in the province of Cilicia, *proconsul* of Sicily, *sodalis Augustalis, quindecimvir sacris faciundis* and *proconsul* of Africa. Mytilene dedicated an honorary inscription and statue to this illustrious citizen, called 'new Theophanes', who cultivated close ties with his homeland. Apparently, he had intervened before the Emperor Antoninus in favor of the 'liberty' of Mytilene, a term denoting perhaps that the city still preserved the status of *civitas libera* at that time. This intervention could have been made necessary by some local disturbances and conflicts in Lesbos, hinted at by Aelius Aristides in one of his speeches of 149 CE,[95] in which the situation in Lesbos is described as the very opposite of *eunomia*, the rule of law.

Regarding the continuity of local legislation in Roman times, only minor traces survive. Potamon, who in spite of cultivating close ties with several Roman emperors did not acquire Roman citizenship, is honoured in Mytilene decrees as *εὐεργέτης* and *κτίστης*,[96] a *terminus technicus* and title attributed to benefactors who secured local autonomy or privileges through their embassies and ties with the Roman rulers. In one inscription Potamon is honoured by the confederation (*koinon*) of the Lesbians as a descendant of Penthilus, the archaic king of the Aeolians,[97] and also as a legislator (*nomothetes*) of Mytilene. Overall, in three decrees of Mytilene Potamon is mentioned as *nomothetes*.[98] As the adoption of laws in Mytilene normally belonged to the competence of the assembly (*ekklesia*), after a probouleutic proposal by the council (*boule*), we do not know if Potamon was named *nomothetes* because new laws were introduced at his proposal, because he had been entrusted exceptionally with the drafting of new laws, or whether the title was merely honorary, although the latter is less likely. The title does, however, reflect that he was the main carrier of innovation in matters of legislation in early imperial times in Lesbos and the driving force behind measures adopted by Roman authorities to the benefit of Mytilene. We can assume that he took an active part in drafting the decrees sent to the emperors and the senate, such as the renewing of the alliance with Rome and the *apotheosis* of Augustus.[99]

[91] Tacitus, *Annales* 1.72. See Syme (1982), 79–80, White (1992).
[92] Buraselis (2001).
[93] Tacitus, *Annales* 6.18.
[94] Hodot (1979).
[95] See Buraselis (2001), 67 ff.
[96] IG XII 2, 159, 160, 161, 162, IG XII Suppl. 43, 44, Charitonides (1968), 43.
[97] Spawforth (2012), 40.
[98] IG XII Suppl. 7, IG XII 2, 255 l. 5, IG XII 2, 9, l. 10–11.
[99] Potamon himself benefited from the highest protection. According to the Suda, Π 1227, when he was to return to Mytilene, Tiberius gave him a letter stating that if anyone was to commit any injustice to him, he should be ready to face the emperor.

The cities of Lesbos, over the first two centuries CE, preserved their local institutions and organs of administration. Members of the imperial family are honorifically nominated as archons, including Augustus, Tiberius and Gaius Caesar as eponymous *prytanes* in Eresos. Agrippina, who had given birth to Julia Livilla in Mytilene, was honoured as *boulaia,* protector of the *boule* and Gymnasiarch in perpetuity, for financing both institutions.[100] Although members of the local elite played an important role, especially in Roman diplomatic missions, important decisions still derived from the local assembly (*ekklesia*). Without being a democracy in the classical sense, popular participation in the assembly remained part of local public life in Lesbos, even if placed under the scrutiny of the Roman authorities. In a decree of Mytilene from the second century CE, the main objective of which is unfortunately lost, it was decided to send a decree to the Roman authorities each year in order to inform them of the city's decisions regarding issues of public interest (ll. 4–6, *ὄππως καὶ αὔτοις φανέραν πόημεν τὰν προαίρεσιν τᾶς πόλιος περὶ τῶν δαμοσίων πραγμ[ά]των*). A relevant prohibition, including a fine, payable to Artemis Thermia is set out in the same decree, and if the generals fail to collect the fine, they are made individually accountable for paying the *duplum*. The measures adopted by the resolution are considered highly important in order 'to save and protect the city's benevolent fate' (*ἐπὶ σαωτηρία καὶ φυλάκα καὶ ἀγάθα τύχα τᾶς πόλιος*), a formula which demonstrates that it belonged to a particularly important category of city decrees. Three *dogmatographoi* bearing Roman names are also mentioned, a terminology that may reflect the Roman practice of witnessing the transcription of the official acts, as attested by the mention of *scribendo adfuerunt* (*γραφομένῳ παρῆσαν*) in the *senatus consulta*.[101] The assembly continued therefore to hold some political role and was still voting on the resolutions (*psephismata)* proposed by the *boule* (in Mytilene they are attested at least until the end of the second century CE). While important political decisions regarding internal policy are missing, or at least have not been preserved in the city decrees of the period, matters of importance treated locally are the conclusion of international agreements, and several administrative, economic, and religious issues, in particular connected to the city's good relations with the Romans.

The council's (*boule*) operation in Mytilene is also attested throughout the early Empire, as it assembled members of the local elite and cultivated close ties with the Romans.[102] Participation in the council may have been hereditary at the time, as evidenced by mentions of being a *bouleutes* as a status symbol in funerary inscriptions. It may also have been honorific, as indicated by the attribution of the title of *bouleutes* to an actor of 'international fame' (*sic*), Tiberius Julius Apolaustus.[103] The *bouleutai* and secretaries of the *boule* mentioned in inscriptions sometime bear Roman names, such as Aurelius Proclus Justus (in a recently discovered and still unpublished inscription from Mytilene). Several inscriptions attest to the intense diplomatic activity and the assignment of specific tasks to ambassadors until at least the end of the second century CE, when Mytilene sent P. Galenius Pollio to Rome to deliver a city decree.[104] Insofar as the subject

[100] IG XII 2, 208.

[101] For this office in other Greek cities, see Rhodes (1997), 494, 557, 560.

[102] Dimopoulou (2015), 608–11.

[103] FD III, 1.551.

[104] IG XII 2, 67.

of such missions was to defend special privileges, such as the renewal of the alliance treaties or tax exemptions, the ambassadors' role was very important and eminently political.

Regarding civic judicial institutions, the information preserved in the sources of the early empire in Lesbos is minimal. An honorary inscription for a public doctor dated to the third century CE mentions among his many offices that he had acted as head of the *boule* and as a *nomophylax*.[105] An honorific inscription mentions a certain Crates as having served among many high offices as ambassador and *ekdikos*, i.e. *defensor civitatis*, the advocate assigned by the city for its representation before the Roman authorities or courts, defending its rights and privileges during litigation or disputes.[106] The name of a *dikastes* from Methymna[107] is attested in an unpublished inscription found in Larissa, dated to the first century CE, stating the names of 6 *metapemptoi dikastai* (foreign judges), coming also from Ilion, Elaia, Smyrna, Adramytteion and Chios, who had been sent to Larissa in order to resolve local disputes, the common form of Hellenistic dispute-resolution procedure for Greek cities. In an honorary inscription from Eresos,[108] dated to the time of Augustus, the word *dikastai* is also preserved, but unfortunately the context is missing. Finally, in the popular novel of Longus, *Daphnis and Chloe*, set on the isle of Lesbos during the second century CE, a dispute between Daphnis and young aristocrats from Methymna, accusing him of the loss of their ship, is first adjudicated *ad hoc* by an old shepherd, acting as a *dikastes* (more as a kind of wise mediator). The dispute which finally ends up with Methymna rallying in the assembly a military assault on the shores of Mytilene.[109] These meager testimonies could tentatively be seen as indications of a certain continuity regarding the local administration of justice in Lesbos.

One piece of evidence regarding Roman jurisdiction in relation to Lesbos comes from the Ephesos inscription, dated to the Flavian period, naming the *conventa iuridicii* of the Province of Asia and indicating that Mytilene came under the district of Pergamon.[110] The inscription lists the communities by national origin (*Μυτιληναῖοι*, *Καλληνεῖς*), and their order is determined by διοικήσεις, corresponding to the *conventa iuridicii*.[111] Each name is followed by a small amount of money expressed in *denarii*. Eresos and Methymna are not mentioned in the surviving part of the inscription. Since it would have been logical to list the Eresians and the Methymnians alongside the Mytilenians, one explanation for their absence is that they were subject to another district (*conventus*), that of Adramyttium, whose city record has not survived.[112] Their classification under a different district from Mytilene is perhaps explained by the fact that the Romans, when establishing the διοικήσεις of the Province of Asia, did not pay much attention to the previous boundaries of the cities. These administrative subdivisions and the respective Roman jurisdiction must have applied, with small variations, from the mid-first century BCE to the early third century CE. So locals from Lesbos did have access to Roman justice and to the tribunal of the proconsul, although this meant they would have to travel a short distance across the Aegean,

[105] IG XII 2, 484. Dimopoulou (2015), 623–6. [106] IG XII 2, 134.
[107] Fournier (2010b), 538, Dimopoulou (2015), 631–2. [108] Charitonides (1968), no. 122.
[109] Longus 2.14.4–2.15.1. [110] Robert (1949), 236–7, n. 6; Robert (1980), 5.
[111] Burton (1975), Fournier (2010b), 60–87, Kantor (2014), 254–9. [112] Habicht (1975), 80.

a boat trip in many aspects admittedly easier than today. To what extend this was practical or accessible for most litigants is another question. Resolving minor disputes before the local authorities may have been a more time-effective and less expensive option.

Finally, under the reign of Diocletian, a Latin dedication (CIL III, 450) to the Tetrarchs dated in 292–305 CE by the *praeses provinciae insularum*, Aurelius Agathus Gennadius, confirms that Lesbos now forms part of the *Provincia insularum*. The most important epigraphic contribution of the era are the fragments of fiscal records on six inscriptions, attesting to the implementation of Diocletian's fiscal reform in Lesbos.[113] The inventories record all kinds of agricultural production and income, the land in *iugera*, including shares in joint properties and the species of the trees of the owner, the number of farm animals (such as horses, cattle, sheep, goats), and the number of his slaves. Some properties are divided into 'parts'. In the village Sykounta for example, the estate consisted of 5½ *iugera* of vines, 60 *iugera* of arable land and of 186 olive trees, and was divided into four parts. These parts constituted shares of joint properties belonging to several co-owners, formed through inheritance. The inventory of Lesbos probably concerned only rural populations. As to the identity of the persons concerned, it seems that everyone is of Lesbian descent and that most are owners of their estates. One of the inscriptions (IG XII 2, 79) includes the term γεωργ(ὸν), denoting the status of *colonus*, a free farmer who leased foreign land for an average duration of lease of five years (*lustrum*).

Overall, the loss of independence that the Roman dominion entailed for Lesbos—once the initial scars of the violent submission of Mytilene healed—opened a new period of prosperity for the island. The conquest of Asia Minor by the Romans moved the borders of the empire further to the east, entailing a loss of strategic importance for Lesbos, but ensuring several centuries of stability and security from military operations. At first, the main focus of the relations of the cities of Lesbos with Roman authorities consisted in a series of diplomatic missions on the highest level. These aimed to secure the citizens' fundamental liberties, immunity from taxation and some privileges related to justice, our understanding of which remains tantalizingly uncertain. Even after the *de facto* integration of Lesbos into the Roman Empire, local life, including the operation of several public Greek institutions, seems to have gone on with the administration of local affairs in the usual manner, relatively undisturbed from Roman official interference, other than in the interest of maintaining stability and order.[114] On the other hand, the endorsement of the imperial cult and the numerous honorific decrees for the Emperors found in Lesbos, mark, other than the importance of cultivating good relations with those in power, the submission to and acceptance of Roman authority. The local elites forged strong bonds with Rome, whereas an important presence of citizens of Roman origin on the island enforced the process of integration. The close interaction of the two ethnic groups, Roman and Greek-Aeolian, must have inevitably generated legal disputes and a need to resolve them

[113] On their discussion and bibliography see Dimopoulou (2015), 662–74.

[114] For the incorporation of Lesbos into the Roman Empire and the absence of references to barbarian raids, see Kaldellis (2002), 17–29.

according to the *ius gentium*. As to their extent and the mechanisms available for their resolution, all we can offer are educated guesses; the same is true of the extent of Roman influence on private transactions. Due to the fragmentary nature of our evidence, very little can be ascertained as to the presence of Roman law and Roman legal administration. Nor do we have any indication on the *Constitutio Antoniniana* as a turning point in the knowledge, application or integration of Roman law in Lesbos, although we must note that, due to the limitations of evidence, very little is known on the private law applied by the island's independent city-states throughout their ancient history.

REFERENCES

Anastasiades, V. 1995. Theophanes and Mytilene's freedom reconsidered. *Tekmeria* 1, pp. 1–14.

Arangio-Ruiz, V. 1942/43. Senatus Consulta Silaniana de Mytilenensibus. *Rivista di Filologia e di Istruzione Classica* 20–1, pp. 124–30.

Bowie, E. 2011. Men from Mytilene. In: T. A. Schmitz and N. Wiater (eds.), *The Struggle for Identity: Greeks and their Past in the First Century BCE*. Stuttgart, pp. 21–49.

Buchholz, H. G. 1975. *Methymna*. Mayence.

Buraselis, K. 2001. Two Notes on Theophanes' Descendants. In: O. Salomies (ed.), *The Greek East in the Roman Context. (Proceedings of a Colloquium Organised by the Finnish Institute at Athens, May 21 and 22, 1999). (Papers and Monographs of the Finnish Institute at Athens, VII)*. Helsinki, pp. 61–70.

Burton, P. 1975. Proconsuls, Assizes and the Administration of Justice under the Empire. *Journal of Roman Studies* 65, pp. 92–106.

Canali De Rossi, F. 2001. *Il ruolo dei patroni nelle relazioni politiche fra il mondo greco e Roma in età repubblicana ed augustea*. Munich.

Carusi, C. 2003. *Isole e Peree in Asia Minore. Contributi allo studio dei rapporti tra poleis insulari e territori continentali dipendenti*. Pisa.

Chankowski, A. S. 2010. *L'Éphébie hellénistique: Étude d'une institution civique dans les cités grecques des îles de la Mer Égée et de l'Asie Mineure. Culture et cité 4*. Paris.

Charitonides, S. 1968. *Αἱ ἐπιγραφαὶ τῆς Λέσβου, Συμπλήρωμα*. Athens.

Chicorius, C. 1889. Ein Bündnissvertrag zwischen Rom und Methymna. *Rheinisches Museum für Philologie* 44, pp. 440–7.

Crawford, M. H. (ed.) 1996. *Roman Statutes*, I. London.

David, E. 1913. *Ἀνέκδοται Ἐπιγραφαὶ Λέσβου*. Mytilene.

DeRose Evans, J. 1987. Sicilian Coinage of Sextus Pompeius. *American Numismatics Society Museum Notes* 32, pp. 124–9.

Dimopoulou, A. 2010. Communiquer avec le pouvoir romain: les lettres de Jules César publiées par la cité de Mytilène. *Revue internationale des droits de l'antiquité* 3ème série, LVII, pp. 33–49.

Dimopoulou, A. 2012. Droits réels et *immunitas* des provinces romaines de l'est, à l'époque républicaine: le cas du *senatus consultum de agris Mytilenaeorum*. In: E. Chevreau, D. Kremer, A. Laquerrière-Lacroix (eds.), *Carmina Iuris, Mélanges en l'honneur de Michel Humbert*. Paris, pp. 259–73.

Dimopoulou, A. 2015. *Λεσβίων Πολιτείαι: Πολίτευμα και δίκαιο των πόλεων της Λέσβου (αρχαϊκοί, κλασικοί, ελληνιστικοί, ρωμαϊκοί χρόνοι)*. Athens.

Dimopoulou, A. 2017. Lesbos sous Auguste. Du renouveau des traités à l'apothéose. In: L. Cavalier and M. C. Ferriès–F. Delrieux (eds.), *Auguste et l'Asie Mineure*. Ausonius Éditions, Scripta Antiqua 97. Bordeaux, pp. 399–412.

Dmitriev, S. 2005. *City Government in Hellenistic and Roman Asia Minor*. Oxford.

Donati, A. 1965. I Romani nell'Egeo. I documenti dell'età republicana. *Epigraphica* 27, pp. 18–20.

Ehrenberg, V. and Jones, A. H. M. 1976. *Documents Illustrating the Reigns of Augustus and Tiberius*. Oxford.

Eilers, C. 2002. *Roman Patrons of Greek Cities*. Oxford.

Evangelides, D. 1924/5. *Ἀνασκαφαί καί ἔρευναι ἐν Λέσβω*. *Αρχαιολογικόν Δελτίον* 9 (*Παράρτημα*), pp. 41–54.

Famerie, E. 2009. Le traité d'alliance Romano-Cnidien de 45 av. J.-C. *Cahiers du Centre G. Glotz* 20, pp. 265–80.

Ferrary, J. L. 1985. La lex Antonia de Termessibus. *Athenaeum* 63, pp. 419–57.

Ferrary, J. L. 1990. Traités et domination romaine dans le monde hellénique. In: L. Canfora, M. Liverani and C. Zaccagnini (eds.) *I trattati nel mondo antico. Forma, Ideologia e Funzione*. Rome, pp. 217–35.

Ferrary, J. L. 1991. Le statut des cités libres dans l'Empire romain à la lumière des inscriptions de Claros. *Comptes rendus des séances de l'Académie des Inscriptions et Belles-Lettres* 3, pp. 557–77.

Ferrary, J. L. 2005. Les Grecs des cités et l'obtention de la *civitas romana*. In: P. Fröhlich and Ch. Müller (eds), *Citoyenneté et participation à la basse époque hellénistique*. Geneva, pp. 55–6.

Fournier, J. 2010a. Entre droit romain et droit grec: la pratique judiciaire dans les provinces hellénophones de l'empire romain (Ier s. av. J.-C.–IIIe s. apr. J.-C. *Revue historique de droit français et étranger* 88, pp. 165–87.

Fournier, J. 2010b. *Entre tutelle romaine et autonomie civique. L'administration judiciaire dans les provinces hellénophones de l'empire romain (129 av. J.-C.–235 ap. J.-C.)*. Paris.

Frija, G. 2012. *Les prêtres des empereurs. Le culte impérial civique dans la province romaine d'Asie*. Rennes.

Garnsey, P. 1968. The Criminal Jurisdiction of Governors. *Journal of Roman Studies* 58, pp. 51–9.

Gaudemet, J., 1982². *Institutions de l'antiquité*. Paris.

Gold, B. 1985. Pompey and Theophanes of Mytilene. *American Journal of Philology* 106, pp. 312–27.

Gruen, E. S. 1984. *The Hellenistic World and the Coming of Rome*. Volume I. Berkeley.

Habicht, C. 1975. New Evidence on the Province of Asia. *Journal of Roman Studies* 65, pp. 64–91.

Hatzfeld, J. 1975. *Les trafiquants italiens dans l'Orient hellénique*. New York.

Hodot, R. 1979. La grande inscription de M. Pompeius Macrinus à Mytilène. *Zeitschrift für Papyrologie und Epigraphik* 34, pp. 221–37.

Hodot, R. 1982. Deux notes sur des inscriptions de Mytilène. *Zeitschrift für Papyrologie und Epigraphik* 49, 187–9.

Jones, A. H. M. 1940. *The Greek City*, Oxford.

Kaldellis, A. E. 2002. *Λέσβος και ανατολική Μεσόγειος κατά τη ρωμαϊκή και πρώιμη Βυζαντινή περίοδο (100 π.Χ.–600 μ.Χ.)*. Athens.

Kantiréa, M. 2007. *Les dieux et les dieux Augustes: le culte impérial en Grèce sous les Julio-Claudiens et les Flaviens: études épigraphiques et archéologiques*, Athens.

Kantiréa, M. 2009. *Τιμητική επιγραφή για τρεις ευεργέτες στη Μυτιλήνη*, 44–36 *π.Χ.* (;). In: S. Aneziri (ed.) *Ανθολόγιο. Επιγραφές και Πάπυροι της Μετακλασικής Αρχαιότητας*. Athens, pp. 161–9.

Kantor, G. 2014. Roman legal administration in the province of Asia: Hellenistic heritage vs. innovation. In: J. Dubouloz, S. Pittia and G. Sabatini (eds.), *L'Imperium Romanum en perspective: Les savoirs d'empire dans la République romaine et leur héritage dans l'Europe médiévale et modern*. Besançon, pp. 243–68.

Kourtzellis, Y., Pappa, M., Kakes, G. 2018. The Roman Aqueduct of Mytilene. In: G. A. Aristodemou (ed.) *Great Waterworks in Roman Greece: Aqueducts and Monumental Fountain Structures.* Athens, pp. 109–130.

Labarre, G. 1996. *Les cités de Lesbos aux époques Hellénistique et Impériale,* Paris.

Magie, D. 1908. The Mission of Agrippa to the Orient in 23 B.C. *Classical Philology* 3, pp. 145–52.

Magie, D. 1939. Rome and the City-States of Western Asia Minor from 200 to 133 B. C. In: W. M. Calder and J. Keil (eds), *Anatolian Studies Presented to W. H. Buckler.* Manchester, pp. 161–185.

Magie, D. 1950. *Roman Rule in Asia Minor to the End of the Third Century After Christ.* Volumes I and II. Princeton.

Mason, H. J. 1995. The End of Antissa. *American Journal of Philology* 116, pp. 399–410.

Mommsen, Th. 1895. Das Potamon-Denkmal auf Mytilene. *Sitzungsberichte der Königlich-Preussischen Akademie der Wissenschaften zu Berlin,* pp. 887–901.

Price, S. R. 1984. *Rituals and Power. The Roman Imperial Cult in Asia Minor.* Cambridge.

Rhodes, R. J. 1997. *The Decrees of the Greek States.* Oxford.

Robert, L. 1937. *Etudes Anatoliennes. Recherches sur les inscriptions grecques de l'Asie Mineure.* Paris.

Robert, L. 1949. Le culte de Caligula à Milet et la province d'Asie. *Hellenica* 7, pp. 206–38.

Robert, L. 1960. Recherches Épigraphiques, IV. Une pierre errante en Écosse. Inscription du Dumbartonshire. *Revue de études anciennes* 62, pp. 276–85.

Robert, L. 1980. Deux poètes grecs à l'époque impériale. In : *ΣΤΗΛΗ εις μνήμην Ν. Κοντολέοντος.* Athens, pp. 1–20.

Rostovtzeff, M. I. 1917. Caesar and the South of Russia. *Journal of Roman Studies* 7, pp. 27–44.

Rowe, G. 2002. *Princes and Political Cultures. The New Tiberian Senatorial Decrees.* Michigan.

Sanchéz, P. 2007. La convention judiciaire dans le traité conclu entre Rome et les Lyciens (P.Schøyen I 25). *Chiron* 37, pp. 363–82.

Sanchéz, P. 2009. 'On a souvent besoin d'un plus petit que soi' le rôle des alliés de moindre importance dans la construction de l'empire romain au IIème siècle av. J.-C. *Cahiers du Centre G. Glotz* 20, pp. 233–47.

Sarikakis, Th. C. 1993–4. *Τα Ρωμαϊκά ονόματα της Λέσβου. Αρχαιογνωσία* 8, pp. 97–105.

Sherk, R. K. 1963. Caesar and Mytilene. *Greek, Roman and Byzantine Studies* 4, pp. 145–53.

Sherk, R. K. 1969. *Roman Documents from the Greek East. Senatus Consulta and Epistulae to the Age of Augustus.* Baltimore.

Sherk, R. K. 1984. *Rome and the Greek East to the Death of Augustus.* New York.

Sherwin White, A. N. 1980. *The Roman Citizenship.* Oxford.

Spawforth, J. 2012. *Greece and the Augustan Cultural Revolution.* Cambridge.

Syme, R. 1982. Tacitus: Some Sources of his Information. *Journal of Roman Studies* 72, pp. 79–80.

Täubler, E. 1913. *Imperium Romanum. Studien zur Entwicklungsgeschichte des Römischen Reichs.* Leipzig.

Welch, K. E. 1995. The Office of Praefectus Fabrum in the Late Republic. *Chiron* 25, pp. 131–45.

White, P. 1992. Pompeius Macer and Ovid. *Classical Quarterly* 42, pp. 210–18.

15

An Outline of Legal Norms and Practices in Roman Macedonia (167 BCE–212 CE)*

Ilias N. Arnaoutoglou

Sometime in the first half of the second century CE the inhabitants of the little known *polis* of Bragylos in the area of Krestonia, north of Thessaloniki, erected at least two stone markers'[1] delimiting the boundaries of their *polis*, according to a pronouncement made originally by the Macedonian king Philip II, and followed up by the Roman proconsul P. Clodius Capito Aurelianus.[2] Boundary stones, despite their ubiquity, usually convey a limited amount of information useful to legal historians. Sometimes they may include a legal term such as the Athenian *πεπραμένου/-ων ἐπὶ λύσει* (i.e. sold under redemption-clause)[3] while in other cases they are mentioned in boundary marking (*ὁροθεσία*) following an agreement between *poleis*, an adjudication by foreign judges or Roman authorities.[4] In Roman Macedonia we know of

* I would like to thank the organizers of the conference and editors of the proceedings, Kimberley Czajkowski and Benedikt Eckhardt, for their generous hospitality at Münster and the formal and informal exchange of perspectives on law in the Roman Empire. Epigraphic publications are abbreviated according to *Guide de l'épigraphiste*, Paris 2010. Translations of Greek and Latin passages are mine unless indicated otherwise.

[1] SEG 39.577 (SEG 30.573; AEp. 1992, 1521; BE 1988, 841) (Bragylos (Krestonia), second cent. CE) *ὅρους ἀπο/κατέστησε κα/τὰ τὴν γεγενημέ/νην ὑπὸ Φι/λίππου τοῦ βα/σιλέως ὁροθεσί/αν Π(όπλιος) Κλώδιος Κα/πίτων Αὐρηλια/νὸς ἀνθύπατος/Βραγυλίοις,/Τιβηρίοις, Κισσυνί/οις· ὅρος [—]/λιος ἡρῷον.* (The boundary stones *(horoi)* were restored, according to the delimitation made by king Philip, by P. Clodius Capito Aurelianus proconsul to the benefit of Bragylians, Tiberians, Kissynians; boundary stone (*horos*) the *heroon* of—lis)

SEG 59.658 (= ZPE 169 (2009) 163–70; AEp. 2009, 1261; BE 2011, 422) (Bragylos (Krestonia), second cent. CE) *ὅρους ἀποκατέσ/τησε κατὰ τὴν γε/γενημένην ὑπὸ/Φιλίππου τοῦ βα/σιλέως ὁροθεσί/αν Π(όπλιος) Κλώδιος Καπίτων/Αὐρηλιανός ἀνθύ/πατος Βραγυλίοις/ὅρος Θράσωνος ἡρῷ/ον.* (The boundary stones *(horoi)* were restored, according to the delimitation made by king Philip, by P. Clodius Capito Aurelianus proconsul to the benefit of Bragylians; boundary stone (*horos*) the *heroon* of Thrason).

[2] For the proconsul and his career see Eck (1981), 238–42.

[3] Attic *horoi*: Fine (1951). Finley (1951: 118–93). Lalonde, Langdon, and Walbank (1991), 22–51. Rhamnous: Petrakos (1999), II, nos 183–92. Eleusis: Clinton (2005), Ia, nos 675–9.

[4] Agreement between *poleis*: FD iii (4) 42 (Skarphieis and Thronieis, late second cent. BCE); adjudication by foreign judges: IG ix (1) 689 (Mondaieis and Azoriastai, 182 BCE); by Roman authorities: FD iii (4) 293 (114 CE), CIL iii 586 and 12306 (Lamia-Hypata, 117–38 CE). See also Ager (1996), Hurlet (2006), 282–3, Camia (2009), and Girdvainyte in this volume p. 213.

Ilias N. Arnaoutoglou, *An Outline of Legal Norms and Practices in Roman Macedonia (167 BCE–212 CE)* In: *Law in the Roman Provinces.* Edited by: Kimberley Czajkowski and Benedikt Eckhardt in collaboration with Meret Strothmann,
Oxford University Press (2020).
DOI: 10.1093/oso/9780198844082.003.0015

three more Greek inscriptions referring to similar processes.[5] The boundary stones mentioned above are significant on another count; they suggest, *prima facie*, a certain degree of legal continuity between royal and Roman Macedonia.[6] It is a fair assumption that these boundary stones were set up following a border dispute resolved by the proconsul, but it is far from certain, since it is possible that the verb ἀποκατέστησε (to restore) means that they were simply restored following some sort of deterioration or destruction.[7] Roman intervention in land and boundary disputes was always rather conservative; such disputes were resolved by Roman magistrates or Greek arbitrators on the basis of the *status quo* when communities entered into an *amicitia* relationship with Rome.[8] Therefore, the reading of continuity between the lines of the inscription should not be considered as self-evident. The envisaged continuity implies an effort to legitimize Roman authority as a natural continuation of royal Macedonia. The standing boundary stones were a reminder of Roman might, guaranteeing peace and respect for the decisions of their predecessors, and a symbol of appropriating the royal Macedonian 'legacy'. Continuity thus could become a political argument. Despite that, two contemporary inscriptions, one from the border between Macedonia and Thessaly and another one from Phrygia in Asia Minor provide a solid basis for the argument on legal continuity. In particular, during Trajan's reign, Virginus Publianus was appointed to settle a boundary dispute between the inhabitants of Doliche and Elimeia. In his decision issued in 101 CE, he mentions that he was shown a *stele* recording a boundary settlement during Amyntas' reign, the father of Philip II.[9] Almost thirty years later, in 129 CE,

[5] Earlier cases: Boundary settlement of Philip II in Mygdonia, SEG 40.542 (Hatzopoulos 1996: ii no. 4) (*c.*357–350 BCE), boundary settlement in Philippoi by Alexander III, SEG 34.664 (Hatzopoulos 1996: ii no. 6) (330 BCE) and the settlement between Pherai and Demetrias in Thessaly, Hatzopoulos (1996: ii no. 11) 206 BCE, Hatzopoulos (2006: 88), and SEG 56.703 (291 BC). Roman Macedonia: EAM 181 (Lynkestis, 114 CE), EKM ii 416 (second–third cent. CE) and an undated from Philippoi, if genuine, Hatzopoulos (1996), App. no. 7. For the communities referred to in the above inscriptions see Hatzopoulos (1996), i. 65–6. See also *AD* 44 (1989) Chron. 367 with BE 1997, no. 346 and 364 for an unpublished boundary settlement concerning *Bocceraeos, Cielaeos,* and *Dolichaeos* in Eordaia. The relevant terminology varies, *termini positi*: IG x (2) (2) 162 (Pelagonia-Vitoliste, 120 CE). *Fines derecti*: CIL iii 591 (101 CE) *inter Dienses et Olossonios*; CIL iii 14406d (117–38 CE) *[inter] r(em) pop(licam) Phil (ippensium) et heredes SPAN—*...; CIL iii Suppl. 14206 (4) (97–101 CE) *inter rempublicam coloniam Philippensem et Claudianum Artemidorum* with CIGLPh 385 no. 5. See discussion in Pikoulas (1999), Burton (2000), Brélaz (2007a), 115, and Bérenger (2014), 307–11.

[6] See Nigdelis and Sverkos (2009) for a detailed discussion of the problems raised by these two inscriptions with copious bibliography. They claim that the king Philip of the inscription should be Philip II (convincing parallel border settlement between Doliche and Elimeia *BSA* 17 (1910/11) 193–204 (= AEp. 1913, no. 2; AEp. 1997, no. 1345) and that the delimitation of SEG 39.577 involved a *trifinium* among three communities.

[7] Similar usage in SEG 43.451 (repair of the statue of Apollo Dekadryos, Pydna, *c.*169 BCE), IK 23 (Smyrna) 721 (restoration of a statue of Athena by the cooperative (συνεργασία) of silversmiths and goldsmiths, late first cent. CE); IK 12 (Ephesos) 519 (repair of a statue); IvP I 62b (repair of a statue?, first cent. BCE/first cent. CE); TAM iv 11 (repair of road, Bithynia, 116 CE).

[8] See IG ix (2) 89 face a, 24–30 and face b, 25–32 (*c.*140 BCE, Narthakion-Thessaly) with Ager (1996), 427–9.

[9] See Wace and Thompson (1910/11) (= AEp. 1913, no. 2 and AEp. 1997, no. 1345) (Doliche, 101 CE): *Descriptum et re/cognitum ex commentario/Vergini Publiani iudicis/dati ab imperatore/Traeiano, quod protulit/C. Aelius Niger, in quo sc/riptum erat id q(uod) infra s(criptum) e(st). Cum/probatum sit mihi in stela lap/idea, quae posita est in for/o Dolichanorum, inscriptos/esse fines conveniente/s definitioni regiae factae/ab Amynta Philippi patr<a>e in/ter Dolichanos et Elemi/otas placet finem*

in Asia Minor, in the area of Aizanoi in Phrygia, Septimius Saturninus primipilarius restored the properties of the sanctuary of Zeus and of the *polis*, after having them measured, originally granted to them in the second century BCE by king Attalos and Prousias.[10]

The aim of this paper is to provide a review of the legal phenomenon (i.e. legal rules and regulations, practices and attitudes to law, as well as legal enforcement) in Roman Macedonia from the Roman conquest in 167 BCE to the extension of Roman citizenship to all free persons in the empire in 212 CE (*constitutio Antoniniana*) and beyond. The timing is opportune for such a task since a significant part of the excavated epigraphic material has been published during the last four decades.[11] At the same time, there is an increased and welcome revisionism among Roman historians in the study of certain aspects of the legal phenomenon during the Empire. The focus of recent investigation has been on the relation of Roman to local administration of law,[12] the role of the provincial governor (ideology and discourse),[13] and the role of custom in the late Empire.[14] In this atmosphere the juridical role of the Roman emperor could not have remained unchallenged; in a recent paper Jonathan Edmondson nuanced Fergus Millar's thesis about the passive juridical role of the emperor.[15] Roman Macedonia looms large by its absence from most of these accounts, largely due to the quality (rather than quantity!) of the surviving pieces of evidence and to the focus of modern scholarship on administration of justice and public law.[16] The article is organized in three parts: the first deals with the salient features of legislation and law in royal Macedonia, in the second part, I review the epigraphic contribution to

esse a ter/mino... (Copied and confirmed from the notebook of Verginius Publianus appointed *iudex* by emperor Trajan, extracted by C. Aelius Niger. It contains what is written in the notebook. Since it was demonstrated to me a stone stele lying in the market of Dolichaioi which contains the formal boundaries between Dolichaioi and Elimiotai following the royal boundary setting by Amyntas father of Philip, it was decided the boundary to be at the *horos*...)

[10] MAMA ix 8: *χώρας Διὶ Κτίστῃ καὶ π]όλει Αἰζανι/[τῶν δοθείσας ὑπὸ Ἀτ]τάλου καὶ Πρου/[σίου βασιλέων ἀποκ]ατέστησεν με/[τροῦντος Σεπτι]μίου Σατουρνεί/[νου πρειμιπιλαρίου κ]αθὼς Προυσίας/ [βασιλεὺς ἤρξατο]*. (lands granted to Zeus Ktistes and to the *polis* of Aizanoi by kings Attalos and Prousias, were restored after measurement by Septimius Saturninus *primipilarius*, when king Prousias was in power).

[11] See IG x (2) (1); IG x (2) (1) Suppl.; IG x (2) (2); EAM; IBeroia, EKM ii; ILeukopetra; IStobi; CIGLPh, IGBulg iv and v, the corpus of the inscriptions from Amphipolis is being prepared for publication by P. Nigdelis, and the relevant entries in BE, SEG, and AEp for the most recent epigraphic publications. Epigraphic documentation as the only available source, Youni (2005), 183; see also the useful anthology of epigraphic texts assembled in Youni (2000), 253–308.

[12] Macedonia: Youni (2000); Asia: Kantor (2014) and (2016); Lycia: the unpublished D.Phil. thesis of Kantor (2007); Egypt: Alonso (2015); Eastern provinces: Fournier (2010). See also Heller (2013) on whether the development of civic institutions in the Greek cities reflect Roman influence or independent, self-induced developments.

[13] Kokkinia (2004). See also Kokkinia (2014) challenging the Roman commitment to large building projects on the example of the port of Ephesos.

[14] Humfress (2011).

[15] F. Millar 'petition-and-response' model was criticized as depicting the imperial administration as simply reacting to petitions, for a defence see Brélaz (2007a); Edmondson (2015) argues for a more pro-active stance, according to which the emperor was intervening in the lives of communities, and the development of a dialogue (with the mediation of the governor) between the emperor and the *poleis*-elites. See most recently Tuori (2016).

[16] Except Kokkinia's (2004) commentary on IBeroia 7.

what the law in 'republican' Macedonia was and in the third part, I reflect, in a more detailed way, on the interplay between local and imported legal traditions, topped up by occasional imperial interventions.

1. LAW IN THE KINGDOM OF MACEDONIA

Legislation in the Macedonian kingdom was introduced through royal *diagrammata* (decrees) and *epistolai* (letters). *Diagrammata* were written regulations of a general character, providing a normative framework for the *poleis* of the kingdom to legislate.[17] *Poleis* were not required to validate royal *diagrammata*; they had to comply with them.[18] In contrast to *diagrammata*, royal letters were addressed to local magistrates (e.g. *epistatai* or *tagoi*) providing responses *cum* orders to questions about particular issues concerning either a geographical area or a particular area of legislation.[19] The Macedonian king had the authority to grant land and other privileges to his officers.[20] Individual *poleis* had an administrative structure similar to that of the southern Greek cities (assemblies, councils, magistrates) and had the authority to pass legislation concerning their affairs, such as the gymnasiarchic law of Beroia and probably the ephebarchic law of Amphipolis.[21] They were not affected by the presence of an *epistates*[22] or of *politarchai* as high ranking officials in Macedonian cities, post 183 BCE.[23] Private

[17] See Hatzopoulos (1996), 405–11 and Mari (2006).

[18] See Table 15.1 in the Appendix.

[19] See Table 15.2 in the Appendix and Hatzopoulos (2009).

[20] See Hatzopoulos (1996), ii. no. 21 (305–297 BCE); SEG 38.620 (305–297 BCE); SEG 38.619 (285/4 BCE).

[21] Mari (2006), 214. Gymnasiarchic law of Beroia: IBeroia 1 (early second cent. BCE); ephebarchic law of Amphipolis: Lazaridou (2015); urban regulation of Kyrrhestos: EKM ii 401 (third cent. BCE). See also the decrees recognizing the Koan Asklepieion as *asylon* SEG 12.373: 1–17 (Kassandreia, 243 BCE), SEG 12.373: 18–34 (Amphipolis), SEG 12.373: 35–55 (Philippoi), and EKM ii 430 (Pella). Honorific decrees: Hatzopoulos (1996: ii nos 37, 39, 44–6, 48–9, 53–5) and IG x (2) (1) 1–2, 1028. For the legislative procedure, the issue of a recommendation by the Council and the ratification process see Hatzopoulos (1996), i. 145.

[22] See Papazoglou (1988) 43 and 49 and Hatzopoulos (1996), I. 371–430. See most recently Raynor (2016) with an extensive discussion of evidence from list of *theorodokoi* and *asylia* decrees as evidence for the autonomy of *poleis* vis-à-vis the Macedonian king. Evidence about magistrates and deliberation organs from the decrees for the acceptance of *asylia* for the Kos sanctuary of Asklepios in SEG 12.372 (Philippoi, *tamias, stratēgoi, ekklēsia*), Amphipolis (*epistatēs, hiereus, ekklēsia*), Pella (243 BCE, *hiereus, tamias*); in the law on *gymnasion* in Beroia (IBeroia 1); in the law about ephebes from Amphipolis (Lazaridou (2015)). Kassandreia: Hatzopoulos 1996: ii nos 44–8 (285–200 BCE) *hiereus* as eponymous archon, *nomophylakes, stratēgoi, tamias, boulē, agoranomoi* (Hatzopoulos (1996: no. 69) (beg. second cent. BCE)). Thessaloniki: Hatzopoulos (1996), ii. nos 50–2 (240–223 BCE) *boulē, dēmos, hiereus* as eponymous archon, *epistatēs, tamias, hypepistatēs, dikastai, agoranomoi* (Hatzopoulos (1996), no. 71 (beg. second cent. BCE)). Moryllos: Hatzopoulos (1996), ii. 53–4 (208–205 BCE) *archontes, stratēgos, mnēmon*; Amphipolis: Hatzopoulos (1996), ii. no. 61 (214/3 BCE) *hiereus* as eponymous archon, *epistatēs* (also in Hatzopoulos (1996), no. 77 (end third cent. BCE), *archontes*, no. 65 (beg. second cent. BCE): *emporiou epimelētai, grammateus*; Pydna, Hatzopoulos (1996), ii no. 55 (beg. second cent. BCE). See also Hatzopoulos (2003/4), Mari (2017), and for the vocabulary of deliberation, Hatzopoulos (2013).

[23] See Papazoglou (1988), 50–1; Hatzopoulos (1996), ii. no. 16.

law transactions recorded on stone include sales (sometimes with a redemption clause) of real estate, securities, loans, and manumissions.[24]

The administration of justice in the Macedonian kingdom may not have been radically different from that in other Greek *poleis*, reflecting to a certain extent the idiosyncracies of the kingdom. The Macedonian king and the assembly of Macedonians retained their jurisdiction especially for offences concerning the army.[25] Various magistrates in the *poleis* were endowed with the power to impose and exact fines; there are circumstantial references to 'common laws' (*koinoi nomoi*) or to particular penalties for offences.[26] The argument is strengthened by three explicit mentions of courts (*dikasteria*) and *dikastai* in the gymnasiarchic law of Beroia, in the narrative of a land sale (EKM ii 425, Tyrissa, beg. 2nd cent. BCE), and in the copy for army recruits from Drama (SEG 49.855).[27] What remains unclear is the identity of these *dikastai*, sometimes called royal (*basilikoi*); their appearance in a document issued by the royal chancellery disassociates them from the legal frame of a *polis*. Instead of regarding them as 'appeal' judges appointed by the king (so EKM ii 425 *ad* p. 561) I would suggest to consider them as a panel of judges appointed with a fixed remit to resolve disputes connected to what was deemed royal interests. In other words, the term 'royal' may not qualify the jurisdiction of the organ but the mode of appointment.[28]

1.1. Submission to Romans

Roman Macedonia's history is marked by two landmark events, i) the battle of Pydna in 168 BCE and its outcome, which changed the whole military and political context in which Macedonians had operated thus far, and ii) the introduction of

[24] Sales of land: Game (2008), Hatzopoulos (2011) (= EKM ii 93 (Mieza, list of sales, third quarter of third cent. BCE), SEG 62.479 (Toronē, mid fourth cent. BCE), possibly SEG 45.60 (Phila-Pieria, third cent. BCE), and in general Velissaropoulos-Karakostas (2011: ii 271–317). Securities: Velissaropoulos-Karakostas (2011), ii. 141–80. Loans: SEG 61.481 (= *Tekmēria* 10 (2011) 71–89, BE 2012, no. 279) and Velissaropoulos-Karakostas (2011), ii. 421–55. Reference to a testament, guardianship and inheritance law in SEG 60.585, 11–19 (222 BCE), SEG 60.605 (*c.*231–29 BCE). Manumissions: IBeroia 45–7 and Velissaropoulos-Karakostas (2011), i. 360–423.

[25] See e.g. Hatzopoulos (1996: i 271–4 and ii no. 12, col. *I*, 4–7) and *IG* xii Suppl. 644, 32–3, 37, 42–6.

[26] See e.g. IBeroia 1 face *B*, 5–6, 8–10, 14–15, 19–23 and Lazaridou (2015: ll. 5, 11–14, 19, 49–51, 107–8, 111–15, 117–23). *Koinoi nomoi*: IBeroia 1, *B*, 44, 87. Particular offences: IG x (2) (1) 3, 16–21 (187 BCE): *Ἐὰν δε τις ποιήσῃ τι τῶν ἀπηγορευμένων, ἔνοχος ἔστω τοῖς ἐπιτίμοις τῆς φωρᾶς.*

[27] IBeroia 1, face B, ll. 29–37; ll. 99–101; ll. 107–9. EKM ii 425, 5–7: *δίκης γενομένης/[πρὸς] τοῖς βασιλικοῖς δικα[σ]/[τ]αῖς*. SEG 49.855, face A, 10–17. See also the words *δικαστὰς* (frg. B, l. 4) and *συνδίκων* (frg. D, l. 2) in SEG 47.885, a *defixio* from early third-cent.-BCE Arethousa.

[28] SEG 43.293 (= *Trikalina* 12 (1992) 115–22) with BE 1995, no. 334, from third-cent.-BCE Pharkadon in Thessaly may provide a useful parallel. It records the decision (l. 1) of two *basilikoi* (*dikastai* in l. 5 according to *editio princeps*) over a dispute between the *koinon* of Pharkadonians and two individuals, Eulykos and Eudemos, for the ownership of land. Menon and Andron, the *basilikoi* (*dikastai*?), having listened to the arguments of the litigants, they convinced them to resign from their claims and compromise; therefore, they have exercised a function like the *metapemptoi dikastai*. Zelnick-Abramovitz (2015: 52 n. 46) entertains the possibility that the expression *martyres dikastōn* attested in third-century BCE Macedonia may be interpreted in the light of Syll³ 279 from Zeleia in Mysia and the *dikastai* elected there to iron out any legal objections to the reclaim of public lands.

the *constitutio Antoniniana*,[29] an imperial initiative granting Roman citizenship to all free inhabitants of the empire and so affecting every free man and woman in it. The significance of the latter is suggested by the change in the way of recording personal names. Greek practice identified a person as X, son of Z (son of Y in some areas) or for a woman X, daughter of Z, wife of Y. For several decades after 212 CE following the addition of the *gentilicium Αὐρήλιος* to the personal name, the patronymic is preceded by the collocation *ὁ πρὶν*.[30] This attitude betrays both a resistance to the new, imposed Roman nomenclature as well as a way to deal with the concomitant uncertainty about the identity of individuals.[31]

Since Roman provinces were not created in a geopolitical *vacuum*, it is vital to discuss, if briefly, the events leading to the imposition of Roman rule in Macedonia. Following three periods of military operations between the Roman *respublica* and the kingdom of Macedonia (known as Macedonian wars, between 214 and 205 (I), 200 and 196 (II), 172 and 168 (III)), the Macedonian army was comprehensively defeated in the battle of Pydna in 168 BCE. The Romans established themselves over the areas controlled previously by the Macedonians, which included Aegean Thrace and Thessaly. The terms imposed on the defeated side were decided largely by the Roman senate who appointed a ten-member committee in cooperation with Aemilius Paullus.[32] They were announced in a ceremony in Amphipolis and according to Livy 45.29–30 and D.S. 31.8.6–9 included the following terms:

[29] P. Giss. 40, 7–9: *Δίδωμι τοί[ν]υν ἅπα/[σιν τοῖς κατοικοῦσιν τὴ]ν οἰκουμένην π[ολιτ]είαν Ῥωμαίων [μ]ένοντος/[οὐδενὸς ἐκτὸς τῶν πολιτευμ]άτων χωρ[ὶς] τῶν [δε]δειτικίων*. See the recent publication and supplement *[ἀδ]δειτικίων* by Purpura (2012: 295–317) and Purpura (2013). See also the discussion in Buraselis (1989), Rocco (2010), Kantor (2016), Bryen (2016), and most recently van Minnen (2016) claims that the issue of the decree extending Roman citizenship should be dated to 11 July 212 CE. It was published in Alexandria on 10 February 213 CE. For an attempt to conceptualize the challenge the 'divine donation' (*theia dōrea*) constituted for the Roman legal system and its integration in it see Ando (2011), 20–2.

[30] Earliest case: *Αὐρήλιος Ποσιδώνιος ὁ [πρὶν] Μέστυος ὁ κὲ Παντακιανός* (ILeukopetra 63, 212/3 CE); latest example: *Αὐρήλιος Παράμονος τοῦ πρὶν Παραμόνου* (ILeukopetra 118, 313 CE). See also EKM ii 64 (Aigai-Blaganoi, 216/7 CE), 144 (Edessa, 225 CE), ILeukopetra 68 (218 CE), 70 (220 CE), 84 (234 CE), 89 (238 CE), 93 (239 CE), 95 (241 CE), 108 (254 CE), 116 (309 or 311 CE), 117 (311 CE), 118 (313 CE), IBeroia 54 (248 CE), and SEG 46.800 (Pydna, 251 CE). Of uncertain date: EAM 168 (Lynkestis); EKM ii 122 (Skydra); IG x (2) (1) 564, 768 with SEG 27.308; IG x (2) (1) Suppl. 1448; SEG 29.584 (Epanomi), and SEG 42.607 (Kalindoia). For various designations of the same meaning see SEG 46.745, 6–9 (Exochi-Eordaia, 223 CE); IGR 3.354 (Sagalassos); MAMA 8.576 (Aphrodisias). In papyri there is a variety of terms and collocations used, M. Chr. 197 (202–3 CE), BGU 2.655 (215 CE), BGU 7.1652 (212 CE), PSI 5.464 (*c*.249 CE), BGU 4.1071 (third cent. CE), SPP 20.19 (217 CE) (refers to a dispute which came to court before 211 CE), P. Oxy. 1458, 2–7 (216–17 CE). For the use of *Αὐρήλιος* in Egypt see SB 20.14116 (212–13 CE), BGU 1.145 (213 CE), P. Gen.^{2} 1.1 (213 CE), SB 14.11705 (213 CE), BGU 1.356 (213 CE), and the discussion in Buraselis (1989: 120–48). Aurelii in Macedonia: Tataki (2006: 112 no. 89); at Dion, Demaille (2016a: 192–3). Blanco-Perez (2016) concludes that appending (M.) *Αὐρήλιος* in the nomenclature is attested since 213 CE; see also Rizakis (2011). For an unusual adaptation in Pamphylia and Bithynia see Feissel (2016). Possible impact of the grant in Ionia, Vujčić (2015).

[31] See already Youni (2000), 34–9 and Youni (2010), 336. Note also the following inscriptions in which no onomastic change is observed: IG x (2) (1) Suppl. 1394 (215 CE), EKM ii 143 (Edessa, 215 CE), and SEG 51.781 (Akropotamos-Thessaloniki, 216 CE).

[32] Livy 45.17–18. For such committees see the recent account by Yarrow (2012).

1. Macedonians were to keep their freedom, that is to preserve their cities, lands, laws and to elect their magistrates; that meant also the abolition of the monarchy and its army. Every person who served the royal dynasty was deported to Italy, and the royal treasures were transported to Rome,
2. Macedonians were to pay half the taxes paid to the king,
3. the kingdom was divided into four regions (*meridai*),[33] each led by an *archēgos* according to D.S. 31.8.9; at their capitals, assemblies were to be convened, magistrates elected and taxes collected,
4. a ban on acquiring property and *epigamia* between individuals of different regions was imposed,[34]
5. closing down of gold and silver mines, while iron and copper mines were permitted to work. It was not allowed to export salt or to exploit the timber.

Much more interesting information survives in Livy 45.31.1 according to which 'after the proclamation of the formula, (Aemilius Paullus) declared that he was going to provide the country with laws' (*Macedoniae formula dicta cum leges quoque se daturum ostendisset*), and again in 45.32.7.[35] Sarikakēs (1962: 109) noted the discrepancy between the license to Macedonians to employ their own laws and the new legislation drafted by Paullus and interpreted it as the adaptation of existing legislation to the new political environment; however, Paullus, on top of modifying existing legislation, may have introduced laws or other rulings on areas not regulated in the royal period, such as the lease of the lands of *ager publicus*, formed of the former royal holdings, or of the monopolies.[36] In this context one

[33] Livy 45.31. *Regio I*, between rivers Strymon (Struma) and Hebros (Marica)-Kypsela excluding Abdera, Maroneia [for which see the treaty with Rome (IAegThrace 168, 167 BCE) and Ainos (declared free by the Romans) notwithstanding their respective *chorai* but including Bisaltia, a region west of Strymon and Herakleia Sintike, with Amphipolis as capital city. *Regio II*, the area between the rivers Strymon (Struma) and Axios (Vardar) and eastern Paionia around Axios, with Thessaloniki as capital. *Regio III*, between Axios (Vardar), south to Peneios rivers, west up to Vermion mountain, Pella was its capital. *Regio IV*, the remaining lands west of Regio III up to border with Illyria at Lychnidos, i.e. Eordaia, Elimeia, Lynkestis, Derriopus, Pelagonia and north Paionia west of Axios river with its capital situated at Pelagonia or Herakleia Lynkestis (for which see Briscoe (2012), 705. See Livy 45.17–18 and 45.29.5–9 with Sarikakēs (1962), 106–13, Papazoglou (1988), 53–70) and Briscoe (2012), 701–6. The administrative division may date back to Antigonids, thus Hatzopoulos (1996), i. 248–54 and the objections raised by Juhel (2011) (BE 2012, no. 265), and it was simply adjusted to the aims of Roman policy. See most recently Ferrary (2018).

[34] The limitation of mobility of the inhabitants among the *meridai* is challenged by Daubner (2014).

[35] *leges Macedoniae dedit cum tanta cura, ut non hostibus uictis, sed sociis bene meritis dare uideretur, et quas ne usus quidem longo tempore, qui unus est legum corrector, experiendo argueret.* ((Paulus) laid down laws for Macedonia with such care as to seem to be giving them not to conquered enemies, but to well deserving allies—laws which do not even experience over a long period, the one best amender of legislation, could prove faulty in actual use). Plutarch, *Aemilius Paullus* 28 with Papazoglou (1988), 53–66. Justin 33.2.7 claims that these laws were still in use in the second century CE. Ferrary (1987–9), 209 considers as probable the imposition of censitarian criteria for the appointment of magistrates. Sarikakēs (1962), 111 argues that Macedonians' contentment with the abolition of monarchy was a convenient Roman myth. Briscoe (2012), 717 understand *leges* as 'the detailed provisions for the government of Macedon; they constituted a *lex data*, drawn by Paullus and the commissioners, not a law passed by the Roman people'. Similar appearance of the Roman general as legislator post 146 BCE, Girdvainyte in this volume p. 225.

[36] AEp. 2014, no. 1168 (= Bouchon (2014), 486–7). See also the *senatus consultum de agro Pergameno* (129 BCE), a decision concerning the dispute between *demosionai* and Pergamon,

should read the recently published inscription AEp. 2014, no. 1168 which includes two letters of Aemilius Paullus to Thessalian Gonnoi about expropriation and transfer of land to, Demophilos, probably a pro-Roman; it is very tempting to see these letters in the context of Paullus' (quasi-)legislative initiatives.

The revolt of Andriskos in 150–148 BCE and its suppression resulted in turning Macedonia into a province.[37] It was significantly increased in comparison to the area controlled by the kingdom, as any further Roman advances in the Balkans were added to the territory of that province; it was extending now from the Adriatic coast in the west to the river Hebros in the east.[38] Subsequently, in 27 BCE Thessaly[39] and Epirus were incorporated into the province of Achaia and the southern border was fixed to the line: estuary of Peneios river–Tempe gorge–Olympos, Chasia and Pindos mountain-range. To the north and east the creation of the provinces of Moesia (15 CE) and Thracia (46 CE) limited Macedonia to the area west of the Nestos (Mesta) river, south of Kresna gorge and Scupi. Thasos was granted the status of *civitas libera* in 196 BCE, which was confirmed by Augustus.[40] No *lex provinciae* was issued but the original arrangement of Aemilius Paullus remained in force. Octavian retained the province among the senatorial ones, but after his death Tiberius turned it into an imperial one, only for it to return under the control of the senate in the reign of Claudius. Nero in 66 CE integrated Thessalia and Epirus into the jurisdiction of the Roman proconsul of Macedonia.[41]

Macedonia was administered by a Roman proconsul (*ἀνθύπατος*) appointed annually by the senate. He had the authority,[42] among other things, to administer and dispense justice in all private and penal law cases involving the inhabitants of the province, apart from the citizens of a *civitas libera* or *foederata*.[43] The regional

IK 24 (Smyrna) 589; IK 13 (Ephesos) 975; *Mouseion* 1 (1873–5) 137 no. 62 and Brélaz (2007a), 137. For the expropriation of lands in Roman colonies see Rizakis (2015).

[37] See, however, Kallet-Marx (1995), 12–18 who has expressed his objection to regarding Macedonia as a province after 148 BCE. Despite that, Roman military commanders are appointed in Macedonia in order to guarantee internal stability and the inviolability of the frontier-line. Provincial administrative structures may have been slowly developed and not imposed top down, something that would explain the lack of information about consistent judicial intervention by the Roman governors. See also Richardson (2008), 16–48 on the use of the terms *provincia* and *ἐπαρχεία* in the legal literature of the Republican period he concluded that they do not mean fixed geographical entity but 'a responsibility allotted to a holder of *imperium*', Richardson (2015), and Jimenez (2016). For the creation of the province of Creta-Cyrenaica see Tzamtzēs (2013), 68–72.

[38] Papazoglou (1988), 81–2 and Fournier (2010), 7–8 on the relation of the proconsul of Macedonia with Achaia before 27 BCE; Fournier (2010), 305–7 on the exceptional character of the proconsul's (of Macedonia) jurisdiction in Achaia.

[39] Apparently Thessaly was attached to the Roman province of Macedonia post-66 CE, when Nero declared the *poleis* of Achaia free, Fournier (2010), 388, n.626.

[40] Papazoglou (1988), 79 and Fournier (2013).

[41] In more detail Girdvainyte in this volume p. 210.

[42] For a concise account and discussion see now Fournier (2010), 19–24.

[43] *Roman Statutes* i 12, Cnidos copy col. IV, 32–9 (100 BCE): *ἐὰν οὗτος ὁ στρατηγὸς ὧι τῆς Ἀσίας Μακεδονίας τε/ἐπαρχεία ἐγένετο τῆς ἀρχῆς αὐτὸν ἀπείπηι ἢ ἀπείπη/ται, ὡς ἐν ἐπιταγῆι ἐξουσία πάντων πραγμά/των ἐπιστροφήν τε ποιεῖσθαι κολάζειν, δικαιοδοτεῖν/κρείνειν κριτὰς ξενοκρίτας διδόναι ἀναδοχων κτημά/των ΤΕ[.]ΓΑΡΟΔΟΣΕΙΣ ἀπελευθερώσεις ὡσαύτως κα/τὰ τὴν δικαιοδοσίαν ἔστω καθὼς ἐν τῆι ἀρχῆι ὑπῆρ/χεν οὗτός τε ὁ ἀνθύπατος ἕως τούτου ἕως ἂν/εἰς πόλιν Ῥώμην ἐπανέλθηι ἔστω* (If the praetor or proconsul to whom the province of Asia or Macedonia shall have fallen abdicate from

division was, perhaps, retained as judicial districts, something corroborated by what seems to be a similar arrangement in the province of Asia, where the Attalid division survived.[44] Macedonians kept their status as citizens of *poleis*, but they were considered *peregrini* by the Roman authorities. Most *poleis* retained their civic institutions (*gymnasia*), deliberation organs (councils, assemblies), and magistracies (e.g. *politarchai, agoranomoi, grammateis, gymnasiarchoi, ephēbarchoi, tamiai, epimelētai*). Thessaloniki was awarded *civitas libera* status in 42 BCE; Amphipolis in the 40s BCE, Stoboi was granted the status of a *municipium* during Augustan times.[45] Roman *coloniae* were created in Kassandreia (43 BCE), Dion (43 BCE?), Pella (*c.*43 BCE), Philippoi (*c.*42 BCE) and were administered as a miniature of Rome.[46] The existing social stratification in the Macedonian *poleis* (citizens, foreigners, freed persons, slaves[47]) and countryside (landowners, smallholders and land-less peasants) was cut across by the installation of Roman *negotiatores*,[48] *veterani* (to whom agricultural land was granted), and military officials accompanying the Roman authorities.

The legal epigraphy[49] of Roman Macedonia consists of three large clusters of about 300 texts, i) epitaphs or other texts on funerary monuments, ii) honorary decrees and inscriptions of *poleis* or other collectivities such as *neoi*, and dedications by had-been magistrates, and iii) manumissions usually associated with a particular sanctuary. But even such a solid 'corpus' of material is marked by a lack

his magistracy, as described in his *mandata* he is to have power in all matters according to his jurisdiction just as it existed in his magistracy, to punish, to coerce, to administer justice, to judge, to appoint *iudices* and *recuperatores*, <registrations> of guarantors and securities, emancipations, and he is to be <immune from prosecution> until he return to the city of Rome—as translated in *Roman Statutes*). See also the treaty between Rome and the Lycian *Koinon* of 46 BCE inscribed on a lead-tablet, SEG 55.1452, 32–43 including rules about local jurisdiction in homicide cases as well as other crimes.

[44] Papazoglou (1988), 66 and Kantor (2014).

[45] Papazoglou (1986) and Papazoglou (1988), 316–17.

[46] For the colonies see Papazoglou (1988), 103–24 (Dion); 137–9 (Pella); 407–13 (Philippoi); 424–6 (Kassandreia). Lands controlled by the Roman in Philippoi, Rizakis (2015) discusses the repercussions of the Roman conquest and installation of *coloniae* on Macedonian soil, that is royal lands turned into *ager publicus* leased out for cultivation or confiscated to be granted to colonists and Brélaz and Tirologos (2016). For the institutions and society of Philippoi see Rizakis (2016) and Brélaz (2016a); for Dion, Demaille (2016b).

[47] Freedmen/women: e.g. EAM 96; IBeroia 31–2; SEG 56.762; IG x (2) (1) 208; 380; IG x (2) (2) 121; 403. Slaves: e.g. IG x (2) (1) 284; SEG 24.496.

[48] *Enkektemenoi* and *(syn)pragmateuomenoi Rhomaioi*: EKM ii 180 (Edessa, first cent. CE); IBeroia 59 (57–55 BCE); IG x (2) (1) 32 and 33 (late first cent. CE); IG x (2) (1) Suppl. 1059 (first cent. BCE/ first cent. CE); IG x (2) (2) 330 (Styberra, first cent. CE); SEG 1.282 (Akanthos, first cent. BCE/ first cent. CE); 19.438 (Idomene(?), 41–4 CE); *GRBS* 57 (2017) 305 no. 2 (Amphipolis, 29/28 BCE) and in an unpublished inscription from Amphipolis, *cives Romanei quei Amphipolis negotiantur.* For the appearance (after 80s BCE), origins and social makeup of Roman *negotiatores* in Thessaloniki and their organization in a *conventus* see Rizakis (1993), Rizakis (2002) with the older bibliography, and Brélaz (2016b). For a general account see van Andringa (2003) and Andreau (2016). Social status revealed through the sarcophagi, Stefanidou-Tiveriou (2010). For the *provincia Achaea* see Girdvainyte in this volume pp. 220–2.

[49] A particular feature of epigraphy in Roman Macedonia is the use of double dating formula that includes, i) the provincial era (starting in 148 BCE) and ii) the *sebastos* (august) era (starting in 27 BCE). Compare Syll^{3} 700, 1 (118 BCE): *ἔτους θʹ καὶ κʹ Πανήμου κʹ* with IBeroia 49, 28–31 (181 CE): *ἐγράψαμεν τὴν ἐπι<σ>το/λήν σοι ἐν Βεροίᾳ ἔτους βισʹ σε/βαστοῦ τοῦ καὶ ηκτʹ*, v *Περειτίου/τετράδι*; see McLean (2002: 174).

of balance; only a fraction of these texts is dated to the first century and a half of Roman conquest. Therefore, we lack significant pieces of information on the earliest institutional accommodation between Roman authorities and the local population, especially the socio-economic elites who effectively controlled most of the civic affairs.[50] Moreover, in that period Roman magistrates were concerned more with military affairs in the north and north east of the province.[51] I suggest, then, to divide the treatment of the epigraphic testimonia between Republican (168–27 BCE) and Imperial (27 BCE–212 CE) Macedonia, although I admit that, as with most chronological divisions, it is both artificial and arbitrary.

2. REPUBLICAN MACEDONIA (168/148–27 BCE)

The epigraphic dossier concerning legal institutions in Republican Macedonia contains twenty inscriptions of which only three[52] concern manumission with no mention of a *paramonē* clause. The surviving references to *skyphos* suggests that there was some continuity in the practice, as dedications of *skyphoi* are mentioned in IBeroia 3 (248 BCE). The remaining sixteen inscriptions record honorific decrees, honorary inscriptions and dedications.[53] Apart from some formulaic elements such as the dating formula, there is little to distinguish between *poleis*-decrees of the royal and of the 'republican' era. Indicative in this respect is the honorary decree IBeroia 2 (second/first cent. BCE) for Harpalos, in which there is reference to the long family pedigree of euergetism and to a recommendation of the council (*probouleuma*) ratified by the assembly.[54] Noteworthy is the appearance of the Roman proconsul as exercising judicial duties in affairs outside Macedonia proper; in particular, in 144/3 BCE Q. Fabius Maximus Servilianus sent a letter to the people of Dyme explaining his course of action once he was informed by a group of councilors under the leadership of Kyllanion that some magistrates conspired to change the constitution granted by the Romans and set the archives of the city on fire.[55] In a fragmentary *senatus consultum* preserved in Delphoi and concerning a dispute between groups of *technitai peri ton Dionyson*,

[50] For the re-composition of elites see Sève (2005).

[51] See Hurlet (2006), 135–42 and the decree Syll³ 700 (anc. Lete, 118 BCE) with Kallet-Marx (1995), 38 and Valverde (2004).

[52] EAM 115 (record of a manumission, 57–55 BCE), IBeroia 31 and 32 (second/ first cent. BCE and beg. first cent. BCE respectively, dedications of a *skyphos* by freed persons).

[53] See Tables 15.3–6 in the Appendix and compare with SEG 62.367 (Doliche, 130–100 BCE), a decree concerning an *epidosis* and the surveillance of the territory of Doliche, in which *tagoi* are mentioned as imposing fines and supervising their exaction.

[54] IBeroia 2, 33–9 (second/first cent. BCE): *ἐπεὶ οὖν ἐν τῶι τῶν ἀρχαιρε/σιῶν και[ρ]ῷι προβουλευσαμένων τῶν/βουλευτῶ̣ν ὅ̣πως ὁ Ἅρπαλος ἀξίως τι/μηθῆι τῶν γεγενημένων ὑπ' αὐτοῦ εἰς/τὴν πατρίδα, ὁ δῆμος ἐπελθὼν ἐπὶ τὸ βου/λευτήρ̣ιον τὴν πλείστην πρόνοιαν ἐ/ποιήσατο περὶ τῆς τιμῆς αὐτοῦ*... (since at the time of elections, when the councilors have recommended to honour Harpalos in a fitting to his benefactions manner to the fatherland, the people, assembled in the council house, showed much care about his honours...). Similarly in Syll³ 700, 2 (118 BCE), honorific decree of Lete for Markos Annios.

[55] Rizakis, *Achaie* III, no. 5 (144/3 BCE) with Girdvainyte in this volume pp. 217–8.

it appears that the Athenian *technitai* brought accusations in front of the Roman general in Macedonia.[56] *A fortiori*, then, one has to deduce that the Roman proconsul exercised the same function in Macedonia, too.

The earliest document of republican Macedonia is apparently a lost honorary inscription put up by the deme of the Amphipolitans, SEG 24.580.[57] Its date is not resolutely fixed and a date later than 167 BCE remains a distinct possibility, especially if we do not identify Gn. Domitius Ahenobarbus of the Livian narrative (45.17.2–3) with *Γν. Δομίτιος Αἰνόβαρβος* the benefactor of the inscription.[58] Two further institutional points are worth noting: the inscription records a decision of the *demos*, while the Council is absent; second, there are five *politarchai* mentioned in this inscription, while earlier inscriptions mention only two.[59] It is a distinct possibility but far from being convincingly demonstrated that due to Roman intervention the number of *politarchai* has increased in, at least, two Macedonian cities from two to five, but there is no need to assume that this was implemented in all the *poleis* of the province.[60] This kind of institutional tinkering may be typical; instead of abolishing an institution and especially one which meant concentration of powers at the hands of few, it was thought expedient to dilute it by either increasing the number of the office-holders or reducing their jurisdiction.

The picture emerging from the above account of the almost 150 years after the abolition of the monarchy raises the question of whether the term Roman Macedonia is meaningful at all; can we speak of Roman Macedonia as one, self-contained, institutional entity, substantially different in the aftermath of Pydna or

[56] Syll³ 705 (112/1 BCE). See LeGuen (2001), I. 98 no. 12, Aneziri (2003), 372 no. C2, and the honorific inscriptions for the priests of Athena by a *koinon techniton*, AEp. 2013, no. 1386 (= *MedAnt* 16 (2013), 223–55) (Amphipolis, 89–88 BCE) and SEG 61.485 (Amphipolis, 85/84 BCE).

[57] *[ὁ] δῆμος Ἀμφιπολειτῶ[ν]/Γ[ναῖο]ν Δο[μί]τιον Γναίο[υ]/[υἱὸ]ν Αἰνόβαρβον τὸν εὐερ/γέτην, πολειταρ χούντων/[Φιλ]οκράτους τοῦ Φιλοκράτους,/[Ἐ]πικράτους τοῦ Σερ[..]ου,/[Θε]οδᾶ τοῦ [———],/Ἑρμοίτου [τ]οῦ Ἁρπάλου,/[Σ]αραπίωνος τοῦ Σαρα/πίωνος* (The people of Amphipolis (honoured) Gnaius Domitius, son of Gnaius, Ainobarbos, benefactor, when politarchs were Philokrates son of Philokrates, Epikrates son of Ser—os, Theodas son of—Hermoitos son of Harpalos, Sarapion son of Sarapion).

[58] The first editor thought that the inscription should be dated at the end of the republican period, Perdrizet (1894), 419–23, no. 2 followed by Papastavru (1936), 83–4. For Gn. Domitius Ahenobarbus, *consul suffectus* in 162 BCE, see Broughton (1951), I. 435 and (1986), III. 81, more recently Carlsen (2006), 34–5 and in a critical mood Nigdelis and Anagnostoudis (2017), 304–5.

[59] Dedication to Artemis Tauropolos by the *demos* of Amphipolis, SEG 31.614 (179 BCE?). A similar inscription from Thessaloniki mentions also two *politarchai*, IG x (2) (1) 28 (Hatzopoulos 1996: ii no. 72 dates it *c.*200–168 BCE): *ἡ πόλις/Διονύσωι/πολιταρχούντων/Ἀριστάνδρου τοῦ Ἀριστόνου,/Ἀντιμάχου τοῦ Ἀριστοξένου*. On the problem of the date *politarchai* were introduced see Hatzopoulos (1996), i. 134–7 and lately Nigdelis and Anagnostoudis (2017), 303–5. The whole discussion relies on the premise of a uniform reform of the apparently same number of *politarchai*, with no regard to the size of the *polis* served by these magistrates. However, important and big *poleis* like Thessaloniki, Amphipolis, and perhaps Beroia may have eventually needed an increased number of *politarchai* to deal with the administration. Smaller *poleis* like Charakoma would not need more than one or two. Therefore, the reform attributed to Roman intervention may not have been but a pragmatist's answer to the increased needs of a *polis*.

[60] Even in the imperial period, Tyrissa (EKM ii 423, 44–5 CE) and Styberra (IG x (2) (2) 300, 95 CE) had two *politarchai's* names recorded on stone. More than two names were probably mentioned in SEG 42.558 (Anthemous, *c.*40 BCE) and in SEG 29.579 (Charakoma, end first cent. CE). In Thessaloniki there is one case in which 6 *politarchai* are named (IG x (2) (1) 126, beg. first cent. CE) and even 9 in IG x (2) (1) 127 dated no more precise than *ante* 212 CE.

even after 148 BCE? My impression is that the pace of change has not yet accelerated; the main players and agents of introducing changes remained the same (i.e. *poleis* and their elites) while the Romans were pre-occupied with dealing with external and internal enemies (Thracian tribes, civil wars).

3. IMPERIAL MACEDONIA (27 BCE–212 CE)

More than 250 inscriptions convey some sort of legal information for this period. They can be divided into four categories; first, inscriptions recording private transactions or providing information about them. For example, we hear of a donation by Tib. Kl. Polycharmos also called Achyrios to the synagogue of Stoboi in 163/4 CE,[61] who explicitly withholds the ownership and possession (τὴν δ' ἐξουσίαν... καὶ τὴν δεσποτείαν ἔχειν ἐμέ) of the flat (ὑπερῷον) above the synagogue. In 95 CE, the council of Styberra accepted by decree an endowment by M. Ouettios Philon,[62] while thirty years later in 126/7 CE the heirs of Anthestia Phouska not only restored statues and a sanctuary but also handed in 5 000 denarii to the council of the same *polis*.[63] Somewhat different is the donation of an amount of money with an explicit clause to be spent on sacrifices (*donatio sub modo*) by the tribes of Alkomena[64] in 192/3 CE. As for buying and selling land there are indirect references from Thessaloniki, in a funerary context despite injunctions against selling a funerary place.[65] In the sphere of obligations, we hear of a broker contracting artists for some sort of performance.[66]

[61] IStobi 19. The donation included the building of four porticoes (*tetrastoon*), a *trikleinon* room and chambers for religious purposes (*oikoi*) adjoining the synagogue. Synagogues in Stobi, IStobi 25, SEG 61.514bis (second/third cent. CE) and 514ter (third cent. CE).

[62] IG x (2) (2) 300. In it there is important information about the working of the local council; it elects its presiding officers (ἀποκληρωθέντων προέδρων), who convene the meeting (συναγαγόντων τὸ βουλευτήριον). The council's decision is described as δόγμα (δόγματος ἀναγραφή). The endowment was provided for in a testament (διαθήκη) and the particular terms of it are described as ἐπί τε ταῖς ὑπ' αὐτοῦ... γεγραμμέναις αἱρέσεσιν. Finally, the receipt of the donated amount of money by the steward of the council (ἐπιμελητὴς τῆς βουλῆς) is acknowledged. Tataki (2006), 443–4, nos 665.3 and 7 for the individuals mentioned. See Youni (2000), 178 and 257 no. 4 and Arnaoutoglou (2012–13).

[63] IG x (2) (2) 336. The five heirs (κληρονόμοι) of Anthestia Phouska (two are *Anthestioi* and one *Ouettios*, Tataki (2006: 94–5 no. 42.4, 9–10 and 443 no. 665.5)) either acted as executors of her testament supervising the fulfilment of her wishes or were charged with a *legatum per damnationem*. See Youni (2000), 175–6 and 297, no. 86.

[64] IG x (2) (2) 348. Roman names in the inscription, Tataki (2006), 74 no. 18.77. The inscription records not only the donation but the handing over of the amount to the four tribes of Alkomena. In case they do not perform the prescribed ritual, the donor's heirs shall recover that amount; effectively they are appointed as executors and supervisors. That the donor is still alive is suggested by the fact that not only he donated the money but paid for the inscription and erection of the stele, ll. 30–3. Donations also in: IGBulg v 5925 with Sharankov (2016), 353–7 (to a *gerousia*, *c.*180 CE); IG x (2) (1) 259 (first cent. CE) and 260 (beg. third cent. CE); a general account in Youni (2000), 234–42.

[65] Despite injunctions against alienating tombs, e.g. *IG* x (2) (1) 608 (147/8 CE), sale of land for funerary purposes was common, see IG x (2) (1) 357 (second cent. CE); IG x (2) (1) Suppl. 1361 (third cent. CE) and Youni (2000), 228–34.

[66] SEG 30.593 (Oreine-Serres, second/third cent. CE): Καπίτων Δέκιμος, Γ[άϊ]/ος Τορκουᾶτ/ος,/ προμισθω[τα]ί,/εὐξάμενοι ἀ[νέθη]/[κ]ạν τὸ ἄγαλμα παλεσ/[τ]ρ(ιώτῃ) Ἡρακλῆδι Ἀγαθί[ου]. The same term appears in the funerary inscription of a certain Σπένδωνος ὀρχηστοῦ, SEG 33.466 (Larissa, first

3.1. Manumissions

The best illustration of an epigraphic cluster in Roman Macedonia is the dossier of nearly 200 manumissions from the sanctuary of the *Meter Thea Autochthon* in modern Leukopetra near Beroia. Similar but considerably smaller clusters, almost contemporary with the Leukopetra one, are attested at Eordaia (EAM 116–17, Enodia), Aigai (EKM ii 63–77, Artemis Blaganitis), Beroia (IBeroia 49 Artemis Agrotera; 53–6 Dionysos Agrios Pseudanor; 51–2 Syria Parthenos), Skydra (*EKM* ii 121–3, Artemis Gazoria), Kyrrhos (*EKM* ii 406–12, Artemis) and Edessa (EKM ii 143–77, Aniketos Ma). The Leukopetra cluster is dated from 141/2 CE to 313 CE. These manumissions usually state the volition of the slave-owners to dedicate (ἀνατίθημι) or donate (δωροῦμαι, χαρίζομαι) their slaves to the deity; sometimes it is accompanied by a clause obliging the freed person to offer some sort of service either to the manumittor or to the sanctuary (*paramonē*-clause).[67] The written manumission agreement was called usually *katagraphē* (καταγραφὴ) or *ōnē* (ὠνὴ) and it was deposited at the sanctuary, at 'the arms of the goddess'.[68] However, the most intriguing information in these texts is the laconic and vague reference to an edict of the *kratistos hēgemōn* (κατὰ κέλευσιν[69] τοῦ κρατίστου ἡγεμόνος μου) Tertyllianus Aquila.[70]

cent. BCE). The term is also attested in a latinized form in the funerary monument of an *archimimos*, CIGLPh 222 (first /second cent. CE).

[67] In Edessa the *paramonē* clause is designated with the collocation ὑφελόμενοι τὴν χρῆσιν παρὰ τὸν τῆς ζωῆς αὐτῶν χρόνον, EKM ii 167 (268 CE), 168 (225 CE), 173 (253/4 CE). For the vexed question of whether the freed under a *paramonē*-clause person remained a slave or a free person see the recent articles by Canevaro and Lewis (2014), Silver (2015), and Sosin (2015). Personal status of *hieroi, hierodouloi and hieroi paides* see Caneva and Delli Pizzi (2015). For a brief account in *provincia Achaea*, Girdvainyte in this volume pp. 228–9.

[68] *Καταγραφή*: Edessa: EKM ii 145 (243 CE); 157 (247–53 CE); 158 (*c*.247/8 CE); 159 (252 CE); 162 (261/2 CE); 167 (268 CE); 171 (post 247 CE); ILeukopetra 94 (239 CE). 'Ωνή: Edessa: EKM ii 151 (246 CE); 168 (225 CE); 169 (252–68 CE); EKM ii 123 (Skydra, late third cent. CE); ILeukopetra 3 (170 CE); 28 (191/2 CE); 33 (192/30 CE); 45 (199/200 CE); 55 (210/11 CE); 69 (219 CE); 73 (229 CE); 93 (239 CE); 98 (243 CE(?)); 129 (post 212 CE).

[69] Note also that all later references to the edict describe it as ἀπόφασις but in the earliest it is designated as κέλευσις. The term ἀπόφασις describes decisions of the emperor, e.g. IG vii 2870 (155 CE) or of Roman magistrates of various levels, ἀπόφασις ἐπάρχου, IEleusis 489 (post 131 CE); of a χειλίαρχος (IOSPE i^2 404 (185/6 or 197–202 CE); of *dikastai* (*IvO* 47 (164 BCE); *IC* 3 iv 9 (112/1 BCE)); of a judge appointed by the governor (IG ix (1) 61 (118 CE). In contrast, the term κέλευσις is usually associated with a divine command (numerous dedications made κατὰ κέλευσιν) or a command of the emperor, MAMA v 60 (117–38 CE), other Roman magistrate, MAMA iv 334 (66/67 CE); MAMA viii 505 (late second cent. AD); IGBulg iii 908 (212–17 CE); SEG 32.1287 (253–60 CE), κατὰ κέλευσιν τῆς πόλεως (AvHierapolis 35), or finally the wishes of the deceased (*BCH* 60 (1936) 336 (second/third cent. CE); IG x (2) (2) 10 (second/third cent. CE); 188 (third cent. CE)). This differentiation suggests that the edict of T. Aquila was perceived as a coercive command and not as the decision over a disputed affair. For the use of the *verb keleuō* (κελεύω) see Katzoff (1982: 212 n.17).

[70] (M. Ulp.) Tertullianus Aquila: PIR^1 v 0572. The proposed identification of M. Ulpius Tertullianus Aquila from Kremna in Pisidia (IK 57 (Central Pisidia) 44: *M. Ulp. Ter/tyllianum/Aquilam/c(larissi-mum) v(irum)/[patri]a sua* (212–*c*.30 CE) and IGR iii 474 (Balboura, *c*.200–12 CE)) with the jurisconsult Tertullianus (Lenel (1889), ii. Cols. 341–4) seems problematic, although it is not excluded by Jones (2005). This identification was first suggested by Sarikakēs (1977), 107 and Youni (2000), 87. Barnes (1971), 22–9 discounts any identification of the jurisconsult with the ecclesiastical author.

This edict is unlikely to have been issued before November 212 CE, since ILeukopetra 61 & 62, dated in November 212 CE, do not mention it and no *Aurelii* feature in it.[71] As to the content of the edict, Maria Youni in a series of articles suggested that it may have included clauses concerning the publication of the manumission. In particular, before the manumission a letter of intention, *pittakion* (πιττάκιον), was put on display for a period of thirty days in Beroia, while the act of manumission referred to sometimes as *ōnē* (ὠνή)[72] was deposited at the sanctuary. If, during that period, no objections were raised concerning the ownership of the slave, the manumittor could proceed with the manumission.

Two elements may be surprising, i) the imposition of the principle of publicity for the manumission, a practice well established in ancient Greek *poleis*, and ii) the lack of any reference to the tax *vicesima libertatis* or any other fiscal burden to the slave, especially after the extension of the Roman citizenship. It is well-known that in neighbouring Thessaly the payment of an amount equal to 22,5 denarii is attested in manumission records of the first century CE.[73] Was a similar payment included in the formalities of publication and incorporated in the *pittakion*?[74]

Did the edict concern the manumissions performed only in Leukopetra? The occurrence of terms like *pittakion* and *grammateion* in inscriptions from Beroia (IBeroia 53–4, 248 CE), Leukopetra (ILeukopetra passim) and Edessa (EKM ii 156, 247 CE), strongly advocate the implementation of the edict not only in Leukopetra. In addition, the collocation καὶ τὴν καταγραφὴν ἔδωκε τὴν θεὸν in EKM ii 157–8 (247–53 CE), 159 (*c*.252 CE), 162 (261 CE), 145 (234 CE) from Edessa may be

[71] ILeukopetra 63 was inscribed in the same year as ILeukopetra 61–2, ἔτους δμσ᾽ σεβαστοῦ τοῦ καὶ ξτ᾽; unfortunately without a reference to a month. In it an *Aurelios* also appears accompanied by the partly restored designation 'formerly' ὁ [πρὶν].

[72] Process of manumission, Youni (2000), 76–85. The term ὠνή appears also in the manumission IG x (2) (2) 233 (Kolobaise-Pelagonia, 200/1 CE), EKM ii 151 (246 CE), 163 (243–62 CE), 169 (252–68 CE) from Edessa, EKM ii 406 (235 CE) and 407 (post 212/3 CE) from Kyrrhos but not in EKM ii 63–77 (*A*igai). Youni (2000), 79–84 and 215–17 distinguishes between, on the one hand the document of slave sale and on the other, the document registering the manumission of the slave. The term ὠνή is used also in Delphoi where it signifies the act of manumission, which is inscribed on the walls of the sanctuary and it is deposited either to the polis archive ot to a trustworthy individual, e.g. FD iii (6) 44 (first cent. CE). The manumittory aspect of these documents has been challenged by Marijana Ricl. Ricl (2001) claimed that the inscriptions from Leukopetra should not be considered as manumissions but as donations of the slaves by their masters to the deity in order to supplement the personnel of the sanctuary. Slave manumission concerns the public and legal sphere of activities, but in the religious sphere slaves remained attached to the sanctuary, Ricl (2001), 146–7. See also Velissaropoulos-Karakostas (2011), i. 379–98. However, the use of the term ὠνή reveals that the transaction had both the character of sale as well as of donation.

[73] In the most recent study Zelnick-Abramovitz (2013), 107 came to the conclusion that in many places the manumitted slave proceeded to a payment or a dedication (*phiale, skyphos, kerata*), independently of the price of manumission (referred to as *lytron* in some areas). That payment could have been a tax on manummisions similar to *vicesima libertatis* or a duty on registering and publicizing it. The dedicated *skyphoi* and *phialai* mentioned in IBeroia 3, 9–13 (248 BCE) belong to this context. A similar payment was introduced in Thessalian cities sometime in the beginning of the second cent. BCE as a duty on registration and publication, e.g. SEG 53.512 (Aiginio, second/third cent. CE), 36.543 (Echinos, mid-second cent. CE) and 34.478 (Atrax, *c*.131 CE). For the payment of 'lytron' and of a duty in Roman Egypt see Taubenschlag (1955), 96–100. *Vicesima libertatis*, Bradley (1984).

[74] See ILeukopetra p. 36 n.8: «La participation active des autorités romaines dans la réglementation de ce type d'affranchissements pose avec encore plus d'acuité la question de leurs aspects financiers, dans la mesure ou elle semble sanctionner la perte de la *vicesima libertatis* prélevée sur les affranchissements selon le droit romain».

restored in ILeukopetra 94, 4–5 (239 CE). Finally, a comparison with manumissions[75] from other areas of Roman Macedonia both before and after the *constitutio Antoniniana* does not suggest tremendous variation. Therefore, it is fair to assume that the edict of Tertyllianus Aquila applied throughout the province.[76]

Why was it thought necessary to have a decree issued almost immediately after the introduction of the *constitutio Antoniniana*? There was the pressing need to establish the status of the individuals manumitted and those who were to be manumitted the Greek way (according to which they were made free but did not acquire any rights to any *polis*), radically different from the Roman way (according to which any lawfully manumitted slave was turned into a Roman citizen). In other words, the Roman governor had to reconcile on the one hand the provisions of the *constitutio* with the status of those manumitted 'à la grecque' and on the other to decide the extent of the rights conferred on those who, at least to Roman eyes, were manumitted in an irregular way. Maria Youni, in a series of articles, has argued that Tertyllianus Aquila most likely proceeded to the functional integration of the Greek manumission[77] performed in Leukopetra in the Roman legal framework about slaves. Greek manumissions were considered identical to informal Roman manumissions (*per epistulam*, *inter amicos*), and therefore the individuals manumitted would not acquire automatically the Roman citizenship but they would be considered as *Latini Iuniani*. I believe we can go a step further and argue that the integration was made possible and perhaps easier thanks to the analogy between the document deposited 'in the arms of the goddess' (attested already in 170 CE, ILeukopetra 3) and the Roman procedure *per epistulam*. Tertyllianus Aquila decided, either through analogy or through constructing a legal fiction, to effectively equate the results of the manumission *per epistulam* with the manumission by consecration particularly in Leukopetra and generally in Macedonia.[78]

3.2. Funerary Monuments

Funerary monuments of the royal period, in verse or in prose, due to their simplicity do not contain any interesting legal information.[79] The situation is different with epitaphs of the imperial period; they usually include: first, information about the erection of the monument by the deceased's heirs (κληρονόμοι, *heredes*) following his/her wishes as they were expressed in a testament.[80]

[75] EAM 59b+c (Elimeia-Elate, 108/9 CE); IG x (2) (2) 233 (Pelagonia-Kolobaise, 200/1 CE); EKM ii 63 (Aigai-Blaganoi, 190 CE); EKM ii 65 (Aigai, 216/7 CE); EKM ii 66 (216/7 CE); EKM ii 146 (Edessa, 238/9 CE); EKM ii 149 (246 CE); EKM ii 151 (246 CE); EKM ii 157–8 (247–53 CE); EKM ii 159 (252 CE); EKM ii 162 (261 CE); EKM ii 428 (Gyrbea, 206 CE).

[76] So Youni (2000), 87. [77] Youni (2003), (2008), (2009).

[78] For what happened to *Iuniani Latini* in the *post* 212 CE period see Corcoran (2011).

[79] Prose funerary monuments, e.g. IBeroia 147–60, 178–81, 196–201, EKM ii 15–48 (Aigai), 424 (Tyrissa), 454–527, 529–34, 542–7 (Pella). In verse funerary monuments, e.g. IBeroia 391, EKM ii 52 (Aigai). See now Kalaitzi (2016).

[80] E.g. *ex testamento*: IG x (2) (1) 927 (first cent. CE); EKM ii 270 (Edessa, second/third cent. CE); IG x (2) (1) Suppl. 1197 (second- first cent. BCE); IG x (2) (2) 160 (Pelagonia-Mariovo, first cent. CE); IStobi 58 (first/second cent. CE *per testamentum*); CIGLPh 59 (first cent. CE); 146 (first–second cent. CE where also the collocation *ex codicillis*); CIL iii 592 (Dion); 672 (Philippoi). Heredes: IG x (2)

The often recurring collocation *κατὰ διαθήκην* is probably a rendering of the Latin expression *ex testamento*, which appears in the first century CE usually in funerary monuments of *veterani*.[81] Second, they may record endowments for celebrations on the tomb or the performance of a ritual.[82] They are similar to civic endowments but the main activity funded is sacrifices on specific dates.[83] Third, they may include fines for violation of the tomb, usually split between the *polis* and the informer.[84] At about the same time, funerary fines abound in Asia

(1) 659 (second/third cent. CE); IG x (2) (2) 160 (first cent. CE); ILGR 191 (Dion). See the recently published IG x (2) (1) Suppl. 1284 (beg. second cent. CE) where the expression, current in Latin inscriptions of the first century CE, *ex testamento arbitratu*, as in CIL iii 546 (Megara), 653 (Doxato-Philippoi) is attested. *Κατὰ διαθήκην*: EAM 11 (Elimeia, 149 CE); EKM ii 574 (Pella); IG x (2) (1) 133 with SEG 26.738 (beg. first cent. CE); IG x (2) (1) Suppl. 1197 (second–first cent. BCE); 1384 (second cent. CE); IG x (2) (2) 130 (Herakleia-Lynkestis (?), second/third cent. CE); SEG 53.664 (Neine, second cent. CE(?)); SEG 56.760 (first cent. CE). For the use of Greek and Latin see Hatzopoulos (2008) and Brélaz (2015). For the use of the collocation *κατὰ διαθήκην* and its repercussions see Youni (2000), 164 and 172–5. However, both testament and endowments were known in the inheritance laws of the various Greek cities, see Velissaropoulos-Karakostas (2011), ii. 477–510 and IK 69 (Priene) 266–75 (third–second cent. BCE). *Κατὰ διαθήκην* and *κληρονόμοι*: IG x (2) (2) 49 (Lynkestis-Resen, third cent. CE), EAM 11 (Elimeia, 149 CE). The phrase *ἐκ τῶν ἐκείνου/ἐκείνης* in funerary monuments perhaps points out the existence of a will or the provision of cash from the testator's property, EKM ii 198 (Edessa, 195/6 CE). *Κληρονόμοι*: *BCH* 56 (1932) 291 (*Spomenik* 71 (1931) 238 no. 636) (Stoboi, 163/4 CE); IG x (2) (1) 478 (second cent. CE); IG x (2) (2) 247 (Pelagonia, second cent. CE); SEG 39.591 (Serrai-Vergi, second/third cent. CE). The anxiety to secure a burial place and a funerary monument is reflected on two inscriptions, IG x (2) (1) Suppl. 1428 (beg. third cent. CE): *ταῦτα δὲ σοί, γαμετή, ἐντέλλομαι τύμβον μου ποιῆσαι καὶ γράμμασι ταῦτ' ἐπιγράψαι*... and IG x (2) (1) 819 (second/third cent. CE): *οὐ τὸ θανῖν σπεύδων τοῦτο ἐποίησα, φίλε, ἀλὰ εἰδὼς κληρονόμων τὴν ἐπιλησμοσύνην*..., for which see also Youni (2000), 164–5. In, at least, one case it seems there is some sort of guaranteed care for surviving children, *Spomenik* 98 (1941–8) 28 no. 68 (Paionia-Izvor, imperial), *Ζωΐλος καὶ Γάϊος/οἱ Διονυσίου οἱ προ/[ν]οοῦντες Ποσειδω/νίου καὶ Ἀμμίας ὀρφα/[ν]ῶν Ποσειδωνίῳ καὶ/Γαΐᾳ τοῖς γονεῦσιν/ αὐτῶν ἐκ τῶν ἐκεί/[νων]*, and similarly in IG x (2) (1) 1004 (second/third cent. CE) and IG x (2) (2) 10 (Lynkestis-Zivojno, second/third cent. CE) with Youni (2000), 160.

[81] IG x (2) (2) 160 (Pelagonia-Mariovo, first cent. CE); 163 (Pelagonia-Vitoliste, beg. second cent. CE); 236 (Pelagonia-Belovodica, first cent. CE); 309 (Derriopos-Pasino Ruvci, 112/3 CE), SEG 53.664 (Sintike-Neine, second cent. CE?)] and later in IG x (2) (2) 218 (Pelagonia, 193–211 CE). See Adams (2003: 76–84) including more cases.

[82] Reference to endowments in the decision of the Roman governor in IBeroia 7 (second cent. CE); IG x (2) (2) 300 (Styberra, 95 CE). Decree of acceptance of an endowment: IG x (2) (2) 322–8 (Styberra, first/second cent. CE). Function of gymnasium relying on endownments: IG x (2) (2) 348 (Derriopos-Alkomena, AD 192/3). Endowments with funerary purpose from the area of Philippoi, second cent. CE or later, BCH 24 (1900) 305 no. 2 (*Καλπαπουρεῖται*) and 60 (1936) 336 (*ποσιασταὶ ἥρωνος*, tranferring the amount of the endowment to a different group in case of non-fulfilment); SEG 50.605 (Serrai-Vergi, second/third cent. CE). Donation *sub modo*?; SEG 31.639 (Serrai-Terpni, second/third cent. CE). Reference to an endowment to a *gerousia* in IGBulg v 5925 (181–8 CE).

[83] Latin: from Philippoi, AEp. 1932, no. 21; 2001, no. 1785; 2012, no. 1382; *BCH* 24 (1900) 312; *BCH* 47 (1923) 50; *BCH* 57 (1933) 347; CIL iii 656, 662, 703–4, 706–7; Nigdelis (2016b), 687; Pilhofer ii. 644/L602. Greek: IG x (2) (2) 166 (Melnica, third cent. CE); 348–9 (Alkomena, 192/3 CE).

[84] E.g. IBeroia 367 (second–third cent. CE), 370 (end first cent. CE); EKM ii 385 (second–third cent. CE); IG x (2) (1) 524 (118 CE); 525 (120 CE); 534, 544, 571, 579, 581–2, 592, 617, 626, 814 etc (second/third cent. CE); IG x (2) (1) Suppl. 1161, 1239, 1270, etc.; IStobi 62–4 (second cent. CE); CIL iii 684 (Philippoi?); SEG 13.401 (Philippoi (?), third cent. CE), SEG 51.806 (Beroia, fourth/fifth cent. CE); AEp. 2001, no. 1785 (Philippoi, second/third cent. CE), AEp. 2014, no. 1185 (Philippoi, second/third cent. CE); CIGLPh 137 (first–second cent. CE). Compare the threat against the violator of the tomb in IG x (2) (1) Suppl. 1434B (= SEG 56.810) of the early third cent. CE: *εἰ δέ τεις ἕτερος τολμήσῃ ἀνῦξε/τὴν ληνὸν χωρεὶς τῶν τέκνων μου, λόγον ὑφέξει/τῷ κατὰ καιρὸν ἡγεμόνει*... (with Nigdelis (2006: 387ff.))

Minor,[85] while they are practically non-existent in royal Macedonia or in other parts of the Greek peninsula.

3.3. Public Domain

Inscriptions are vocal supporters of the institutional autonomy of the *polis* in Roman Macedonia; most *poleis* have retained their council and magistrates, but the role of the assembly seems reduced. Throughout the Imperial period in Thessaloniki and in other cities the council (*boulē*) and the popular assembly (*dēmos*) were operating, probably on a censitarian basis, their decisions called *dogma* (*δόγμα*) or *doxan* (*δόξαν, τὰ δόξαντα*).[86] Apart from several honorary decrees in various states of preservation, there are only two normative texts, one from the area of Gazoros in the East and one from Battyna in the West of the province, pertaining either to long term leases of agricultural land belonging to the communities, or to dealing with disturbances in enjoying landed property.[87]

Roman intervention in private law was much more limited in comparison to the administration of justice. The development of the *cognitio extra ordinem* procedure alone cannot explain that trend; individuals from *civitates liberae* and *stipendiariae* treated the court of the governor as another tribunal for having their disputes resolved in the most beneficial way. For the *coloni* in, e.g., Philippoi, jurisdiction for dispute resolution and for keeping the peace lay with *duumviri*

while in IG x (2) (1) Suppl. 1351 (= SEG 53.633) of the early fourth cent. CE the violator is threatened not with a fine but: *τοῦτον αὐτὸν μὲν σταυροῦ ὑποκῖστε κινδύνου, τὰ δ᾽ἐκείνου τῷ ταμείῳ*. Of particular importance is a third cent. CE inscription IG x (2) (1) Suppl. 1430 (= SEG 13.401) in which there is an explicit reference to the prohibition to bury and the accompanying fine in the text of a testament: *[διέθ]ετο ἐν τῇ διαθήκῃ Λούκιος Οὐαλέριος Μάξιμος μηδένα/[εἰς τὴ]ν σορὸν ἑαυτοῦ τεθῆναι μηδὲ εἰς τὸν κύβον, εἰ μὴ μόνον ἑαυτὸν/[ἀ]ρχικόν, καὶ προσέταξε εἴ τις ἂν τολμήσειεν πτῶμά τινος/[κατ]αθέσθε ἤτε ἰς τὸν κύβον ἢ ἰς τὸ ἀνγεῖον, δώσι εἰς τὸ ταμεῖον/δηνάρια δισχίλια πεντακόσια*; meaning of the term *κύβος*, Nigdelis (2016a). Latin inscriptions with a fine for tomb violation: AEp. 2006, no. 1342–3; CIL 3.14206 (26), CIL 3.687+14206(29), CIL 3.669 with the remarks of J. Bartels, *ZPE* 157 (2006) 199 no. 1, 206 no. 10, 207 no. 11. Latin influence is more than evident (CIL 3.684; BCH 61 (1937) 418 no. 12 = AEp. 1938, no. 50) in the use of the term *delator*, sometimes hellenized as *δηλάτωρ* instead of the Greek *μηνυτὴς* (for which see IK 56 (Anazarbos) 95 and 111 (third cent. CE), IPorto 92 with SEG 36.922 (5)), in the area of Philippoi, *BCH* 24 (1900) 313; 59 (1935) 152 no. 45; 60 (1936) 336; CIGLPh 91 (third cent. CE) and Kallipolitēs and Lazaridēs (1946: 17 no. 10) with BE 1948, no. 102 (Philippoi, third/fourth cent. CE). See also Strubbe (1997).

[85] Earliest piece of evidence from Thessaloniki: IG x (2) (1) 524. Asia Minor: Harter-Uibopuu and Wiedergut (2014).

[86] E.g. decisions of the council, IBeroia 108 (mid third cent. CE); EKM ii 181 (Edessa, 180/1 CE)); IG x (2) (1) 201–3 (third cent. CE); IG x (2) (2) 300 (Styberra); 53 (Herakleia Lynkestis); IStobi 37 and 39 (second cent. CE); IGBulg iv 2265 (Parthikopolis, 209/10 CE); SEG 1.276 (Mygdonia-Lete,121/2 CE); SEG 12.349 (Krestonia-Bragylos, 117–32 CE); SEG 48.800 (Eordaia-Philotas, first/second cent. CE). Decisions of the assembly, e.g. IG x (2) (1) 5 with SEG 50.637 (60 BCE); 179 and 180 (second half of third cent. CE); 192 (first half of third cent. CE); SEG 59.700; IStobi 34 and 41–2 (second–third cent. CE). *Probouleusis* in SEG 56.743 (Thessaloniki, *c.*133 CE). See Rhodes and Lewis (1997), 187–94, Sverkos (2000), 48–9, and for the province of Achaia Girdvainyte in this volume pp. 227–8.

[87] SEG 30.570 (Gazoros(?),158/9 CE); EAM 186 (Battyna, 192/3 CE). See Sartre (1991), 214–15, Buraselis (1993), Youni (2000), 193–7 and 254, no. 3), and Rizakis (2004).

iure dicundo.[88] In *Acts* 16.19–24, Paul and his companions, while in Philippoi, were accused of unrest; they were arrested and detained on orders of the *strategoi*, alias *duumviri iure dicundo.*[89] The *rabdouchoi* in the same episode are probably lower ranking officials responsible for executing the orders of the *strategoi*. In Thessaloniki, a *polis* enjoying the status of a *civitas libera*, similar accusations were addressed to the *politarchai* (*Acts* 17.6–9). Antoninus Pius in a letter to Parthikopolis fixes (or alludes to?) the jurisdiction of local magistrates over those possessing land, according to the value of the dispute.[90] These landowners (*hoi enkektemenoi*) probably claimed that they were subject to a special jurisdiction or, at least, not to the jurisdiction of the *polis* magistrates. With the *epistula*, Antoninus responds probably to a petition of the authorities from Parthikopolis and confirms their view that for disputes up to 250 *denarii*, the case would have been heard by the local magistrate with judicial authority. What, however, is left out is who decides about disputes above that threshold;[91] could it have been the Roman governor? Finally, in the proconsular decree IBeroia 7, C, 9 there is a passing reference to a trial, [- - - - - - *τῶν τῇ* (;)] *πόλει συμφερόντων καταλιπεῖν δίκην τὴν* [- - - - -]. We may assume that there is some sort of connection to a contractor and to an agreement, terms appearing earlier in the fragment (ll. 4–6, *ἐργολάβον*, *συνγραφή*, [*σύ*]*μφωνον*).[92]

Imperial interference in the form of *epistulae* is rather limited; there are two letters by Hadrian, one addressed to the *koinon Makedonōn* about the duties of their magistrates and their successors, fragmentary letters of Antoninus Pius to Beroia, to Thessaloniki and to Parthikopolis (for which see above), a fragmentary letter of Septimius Severus concerning the fiscal affairs of an unknown city, perhaps Idomene, one from Gallienus, and three more fragmentary letters from Beroia.[93] Almost all the proconsular edicts are in a very bad state of preservation; in Beroia two edicts were found, one well-known concerning the reorganization of the finances of the *gymnasium* on a sounder basis with rerouting cash from various endowments and other sources of income to a fund (*enthēkē*, *ἐνθήκη*) of 100 000 *denarii* and the other less known, although more significant

[88] For that office there are brief references in the *cursus honorum* of certain Philippesians, e.g. CIGLPh 50 (first/second cent. CE); 59 (beg. first cent. CE); 125, 136, 145–6, 152 (first–second cent. CE), 133–4 (second/third cent. CE), 162–3 (second–third cent. CE).

[89] So Rizakis (2016), 179. For *eirenarchai* in Philippoi, Brélaz, and Rizakis (2003), 160, Brélaz (2007b), and Rizakis (2008).

[90] IGBulg iv 2263 = v 5895 (157/8 CE): *οἱ ἐνκεκτημένοι παρ' ὑμ*[*ῖ*]*ν ὑπακουέ/τωσαν τοῖς ἄρχουσι πρὸς τὰς δίκας καὶ διώκοντες καὶ φεύ/γοντες μέχρι διακοσίων πεντήκοντα δηναρίων* (the landholders residing in your city shall obey the magistrates responsible for the trials when they sue and when they are sued for a dispute worth up to two hundred and fifty *denarii*); see the new readings in ll. 3–4, 6 and 18 by Sharankov (2016), 341–2 and Fournier (2010), 350–3. Payment for obtaining a place in the local Council, Garnsey (1971), 312 and Hurlet (2016), 69–70.

[91] For local courts see Bérenger (2014), 183–6.

[92] See commentary in Nigdelis and Souris (2005), 99–101.

[93] Hadrian: IBeroia 5–6 (*c.*127 CE), SEG 42.593 (Beroia, 137 CE); Antoninus Pius: IGBulg iv 2263 = v 5895 (Parthikopolis, 157/8 CE), IBeroia 8 (165 CE), 9 (161–9 CE), IG x (2) (1) 15 (143–61 CE), SEG 42.573 (Beroia, 161 CE); Septimius Severus: SEG 56.708 II (196/7 CE); Gallienus: IBeroia 15 with AEp. 2001, no. 1758 (267 CE); and IBeroia 488 (second–third cent. CE) an *epistula* addressed to the *koinon* of Macedonians, Brélaz (2007a), 126.

and challenging, since it seems to reaffirm certain rules about the sale of slaves.[94] From Herakleia in Lynkestis there survives a proconsular edict settling fiscal disputes, while recently an interesting dossier of four documents in Greek and Latin pertaining to the *cursus publicus* from the early third-century-CE Pella was published.[95] It is more than clear that the proconsuls of Macedonia fulfil their duties as prescribed by Ulpian, paying attention to the infrastructure of the *poleis* and smoothing any possible rough edges in legal processes.[96]

4. CONCLUDING REMARKS

The legal landscape of Roman Macedonia as it emerges from the epigraphic dossier is dotted with pockets of continuity but also clusters of innovative practices. There is not a continuous line extending from the royal to imperial period in all the fields regulated by law; continuity is much more prominent in 'republican' Macedonia and in the autonomy enjoyed by some *poleis*, even if it is sometimes diluted. In imperial Macedonia there is increasing evidence that the adoption and adaptation of practices from the Latin speaking world as well as from Asia Minor was rife.[97] While *poleis* continued to hold business as usual, innovations in the legal and quasi-legal vocabulary, insignificant at first, surge in the epigraphic record.[98] They are mainly detected in funerary monuments of non-Macedonians, traders, itinerant craftsmen or retired army personnel, soldiers and officers who, attracted by the country and its people, decided to settle there.[99] While manumissions continued to be performed in a similar but not identical way, funerary endowments, fines and references to testaments and heirs appear for the first time; is it mere coincidence that in most endowments persons with *tria nomina* are involved? Or that the earliest references to a funerary monument built according to the provisions of a testament occur in the circles of retired army officers? Laws

[94] IBeroia 7, for which see Kokkinia (2004), 1–6 and Nigdelis and Souris (2005). IBeroia 13 with Youni (2000), 230–1 and 253, no. 1, proposed restorations by Müller (2001) (= SEG 48.750) and Souris (2009) (= SEG 58.561). Sharankov (2016), 337 n.64 identifies *ὑπατικό Καυαρ- - - -ων* with *Καυάριος Φρόντων* attested in IGBulg iv 2057 (117–38 CE); therefore, the reference to the decree is of a post-Hadrianic date.

[95] IG x (2) (2) 52 (Herakleia Lynkestis, beg. second cent. CE). The dossier republished in EKM ii 432 (= Nigdelis (2014) = AEp. 2014, no. 1178) includes a petition of the Council of Pella to the governor Messala Rutilianus, his correspondence with the *prefectus praetorium* in Rome and a copy of an edict.

[96] See *D.* 1.16.7, 1 (Ulpianus libro secundo *de officio proconsulis*).

[97] Artistic influences from Asia Minor: Stefanidou-Tiveriou (2001); from Italian peninsula: Papagianni (2017).

[98] See the reference to a *τούτωρ αὔκτωρ* (Lat. tutor auctor) accompanying *Αἰλία Σοτηρὶς* in the manumission ILeukopetra 51 (208/9 CE). In the same climate one must situate the collocation *τριῶν τέκνων δίκαιον* (*Lat. ius trium liberorum*) in EKM ii 143 (Edessa, 215 CE); IBeroia 51 (240 CE); 52 (262 CE); 53 (248 CE); IG x (2) (2) 18A (Lynkestis-Suvodol, 282 CE), and ILeukopetra 6 (172 CE?); 52 (208/9 CE); 73 (229 CE); 76 (230 CE); 89 (238 CE); 91 (239 CE); 92 (239 CE); 94 (239 CE). See Youni (2000), 47–9 who argues for a superfluous use of the collocation with no legal consequences and in general Kaser (1955), 273 and Dimopoulou-Piliouni (2013).

[99] See, for example, the funerary monument of *Klemes* (Lat. *Clemens*) from Herakleia in Lynkestis, *IG* x (2) (2) 121 (first/second cent. CE): *Εὐρώπη λει/βέρτα ❦ Μα/νικοῦ Τ(—) Κλή/μ̣ε̣ντι[.] ἀννώ/ρουμ οὐειγ̣έντι.*

or other normative texts like the gymnasiarchic law of Beroia or the ephebarchic law from Amphipolis may have remained unaltered, but the social context rendered them useless, if e.g. the *gymnasion* of Beroia could not operate due to lack of funds. The picture painted so far brings forward the question of the agent of legal transfer(s) and this may be perhaps the most profitable line of further investigation. Individuals, locals and immigrants (from the Italian peninsula or Asia Minor) were involved in the system of the administration of justice at *poleis*-level and/or at province-level and knowledge of Roman law was praised.[100] Communities of Italian and Roman merchants who settled in Macedonia in the early first century BCE brought with them patterns of business transaction and networks, marital and inheritance strategies and practices. Soldiers and veterans, of Roman and provincial background, had their activities limited due to impediments imposed by law or privileges granted to them. It seems as if elements of Roman law slip in slowly but steadily in the realm of regulating social relations, not in a top down direction but spreading horizontally in the middle and lower social strata. Finally, what is worth investigating further is the role of the local elites[101] involved in the legal realm, including not only the administration of public affairs under Roman supervision (defenders of the interests of the *polis*, *ekdikoi*, *syndikoi*, or *nomikoi*) but also the extent to which Roman legal practices were adopted in everyday interactions.

[100] See the epigram on the basis of Poseidippos' statue, IBeroia 97 (beg. third cent. CE): *τῆδε Ποσείδιππον/χαλκήλατον Ἠμαθιῆες/στῆσαν Ἰουλίῃ/μητρὶ χαριζόμενοι/καὶ δ' αὐτὸν τείοντες/ἐπεὶ καὶ φέρτατος ἦεν/θεσμῶν Αὐσονίων/ἴδριδα μῆτιν ἔχων* (This bronze statue of Poseidippos was erected by the Emathians (= Macedonians) to console his mother and honour him, since he was the best, having a deep knowledge of Roman rules) and the honorific inscription for Licinius Rufinus, IBeroia 101 (*c.*254 CE): *ἀγαθῆι τύχηι./<κατὰ τὸ δόξαν τῷ>/<λαμπροτάτῳ συνε>/δρίῳ Λικίνιον/Ῥουφεῖνον, τὸν ὑ/πατικόν, συναγο/ρεύσαντα τῇ ἐπαρ/χείᾳ περὶ τῆς συντε/λείας τῶν Θετταλῶν,/Δομίτιος Εὐρύδικος/ὁ μακεδονιάρχης/ἐκ τῶν ἑαυτοῦ.* (Good luck. According to a decision of the most splendid council, *Domitios Eurydikos* the leader of the *koinon* of Macedonians (*makedoniarchēs*) has honoured, from his own resources, Licinius Rufinus, consul, for his assistance to the province in the litigation concerning the taxation of Thessalians). See Fournier (2010), 530, n.106 and Girdvainyte in this volume p. 224.

[101] For the form and structure of the Macedonian elite see Bartels (2008).

APPENDIX

Table 15.1. Royal *diagrammata* on stone

IPArk 5	Decision of Alexander III regarding the return of exiles in Tegea	Tegea	324 BCE
IG xii Suppl. 644 = Hatzopoulos (2001: App. 1 I)	Military *diagramma* of Philip V	Chalkis	*c.*200 BCE
SEG 51.640bis = Hatzopoulos (2001: App. 1 II)	copy of the previous	Kynos	*c.*200 BCE
IG x (2) (1) 3 = Hatzopoulos (1996: ii no. 15)	Decision of Philip V regarding Serapeum in Thessaloniki	Thessaloniki	187 BCE
SEG 49.722 = Hatzopoulos (2001: App. 2.II)	Copy of the decree concerning military service of Philip V	Kassandreia	
SEG 49.855 = Hatzopoulos (2001: App. 2.I)	Copy of the decree concerning military service of Philip V	Drama	
Hatzopoulos (1996: ii no. 12)	Copy of the decree concerning military service of Philip V	Amphipolis	
SEG 43.369 & SEG 46.717 = Hatzopoulos (1996: ii no. 16)	Fragmentary decree for service in expeditionary force		183/2 BCE
Hatzopoulos (2001: App. 4)	Fragmentary decree concerning registration in army registers[102]		
Hatzopoulos (1996: ii no. 16)	*Diagramma* of Philip V concerning the *gymnasion* in Amphipolis	Amphipolis	183/2 BCE
Hatzopoulos (1996: ii no. 56)	Fiscal law	Dion	fourth cent. BCE

Table 15.2. Royal letters on stone

SEG 56.703 = Hatzopoulos (1996: ii no. 11)	Letter of Demetrios Poliorcetes to Ladamas	291 BCE?
SEG 48.783 and SEG 51.796	Two copies of a letter of Antigonos Gonatas to Agasikles	*c.*277–239 BCE
IBeroia 3	Letter of Demetrios to Beroians	248 BCE
SEG 60.605	Letter of Demetrios II to Therson	*c.*234–230 BCE
IBeroia 4	Letter of Antigonos Doson to Beroia	223 BCE
SEG 60.585	Letter of Antigonos to Megalokles	222/1 BCE
SEG 60.586	Letter of Antigonos to Megalokles and the *koinon* of Tripolitai	*c.*222/1 BCE
EKM ii 431	Letter of Philip V to a Pellaean magistrate	221–197 BCE
SEG 27.245 = Hatzopoulos (1996: no. 9)	Letters of Philip V to Amphipolis	218 BCE
Hatzopoulos (1996: no. 10)	Letter of Philip V to Beroia	215–214 BCE
IG ix (2) 517	Letter of Philip V to the Lariseans	214 BCE
Hatzopoulos (1996: no. 11)	Letter of Philip V and boundary settlement between Pherai and a Thessalian city	206–205 BCE
SEG 46.716 (partly in Hatzopoulos (1996: ii no. 14)	Two letters of Philip V to Amphipolitans	197 and 191 BCE
EAM 87	Letter of Philp V concerning the grant of lands	181 BCE
SEG 48.785	Letter of Philip V concerning a grant of asylia to Kyzikos	*c.*180 BCE
IG x (2) (2) 347 = Hatzopoulos (1996: ii no. 19)	Letter of Perseus	173 BCE?

[102] See also Chrysafis (2014) for an interpretation of the term *pyrokausis* as a military squad.

Table 15.3. Honorary decrees, inscriptions and dedications: *polis* to officials

IBeroia 2	Beroia	second/first cent. BCE
IG x (2) (1) 7	Thessaloniki	first cent. BCE
SEG 42.558	Anthemous	*c.*40 BCE
GRBS 57 (2017) 295 no. 1	Amphipolis	167–148 BCE
GRBS 57 (2017) 305 no. 2	Amphipolis	29/28 BCE

Table 15.4. Honorary decrees, inscriptions and dedications: *polis* to benefactors

IBeroia 59	Beroia	57–55 BCE
IG x (2) (1) 5 with SEG 50.637	Thessaloniki	60 BCE
IG x (2) (1) 135	Thessaloniki	105 BCE?
SEG 24.580	Amphipolis	167 BCE?
Syll[3] 700	Lete	118 BCE
GRBS 57 (2017) 314 no. 3	Amphipolis	11–9 BCE

Table 15.5. Honorary decrees, inscriptions and dedications: Collectivities

IG x (2) (1) 4	Thessaloniki	95 BCE
SEG 51.786	Amphipolis	105/4 BCE
SEG 43.371	Amphipolis	second/ first cent. BCE

Table 15.6. Honorary decrees, inscriptions and dedications: Honorary inscriptions

IG x (2) (1) 27	second cent. BCE	*politarchai*

Table 15.7. Honorary decrees, inscriptions and dedications: Dedications

IBeroia 24	Beroia	end second cent. BCE	*agoranomoi*
SEG 42.561	Anthemous	106/5 BCE	*agoranomoi*
SEG 47.1002	Velvendos-Elimeia	second/first cent. BCE	*agoranomos*

REFERENCES

Adams, J. 2003. *Bilingualism and the Latin language*. Oxford.

Ager, S. 1996. *Interstate arbitrations in the Greek world, 337–90 B.C.* Berkeley.

Alonso, J.-L. 2015. The status of peregrine law in Egypt: 'Customary law' and legal pluralism in the Roman empire. *Journal of Juristic Papyrology* 43, pp. 351–404.

Andreau, J. 2016. Qu'est-ce qu'un *negotiator* à la fin de la République?. In: A.-F. Baroni et al., (eds.), *Echanger en Méditerranée. Acteurs, pratiques et normes dans les mondes anciens*. Rennes, pp. 19–35.

van Andringa, W. 2003. Cité et communautés d'expatriés installées dans l'empire romain: Le cas des *cives Romani consistentes*. In : N. Belayche and S. C. Mimouni (eds.), *Les communautés religieuses dans le monde gréco-romain. Essais de définition*. Turnhours, pp. 49–60.

Aneziri, S. 2003. *Die Vereine der dionysischen Techniten im Kontext der hellenistischen Gesellschaft. Untersuchungen zur Geschichte, Organisation und Wirkung der hellenistischen Technitenvereine*. Wiesbaden.

Arnaoutoglou, I. 2012–13. Dorees, klērodosies kai 'hidrymata' stēn hellēno-romaikē archaiotēta. Problēmata orologias. *EHHD* 44, pp. 59–85.

Barnes, T. 1971. *Tertullian. A historical and literary study*. Oxford.

Bartels, J. 2008. *Städtische Eliten im römischen Makedonien. Untersuchungen zur Formierung und Struktur*. Berlin.

Bérenger, Agnès. 2014. *Le métier de gouverneur dans l'empire romain, de César à Dioclétien*. Paris.

Blanco-Perez, A. 2016. Nomenclature and dating in Roman Asia Minor: M. Aurelius/a and the 3rd century AD. *Zeitschrift für Papyrologie und Epigraphik* 199, pp. 271–93.

Bouchon, R. 2014. Démophilos de Doliché, Paul-Emile et les conséquences de la troisième guerre de Macédoine à Gonnoi. *Topoi* 19, pp. 483–513.

Bradley, K. 1984. The *vicesima libertatis*: Its history and significance. *Klio* 66, pp. 175–82.

Brélaz, C. 2007a. Motifs et circonstances de l'ingérence des autorités romaines dans les cités grecques sous le Principat. In : A. Baroni (ed.), *Amministrare un impero: Roma e le sue province*. Trento, pp. 109–43.

Brélaz, C. 2007b. Les irénarques de la colonie romaine de Philippes. In : *Actes du XIIe Congrès international d'epigraphie grecque et latine* (Barcelona, 3–8 septembre 2002). Barcelona, pp. 1217–19.

Brélaz, C. 2015. La langue des *incolae* sur la territoire de Philippes et les contacts linguistiques dans les colonies romaines d'Orient. In: Fr. Colin et al. (eds.), *Interpretatio. Traduire l'alterité culturelle dans les civilisations de l'antiquité*. Paris, pp. 371–405.

Brélaz, C. 2016a. Le faciés institutionnel, social et religieux d'une colonie romaine dans la province de Macédoine. In : J. Fournier (ed.), *Philippes, de la préhistoire à Byzance. Études d'archéologie et d'histoire*. Paris, pp. 199–214.

Brélaz, C. 2016b. Des communautés de citoyens romains sur le territoire des cités grecques: statut politico-administratif et régime des terres. In : Fr. Lerouxel and A-V. Pont, eds. *Propriétaires et citoyens dans l'Orient romain*. Bordeaux, pp. 69–86.

Brélaz, C. and Rizakis, A. 2003. Le fonctionnement des institutions et le déroulement des carrières dans la colonie de Philippes. *Cahiers du Centre Gustave Glotz* 14, pp. 155–65.

Brélaz, C. and Tirologos, G. 2016. Essai de reconstitution du territoire de la colonie de Philippes: Sources, méthodes et interprétations. In: H. Bru et al. (eds.), *Espaces et territoires des colonies romaines d'Orient* (Journée d'études à Besançon, 3 octobre 2013). Besançon, pp. 119–89.

Briscoe, J. 2012. *A commentary on Livy. Books 41–45*. Oxford.

Broughton, T. 1951. *The magistrates of the Roman Republic*. I. New York: and III, Atlanta 1986.

Bryen, A. 2016. Reading the citizenship papyrus (*P. Giss*. 40). In: C. Ando (ed.) *Citizenship and Empire in Europe 200–1900. The Antonine constitution after 1800 years*. Stuttgart, pp. 29–43.

Buraselis, K. 1989. Theia dorea. *Meletes panō stēn politikē tēs dynasteias tōn Sevērōn kai tēn* Constitutio Antoniniana. Athens.

Buraselis, K. 1993. Bemerkungen zum Dekret der Battynäer. In: *Ancient Macedonia* V (Papers read at the Fifth International Symposium held in Thessaloniki, October 10–15, 1989). Thessaloniki, pp. 279–92.

Burton, Gr. 2000. The resolution of territorial disputes in the provinces of the Roman empire. *Chiron* 30, pp. 195–215.

Camia, F. 2009. *Roma e le* poleis. *L'intervento di Roma nelle controversie territoriali tra le comunità greche di Grecia e d'Asia Minore nel secondo secolo a.C.: le testimonianze epigrafiche*. Athens.

Caneva, S. and Delli Pizzi, A. 2015. Given to a deity? Religious and social reappraisal of human consecration in the Hellenistic and Roman East. *Classical Quarterly* 65, pp. 167–91.

Canevaro, M. and Lewis, D. 2014. *Khoris oikountes* and the obligations of freedmen in late classical and early Hellenistic Athens. *Incidenza dell'Antico* 12, pp. 91–121.

Carlsen, J. 2006. *The rise and fall of a Roman noble family: The Domitii Ahenobarbi, 196 BC–AD 68*. Odense.

Chrysafis, Ch. 2014. *Pyrokausis*: Its meaning and function in the organisation of the Macedonian army. *Klio* 96, pp. 455–68.

Clinton, K. 2005. *Eleusis. The inscriptions on stone. Documents of the sanctuary of the two goddesses and public documents of the deme*. Athens.

Corcoran, S. 2011. «Softly and suddenly vanished away»: The Junian Latins from Caracalla to the Carolingians. In : K. Muscheler, ed. *Römische Jurisprudenz–Dogmatik, Überlieferung, Rezeption. Festschrift für Detlef Liebs zum 75. Geburtstag*. Berlin, pp. 129–52.

Daubner, F. 2014. Makedonien I bis IV. Verhinderte Mobilität oder Forscherkonstrukt? In: E. Olshausen and V. Sauer, eds. *Mobilität in den Kulturen der antiken Mittelmeerwelt* (Stuttgarter Kolloquium zur historischen Geographie des Altertums II, 2011). Stuttgart, pp. 113–24.

Demaille, J. 2016a. Frontières juridiques et frontières linguistiques dans la colonie romaine de Dion. In: H. Berthelot et al. (ed.), *Vivre et penser les frontières dans le monde méditerranéen antique*. Bordeaux, pp. 187–97.

Demaille, J. 2016b. The territory of the Roman colony of Dion. Extension and cadastration. In : H. Bru, ed. *Espaces et territoires des colonies romaines d'Orient* (Journée d'études à Besançon, 3 octobre 2013). Besançon, pp. 93–117.

Dimopoulou-Piliouni, A. 2013. *Ius trium liberorum*: pronomio tōn oligōn ē dikaiōma tōn pollōn. In: Vassiliki Leontaritou et al. ed. *Antecessor. Festschrift für Spyros N. Troianos*, I. Athens, pp. 493–510.

Eck, W. 1981. Miscellanea prosopographica. *Zeitschrift für Papyrologie und Epigraphik* 42, pp. 227–56.

Edmondson, J. 2015. The Roman emperor and the local communities of the Roman emperor. In: J.-L. Ferrary and J. Scheid, eds. *Il princeps romano: autocrate o magistrato? Fattori giuridici e fattori sociali del potere imperiale da Augusto a Commodo*. Pavia, pp. 701–29.

Feissel, D. 2016. Citoyenneté romaine et onomastique grecque au lendemain de la *constitutio Antoniniana*: les cognomina en *-ιανὸς* dans les inscriptions de Pamphylia et de Bithynie. In: B. Takmer et al. (eds.) *Vir doctus Anatolicus. Studies in memory of S. Şahin*. Istanbul, pp. 349–55.

Ferrary, J.-L. 1987–9. Les Romains de la République et les démocraties grecques. *Opus* 6–8, pp. 203–16.

Ferrary, J.-L. 2018. Le passage de la Macedoine et des regions adjacentes sous la domination romaine. In: M. Kalaitzi, P. Paschidis, C. Antonetti and A.-M. Guimier-Sorbets (eds.), *Boreioelladika. Tales from the lands of ethne. Essays in honour of Miltiades B. Hatzopoulos* (Proceedings of the international conference held in Athens, February 2015). Athens, pp. 299–308.

Fine, J. 1951. Horoi: *Studies in mortgage, real security and land tenure in ancient Athens*. Baltimore.

Finley, M. 1951. *Studies in land and credit in ancient Athens*. Reprinted 1985. Oxford.

Fournier, J. 2010. *Entre tutelle romaine et autonomie civique. L'administration judiciaire dans les provinces hellénophones de l'Empire romain (129 av. J.-C.–235 apr. J.-C.)*. Athènes-Paris.

Fournier, J. 2013. Entre Macédoine et Thrace: Thasos à l'époque de l'hégémonie romaine. In: M-G. Parissaki (ed.), *Thrakika Zetemata II. Aspects of the Roman province of Thrace*. Athens, pp. 11–63.

Game, J. 2008. *Actes de vente dans le monde grec. Témoignages épigraphiques des ventes immobilières*. Lyon.

Garnsey, P. 1971. Honorarium decurionatus. *Historia* 20, pp. 309–25.

Harter-Uibopuu, K. and Wiedergut, K. 2014. 'Niemand anderer soll hier bestattet werden…'Grabschutz im kaiserzeitlichen Milet. In: G. Thür, ed. *Tod und Jenseits in Frühgeschichte und Altertum* (Akten der 3. Tagung des Zentrums Archäologie und Altertumswissenschaften an der Österreichischen Akademie der Wissenschaften, 21.–22. März 2010). Vienna, pp. 147–65.

Hatzopoulos, M. 1996. *Macedonian institutions under the kings*. Athens–Paris.

Hatzopoulos, M. 2001. *L'organisation de l'armée macédonienne sous les Antigonides. Problèmes anciens et documents nouveaux*. Athens–Paris.

Hatzopoulos, M. 2003/4. *Quaestiones Macedonicae*: lois, décrets et epistates dans les cites Macédoniennes. *Tekmeria* 8, pp. 27–60.

Hatzopoulos, M. 2006. *La Macédoine. Géographie historique—Langue—Cultes et croyances—Institutions*. Paris.

Hatzopoulos, M. 2008. Le grec et le latin dans les inscriptions de Beroia. In : F. Biville et al., ed. *Bilinguisme gréco-latin et épigraphie* (Actes du colloque, 17–19 mai 2004). Lyon, pp. 129–39.

Hatzopoulos, M. 2009. Some new documents from the Macedonian chancery. Problems of form and content. In: S. Drougou, ed. *Kermatia philias. Timētikos tomos gia ton I. Touratsoglou II. Epigraphikē, Archaiologia, Varia*. Athens, pp. 47–55.

Hatzopoulos, M. 2011. A list of sales from Mieza and the constitution of extensive landed properties in the central Macedonian plain. *Tekmeria* 10, pp. 47–69.

Hatzopoulos, M. 2013. Le vocabulaire de la prise de décision dans les sources littéraires et épigraphiques de la Macédoine antique. *Studi ellenistici* 27, pp. 61–70.

Heller, A. 2013. Les institutions civiques grecques sous l'Empire: romanisation ou aristocratisation? In: P. Derron (ed.), *Les Grecs héritiers des Romains*. Genève, pp. 207–47.

Humfress, C. 2011. Law & custom under Rome. In: A. Rio (ed.) *Law, custom, and justice in late antiquity and the early Middle Ages*. London, pp. 23–47.

Hurlet, F. 2006. *Le proconsul et le prince d'Auguste à Dioclétien*. Bordeaux.

Hurlet, F. 2016. Entre juridiction civique et juridiction impériale. La sphère de compétences du proconsul. In: R. Haensch (ed.), *Recht haben und Recht bekommen im Imperium Romanum. Das Gerichtswesen der römischen Kaiserzeit und seine dokumentarische Evidenz*. Warsaw, pp. 63–88.

Jimenez, A. 2016. 'What is a province?'. In: S. Alcock et al. (eds.), *Beyond boundaries. Connecting visual cultures in the provinces of ancient Rome*. Los Angeles, pp. 16–30.

Jones, C. 2005. Culture in the careers of Eastern senators. In: W. Eck and M. Heil (eds.), Senatores populi Romani: *Realität und mediale Präsentation einer Führungsschicht* (Kolloquium der Prosopographia Imperii Romani vom 11.–13. Juni 2004). Stuttgart, pp. 263–70.

Juhel, P. 2011. Un fantôme de l'histoire hellénistique: le 'district' macédonien. *Greek, Roman and Byzantine Studies* 51, pp. 579–612.

Kalaitzi, M. 2016. *Figured tombstones from Macedonia, fifth–first century BC*. Oxford.

Kallet-Marx, R. 1995. *Hegemony to empire. The development of the Roman imperium in the East from 148 to 62 BC*. Berkeley.

Kallipolitēs, B. and Lazaridēs, D. 1946. *Archaiai epigraphes Thessalonikēs*. Thessaloniki.

Kantor, G. 2007. *Ancestral laws under the Roman rule: The case of Lycia*. Oxford users.ox.ac.uk/~ball1674/lycian_text.rtf (last consulted on 18/12/2017)

Kantor, G. 2014. Roman legal administration in the province of Asia: Hellenistic heritage vs. innovation. In: J. Dubouloz et al. (eds.), *L'imperium Romanum en perspective. Les savoirs d'empire dans la République romaine et leur héritage dans l'Europe médiévale et moderne*. Besançon, pp. 243–68.

Kantor, G. 2016. Local law in Asia Minor after the *Constitutio Antoniniana*. In: C. Ando (ed.), *Citizenship and empire in Europe 200–1900. The Antonine constitution after 1800 years*. Stuttgart, pp. 45–62.

Katzoff, R. 1982. Prefectural edicts and letters. *Zeitschrift für Papyrologie und Epigraphik* 48, pp. 209–17.

Kaser, M. 1955. *Das römische Privatrecht*. I. Munich.

Kokkinia, C. 2004. Ruling, inducing, arguing. How to govern (and survive) a Greek province. In: L. de Ligt et al. (eds.), *Roman rule and civic life: Local and regional perrspectives*. Amsterdam, pp. 1–18.

Kokkinia, C. 2014. Rome, Ephesos, and the Ephesian harbor: a case study in official rhetoric. In: A. Kolb (ed.), *Infrastruktur und Herrschaftsorganisation im Imperium Romanum*. Berlin, pp. 180–96.

Lalonde, G. V., Langdon, M. K. and M. B. Walbank. 1991. *The Athenian Agora 19: Horoi. Poletai records. Leases of public lands*. Princeton.

Lazaridou, K. 2015. Ephēbarchikos nomos apo tēn Amphipolē. *AEph* 2015, pp. 1–48.

LeGuen, B. 2001. *Les associations de technites dionysiaques à l'époque hellénistique*. Nancy.

Lenel, O. 1889. *Palingenesia iuris civilis*. Leipzig.

Mari, M. 2006. L'activité législative du roi et des cités en Macédoine. In : A-M. Guimier-Sorbets, M. Hatzopoulos and Y. Morizot (eds.), *Rois, cités, necropoles. Institutions, rites et monuments en Macédoine*. Athens, pp. 209–25.

Mari, M. 2017. Istituzioni cittadine della Macedonia preromana. Alcune novità epigrafiche. *Historika* 7, pp. 345–64.

McLean, B. 2002. *An introduction to Greek epigraphy of the Hellenistic and Roman periods from Alexander the Great down to the reign of Constantine (323 B.C.–A.D. 337)*. Ann Arbor.

van Minnen, P. 2016. Three edicts of Caracalla? A new reading of *P. Giss.* 40. *Chiron* 46, pp. 205–21.

Müller, H. 2001. Makedonische Marginalien. *Chiron* 31, pp. 417–55.

Nigdelis, P. 2006. *Epigraphika Thessalonikeia. Symbolē stēn politikē kai koinōnikē historia tēs archaias Thessalonikēs*. Thessaloniki.

Nigdelis, P. 2014. Ho *cursus publicus* stē Makedonia: ena neo dossie dēmosiōn engraphōn apo tēn rōmaikē apoikia tēs Pellas. In: A. Chrysostomou and P. Chrysostomou (eds.) *Hē Edessa kai hē periochē tēs. Istoria kai politismos* (Praktika 3ou panellēniou epistēmonikou symposiou, 11–12 Dekembriou 2010). Edessa, pp. 85–104.

Nigdelis, P. 2016a. *Κύβος*: on the funerary vocabulary of Thessaloniki. *Zeitschrift für Papyrologie und Epigraphik* 200, pp. 198–204.

Nigdelis, P. 2016b. *Harpaliani*: A new village of the Roman colony of Philippi. In: B. Takmer et al. (eds.) *Vir doctus Anatolicus. Studies in memory of S. Şahin*. Istanbul, pp. 640–50.

Nigdelis, P. and Anagnostoudis, P. 2017. New honorific inscriptions from Amphipolis. *Greek, Roman and Byzantine Studies* 57, pp. 295–324.

Nigdelis, P. and Souris, G. 2005. *Anthupatos legei. Ena diatagma tōn autokratorikōn chronōn gia to gymnasio tēs Beroias*. Thessaloniki.

Nigdelis, P. and Sverkos, E. 2009. Zur Neudefinition des Territoriums eines makedonischen Polis der Kaiserzeit: Der Fall von Bragylos in Krestonia. *Zeitschrift für Papyrologie und Epigraphik* 169, pp. 163–72.

Papagianni, E. 2017. *Ingenui* kai *liberti* se epitymbia anaglypha tēs hysterēs hellēnistikēs kai tēs prōimēs autokratorikēs epochēs apo tē Thessalonikē. In : E. Voutyras et al. (eds.) *Bonae Gratiae. Meletes rōmaikes glyptikēs pros timēn tēs kathēgētrias Theodosias Stephanidou-Tiberiou*. Thessaloniki, pp. 249–60.

Papastavru, J. 1936. *Amphipolis. Geschichte und Prosopographie*. Leipzig.

Papazoglou, F. 1986. *Oppidum Stobi civium Romanorum* et *municipium Stobensium*. *Chiron* 16, pp. 213–37.

Papazoglou, F. 1988. *Les villes de Macédoine à l'époque romaine*. Paris.

Perdrizet, P. 1894. Voyages dans la Macédoine première. *Bulletin de Correspondance Hellénique* 18, pp. 416–45.

Petrakos, B. 1999. *Ho demos tou Rhamnountos, II. Hoi epigraphes*. Athens.

Pikoulas, G. 1999. Termonismoi Makedonias, synbolē prōtē. In: *Ancient Macedonia* VI. Thessaloniki, pp. 893–902.

Purpura, G. 2012. *Revisione ed integrazione dei Fontes Iuris Romani Anteiustiniani (FIRA). Studi preparatori I. Leges*. Torino.

Purpura, G. 2013. Il *P. Giss.* 40, I. *Iuris Antiqui Historia* 5, pp. 73–85.

Raynor, B. 2016. *Theorodokoi*, *asylia*, and the Macedonian cities. *Greek, Roman and Byzantine Studies* 56, pp. 225–62.

Rhodes, P. and Lewis, D. 1997. *The decrees of the Greek states*. Oxford.

Richardson, J. 2008. *The language of empire. Rome and the idea of empire from the third century BC to the second century AD*. Cambridge.

Richardson, J. 2015. Roman law in the provinces. In: D. Johnston (ed.) *The Cambridge companion to Roman law*. Cambridge, pp. 45–60.

Ricl, M. 2001. Donations of slaves and freeborn children to deities in Roman Macedonia and Phrygia: A reconsideration. *Tyche* 16, pp. 127–60.

Rizakis, A. 1993. Hē koinotēta tōn 'synpragmateuomenōn Rhōmaiōn' tēs Thessalonikēs kai hē rōmaikē oikonomikē dieisdusē stē Makedonia. In: *Ancient Macedonia V* (*Papers read at the Fifth International Symposium held in Thessaloniki, October 10–15, 1989*). Thessaloniki, pp. 511–24.

Rizakis, A. 2002. L'émigration romaine en Macédoine et la communauté marchande de Thessalonique: Perspectives économiques et sociales. In: C. Müller and C. Hasenohr, eds. *Les Italiens dans le monde Grec, IIe siècle av. J.-C.–Ier siècle ap. J.-C. Circulations, activités, intégration* (Actes de la table ronde, École Normale Supérieure, Paris 14–16 mai 1998). Paris, pp. 109–32.

Rizakis, A. 2004. L'emphytéose sous l'Empire en pays grec. In: Follet, S. ed. *L'Hellénisme d'époque romaine. Nouveaux documents, nouvelles approches (Ier s. a. C.–IIIe s. p. C.)* (Actes du colloque international à la mémoire de Louis Robert, Paris, 7–8 juillet 2000). Paris, pp. 55–75.

Rizakis, A. 2008. Hē dioikētikē organōsē tēs rōmaikēs apoikias tōn Philippōn: Hē periptōsē tōn *praefecti fabrum*. In : E. Sverkos (ed.), *Praktika B' panellēniou synedriou epigraphikēs* (Thessalonikē, 24–5 Noemvriou 2001). Thessaloniki, pp. 189–97.

Rizakis, A. 2011. La diffusion des processus d'adaptation onomastique: les *Aurelii* dans les provinces orientales de l'Empire. In: M. Dondin-Payre (ed.), *Les noms de personnes dans l'Empire romain. Transformations, adaptation, évolution*. Bordeaux, pp. 253–62.

Rizakis, A. 2015. Expropriations et confiscations des terres dans le cadre de la colonisation romaine en Achaïe et en Macédoine. *Mélanges d'archéologie et d'histoire de l'École française de Rome* 127, pp. 469–85.

Rizakis, A. 2016. Société, institutions, cultes. In: J. Fournier (ed.), *Philippes, de la préhistoire à Byzance. Études d'archéologie et d'histoire*. Paris, pp. 175–97.

Rocco, M. 2010. The reasons behind *Constitutio Antoniniana* and its effects on the Roman military. *Acta classica universitatis scientiarum Debreceniensis* 46, pp. 131–55.

Sarikakēs, T. 1962. *Leukios Aimilios Paulos. Synbolē eis tēn historian tou III Makedonikou polemou*. Athens.

Sarikakēs, T. 1977. *Rhōmaioi archontes tēs eparchias tēs Makedonias B': apo tou Augoustou mechri tou Dioklētianou (27 p.Ch.–284 m.Ch.)*. 107. Thessaloniki.

Sartre, M. 1991. *L' Orient romain. Provinces et sociétés provinciales en Méditerranée orientale d'Auguste aux Sévères (31 avant J.-C.–235 après J.-C.)*. Paris.

Sève, M. 2005. Notables de Macédoine entre l'époque hellénistique et le Haut-Empire. In: P. Frölich and C. Müller (eds.) *Citoyenneté et participation à la basse époque hellénistique* (Actes de la table ronde des 22 et 23 mai 2004 Paris BNF). Genève, pp. 257–73.

Sharankov, N. 2016. Notes on Greek inscriptions from Bulgaria. In *Monuments and texts in antiquity and beyond. Essays for the centenary of G. Mihailov (1915–1991)*. Sofia, pp. 341–2 (= *Archeologia Bulgarica* 20 (2016), pp. 57–74).

Silver, M. 2015. «Living apart», *apeleutheroi* and *paramone*-clause. A response to Canevaro and Lewis. *Incidenza dell'Antico* 13, pp. 139–62.

Sosin, J. 2015. Manumission with *paramone*: Conditional freedom? *Transactions of the American Philological Association* 145, pp. 325–81.

Sourēs, G. 2009. To rōmaiko engrapho me kanonismous agorapōlēsias doulōn apo tē Beroia (*I. Beroia* 13). In : E. Sverkos, ed. *Praktika tou B' panellēniou synedriou epigraphikēs* (Thessalonikē, 24–5 Noemvriou 2001). Thessaloniki, pp. 217–30.

Stefanidou-Tiveriou, T. 2001. Kleinasiatische Einflüsse bei römischen Sarkophagen in Makedonien. In : C. Reussner (ed.), *Griechenland in der Kaiserzeit. Neue Funde und Forschungen zu Skulptur, Architektur und Topographie* (Kolloquium zum sechzigsten Geburtstag von Prof. Dieterich Willers, Bern 12.–13. Juni 1998). Bern, pp. 115–23.

Stefanidou-Tiveriou, T. 2010. Social status and family origin in the sarcophagi of Thessalonikē. In: L. S. Nasrallah et al. eds. *From Roman to early Christian Thessalonike: studies in religion and archaeology*. Cambridge, MA, pp. 151–88.

Strubbe, J. 1997. Arai epitymbiai. *Imprecations against desecrators of the grave in the Greek epitaphs of Asia Minor. A catalogue*. Bonn.

Sverkos, E. 2000. *Synbolē stēn historia tēs Anō Makedonias tōn rōmaikōn chronōn (politikē organōsē—koinōnia—anthrōponymia)*. Thessaloniki.

Tataki, A. 2006. *The Roman presence in Macedonia. Evidence from personal names*. Athens.

Taubenschlag, R. 1955. *The law of Greco-Roman Egypt in the light of the papyri, 332 B.C.–640 A.D.* Second edition. Warsaw.

Tuori, K. 2016. *The emperor of law: the emergence of Roman imperial adjudication*. Oxford.

Tzamtzēs, I. 2013. Creta Romana. *Pēges dikaiou, politikoi kai koinōnikoi thesmoi stēn Krēte kata tē rōmaikē periodo [67 p.Ch.–235 m.Ch.]*. Chania.

Valverde, L. 2004. Sexto Pompeyo, gobernador de Macedonia, y las incursiones escordiscas ca. 120–100 a.C. *Iberia* 7, pp. 19–38.

Velissaropoulos-Karakostas, J. 2011. *Droit grec d'Alexandre à Auguste*. Athènes–Paris.

Vujčić, N. 2015. The edict of Caracalla and the cities of Ionia. *Journal of Classical Studies Matica Srpska* 17, pp. 99–108. (in Serbian)

Wace, A. J. B. and Thompson. M. S. 1910/11. A Latin inscription from Perrhaebia. *Annual of the British School at Athens* 17, pp. 193–204.

Yarrow, L. 2012. *Decem legati*: A flexible institution, rigidly perceived. In: Chr. Smith and L. Yarrow (eds.) *Imperialism, cultural politics, and Polybius*. Oxford, pp. 168–83.

Youni, M. 2000. Provincia Macedonia. *Thesmoi idiōtikou dikaiou stē Makedonia epi Rōmaiokratias*. Thessaloniki.

Youni, M. 2003. Ho anthypatos Tertyllianos Akylas kai hē kodikopoiēssē tōn apeleutherōtikōn praxeōn stēn romaikē Makedonia. *EHHD* 37, pp. 29–45.

Youni, M. 2005. Maîtres et esclaves en Macédoine hellénistique et romaine. In : V. Anastasiadis and P. Doukellis (eds.) *Esclavage antique et discriminations socio-culturelles*. Bern, pp. 183–95.

Youni, M. 2008. Sur le statut juridique de l'affranchi grec dans le monde gréco-romain. In : A. Gonzalez (ed.), *La fin du statut servile? Affranchissement, libération, abolition. Hommage à Jacques Annequin*. Besançon, pp. 161–74.

Youni, M. 2009 L'aspect juridique des affranchissements de la Macédoine romaine. In : E. Sverkos, ed. *Praktika B' panellēniou sunedriou epigraphikēs* (Thessaloniki, 24–5 Noemvriou 2001). Thessaloniki, pp. 73–84. (in Greek)

Youni, M. 2010. Transforming Greek practice into Roman law: manumissions in Roman Macedonia. *Tijdschrift voor Rechtsgeschiedenis* 78, pp. 313–42.

Zelnick-Abramovitz, R. 2013. *Taxing freedom in Thessalian inscriptions*. Leiden.

Zelnick-Abramovitz, R. 2015. Public registers of land sales in ancient Greece. In: E. Jakab (ed.), *Sale and community. Documents from the ancient world. Individual's autonomy and state interference in the ancient world* (Proceedings of a colloquium supported by the University of Szeged, Budapest, 5.–8.10.2012) Trieste, pp. 41–65.

Part III
Africa and the West

16

The *leges municipales* as a Means of Legal and Social Romanization of the Provinces of the Roman Empire*

Werner Eck

When the text of the *lex Irnitana* was published in the *Journal of Roman Studies* at the end of 1986, this new epigraphic text, although a scholarly sensation, did not come as a complete surprise when one considers its contents as a whole. The subtitle of the publication itself gave an indication of this: 'A New Copy of the Flavian Municipal Law'.[1] The new law was passed specifically for the town of Irni. The majority (namely six) of the original ten bronze tablets are preserved in their entirety. In addition, a few fragments of a seventh tablet have been found.[2] The *lex* was proclaimed to the population of the *municipium* during the Domitianic period, certainly before 10 October AD 91, before being presented on the metal tablets to the public. In total, almost two thirds of the original text of the *lex* have come down to us, that is, 63 of 97 chapters.[3] Yet the content was not new in its totality, only in part. This is because parts of this municipal law had already been familiar for a long period of time from other cities in Baetica, which encompassed a significant number of chapters. Above all, the fragments for the two *municipia* of Malaca and Salpensa are quite extensive, although not nearly as long as in the case of the *lex Irnitana*. For in Irni, a total of sixty-three *rubricae* (as the paragraphs in the *lex* are named) have been preserved, whereas in Malaca nineteen survive, and in Salpensa nine. As of now, some paragraphs from the authoritative version of

* This chapter was translated from the German by Julian Wagstaff, with revisions by the author, Kimberley Czajkowski, and Benedikt Eckhardt.

[1] González and Crawford (1986). For comprehensive information on municipal laws and the questions arising from them see the collection in Capogrossi Colognesi and Gabba (2006).

[2] Fernández Gómez and Del Álamo y De La Hera (1990), 35ff., 49ff.; see also Lamberti (1993), 269; Wolf (2011), 149 ff.

[3] The last two chapters (numbered 98 and 99 in the publications) are not part of the legal text. Chapter 98 is a letter from Domitian, which resolves a contentious question, while Chapter 99 provides information only about the two officeholders who had arranged for the text of the law to be displayed on the bronze tablets.

Werner Eck, *The* leges municipales *as a Means of Legal and Social Romanization of the Provinces of the Roman Empire* In: *Law in the Roman Provinces.* Edited by: Kimberley Czajkowski and Benedikt Eckhardt in collaboration with Meret Strothmann, Oxford University Press (2020). © Oxford University Press.
DOI: 10.1093/oso/9780198844082.003.0016

the Flavian municipal law have actually come down to us twice, once in the *Irnitana* and then once again in the *lex Malacitana* or the *Salpensana*. In addition to these three central copies, further fragments extend the historical record of the municipal law. These have been found in other smaller and larger cities, including Ostippo, Conobaria, and Hispalis. These fragments could hardly have been correctly expanded or classified were it not for our knowledge of the preserved parts of the first three copies.[4] Nonetheless, these small remnants are also of great significance, as they demonstrate unambiguously that a large number of municipalities in Baetica had not only been granted Latin municipal legal rights by the Flavian emperors, but, more importantly, that this municipal law had the same wording for all municipalities, with the exception of small sections which were specific to the municipality in each case (for example the number of decurions to be elected in the individual city). Apart from that, the many small fragments from the different places are important because they show that publication for the benefit of the general populace was practiced everywhere in the province. It appears that hardly any municipality in Baetica shied away from the costs of publishing their own constitution ostentatiously on bronze tablets. This was a question of prestige. No town wanted to stand in the shadow of another. Whatever another could do, one's own municipality could do just as well. Thus a city's constitution was made publicly accessible for all inhabitants. It was a law which applied to everyone, to their own citizens and to the *incolae*, who often only lived in the municipality for a limited period of time.

The majority of the municipal laws from Baetica which we know of date from the Flavian period. Yet the enactment of such laws was nothing new after 70 CE. An important piece of evidence for this is the *lex coloniae Genetivae Iuliae*, also often known as the *lex Ursonensis* after the name of the municipality found in other inscriptions: *res publica Ursonensium*. Today Urso bears the name Osuna.[5] Fifty chapters of the *lex* have been known since the nineteenth century, while a further seven chapters were first published in 2006.[6] This law was written as early as the Caesarian period. It is therefore not so surprising that the text differs substantially from the Flavian *lex municipalis*, which we know from Baetica. In general it may be assumed that its transfer onto bronze tablets did not occur until many decades later.

This concentration of finds from the Iberian Peninsula has almost led us to forget that Roman-Latin municipal laws were not a Spanish peculiarity, but rather a phenomenon with repercussions right across the Imperium Romanum—in every place where the establishment of Roman or Latin-organized municipalities had occurred. This means that the phenomenon must have existed more or less everywhere, even if in many provinces of the east it was not the Roman forms of municipal law which dominated, but rather the *polis* was the predominant organisational form. But even in Achaea, *illa vera et mera Graecia*, as Pliny the Younger called it,[7] Roman colonies were established at Corinth and Patras, also in Macedonia and some regions of Asia Minor, in Syria,[8] and also in Judaea, where

[4] See the impressive compilation in Caballos Rufino (2009), 131ff., esp. 141–57.

[5] CIL I 594 = CIL II 5439 = II/5, 1022; Crawford (1996), I. 393–454. Also Galsterer (1988) and Galsterer (2006), 31–53.

[6] Caballos Rufino (2006) = AE 2006, 645; Caballos Rufino (2010).

[7] Pliny, *Epistulae* 8.24.2.

[8] See also numerous contributions in Brélaz (2017).

the colonia Flavia Prima Caesarea and the colonia Aelia Capitolina were founded.[9] Thus, Roman colonies and corresponding municipalities existed throughout the empire, and so must have the *leges municipales*, because in the Imperium Romanum no municipality could exist without a constitutional order, particularly if it had been founded as a new municipality. This was about Roman citizens, and Rome did not leave their organisation to the fates when they established self-administering municipalities.

And yet, until a relatively short while ago, whenever we discussed the effects of the municipal laws which regulated life in the municipalities of the Roman provinces, we had to refer to the Spanish provinces or even just to Baetica. This created the impression that everything contained in these legal documents was a phenomenon specific to the southern part of the Iberian Peninsula, namely the province of Baetica.

This was, of course, never the reality, and this was always known in theory. However, it is now increasingly demonstrable through concrete evidence in the form of epigraphic documents from Alpes Cottiae, Noricum, Moesia Superior, and Moesia Inferior. The Danubian provinces in particular, whose appearance is strongly determined by the military, may thus now be viewed in a very different light, characterised by Roman law and the social order with which this law was bound up.

One of these pieces of evidence, which replace the Baetica-centric view but which do not originate in the Danubian provinces, has been known for an even longer period of time. However, its significance had been overlooked, precisely because the fragments preserving the remnants of a municipal law are so small. These are two bronze fragments from Susa in the Alpes Cottiae, which were found as far back as the early twentieth century. Only since the *lex Irnitana* offered a broad textual foundation for the basic contents of the Flavian municipal laws was it possible to identify epigraphic texts of such fragmentary character, which were created according to a similar pattern. In Susa (Segusio), the capital of the Alpes Cottiae, sections of three paragraphs of a municipal law have been preserved, although the content of the regulation is more precisely discernible from only one of them. Therein it is determined how the parties may reject individual judges during their election, and how they are finally appointed.[10] In the *lex Irnitana* this regulation is to be found in *rubrica* 87. It cannot be determined whether this paragraph also carried this number in Susa—if, indeed, it was even given a number. However, it is rather improbable when one considers the amount of time which had lapsed between the formulation of the two laws. For the law for the province of Alpes Cottiae, immediately bordering Italy, probably dates from the Augustan period, in other words more than seventy years before the Flavian law for the towns in Spain. Although the pace of development of laws in the Roman empire was slower than it is today, this span of years is long enough to allow us to suppose that, by the Flavian period, developments in content may have occurred, and certainly linguistic developments at the very least. In the case of the *lex Troesmensium* (see below), such developments are very clearly discernible in the time between the Flavian period and the end of the rule of Marcus Aurelius,

[9] Isaac (2017). [10] Letta (2007), 145 = AE 2007, 891.

and similarly in the case of the *lex Ursonensis* and the Flavian *lex municipalis* for the Iberian Peninsula.

In Lauriacum in Noricum it had been possible to identify a number of inscribed bronze fragments as being part of a municipal law even before the publication of the *lex Irnitana*.[11] The reconstructible portion is even smaller in this case than at Susa, due to its very fragmentary condition. Nonetheless it can be discerned that here a regulation is to be found for the case when a *IIvir* has to leave the city and must not return until nightfall. In this case a *praefectus* must be appointed as his representative, who has to be at least 35 years of age. This regulation is important because it specifies an age for the assumption of an office which is greater than 25, the customary minimum age for normal municipal magistrates, as set down not only for the Roman-organized cities, but also in Rome for the quaestors. The regulation stipulating 35 years is also found in *rubrica* 25 of the *lex Salpensana* and *lex Irnitana*.

Just as the settlement of Lauriacum developed around a legionary camp, which in the early third century received the status of a—probably Roman—*municipium*, there were other towns in the Danube region which emerged next to or in place of a legionary camp. Thus under Hadrian, Carnuntum received the status of a *municipium*, and the same happened in Aquincum and Viminacium, while Oescus was raised to colonial status as early as Trajan's time. The town of Troesmis, situated the furthest east, also belongs to these municipalities. Continuing into the time of Marcus Aurelius, the *legio V Macedonica*, which had previously been stationed in Oescus, had its base there, around which extensive *canabae* and a *vicus* developed.[12] Yet Marcus Aurelius initially deployed the legion in the Roman–Parthian war. When it ended, the legion did indeed return to the Danube area, but probably not to Troesmis, at least not for an extended period. It is more probable that it was transferred immediately to Dacia north of the Danube, where it remained stationed until the province there came to an end.[13] It is not known who suggested the idea to the emperor of turning the long-established settlements in Troesmis into an autonomous city. Perhaps it required no particularly intensive impetus because the founding of similar municipalities already enjoyed a long tradition.[14]

The fact that in Troesmis a *municipium* had emerged has long been evidenced by a large number of inscriptions, in which the *municipium Troesmensium* and its magistrates were referred to.[15] The more precise point in time at which the founding occurred has only recently been determinable. A few years ago, two inscribed bronze tablets became known, which made it clear that between 177 and 180, when Commodus was already acting alongside his father as Augustus, a *municipium* was created there. In other words, the existing settlements received

[11] AE 1907, 100; 1953, 124; Weber in Ubl (1997), 96–8; Wedenig (1997), 182ff. No. L 2; AE 2003, 1323.

[12] See also Eck (2016a). Also additional contributions in the same including the results of extensive surveys.

[13] Piso (2000), 213ff.

[14] See the seminal articles by Vittinghoff (1994); Vittinghoff (1977).

[15] See merely for example CIL III 6172, 6173, 6199, 7504, 7509.

the status of a town, which was to be autonomous, i.e. self-administering.[16] What is important, however, is that this *municipium* did not receive Latin law (a kind of preliminary stage on the way to full Roman law), as was the case with nearly all municipalities on the Iberian Peninsula and probably also Susa. Rather, Troesmis became a *municipium civium Romanorum*, a municipium of Roman citizens, as was likely the case with Lauriacum. The specific content of the three chapters of the *lex Troesmensium*, parts of which are preserved on the two bronze tablets, shows this clearly, including regulations from the Augustan period, which only applied to Roman citizens.[17]

The *leges*, which we—again, until recently—knew from the period between Augustus and the beginning of the third century were all intended for *municipia*, mainly for Latin ones, but in the case of Troesmis (and probably for Lauriacum) a Roman one. However, what was missing from these centuries hitherto was evidence of a *lex* intended for a *colonia civium Romanorum*, which of course must have existed.[18] This blank spot has also been filled to some extent in the meantime. For, it can now be proven that a municipality with this legal status, the *colonia Ulpia Ratiaria*, had a *lex coloniae*, which it also brought to the attention of its own citizens on bronze tablets, as we know from the sites already mentioned.[19] Up until the early Trajanic period, the *legio IV Flavia* had its encampment near Ratiaria in the central Danube region. When, with the conquest of Dacia, the legion was transferred to the new province because it was no longer required at its previous location, the settlement, which there too had developed around the camp, was made into a town. But here it was declared a *colonia civium Romanorum*, named after Trajan: *colonia Ulpia Ratiaria*. However, only three small fragments of the *lex coloniae* which was issued for the new community have been preserved. These provide no unambiguous content-specific details on the regulations beyond the mere fact of the existence of the *lex*. Nonetheless, through a comparison with the municipal laws on the Iberian Peninsula it can be shown that one of the fragments, despite the meagreness of the remnants, may probably be correlated with *rubrica* 26 of the *lex Irnitana*, where reference is made to the oath-taking of the magistrates.[20] The other remnants are too scant to allow a correlation to be made with any specific paragraph of the known municipal laws with any degree of certainty. Still, the limited fragments show that Roman colonies were no different from municipalities in presenting their basic law to their citizens in an elaborate and costly fashion.

If any further evidence were required to demonstrate that municipal laws, formulated in detail according to Roman principles, could influence substantial swathes of the lives of the people in all Roman and Latin cities, be they *municipia* or *coloniae*, then this has been shown clearly through the remnants of *leges* that

[16] On the *lex Troesmensium* see Eck (2013a); Eck (2014a); Eck (2014b); Eck (2015); Eck (2016b).

[17] See the literature in n.16 with the explanatory notes on the *lex Iulia de maritandis ordinibus* as well as on the *lex Papia Poppaea*. In the case of Lauriacum one can probably deduce the Roman status of the *municipium* from the fact that it was likely conceived as a settlement primarily for Roman veterans.

[18] The *lex coloniae Ursonensis* was passed when Caesar was still in power.

[19] Eck (2016c). [20] See the contribution by Rafetseder (2018).

have been fortuitously preserved in various different provinces.[21] This is because the texts did not simply languish in the town archives but were visible and accessible to all. Admittedly, we know nothing about the actual locations where the documents were set up. Yet merely on account of the quantity of text and the number of tablets on which they appeared, they could not have gone unnoticed by the general public. In Irni, for example, the ten law tablets formed a wall more than 9 metres wide. In Troesmis the tablets presumably extended over more than 50 meters,[22] an imposing presence of Roman law at the borders of the empire in close proximity to the world of the 'barbarians'.

The bestowal of these municipal rights is, however, not to be viewed in isolation. It rather forms part of the process of Romanization, through which Roman citizenship became more and more widespread in the provinces by various means since the time of Caesar, and even more after Augustus.[23] While the founding of *coloniae* was still thoroughly associated with the settlement of Roman citizens up until the late second century, the raising of an existing settlement to a Roman *municipium* already required Roman citizens who lived on site—as was the case, for example, with the abovementioned *municipium Troesmis*. There, many inhabitants of the *canabae* and also of the *vicus* were already *cives Romani*, as the many inscriptions preserved from the pre-municipal period show. From this one can infer that even before the latter part of Marcus Aurelius' reign, it was primarily veterans from the legions who lived there. Similarly, there were also significant numbers from the auxiliary units, from which many thousands of soldiers were released every year and who received Roman citizenship after 25 or more years of service. This is evidenced by the *diplomata militaria*, of which many more than a thousand are now known. And as in the case of Troesmis, the same phenomenon may be observed at other locations, for example in the Roman cities of the Dacian provinces.[24] Many soldiers settled down near to their place of deployment following their *honesta missio*, and, when a new polity was formed along Roman or Latin organisational lines, they were then incorporated into that polity as citizens. And in the same way, many veterans integrated themselves into other existing polities of this kind on their own initiative, because in general it was up to the individual soldier where he made his new home following his service in the army. Not everyone wanted to return to their old region of origin following their discharge. The settlement of entire units or even larger parts of a unit was no longer customary by the second century. The *missio agraria*, i.e. discharge with an ensuing settlement on open land to guarantee a living in old age, had long been replaced by the *missio nummaria*, i.e. a monetary payment. This shift had already begun during the Augustan period.[25]

The soldiers for the army were originally recruited from the most varied regions of the empire. While legionaries in the first century, at least until the Flavians, still

[21] Besides, one must also presuppose this in the case of the poleis, which were founded in the Greek east during the Roman period. The only question would be whether the basic order of these poleis came from the emperors, or whether the inhabitants of the poleis could decide on it themselves.

[22] Eck (2016b), 601.

[23] See most recently Eck (2018).

[24] See, for example, Cupcea (2014), 70ff., 110ff.

[25] There were, however, clearly also later cases of settlements, for example in Peraia beyond the Jordan in the province of Iudaea, see Eck (2000).

came from Italy, but even more from regions which had long been part of the Imperium (such as the Iberian Peninsula, southern France or the cities of the Dalmatian coast), in the later period even the Roman citizen-legions were increasingly populated by recruits from the less Romanized provinces. This applied even more to the auxiliary units, and to the fleets in Italy or in the provinces. Even in the case of the praetorians, who from Augustus onwards had to be Roman citizens by definition, and in the second century still came predominantly from Italy, it could happen that individuals, and sometimes not just a few individuals, who did not have Roman citizenship, were taken on. A case in point is supported by evidence from as early as Claudius's time,[26] when recruits from the peregrine tribes of the Italian Alpine foothill regions were able to join the imperial guard. Far more pressing was the situation at the end of Trajan's reign, when in the east the gaps in the *cohortes praetoriae*, which probably emerged during the Parthian war and due to the horrendous Syrian earthquake in AD 115, had to be filled quickly with soldiers from auxiliary units. The officers probably did not look too closely at the legal status of the personnel. Hadrian had to tackle the thorny situation officially in February 119 through an edict passed at a people's assembly in Rome. He made the affected members of his guard Roman citizens retrospectively. At the same time he remedied all legal acts which these praetorians had concluded previously with Roman citizens, in which the parties to the contract had assumed that the soldiers were similarly Roman citizens.[27] Legionaries could sometimes in fact possess Roman citizenship when they were admitted into a legion, without being too much affected by Roman culture; however, it was also possible in particular situations for them to be granted citizenship only immediately prior to their entry into the citizens' unit, as happened in AD 133, for example, in the case of several thousand fleet soldiers, in order to plug the gaps left by the Bar Kokhba revolt in the two legions in Judaea.[28]

All of these veterans, if they settled in a Roman or Latin polity in the province, or if a settlement was made into such a polity for the first time, had around twenty-five years' worth (or even slightly more) of Roman-structured socialisation behind them within the army.[29] As a matter of necessity, they had all learned more or less perfect Latin, which was an absolute prerequisite for life in a polity organised along Roman lines.[30] They had also concluded contracts according to Roman legal regulations insofar as these were relevant within a military context, or had made purchases.[31] Similarly, they had become conversant with the Roman social structure, at least through their officers and their families, even if that could only occur at the natural distance between officers and the ordinary soldiers. In addition, all were in one way or another involved in Roman cults, although they were in no way exclusively geared towards Roman gods. Thus the soldiers were

26 See the so-called *tabula Clesina*: CIL V 5050 = Dessau 206; most recently also Faoro (2014).

27 Eck, Pangerl, and Weiß (2014a); Eck, Pangerl, and Weiß (2014b) = AE 2013, 2183 ff.; see also Eck (2017).

28 Eck and Pangerl (2006); Eck (2012).

29 See also Speidel (2007).

30 See also the discussion surrounding Latin in Caesarea Maritima and other colonies in the east of the empire: Eck (2009) and with a different viewpoint Isaac (2009).

31 See e.g. the purchase agreement, relating to a slave, between soldiers from the Fleet of Misenum stationed in Syria, in which all legal certainties are formulated in accordance with the aediles' edict: P. Lond. 229 = FIRA III 132 = Eck and Heinrichs (1993), No. 47, p. 33ff.

indeed familiar with everything 'Roman' in a military context, that is, with a life in which a great deal was bound up with obedience to one's superiors. To what extent this also applied to the wider arena of marriage, family and children, in other words to a significant part of normal existence for citizens within a polity, is hard to estimate. For the fact that many soldiers were associated with a woman, although they were forbidden from entering into marriage from the standpoint of the law, is backed up by a large amount of evidence, and of course such relationships also produced progeny. In many Roman military diplomas that grant citizenship, particularly from the Trajanic–Hadrianic period, auxiliary veterans not only included the woman with whom they already lived, for the *conubium*, but also children. It was not uncommon that five or more children were mentioned in the diplomas.[32] Here, too, much that reflected Roman legal rules was probably already practiced. Other aspects of Roman legal rules probably remained somewhat foreign to soldiers up until the end of their period of service, primarily those which, within a Roman or Latin polity, would have been self-evident, as they concerned those rules governing the public sphere and the communal activity of the citizenry. For a very large portion of the troops hailed from peregrine municipalities. Others, who had perhaps grown up in cities organised along Roman or Latin lines, may have long become estranged from communal life following decades of military service with its very different imperatives, if they had not entirely forgotten how the inner life of such polities was constructed, and how one was to act in such settings. It is no coincidence that for soldiers, those who lived beyond the camp on the territory of the polity belonged to an alternate world. It was the world of the *pagani*, the civilians, from which the world of the soldiers differed significantly.[33]

On settling in a *municipium* or a *colonia*, veterans had to orientate and organise themselves anew; they were now themselves half civilians. They brought with them a number of important prerequisites for life within these polities, while other necessities they had first to learn, as required by the legal framework of the municipal law. At the same time it was certainly of particular advantage for the veterans of the legion that they were financially well catered for through the bursary that they received at the time of their honourable discharge (*honesta missio*), and that they could thus find their way in civilian life without any economic pressures. They received a payment of at least thirteen times their annual pay, which also applied to the higher ranks such as *centuriones*, and at least approximately to the *primipili*. The latter had an annual pay of 72,000 sestertii in the middle of the second century,[34] and on leaving service a severance payment of 600,000 sestertii was granted.[35] They thereby surpassed many equestrian families. But even the humble centurions were not badly off with an annual pay of 18,000 and a severance payment of 234,000 sestertii. All of them belonged to the foremost social stratum of a city, at least from a financial point of view. They easily exceeded the necessary minimum level of wealth, which one had

[32] See e.g. RMD IV 223. 227. 235. 241. 248; V 344. 351 + AE 2005, 1703 + AMN 41/2, 2004/5, 61 ff. 357. 385; AE 2005, 1724; 2007, 1783.

[33] Eck (2010).

[34] According to Speidel (1992), esp. 106 [=Speidel (2009), esp. 380].

[35] See Dobson (1978), 116.

to demonstrate in Irni to be appointed as a judge, for example. There it was 5000 sestertii,[36] although elsewhere it was certainly much more. Veterans of the legion, however, could easily keep pace. In addition, many of the former soldiers had been employed within the *officia*, the unit's scriptoria, during their military service, and therefore had gained experience in bureaucratic work, which could be advantageous for them in civil and municipal life. Of course, they were all as veterans in the first instance released from obligations towards the municipality in which they lived. No one could demand services from them for the city—these had to be provided voluntarily.[37] If they did undertake them, this was recognised as all the more meritorious by their fellow citizens. However, most of these new municipal citizens did not keep themselves aloof, even if civilian life made some not inconsiderable demands on them following a long period of military service. The municipal law set the framework for all.

The majority of citizens who lived in the Roman-Latin cities of the provinces were of course not military people. They came from the indigenous population who lived where Roman-Latin towns emerged, or they were immigrants from other provinces. This of course applied to all *municipia* on the Iberian Peninsula, which received Latin laws and rights through Vespasian and his sons, no differently from, for example, the communities in Gaul, who perhaps received the same privilege from Claudius or later also from Galba due to political support following his revolts against Nero.[38] But even when colonies were founded in communities that had long existed, portions of the earlier population were incorporated into the citizenry of the colony alongside the colonists who had settled there, in that they received Roman citizenship. This must have happened, for example, in the Ubii settlement, when a veteran colony was founded there on the initiative of Claudius's wife Agrippina in the year AD 50. While not all Ubii received the *civitas Romana*, a portion of the Ubii must have done, otherwise, 19 years later when the rebelling Germanic people from the right bank of the Rhine laid siege to the colony demanding the murder of the Romans who had settled there, they would not have answered that they could not demand of them that they kill their 'parents, brothers, or children'. This was because they were joined through bonds of marriage with the colonists who had settled there.[39] This attitude on the part of the leading Agrippinenses was only possible, however, if parts of the Ubii had also become citizens of the *colonia* in the year AD 50, after the emperor had granted them Roman citizenship. In a similar manner, many inhabitants of the *polis* Caesarea Maritima in Judaea must have become Roman citizens when in

[36] *Lex Irnitana, rubrica* 86:... *non minores quam XXV annorum, quibus ip[si]s quorumv[e] cui[u]s patri avove paterno proavove paterno aut patri cuius in potestate erit non minor quam HS V(milia) res sit* (not younger than 25, whose own property is worth not less than 5,000 sesterces, or whose father or paternal grandfather or paternal great-grandfather or father in whose power they are has such property). English translations of the *lex Irnitana* are all from González and Crawford (1986).

[37] On veterans' privileges, see Wolff (1986).

[38] See, for example, Raepsaet-Charlier (1998), 174 ff.

[39] Tacitus, *Historiae* 4.65.2: *deductis olim et nobiscum per conubium sociatis quique mox provenerunt haec patria est; nec vos adeo iniquos existimamus ut interfici a nobis parentes fratres liberos nostros velitis* (As for those who in former days settled here, and have been united to us by marriage, and as for their offspring, this is their native land. We cannot think you so unjust as to wish that we should slay our parents, our brothers, and our children).

AD 70/71 Vespasian raised the town that had supported him during the war against the rebellious Jews to the status of a colony,[40] regardless of the question whether he also settled veterans there at the same time, in order to strengthen the Latin-Roman element in the city. All of these people, who prior to incorporation into a Roman-Latin city had been socialised very differently, had to fit into the new legal and political order of the community to which they now belonged and adopt the new rules in order to not only belong in a legal sense but also to live with and within the new community. These were rules that applied to Roman citizens everywhere, but also specifically to the polity in question.

If one moved as a Roman citizen into such a polity, then of course one already bore a Roman name. However, those who only received Roman or Latin citizenship through their acceptance into the polity also had to assimilate with regard to their name, in other words to adopt a three-part Roman form of their name. The specifics of how this was to happen were not regulated. Sometimes, new citizens took the *praenomen* and *nomen gentile* of an emperor, if they had received citizenship through a special imperial act, as happened in AD 106 in the context of the Second Dacian War, when Trajan honoured all the members of the *cohors I Brittonum* with the *civitas Romana*. Then all soldiers of the unit bore the name Marcus Ulpius, while the previous, usually peregrine personal name of the individual soldier became the cognomen which continued to be the primary designation of the person. From then on one of these soldiers' full name was M. Ulpius Novantico,[41] another's was M. Ulpius Longinus.[42] In Pesch, one of the *matres* shrines of the Ubii, very varied names are found after approximately the middle of the second century. While some dedicants still used their simple names of Roman or Ubian origin, for example a Verecundus together with a Leubasn[a],[43] most already bore a tripartite Roman name; thus one was called Q. Veranius Verecundus, another C. Verinius Natalis, while one woman was called Flaccinia Lefa.[44] The majority of these dedicants were of Ubian origin, most of whom probably had not immediately received Roman citizenship in AD 50 along with the elite of their tribe. However, over the course of the next century, citizenship appears to have been granted to many, if not all, of these ethnic Ubii, who then also assimilated to the Roman naming system.[45] With these new names they were then recorded in the citizens' lists of the municipality and also in the tax registers, which were held by the financial procurators and publicans.

In the previously peregrine communities, which were raised to the level of a *municipium*, or in poleis, which were raised to a *colonia*, there had already existed a municipal organisation, with people's assembly, town council and magistrates.

[40] Pliny, *Naturalis historia* 5.69: *Caesarea ab Herode rege condita, nunc colonia Prima Flavia a Vespasiano Imperatore deducta*; (Caesarea, founded by King Herod, but now the colony called Prima Flavia established by the Emperor Vespasian) D.50.15.8.7: *Divus Vespasianus Caesarienses colonos fecit non adiecto, ut et iuris italici essent, sed tributum his remisit capitis: sed divus Titus etiam solum immune factum interpretatus est* (The Divine Vespasian made the Caesarienses *coloni* without adding the *ius Italicum*, but remitted the poll-tax; but the Divine Titus decided that the soil had been made immune also). See Eck (2013b).

[41] CIL XVI 160. [42] CIL XVI 163. [43] CIL XIII 12019.

[44] CIL XIII 12031. 12032. 12024.

[45] In RGZM 8 an Ubian auxiliary receives citizenship: *gregali Primo Marci f(ilio) Ubio*; father and son already bear Roman names, but not yet the *tria nomina*.

These were now configured according to Roman criteria, which probably not infrequently differed considerably from the previous ones. While everyone cast their individual vote in the people's assembly, which also had to elect magistrates, it now counted only within the *curia* in which the individual citizen was registered. In Irni, for example, there were presumably eleven *curiae*; more were not permitted to be established. In the end the majority in the *curia* decided by means of a vote which candidate was elected by the *curia* members.[46] The individual vote, which a citizen cast for a different candidate, did not then count. This may initially have appeared strange to a new citizen, though this corresponded with Roman custom in respect of elections. Similarly new for many was surely the fact that they, if they possessed a fortune which had been in the family for three generations, had to serve as a judge, for it was not the elected magistrates who sat in judgement on legal disputes, but citizens who had been appointed *iudices*. One could be elected to this judicial office even if one did not belong to the decurion council, and there was no right of appeal.[47] Some may have been filled with pride when they saw their name in the list of judges on public display, while others felt it to be a burden. The same applied to the appointment of those who were called upon to pursue communal matters as envoys, beyond the territory of the town itself. This might apply to assignments which had to be concluded before the governor of the province. Sometimes, however, the matter went beyond the competence of the governor. Then envoys had to travel to Rome to receive the required decisions—from the senate, or increasingly from the emperor. Some may have appreciated carrying out assignments of this kind as a *legatus*. However, five citizens of the Trajanic colony Sarmizegetusa in the province of Dacia, who undertook a journey to Rome for the accession as consul of their former governor Severianus, were appointed to this task, for they say they had been dispatched to the accession. When they returned *incolumes* they thanked *Diis et Numinib(us) Aquarum*.[48] For such journeys were stressful and could be dangerous, for which reason many citizens preferred to evade such requests. This can be seen from the regulations of the *lex Irnitana* regarding the appointment of municipal envoys and their responsibilities.[49] However, following the enactment of this Flavian municipal law, the officials in Rome, who formulated the municipal laws, realised that the sanctions envisaged at that time were not sufficient. Thus the regulations proscribing such dereliction of duty in the *lex municipalis Troesmensium* were made significantly more precise in order to enforce the interests of the wider community.[50] In this matter, as in many others, the Roman-Latin *leges* demonstrated that everyone had to play their part for the benefit of the community, the *communis res municipum*. Wherever necessary, the municipal laws demanded that those who undertook or were compelled to undertake an assignment on behalf of the community had to swear an oath to *Iupiter*, the *divi imperatores*, and

[46] *Lex Malacitana, rubrica* 55 ff.

[47] *Lex Irnitana, rubrica* 86.

[48] CIL III 1562 = Dessau 3896: *Dis et Numinib(us) Aquarum Ulp(ius) Secundinus, Marius Valens, Pomponius Haemus, Iul(ius) Carus, Val(erius) Valens legati Romam ad consulatum Severiani c(larissimi) v(iri) missi incolumes reversi ex voto.* How dangerous journeys were is shown vividly by an epigram published by Sharankov (2017).

[49] *Lex Irnitana,* chapters 44–7.

[50] See *kaput XI* in the *lex Troesmensium*: Eck (2016b), 579 ff.

the *dei Penates*, which would serve to bind those persons to fulfilling the demands of the municipal law.[51]

Above and beyond the public sphere, life in communities that were subject to Roman-Latin law also required of its citizens that the lives of families be shaped in accordance with the provisions of Roman private law, including in their actions with respect to fellow citizens. Its validity was specifically established in the *lex Irnitana*, which indeed applied to a Latin *municipium*.[52] This *ius privatum* applied to children as well as to wives, but also to slaves or freedmen. The local peregrine communities surely lived according to their own rules in this sphere of life, which were not the same as those of Roman private law. Some of these may have persisted even in the Roman-Latin municipalities, without being negated by the different Roman legal norms—as long as conflicts did not arise. For example, how far the rights of a father extended in respect to his children, and in particular female children, was surely often determined in internal family practice by the origins of the individual participants and the rules to which they were accustomed. Presumably, and not only in Egypt, fathers continually attempted to not only arrange the marriages of their daughters, but also to mould them in accordance with their own perceptions and/or local rights on an ongoing basis. Thus, for example in Egypt, a father could dissolve the marriage of his daughter even against her will, according to common law applicable there.[53] If a conflict emerged in such cases which came before a Roman judge, then the father would have to comply with Roman law, even if he still adhered *de facto* to a different conception of the law. For, since Antoninus Pius at the latest, such an intervention on the part of the father was no longer permitted by Roman civil law.[54] Everyone had to submit themselves to this law. And the more frequently disputes occurred, the more everyone became aware of how mandatory Roman norms in the municipalities were. In the paragraphs of the *leges municipales*, which were publicly accessible everywhere, everyone could see to which norms they were required to subject themselves, including in daily life, even if the *ius privatum* was to be found only in rudimentary form within its paragraphs.[55] In any case, these laws also contained several regulations that we today would surely assign to the realm of private law, such as the freeing of slaves from the authority of their masters. Of course, it made sense that appropriate provisions were incorporated into the municipal laws because Latin or Roman citizenship was transferred through orderly manumission. Thus everyone, i.e. the general public, must have had an interest of some form or other in having such acts carried out in accordance with law. At the end of

[51] See e.g. *rubrica* 25 of the *lex Irnitana*: a *praefectus iure dicundo* employed in place of an absent *IIvir* is to swear: *ut is iuret per Iovem et divom Aug(ustum) et divom Claudium et divom Vespasianum Aug(ustum) e[t] divom Titum Augustum et Genium Imp(eratoris) Caesaris Domitiani Au[g(usti)] deosque Penates, quae IIvirum, qui iure dicundo praeerit, hac lege [f]acere oporteat se, dum praefectus erit.* (by Jupiter and the Divine Augustus and the Divine Claudius and the Divine Vespasian Augustus and the Divine Titus Augustus and the genius of the Emperor Caesar Domitian Augustus and the Penates, that he will do what it is appropriate for a duumvir who is in charge of the administration of justice to do under this statute, while he is *praefectus*).

[52] *Lex Irnitana, kaput* 93.

[53] See the famous case of Dionysia, who prevailed against her father, P.Oxy. II. 237, also discussed in the introduction to this volume.

[54] Kaser (1959), 322.

[55] From a different perspective, on this subject: Eck (2018).

the day, freedmen were to become their own fellow citizens following the act of manumission. Decisions were therefore to be taken with proper consideration and in accordance with the expectations of society at the time. Minors who had not yet reached the age of twenty did not have the right to participate in the public life of a municipality. In general, women did not have the right to do so either. Thus it was only consistent that minors and women of any age could only release a slave in the presence of their *tutor*, which in the case of women applied not only to this legal act but to all legal acts.[56] At the same time there were, of course, exceptions, which in turn appeared thoroughly logical in the wake of Augustus's 'social legislation'. After the birth of three children, through which the future life of the community was strengthened, women had the right to appear and act without their *tutor (ius trium liberorum)*; freedwomen received this right if they had four children. Corresponding rules had therefore rightly found their way into the municipal laws, no differently from the appointment of legal guardians.[57]

The provisions of the municipal laws applied primarily to the citizens of the corresponding municipalities everywhere. However, many members of society in the Roman provinces were highly mobile, and a not inconsiderable number lived in municipalities of which they were not citizens. Roman Cologne, for example, had residents from the Gallic tribes of the Nervii and Viromandui,[58] as well as from tribes in Britain[59] and the Greek east.[60] Yet they all had to abide by the legal conditions of the citizens of the *colonia* in coexistence with them, be they Italic or Ubian. Thus they necessarily grew into the world shaped by the Romans through their life in the CCAA. The same applied to the Ubii, who had not become citizens at the time the colony was founded, but who continued to live as *peregrini* on the territory of the new civic community, which is demonstrable until at least the end of the first century CE. However, one must assume that they were subject to the magistrates of the colony from the start. If a conflict arose, for example at the town's market, between a male Agrippinensian—whether the offspring of a veteran or one of the Ubii granted citizenship in AD 50—and a female peregrine Ubian, who had come to the central town to sell her agricultural produce, then the dispute would be settled before the colony's aediles, and almost inevitably according to Roman legal rules. And of course the Ubian would have to be assisted by her *tutor*,[61] even if such a legal escort would perhaps not have been necessary among her peregrine tribespeople. How mandatory this provision was in Roman-influenced societies can be seen, for example, in the fact that even in the Greek east, where women were legally competent according to Hellenistic and also Jewish law, an *epitropos—tutor* was appointed for them if they wished to seek a decision before Roman officeholders.[62] People had learned to what extent this assimilation with the Roman legal system could aid the furtherance of their own interests. The peregrine Ubii also learned this lesson, as many others did, and in all probability assimilated themselves quickly, in order to be able to assert their rights

[56] *Lex Salpensana kaput* 28. [57] *Lex Salpensana kaput* 29.

[58] CIL XIII 8339–42 = IKöln² 410. 416. 417. 430. [59] CIL XIII 8314 = IKöln² 381.

[60] CIL XIII 8343 = IKöln² 406. [61] See above nn. 56 and 57.

[62] See comprehensive discussion by Cotton (1997); Cotton (2007), esp. 247 ff. with reference to further statements on this phenomenon. See also Eck (2018).

in comparable situations and avoid the otherwise foreseeable complications. If these formerly peregrine Ubii became citizens of the colony in the course of time, they would enter a world which was not entirely alien to them. They would probably already have gained a certain knowledge of the Latin language, the *lingua franca* in the colony, and certainly in most cases before the municipal court, especially before the governor. And this holds true even though the Ubian idiom probably persisted at least until well into the second century, if not longer, as a common language in the narrower sphere of life. The dedications to the Matres, the deities particularly revered by the Ubii, indicate this clearly, for here a number of linguistic peculiarities of the Ubian language are preserved more than one hundred years after the founding of the Roman colony.[63] In other regions of the empire, primarily in the east, Latin did not succeed in establishing itself as a *lingua franca*. In its place, general communication was dominated by Greek.

Assimilation to Roman law and the Latin language did not, therefore, entail a complete overpowering or extinguishing of ethnic characteristics within a local society, not only in the west. Rather, we are dealing with a gradual assimilation to Roman social norms, which had their concrete legal foundations in the *leges municipales*. By these means, the way had in many respects been paved for the general grant of citizenship by Caracalla in the year 212. It could no longer be a truly revolutionary act. Rather, it was the logical end point of a development which had been substantially promoted by the Roman-Latin municipal laws.

REFERENCES

Brélaz, C. (ed.) 2017. *L'héritage Grec des colonies Romaines d'Orient. Interactions culturelles dans les provinces hellénophones de l'empire romain*. Paris.

Caballos Rufino, A. 2006. *El nuevo bronce de Osuna y la política colonizadora romana*. Sevilla.

Caballos Rufino, A. 2009. Publicación de documentos públicos en las ciudades del Occidente Roman: el ejemplo de la Bética. In: R. Haensch (ed.), *Selbstdarstellung und Kommunikation. Die Veröffentlichung staatlicher Urkunden auf Stein und Bronze in der Römischen Welt. Internationales Kolloquium an der Kommission für Alte Geschichte und Epigraphik in München (1. bis 3. Juli 2006)*. München, pp. 131–72.

Caballos Rufino, A. 2010. Colonizzazione cesariana, legislazione municipale e integrazione provinciale: la Provincia Hispania Ulterior. In: G. Urso (ed.), *Cesare: Precursore o visionario?* Pisa, pp. 63–84.

Capogrossi Colognesi, L. and Gabba, E. (eds.), 2006. *Gli Statuti Municipali*. Pavia.

Cotton, H. M. 1997. The Guardian of a Woman in the Documents from the Judaean Desert, *Zeitschrift für Papyrologie und Epigraphik* 118, 267–73.

Cotton, H. M. 2007. Private international law or conflict of laws: Reflections on Roman provincial jurisdiction. In: R. Haensch and J. Heinrichs (eds.), *Herrschen und Verwalten: Der Alltag der römischen Administration in der hohen Kaiserzeit*. Köln, pp. 234–55.

Crawford, M. H. 1996. *Roman Statutes*. Two volumes. London.

Cupcea, G. 2014. *Professional Ranks in the Roman Army of Dacia*. Oxford.

Dobson, B. 1978. *Die Primipilares. Entwicklung und Bedeutung, Laufbahnen und Persönlichkeiten eines römischen Offiziersranges*. Köln and Bonn.

[63] See also Eck, Die Ubier.

Eck, W. 2000. Der Bar Kochba Aufstand, der kaiserliche Fiscus und die Veteranenversorgung. *Scripta Classica Israelica* 19, pp. 139–48 [= in: W. Eck, 2014. *Judäa—Syria Palästina. Die Auseinandersetzung einer Provinz mit römischer Politik und Kultur.* Tübingen, pp. 275–83]

Eck, W. 2009. Presence, role and significance of Latin in the epigraphy and culture of the Roman Near East. In: H. M. Cotton, R. G. Hoyland, J. J. Price, and D. J. Wasserstein (eds.), *From Hellenism to Islam: Cultural and Linguistic Change in the Roman Near East.* Cambridge, pp. 15–42.

Eck, W. 2010. *Milites et pagani.* Die Stellung der Soldaten in der römischen Gesellschaft. In: A. Corbino, M. Humbert and G. Negri (eds.), *Homo, caput, persona. La costruzione giuridica dell'identità nell'esperienza romana*, Pavia, pp. 597–630.

Eck, W. 2012. Der Bar Kochba-Aufstand der Jahre 132–136 und seine Folgen für die Provinz Judaea/Syria Palaestina. In: P. Urso (ed.), *Iudaea socia—Iudaea capta.* Pisa, pp. 249–65.

Eck, W. 2013a. La loi municipale de Troesmis: données juridiques et politiques d'une inscription récemment découverte. *Revue historique du droit français et étranger* 91, pp. 199–213.

Eck, W. 2013b. Wie römisch war das caput Iudaeae, die Colonia Prima Flavia Caesariensis? In: R. Boustan, K. Hermann, R. Leicht, A. Yoshiko Reed and G. Veltri (ed.), *Envisioning Judaism: Studies in Honor of Peter Schäfer on the Occasion of his Seventieth Birthday* Vol. I. Tübingen, pp. 91–105.

Eck, W. 2014a. Das Leben römisch gestalten. Ein Stadtgesetz für das Municipium Troesmis aus den Jahren 177–180 n. Chr. In: St. Benoist and G. de Kleijn (eds.), *Integration in Rome and in the Roman World.* Leiden, pp. 75–88.

Eck, W. 2014b. Der Stolz des municipium Troesmensium: das Stadtgesetz. In: W. Eck and P. Funke (eds.), *Öffentlichkeit—Monument—Text. XIV Congressus Internationalis Epigraphiae Graecae et Latinae—Akten.* Berlin, pp. 708–10.

Eck, W. 2015. Akkulturation durch Recht: Die lex municipalis Troesmensium. In: L. Zerbini (ed.), *Culti e religiosità nelle province danubiane. Atti del II Convegno Internazionale Ferrara 20–22 Novembre 2013.* Bologna, pp. 9–18.

Eck, W. 2016a. Die Lex municipalis Troesmensium: Ihr rechtlicher und politisch-sozialer Kontext. In: C.-G. Alexandrescu (ed.), Troesmis—A changing landscape. Romans and the Others in the Lower Danube Region in the First Century BC–Third Century AD. *Proceedings of an International Colloquium Tulcea, 7–10 October 2015.* Cluj-Napoca, pp. 33–46.

Eck, W. 2016b. Die lex Troesmensium: ein Stadtgesetz für ein municipium civium Romanorum. Publikation der erhaltenen Kapitel und Kommentar. *Zeitschrift für Papyrologie und Epigraphik* 200, pp. 565–606.

Eck, W. 2016c. Fragmente eines neuen Stadtgesetzes—der lex coloniae Ulpiae Traianae Ratiariae. *Athenaeum* 104, pp. 538–44.

Eck, W. 2017. Rechtsunsicherheit heilen: Hadrian und seine Prätorianer am Beginn seiner Regierung. In: J. C. Bermejo Barrera and M. García Sánchez (eds.), *ΔΕΣΜΟΙ ΦΙΛΙΑΣ. Studies on Ancient History in Honour of F. Javier Fernández Nieto.* Barcelona, pp. 137–44.

Eck, W. 2018. Die Wirksamkeit des römischen Rechts im Imperium Romanum und seinen Gesellschaften. In: E. Lo Cascio and D. Mantovani (eds.) *Diritto romano e economia. Due modi di pensare e organizzare il mondo (nei primi tre secoli dell'Impero).* Pavia, pp. 237–55.

Eck, W. Die Ubier und ihre autochthone Religion. To be published in: E. Dupraz and M. J. Estarán (eds.), *Parole per gli dèi. Dediche religiose in lingue epicoriche del Mediterraneo Occidentale.* Roma.

Eck, W. and Heinrichs, J. 1993. *Sklaven und Freigelassene in der Gesellschaft der römischen Kaiserzeit.* Darmstadt.

Eck, W. and Pangerl, A. 2006. Die Konstitution für die classis Misenensis aus dem Jahr 160 und der Krieg gegen Bar Kochba unter Hadrian. *Zeitschrift für Papyrologie und Epigraphik* 155, pp. 239–52.

Eck, W. Pangerl, A. and Weiß, P. 2014a. Edikt Hadrians für Prätorianer mit unsicherem römischen Bürgerrecht. *Zeitschrift für Papyrologie und Epigraphik* 189, pp. 241–53.

Eck, W. Pangerl, A. and Weiß, P. 2014b. Ein drittes Exemplar des Edikts Hadrians zugunsten von Prätorianern vom Jahr 119 n. Chr. *Zeitschrift für Papyrologie und Epigraphik* 191, pp. 266–8.

Faoro, D. M. 2014. Appuleius, Sex. filius, legatus. Augusto, Tridentum e le Alpi orientali. *Aevum* 87, pp. 99–124.

Fernández Gómez, F. and Del Álamo y De La Hera, M. 1990. *La lex Irnitana y su contexto arqueológico*. Servilla.

Galsterer, H. 1988. Municipium Flavium Irnitanum. A Latin town in Spain. *Journal of Roman Studies* 78, pp. 78–90.

Galsterer, H. 2006. Die römischen Stadtgesetze. In: L. Capogrossi Colognesi and E. Gabba (eds.), *Gli Statuti Municipali*. Pavia, pp. 31–56.

González, J. and Crawford, M. H. 1986. The Lex Irnitana, a New Flavian Municipal Law. *Journal of Roman Studies* 76, pp. 147–243.

Isaac, B. 2009. Latin in Cities of the Roman Near East. In: H. M. Cotton, R. G. Hoyland, J. J. Price, and D. J. Wasserstein (eds.), *From Hellenism to Islam: Cultural and Linguistic Change in the Roman Near East*. Cambridge, pp. 43–72 [= In: B. Isaac, 2017. *Empire and Ideology in the Graeco-Roman World*. Cambridge, pp. 257–84].

Isaac, B. 2017. Caesarea-on-the-Sea and Aelia Capitolina: Two Ambiguous Roman Colonies, In: C. Brélaz, (ed.) *L'héritage Grec des colonies Romaines d'Orient. Interactions culturelles dans les provinces hellénophones de l'empire romain*. Paris, pp. 331–43.

Kaser, M. 1959. *Das römische Privatrecht 1: Das altrömische, das vorklassische und klassiche Recht* (Handbuch der Altertumswissenschaft 10.2.2.1). München.

Lamberti, F. 1993. *Tabulae Irnitanae. Municipalità e 'ius Romanorum'*. Napoli.

Letta, C. 2007. Fragmentum Segusinum. Due frammenti a lungo ignorati della *lex municipalis* di Segusio. In: G. Paci, ed. *Contributi all'epigrafia d'Età augustea. Actes della XIIIe rencontre franco-italienne sur l'épigraphie du monde romain*. Tivoli, pp. 145–69.

Piso, I. 2000. Legiones Daciae. In: Y. Le Bohec and C. Wolff (eds.), *Les légions de Rome sous le Haut-Empire*. Paris, pp. 204–25.

Raepsaet-Charlier, M.-Th. 1998. Les Gaules et les Germainies. In: C. Lepelley (ed.), *Rome et l'integration de l'Empire 44 av. J.-C.–260 ap. J.-C. Tome 2: Approches régionales du Haut-Empire romain*. Paris, pp. 143–95.

Rafetseder, N. 2018. Die Stadtgesetzfragmente der *colonia Ulpia Traiana Ratiaria*: Ein Ergänzungsversuch, *Zeitschrift für Papyrologie und Epigraphik* 207, pp. 274–7.

Sharankov, N. 2017. A Verse Epitaph and Other Unpublished Inscriptions from *Heraclea Sintica*. *Archaeologia Bulgarica* 21:1, pp. 15–38.

Speidel, M. A. 1992. Roman Army Pay Scales. *Journal of Roman Studies* 82, pp. 87–106 [= In: M. A. Speidel, 2009. Herr und Herrschaft im römischen Reich der hohen Kaiserzeit. Stuttgart, pp. 351–80].

Speidel, M. A. 2007. Honesta missio. Zu Entlassungsurkunden und verwandten Texten. In: M. A. Speidel and H. Lieb (eds.), *Militärdiplome. Die Forschungsbeiträge der Berner Gespräche von 2004*. Stuttgart, pp. 293–326.

Ubl, Hannsjörg (ed.) 1997. *Katalog zur Schausammlung 'Römerzeit' des Museums Lauriacum-Enns* 2. Enns.

Vittinghoff, Fr. 1994. Die Bedeutung der Legionslager für die Entstehung römischer Städte an der Donau und in Dakien. In: Vittinghoff, Fr. (W. Eck (ed.)) *Civitas Romana. Stadt und politisch-soziale Integration im Imperium Romanum der Kaiserzeit*. Stuttgart, pp. 89–105.

Vittinghoff, Fr. 1977. Zur römischen Municipalisierung des lateinischen Donau-Balkanraumes. Methodische Bemerkungen. *Aufstieg und Niedergang der römischen Welt* II.6, pp. 4–51.

Wedenig, R. 1997. *Epigraphische Quellen zur städtischen Administration in Noricum.* Klagenfurt.

Wolf, J. G. 2011. *Die Lex Irnitana. Ein römisches Stadtrecht aus Spanien. Lateinisch und Deutsch.* Darmstadt.

Wolff, H. 1986. Die Entwicklung der Veteranenprivilegien vom Beginn des 1. Jh. v. Chr. bis auf Konstantin d. Gr. In: W. Eck and H. Wolff (eds.) *Heer und Integrationspolitik. Die römischen Militärdiplome als historische Quelle.* Köln, pp. 44–115.

17

Roman City-Laws of Spain and their Modelling of the Religious Landscape

Meret Strothmann

1. PRELIMINARY OBSERVATIONS

City-laws represent the political order; they model social relations and ensure the transparency of duties and responsibilities in urban societies. The rules contained in city-laws concern both Roman citizens and *incolae*. However, in the case of cultic matters, it is interesting that, while many rules deal with official Roman civic cults, only a few concern the cults of the indigenous population. The main purpose of this paper is to consider whether this gap reflects the intention of the founder of *municipia* and *coloniae*, i.e. the Roman state, or if it is due to the incomplete nature of some of our texts.

My assumption is that the Roman state, which formulated the city-laws, was aware of the *incolae* and of their indigenous cults, and that the lack of specific regulations was intentional; for the handling of indigenous cults could prove problematic for the city-state and the *incolae* themselves. Spain is a region with an exceptional density of city laws,[1] and therefore is the natural starting point for research on this subject. The aim of the Roman state was to romanize the Iberian peninsula as a whole, with its very diverse cultural contexts, but it had to operate carefully and with due consideration of the specifics of each region.[2]

In general, cities played a central role in the making of the Roman Empire as an integrated political and even social space,[3] and, in terms of organizing life in the

[1] From Baetica we know the *lex Ursonensis* (ILS 6087, FIRA I 21, Crawford (1996) vol. 1, no. 25), the *lex Malacitana* (ILS 6089, FIRA I 24), the *lex Salpensana* (ILS 6088, FIRA I 23), and the *lex Irnitana* (see Wolf (2011)). Panzram (2002) refers to the list of the city-laws which were found in Beltrán Lloris (1999), esp. 29–35.

[2] For the organization of the provinces of the Iberian peninsula cf. Alföldy (2007). He mentions two new provinces, *Transduriana provincia* and *provincia Hispania superior* existing in the time of the princeps Augustus. Both are known from recent inscriptions. See Alföldy (2007), especially at 327–8. For the fourteen *conventus* in Spain see Kulikowski (2006), especially at 130–1; see also Beltrán Lloris (2015).

[3] Liebeschuetz (2001); for euergetism as a system that divided the social classes while at the same time transcending them, see Goffin (2012).

Meret Strothmann, *Roman City-Laws of Spain and their Modelling of the Religious Landscape* In: *Law in the Roman Provinces.* Edited by: Kimberley Czajkowski and Benedikt Eckhardt in collaboration with Meret Strothmann,
Oxford University Press (2020). © Oxford University Press.
DOI: 10.1093/oso/9780198844082.003.0017

provinces, it was the main task of Roman magistrates to model communication between Rome and her subjects. This specifically Roman project was not invented by the emperors, but as it helped to bolster their own position, it did become one of their priorities. We see this reflected in numerous inscriptions, cults and coinage. The foundation itself of new political units like the *municipia* and colonies with Latin or Roman right originally had this function.[4] While living in their own, distinct social sphere, people were bound to urban spaces that provided room for the representation of the imperial project—like fora, graves, or official cult-places, to name but a few.

Within this setting, local elites were respected with regard to their social rank. They were either grouped together with Roman citizens in a typical Roman colony of soldiers, or they were placed as now newly made Roman elites into a Roman *municipium*, sometimes also together with Roman citizens. They were thus integrated into the Roman world, along with its structure of political participation, and organization of space and time. Their main problem was how to deal with indigenous cultural and religious settings, and how to further maintain their status as local elites vis-à-vis the non-elite indigenous inhabitants.

These newly formed elites therefore became the binding link between Rome and the local population. This is relatively well known for Gaul, which became an integral part of the Roman Empire within a very short period of time. About a hundred city-states were founded in the course of the first century of Roman rule. For Gaul we can confidently state that by means of these city-states, the landscape as a whole was brought into the imperial domain.[5] For Spain the situation is much more complex.[6] While we know some city-laws from Spain, none survive from Gaul.

Strabo tells us about the Iberian situation in the Augustan era, when for the first time the entire peninsula belonged to the Roman Empire.[7] There are two points in his description of Spain that seem characteristic of the region. First, he states that there are very different cultural spaces in the region, and secondly, that the level of civilization differs greatly from place to place. There are some overarching reasons behind this: first, geographical factors played a large role in this variation, as the Iberian space was divided into large regions where resources were scarce, and some others of considerable wealth. Secondly, the region encompassed both Iberian and Celtic culture without any clear differentiation. The history of different places within the region therefore varies immensely. In the south, at the coast of the Mediterranean sea, wealthy political units emerged, and indeed before the Roman occupation the Carthaginians had controlled the cultural and political

[4] In general, see Lintott (1993); Galsterer (2000).

[5] For the political units, organized in towns or *vici* in Gaul, see Loseby (2006), especially at 103. He demonstrates that the towns in Gaul changed radically, which is an important indicator of the extraordinary rank of towns in Gaul. For the *conventus* at Gaul cf. Haensch (1997).

[6] For the cities in Spain and their importance see Curchin (1991) and Kulikowski (2004); Kulikowski (2006). A list of the *oppida* in Spain may be found at Pliny, *Naturalis historia* 3.7; 3.24–5; 4.117. On the Latin colonies in Spain and their communication with Rome, see Garcia Fernandez (2015).

[7] Strabo 3.17–20 reports about the structure of land and society on the Celtiberic peninsula. See also Pliny, *Naturalis historia* 3. 7–30, cf. Pliny's description of Baetica as a country of high civilization and culture (Pliny, *Naturalis historia* 3.7).

space of this southern area. The integration of Spain into the Roman Empire was not a fast process; it took about 150 years overall.[8]

To sum up: Spain as a whole did not exist, neither as a cultural space nor as a political unit. This was presumably the reason why the Romans divided Spain into very different and unequal provinces, even in terms of their size.

2. THE CITY-LAWS

The city-laws of Spain all belong to only one of these provinces, namely Baetica. To the south of the Tarraconensis, Baetica was the most civilized region of Spain.[9] There were many Roman cities, presumably all of them with a territory that they controlled. So Baetica was organized more like Gaul than most of the rest of Spain. We shall see shortly what this meant with respect to their religious landscape.

While city-laws have been found only at very few places, they were supposed to have universal relevance; they did not aim to capture the diversity of the civilization and cults of the Iberian provinces. We may assume that such laws must have existed for cities in Gaul and elsewhere too with little variation. There must be a reason why the diversity of cults and sacred concepts is not mirrored in the city-laws: one solution might be that only those matters that were important for the effective administration of the region were regulated, but many other things were by intention not dealt with.

The text of later Iberian laws can be completed by setting the various *leges* alongside each other: the Flavian *Lex Irnitana* may be supplemented with the *Lex Malacitana* and with the *Lex Salpensana* from about the same time. These city-laws are historical sources with two very important features: first, they show the principles of communication between Rome and cities in the West that governed themselves according to a Roman legal framework; and secondly, they provide a basis for empire-wide communication about some of the essentials of the Roman cultural and political sphere.

2.1. *Religion, Magistrates, and Priests in the City-Laws: the* Lex Ursonensis

Only one of these city-laws tells us anything concrete about modelling the religious landscape, but we can assume that the lack of such instructions in other laws is merely due to a lack of preservation. The relevant text is the *Lex Ursonensis*, a law given by Caesar at the very end of his life.[10] Caesar's first purpose

[8] See especially Richardson (1996); Curchin (2004), 69–95; Curchin (1991), 10–39; Keay (1988), 8–24.

[9] Alföldy assumes that the province was under imperial and not under senatorial government in the mid-third century, because A. Caecina Tacitus undertook his tasks as *legatus principis* and not as a regular *proconsul*. He also practised as *sacerdos VIIvir epulonum*: see Alföldy (1995), especially at 40–1.

[10] ILS 6087 (CIL II 5439; FIRA 1, 21). See Crawford (1996), vol. I, 393–454 on the *Lex Coloniae Genetivae*; he argues that 'the style of the letters makes it clear that the text was engraved in the Flavian

in founding this Roman colony was to settle veterans, but it is also evident that—perhaps more than in later laws—he tried to leave the social and political system of Urso autonomous as far as possible. If the assumptions outlined above are correct, this is relevant for modelling the landscape of the area. We know that religion was a central theme of communication in the Roman empire, as may be seen in its function within the provincial councils, and in the important role of religious communication with and about the emperor.

The organization of cults within a Roman framework was a central task for the political units themselves, especially when creating the local calendar. Some paragraphs in the *lex Ursonensis* are central for our understanding of how the religious landscape was mapped in these laws. The passages from § 64 to § 72 and § 91 deal with priests and their duties. The first thing to note is the combination of the tasks and the election of magistrates and priests.[11] There was no attempt to differentiate priests from magistrates and preserve religious authority as authority *sui generis*, as Jörg Rüpke has pointed out.[12] Some special priests, the pontiffs and augurs, were selected—when they were not coopted—in the same manner as magistrates, following a completely different practice from standard Roman procedure; in addition, the magistrates undertook tasks for which the priests were usually responsible. Thus, in the law of the colony of Urso the first *duumviri* had to propose to the decurions the festival days and the sacrifices to be performed in the public sphere.[13] This amounts to no less than the city's competence not only to formulate the calendar for the year, but also to decide which cults should become public and who would be able (and have the responsibility) to carry out official sacrifices. The nomination had to be accepted by the decurions in order to

period and not in the Caesarian age. But this is not in itself a reason for supposing that the text was substantially altered in the course of the intervening century or so' (at 395, introduction to the Lex). See also Rüpke (2006), especially at 34–5.

[11] Tasks of the magistrates in general: The IIviri, aedile or prefect during his own year is to act and see that *magistri* be appointed for the *fana*, temples and shrines;... and that they... see that games in the circus, sacrifices, and preparing of couches for the gods take place (§ 128). They also took care of the *loca religiosa*: The IIviri or aediles are also to see to the demolishing of a *monumentum mortui* built in the boundaries of the town or the colony. No one is allowed to bring a dead person within the boundaries of a town or of a colony, to bury him there or to burn him in the boundaries of the town. If a dead person shall have been brought in or deposited contrary of these rules, they are to make expiation as shall be appropriate (§ 73).

[12] Rüpke (2006), especially at 44. The following remarks on the *lex Ursonensis* mainly refer to Rüpke's paper.

[13] § 64 *IIviri quicumque post colon(iam) deductam erunt ii in die/bus X proxumis quibus eum mag (istratum) gerere coeperint at/decuriones referunto cum non minus duae partes/aderunt quos et quot dies festos esse et quae sacra/fieri publice placeat et quos ea sacra facere place/at quot ex eis rebus decurionum maior pars qui/tum aderunt decreverint statuerint it ius ratum/que esto eaque sacra eique dies festi in ea colon(ia)/sunto* (All duumvirs holding office after the establishment of the colony shall bring, within ten days next following the commencement of their magistracy, before the decurions, when not less than two thirds are present, the question as to the dates and the number of festal days, the sacrifices to be publicly performed, and the persons to perform such sacrifices. Whatever a majority of the decurions present at such meeting decree or determine concerning the said matters, it shall be lawful and valid, and such sacrifices and such festal days shall be observed in the said colony).

become valid. The *duumviri* were competent for another important task which, at Rome, was usually taken over by the priests:

> Whatever sum shall have been brought into public hands as a penalty on account of the revenues which shall belong to the *colonia Genetiva Iulia*, no-one is to have the power to pay it out or to give or assign it to anyone, except for those sacrifices which may be performed in the colony or any other place in the name of the colonists. (…) And the IIviri without personal liability are to give and assign that money for those sacrifices,…and they are to have the right and power to do it. (§ 65)[14]

There is more: the *duumviri* are directly connected to the cult of Jupiter, Juno and Minerva, because 'during their magistracy [they] are to organize a show or dramatic spectacle for Jupiter, Juno and Minerva, and the gods and goddess (*deis deabusq(ue)*)' (§ 70).[15] This also applies to the aediles, who must likewise organize shows or spectacles to Jupiter, Juno and Minerva, albeit for only three days (§ 71);[16] the spectacles of the *duumviri* had to last for four. The aediles are not instructed to celebrate 'gods and goddesses'; only the IIviri had the opportunity to choose and include them. The following chapter is rather unclear in its definitions:

> Whatever sum shall have been given or brought in to the sacred temples,…, whatever of that sum shall be left over from those sacrifices, which sacrifices shall have been performed, as it shall be appropriate for them according to this statute, for that god or goddess (*deo deaeve*), whose temple it shall be, no one is to act or see or to intercede to the effect that it may not be spent in that temple, to which temple that sum shall have been given or brought together under the character of an offering, nor is anyone to spend that money for any other purpose nor is anyone to the effect that it rather be spent on any other matter. (§ 72)[17]

Both passages use the terms 'god' and 'goddess'; the deities are intentionally left unnamed. The second case raises the scenario of someone who wanted to bring an offering to a god or goddess of his choice being prevented from doing so. The terms *facito—curato—intercedito* show that there are juridical concepts behind this. The actor here is a *civis*, but does this mean that the one bringing an offering was conclusively in every case a *civis*, or should non-citizens also be protected?

Besides the lictors, scribes and messengers, whoever acted as *duumvir* also had the right to have a haruspex and a flute-player. The aedile was also allowed to have these servants, in the same number. The naming of these priests in this context is interesting because they are directly subordinated to the magistrates; we know nothing about their official tasks. In the year in which he serves, the haruspex and all the other servants cannot be forced to administer an oath, nor is he to be requested to be bound by the regular military oath, except in the case of a *tumultus Italicus Gallicusve*.[18]

[14] Translation from Crawford.

[15] Translation from Crawford; see Crawford, *comm. ad locum*. It has also been suggested that in Chs. 70–71 *dies deabusq(ue)* has been added, but the occurrence of dedications *sei deo sei deae* does not support the view that sacrifices *dies deabusque* could not be described in a Caesarean statute (Crawford (1996), vol I, 395).

[16] Curchin (1991), 173. [17] Translation from Crawford.

[18] § 62, Crawford (1996), vol. 1, 433, comm. to § 62.

But what tasks are left to the regular priests and what sorts of priests do we encounter in the *lex*? Chapters 66 to 68 inform us about the priests, namely pontiffs and augurs, but the contents mainly concern priestly privileges, and few details are given about their tasks:

> Whichever pontiffs or whichever augurs C. Caesar shall have appointed... they are to be in the college of pontiffs or augurs in the same way as those who are or shall be pontiffs or augurs with the best conditions and the best status in any colony. For those and for their children is to be exemption from military service and compulsory public service. And those pontiffs and augurs at the games, whenever the magistrates shall give them publicly and when those pontiffs' augurs shall perform the public sacrifices..., are to have the right and power wearing togae praetextae.... and they have the right and power to watch the games and combats of gladiators among the decurions. (§ 66)

But some functions of the augurs are mentioned. We know from § 66 that 'Concerning auspices and whatever things shall pertain to those matters, jurisdiction and right of judgement are to belong to the augurs.' Their function therefore included *iuris dictio* and *iudicatio* (*auspiciorum*).[19] After the death or condemnation of a pontiff or augur, whoever was chosen or coopted to replace him was augur or pontiff in this college in the same way, and with all the corresponding rights that were attached to such roles in every colony.[20] No one was to be chosen or received or coopted as replacement except at a time when there were fewer than three pontiffs; the same applied to the augurs.[21] The peculiarity of this instruction has been discussed by Jörg Rüpke: he argues that there was no attempt to reproduce original Roman practice, but that there was instead a restriction of the college to the very minimum of what could be classified as a *collegium*. He also raises doubts about the adoption of the Roman procedure of *nominatio* by the college, because the remaining two members would not be strong enough to make the pre-selection of candidates socially acceptable.[22]

The term *sacerdos* is used only once, in Chapter 91 concerning the domicile of the pontiffs, augurs and decurions, appointed or elected.[23] The IIviri are to see that the names of the *sacerdotes* and decurions who failed to follow this instruction were removed from the public records. The sentences on public priests are also interesting in this respect. They follow Roman custom, but in the case of the pontiffs the possibility of caring for indigenous or new cults from another region is not ruled out.

It emerges from this discussion that at Urso, the priesthoods were partially subordinated to magistral power.[24] However, this applies only to the priests and tasks which are explicitly named. Thus, some matters were strictly regulated, but there are gaps to be filled with regard to non-public *sacra*. Private *sacra* were not mentioned and hence not regulated,[25] and it seems that these gaps were

[19] § 66, Crawford (1996), vol.1, 435, comm. to § 66. Linderski (1986), 2146–51, 2158–61.

[20] cf. *Lex Ursonensis* § 67.

[21] cf. *Lex Ursonensis* § 67.

[22] Rüpke (2006). 44. Mangas (1986), 339 assumed that the prescribed number of three *pontifices* was often reduced. For the priests see Curchin (1991), 166–70 and Mangas (1986), 338–40.

[23] *Lex Ursonensis* § 91.

[24] Rüpke (2006), 45.

[25] Rüpke (2006), 36: private religion is not regarded as an object of public legislation.

intentional. Anything that was not explicitly mentioned, and thus not expressly forbidden, must be considered allowed, as long as it did not directly contravene the instructions of the *lex*. These chapters of the law—if we understand them correctly—grant the city the ability to allow for religious diversity, and so would have enabled acculturation in one very important area.

2.2. *Religion, Cults, and Pontiffs in the City-Laws of the Principate: the* Lex Irnitana

After these remarks on religious practice and on priests and their duties we should now turn to the city-laws of the imperial period. Which sacred regulations do we know of, and what do they tell us about indigenous cults? Although very large parts of the *Lex Irnitana* have survived[26] that can be supplemented with passages from the *Lex Malacitana*[27] and the *Lex Salpensana*,[28] the laws tell us nearly nothing about indigenous cults. Julián González, in considering CIL VII 769 on the election of priests, argues that in the lost tables one might have found instructions concerning priesthoods in the Roman Empire,[29] and regulations on interactions between the priests, including definitions of their duties, as an expression of the priestly hierarchy. But in line with the theory outlined above concerning the lack of instructions in the *lex Ursonensis*, we might also assume that there was no fixed information about regulating cult and priestly hierarchy in the *Lex Irnitana*, with the exception of a few traces of matters concerning religion in §§ 77 and 79.

§77 deals with expenses for the religious observances, games and dinners which were to be provided. It is the only text about financial regulations for the *sacra*,[30] and besides §79 the only passage dealing with religion at all. The IIviri asked for the *inpensa ludorum sacrorum* and the decurions decided on the costs for the public religious festivals for the following year. In §79, one passage concerns the money for public religious festivals, meals and games where the decurions, the *conscripti* or the *cives* are to be invited. The *conscripti* or decurions had to decide on the sum of these costs. In general, this is all we find in the *lex* concerning religion.

The priesthoods of the augurs and pontiffs as mentioned in the *lex Ursonensis* are not found in the *lex Irnitana*. We have another *lex* from Gaul in the time of the principate: the *lex de officiis et honoribus flaminis provinciae Narbonensis*.[31] In this *lex*, we see *sacerdotes* worshipping the emperor,[32] but in the *lex Irnitana* we do not even find the term *sacerdos*. So no priests at all appear in the extant parts of the *lex*

[26] For the text see Wolf (2011). For the senatorial elite in the *lex Irnitana*, see Mentxaka (1993); on the meaning of the *lex* for integration into the Roman Empire, see Wolf (2006).

[27] *Lex Malacitana*, ILS 6089 (CIL II 1964, FIRA I 24).

[28] *Lex Salpensana*, ILS 6088 (CIL II 1963, FIRA I 23).

[29] González (2005), 85.

[30] See the commentary by González on this paragraph with hints at expenses for *sacra* in general and their administration, González (2005), 109–10.

[31] ILS 6964; CIL XII 6038; AE 1987, 749.

[32] On *sacerdotes* for worshipping the deified emperor in the Iberian provinces, see Alföldy (2007), 336–8.

Irnitana. We can assume that priests were mentioned in the *lex Irnitana* as in the *lex de officiis*, but were there also 'intentional gaps', as we have postulated for the *lex Ursonensis*? A door was certainly left open for emperor worship,[33] and Romans could take up high priestly positions as *VII epulonum*, as *sodalis*, as *sevir Augustalis* or at least as *flamen*, all of which are mentioned in inscriptions from the province.[34]

It is possible that the *lex de officiis et honoribus* was in some way connected with the *ius Latii*. If this *ius* applied in the whole peninsula,[35] a large number of people in the province would have had the chance to obtain the position of a priest for the imperial cult, as *sodalis* or *VIIvir epulonum*. If the *ius Latii* was given in the time of Vespasian through an *edictum*,[36] there might be a connection with the institution of emperor worship, the flaminate, and also with the *lex Salpensana* and *lex Malacitana*, as Sabine Panzram supposed.[37] There is another 'if': Estela Garcia Fernandez has argued that the *ius Latii* was granted as early as the Augustan era,[38] not under Vespasian, with consequences for the establishment of the highest priesthood of the province. Nothing certain is known about how to become a *flamen provincialis*. An inscription from Spain informs us about appointing the *flamines*,[39] and the earliest known *flamen* for the province of Baetica is Sempronius Speratus in 98 CE.[40] Perhaps the grant of the *ius Latii* to Spain was connected with the priesthood of the *flamines*. We are informed about the honours and privileges of these priesthoods by the *lex de officiis et honoribus flaminis provinciae Narbonensis* (above), issued in Gaul but probably followed in Spain as well. Unfortunately, it is not certain whether the name of Augustus or of Vespasian is to be supplied in the gap in lines 13 and 26, so once again we cannot be sure about the date of this document. The special honours and privileges given to the *flamen* priesthood are remarkable, and included the following: the right to erect a statue for oneself (l. 11), to be *praetextatus* during a sacrifice (ll. 15–16), and to have lictors in accordance with political competences. The *flaminica* is also mentioned (l. 6), and there are some instructions about touching a dead person (l. 7). We can

[33] On the beginning of the ruler cult and its starting point in Augustan time see Curchin (1991), 161–3.

[34] Some examples can be given: for *sacerdos*:

- *L. Cornel[ius] Heracla[nus] sa[ce]rd[os]*, AE 2009, 528 from the end of the first century CE.
- Q. Pomponius Munatianus Clodianus was a *sodalis Titiali* (see Alföldy (1995), 41).
- A pontifex from Barcino: C. Cilnius Pomptina Ferox, *pont.; cos. suff.* from 87 CE. He was a member of the Roman collegium of the pontiffs; see Alföldy (1969), 126.
- For *VII epulonum: L. Funisulanus L.f. Ani Vettonianus VII epulonum*, probably *cos. suff.* in 87 CE; see Alföldy (1969), 126. The other *VII epulonum* is interesting. A. Caecina Tacitus was an imperial *legatus*, but he is not a proconsul. Alföldy gave a new reading of the inscription AE 1929, 158 set up by Rutilius Prudens Crispinus and presumed a change in the status of the Province Baetica in the middle of the third century CE. Baetica was no longer a senatorial province, but now one that belonged to the emperor. See Alföldy (1995), especially at 40.

[35] Panzram (2002), 177.

[36] Plin. *Nat.* 3.30. For the date of the *lex*, see Panzram (2002), 177 including more literature and further arguments at n. 253; Kulikowski (2006), 131 discusses the function of the *lex Flavia municipalis* for the Romanization and integration of the towns into the Roman society *in toto*.

[37] The connection between the *edictum* and the *lex* is denied by Millar (1977), 404–405. See also Panzram (2002), 177, n. 248.

[38] Garcia Fernandez (2015), especially at 116.

[39] CIL II 5124.

[40] CIL II^2 7.799, see Panzram (2002), 173 n. 230.

assume some parallels to the *flamines* in Rome. We are also informed about the honours and privileges of the *seviri Augustales*. They are allowed to receive *decurionalia ornamenta*, to receive a *funus publicum*, to have a *subsellium* and sometimes *immunitas*.[41] But again we have no specifics remarks on the defined tasks and functions either of the *flamines* or of the *Augustales*.[42] The *Augustales* represent a special group of participants because they often were freedmen: they were below the level of imperial representatives, but above the ordinary *plebs*; perhaps they sometimes followed the decurions in making decisions. Thus, we can see a few overlaps with the tasks of the decurions, as seen in the *lex Ursonensis*, where the decurions in some cases took over the tasks of the priests.

In the city-laws, there are no regulations on ruler-cult, just as there are none on indigenous and private cults. This fits our theory that such regulations are not simply lost because of the fragmentary state of the inscriptions. Ruler-cult was little regulated, because creativity was an essential part of it: local initiatives gave elites opportunities to communicate with the emperor in ways appropriate to their situation. The regulations about priests were presumably more synchronized with central Roman practice than the opportunities to honour the ruler. Indeed, there are only a few redactional hints at ruler-cult, especially in §§ 31 and 92. The *Lex* confirms that business will not be conducted during festivals of the imperial cult.[43] But there is one element that clearly indicates a modelling of the religious landscape. This is the new formula of the oath, sworn by various groups and demanded on two occasions: when a decision pertains to the whole community of the *municipium*,[44] and when a rule is not firmly fixed and leaves some space for individual decisions.[45] This fits our theory perfectly. Decisions had to be made but there were intentionally open spaces for individual actions. People had to be aware that they had responsibilities to the Roman government. The responsibility would be acknowledged by swearing an oath: this was a specific, religious element, so the oath had to be repeated *in toto* whenever necessary, and was sworn by the prefect, the magistrates, the *legatus*, the elected candidates, the *scriba*, and the *IIviri*. In such cases the people who were responsible had to justify their actions and their decisions. The oath was sworn by Jupiter, by the *divus Augustus, divus Claudius, divus Vespasianus, divus Titus*, the Genius of Domitian and the *penates* (of the imperial household). The oath appears six times in the municipal legislation.[46] Furthermore, the oath emphasized the differentiation between the worship of an emperor who was dead and one who was alive. It was not the same thing to worship a dead, deified emperor and a living one—not even under Domitian. This part of the *lex* tied gods and *cives* together directly, and added a juridical aspect to the oath.

In what ways were the indigenous inhabitants who wanted to perform their own cults subjected to the regulations of this law? Like the god in the *lex Ursonensis*, the

[41] Vandevoorde (2012), especially at 413.

[42] Vandevoorde (2012) tells us much about the symbolic capital while Duthoy (1974) discusses the social function, but neither offers information about concrete tasks.

[43] Curchin (1991), 172–73.

[44] *Lex Irnitana* § 26; *Lex Malacitana* § 59, *Lex Irnitana* § 79, 50–6.

[45] *Lex Irnitana* § 25, 25–6; § 45; § 73.

[46] At §§ 25, 26, 45, 59 (*lex Mal.*), 73 and 79; Wolf (2011), 31.

term *incolae* remained vague. They were conceived as part of the whole population of the city, as mentioned in the oath above. In one further instance we can see how the Roman government thought about integration, and how it allowed space for local ideas and concepts, in sacral as in legal respects. §§ 93 and 94 give specific insights into the juristic interaction between the *incolae* and the Romans, and on how to apportion jurisdiction between the two.[47] Paragraph 93 deals with matters that are not covered in the law, and orders the *municipes* to use the *ius civile* of the Romans. On first sight there seems to be a contradiction between the passages in this *lex* that intentionally do not stipulate to which law the *municipes* are bound and the paragraphs in which they are directed to follow the *ius civile.* We have to be aware that Roman law was not strictly fixed in detail, and so each juridical actor in the Roman Empire had to find a way of solving problems within the limits of the law. In addition, all juristic matters that were not carried out in direct opposition to the regulations of the Flavian Law would have been allowed and accepted. In fact, this is an invitation for autonomous action as long as it did not contravene the law. Many matters were intentionally not fixed in the law, so the *municipes* had to decide on their own what course to follow. This was entirely deliberate. Like the *municipes* in §93, the *incolae* had to obey these regulations, as emerges from §94. The instruction might be seen as a privilege, allowing the *incolae* to be equal to the *municipes,* since they could also act autonomously when they conformed with the law. They are, like the *municipes*, subject to the authority of the aediles and *IIviri.* The *incolae* are liable to *operae* (§ 83), but have no access to manumission or *tutela* (§§ 28, 29).[48]

3. HOW TO MODEL THE RELIGIOUS LANDSCAPE

3.1. *Spain as an Amalgamation of Roman and Indigenous Gods*

150 years separate the city laws of Urso and Irni. It is surprising—but only on initial consideration—that control over sacred rites changed very little in this long period of time. The terms remained relatively vague, with the exception of the formula for the oath for the Roman emperor. The connections between ruler cult

[47] § 93: *R de iure municipum. Quibus de rebus in H L nominatim cautum[ve] scriptumve non est quo iure inter se municipes municipi Flavi Irnitani agant de iis rebus omnibus ii inter se <eo i>ure agunto quo cives Romani inter se iure civili agunt. Agent quod adversus H L non fiat quodque ita actum gestum conprehensumque erit id ius ratumqze esto. § 94 R de incolis. Huic legi uti municipes parere debebunt ita eius municipi* incolae *parento* (Rubric. Concerning the law of the *municipes.* On whatever matters there is no explicit provision or rule in this statute, concerning the law under which the *municipes* of the Municipium Flavium Irnitanum should deal with each other, they are to deal with each other in all these matters under the civil law under which Roman citizens deal or will deal with each other. Whatever does not take place contrary to this statute and whatever is done in such a way that it does not take place or is not done with wrongful intent, is to be legal and valid. § 94 Rubric. Concerning *incolae.* As the *municipes* should obey this statute, so the *incolae* of that *municipium* are to obey (it).). Translation from Gonzalez (1986).

[48] These results are from González (2005), 122–3.

and the oath for the emperor has not yet been discussed in detail.[49] The oath to the emperor surely shows some orientation around the current *princeps*; it offered an opportunity to attribute the prosperity of the present to him. How declarations of loyalty were managed and organized in practice and how different the forms could be is left to our imagination. It is, however, clear that whatever was not in opposition to the existing law was permitted; the people who held positions of responsibility therefore had to decide how to proceed on a case by case basis. And all who performed these functions had to be aware that they were obliged to the gods while swearing their oath of office. Detailed regulations and arrangements for the ruler-cult were only made by the *collegia* of the priests and were derived from the special duties and functions of these *collegia* as *sodales*, *flamines*, and *VIIviri epulonum*; they were not specified in the *lex de officiis*. Thus the ruler cult offered a proper way to put on display hierarchical differences between civic communities.

The collective veneration of the single emperor made the people of Spain part of a common whole, side by side with others, in the context of becoming Roman with the same rights as Romans themselves. With this it became possible to accelerate the process of religious synchronization of all regions, and of the centre itself. For Spain it seems that this was not as easy as in other provinces, because of the rather different religious concepts that Rome encountered. The Celto-Iberian religious belief consisted not only of special gods that were comparable to Roman gods, but also included a veneration of some animal-gods, as well as some mystic elements.[50] We also have testimonies of the influence of oriental gods[51] and mystery cults.[52] One can assume that this process of synchronization occurred in different ways and was reliant on the ability of the indigenous peoples to make changes in their own religious concepts or even in their manner of veneration.

3.2. Deus et dea

There is very little evidence as to what might lie behind the terms *deus et dea* as mentioned in the *lex Ursonensis*. Which deities were meant, or could have been meant, and who the people responsible for their cult were, shall be investigated shortly. For the moment, we can assume that indigenous gods and cults were meant. These were mostly venerated in private spaces, and sometimes they had to share the public sphere with Roman deities. In some Hispanic regions Roman inscriptions show only a few indigenous cults—Baetica, for example—, whereas in other regions indigenous cults stayed alive for a long time.[53] We should here recall

[49] The contribution of Cancik (2003) discusses the function of the oath as a sign of loyalty towards the emperor and an instrument to control the inhabitants of the provinces. The first oath given by citizens of the provinces of 'Gallia, Hispania' and others is mentioned in the *Res Gestae* 25. Because there was the same formula in the West and East of the empire, Cancik (2003), 35 assumes that the oath was not a local initiative but imposed from above.

[50] On religion in Spain in general, see Keay (1988), 145–71 and Blázquez (1986), 164–275. The literary evidence is very scarce: see the remarks on Strabo and Cicero by Blázquez (1986), 168–9.

[51] Bendala Galán (1986), 345–402.

[52] Curchin (1991), 163–5; Bendala Galán (1986), 380–93.

[53] On the inscriptions that mention indigene goddesses see Blázquez (1986), 167–73. He reports about the few inscriptions in highly Romanized regions like the Baetica and more in the less Romanized provinces in the North, central area, and the West.

that the surviving city laws originated from Baetica. One may therefore ask whether in other regions there was no such legal capacity for religious modelling, whether no religious modelling was necessary in these regions, and why the indigenous cults became less attractive in this particular province.

It is interesting that evidence for public cults of indigenous gods is very rare or even missing for Spain as a whole. From inscriptions we know of just a few centres where indigenous gods were worshipped: for example, the god Velicus from Postoloboso, in the area of Avila in Lusitania.[54] But many other apparently genuine native gods are honoured, and we know of approximately 320 indigenous gods.[55] Other dedications are to native gods 'covered' by Roman names, Matres, Nymphae and I.O.M.[56] It is clear that less acculturated natives tended to dedicate to native gods. The names in inscriptions from Postoloboso confirm this. No non-native names appear on such dedications. In dedications to 'covered' deities, native names again occur, but with a mixture of freedperson or slave names: perhaps they picked up the Roman practice and combined two concepts of religion.[57] The region of Avila shows many indications of strong native influences on the life of its inhabitants, and the second century CE in particular shows an interesting amalgamation of native and Roman ideas, recorded on grave-stones with the Roman formula *D(is) M(anibus)*. According to the argument advanced above concerning the priests and rules mentioned in the *lex Ursonensis*, indigenous cults are left out.[58] As we can assume that native cults were cared for by natives, perhaps the cults which had a public aspect are dealt with in the law, but private cults are set aside.

A possible dividing line can thus be reconstructed between public and private. But what is 'private'—is it always the unmentioned? Again, an inscription casts some light on the matter, connecting public–Roman and private–native in a special context. The *cives et incolae* the Municipium Liberum Singiliense,[59] south-east from Irni, dedicated an inscription to Marcus Valerius Proculinus, one of the duumviri. The duumvir in his current year of office (109 CE) celebrated *publicos ludos* et *totidem dierum privatos*. He also took care of providing oil and baths for the *populus universus* living in the *municipium*, as well as for the *incolae*. On the last day of his magistracy, *cives* and *incolae huic gratias egerunt ob rem publicam bene administratam consensu omnium* and dedicated a statue. The *ordo decurionum* granted permission to choose this place. The *cives* and *incolae*

[54] The following observations are taken from Knapp (1992), 405–408.

[55] Blázquez (1986), 167.

[56] On the transition to Roman deities see Curchin (2004), 177–92 and on the Romanization of beliefs, the chapter in Curchin (1991), 154–77. For details of a goddess like Minerva, see Blázquez (1986), 258–60; for the veneration of Jupiter Optimus Maximus in detail see Mangas (1986), especially at 289–94.

[57] Curchin (2004), 177: 'The persistence, without conscious paradox, of indigenous deities alongside Roman deities can be interpreted as an integration of old and new memes, as well as an illustration that religion is resistive to cultural convergence.' For the veneration of Roman gods in general, see Mangas (1986), 276–344.

[58] I am in complete agreement with Rüpke (2006), 37, who argues that 'there is religion outside public religion'; otherwise, the author would not need to emphasise *quae sacra fieri publice placeat* (*Lex Ursonensis* § 64).

[59] AE 1989, 420 with a photo, at Gómez-Pantoja (2009), 87–8.

explicitly honoured the duumvir concerning the festivals which were held publicly and privately, for an equal number of days. The specific term *totidem* could be understood as a differentiation between public festivals for the *cives* and private ones for the natives. The *populus universus* named later includes the *cives* and *municipes* living in town and the *incolae* in the city and its surroundings. All groups of the population had a reason to be thankful to the magistrate. The question remains how indigenous cults were related to the public sphere or even to some private or social spaces. If the public sphere itself were mainly based on Roman gods, people may have preserved cults for their own gods in other contexts. And in those other spheres, native gods could either disappear in the course of intensive acculturation, or remain present as happened in the north of Spain. As some religious concepts were compatible with both societies, like the veneration of a genius[60] or of springs, opportunities for acculturation would still have been available.

* * *

Since the inhabitants of the region were given the opportunity to act autonomously as long as they conformed with the *lex*, we may reach the following conclusion with respect to the intention of the municipal law, and the realities as evidenced by the inscription mentioned above: in religious practice, the communities of citizens and *incolae* were grouped together. The Romans offered to regulate their communication—but with permeable boundaries and complete integration of native customs. Thus the Romans decided that festivals connected with Roman magistracies should be celebrated together. But otherwise, their modelling of the religious landscape intentionally left many gaps that could be filled by the natives themselves.

REFERENCES

Alföldy, G. 1969. *Fasti Hispanienses. Senatorische Reichsbeamte und Offiziere in den spanischen Provinzen des römischen Reiches von Augustus bis Diokletian*. Wiesbaden.

Alföldy, G. 1995. Der Status der Provinz Baetica um die Mitte des 3. Jh. In: R. Frei-Stolba and M. Speidel (eds.), *Römische Inschriften—Neufunde, Neulesungen und Neuinterpretationen*. Basel and Berlin, pp. 29–42.

Alföldy, G. 2007. Fasti und Verwaltung der hispanischen Provinzen. Zum heutigen Stand der Forschung. In: R. Haensch and J. Heinrichs (eds.), *Herrschen und Verwalten. Der Alltag der römischen Administration in der Hohen Kaiserzeit*. Cologne, pp. 325–56.

Beltrán Lloris, F. 1999. Inscripciones sobre bronce: ¿un rasco característico de la cultura epigráfica de las ciudades hispanas? *Atti XI Congresso Internazionale di Epigrafia Greca e Latina. Roma, 18–24 settembre 1997*. Rome, pp. 22–37.

Beltrán Lloris, F. 2015. The Hospitium publicum of Gades and Cornelius Balbus. In: M. Jehne and F. Pina Polo (eds.), *Foreign Clientelae in the Roman Empire. A Reconsideration*. Stuttgart, pp. 142–51.

Bendala Galán, M. 1986. Die orientalischen Religionen Hispaniens in vorrömischer und römischer Zeit. *Aufstieg und Niedergang der römischen Welt* II.18.1, pp. 345–402.

[60] On the veneration of the Genius, see Blázquez (1986), 257–8.

Blázquez, J. M. 1986. Einheimische Religionen Hispaniens. *Aufstieg und Niedergang der römischen Welt* II 18.1, pp. 164–275.

Cancik, H. 2003. Der Kaiser-Eid. Zur Praxis der römischen Herrscherverehrung. In: H. Cancik and K. Hitzl (eds.) *Die Praxis der Herrscherverehrung in Rom und seinen Provinzen*. Tübingen, pp. 29–46.

Crawford, M. H. 1996. *Roman Statutes*. Two volumes. London.

Curchin, L. A. 1991. *Roman Spain*. London and New York.

Curchin, L. A. 2004. *The Romanization of Central Spain. Complexity, diversity and Change in a Provincial Hinterland*. London and New York.

Duthoy, R. 1974. La fonction sociale de l'augustalité *Epigraphica* 26, pp. 134–54.

Galsterer, H. 2000. Local and provincial institutions and government. In: A.K. Bowman, P. Garnsey, and D. Rathbone (eds.), *Cambridge Ancient History* XI, Cambridge, pp. 344–60.

Garcia Fernandez, E. 2015. Client Relationship and the Diffusion of Roman Names in Hispania. In: M. Jehne and F. Pina Polo (eds.). *Foreign Clientelae in the Roman Empire. A Reconsideration*. Stuttgart, pp. 107–18.

Goffin, B. 2012. *Euergetismus in Oberitalien*. Bonn.

González, J. 2005. *Epigrafía Jurídica de la Bética*. Rome.

González, J. 1986. The Lex Irnitana: A New Copy of the Flavian Municipal Law. *Journal of Roman Studies* 76, 147–243.

Gómez-Pantoja, J. L. 2009. *Epigrafia anfiteatrale dell'Occidente Romano, vol. VII. Baetica, Tarraconensis, Lusitania*. Rome.

Haensch, R. 1997. *Capita provinciarum. Statthaltersitze und Provinzialverwaltung in der römischen Kaiserzeit*. Mainz.

Keay, S. J. 1988. *Roman Spain*. London.

Knapp, R. C. 1992. *Latin inscriptions from Central Spain*. Berkeley.

Kulikowski, M. 2004. *Late Roman Spain and its Cities*. Baltimore.

Kulikowski, M. 2006. The Late Roman City in Spain. In: J.-U. Krause and C. Witschel (eds.), *Die Stadt in der Spätantike*. Stuttgart, pp. 129–52.

Liebeschuetz, J. H. W. G. 2001. *The Decline and Fall of the Roman City*. Oxford.

Linderski, J. 1986. The Augural Law. *Aufstieg und Niedergang der römischen Welt* II.16.3, pp. 2146–312.

Lintott, A. 1993. *Imperium Romanum: Politics and Administration*. London.

Loseby, S. T. 2006. Decline and Change in the Cities of Late Antique Gaul. In: J.-U. Krause and C. Witschel (eds.), *Die Stadt in der Spätantike—Niedergang oder Wandel*. Stuttgart, pp. 67–104.

Mangas, J. 1986. Römische Religion in Hispanien. *Aufstieg und Niedergang der römischen Welt* II 18.1, pp. 276–344.

Mentxaka, R. 1993. *El senado municipal en la Bética hispana a la luz de la Lex Irnitana*. Vitoria.

Millar, F. G. B. 1977. *Emperor in the Roman world*. Ithaca.

Panzram, S. 2002. *Stadtbild und Elite: Tarraco, Corduba und Augusta Emerita zwischen Republik und Spätantike*. Stuttgart.

Richardson, J. 1996. *The Romans in Spain*. Oxford.

Rüpke, J. 2006. Religion in the *lex Ursonensis*. In: C. Ando and J. Rüpke (eds.), *Religion and Law in Classical and Christian Rome*. Stuttgart, pp. 34–46.

Vandevoorde, L. 2012. Augustales and Decuriones. Sixteen Inscriptions from Narbonese Gaul. Latomus 71, pp. 404–23.

Wolf, J. G. 2006. The Romanization of Spain: The Contribution of the City Laws in the Light of the Lex Irnitana. In: A. Burrows and A. Rodger (eds.), *Mapping the Law. Essays in memory of Peter Birks*. Oxford, pp. 439–54.

Wolf, J. G. 2011. *Die Lex Irnitana. Ein römisches Stadtrecht aus Spanien. Lateinisch und Deutsch*. Darmstadt.

18

Public Law in Roman North Africa

Clifford Ando

1. INTRODUCTION

This volume studies the legal cultures of the provinces of the empire in historical perspective. Its primary focus concerns that which Ulpian denominates private law, or what in vernacular terms is called civil law.[1] The inquiry is historical in the broad sense, both as regards change in time and as regards the form of legal-historical inquiry. The focus of the project overall is therefore on socio-legal questions such as the scope of social relations subject to legal regulation, the interaction of Roman with indigenous legal traditions and their relative importance across time, the issue of knowledge of law, and the social position and origin of legal experts.

For the Romans, the histories of substantive law and law-making and law-applying institutions were inseparable from those of public law. To simplify, and put the matter another way, no question concerning what rule applied can be divorced from the questions of who had the power to make rules, who held jurisdiction, and on what basis. The paired chapters on Roman law in Africa are therefore divided in responsibility, between public law and administration (this chapter) and knowledge of law, legal experts and legal practice (that of Anna Dolganov).

For obvious reasons, public law is not typically a site of investigation for work on knowledge of law in colonial and imperial legal systems: structures of magistracy, rights and powers of law-making, rules of both jurisdiction and choice of law tend to be imposed by the metropole. This is a mistake, because premodern empires tended to be infrastructurally weak and therefore relied heavily on the cooptation and adaption of pre-existing institutions to actualize social orders—and, as a related matter, they tended to develop ideologies of sovereignty and law that recognized certain forms of diversity as constituent of imperial rule. To ignore the history of public law in writing the legal history of the Roman provinces is also a mistake because issues like municipalization, the spread of citizenship, and the history of mobility are so discrepant from one context to another.

In what follows, I first review aspects of the administration of Africa as bear on the development of public law institutions (section II). I then give detailed

[1] Ulpian, *Institutes*, Book 1 (D.1.1.2), fr. 1908 Lenel.

Clifford Ando, *Public Law in Roman North Africa* In: *Law in the Roman Provinces*. Edited by: Kimberley Czajkowski and Benedikt Eckhardt in collaboration with Meret Strothmann, Oxford University Press (2020). © Oxford University Press.
DOI: 10.1093/oso/9780198844082.003.0018

consideration to two instruments of public law, the *lex agraria* of 111 BCE (section III) and a *lex sacra* (or perhaps a *feriale*) from the colony of Carthage of the high imperial period (section IV). The one is a metropolitan enactment that looks toward the province, with a fantasy of control and an anxiety about knowledge; the other is a local enactment, which combines an informed nostalgia for the metropole with evident local pride.

2. AFRICA PROCONSULARIS UNDER ROMAN RULE

The surviving evidence now available for the scientific study of Roman North Africa, and the province of Proconsularis in particular, is extraordinarily robust. For reasons having to do with the history of modern empire, the archaeology and epigraphy of Algeria advanced rapidly in the earliest days of modern historical research, and the early twentieth century saw the production of two exemplary histories, Stéphane Gsell's monumental *Historie ancienne de l'Afrique du Nord* and T. R. S. Broughton's *The Romanization of Africa Proconsularis*.[2] The pace of both interpretive and empirical work has been remarkable, and it is now possible to write very sophisticated histories of Roman North Africa with nearly non-convergent agenda and, indeed, bibliographies. Cases in point include the recent survey by Yann Le Bohec (2005) and the interpretive monograph by David Mattingly (2011). Le Bohec periodizes his work in relation to temporality of metropolitan politics and assumes that policy and practice emanating from Rome drove aspects of local social and economic conduct, not least as regards the monumentalization of the landscape. Mattingly, by contrast, seeks to understand the experience of the victims of Roman imperialism. He seems to assume that recuperation of the memory and agency of those peoples requires one to set aside as without relevance (and, presumably, effect) the gloss of imperial institutions, not least those of public memory, that claimed to organize social life in the municipalities of Africa. What is more, rare is the work on Roman Africa that gives appropriate recognition to the historical imbrication of systems of conquest and control in the region: Africa was Carthaginian before it was Roman, and the nature and extent of Roman influence is perhaps best revealed by understanding first the nature and limits of social change under Carthage before one turns to social, material, demographic and agricultural change under Rome.[3]

Perhaps the most notable features of the history of Africa Proconsularis under Roman rule as it bears on legal institutions and legal practice are the belatedness of the flourishing of municipal life, and then its long history. In imperial perspective, Africa was subject to several moments of public law regulation and distinct waves of colonization. These last occurred in the aftermath of the annexation of Carthaginian territories in the second half of the second century BCE, under the influence of Julius Caesar, and in the reign of Augustus. However, in the case of North Africa (as sometimes elsewhere), the introduction of Roman colonists into

[2] Gsell (1914–30); Broughton (1929).

[3] Fentress (2006); see also Toynbee (1965), 1:28–38; Lancel (1995); Pilkington (2013).

pre-existing settlements often did not result in a change in the public law status of the community or the status of its inhabitants. Instead, as it seems, the community of Roman citizens was constituted as a public-law entity of its own (an *oppidum*, *pagus*, *conventus*, or what have you), spatially integrated but legally apart from the indigenous population.[4] Several consequences follow that are of relevance to this inquiry.

First, although it is possible to write a history of urbanism as an archaeological matter under the Julio-Claudians, such a history fails to capture the complexity of the legal and social relations that both united and disjoined the populations under Roman rule.[5] This is so in part because so many populations continued to be categorized as sub-municipal in their complexity and autonomy. Second, in many places, civic life becomes visible to us in North Africa comparatively late, in the second century CE, at which time many places still carry indigenous toponyms and elect magistrates under the Punic title *sufetes*.[6] (In some places, *sufetes* and *magistri* appear to be attested simultaneously.) It is only very late in the second century, above all under Septimius Severus, that many places are endowed with the status of autonomous city and their public institutions are reorganized accordingly.[7] This is not to say that there was not significant social interaction among populations, including intermarriage,[8] but it has implications for the status and use of local norms, as well as the use of law-applying institutions. (One should be wary about how one interprets this chronological pattern: evidence for the organization and holding of assizes by the governor also derives nearly wholly from the late second century CE.[9]) Third, one significant Roman practice, tightly and essentially related to institutions of law, that did penetrate local life throughout the area very early was so-called centuriation: the imposition of a Roman-style cadastral grid and the concomitant use of Roman systems of land tenure. The disruptions caused by appropriation, but perhaps also by the new system of title—in atomizing populations and monetizing land-tenure—were significant enough to motivate widespread revolt under Tiberius, about which the surviving narratives focus on the figure of Tacfarinas.[10] Fourth and last, these patterns, and many other factors besides, contribute to a remarkable efflorescence in both civic life and material culture more generally in high imperial and late antique North Africa, visible not only in a massive increase in urbanization but also in the penetration of Roman material cultures into the countryside.[11] The remarkable history of late ancient North Africa is, however, not part of this survey, as its apex falls well after the passage of the Antonine Constitution and legal revolution that the Constitution set in motion.

In what follows, I concentrate on two documents: the *lex agraria* of 111 BCE, namely, the first surviving public-law document concerned with Africa; and what has been published as a *lex sacra* of the cult of the Cereres from Carthage, but which might well be a *feriale* of the colony. In the one case, namely, the *lex agraria*,

4 Gascou (1982a). 5 Bullo (2002); see also Gascou (1981); Gascou (1982b).

6 Belkahia and Vita-Évrard (1995). 7 Gascou (1972), (1979), (1982b), and (1982c).

8 A topic studied in Cherry (1998), with attention to microregional patterns.

9 Lepelley (2001), 55–68.

10 Le Bohec (2005), 57–9; Fentress (2006), esp. 28–9, but her entire argument is apposite.

11 Lepelley (1979–81); Dossey (2010).

we have an example of metropolitan law-making but one that displays multiple kinds of deference *both* to pre-existing conditions and to local interpretive authorities; the other is a piece of local law-making that exhibits a remarkable sensitivity to a specifically Roman vocabulary and practice of cult, and at the very same directs worship to gods that had been taken up by colonial authorities from practices with roots far older than Roman control in the area.

3. PUBLIC LAW IN AFRICA PROCONSULARIS: THE FIRST THIRTY-FIVE YEARS. THE *LEX AGRARIA* OF 111 BCE

Writing the history of public law in the first decades of Roman control in North Africa is valuable and interesting for a number of reasons. First, thanks to the *lex agraria* of 111 BCE especially, but also the narrative of Appian, we are unusually well informed about the early history of Roman control.[12] Indeed, the *lex agraria* also provides extremely valuable information about the content of the *leges Livia* and *Rubria*, the first being the statute that confirmed the arrangements made by Scipio and the ten advisors dispatched by the Senate after the defeat of Carthage, the second being the statute passed at the urging of Gaius Gracchus in 122 to found a colony near the site of Carthage.[13] What is more, this overall information allows us to confirm some number of the significant details contained in Appian's narrative and enhances our degree of confidence about the rest. (Of course, the quality of Appian's information regarding the Third Punic War and the age of the Gracchi in particular is generally extremely high.)

Second, recent decades have witnessed a profound deepening in our knowledge of the early history of the province of Asia in particular: this is due above all to the inscriptions for Menippos and Polemaios of Colophon published by Jeanne and Louis Robert,[14] the *lex portorii Asiae*,[15] and the Pergamene text of 133 BCE published by Michael Wörrle in Chiron in 2000.[16] To this, one might add the now-earliest contemporary attestation for the delivery of *leges*—meaning, perhaps, a charter—to a Roman colony, to wit, a text from the supplementary deduction of colonists to Aquileia.[17] All this allows for a better appreciation of the information provided by Livy via Polybius regarding the public-law arrangements imposed by Rome on Macedonia after Pydna, and on Achaea after 146. To all this one might add the very significant evidence for Roman conceptions of provincial jurisdiction and of sovereignty over territory provided by Cicero's

[12] The *lex agraria* is cited from its edition in RS no. 2. The bibliography and commentary there may be supplemented by that in Lintott (1992).

[13] The *lex Livia*: *lex agraria* l. 77. The *lex Rubria*: *lex agraria* ll. 59–60. For the context see Appian, *Lib*. 135.639–136.645.

[14] Robert and Robert (1989).

[15] SEG 39, no. 1180; a translation (and text) is available in Cottier et al. (2008).

[16] Wörrle (2000).

[17] AÉ 1996, 685: *T(itus) Annius T(iti) f(ilius) tri(um) vir. | Is hance aedem | faciundam dedit | dedicavitque, legesq(ue) | composivit deditque, | senatum ter coptavit* (Titus Annius, son of Titus, triumvir. He provided for the construction of this temple and dedicated it. He formulated and enacted the laws. He recruited the senate three times.).

account of the *lex Rupilia*. In short, the decades from 167 to 111 BCE are the first era for which we can provide a significant history of Roman public law in the provinces. Indeed, the extraordinary care with which the legislation of this era makes reference to prior enactments—and, therefore, its silence in respect of enactments prior to this era—could well induce the belief that few if any significant public law enactments in regard to provincial administration existed before this period.[18]

As for what the *lex agraria* reveals about the history of law, to begin with, in the initial years of Roman control, not simply sovereignty over Africa, but legislation was understood to originate at Rome. This is clear from the prior public law enactments to which the *lex agraria* refers, including the *lex Livia*, which established the commission of ten advisors for Scipio after the defeat of Carthage (ll. 77–8; 78–82); the *lex Rubria* of 122, establishing the colony of Junonia (*lex agraria* ll. 55, 58–61); the institution of a schedule for the recording of property, its value and tax liability by the censors Lucius Caecilius and Cn. Domitius (115–114 BCE) (*lex agraria* ll. 85–7, 87–9); and the letting of a contract for those taxes by the consul of 113, Cn. Papirius (*lex agraria* l. 89). This fact is further emphasized by the occasional juxtaposition of references to land in Africa with locatives that situate authority at Rome, the most concise of which occurs in the first legible reference to Africa, but whose substantive import is not clear: *quei ager locus in Africa est, quei Romae publice*.... The coupling of the locative *Romae* with the legalitarian specification *publice* makes the stakes quite clear (*lex agraria* l. 48).

As a related matter, Roman-style government at this period generated knowledge, and it relied on knowledge. (Some of what I shall say at this juncture has implications for the now-popular position that the concept of the 'province' as a territorial unit of rule did not yet exist.) The information cited or required for the operation of the *lex agraria* includes the boundaries of lands assigned to free cities (*lex agraria* ll. 74–7, 78–82); lists of colonists and those enrolled among the citizens (*lex agraria* ll. 53, 55, 58–61, 66–7, etc.; more on this topic below); cadastral records of private property holdings by Roman colonists as well as those subject to poll taxes and taxes on land, and the information about persons and property clearly takes the form of both lists and maps (*lex agraria* ll. 58–61, 61–6, 70–2, 77–8, 78–82; implied at l. 89). Crucially, where specification is made, the records are to be held in Rome. Students of boundary disputes will immediately think of the famed decree of Lucius Helvius Agrippa from Sardinia regarding the boundary dispute between the Patulcenses and Galillenses, which records that a delay in the proceedings of three months was granted so that one party could consult the relevant *forma*, the map, kept in the *tabularium principis* at Rome.[19]

Some of the information that I have itemized is of the sort that one would expect to be included in the *forma* and *formula provinciae*. The word *formula* is not used in the *lex agraria*, though the IIvir appointed in consequence of it is charged with producing a *ratio* of the lands for which he affirms title or which he privatizes. I have already stressed that maps were very likely generated by the

[18] For the data on provincial administration in the republican period, Díaz Fernández (2015) is now essential.

[19] ILS 5947.

senatorial commission appointed *ex lege Livia*. The use of such instruments to specify land within a province exempt from taxation is clearly attested for Asia in letters of Trajan and Hadrian to Aphrodisias and is implied already in the decree in honor of Menippos, as well as in the *lex portorii Asiae*, although in the later clauses of that document, tax-free lands are separated from the relevant diocese and not the province.[20] As regards Africa, something like a schedule or taxonomy of types of persons and property was generated by Scipio and the senatorial commission appointed to assist in the organization of the province, or at the very latest by the censors of 115–114, whose *lex*, presumably containing what Ulpian called the *forma censualis*, is cited in the *lex agraria*.[21] There seems to me no other way to explain the fact that the linguistic formula used in Proconsularis to describe resident alien Romans living in non-Roman communities is used uniformly throughout the province but also used in no other province: they, I believe, are always called *cives qui <locative> morantur*.[22]

In similar fashion, the *lex agraria* preserves as public the roads and ways that existed in the *ager* in Africa before Carthage was captured (*lex agraria* ll. 89–90). In the *lex portorii Asiae*, the entire administration of the customs tax is topographically and materially calqued on Attalid infrastructure (see, e.g., SEG 39, 1180: §28), and much the same is true of the taxation system imposed on Macedon after Pydna, which was arranged only after Aemilius and the ten senatorial commissioners had examined all the documents and materials stored in the *poleis* of the kingdom (Livy 45.29.1).

It is of course a truism to say that Roman practice in any given area, in the aftermath of annexation, rested upon the cooptation and exploitation of preexisting institutions, including both depersonalized institutions of government as well as those of politics, to wit, systems of political and social dependency. Roman sources often acknowledge this fact, but cashing this out in a granular way in historical terms would require detailed knowledge of pre-Roman government that we often do not have. For example, Strabo says that on the eve of the Third Punic War, the territory of Carthage contained 300 *poleis* (Strabo 17.3.15). By *polis* does he mean nothing other than substantial conurbation? Or does he mean a city-state employed as a nodal point by Carthage as metropole in the extension of imperial power over its territory? Without the ability to consider these and other possibilities, Strabo tells us little about Africa under Carthage and therefore little about how the Romans did or did not leverage Carthaginian institutions in the early years of Roman rule. There is also the fact, which I have already stressed, that much appears to have changed in Roman ambitions for provincial government in the mid-second century BCE: the imposition of a system of jurisdiction on Sicily in the form of the *lex Rupilia* 110 years after the island's annexation is a case in point.[23] About what had happened prior to 132, we are nearly wholly ignorant.

The process by which any given area passed into Roman control is also crucial. In Africa, according to Appian, Rome 'decided to destroy' (ἔδοξε καθελεῖν) all the

[20] Aphrodisias: Reynolds (1982): no. 14, l. 3, and no. 15, ll. 13–14. Menippos: Robert and Robert (1989), Menippos col. 1, ll. 37–40. The tax law of Asia: *lex portorii Asiae* = SEG 39, 1180: §10, §39.

[21] Ulpian, *On taxes* 3 (D.50.15.4), fr. 22 Lenel.

[22] AÉ 1974, 691; ILS 6777 = AÉ 1894, 63; AÉ 1915, 21 = ILAfr 243; AÉ 1937, 71 = ILTun 682.

[23] For the data on the *lex Rupilia* see Broughton, *MRR* sub anno 132 (vol. 1: 498).

poleis that had fought with Carthage.[24] But existing *civitates* were the nodal points through which Roman government operated: the Roman claim to fiscal and juridical sovereignty over Sicily is expressed through the insistence that a network of *civitates* can account for the totality of persons and territory in the province.[25] How did Rome govern without local institutions? The *lex agraria* speaks only of the conditions in which it intervenes and so makes no reference to any such destruction, beyond the category of city of Carthage itself, which is cited as no longer extant (*lex agraria* ll. 78–82). That said, it is notable that no other political community is mentioned, either by name or type, whether of a conurbation or population: no *civitas, municipium, oppidum, vicus, pagus, conciliabulum, castellum, forum, natio*, or *gens*, to name the terms used elsewhere in Roman legislation. Instead, Appian tells us that the Romans imposed a tax on land and individuals, men and women alike (Appian, *Lib.* 135.641: *τοῖς δὲ λοιποῖς φόρον ὥρισαν ἐπὶ τῇ γῇ καὶ ἐπὶ τοῖς σώμασιν, ἀνδρὶ καὶ γυναικὶ ὁμοίως*). It is in this light striking that the *lex agraria* discusses taxation and always refers to deserters who were granted ownership of land using collective plurals of individual human beings (see, e.g., *lex agraria* ll. 74–7, 78–82: *eis hominibus, quei ad imperatorem populi Romanei bello Poinicio proxsumo perfugerunt* . . .); this is in contrast to the communities declared free and self-governing, who are called *populi* (*lex agraria* ll. 74–7). The possibility that the territory formerly controlled by Carthage was at the start, at least, conceived as a uniform and undifferentiated political space is perhaps affirmed by the extraordinary fact that all the earliest Roman settlers belonged to a single voting tribe (the Arniensis), although they inhabited an area covering thousands of square kilometers.

The writing of the *lex Rupilia* in just these years establishes a context and invites us to pose the question how the Romans imagined jurisdiction to work, in a region that they had deprived of civic institutions. One answer might lie in the two invocations of the *praetor qui inter ceives Romae ious deicet*: both appear to concern the selling-off of land for which liabilities to the Roman people are not paid within 120 days of the passage of the statute. That said, to my mind, the language also suggests that a rule of personality applied in choice of law: the urban praetor was assigned the task of ruling in matters involving Roman citizens.[26] In Africa itself, beyond a reference to magistrates or those functioning in the place of magistrates holding *imperium, iudicium* and *potestas* (*lex agraria* ll. 87–9), there is a tantalizing reference to prefects, so far as I know the earliest use of the term in contemporaneous language in public law (*lex agraria* l. 55: *praefectus milesve in provinciam erit*). Of course, the Romans had experience supervising private-law relations in the absence of any civic institutions: this was exactly the situation for which the *praefectus iure dicundo* was apparently devised, in the punishment of Capua during the Second Punic War.

Allow me to close my discussion of the *lex agraria* by comparing the language employed in its clauses on Africa to discuss colonists with the language employed in its clauses on Italy to discuss communities. In Africa, reference is repeatedly made

[24] Appian, *Lib.* 135.640.

[25] For an elaboration of this point in respect to an ancient language of territoriality see Ando (forthcoming).

[26] Ando (2016).

to 'colonists and those enrolled in the number of a colonist' (*colonus isve quei in colonei numero scriptus est*). The standard interpretation is that more persons were enrolled as colonists under the *lex Rubria* than had in fact been allowed by that statute. In the clauses on Italy, claims are made in respect of colonies and municipalities, and communities that are not colonies or municipalities but which are to be treated as if they were (*lex agraria* l. 31: *quibus colonieis seive moinicipieis, seive quae pro moinicipieis colon[ieisve*...). We have no idea what these latter communities might be, nor the criteria according to which one might assimilate a non-colony to a colony. What we have here is statutory language that attempts to capture the totality of a social reality, by way of asserting sovereignty over it, while handing off interpretive power to those on the ground. The language on Africa does the same, retrospectively: it declines to name as 'colonists' those who were enrolled in supernumerary fashion, but it respects the power of local officials to have created legal facts, regardless.

4. RELIGION IN ROMAN CARTHAGE: ROMAN WORSHIP, LOCAL GODS

The second text that I wish to discuss derives not from Italy but from Africa, and not from the second century BCE but the second or third century CE. The text in question has been identified by its editors as a *lex sacra* of the cult of the Cereres. The initial discovery was made by Liliane Ennabli in the course of excavating the so-called basilica of Carthagenna and consisted of fragments of a marble plaque deposited in a cistern, which was later filled in to serve as the foundation for a column of the basilica. The *editio princeps* was published in 1999.[27] A few further fragments were later located in the archaeological museum in Carthage; Ennabli and John Scheid then collaborated on a somewhat fuller publication in 2007–8, though the overall interpretation of the content, and of the genre of the text, remains unchanged.[28]

Since the text has not attracted anything like the attention it deserves, I will discuss some of its details in a more systematic fashion than I employed regarding the *lex agraria*; its fragmentary condition also constrains the interpretive acts that one can perform. But I will ultimately stress two points. First, it is an extraordinarily Roman document, in the sense that its language, and the ritual practices it enjoins, are those of a learned Roman religion. Second, it is also the product of colonial law-making: the local pantheon it invokes is that of a specific colony. Indeed, I suggest that rather than a *lex sacra* for a particular cult, what we have in this text is a *feriale* approved by the local council for a specific year, such as we know colonies were enjoined to produce every year shortly after the entry into office of that year's magistrates.[29]

[27] Ennabli (1999). The most significant fragments were republished as AÉ 1999, 1835–41.

[28] Ennabli and Scheid (2007–8) (catalogued in AÉ 2007).

[29] See above all *Lex coloniae Genetivae Iuliae* (RS no. 25), ch. 64: 'Whoever shall be IIviri after the foundation of the colony, they, within the ten days next after that on which they shall have begun to hold that magistracy, are to raise with the decurions when not less than two-thirds shall be present,

To begin with, two coincidences of the text's preservation present us with a challenge: it just so happens that the extant fragments contain a single finite verb, *secuntur* (fr. 12). Many kinds of texts record (or prescribe) chronological orderings of ritual actions. In this case, the tense and mood of the verb at least operate so as to preclude the possibility that the text was a set of *acta*, a record of acts performed in the past. On the contrary, it must be a *lex* or *feriale*, to wit, a listing of acts to be performed in the future. Second, *if* this text is a *lex sacra*, as the editors suppose, then we do not know the identity of the god or goddess (or goddesses) to whom the cult was directed: the most likely candidate might be the Cereres, but they are entirely unmentioned in the extant fragments.

The condition of the text being what it is, I proceed by remarking on some matters of detail, fragment by fragment. In doing so, I draw freely on the commentary provided by Ennabli and Scheid. I focus on those aspects of the text that highlight its status as a piece of colonial law-making, in which the law serves as a vehicle for asserting the status of the community as both Roman and provincial, as a colony must perforce be. To achieve this, I have sought above all to ascertain whether the vocabulary of this text is commonly employed in epigraphy, and, if so, where the relevant inscriptions were produced. The observations below rely on the Manfred Clauss databank and the TLL. I close this section by offering two interpretive claims.

In fragment 1, the term *megaro* (from *megarum*) is attested at Ostia and Rome in the forms *megarum* and also *magar*, where it refers to the inner room of a temple of Isis.[30] (Ennabli and Scheid associate it also with the term μέγαρον, used in the cult of Demeter, and the verb μεγαρίζουσι, of women throwing offerings into the hole.) *Sarmenta* (from *sarmentum*), 'vine twigs,' is unattested epigraphically. *Triclas* (also found *trichla, triclia, trichila*, etc.), 'bowers, summer houses,' is used of dining spaces under four-poled tents. Plutarch, *Caesar* 9.3 explains that feasts associated with the worship of *Bona Dea* involved dining in tents decorated with branches of vine. *Triclae* are attested at Rome, Roman colonies (e.g., Augusta Emerita) and at one *municipium civium Romanorum*, namely, Olisipo; and the word is restored in the great inscription of the Fundus Aufidianus.

In fragment 2, the term *libos*, 'sacrificial cakes,' is at most very rarely attested on inscriptions—this might be the only occurrence. Likewise, the term *lampadas*, 'light, torch,' is very rare in inscriptions but is well attested in learned Roman writings on ritual practice.

In fragment 3, Ennabli and Scheid restore *per sacerdotes summas* in order to align the language of this text with the so-called *sacerdotes magnae* described as instituted at Carthage for the worship of the *Cereres*. If they are correct, we might have proof of the taking up by the colony of the religious obligation attributed by Macrobius to the *evocatio* of Carthage in 146, in which case it might date to the establishment of the colony in 44/38.[31] The term *pultes* (also restored in fragment 6) is otherwise attested epigraphically only in the acts of the

which and how many days it may be agreed shall be festivals and which sacrifices shall be publicly performed and who shall perform those sacrifices.' On the establishing of the calendar in Roman colonies see Rüpke (2006); in municipalities, Scheid (1999a).

[30] See, e.g., CIL 14, 19.

[31] Macrobius, *Saturnalia* 3.9, on which see Ando (2008), 120–48.

arval brethren.[32] Finally, the term *publice* would seem to affirm that this text has to do with the colony as corporate entity.

In fragment 5, *Abbadiri*, 'Abbadir,' is described in late sources as either a god or a *baityl*. It is in any event an indigenous god.

In fragment 10, two locations are named, *in Capitolium* and *fastigi Isidis*. Scheid has suggested elsewhere than his study of this text that Isis was widely taken up by Roman colonies as a matter of public cult in response to the initiation of public cult to Isis at Rome under Vespasian.[33]

In sum, perhaps five, six or seven gods are identified as objects of ritual action in this text: Spes (fr. 1), Volcanus (fr. 1), implicitly the Cereres, Abbadir (fr. 5), the Capitoline triad (fr. 10, implicit in reference to Capitolium), and Isis (fr. 10), and perhaps Bona Dea, implied by use of *triclae*. In addition, at least four locations are named: the shore, two temples, which are cited as a pair, the Capitolium, and perhaps a temple of Isis.

Let me now advance two interpretive claims, one about the genre of the text, the second a wholly uncontroversial assertion about its vocabulary.

First, I wonder if this really is a *lex sacra* for a specific cult. I suggest instead it might be an extravagant act of a single year, to wit, the inscription of that year's *feriale*, following the specification in colonial and municipal charters that ritual obligations are to be settled by the council at the start of each year, as required, for example, in chapter 64 of the *lex Ursonensis* (*RS* no. 25). Otherwise, it seems to me very hard to explain the way the gods are named. In the *commentarii* of the Arvales, for example, the totality of the gods that were worshipped in any given action are always named.[34] Here, we must somehow believe that only contingent actions are specified while the identity of the main recipient(s) of cult is (are) simply assumed. In brief, I suggest that this text should be understood on analogy with the *feriale Duranum* and not, e.g., the *lex sacra* of the altar at Narbo.

Second, the extraordinary Romanness of its vocabulary represents a spectacularly learned attempt by a Roman community to be Roman or, perhaps, perform Romanness. At the same time, the worship of *Cereres* and *Abbadir* mark this out as a Roman colony in a very specific sense, namely, in its taking up of cultic obligations from the prior inhabitants of its territory.

5. CONCLUSION

Broadly speaking, in the Roman world, public law set the conditions of possibility for the existence and purview of law-making and law-applying institutions. In the case of Africa Proconsularis in particular, we are unusually well-positioned in our knowledge of public-law provisions for the province. The *lex agraria* clearly assumes a landscape relatively devoid of juridically constituted political communities, such as might serve as nodal points for the generation or transmission of

[32] Scheid, *CFA* no. 101 line 1; no. 107, col. I, line 5.

[33] Scheid (2009); see also Scheid (2016), 131–2.

[34] Scheid (1999b) = Scheid (2005), 58–83, 301–5.

norms or the provision of institutions of dispute resolution. This is not to say that no towns existed, nor that these lacked structured systems of public powers. Rather, the *lex agraria* suggests quite powerfully that Rome did not recognize these, and in an imperial context, this lack of recognition by metropolitan authorities is a significant fact. Certainly we are scarcely in a position to write a history of political and juridical life in those indigenous communities of North Africa that were directly subordinated to Roman administration until the first century CE. Indeed, it is only in the second century CE that we witness the flowering of institutions of public power and, in the latter part of the second century, a sudden and startling municipalization of civic life. This history is roughly covariant with the evidence for knowledge of law and the activity of advocates in the province, as Anna Dolganov's chapter makes clear. But we should beware the temptation to regard this pattern as somehow late, as though the actions taken by Rome in respect of Carthage and its allies somehow retarded the development of political and legal institutions, of the sort that would be recognized in Rome and commemorate themselves using Roman cultural forms. One of the more startling patterns now emerging in the study of legal history in the provinces of the empire—including both the operation of Roman courts but especially the presence of experts in local law—is their belatedness when compared with the evidence for other institutions of public power. Confirming such patterns, and explaining them, are tasks that can only be commenced when volumes like this assemble and render visible the evidence in systematic fashion.

REFERENCES

Ando, C. 2008. *The Matter of the Gods. Religion and the Roman Empire.* Berkeley.

Ando, C. 2016. Legal pluralism in practice. In: P. du Plessis, C. Ando and K. Tuori (eds.), *The Oxford Handbook of Roman Law and Society.* Oxford, pp. 283–93.

Ando, C. Forthcoming. Hannibal's Legacy. Sovereignty and territoriality in republican Rome. In: K.-J. Hölkeskamp and R. Roth (eds.), *Empire, Hegemony or Anarchy? Rome and Italy, c.200–30 BC.* Stuttgart.

Belkahia, S. and Di Vita-Évrard, G. 1995. Magistratures autochtones dans les cités pérégrines de l'Afrique proconsulaire. In: P, Trousset (ed.) *L'Afrique du Nord antique et médiévale: Monuments funeraires, institutions auctochtones.* Paris, pp. 255–74.

Broughton, T.R.S. 1929. *The Romanization of Africa Proconsularis.* Baltimore.

Bullo, S. 2002. *Provincia Africa: le città e il territorio dalla caduta di Cartagine a Nerone.* Rome.

Cherry, D. 1998. *Frontier and society in Roman North Africa.* New York.

Cottier, M., Crawford, M. H., Crowther, C. V., Ferrary, J.-L., Levick, B. M., Salomies, O. and Wörrle, M. (eds.), 2008. *The customs law of Asia.* Oxford.

Díaz Fernández, A. 2015. *Provincia et Imperium: El mando provincial en la República Romana (227–44 a.C.).* Sevilla.

Dossey, L. 2010. *Peasant and Empire in Christian North Africa.* Berkeley.

Ennabli, L. 1999. À propos de Mégara. In: S. Lancel (ed.) *Numismatique, langues, écritures et arts du livre, spécificité des arts figurés. Actes du VIIe colloque international sur l'histoire et l'archéologie de l'Afrique du Nord.* Paris, pp. 193–210.

Ennabli, L. and Scheid, J. Une 'lex sacra' de Carthage relative au culte des Cereres?: nouvelles observations sur les fragments découverts dans la basilique de Carthagenna. *Atti della Pontificia Accademia Romana di Archeologia* 80 (2007–8), pp. 37–75.

Fentress, E. 2006. Romanizing the Berbers. *Past & Present* 190, pp. 3–33.

Gascou, J. 1972. *La politique municipale de l'empire romain en Afrique proconsulaire de Trajan à Septime-Sévère*. Rome.

Gascou, J. 1979. L'emploi du term *respublica* dans l'épigraphie latine d'Afrique. *Mélanges de l'école française de Rome Année* 91, pp. 383–98.

Gascou, J. 1981. Tendances de la politque municipale de Claude en Maurétanie. *Ktema* 6, pp. 227–38.

Gascou, J. 1982a. Les pagi carthaginois. In: P.A. Février and Ph. Leveau (eds.) *Villes et campagnes dans l'empire romain. Actes du Colloque organisé à Aix en Provence par l'U.E.R. d'Histoire, les 16 et 17 Mai 1980*. Aix-en-Provence, pp. 139–75.

Gascou, J. 1982b. La politique municipale de Rome en Afrique du Nord I: De la mort d'Auguste au début du IIIe siècle. *Aufstieg und Niedergang der römischen Welt* 10.2, pp. 136–229.

Gascou, J. 1982c. La politique municipale de Rome en Afrique du Nord II: Après la mort de Septime-Sévère. *Aufstieg und Niedergang der römischen Welt* 10.2, pp. 230–318.

Gsell, S. 1914–30. *Histoire ancienne de l'Afrique du Nord*. 8 vols. Paris.

Lancel, S. 1995. *Carthage: a history*. Translated by Antonia Nevill. Oxford.

Le Bohec, Y. 2005. *Histoire de l'Afrique romaine: 146 avant J.-C.–439 après J.-C.* Paris.

Lepelley, C. 1979–81. *Les Cités de l'Afrique romaine au Bas-Empire*. Paris.

Lepelley, C. 2001. *Aspects de l'Afrique romaine: les cités, la vie rurale, le Christianisme*. Bari.

Lintott, A. 1992. *Judicial reform and land reform in the Roman Republic. A new edition, with translation and commentary, of the laws from Urbino*. Cambridge.

Mattingly, D. J. 2011. *Imperialism, Power, and Identity: Experiencing the Roman Empire*. Princeton.

Pilkington, N. 2013. An Archaeological History of Carthaginian Imperialism. Dissertation, Columbia University.

Reynolds, J. 1982. *Aphrodisias and Rome*. London.

Robert, L. and Robert, J. 1989. *Claros I. Décrets hellenistique*. Paris.

Rüpke, J. 2006. Religion in the lex Ursonensis. In: C. Ando and J. Rüpke (eds.), *Religion and law in classical and Christian Rome*. Stuttgart, pp. 34–46.

Scheid, J. 1999a. Aspects religieux de la municipalisation. Quelques réflexions générales. In: M. Dondin-Payre and M.-T. Raepsaet-Charlier (eds.), *Cités, Municipes, Colonies. Les processus de municipalisation en Gaule et en Germanie sous le Haut Empire romain*. Paris, pp. 381–423.

Scheid, J. 1999b. Hiérarchie et structure dans le polythéisme romain. Façons romaines de penser l'action. *Archiv für Religionsgeschichte* 1, pp. 184–203. Translated by Philip Purchase as, 'Hierarchy and Structure in Roman Polytheism: Roman Methods of Conceiving Action,' in C. Ando (ed.), *Roman Religion*. Edinburgh, pp. 164–89.

Scheid, J. 2005. *Quand faire, c'est croire. Les rites sacrificiels des Romains*. Paris.

Scheid, J. 2009. Le statut du culte d'Isis sous le Haut-Empire. In: C. Bonnet, V. Pirenne-Delforge, and D. Praet (eds.), *Les Religions orientales dans le monde grec et romain: Cents ans après Cumont (1906–2006)*. Rome, pp. 173–86.

Scheid, J. 2016. *The Gods, the State, and the Individual. Reflections on Civic Religion in Rome*. Translated by Clifford Ando. Philadelphia.

Toynbee, A.J. 1965. *Hannibal's Legacy. The Hannibalic War's Effects on Roman Life*. Oxford.

Wörrle, M. 2000. Pergamon um 133 v. Chr. *Chiron* 30, pp. 543–76.

19

Nutricula causidicorum

Legal Practitioners in Roman North Africa

Anna Dolganov

In his seventh satire, composed most probably in the 120s CE, the Roman poet Juvenal pokes fun at individuals who have laboriously pursued a rhetorical education and are now struggling to make a living in the city of Rome. Among these poor wretches are forensic pleaders (*causidici*) who have trouble finding clients and receive only meager payment for successful cases.[1] According to the satirist, success in Roman courts is entirely a function of social status. Although Aemilius the nobleman is no brilliant orator, his rank and wealth earn him the highest fees (7.124–128). By contrast, a superior pleader of low status can expect to be rewarded with a dry ham or bad local wine (7.119–121). In Juvenal's Rome, not even Cicero would be able to bring in high fees without a gigantic gold ring on his finger, a magistrate's chair and a retinue of slaves, assistants and distinguished friends (7.139–143). Accordingly, Juvenal's advice to the humble *causidicus* who seek to make a living by pleading cases is to go to Gaul, or better yet to Africa, the 'nursemaid of pleaders' (*nutricula causidicorum*, 7.148).

On one level, the satirist seems to be expressing a general stereotype about the provinces as lacking the refinements of the imperial capital. Unlike fastidious Roman clients, who prefer to engage elite orators to represent them, Gallic and African provincials are happy to hire an ordinary *causidicus*—which is to say that provincial sensibilities with regard to status and prestige are less developed than they are at Rome. The phrase *nutricula causidicorum* evokes an image of Roman North Africa as a particularly rich and litigious place, where ample private wealth is available to be spent on litigation. Just as interesting is what Juvenal takes for granted, namely that a *causidicus* trained at Rome would be perfectly capable of pleading in Gallic or African courts, which implies that these courts employed Roman-style litigation and by implication Roman law. This impression is reinforced by a passage in Juvenal's fifteenth satire, where the poet comments on the spread of forensic oratory in the provinces as a process of cultural globalization

[1] See Juvenal 7.106–49. For a critical overview of scholarly interpretations of this passage, see Vössing (1997a), 388–90. On the date of Juvenal's satires, see the introduction to the commentary of Courtney (1980).

Anna Dolganov, Nutricula causidicorum*: Legal Practitioners in Roman North Africa* In: *Law in the Roman Provinces*. Edited by: Kimberley Czajkowski and Benedikt Eckhardt in collaboration with Meret Strothmann, Oxford University Press (2020).

DOI: 10.1093/oso/9780198844082.003.0019

effected by Roman rule: 'now, the whole world has its own Greek and Roman Athens, eloquent Gaul has been training pleaders (*causidici*) from Britain and even Thyle speaks of hiring a teacher of rhetoric!' (15.110–12). The image of Thyle, the semi-legendary *terra incognita* of the north seas, hunting for a teacher of rhetoric is a humorous illustration of the impact and reception of Roman models by provincial elites.

The remarks of Juvenal hint at the profound cultural impact of the Roman imperial court system. A key factor in this process were the annual assizes (*conventus*) held by Roman governors throughout each province, where governors and other high-ranking Roman officials received numerous petitions and admitted hundreds of litigants into their courts.[2] The Roman assize system gave rise to a vibrant sphere of litigation in the provinces. In particular, provincial sources illustrate the rise of legal practice as a prestige-activity of provincial elites, in line with its traditional function for the political elite at Rome, for whom the courts were an important venue for display and social performance and whose traditional duty it was to furnish their clients and friends with advocacy and legal advice.[3] Accordingly, members of the Roman elite engaged in different forms of legal practice, pleading and adjudicating cases, serving as judicial advisors and dispensing legal opinions.[4]

In Roman North Africa, numerous inscriptions show members of the African civic elite identifying themselves as forensic orators (*advocati, togati*), legal experts (*iurisperiti, iuris studiosi*) and judicial advisors (*assessores*), while epitaphs for young men from wealthy families depict them as students of rhetoric and law and praise their eloquence and legal expertise.[5] Epigraphic evidence for legal practice in the African provinces surges at the turn of the third century, a development that is mirrored by the rise of Greek epigraphic testimonia for legal practitioners (*rhētores, nomikoi, sumboulētai, synkathēdroi*) and students of rhetoric and law in the East.[6] Overall, the epigraphic record appears to indicate that the Roman assize system delivered its transformative impact on provincial legal culture in the Roman provinces in the Severan age.[7]

[2] On the Roman assize system, see Burton (1975) and Haensch (1997).

[3] The impact of Roman models of elite legal culture in the provinces is discussed in detail in Dolganov (2018a), 358–91.

[4] On the Roman tradition of forensic oratory, see Crook (1995), 119–71, Frier (1985), 95–138 and David (1992). On the traditional Roman practice of elite legal experts issuing authoritative legal opinions (*responsa*), see Kunkel (1967^{2}), 38–62, Frier (1985), 139–70 and now Lehne-Gstreinthaler (2019). On the impact of Roman models of legal practice in the provinces, see Heath (2004) on forensic oratory and Humfress (2007), 29–134 on oratory and legal science in the late Empire.

[5] See my detailed discussion of the African epigraphic evidence below.

[6] On orators and sophists in Greek inscriptions, see Puech (2002). On *nomikoi* in the Greek East, see Jones (2007). Testimonia for young men from the Greek East traveling to Rome to study Roman law include CIL VI 8991 = AE 2000, +132 (a student of rhetoric or law who died at Rome at the age of 16) and CIL VI 33868 (a *iuris studiosus* from Nicomedia who died at Rome). See also SEG 36.1456 (a man from Pamphylia who had studied law at Berytus) and the journey of Gregory Thaumatourgos from Pontus to Rome, ultimately diverted to Berytus, in the early third century (*In Origenem oratio panegyrica* 1 and 5), discussed further below.

[7] As a consequence, the rise of Roman-style forensic culture in North Africa—and other Roman provinces—tends to be discussed as a phenomenon of the third and fourth centuries, see for example Liebs (1993), Heath (2004), Vössing (1997a) and Humfress (2007).

In chronological terms, this is not what we would expect. The activity of legal practitioners in connection with Roman assizes considerably predates their emergence in the epigraphic record in the mid-second century. Already in the 70s BCE, Cicero's account of Verres' governorship of Sicily shows Sicilian provincials pleading cases as forensic orators and serving as judges and judicial advisors at the Roman *conventus*.[8] Similarly, papyri from Roman Egypt show forensic orators of Egyptian origin pleading at the *conventus* within a few decades of the annexation of Egypt as a Roman province in 30 BCE.[9] As soon as court proceedings begin to be attested in papyri in the Flavian period, we observe the ubiquitous presence of legal practitioners at all levels of the Roman court system: forensic orators (*rhētores*) pleading each side of the case, judges sitting with councils of judicial advisors (*symbouloi, synēdroi, parēdroi*) and legal experts (*nomikoi*) dispensing authoritative legal opinions.[10] In Africa, one of the oldest Roman provinces, it can be presumed that legal practitioners were similarly active at Roman assizes in the late Republic and early Principate. Accordingly, their prominence in the African epigraphic record at the turn of the third century seems unlikely to reflect the emergence of new practices, all the more so considering that the literary evidence for legal practice in Roman North Africa predates the epigraphic record by at least half a century. In an effort to explore possible explanations for this phenomenon, this chapter will present the epigraphic evidence for legal practitioners in Roman North Africa, comparing it with what can be gleaned from literary sources, and analyze the cultural and institutional developments that the chronology of the evidence appears to reflect.

1. LEGAL PRACTITIONERS IN ROMAN NORTH AFRICA: THE EPIGRAPHIC EVIDENCE

From the perspective of surviving documentary evidence, the world of courts and legal practice in the African provinces is largely invisible to us before the turn of the third century. A rare exception is a unique inscription from the city of Lepcis Magna *c.*120 CE, approximately contemporary with Juvenal's seventh satire, where a priest named Tullus makes a votive dedication to Mercury and Minerva in thanks for his victory in a lawsuit against a tavern-keeper named Boccius at the Roman governor's court.[11] After losing the initial hearing, Boccius had paid Tullus off in a private settlement so that Tullus would not file a second lawsuit for insult and injury (*iniuria*) available to him under Roman law. If such a lawsuit were successful, Boccius would incur public ignominy (*infamia*) accompanied by

[8] See for example Cicero, *In Verrem* 2.2.23, 69–73, 102, 106–108.

[9] See P. Oxy. XII 1479 (Alexandria, late 1c. BCE), BGU XVI 2631 (Herakleopolite nome, 2 March 9 BCE), CPR XV 15 and P. Lond. III 354 (Soknopaiou Nesos, 7–4 BCE).

[10] On Roman court proceedings in papyri, see Coles (1966) and Palme (2014).

[11] IRT 304 (c. 120 CE). For the identification of the *proconsul* with Marcus Vitorius Marcellus (*cos. suff.* in 105, PIR[1] V 519) see Syme (1980), 4–6 and Eck (1983), 154 and 179. A judicial sentence of the same governor is attested in a contemporary inscription from the hinterland of Carthage, which records a border dispute between the community of the Aunobaritani and an individual named Iulius Regillus, see ILAfr 591 = AE 1921 38 (*c.*120 CE) with Burton (2000).

numerous legal penalties for bringing false accusations (*calumnia*).[12] Having accepted the private settlement, Tullus used the money to finance the inscription, thereby indirectly achieving the public defamation that Boccius had wished to avoid.[13] It can be presumed that both Tullus and Boccius had advocates to plead their cases at the governor's court—a standard practice in Roman courts that is documented virtually without exception at the court of the Roman prefect of Egypt.[14] Important evidence for legal advocacy in Africa is provided by lead curse tablets excavated from graves in the necropoleis of Carthage, in which individuals seek to 'bind the tongues' of adversaries and their advocates in imminent legal proceedings. The resemblance of these African curse-texts to a curse tablet from Aquitania suggests that judicial curses were an established genre in major judicial centres of the Roman Empire.[15] The agency of African legal practitioners can also be inferred from the numerous civic endowments and testamentary bequests attested in North African inscriptions.[16] These testimonia suggest that the survival of ephemeral documentation of the sort that is preserved in Roman Egypt would reveal a no less dynamic sphere of legal practice in Roman North Africa, already in the first and second centuries.[17] Due to the absence of this sort of evidence, however, African legal practitioners remain invisible to us.

The African epigraphic record begins to yield testimonia for legal practice in the late second century. Of the approximately eighty inscriptions where individuals are identified as legal practitioners (*advocati, defensores, iụrisperiti, assessores*) or praised for their eloquence and legal expertise, only one can be securely dated before the mid-second century.[18] While some inscriptions lack a precise date and fall into the interval between the second and third centuries on the basis of epigraphic formulae (such as *DMS* and *Dis Manibus*), an overwhelming majority of datable inscriptions date to the third century and some to the fourth century. This pattern, together with approximate dating criteria such as nomenclature and letter forms, strongly favor a third-century date for most of the undated material, as will be noted with reference to individual inscriptions below.[19] Thus, the

[12] On *infamia* as an automatic consequence of a successful *actio iniuriarum*, see Buckland (1921), 588. See also D.3.5 on *calumniatores* and D.47.15 on *praevaricatio*.

[13] One suspects a similar sort of extra-legal reckoning 'in the shadow' of Roman imperial courts in the so-called confession inscriptions attested in rural sanctuaries in Roman Asia Minor, in which the offenses of individuals are made public, see Petzl (1994) and (1998) and Chaniotis (1997) and (2005).

[14] On forensic oratory in papyri, see Crook (1995), 58–118 and my discussion in Dolganov (2018a), 323–404 and 451–76.

[15] For judicial curses from Carthage, see DefTab 217–26 and 303 = Kropp 11.1.1.3–12 and 32 (2–3c). See also a very similar curse from Aquitania, CIL XIII 11069–70 = DefTab 111–112 = Kropp 4.3.1.1–2. On 'agonistic' curses, see Gordon (2013) on curse tablets from Carthage and Hadrumetum pertaining to chariot races; these observations can be extended to judicial curses as well.

[16] Some of the abundant evidence for civic bequests *ex testamento* in Roman North Africa is discussed in general studies of civic patronage and munificence, see Duncan-Jones (1962), Wilkins (1990) and Nicols (2014), 239–78. Even in small communities in the deep hinterland, individuals had access to notaries who composed Roman wills, as evidenced by AE 1974, 691 = AE 1975, 875, Ureu (mid-2c).

[17] For a detailed analysis of the papyrological evidence for legal practice, see Dolganov (2018a), 297–435.

[18] See [A4], discussed below.

[19] A late second- or third-century date for most of the undated epigraphic testimonia for legal practitioners is argumented by Vössing (1997a), cited below where relevant. On the dating of funerary epitaphs in Roman North Africa, see Lassère (1973).

African epigraphic evidence for legal practitioners effectively begins in the late Antonine period and then rises significantly in the Severan age. The evidence can be classified into the following categories:

A. individuals acting as legal representatives (*advocati, defensores*) of civic communities
B. legal practice in honorific and funerary inscriptions of the officeholding elite
C. eloquence and legal expertise as virtues attributed to young men pursuing their studies
D. legal practice in funerary inscriptions of individuals without an officeholding career
E. individuals who received appointments as legal representatives of the *fiscus* (*advocati fisci*)

In what follows, I will examine the evidence from each category (A–D), with special attention to its chronological distribution. The final category (E) will be examined in the final section of the chapter. The inscriptions will be cited with reference to the relevant appendices (A–E) of epigraphic testimonia.

A. *Honours for* advocati *and* defensores *of Civic Communities*

A handful of second-century inscriptions honour individuals for their activity as advocates (*defensores, advocati*) on behalf of civic communities. The earliest datable example is a dedication from the reign of Trajan (98–117 CE) by the Carthaginian satellite-community (*pagus*) of Thugga to a senatorial *patronus* of the town, who is praised as a defender (*defensor*) of its tax-privileges [A4].[20] Apparently, an embassy had been sent from Thugga to Rome to argue for the protection of the privileged tax-status of the territory (*pertica*) of Carthage, which was shared by all Carthaginian *pagi*. The precise context is unknown: it may have been a new tax imposition or possibly a conflict between the *pagus* and the adjoining Punic *civitas*, which did not enjoy the same privileges. The term *defensor* conveys the role of the *patronus* in pleading on behalf of the *pagus*, presumably before the Roman senate, the emperor or both.[21] The fact that the ambassadors from Thugga required additional assistance from a senatorial *defensor* was probably due to the high prestige of the hearing at Rome.[22] This appears to be the only epigraphic testimonium for legal practice in Africa that predates the mid-second century. The term *defensor* occurs in another second-century

[20] On civic patronage in the Roman Empire, see Nicols (2014); on civic patronage in Africa, see Warmington (1954) and Wilkins (1990).

[21] On the interaction between provincial communities and the emperor, see Millar (1977), 375–455. Some requests were heard by the Senate without the emperor, as evidenced by CIL VIII 270 = XI 451 (*Saltus Beguensis*, 138 CE) where a senatorial landowner had requested market-rights, see Shaw (1981) and more recently Chaouali (2002–2003).

[22] A parallel example is furnished by the court hearing recorded in the inscription from Dmeir in Syria (SEG 17.759) where the grievances of Syrian villagers against a tax farmer were heard by the emperor Caracalla at Antioch in 216. At the hearing, both the tax farmer and the legal representative (*defensor*) sent by the villagers were represented by eminent senatorial *advocati*. On the orchestrated nature of the proceedings, see Stolte (2003) and my discussion in Dolganov (2018a), 388–91.

inscription from Thugga, where the *pagus* and *civitas* collectively honour a *patronus* of unknown rank for his activity as *defensor causae publicae* [A3]. Elsewhere, the *pagus* and *civitas* honour an equestrian *patronus* of local origin for his role as a 'most eloquent advocate' (*advocatus eloquentissimus*) on their behalf [A5].[23]

The role of *defensor*, in addition to being taken on by civic *patroni* of senatorial or equestrian rank, was also a civic duty (*munus*) to which communities appointed members of their own curial class.[24] In a second-century inscription from the African *municipium* of Vallis, a senior officeholder (*omnibus honoribus functus*) is praised for his activity as *defensor causarum publicarum municipii* [A2]. An epitaph from the Numidian city of Cuicul commemorates Lucius Gargilius Praetorianus, a legal expert (*iuris peritus*) and senior officeholder (*omnibus honoribus functus*) who was serving as *advocatus rei publicae* when he died at the age of forty [A1/B11]. It is implicit that Praetorianus died during a mission as a legal representative of his city. Additional evidence for advocacy on behalf of civic communities is indirectly provided by numerous second-century inscriptions honouring Africans for financing embassies to Rome.[25]

These second-century testimonia for *advocati* and *defensores* of communities, some of whom are explicitly praised for their eloquence, provide direct evidence for the training of North African civic elites in forensic oratory, which was an essential skill in the interaction between provincial communities and Roman imperial authorities.[26] These inscriptions can also be regarded as indirect evidence for the broader involvement of African elites in legal practice at Roman assizes, along the lines of the papyrological evidence from Egypt, which shows members of the Alexandrian elite pleading cases and dispensing

[23] The same *patronus* appears in a dedication made by his father (CIL VIII 26594 = AE 1893, 102), which reveals that his name was Q. Calpurnius Rogatianus and that the family was local, see Vössing (1997a), 395 n. 1316. On the origins of civic *patroni* and their ties to their client communities, see Warmington (1954).

[24] The *advocatio/defensio civitatis* is described as a *munus personale* in the *iuris epitomae* of Hermogenian (D.50.4.1) at the turn of the fourth century. The liturgical nature of this function is also implied by Paul, *Sentences* 1 (D.50.4.16.3). The *advocatio civitatis* may have been an aspect of the public role of senior officeholders that gradually evolved into a formal liturgical duty, see Neesen (1981) on this process. On the Roman system of *munera publica*, see Charbonnel (1974) and Drecoll (1997) on the third century and Grelle (1986) and (1999) on late antiquity.

[25] See for example CIL VIII 22737 = ILS 6780 = ILTun 41 (Gigthis, 2c.), ILAfr 21 = AE 1915, 43 (Gigthis, 2c.) and ILAfr 478 = ILS 9508 = AE 1912, 30 (Thuburnica, 2–3c.?). Both inscriptions from Gigthis explicitly thank ambassadors for financing their journey to Rome. The inscription from Thuburnica commemorates an individual who had already sponsored numerous embassies before he died at Ostia at the age of thirty-two. On the appointment of ambassadors and the financing of embassies, see Millar (1977), 383–85.

[26] See Millar (1977), 385: 'The sheer volume of evidence for embassies from provincial communities to the emperor must make us realize that we are dealing with an essential aspect of the life of the empire.' The importance for communities to have eloquent *defensores* is illustrated by an amusing episode recounted by Philostratus, where the sudden death of the sophist Polemo leaves an embassy from Smyrna to fend for themselves at the court of the emperor. Their oratory is so abysmal that the emperor refuses to listen to them and asks for a draft of Polemo's speech to be recited instead, see Philostratus, *Vitae sophistarum* 539–40. On the enduring importance of oratory in public life in the late Roman world, see Brown (1992).

legal opinions to Roman officials at the *conventus*.[27] While forensic activity of this sort is not visible in African inscriptions from the first and second centuries, it emerges as a prominent element of elite self-representation in the epigraphy of the Severan age.

B. Advocati *and* iurisperiti *in Inscriptions of the Officeholding Elite: the Severan Shift*

At the turn of the third century, elite Africans begin to identify themselves epigraphically as forensic orators (*advocati*), legal experts (*iurisperiti, iuris studiosi*) and judicial advisors (*assessores*). This development is illustrated by a series of inscriptions from the Numidian capital of Lambaesis in the early third century. The earliest is a dedication from *c.*200 CE where a civic officeholder named Marcus Sedius Rufus identifies himself as an *advocatus* and honours the governor Anicius Faustus as his *patronus* [B1a]. The context implies that Rufus was a leading orator at the court of Faustus. Additionally, Rufus mentions his officeholding career in the city of Lambaesis, which spanned the full *cursus honorum*, culminating in the offices of *duovir quinquennalis* and *flamen perpetuus*. Another inscription documents the construction of a shrine to the *genius* of Lambaesis on the premises of the *capitolium*, financed by the same Rufus through an impressively large *fideicommissum* of 600,000 HS [B1b].[28] In this inscription, Rufus is posthumously described as a 'man of honest reputation, *flamen perpetuus* and *advocatus*.' The prominence of *advocatus* underscores the prestige of Rufus' activity as a forensic orator, on par with his officeholding career. This is the first firmly dated instance of *advocatus* as a title in an African career inscription.

On the base of an honorific statue from Lambaesis, two brothers named Sextus Sinicius Rufus and Sinicius Fortunatus identify themselves as *advocati* and honour the governor Pollienus Auspex as their *patronus* [B6]. Like Marcus Sedius Rufus, Sinicius Rufus was a high-ranking civic officeholder (*flamen perpetuus*).[29] Similarly, the governor Cominius Cassianus is honoured for his judicial activity by an *advocatus* of equestrian rank, a *duovir* and a *flamen perpetuus*, 'who so often [admired his *iustitia* and] judgments in the *forum*' [B5]. The context implies that the *advocatus* was active at the governor's court. As high-ranking civic officials, the *duovir* and *flamen perpetuus* would likewise have participated in the governor's judicial activity—for example, as judges to whom the governor delegated cases. They may also have pleaded as *advocati* while holding office, a practice that

[27] On the involvement of provincial elites in legal practice in Roman imperial courts, see my discussion in Dolganov (2018a), 228–334. On forensic culture in the late Empire, see Heath (2004), 277–332 and Humfress (2007), 29–134. On elite orators in papyri, see Dolganov (2018a), 358–91; on elite legal experts in papyri, see *ibid.*, 417–31.

[28] On the shrine, see Eingartner (2005), 151, 219–21. The bequest of Rufus is the largest known sum to be spent on a temple in the Roman Empire, see Duncan-Jones (1982), 90.

[29] As revealed by another inscription: ZPE 69, 208 = AE 1987, 1064.

is attested for Alexandrian officeholders in the third century.[30] The same governor is honoured with a statue by Lucius Valerius Optatianus, another *advocatus* of equestrian rank [B2a].[31]

The inscriptions from Lambaesis likewise furnish us with two testimonia for legal experts serving as judicial advisors to the governor. The first is a funerary inscription from the 180s CE that commemorates Gaius Vibius Romulus, a judicial councilor (*assessor*) of the governor Maximianus [B8].[32] It is possible that the *assessor* came to Numidia from another province as a member of the personal staff of Maximianus. A parallel example is furnished by a Greek epitaph from Sicca Veneria for the legal expert and *assessor* (*nomikos, synkathedros*) Pinnius Justus of Amastris, who had traveled from Pontus to Numidia to serve on the staff of the governor Ulpius Arabianus and then died 'on the job' in Numidia *c.*200 CE [B4].[33] It is also possible, however, that Romulus was a local legal expert from Lambaesis who had been invited by Maximianus to serve on his *consilium*.[34] In another funerary inscription from Lambaesis, we find Gaius Fabius Clodianus, a 'most dedicated scholar of the law' (*iuris studiosus constantissimus*) [B15].[35] The location of the epitaph in the entrance hall of the governor's headquarters (*principia*) suggests that the *iuris studiosus* was active at the governor's court. Again, while it is conceivable that Clodianus was an *assessor* on the governor's personal staff who came to Numidia from elsewhere and then died there, the absence of any reference to his origins may rather suggest that he was a legal expert of local origin.[36] An African origin for Clodianus and Romulus would place these inscriptions in line with other testimonia for elite Africans being identified as legal practitioners in the epigraphy of the Severan age.

[30] On the role of local elites as *advocati* and delegated judges at the *conventus*, see my discussion in Dolganov (2018a), 115–29, 367–72.

[31] The same *advocatus* erects a statue for the governor Tertullus Antiochus, see [B2b]. See also [B10] where an *advocatus* honors the governor Petronius Probatus (Thomasson (1996), 184 no.62, *c.*222–35 CE) as his *patronus*.

[32] This inscription is not discussed by Liebs (1993).

[33] See Liebs (1993), 22 and Vössing (1997a), 424–25. The *proconsul* Ulpius Arabianus was a native of Pontus and had evidently chosen one of his compatriots to serve as his *assessor*. See the very similar story told by Gregory Thaumatourgos of his brother-in-law being appointed *assessor* by a third-century governor who was a native of Pontus (Gregory Thaumaturgus, *In Origenem oratio panegyrica* 1–5). On the assessorate, see Kunkel (1967²), 332–34 and Behrends (1969). Generally on the Roman institution of judicial advisory councils, see Crook (1954) and now Kantor (2017).

[34] On the *consilia* of Roman governors, see Kantor (2017) with evidence for the participation of provincial elites discussed at 70–3. On elite Alexandrian *nomikoi* in Roman Egypt, who traveled with the governor, advised him in court and issued written legal opinions, see my discussion in Dolganov (2018a), 417–31.

[35] See Liebs (1993), 22–4 and Vössing (1996), 129–30 and (1997a), 424.

[36] Here, I agree with Liebs (1993), 23–4, who argues for a local origin. This is supported by other evidence for provincial legal experts advising governors, see Kantor (2017), 70–3 and Dolganov (2018a), 417–31. The widely accepted notion that *assessores* were not permitted to serve in their home provinces (see for example Kunkel (1967²), 333 and Vössing (1996), 130 to this effect) does not have a firm evidentiary basis. In Paul, *On the lex Iulia et Papia* 3 (D. 4.6.37) and Ulpian, *On the lex Iulia et Papia* 6 (D.4.6.38*pr.*) it is merely stated that *assessores* who serve in their home provinces beyond a certain period or without special permission lose the privileges of *absentes rei publicae causa*, while Macer, *On the office of the governor* 1 (D.1.22.3) states that, if a province is subdivided, the *assessores* serving in it should be transferred away from their province of origin to the neighboring province. All three passages, in fact, imply that *assessores* were serving in their home provinces.

In a marble inscription from the wall of the theater of Lepcis Magna, Quintus Marcius Pudens is honoured by his son as a 'legal expert (*iuris peritus*) and excellent father' by decree of the *ordo decurionum* [B21].[37] The quality and prestigious location of the inscription suggest that Pudens belonged to a prominent officeholding family at Lepcis. The public context also suggests that *iuris peritus* corresponded to an official function. One may imagine that Pudens, like the elite *nomikoi* attested in Roman Egypt and Asia Minor, was a high-profile legal expert who served on judicial *consilia*, issued *responsa* and advised the governor when he held his annual assizes on the Tripolitanian coast. The choice of the theater of Lepcis for the inscription may have been due to its function as a judicial venue.[38] It is noteworthy that the son of Pudens chose to have his father commemorated as a *iuris peritus*. If, as one would imagine, Pudens was a local officeholder and member of the *ordo decurionum*, his public representation as *iuris peritus* underscores the social prestige of this function.

Forensic oratory and legal expertise also find their way onto private funerary monuments. An epitaph from the Numidian city of Cuicul, most probably dating to the third century, commemorates Lucius Turpilius Victorinus Marianus, *eques Romanus* and *advocatus*, a man 'of all letters and virtues' who 'pleaded cases to great acclaim' and died at the age of thirty-two [B16]. It is noteworthy, in view of his age and equestrian rank, that no public offices are mentioned. It may be that Victorinus had not yet held political office or that his officeholding career was elided in the epitaph. This would constitute very powerful evidence for the prestige of his position as *advocatus* at the court of the Numidian governor (so it may be presumed) as the career achievement most worth mentioning in his funerary inscription. The same is suggested by the epitaph of Marcus Valerius Valerianus [B7]/[D2], a native of Lambaesis who died at the age of thirty-five and is commemorated by his mother as an *advocatus* at Carthage.[39]

A cemetery of the *municipium* of Thubursicu Numidarum—a town in the vicinity of Madauros, the birthplace of Apuleius—presents us with several tombstones of the prominent local family of the Vetidii, most probably dating to the first half of the third century. The head of one branch of the family, Quintus Vetidius Iuvenalis, lived to the impressive age of 87 and is described as 'holding all civic offices (*omnibus honoribus functus*), the father of three *equites Romani*, a legal expert in the forum (*in foro iuris peritus*) and a good farmer (*agricola bonus*)' [B20].[40] This epitaph offers revealing insight into the social imaginaire of African municipal elites. Iuvenalis is described as embodying a number of traditional Roman ideals, including *concordia*, marital harmony, as well as the ideal of a *bonus agricola*.[41] His long list of achievements, particularly his ability

[37] See Liebs (1993), 24. The Punic-derived name of Pudens, in itself, suggests the local origin of the family, see Bradley (2012), 45 and 299.

[38] On theaters as judicial venues, see Färber (2014), 138 and 201–203.

[39] Briefly discussed by Vössing (1997a), 420.

[40] See Liebs (1993), 25–6 and Vössing (1996), 133–34.

[41] The phrases *agricola bonus* and *in foro iuris peritus* look like generic references to Roman social ideals. Similarly, an epitaph from Aquileia commemorates someone as *iurisperitus* and *vir bonus*, see CIL V 1026 = CIL V 429 = Inscr. Aqu. I 705 = Grabalt. 119, dated archaeologically to the period between 76–125 CE. On the Roman ideal of the *bonus agricola* in African inscriptions, see Stone (1998).

to bestow sufficient wealth on his three sons to enable them to enter the equestrian order,[42] proudly showcases his rise in African society. Alongside *agricola bonus*, the expression *in foro iuris peritus* does not suggest that Iuvenalis had a formal position as a legal expert who issued *responsa* to officials. Instead, it is more likely to be a stock-expression for forensic activity.[43] The epitaph of Iuvenalis *peritus* further highlights the prestige of the forum and legal expertise in Africa in the Severan age.

Legal expertise also receives monumental commemoration on the tomb of the Gargilii Praetoriani, a prominent officeholding family in the Numidian *colonia* of Cuicul in the Severan age. The sponsor of the monument honours his deceased brother Lucius Gargilius Praetorianus, who had completed the full municipal *cursus honorum* (*omnibus honoribus functus*) and was also a *iuris peritus* who happened to be serving as *advocatus rei publicae* when he died at the age of forty [B13/A1].[44] Evidently, in line with the social role of eminent citizens described above, Praetorianus represented his city at the court of the Numidian governor—and possibly at the court of the Severi, who toured the African provinces in 202–3. In the context of his career, the phrase *iuris peritus* suggests that, like the elite *iurisperiti* and *nomikoi* attested elsewhere, Praetorianus dispensed legal opinions and served as a judicial advisor to officials. His activity as *advocatus rei publicae* shows that Praetorianus was also skilled in oratory. He may be an example of what Greek sources refer to as a *nomikos rhētōr*, possessing expertise in both oratory and law.[45]

A verse epitaph from the area of Timgad commemorates a legal practitioner named Quintus Maior, who is described as 'serving the statutes and expertly defending the laws' (*adseruit leges, defendit iura peritus*) [B3].[46] What precisely is meant by this phrase has been debated. The term *defendit* indicates that Maior

[42] On the sons of Iuvenalis, see [C26–7] discussed in the next section. On mechanisms of entry into the equestrian order, see Duncan-Jones (2016), 94–7 for an overview of the scholarly debate. The categories *eques equo publico* and *eques Romanus* appear to have been distinct, the former denoting a more prestigious status with a formal adlection procedure (see for example the anecdote preserved in the *Hermeneumata Pseudodositheana*, Goetz, *Corp. Gloss. Lat.* 3: 32, cited by Duncan-Jones (2016), 96 n. 43), the latter most likely signifying that the individual possessed property worth at least 400,000 HS and was registered in the equestrian *census* class. This is, in my view, the most plausible explanation for the equestrian status of the young sons of Iuvenalis. I am grateful to Brent Shaw for discussing this issue with me.

[43] On the judicial activity of local magistrates in Africa, see for example the *acta* of Marian and James in Rébillard (2017) and the municipal *acta* attached to the treatise against the Donatists by Optatus of Milev (CSEL 26, Ziwsa (1893), 185–204). On the role of African magistrates in instructing cases, see Lepelley (1979), 1.216–22. On their law enforcement activity, see Lopuszanski (1951) and Fuhrmann (2011), 58–82.

[44] See Liebs (1993), 21–2 and Vössing (1996), 130–31 and (1997a), 385–86 n. 1316. On the *gens* of the Gargilii and other elite families in Cuicul, see Jacques (1984), 549–53.

[45] The argument of Vössing (1997a), 385–86 n. 1316 that Gargilius was not a 'professional *advocatus*' but a legally knowledgeable member of the local elite seems a misleading distinction. For forensic orators who are simultaneously described as legal experts (*iurisperiti, nomikoi*), see Philo of Byblos FgrHist 790 F 34 (*rhētōr* and *nomikos* from Gerasa, early 2c.), Radet, G. *BCH* 14, 1890 no. 2 = Jones (2007), no. 20 (individual from Nysa praised for his oratory and legal expertise) and CIL VI 9487 = ILS 7743 (*advocatus* and *iurisperitus* from Rome, 2–3c.). See my discussion in Dolganov (2018a), 313–23.

[46] See Liebs (1993), 27–9 and Vössing (1996), 134–35 and (1997a), 424 n. 1437.

was active in the courts, presumably at Timgad, a major assize centre of the Numidian governor. While it has been argued that Maior was a forensic orator and therefore not a legal expert in the true sense, the two activities were not mutually exclusive. The poetic formulation *defendit iura peritus* may convey that Maior was a legal expert (*iuris peritus*) who 'served' and 'defended' the law by advising officials in court. Alternatively, *defendit iura peritus* could also be a reference to forensic oratory, in line with Philo's description of Plato of Gerasa as an orator who 'safeguarded the laws in his court speeches.'[47] Maior may be yet another example of a *nomikos rhētōr*, renowned for his legal expertise on par with his rhetorical abilities.

The emergence of legal practice in third-century African inscriptions reaches beyond the provinces of Africa and Numidia to Mauretania, where a funerary monument from Sitifis honours Marinus, *eques Romanus,* who was 'highly expert in the law' (*iuris peritissimus*) and died at the age of twenty-five [B11].[48] Also included in the epitaph is Fabius Donatus, *eques ex numero officialium,* a cavalry officer who had been appointed to the bureaucratic staff (*officium*) of the governor. In view of their being commemorated together, it is possible that, like the *officialis* Fabius Donatus, Marinus the legal expert had a position on the governor's staff. The city of Sitifis was a major assize centre that became the capital of the new province of Mauretania Sitifensis in the last decades of the third century.[49] The transformation of Sitifis into a provincial capital and seat of the governor provides a plausible context for our inscription. The reference to a *numerus officialium* conveys the exclusive nature of appointments to the *officium*, evidently perceived as a mark of distinction and a major career achievement. This is a good illustration of the role of prestige—in this case, the prestige attached to an official position or appointment—determining whether a particular activity shows up in an inscription, a point that will be developed in the final section of this chapter.

An epitaph from the coastal city of Gigthis in Africa Proconsularis documents a *iurisconsultus* (inscribed on the stone as *ius consultum*) named Iunius Urbanus, who is commemorated as a 'beloved son' [B12]/[D4].[50] This epitaph, dating most likely to the late third or early fourth century, appears to be the earliest epigraphic attestation of *iurisconsultus* with reference to a legal expert in the provinces.[51] In two inscriptions from 361 CE, we encounter another African

[47] See Philo of Byblos *FGrHist* 790 F 34.

[48] See Liebs (1993), 29–31 and Vössing (1996), 135–36.

[49] The creation of Mauretania Sitifensis took place between 288 and 290 CE: a dedication by the *praeses* of Caesariensis (CIL VIII 8474, Sitifis) shows the province still undivided in 288, while a dedication by another *praeses* of Caesariensis at Saldae (CIL VIII 8924) mentions Sitifensis in 290 CE. On the *officia* of governors, see Palme (1999).

[50] See Liebs (1993), 33–4 and Vössing (1996), 131–32 and (1997a), 79.

[51] The emergence of provincial *iurisconsulti* in the fourth century has been taken to mean that the term lost its traditional meaning of 'legal expert with the *ius publice respondendi*' and became synonymous with *iurisperitus*, see Kunkel (1967^2), 348 n. 735 and Vössing (1996), 131 and (1997a), 79, 134, 231 and 387. *Iurisperitus* and *iurisconsultus* are treated as interchangeable by Humfress (2007). An examination of the late Roman testimonia for *iurisconsultus* suggests, however, that the term

iurisconsultus: a civic officeholder (*flamen perpetuus*) named Annius Namptoivius, who had held the post of *magister studiorum* and was serving as *curator rei publicae* in Thuburbo Maius where he supervised the reconstruction of a bathhouse [B19].[52] It has been suggested that *magister studiorum* should be understood, not in the usual way as referring to the imperial secretariate *a studiis* at Rome, but as a reference to the teaching of the liberal arts and in this context specifically to the teaching of Roman law.[53] Similarly, the late third-century epitaph of Marcus Picarius Turranius describes him as a 'chaste and extraordinary man during his lifetime' who was 'moreover a teacher of the law (*magistro etiam iuris*)' [B14].[54] Alternatively, *magister studiorum* could have been a post in the *officium* of the proconsul of Africa.[55] If this inference is correct, Namptoivius would be yet another example of a provincial legal expert at the court of the governor.[56]

The epigraphic trend whereby members of the African officeholding elite begin to be commemorated as forensic orators, legal experts and judicial advisors at the turn of the third century suggests a surge in the public prestige of legal practice. Even expressions of patronal relations between Roman governors and members of the local elite—a well-established epigraphic genre—begin to be articulated through the vocabulary of legal practice in the third century. Particularly striking is the emergence of *advocatus*—a general term for a courtroom role—as a title in career inscriptions, where it appears alongside public offices and even seems to eclipse references to officeholding careers. The presence of *advocatus* and *iurisperitus* in private funerary contexts, including poetic descriptions of individuals 'pleading cases to great acclaim' and 'serving and defending the law,' further underscores the rise of legal practice as an element of elite self-representation in Roman North Africa in the Severan age.

retained its specific association with legal experts whose *responsa* had an official authority. This is explored by me in a separate paper.

[52] The text is attested in two non-identical copies, see Liebs (1993), 31–3, see also Lepelley (1979), 2.200–201, Kaster (1988), 134 no. 103 and Vössing (1996), 129 and (1997a), 284–85. The name Namptoivius is derived from the Punic Namphamo, see Shaw (2011), 236–37, I am grateful to Brent Shaw for pointing this out to me. On *curatores rei publicae* in Africa, see Jacques (1984), 221–48.

[53] Both Lepelley (1979), 2.200 and Kaster (1988), 134 argue that *magister studiorum* in this inscription is unlikely to refer to the imperial secretariate *a studiis*, a post that is still attested in the reign of Constantius (CIL VI 1704, Rome, 325–37 CE), held by a *clarissimus* who had previously served as *advocatus fisci*, *a consiliis* and *a libellis*. That *magister studiorum* could refer to the teaching of the liberal arts has been suggested by Lepelley (1979) and Kaster (1988) 134 and 303 on the basis of *CTh* 13.3.5 (362 CE) and a fourth-century inscription from Trier for a *magister studiorum* who was also a *grammaticus* and a teacher of rhetoric (Schillinger 2 = *MEFR* 1994: 685 = AE 1978, 503, 4c. CE).

[54] See Liebs (1993), 26–7 and Vössing (1996), 132 and (1997a), 283–84.

[55] This inference is supported by papyrological evidence for a secretary *ab epistulis* in the service of the Roman prefect of Egypt, see SB XVI 12749 = P. Daris 2 = P. Strasb. IV 179 (Arsinoe, 176–9 CE) where a certain Messius Bassus, ἐπὶ τῶν ἐπιστολ(ῶν) Ἑλληνικῶν, serves on the *consilium* of the prefect. The ἐπιτηρητὴς ἡγεμονικῶν ἐπιστολῶν mentioned in two further papyri (P. Oxy. LI 3615, 214–48 CE; SB XVIII 13175 = W.Chr. 52, 194 CE) may be the same official.

[56] See also [B18] (4c. CE) where father and son had worked together as legal scholars and *assessores* at Carthage.

C. Eloquence and Legal Expertise in Funerary Inscriptions of Young Men Pursuing Their Studies

In the city of Mactaris, a Roman *colonia* in the hinterland of Africa Proconsularis, we find an elaborate mausoleum belonging to the family of the Iulii dating to the first half of the third century. One of several iambic verse epitaphs commemorates Gaius Iulius Proculus Fortunatianus, a son of the head of the family, who died at the age of twenty-two [C2].[57] Despite his young age, the epitaph emphasizes the achievements of Fortunatianus as far outstripping his years. He is poignantly portrayed as a 'clever boy and a modest youth, who grew up to be a young orator and delighted the ears of the public with his skills as a *togatus*' to great acclaim (*multis laudibus*). The term *togatus* may refer to Fortunatianus giving declamatory performances, as the references to *studia* and public entertainment (*publicas aures togatus studiis delectavit suis*) may also suggest. Alternatively, this could be a reference to him pleading as a forensic orator (*togatus*) in the courts.[58] Fortunatianus of Mactaris clearly belonged to a very wealthy local family. One wonders whether he was pursuing his rhetorical education at Mactaris, as his epitaph seems to suggest, or whether his family had opted for him to receive superior rhetorical training in the provincial capital.[59] This was the path taken by Lucius Baebius Barbarus, a young man from the town of Agger in the vicinity of Mactaris, who was a student at Carthage when he died at twenty [C13].[60] Another epitaph from Agger commemorates Marcus Antonius Faustianus Nepos Principinus, a young man who was 'recognized as an expert orator in his community' (*acceptus patriae dicendi peritus*) before he died at eighteen [C14].[61] The phrase *dicendi peritus* echoes a well-known dictum ascribed to Cato the Elder (*vir bonus dicendi peritus*).[62] Considering that the Punic *civitas* of Agger achieved the status of a Roman *municipium* at a late stage, not before the Severi, the reference to Cato may reflect oratory being proudly showcased by its Romanized elite into the third century as a hallmark of Roman culture.[63]

We find another aspiring student of oratory in the cemetery of Thubursicu Numidarum among the sons of the wealthy landowner and officeholder Quintus Vetidius Iuvenalis, mentioned earlier. Of his three sons, all of whom were *equites Romani,* two died at a young age. One of them, Lucius Vetidius Maternus Vetidianus, was studying at Carthage when he died at eighteen [C26].[64] His tombstone mentions that his family received special permission from the governor to convey his remains back to his hometown. A similar dispensation was

[57] See Vössing (1997a), 148–51.

[58] All three possibilities are entertained by Vössing (1997a), 149–50.

[59] On the enduring role of Carthage as an educational center in Roman North Africa, see Vössing (1997a), 268–324.

[60] See Vössing (1997a), 287–88.

[61] See Vössing (1997a), 217–19.

[62] See Quintilian, *Institutio oratoria* 12.1 with Winterbottom (1964).

[63] On the municipalization of Roman North Africa, see Gascou (1982a–b). On the civic status of Agger, see Gascou (1982b), 301 and Vössing (1997a), 117–18.

[64] See Vössing (1997a), 288–89.

granted to the Caecilii Frontones, a wealthy family from Volubilis in Mauretania, whose son Lucius Caecilius Fronto had died while studying at Rome [C24].[65] The brother of Maternus, Quintus Vetidius Felix Honoratianus, died in his hometown of Thubursicu Numidarum at the age of twenty-one [C27]. It is possible, although not specified, that he had studied rhetoric at Carthage as well. Additionally, both brothers are praised as *utraque lingua eruditi,* reflecting their sophisticated literary education in Latin and Greek. In advertising their bilingual education, the epitaphs of the Vetidii reflect a broader trend in African funerary epigraphy, where multiple *utraque lingua eruditi* are attested in the first half of the third century.[66]

It is clear from the epitaphs of the Vetidii that Iuvenalis and his wife were showcasing their ability to provide their sons with an expensive education, in spite of the fact that fate had dealt them a cruel hand. By contrast, in an epitaph from Calama, a distraught father describes how he nurtured his two sons in their early years, sent them off to pursue their studies, and then, after many expenses and with none coming to fruition, buried them both [C6].[67] Other families were more fortunate: a verse inscription from a floor mosaic in a large third-century villa at Cuicul proclaims that 'the young men born into this house, brothers and colleagues whom illustrious [Cuicul] marvels to have produced with the great favor [of the gods], are now attending the auspicious tribunals of Libya, together and decorated by everlasting honour. Fortunate are the parents who have merited this . . . ' [C29].[68] Evidently, both sons had attained prestigious positions in the high courts of the province, as high-profile orators or legal experts or both. The phrases *tribunalibus adsunt* and *honore perenni* suggest that, like the elite *rhētores* and *nomikoi* in Greek inscriptions and papyri, they belonged to an inner-circle of elite legal practitioners at the court of the governor who traveled with him to the *conventus.* The floor inscription vividly attests to the contemporary perception of legal practice as a pinnacle career achievement in Roman North Africa in the third century.

It is a logical tendency for epitaphs of young men who died without attaining public careers to be superlative with regard to their innate talents and educational achievements. In a Severan epitaph from Cirta, we encounter a young 'master of all disciplines' (*peritissimus omnium studiorum*) who died at the age of twenty [C8].[69] In a funerary inscription from the vicinity of Masculula in the region of Sicca Veneria, a young aedile named Quintus Pomponius Fortunatus is described as 'a just and sober youth, constant in his upright and equitable habits, an expert in the law (*iuris peritus,* inscribed on the stone as *ruris peritus*) who in his earliest years displayed the modesty (*frugalitas*) of his ancestors and showed himself to be

[65] See Vössing (1997a), 165 n. 599. The remains of Fronto were conveyed back to Mauretania for a state funeral, which had been voted by the city council.

[66] For *utraque lingua eruditi* in African inscriptions, see [C9], [C26], [C27], and [C28]; see also [C5] and [C20] with Kotula (1969). Vössing (1997a), 288 assumes that the Vetidii learned Greek with a *grammaticus* at Carthage.

[67] See Vössing (1997a), 214–16.

[68] On the so-called 'house of Castorius'—see Blanchard-Lemée (1975), 153–70; the floor inscription is discussed at 167–8.

[69] See also [C9] with Vössing (1997a), 392 n. 1337, [C3] with Vössing (1997a), 120–1 and [C17].

their equal' [C22].[70] In view of his young age, one wonders whether *iuris peritus* should be understood in a technical sense, as referring to the activity of advising judges and issuing *responsa*, or whether this was an attribution of legal expertise to a young man who was, perhaps, studying the law and beginning to engage in forensic activity.[71]

In some epitaphs, the depiction of young men as illustrious orators and legal experts appears somewhat exaggerated, a reflection perhaps of the emotions of grief-stricken families and the wishful aspirations of small-town elites. Certain epitaphs, however, appear to document the start of an eminent career cut short by an untimely death. A third-century inscription from the base of a funerary statue in Thibilis—a small town in the hinterland of Cirta that was the birthplace of several Roman senators—commemorates a young man as a 'kinsman of Roman senators and equestrians, fluent and endowed with a marvelous eloquence, in [pleading] a noble orator and a declaimer effortless in improvisation, an author of dialogues, letters and bucolic poems' [C7].[72] The literary and rhetorical education of this young man, who died in his teens or early twenties, was clearly of the most expensive and prestigious sort, which accords with the manifest wealth of his family, who erected a funerary statue in his honour. One would imagine that the scion of such a family was being groomed for a public career at Cirta and entry into the equestrian civil service. An apparent reference to forensic oratory suggests that he had already started pleading in the courts—at Cirta, so it may be presumed, possibly as a young *protégé* of one of the eminent men alluded to in the epitaph.

We also find the virtues, ambitions and career achievements of adult members of the civic elite being projected onto very young children.[73] In a verse epitaph from Carthage, a boy (*puer*) named Annaeus Mussius is praised for his education (*disciplina*) [C30]. The phrase *agens bonus* appears to represent Mussius as already practicing forensic oratory. Several epitaphs for boys (*pueri*) as young as six praise them for their intellect (*ingenium*) and 'extraordinary talent' (*egregia indoles*).[74] In a Severan verse epitaph from Caesarea in Mauretania, which glosses a famous line of Vergil's fourth eclogue, the young son of a governor is exhorted to 'begin outstripping your father in your studies and decorate your illustrious stock

[70] See Liebs (1993), 19–21, who reads *iuris peritus* in place of *ruris peritus*. Vössing (1997a), 119 n. 399 favors *ruris peritus*. In view of the numerous orthographical errors in the inscription (due in part to the stonecutter's creative use of ligatures), *ruris peritus* seems to me less plausible; this expression has no parallel and does not fit the context.

[71] The same question arises with regard to Greek funerary inscriptions for very young men who are commemorated as skilled *nomikoi*, see Dörner (1952), 58 no. 64 = Jones (2007), no. 33 and Jones (2007), no. 22 (224 CE).

[72] See Vössing (1997a), 454–5 n. 1533. In my view, the reconstruction *i[n agen]/do orator nobilis* is preferable to *i[n dicen]/do orator nobilis* (Pflaum, ILAlg) which seems tautological, especially since it follows *mira eloquentia facundus*. For a similar formulation comparing forensic and epideictic oratory, see Seneca the Elder on the rhetorical style of Asinius Pollio (Sen. *contr.* 4 *praef.* 3).

[73] On the Roman representation of children as miniature adults, see Vössing (1997a), 602–603 with an overview of the scholarly literature.

[74] For boys being praised for their *ingenium* and *indoles*, see [C1], [C3], [C11], [C19], [C23], [C30], [C31], [C32].

with your own achievements' (*incipe parve puer studiis superare parent(em) egregiumque genus propriis virtutibus orna*) [C33].[75]

It is a clear and significant chronological pattern that references to education (*studia, disciplina, eruditio*), rhetorical skill and legal knowledge emerge in African funerary inscriptions for boys and young men at the turn of the third century. In line with the rise of epigraphic testimonia for *advocati* and *iurisperiti*, attested in twenty-three inscriptions from the third and fourth centuries, all eleven references to oratory and law in funerary inscriptions of young men can be firmly dated to the third century.[76] Likewise, four of the five epigraphic testimonia for bilingualism in Latin and Greek (*utraque lingua eruditio*) date to the Severan age.[77] From a total of approximately fifteen references to *ingenium* (intellect) and *indoles* (talent), seven date to the third and fourth centuries, while the rest most probably date to the late second or third century.[78] From approximately twelve references to *studia*, nine date to the third century and one to the fourth or fifth century. The remaining two most probably date to the late second or third century.[79] To these we may add a Severan inscription from Calama for a seasoned Roman *eques* who had held all local civic offices and is commemorated by his children as *amator studiorum*.[80] A fourth-century inscription from the base of an honorific statue in the Severan forum of Lepcis Magna honours Aurelius Sempronius Serenus, a Roman *eques* and leading citizen (*principalis*) of Alexandria who was also a member of the local *ordo decurionum*. He is praised for his 'outstanding and admirable genius in his scholarly pursuits' (*insigne et admirabile ingenium studiorum*). By the standards of the fourth century, this implicitly included oratory and possibly law.[81] Altogether, the evidence shows a dramatic surge of references to education, oratory and legal expertise in African epigraphy in the third and fourth centuries. A clear turning point for this development was the Severan age.

[75] See Vössing (1997a), 42–4.

[76] For references to oratory, see [C2], [C7], [C9], [C10], [C13], [C14], [C18], [C26], [C30] (3c. CE); see also [B1ab], [B2ab], [B5], [B6], [B7], [B10], [B13], [B16], [D1], [D5], [D6] (3c. CE) and [D3] (2c.–3c. CE). For references to legal expertise, see [C22], [C29] (3c. CE); see also [B8] (late 2c.), [B21] (2c.–3c.), [B3], [B4], [B11], [B12], [B13], [B14], [B15], [B20] (3c. CE), [B18], [B19] (4c. CE).

[77] For references to *utraque lingua eruditi*, see [C5] (3c. CE?), [C9], [C26], [C27] [C28] (3c.); see also [C20] (3c. CE).

[78] For references to *ingenium*, see [C4], [C5], [C14], [C16] (2c.–3c. CE), [C15] (3c. CE) and [C31] (4c. CE). For references to *indoles*, see [C12], [C19], [C21], [C24] (2–3c. CE), [C11], [C23], [C25] (3c. CE) and [C33] (3–4c. CE). See further Vössing (1997a), 165 n. 599.

[79] For references to *studia*, see [C13], [C17] (2c.–3c. CE) and [C2], [C6], [C8], [C18], [C26], [C32] [E6] (3c. CE), see also CIL VIII 5373 = CIL VIII 17498 = ILAlg 1, 330 (a sixteen-year-old *studiosus* from Calama, 3c. CE), ILAlg 1, 2769 = ILCV 4736 = CLEAfr 2, 122 = AE 2014, 1545 (a *puer* pursuing his studies, Madauros, 4c.–5c. CE) and CIL VIII 8870 = CLE 501 = CLEAfr 143 (a poet whom the learned muse Thalia has decorated with literary achievements (*studia*), Tubusuctu, 3c. CE).

[80] CIL VIII 5367 = CIL VIII 17496 = ILAlg 1, 288 = Louvre 117 = AE 2000, +68 (Calama, *c*.200–50 CE).

[81] IRT 559 = AE 2003, 1917 = AE 2007, +1692 = AE 2007, +1694 (Lepcis Magna, 4c. CE). On *studere* with reference to forensic oratory, see the sources cited in Vössing (1997a), 43 n. 112. On *studere* with reference to legal experts (*iuris studiosi*), see Liebs (1993), 22–4 and Vössing (1996), 129–30 and (1997a), 424.

D. Legal Practice in Funerary Inscriptions of Individuals without an Officeholding Career

African inscriptions offer a few testimonia for individuals who engaged in legal practice but did not, as far as we can tell, belong to the officeholding elite or pursue a public career. At Lambaesis, a small funerary stele records the vicissitudes of Lucius Calpurnius Flamininus, a seasoned orator who 'pleaded cases happily' (*oravi causas felix*) before a sudden catastrophe swept away his entire family. He had the inscription made during his lifetime and died at the age of seventy-five [D3]. The very fact that Flamininus wrote his own epitaph, in which he simply refers to himself as 'pleading cases,' in itself suggests his non-elite status. In contrast to members of the curial class, for whom forensic oratory was part of a public career, the tombstone of Flamininus suggests that he spent his years pleading cases as a source of income. In this respect, Flamininus can be compared to the more humble sort of orators attested in the hinterland of Egypt, who pleaded cases and performed legal services for local families and clients of modest means.[82]

An epitaph from Thamugadi documents a family tomb erected by Gaius Iulius Silvanus, whose stylized name *Cicero Thabudeiensis* ('Cicero of Thabudeos') suggests that he was a forensic orator or teacher of rhetoric in the nearby town of Thabudeos [D1].[83] In an epitaph from the area of Bisica, the deceased Agmina Secunda laments being separated from her beloved husband Gaius Modius Silvanus Ciceronianus whom she refers to as 'my Cicero,' suggesting likewise that the man was a teacher or practitioner of oratory who had adopted Ciceronianus as an artistic name.[84] It is possible that the *advocatus* Valerius Valerianus [B7]/[D2] and the *iurisconsultus* Iunius Urbanus [B12]/[D4], both of whom died in their thirties and were buried by their mothers, were not members of the civic elite but more humble individuals who made a living by pleading cases, drafting legal documents and giving litigants legal advice.[85]

The relative paucity of such testimonia in the African epigraphic record throws into relief the extent to which epigraphic evidence for legal practice predominantly documents the activity of the elite, providing us with a rather limited view of the broader world of litigation and legal culture in the African provinces. Among the chance epigraphic attestations that shed light on this world, we can cite a third-century funerary monument from the Roman colony of Ammaedara in Numidia, where an individual proudly states: 'throughout the seventy years that I have lived, neither the crowds of the forum nor the laws were of any concern to me' [D6]. This statement suggests just how much other individuals around him *were* concerned with the laws and the activity of the forum.

[82] See for example the *rhētōr* Pasion, active in the Arsinoite nome: P. Fam. Tebt. 24 ll. 82–102 (Arsinoite nome, August 15, 114 CE); P. Fam. Tebt. 24 ll. 22–40 (Arsinoite nome, 124 CE) and P. Phil. 3 (Arsinoite nome, 123 CE). See my discussion in Dolganov (2018a), 352–53. One suspects that the profile of Calpurnius Flamininus was akin to that of the *causidici* mocked by Juvenal in his seventh satire.

[83] See Vössing (1997a), 401–402 n. 1370.

[84] See Vössing (1997a), 401–402 n. 1370.

[85] See my discussion above with nn. 39 and 50.

2. LEGAL PRACTITIONERS IN ROMAN NORTH AFRICA: LITERARY AND LEGAL SOURCES

As one might expect, the African perspective on forensic culture in Roman North Africa was more complimentary than Juvenal's satirical description—not the 'nursemaid of pleaders' (*nutricula causidicorum*) but the 'muse of orators' (*camena togatorum*), in the words of Apuleius in a speech praising Carthage to the Roman governor in the 160s.[86] In his autobiographical self-defence against charges of black magic at the governor's court in 158, Apuleius sheds light on the educational pursuits of wealthy elites in the African hinterland. Apuleius himself was a native of Madauros, a Roman *colonia* in the hinterland between Africa and Numidia. The son of a municipal officeholder (*duumvir*), he received his primary education in both Latin and Greek and was subsequently sent to Carthage for his rhetorical training.[87] He traveled to Athens to study philosophy and finally to Rome to study (and, presumably, practice) oratory. Apuleius ultimately returned to Africa, where he became an acclaimed orator and pursued an officeholding career.[88] A similar path was taken by Apuleius' younger friend Sicinius Pontianus, the scion of a wealthy family of equestrian rank from Oea on the Tripolitanian coast (69, 72, 94). By contrast, Sicinius Pudens, the young brother of Pontianus, is mocked by Apuleius for his rudimentary Latin and Greek and lack of a literary education (98).[89] Throughout his speech *De magia*, Apuleius showcases his own mastery of both languages (9, 12, 36, 38–9, 82).[90] Two centuries later, the young Augustine would follow in the footsteps of Apuleius, traveling from his native town of Thagaste to Madauros for his primary education, then to Carthage for his rhetorical training. Like Apuleius, Augustine traveled to Rome to advance his

[86] See Apuleius, *Florida* 20. In his commentary to the *Florida*, Hunink (2001), 109 and 206 takes *togatus* to mean 'erudite' whereas it seems to me to be a clear reference to forensic activity, as illustrated by *Florida* 9 where a toga-clad herald (*praeco togatus*) speaks from the tribunal of the *proconsul*. This meaning of *togatus* is corroborated by a contemporary epigraphic reference to an association of forensic orators (*corpus togatorum a foro*, CIL XIV 409 = ILS 6146, Ostia, 100–50 CE). This is consistent with the late Roman meaning of *togatus* = *advocatus*, see the sources discussed in Weiling (1996).

[87] On the Roman rhetorical curriculum, see Heath (2004). For a general account of education in the Roman Empire, see Vössing (1997a) and the still useful study of Marrou (1981) vol. 2 (sixth edition of the 1948 original). The more recent survey of Vössing downplays legal training for orators, citing a lack of evidence for provincial law schools beyond Rome and Berytus, see Vössing (1997a), 367–410. More convincing on this point is Humfress (2007), 81–6, who emphasizes private study and *tirocinium* as modes of legal training, see Kunkel (1967^2), 335–45 on the tradition of *tirocinium* among legal experts.

[88] On Apuleius' self-defence *De magia*, see Bradley (2014) and (2012), 3–22 and 147–63. Regarding Apuleius' career, Augustine states in *Ep.* 138.19 that Apuleius held the provincial priesthood of the imperial cult, the highest civic office in the province. This is corroborated by a statement of Apuleius in *Florida* 16 that he 'accepted a priesthood' and thereby 'attained the greatest honor at Carthage' (*suscepti sacerdotii summum mihi honorem Carthaginis adesse*). In the same letter, Augustine points out that Apuleius never achieved a *iudiciaria potestas*, an imperial administrative appointment, by which he presumably meant that his career never reached the equestrian *cursus honorum*.

[89] See *De magia* 8, 28, 94 and 98. As cogently stated by Bradley, 'the Sicinii, although prosperous, cannot all be assumed to have been well educated or committed to metropolitan culture,' see Bradley (2012), 162.

[90] See also *Flor.* 18, where Apuleius refers to his own ability to extemporize in Latin and Greek (*utraque lingua*) and describes a dialogue composed by him with Latin and Greek speaking parts that will be performed by the orators Sabidius Severus and Iulius Persius, respectively.

career as a rhetorician and ultimately returned to establish himself in his home province. The remarkably similar paths taken by Apuleius and Augustine reflect the stability of Roman models of education and civil career paths followed by civic elites in Roman North Africa (and other provinces) from the high Empire to late Antiquity.[91]

After spending some years at Rome, some provincials stayed on to pursue careers in the imperial capital.[92] For Africans from senatorial families—such as Marcus Cornelius Fronto, the eminent orator and statesman from Cirta who came to Rome in his youth,[93] or Salvius Iulianus [B17] the eminent legal expert from a small village near Hadrumetum who studied law at Rome under Iavolenus Priscus[94]—forensic activity in the imperial capital opened the door to a senatorial career. In a letter to the councilors of Cirta in 158 CE, Fronto mentions numerous Roman senators from Numidia who had achieved renown as orators and legal experts at Rome.[95] Several of these Numidian *clarissimi* were ranked among the best orators (*nunc fori principem locum occupant*) while another had been granted the right to issue public legal opinions (*ius publicum respondentem*) by the emperor. This man can be identified as the *iurisconsultus* Publius Pactumeius Clemens [B9ab], a native of Cirta whose senatorial career is attested in three inscriptions and whose legal writings are briefly quoted by Pomponius in the *Digest*.[96] As a member of an established senatorial family, Clemens is likely to have received some of his rhetorical and legal training at Rome. The courts at Rome also offered career opportunities for less illustrious individuals, such as Praetextatus, a 'most noble legal expert from Africa' (*iuris peritus nobilissimus ex Africa*) who died at Rome in his sixties in the second or third century.[97] The third-century Christian apologist Minucius Felix was a forensic orator (*causidicus*) from Africa active at Rome. The dramatic setting of his apologetic treatise *Octavius* is a debate (*controversia*) in Ostia between two orators who are on vacation (*feriae*) from the

[91] On the education and early life of Augustine, see Brown (1967), 7–63.

[92] On career paths and mechanisms of social mobility among North African elites in the high Empire, see Garnsey (1978). On the growing importance of education as a factor of mobility, see Hopkins (1961) and Vössing (1997a), 590–95 on the late Empire.

[93] On Fronto, see Champlin (1980), who assumes that he was mostly educated at Rome. On the careers of Fronto and Apuleius, see Keulen (2014).

[94] On Salvius Iulianus (PIR^2 S 136, Thomasson (1996), 68–9 no. 85), see Kunkel (1967^2), 157–66, Bund (1976) and Liebs (1997a).

[95] See Fronto, *Ad. Am.* II 11 with van den Hout (1999), 458–61. Among the orators mentioned by Fronto are Servius Silanus from Hippo Regius (PIR^1 S 428) and M. Postumius Festus from the region of Cirta (PIR^1 Postumius 660, RE 22.95 M. Postumius Festus). The latter is posthumously commemorated at Rome by his great-grandson as *orator utraque facundia maximus* in CIL VI 1416, 3805, 4694, 4774 = CIL VI 31649 = ILS 2929 (Rome, mid-3c. CE).

[96] On Pactumeius Clemens (PIR^2 P 37), see Kunkel (1967^2), 154–57, Champlin (1980), 13–5 and Eck (1983), 179–84. The career of Clemens is attested in two inscriptions from Cirta, see CIL VIII 7059 = ILAlg 2.1 645 = ILS 1067 and CIL VIII 7060 = ILAlg 2.1 646. A citation from his legal works occurs in Pomponius, *On Plautius* 7 (D.40.7.21.1).

[97] CIL VI 33867 (2–3c. CE). See also the epitaph for Aemilius Pollio, an *advocatus* of 'good talent' (*bonae indolis*) from Tripolitania, who pleaded at Rome in the fourth century and died there at the age of twenty eight, CIL VI 33829 = ICUR 3 6537 = ILCV 745 (Rome, 3–4c. CE). On Africans attested in inscriptions at Rome, see Ricci (1994), with Pollio and Praetextatus discussed at 192, 194 and 202.

courts at Rome. Both orators, as well as Minucius Felix who arbitrated the *controversia*, were African provincials.[98]

Other elite provincials, after completing a period of training and networking at Rome, sought their fortune in major provincial cities[99] or returned to their home provinces to pursue local careers. In his *Apology*, Apuleius describes how, after coming back from Rome, Pontianus wished to begin his *tirocinium orationis* and asked Apuleius to recommend him to the *proconsul* Lollianus as a promising young orator. The phrase *tirocinium orationis* implies that Pontianus was seeking to apprentice himself to orators at the governor's court. The fact that Apuleius was in a position to write him a letter of recommendation implies that he had already made a name for himself at the court of the *proconsul*.[100] In this brief remark, Apuleius provides us with important information about the progress of provincial careers: both men spent some years at Rome, then returned to Africa and proceeded to advance their careers through forensic activity at the court of the provincial governor. Through the patronage of influential men, such as the *proconsul* and his *legati*, they could rise to top offices in the provincial capital and even be adlected into the equestrian civil service. The wealthy equestrian family of Pontianus was well-positioned to enter the imperial ruling elite and successfully did so in the course of the second century.[101] By contrast, according to Augustine, Apuleius never managed to achieve an equestrian career.[102] Another area of forensic activity through which provincials could achieve distinction and promotion was the law. While some legal experts from Africa—such as Pactumeius Clemens [B9ab], Salvius Iulianus [B17], Messius Saturninus [E13], and possibly Papinian [E14]—pursued their careers at Rome, others were active in major African cities.[103] The activity of one such legal expert is documented by the letter of Augustine to Eustochius, whom Augustine asks for a written legal opinion (*responsum*) on of the law of slavery.[104] It is evident that Eustochius had an official authority to issue *responsa*, which Augustine could proceed to

[98] On Minucius Felix as a forensic orator at Rome, see Lactantius, *Divinae Institutiones* 5.1.22, Jerome, *Epistulae* 70 and *De viris illustribus* 58. On the dramatic setting of the dialogue, see *Octavius* 2.3. Vössing (1997a), 387 n. 1323 remarks that the two disputants—the Christian Octavius and the pagan Caecilius Natalis—were implicitly orators from Africa and suggests that they were in a relationship of *tirocinium fori*.

[99] See for example the wandering African *rhētor* who ended up in Dalmatia (CIL III 2127 = ILS 7774, Salona, 2c.–3c. CE). See also Fronto's letter of recommendation for the Greek rhetorician Aquila, who was seeking employment in Gaul (*Ad amicos* 1.7).

[100] See Apuleius, *De magia* 94.3–5 with Hunink (1997), 2.232–33, who rightly emphasizes the implications regarding Apuleius' own forensic activity at the governor's court.

[101] The second-century rise of Pontianus' family may be illustrated by the career of L. Aemilius Frontinus (PIR² A 348), possibly a kinsman of Pontianus' mother Pudentilla, who was consul in the 160s and *proconsul* of Asia under Commodus. Subsequently, at the turn of the third century, a Q. Sicinius Clarus (PIR² S 699, Thomasson (1984–90), 1.170 no. 45; *id.* (2009), 67) is attested as governor of Thrace, see Bradley (2012), 5.

[102] See Augustine, *Epistulae* 138.19 with n. 79 above.

[103] See [B8], [B11], [B12] [B15], [B18], [B19], [B21] and [C22]. Additionally, several legal writers in the *Digest* are suspected by Liebs to be Africans active in Africa: Tertullianus, Claudius Saturninus and Aemilius Macer, see Liebs (1993), 37–58. Regarding his more tentative attribution of the *Sententiae Pauli* to an African jurist, see the critical comments of Vössing (1997b).

[104] See Augustine, *Epistulae* 24* (422 CE) with Liebs (1993), 34–5, Vössing (1996), 136–38 and Humfress (2007), 73–4.

employ in his episcopal court. In view of the evidence for elite *nomikoi* giving *responsa* in Egypt in the Flavian period, it can be presumed that this practice already existed in Africa by the second century.

A curious commentary on the Roman model of rhetorical training and legal practice as the basis of elite careers can be found in Apuleius' *Golden Ass.* Lucius, the protagonist of the novel, is a Greek provincial from a senatorial family who travels to Rome to study Latin oratory and Roman law (1.1–2). After completing his studies, Lucius returns to his home province where he is transformed into an ass and takes part in a series of traumatic events that resemble the contrived plots of rhetorical exercises. As soon as he regains human form, Lucius returns to Rome to become an immensely successful forensic orator (*advocatus*) (11.28, 30).[105] Apuleius' depiction of a provincial landscape obsessed with Roman trials, crime and punishment can be read as a satirical commentary on legal culture in the African provinces. Even more significantly, Apuleius' pervasive legal references suggest a high degree of familiarity with Roman law on the part of his audience.[106] An even more remarkable density of legalisms occurs in the writings of the Severan Christian writer Tertullian of Carthage, where Roman legal doctrine plays a central role in theological arguments. Tertullian's elaborate use of legal language suggest that his African audience was well-acquainted with Roman law, use of legal contexts as dramatic settings for his treatises—the composition of a petition, the execution of a contract—suggests a high degree of familiarity with Roman courts and legal practice.[107]

In his apologetic treatise *Ad Scapulam*, Tertullian speaks of the Roman *proconsul* delivering judgment 'among the *advocati* and *assessores.*' He also reminds the governor Julius Scapula of earlier policies with regard to the Christians: 'all of this can be cited to you by the staff in your *officium,* as well as the *advocati,* who, proclaiming what they will about us, have themselves received favors from the Christians.'[108] Tertullian's reference to *advocati* alongside the *officium* and *assessores* suggests that these orators were 'regulars' at the governor's court. Tertullian goes on to describe how the assistants and family members of these *advocati* are frequently afflicted by demons, including a stenographer (*notarius*) struck down during a court hearing.[109] As the implicit source of these demons, one suspects that Tertullian intended for his audience to think of judicial curses, precisely of the sort that have been discovered in the necropoleis of Carthage.[110]

[105] On the link between declamation and the Roman novel, see van Mal-Maeder (2007), 115–46. My interpretation of the *Golden Ass* from the perspective of Roman elite education is the subject of a forthcoming paper.

[106] On trials in the *Golden Ass*, see Bodel (2010). For Roman legal jokes in the *Golden Ass*, see for example 2.28, 6.22–3, 6.29 and 9.27.

[107] On Roman legalism in Tertullian, see Beck (1967) and Vitton (1924). For a balanced assessment of the debate whether Tertullian was a 'jurist' (and whether this is a useful question) see Rankin (1997). The significance of Tertullian's legalism is explored by me in several forthcoming papers.

[108] See Tertullian, *Ad Scapulam* 4.3.

[109] Tertullian, *Ad Scapulam* 4.5.

[110] On judicial curses from Carthage, see n. 15 above.

3. FACTORS OF CHANGE: INSTITUTIONAL DEVELOPMENTS AND THE GROWING PRESTIGE OF LEGAL PRACTICE

The testimony of Fronto and the works of Apuleius and Tertullian illustrate the profound impact of the Roman judicial system on legal culture in Roman North Africa by the Antonine age. The career of Apuleius, who traveled from Madauros to Carthage and Rome to study oratory, suggests widespread adoption of Roman models of education and civil careers by African municipal elites. In view of the evidence for Roman forms of legal practice in first-century Egypt, one can only imagine that forensic culture in the cities of Africa and Numidia was strongly influenced by Roman models by the Flavian period. Consequently, the emergence of *advocati* and *iurisperiti* in African inscriptions at the turn of the third century is unlikely to reflect the adoption of Roman forms of legal practice where they did not exist before. The final task of this investigation, accordingly, will be to explain the surge in evidence for legal practice—predominantly, in the self-representation of the officeholding elite—in the Severan age.

In general terms, we are observing a change in the commemorative habits of North African elites. The question is, what spurred on this change. A perspective on this question is offered by second-century honorific inscriptions for five renowned figures in Roman jurisprudence. The first is an inscription from Dalmatia *c.*100 honouring the senator Iavolenus Priscus, which gives a full account of his senatorial career without any reflection of his activity as a leading legal expert who gave public *responsa* at Rome and led the so-called 'Sabinian' school of jurisprudence.[111] Similarly, the senatorial career inscription of Publius Iuventius Celsus, a prolific and influential jurist who led the so-called 'Proculian' school, makes no mention of his status as a leading legal expert.[112] Neither does the lengthy African inscription honouring Salvius Iulianus as *proconsul* of Africa in the 160s [B17], which describes his senatorial career in detail without any mention of his legal expertise—a noteworthy fact, considering that Iulianus was a leading jurist during three imperial reigns and one of the most influential figures in Roman jurisprudence in his generation.[113] By contrast, two African inscriptions

[111] On Iavolenus Priscus (PIR² I 14), see Kunkel (1967²), 138–40 and Liebs (2010), 130–31. The inscription in question is CIL III 2864 = CIL III 9960 = ILS 1015 (Dalmatia, *c.*100 CE). In one of his letters, Pliny states that 'Priscus is altogether of doubtful sanity of mind. Nevertheless, he is involved in public affairs and is invited to participate in judicial *consilia* and even gives public *responsa* on the *ius civile*' (*est omnino Priscus dubiae sanitatis, interest tamen officiis, adhibetur consiliis atque etiam ius civile publice respondet*, Pliny, *Ep.* 6.15.3). In his *Digest*, Salvius Iulianus mentions that Iavolenus was his teacher (*praeceptor*) of Roman law, see Iulianus, *Digest* 42 (D.40.2.5).

[112] On Celsus (PIR² I 882) see Kunkel (1967²), 146–47 and Liebs (2010), 24. The inscription in question is AE 1978, 292 (Sentinum, 114–117 CE). See also the letter to Celsus preserved in CIL VI 2120 = ILS 8380 = AE 1999, +24 = AE 2002, +135.

[113] On Iulianus, see [B17] and n. 94 above. The statement that Iulianus was honored by Hadrian with a double salary as *quaestor principis* on account of his 'great learning' (*cui divos Hadrianus soli/salarium quaesturae duplicavit/propter insignem doctrinam*) may be an indirect allusion to his legal work. One wonders whether Iulianus' great fame as a jurist itself prompted the laconic, understated reference to his *insignis doctrina*. Instead, the inscription focuses on his spectacular senatorial career.

from the 160s honouring Publius Pactumeius Clemens [B9ab] place the title *iurisconsultus* in a prominent position at the end of his senatorial career.[114] Likewise, a contemporary inscription from Ostia for Volusius Maecianus places *iurisconsultus* above Maecianus' most prestigious office of *praefectus Aegypti*.[115]

The emergence of *iurisconsultus* as a title in senatorial and equestrian career inscriptions in the 160s is a conspicuous shift that requires explanation.[116] A plausible inference would be that this status became more official or more exclusive (and, consequently, more prestigious) in the mid-second century. This would accord well with what Antonine legal writers have to say about the *ius publice respondendi* ('right to issue public legal opinions') as an exclusive privilege bestowed by the emperor on select legal experts.[117] In particular, we may note Pomponius' reference to an exchange between Hadrian and a legal expert who petitioned him for the *ius respondendi*, to whom the emperor sharply replied that the privilege was 'not to be asked for, but to be bestowed' (*non peti, sed praestari solere*).[118] It may be that Hadrian sought to make the *ius publice respondendi* a more narrow privilege, conferred on a small number of legal experts who thereby acquired a highly influential role within the imperial court system. This would be in line with Hadrian's well-known efforts to increase the legal competence of the *consilium principis* and the imperial bureau of petitions (*a libellis*). The increasingly prominent role of legal experts in the administration of the empire and the legal activity of the emperor under Hadrian and his successors are additional factors favoring the development of *iurisconsultus* into a prestigious title in the mid-second century.[119]

As with *iurisconsultus* in senatorial and equestrian careers, the emergence of *advocatus* and *iurisperitus* in African career inscriptions indicates that these terms corresponded to an official status or function that could be regarded as a career achievement of the elite. In Numidia, this development can be dated with precision to the reign of Septimius Severus, as illustrated by the inscriptions from

By contrast, the less illustrious career of Pactumeius Clemens and the equestrian career of Maecianus may have received a welcome boost from *iurisconsultus*.

[114] On Clemens, see [B9ab] and n. 96 above.

[115] CIL XIV 5348 = SdOstia 11 no. 42. On Maecianus, see Kunkel (1967^2), 174–76, Liebs (1997b) and Pflaum (1960–1961), no. 141. For a further instance of *iurisconsultus*, see CIL VI 41294 = CIL VI 1628 = ILS 1456 = Bagno 73 (Rome, 231–300 CE), plausibly attributed to Herennius Modestinus, see Magioncalda (2009).

[116] For a useful (although not exhaustive) list of testimonia for *iurisconsultus*, see Tuori (2004), 306.

[117] On the *ius publice respondendi*, see Pomponius, *Enchiridion* (D.1.2.2.48–9), Gaius, *Inst.* 1.7 and Justinian's *Inst.* 1.2.8. For a useful overview of the scholarly debate, see Tuori (2004). In my view, Magdelain (1950) and Kunkel (1967^2), 271–304 remain the most cogent discussions of the ancient sources on the *ius respondendi*.

[118] On Hadrian and the *ius respondendi*, see Pomponius, *Enchiridion* (D. 1.2.2.49) with Kunkel (1967^2), 295–300.

[119] On the role of legal experts in the legal activity of the emperor, see Kunkel (1967^2), 272–304 and Honoré (1994^2), 1–32. Regarding the more recent study of Tuori (2016), see my remarks in Dolganov (2018b). For Kunkel, *iurisconsultus* was an exclusive title of legal experts with the *ius publice respondendi* since the early Principate. It is not possible to demonstrate this conclusively. A strong link between the title *iurisconsultus* and the *ius publice respondendi*, corresponding to an official function within the court system, may very well have been a second-century development. This is explored by me in a forthcoming paper. On legal experts in the Roman imperial administration, see Peachin (2016).

Lambaesis (mentioned above) where African officeholders refer to themselves as *advocati* and honour governors as their *patroni*. There is a total of six dedications to five different Numidian governors attested during the period from 200–48 CE [B1a], [B2ab] [B5], [B6] and [B10]. While some *advocati* mention their highest civic offices (*duovir, flamen perpetuus*), others do not mention their careers at all but represent themselves simply as *advocati*. In two dedications from the 240s, an equestrian *advocatus* named Lucius Valerius Optatianus thanks two different governors for the 'extraordinary favor' bestowed upon him (*ob insignem erga se dignationem*) [B2ab]. The Severan jurist Ulpian uses a similar formulation with reference to the special status (*dignitas*) of certain *advocati* who frequently plead before the governor.[120] In both contexts, the terms *dignatio* and *dignitas* appear to refer to an inner-circle of elite orators at the governor's court. That the dedications of Optatianus were made in two different cities (Lambaesis and Timgad) suggests, in line with the evidence from Egypt and Asia Minor, that this group of elite orators traveled with the governor on his assize tour.[121]

These Numidian inscriptions are contemporary with the first clear evidence from Roman Egypt for the affiliation of elite orators to the courts of specific officials. During an assize held by the prefect of Egypt in the early third century, a *rhētōr* exclaims: 'this is a powerful man, a *rhētōr* of the *epistratēgos*. For this reason, I cannot plead against him at that court but only before you.'[122] Another third-century papyrus documents a hearing before the prefect where all parties are represented by *rhētores*, except for three wealthy villagers who are represented by a *synēgoros* with the dazzling name of Seleukos. This Seleukos speaks to the prefect in a confident tone and aggressively assails his opponents. As soon as he reads out a pronouncement of Septimius Severus, the prefect declares his determination to uphold it. The dynamics of the hearing strongly suggest that Seleukos was an elite orator with a special status at the prefect's court. Considering that *synēgoros* was a technical term for *advocatus*, the status of Seleukos as a *synēgoros*—distinct from the ordinary *rhētores*—may have been analogous to that of Marcus Sedius Rufus and other leading *advocati* at court of the Numidian governor.[123]

[120] See Ulpian, *On the duties of proconsul* 1 (D.1.16.9.4).

[121] On elite legal practitioners traveling with the governor, see nn. 33–34 above.

[122] See SB I 5676 (232 CE) with my discussion in Dolganov (2018a), 378–80. The fearsome *rhētōr*, whose name is Claudius Dionysius, is attested pleading in another papyrus, see SB XX 15827 (3c. CE).

[123] See SB V 7696 (249 CE) with Crook (1995), 98–9, who does not comment on the significance of *synēgoros*. Contrary to the *editio princeps* (Skeat and Wegener (1935), 227), *synēgoros* and *rhētōr* are not synonyms in Roman judicial records, where *rhētōr* is the standard term whereas *synēgoros* is rare and always designates a special status such as *advocatus fisci* (*synēgoros tameiou*, see PSI XV 1549, 249–50 CE). An orator named Isidoros is described as *apo synēgoriōn* in P. Sakaon 31 = P. Thead. 15 (Arsinoite nome, 280–1 CE), see Crook (1995), 101–102 and Dolganov (2018a), 377–78. Crook interprets *apo synēgoriōn* as 'former *advocatus fisci*' (see *apo synēgoriōn tameiou* in IG II^2 3704, Attica, mid-3c. CE). I suspect that Isidoros, like Seleukos, belonged to an elite pool of *advocati* (= *synēgoroi*) affiliated with the court of the governor. This terminology looks forward to *synēgoros forou* as the technical term for statutory advocates affiliated with specific courts in late Antiquity, to be discussed further below. For *synēgoros forou* in late Roman papyri, see P.Princ. II 82 (481 CE) and P.Oxy. LXIII 4394 (494 CE).

The combined evidence from Numidia and Egypt suggests a broader development in the institutional organization of forensic oratory in the Severan age. What we seem to be observing is the creation of a formal status for elite orators pleading in major imperial courts. This appears to have involved singling out a small number of leading *advocati* (in Greek, *synēgoroi*) who received a privileged status—*dignitas*, in the words of Ulpian. A development of this sort would explain why *advocatus*, a broad term for a courtroom role, emerges as a title in third-century career inscriptions, where *advocati* advertise their relationship to the governor. It would also account for the emergence of *synēgoros* as distinct from *rhētōr* in Roman judicial records in the third century.

The evidence for legal experts may reflect a similar sort of development. Of the approximately sixteen legal experts attested in African inscriptions, at least twelve show a clear connection to the court of the governor: there are six *assessores* (one foreign [B4], one of unclear origin [B8], four African: [B18], [C22]), one *iurisperitus* [B21] and one *iuris studiosus* [B15] who are commemorated in public locations that probably functioned as judicial venues, three *iurisconsulti*: one active at Rome [B9ab], two in Africa [B12, B19]) and a *iuris peritissimus* commemorated alongside an *officialis* of the governor [B11]. A rescript of Antoninus Pius, which refers to *iuris studiosi* being entitled to seek remuneration (*salaria*) for their services, shows that there were salaried legal experts in the service of imperial officials by the mid-second century.[124] As we discover in an inscription from Antium, by the reign of Marcus Aurelius there were legal experts with procuratorial salaries of 60,000 HS and 100,000 HS serving on the advisory council (*consilium*) of the emperor.[125] A remark of Ulpian, who draws an analogy between *comites* who are eligible to receive *salaria* and public teachers of the liberal arts (*professores*), can be taken to imply that the *salaria* of *assessores* were paid out of the public purse.[126] Altogether, our sources appear to be documenting a process whereby legal experts acquired a formal status as salaried officials within the Roman imperial administration by the turn of the third century.

An important perspective on these developments is provided by the bureaucratization of the courts in late Antiquity. As documented by legal sources and papyri from the fourth and fifth centuries, the late Roman court system had a *numerus clausus* of orators (*advocati* or *scholastici fori*, in Greek *synēgoroi*

[124] See Paul, *On Plautius* 4 (D.50.13.4) with Behrends (1969), 217.

[125] The inscriptions in question document the equestrian career of a legal expert (*iurisperitus*) named Papirius Dionysius (PIR I^2 320ff. and Pflaum (1960–1), 1.472–76 no. 181). See CIL X 6662 = ILS 1455 and IG XIV 1072 = IGR I 135 = IGUR 59 with Kunkel (1967^2), 222–24 and Liebs (2010), 35.

[126] See Ulpian, *On all tribunals* 8 (D. 50.13.1.8) with Behrends (1969), 218. Behrends rightly points out that Ulpian's remarks about *professores iuris civilis* not being entitled to sue for salaries (Ulpian, *On all tribunals* 8 (D. 50.13.1.5)) do not apply here. Instead, the analogy is to *professores* of the liberal arts, who *were* entitled to sue. See also Ulpian, *On the Edict* 32 (D. 19.2.19.10) where Ulpian cites Papinian on the necessity to pay *salaria* to *comites* for the remaining period if a governor happens to die in office. The creation of public *salaria* for *assessores* is attributed to Pescennius Niger and Severus Alexander in the *Historia Augusta*, see *HA Pescennius Niger* 7.5 (which seems to imply that the *consiliarii* had previously been paid privately by the judge) and *HA Alexander Severus* 46 with Behrends (1969), 218–19.

or *scholastikoi forou*) who were authorized to plead in a specific imperial court.[127] The hierarchy of orators at each court was determined by factors of seniority and skill. At the top of the hierarchy was a small number of positions for legal representatives of the imperial treasury (*advocati fisci*), a prestigious salaried post that individuals could hold for a limited number of years.[128] Already in the fourth century, literary and legal sources document the role of the courts as a recruiting ground for officials at all levels of the imperial administration. Thus, the rise of the late Roman 'Bar' was integral to the development of the late Roman system of civil administration as a whole.[129] The Severan sources appear to be documenting an important earlier phase of this process, whereby elite legal practitioners began to acquire institutional ties to imperial courts.[130]

To contextualize these developments, we can look to the broader evolution of the Roman sphere of civil administration in the second and third centuries progressively contributing to the rise of legal practice as an avenue into imperial careers. Instituted under Hadrian, the *advocatio fisci* evolved in the course of the second century into an important entry-level position into the equestrian *cursus honorum*. By serving as *advocati fisci*, equestrians could dispense with military service and progress from the courts directly to administrative posts. Thus, the *advocatio fisci* created a formal mechanism—unique, as far as we can tell—for pursuing purely civil administrative careers.[131] The second-century creation of equestrian posts in the imperial bureaux of petitions (*a libellis*), court hearings (*a cognitionibus*), archives, libraries and judicial records (*a studiis, a bibliothecis, a*

[127] Only orators who had the license to plead (*potestas agendi*) in a particular court could plead there, and nowhere else, see *CTh*. 2.10.1–2 (319 CE). The reference an imperial *iussio* implies that this order had been issued in relatively recent memory. It most probably emanated from the Tetrarchic reforms at the end of the third century. On the significance of the reforms for the courts and *officia* of provincial governors, see Palme (1999), 96–7.

[128] The evolution of the *advocatio fisci* into a position at the top of the hierarchy of forensic orators at each imperial court is documented by legal sources from the fifth and sixth centuries, see *CJ* 2.7 sections 8, 10, 12–13, 22 and 24.

[129] On the rise of a 'Bar' of statutory advocates in major imperial courts in late Antiquity and its role as a recruiting ground for imperial administrators, see the classic chapter of Jones (1964), 1.470–522 with more recent discussions by Weiling (1996) and Humfress (2007), 99–106. See also Chastagnol (1979) on *advocati* in fourth-century Numidia.

[130] It is curious that the *Historia Augusta* credits Severus Alexander with 'bestowing many privileges on forensic orators in the provinces, even granting the *annona* to those whom he appointed to plead without remuneration (*quos constitisset gratis agere*),' *HA Alexander Severus* 44.4–5. The contrast between *militares* and *litterati* clearly reflects the *HA* author's fourth-century perspective. In view of the results of this investigation, however, one wonders whether there may be a factual core to this anecdote. On the separation of the civilian and military spheres (*militia officialis* and *militia armata*) under Diocletian and Constantine, see Speidel (2006), 263–68; Demandt (1989), 77 and 87 and Jones (1964), 1.42–5, 101 and 2.566.

[131] On the *advocatio fisci*, see de Ruggiero (1895), 1.125–31, Pflaum (1950), 89, Jones (1964), 509–11 and Vössing (1997a), 427–9. See also the unpublished dissertation of Avon (1972). On civil careers in the imperial administration, see the remarks of Pflaum (1950), 229, 245, 258 and 268 and (1960–1961), 219–24 on the career of Suetonius (no. 96). It is somewhat surprising that Pflaum, in his emphasis on military service as the enduring basis of imperial careers, does not comment on the significance of the *advocatio fisci* as marking the creation of purely civil career paths.

commentariis) and the emperor's Greek and Latin correspondence (*ab epistulis*) created further career opportunities in civil administration.[132] The evolution of the assessorate into a salaried post for legal experts, including equestrian appointments to the *consilium* of the emperor, can be regarded as a parallel development. From the reign of Hadrian, the imperial bureaux *a studiis* and *a libellis* were staffed by leading legal experts at Rome.[133] Similarly, the equestrian post *a commentariis* at the court of the praetorian prefects tended to be held by individuals with forensic expertise, either as former *advocati fisci* or as managers of the judicial records of officials.[134] This trend reached a high point under the Severi, when a number of legal experts progressed from the imperial bureaux to top administrative posts such as the praetorian prefecture. The variety of *advocationes fisci* documented by provincial sources indicates that their ranks diversified and multiplied in the provinces. The overwhelming majority of this evidence dates to the third century.

The significance of the Severan age for the rise of rhetorical and legal careers is clearly illustrated by the African epigraphic evidence for *advocati fisci* (Appendix E). From a total of approximately fourteen testimonia, thirteen have a third-century date. The one exception is an inscription from the 160s honouring Sextus Caecilius Crescens Volusianus, a native of an African *municipium* who had progressed from the *advocatio fisci* at Rome to the imperial secretariate *ab epistulis* [E3].[135] There is no information about Crescens pursuing any part of his career in Africa. In contrast to the Italian career of Crescens, third-century inscriptions show Africans progressing to *advocationes fisci* through local careers. The *eques* Marcus Herennius Victor from Thibilis began his career as a magistrate at Cirta before receiving an appointment as *advocatus fisci* at Rome, followed by a series of procuratorships posts in Italy and eventually in his home province of Numidia [E9]. The *eques* Aulus Vitellius Felix Honoratus from Thugga was first appointed *advocatus fisci* at Carthage, then progressed to *advocationes fisci* in Numidia and Noricum and ultimately to an *advocatio fisci* and procuratorial posts in Italy [E11].[136] Similarly, Pomponius Lemurianus from Sufetula began as *advocatus fisci* at Carthage, then progressed to an *advocatio fisci* in the Spanish provinces, served as *a commentariis* of the praetorian prefects at Rome and finally returned to Africa as a ducenariate procurator of the administrative

[132] On the proliferation of equestrian posts in the imperial bureaux in the Antonine and Severan age, see Pflaum (1950), 64–5, 70–1, 80–2 and 90–2.

[133] On legal experts in the imperial bureaux, see Honoré (1994^2).

[134] On the equestrian post *a commentariis* of the praetorian prefects, see Haensch (1995). Surviving testimonia for the equestrian careers of *a commentariis* include one former *advocatus fisci* (CIL VIII 11341 = ILS 9016 = ILTun 362 = AE 1908, +64 = Pflaum (1960–1961), no. 320, Sufetula, 3c. CE) one former manager of judicial records (*archistator*) for the prefect of Egypt (AE 1960, 245 = AE 1961, 227, Caesarea in Mauretania, *c.*167 CE) and one procurator who went on to govern several provinces (CIL VIII 8328 = ILAlg 2.3 7912 = AE 1912, 132 = AE 1941, 175 = AE 1949, +11= Pflaum (1960–1961), no. 331 (Cuicul, 3c. CE), *contra* Jarrett (1962) who sees the latter as a failed military career.

[135] For another African *advocatus fisci* who became *ab epistulis*, see [E12].

[136] For another African *advocatus fisci ad patrimonium Carthaginis*, see [E10].

region (*dioecesis*) of Hadrumetum [E7].[137] A third-century cursus from Lambaesis shows a *flamen perpetuus* who was 'thrice promoted to the *advocatio fisci*' in three different regions of Africa and Numidia [E5].[138] To obtain their first appointments as *advocati fisci* at Carthage and Lambaesis, these *equites* had presumably first distinguished themselves as forensic orators at the court of the governor. This is illustrated by another inscription from Lambaesis, where an *eques* and municipal officeholder (*flamen perpetuus*) named Gaius Vibius Maximus honours the deputy governor for nominating him to the *advocatio fisci* in Numidia [E1].[139] One can immediately note the resemblance between this inscription and other third-century Numidian inscriptions where elite *advocati* thank governors for their patronage [B1a], [B2ab] [B5], [B6], [B10]. One would imagine that these *advocati* constituted an elite pool of orators from which governors made nominations to the *advocatio fisci*. Such careers could lead to the very top, as exemplified by the career of Publius Messius Saturninus [E13], a native of Pheradi Maius who served in the imperial bureau *a studiis*, was appointed *advocatus fisci* at the imperial court (*sacrum auditorium*) and ultimately rose to a post *a declamationibus Latinis* under Septimius Severus with an impressive salary of 300,000 HS.[140] Another third-century *eques*, from a *municipium* in the hinterland of Carthage, served as *advocatus fisci* in eleven provinces, then received a series of procuratorial appointments that culminated in the praetorian prefecture [E2]. For Opellius Macrinus [E16], a native of Caesarea in Mauretania, activity as an *advocatus* in Africa was followed by an appointment to the *advocatio fisci* at Rome, which led to the praetorian prefecture and ultimately to his proclamation as emperor in 218. If we are to trust late Roman sources, the careers of the Severan legal expert and praetorian prefect Papinian [E14] and the emperor Septimius Severus [E15] likewise began with the *advocatio fisci* at Rome.

The growing nexus between legal practice and career opportunities had the logical consequence of enhancing the prestige-value of rhetorical and legal

[137] This inscription was erected for Lemurianus by another *eques* from Sufetula, who had studied together with him. The term *condiscipulatus* may refer to their primary education with a *grammaticus* or possibly to their rhetorical studies. Another third-century African *eques*, a native of the Severan *municipium* of Thubursicum Bure, was appointed by the emperor to the *advocatio fisci* at Rome and progressed to a procuratorial career in Italy see [E4]. For another third-century *advocatus fisci* who progressed to an equestrian career in Italy and the West see [E8].

[138] He is honored by his brothers, who had both held top civic offices and were themselves engaged in the pursuit of equestrian careers (*a militiis*).

[139] The appointment of *advocati fisci* is humorously illustrated by two anecdotes in Philostratus, where Caracalla appoints two sophists after being stunned by their superb rhetorical abilities, see Philostratus, *Vitae sophistarum* 621 and 626.

[140] On the career of Saturninus (PIR^2 M 527), see Pflaum (1960–1), 613–20 no. 231 and most recently Peachin (2016), 174 n. 30. He may be the same person as the Messius who serves together with Papinian on the *consilium* of the emperor Septimius Severus, see Paul Decrees 3 (D.49.14.50). This identification, already suggested by Poinssot (1932) (CRAI 1932, p. 69 = AE 1932, 34) and accepted by Pflaum (1960–1), is not taken into account by Kunkel (1967^2), 229–30. See also career of Nepotianus of Sicca Veneria (CIL VIII 27573 = ILS 9020 = AE 1906, 23, Sicca Veneria, *c.*200–50 CE; Pflaum (1960–1), no. 243) whose rhetorical skills earned him the first chair of rhetoric (*prima cathedra*) at Rome.

education and making them more visible in elite self-representation—as illustrated by an honorific inscription for Licinius Donatus, a *decurio* from the Roman colony of Rusguniae in Mauretania, which spells out how 'by virtue of his studies in the early years of his youth' he was selected to defend the *fiscus* in Baetica, then through his merits as a forensic orator promoted to the *defensio populi* at Rome [E6]. The developing link between rhetorical and legal training and prestigious career prospects arguably provides the strongest explanation for the proliferation of references to education, oratory and legal expertise in funerary inscriptions for young men at the turn of the third century. It is most probably by virtue of the same trend that teachers of rhetoric and law emerge in third-century African inscriptions as well.[141] When a young senator from Thibilis was appointed to the quaestorship in the early third century, he immediately sponsored an honorific statue to Cornelius Rusticus, his 'most faithful and extraordinary teacher'—of rhetoric, it may be presumed, which evidently played an instrumental role in the senator's successful entry upon a senatorial career.[142] A late Roman epitaph from Mactaris commemorates a teacher of rhetoric who died at the ripe age of eighty having been 'a master of speaking, as well as a master of life' (*fandi quondam vitaeque magister*), which gives a sense of the lofty light in which rhetorical skill was regarded at Mactar.[143] As with the evidence for *advocati* and *iurisperiti*, epigraphic testimonia for *magistri* provide only a small glimpse of the rhetorical and legal instruction that actually took place in the African provinces. The fact that these testimonia emerge in the epigraphic record at all reflects the immense importance and prestige that forensic activity had progressively acquired.

The trends illustrated by African inscriptions are mirrored by epigraphic evidence elsewhere in the Empire. Among the firmly datable epigraphic testimonia for legal experts in the Greek East, only two predate the turn of the third century.[144]

[141] A useful list of testimonia for teachers in Roman North Africa—ranging from *paedagogi* to *magistri, grammatici* and *rhetores*—has been compiled by Vössing (1997a), 659–61. Of the approximately three dozen epigraphic testimonia on this list, only three have been dated earlier than the third century: a *ludi magister* from the area of Lepcis Magna (IRT 850, 2c. CE), a *grammatica* from Caesarea in Mauretania (AfrRom 11.1, 164 = BCTH 1993/95, 101 = MEFR 1994, 710 = AE 1994, 1903 = AE 1996, 1903, 2c. CE) and a *paedagoga* from Thugga (CIL VIII 1506 = Dougga 102 = MAD 263 = AntAfr 1973: 133, 1c. CE).

[142] CIL VIII 5528 = CIL VIII 18862 = ILAlg 2.2, 4687 (Thibilis, *c.*200–50 CE). On the role of teachers of rhetoric in promoting the careers of their students, see Petit (1957) and Cribiore (2007), 197–228 on the students of Libanius. For other teachers of rhetoric and law in North African inscriptions, see [B14], [B19], and CIL VIII 26672 = ILTun 1447 = MAD 1191 = Dougga 158 = CLE 107 = ILS 7772 = AE 1892, 121 (Thugga, 3–4c. CE) with Vössing (1997a), 220–21.

[143] BCTH 1950, 160 = Zarker 53 = ICMactar 12, 1 = *AE* 1953, 49 = AE 1964, +140 (Mactaris, 4–5c. CE), see Vössing (1997a), 151–53.

[144] The two testimonia are Jones (2007), no. 35 (Amastris, Bithynia, 144 CE) and no. 36 (Amisos, Paphlagonia, 144/145 CE). The *nomikos* from Bithynia died young at Alexandria Troas, which suggests that he was a law student. The *nomikos* from Paphlagonia has Latin names (Silvanus son of Fronto) that may suggest Western provincial origins.

4. CONCLUSION

The goal of this chapter has been to trace the rise of Roman forms of legal practice and the adoption of Roman models of forensic culture in the provinces through a regional study of Roman North Africa. In Africa as elsewhere in the Empire, documentary evidence composed mostly of funerary inscriptions might at first suggest that provincial elites were discovering and enthusiastically embracing Roman-style forensic practice in the Severan age. In fact, the cultural process clearly began much earlier: papyri from Egypt show forensic orators and legal experts of Egyptian origin active at Roman assizes by the Flavian period, while African literary sources indicate that Roman rhetorical and legal culture had been widely embraced by municipal elites by the Antonine age. Accordingly, what we seem to be observing in Severan inscriptions is a shift in elite self-representation, which ostensibly had to do with the developing role of legal practice as an avenue into high-profile careers. As I have argued, the emergence of *advocati*, *iurisperiti*, and *assessores* in the epigraphic record can be linked to the creation of official posts for legal practitioners in major imperial courts, including the *advocationes fisci*, which are attested in growing numbers in third-century inscriptions. Taken together, the evidence suggests that, more than a century before the formal separation of the civil and military spheres of the empire through the Tetrarchic reforms, oratory and law were progressively gaining traction for imperial careers and coming to constitute specialized career patterns. It would not be an exaggeration to say that the *advocatio fisci*, which enabled individuals to rise through the courts to administrative careers, marks the emergence of a new imperial career model that looks forward to the imperial bureaucracy and civil service (*militia officialis*) of late Antiquity. It appears as though the developing institutional link between legal practice and prestigious career opportunities constituted the decisive factor of change that caused oratory and law to 'spill' into the epigraphic record in the third century.

The results of this investigation underscore the striking extent to which the epigraphic self-representation of elites in the Roman Empire came to be configured according to specific, socially accepted and relatively homogenous models of prestigious public careers. At the same time as members of the officeholding elite became eager to represent themselves as forensic orators and legal experts, they took care to commemorate their young children as the orators and legal experts they would have become, had fate not intercepted them. While we already observe Apuleius showcasing his bilingualism at the court of the proconsul in the mid-second-century, it is not until the Severan age that Africans would flaunt their bilingualism in funerary inscriptions. As legal practice acquired an increasingly prominent and well-defined role in elite careers—and, one can infer, became a progressively more competitive field—education became an increasingly valuable and celebrated asset. Accordingly, students and teachers of rhetoric and law emerge in the epigraphic record as well. By the time Augustine followed in the footsteps of Apuleius, setting out from Thagaste to Madauros and thence to Carthage and Rome in the late fourth century, it had become possible for a talented schoolmaster to be appointed to a chair in rhetoric and thence to top posts in the imperial administration.[145]

In the age of Domitian, the African grandfather of the emperor Septimius Severus is praised by the Roman poet Statius in the following terms: 'your language and dress are not Punic nor is your mentality foreign—you are Italian, Italian!' The poet elaborates: 'even when the Forum is roaring your voice resounds cheerfully, but your eloquence is not for sale!'[146] In line with Roman cultural models, eloquence and forensic oratory were key elements that defined an elite provincial as a legitimate member of a Roman imperial ruling class. In the age of Augustine, the life of Septimius Severus himself could be playfully imagined as the following sequence of events: 'born into a family of middling wealth, imbued first in letters then in the activity of the *forum* but not displaying a particular talent for either (as may happen with the arts), he tried and sought after different and better things and ultimately ascended the imperial throne.'[147] The punchline appears to be that Septimius Severus rose to supreme power in spite of his failure to succeed in what, by the fourth century, had become a stable trajectory of provincial elites from the rhetorical schoolroom to the imperial courtroom to direct involvement in the business of imperial rule.

[145] See Hopkins (1961) and Sivan (1993), 83–93 on the career of Ausonius of Bordeaux.

[146] Statius, *Silvae* 4.45–6, 49–50: *non sermo Poenus, non habitus tibi, externa non mens: Italus, Italus!... est et frementi vox hilaris foro; venale sed non eloquium tibi...*

[147] Aurelius Victor, *De caesaribus* 22.28: *Ortus medie humili, primo litteris, dehinc imbutus foro; quo parum commodante, uti rebus artis solet, dum tentat aut exquirit varia melioraque, conscendit imperium.*

APPENDICES

Appendix A

Table 19.1. Civic honours for *advocati publici*

	Inscription	Place	Date	Description
A1.	*CIL* VIII 10899 = *CIL* VIII 20164 = *ILAlg* 2.3 7943b	Numidia: Cuicul	late 2c.–early 3c. CE	Epitaph from the family tomb of the Gargilii for Lucius Gargilius Praetorianus, *advocatus rei publicae*, see [B13].
A2.	*CIL* VIII 14784	Africa Proconsularis: Vallis	late 2c.–early 3c. CE Vallis was already a *municipium* but not yet a *colonia* (on which see *CIL* VIII 1285 = *CIL* VIII 14781).	Inscription from the base of an honorific statue of a municipal officeholder (*omnibus honoribus functus*) for his acts as *defensor causarum publicarum*.
A3.	*CIL* VIII 26597 = *Dougga* 52	Africa Proconsularis: Thugga	ca. 150–205 CE The date is determined by the phrase *utriusque ordinis*, which emerges in the mid-second century and disappears after the unification of the *pagus* and *civitas* into a *municipium* in 205 CE.	Inscription from the base of an honorific statue erected by the *pagus* and *civitas* of Thugga for Marcus Galbinus Clemens Clodianus, *patronus* and *defensor causae publicae*.
A4.	*Dougga* 50 = *AntAfr* 1970, 75 = *AE* 1963, 94	Africa Proconsularis: Thugga	ca. 100–117 CE (reign of Trajan) The *patronus* had served as *legatus Augusti* of Aquitania under Trajan.	Honorific dedication by the *pagus* of Thugga to a senatorial *patronus*, who had acted as *defensor* on behalf of a local embassy to Rome to protect the fiscal immunity of the *pertica* of Carthage.
A5.	*ILTun* 1514	Africa Proconsularis: Thugga	160s–170s CE (reign of the *divi fratres*)	Honorific dedication by the *pagus* and *civitas* of Thugga to a Roman *eques*, *patronus* of Thugga and *advocatus eloquentissimus*. He is most probably to be identified with Q. Calpurnius Rogatianus, *eques equo publico*, attested on an honorific statue base: CIL VIII 26594 = *AE* 1893, 102.

Appendix B

Table 19.2. *Advocati, iurisperiti,* and *assessores* in inscriptions of the officeholding elite

	Inscription	Place	Date	Description
B1a.	*AE* 1911, 99 = *AE* 1913, +10	Numidia: Lambaesis	*c.*200 CE On Anicius Faustus, the first governor of Numidia as an independent province, attested in office in 197–201 CE, see Thomasson 1996: 170–6 no. 50.	Honorific dedication by Marcus Sedius Rufus, municipal officeholder (*flamen perpetuus, flamen Commodianus et Herculaneus*) and *advocatus,* who honors the governor Anicius Faustus as his *patronus.* For other dedications by *advocati* to governors, see [B2ab], [B5], [B6] and [B10].
B1b.	*CIL* VIII 18227 = *LBIRNA* 533	Numidia: Lambaesis	early 3c. CE	Dedicatory inscription of a shrine to the *genius* of Lambaesis within the *capitolium,* financed through a testamentary bequest (*fideicommissum*) of 600,000 HS by Marcus Sedius Rufus, *flamen perpetuus* and *advocatus.*
B2a.	*AE* 1917/18, 73	Numidia: Lambaesis	*c.*246–8 CE On Comminius Cassianus, attested as governor in 246–8 CE, see Thomasson 1996: 186 no. 66.	Inscription from the base of an honorific statue erected by Lucius Valerius Optatianus, *eques Romanus* and *advocatus,* who honors the governor Cominius Cassianus as his *patronus* and thanks him for the outstanding honor bestowed upon him (*ob insignem eius erga se dignationem*). For other dedications by *advocati* to governors, see [B1a], [B2b], [B5], [B6] and [B10].
B2b.	*CIL* VIII 2393 = *AE* 1923, +96	Numidia: Thamugadi	*c.*242 CE On Tertullus Antiochus, attested as governor in 242 CE, see Thomasson 1996: 185–6 no. 64.	Inscription from the base of an honorific statue erected by Lucius Valerius Optatianus, *eques Romanus* and *advocatus,* who honors the governor Tertullus Antiochus as his *patronus* (describing himself as his *cliens*) and thanks him for the outstanding honor bestowed upon him (*ob insignem in se dignationem*). For other dedications by *advocati* to governors, see [B1a], [B2a], [B5], [B6] and [B10].

B3.	AE 1926, 29 = *CLEAfr* 109 = *Zarker* 42 = *PCV* 17 = *CLEAfr* 1, 87 = *CLEAfr* 2, 115	Numidia: area of Thamugadi (Bir Abd er-Rahman)	3c. CE or later Regarding the date, Vössing 1996: 135 notes that verse epitaphs for members of the African curial class are uncommon before the fourth century, see Pikhaus 1981.	Verse epitaph for Quintus Maior, who 'protected and expertly defended the law' (*adservit leges, defendit iura peritus*) and died at 45.
B4.	*CIL* VIII 1640 = *CIL* VIII 15876	Africa Proconsularis: Sicca Veneria	*c.*200 CE On Ulpius Arabianus, attested as governor *c.*200 CE, see Thomasson 1996: 81–2 no.109.	Epitaph for Pinnius Iustus, a legal expert (*nomikos*) from Amastris in Bithynia, who died at 37 while serving as *assessor* of the *proconsul* Ulpius Arabianus, himself a native of Bithynia.
B5.	*CIL* VIII 2734 = *CIL* VIII 18125	Numidia: Lambaesis	*c.*246–8 CE On Comminius Cassianus, attested as governor in 246–8 CE, see Thomasson 1996: 186 no. 66.	Honorific dedication by Titus Flavius Silvanus, *eques Romanus* and *advocatus*, Quintus Pinarius Urbanus *II vir* and Lucius Gargilius Felix *flamen perpetuus*, who honor the governor Cominius Cassianus as their *patronus*, having 'so often [admired his *iustitia* and] judgments in the *forum*.' For other dedications by *advocati* to governors, see [B1a], [B2ab], [B6] and [B10]. The editorial reconstruction *qui iu[dicia] eius/for[i iustitiamque]/tot[ies admirati sunt]* is tentative but plausible, see Panciera 2006 on *iustitia* and other judicial virtues in honorific inscriptions for governors.
B6.	*CIL* VIII, 2743	Numidia: Lambaesis	*c.*212–22 CE On Pollienus Auspex, governor in the reign of Caracalla or Elagabalus, see Thomasson 1996: 180–1 no.57.	Inscription from the base of an honorific statue erected by two brothers and *advocati*, Sextus Sinicius Rufus and Sinicius Fortunatus, who honor the governor Pollienus Auspex as their *patronus*. Sextus Sinicius Rufus is elsewhere attested as *flamen perpetuus* (*ZPE* 69: 208 = *AE* 1987, 1064, Lambaesis). For other dedications by *advocati* to governors, see [B1a], [B2ab], [B5] and [B10].

(*continued*)

Table 19.2. Continued

	Inscription	Place	Date	Description
B7.	CIL VIII 2775	Numidia: Lambaesis	3c. CE? Although the inscription is not discussed by Lassère 1973, it resembles other epitaphs from Lambaesis with the formula *DM* that are dated by Lassère to the Severan age, see for example CIL VIII 2816 and 2823. A third-century date is further supported by the lack of firmly dated epigraphic testimonia for *advocatus* before the turn of the third century.	Epitaph for Marcus Valerius Valerianus, an *advocatus* at Carthage, who died at 35 and was buried by his mother at Lambaesis. It is likely that Valerianus belonged to the curial class and possibly pursued an officeholding career that is elided in the epitaph. It remains possible, however, that he was not a member of the curial class, see [D2].
B8.	*CIL* VIII 2777 = *CIL* VIII 18134 = *AntAfr* 1973, 133	Numidia: Lambaesis	*c.*183–5 CE On Maximianus (PIR III[1] 361), attested as governor in 183–5 CE, see Thomasson 1996: 164–166 no. 43.	Epitaph for Gaius Vibius Romulus who had served as *assessor* to the governor Maximianus. He died at 50.
B9a.	CIL VIII 7059 = *ILAlg* 2.1, 645 = *ILS* 1067 = *AE* 2007, +106	Numidia: Cirta	160–1 CE On Rosianus Geminus (PIR[2] P 939), attested as governor in 160–1 CE, see Thomasson 1996: 64–65 no. 79.	Inscription from the base of an honorific statue of Publius Pactumeius Magnus Clemens (PIR[2] P 37), *legatus* of the *proconsul* and *patronus* of the Cirtensian confederacy, whose senatorial career culminates in the title *iurisconsultus.*
B9b.	CIL VIII 7060 = *ILAlg* 2.1, 646 = *AE* 2007, +106	Numidia: Cirta	160–1 CE On Rosianus Geminus (PIR[2] P 939), attested as governor in 160–161 CE, see Thomasson 1996: 64–5 no. 79.	Fragmentary honorific inscription for Publius Pactumeius Magnus Clemens (PIR[2] P 37), *legatus* of the *proconsul* and *patronus* of the Cirtensian confederacy, whose senatorial career culminates in the title *iurisconsultus.*
B10.	*CIL* VIII 8327 = *ILAlg* 2.3 7911 = *AE* 2006, +1808	Numidia: Cuicul	*c.*222–35 CE On Petronius Probatus, attested as governor in the reign of Severus Alexander or shortly thereafter, see Thomasson 1996: 184 no. 62.	Inscription from the base of an honorific statue erected by an *advocatus,* who honors the governor Petronius Probatus as his *patronus.* Curiously, the relevant lines have been chiselled out of the inscription. Nevertheless, *advocatus* remains clearly discernible. For other dedications by *advocati* to governors, see [B1a], [B2ab], [B5] and [B6].

B11.	*CIL* VIII 8489	Mauretania Caesariensis: Sitifis	3c. CE The third-century date is determined by the title *eques Romanus*, which first emerges in African inscriptions *c.*198 CE (Duncan-Jones 2016: 95) and ceases to be attested in the early fourth century (Vössing 1996: 136).	Epitaph for Marinus, a Roman *eques* and 'outstanding legal expert' (*iuris peritissimus*) who died at 25. Another name on the monument is Fabius Donatus, a cavalry officer on the bureaucratic staff of the governor (*eques ex numero officialium*) who died at 35.
B12.	*CIL* VIII 10490 = *CIL* VIII 11045	Africa Proconsularis: Gigthis	3c.–early 4c. CE The absence of a *praenomen* suggests a date in the late third or early fourth century, as noted by Vössing 1996: 131.	Epitaph for Iunius Urbanus, 'beloved son and legal expert (*ius consultum*)' who died at 28 or 38. The *editio princeps* gives the age of Urbanus as LXXXVIII, which is implausible if he was buried by his mother. As suggested by Liebs 1993: 33–34, the initial L or LX probably belongs to the preceding text, which leaves XXXVIII or XXVIII as the age of Urbanus. It is likely that Urbanus belonged to the curial class and possibly pursued an officeholding career that is elided in the epitaph. It remains possible, however, that he was not a member of the curial class, see [D4].
B13.	*CIL* VIII 10899 = *CIL* VIII 20164 = *ILAlg* 2.3 7943b	Numidia: Cuicul	late 2c.–early 3c. CE Other evidence for the Gargilii of Cuicul favors a third-century date, see Jacques 1984: 549–53 and Vössing 1996: 130–1 and 1997: 385–6 n.1316.	Epitaph from the family tomb of the Gargilii Praetoriani for Lucius Gargilius Praetorianus, municipal officeholder (*omnibus honoribus functus*) and legal expert (*iuris peritus*) who was serving as *advocatus rei publicae* when he died at 40, see also [A1].
B14.	*CIL* VIII 12418 = *ILS* 7748	Africa Proconsularis: area of Carthage (Abthungi, Thuburbo Maius or Semta)	late 3c. CE The lack of a *tribus* suggests a date in the second half of the third century, see Forni 1979.	Epitaph (reused in an aqueduct) for Marcus Picarius Turranianus, who was *magister iuris* and died at 70.
B15.	*CIL* VIII 18348 = *AntAfr* 1973, 140	Numidia: Lambaesis	3c. CE The combination of *memoriae* and *DMS* suggests a date in the third century, see Lassère 1973: 103–7 and 140.	Epitaph in the *praetorium* of Lambaesis for Gaius Fabius Clodianus, a 'most dedicated scholar of the law' (*iuris studiosus constantissimus*).

(*continued*)

Table 19.2. Continued

	Inscription	Place	Date	Description
B16.	*CIL* VIII 20162 = *ILAlg* 2.3 8324a = *ILS* 7744 = *ILCV* +280 = *ILCV* 746	Numidia: Cuicul	late 2c.–mid-3c. CE The formula *memoriae* suggests a third-century date, see Lassère 1973: 103–7. This epitaph appears to have belonged to a family memorial, as suggested by another epitaph for a L. Turpilius Victorinus, *eques Romanus* (*CIL* VIII 20163 = *ILAlg* 2.3 8324). A reference to the *tribus* dates this inscription before the mid-third century, see Forni 1979.	Epitaph for Lucius Turpilius Victorinus Marianus, *eques Romanus* and *advocatus*, who pleaded cases to great acclaim (*magna cum laude actus*) and died at 32.
B17.	*CIL* VIII 24094 = *ILPBardo* 1 417 = *ILS* 8973 = *ILTun* 797 = *AE* 1899, 125 = *AE* 1899, +162 = *AE* 1899, +195 = *AE* 1901, +55 = *AE* 1903, +200 = *AE* 1904, +147 = *AE* 1956, +124	Africa Proconsularis: Pupput	160s CE	Inscription from the base of an honorific statue of Lucius Octavius Cornelius Salvius Iulianus Aemilianus, native of Pupput, whose senatorial career includes a reference to his being singled out by Hadrian with a double salary as *quaestor principis* on account of his 'great learning' (*insignis doctrina*). Despite his role as a leading jurist at Rome during three imperial reigns, Iulianus is not explicitly referred to as a legal expert.
B18.	*CILPCart* 302 = *AE* 2011, 1739	Africa Proconsularis: Carthage	4c.–early 5c. CE A reference to the *dioecesis* of Carthage dates this inscription after the tetrarchic reforms, while the formula *DMS* provides a *terminus ante quem* in the early fifth century.	Epitaph from a funerary monument erected by Titus Iulius Pyrattianus for his son, Titus Iulius Celsus, whom he calls his *constudiosus* and *consessor*, presumably a reference to their being legal experts (*iuris studiosi*) and judicial advisors (*assessores*) at Carthage.
B19.	*ILAfr* 273a and b = *ILPBardo* 357 = *LBIRNA* 714–715 = *AE* 1916, 20b = *AE* 1916, 87–88	Africa Proconsularis: Thuburbo Maius	361 CE The inscription is dated by the proconsulship of Hermogenianus, see Barnes 1985: 152.	Inscription documenting the reconstruction of the city baths undertaken by Annius Namptoivius, *curator civitatis* and civic officeholder (*flamen perpetuus*) who was also a legal expert (*iurisconsultus*) and had served as *magister studiorum*.

B20.	*ILAlg* 1 1362 = *AE* 1903, 319 = *AE* 1904, +58 = *AE* 1904, +81	Africa Proconsularis: Thubursicu Numidarum	*c.*200–50 CE An earlier inscription by Iuvenalis (*ILAlg* 1 1236 = *AE* 1904, 82) mentions his *tribus Papiria* and therefore predates the mid-third century, see Forni 1979. The presence of *signa* in the epitaphs of Iuvenalis and his sons (*ILAlg* 1 1363–4), which begin to be attested in the late second century, supports a date in the first half of the third century, see Kajanto 1966: 42ff. A further criterion for dating the inscription is the term *praeses* for *proconsul* in the epitaph of Iuvenalis' son Maternus (*ILAlg* 1 1363), a usage that emerges in Severan legal writers.	Epitaph from the family tomb of the Vetidii, erected by Quintus Vetidius Iuvenalis, *omnibus honoribus functus*, father of 3 *equites Romani*, legal expert in the forum (*in foro iuris peritus*) and proficient farmer (*agricola bonus*) who died at 87.
B21.	*IRT* 647	Africa Proconsularis: Lepcis Magna	2c.–3c. CE The monumental letters of the inscription suggest an Antonine or Severan date, see Vössing 1996: 132.	Honorific inscription in the theater of Lepcis Magna honoring Quintus Marcius Pudens, a legal expert (*iuris peritus*) and excellent father, erected by his son *decreto decurionum.*

Appendix C

Table 19.3. Eloquence and legal expertise in funerary inscriptions of young men pursuing their studies

	Inscription	Place	Date	Description	Emendations
C1.	BCTH-1934/35-104	Mauretania Caesariensis: Tubusuctu	2c.–3c. CE The formula *DMS* dates this inscription to the second century at the earliest, see Lassère 1973: 119–26. The formula becomes progressively more common in the second half of the 2c.	Epitaph for Lucius Gessius Optatus, a boy (*puer*) who is praised for his 'extraordinary talent' (*egregia indoles*) and died at 8. For other references to *indoles*, see [C12], [C19], [C21], [C24] (2-3c. CE); [C11], [C23], [C25] (3c. CE); [C33] (3-4c. CE).	
C2.	*CIL* VIII 646 = *CIL* VIII 11786 = *ILTun* 517 = *CLE* +116 = *AfrRom* 17.4, 2383 = *CLEAfr* 23b	Africa Proconsularis: Mactaris	*c.*230–50 CE The mausoleum is dated to the 230s or 240s by Picard on the basis of letter-forms, iconography and its chronological relationship to other epitaphs at Mactar, see Picard, Bonniec and Mallon 1970: 149 n.1. For a valuable nineteenth-century description of the mausoleum, see Guerin 1862: 412–16.	Epitaph from the mausoleum of the Iulii for Gaius Iulius Proculus Fortunatianus, a young man who died at 22, having been an orator and *togatus* who 'delighted the ears of the public with his skills' (*publicas aures togatus studiis delectavit suis*).	
C3.	*CIL* VIII 724 = *CIL* VIII 12135 = *ILTun* 590 = *CLE* 1612 = *ILS* 7759 = *CLEAfr* 34	Africa Proconsularis: Municipium Avula	3c. CE The inscription is dated on the basis of letter forms, see Vössing 1997a: 120.	Epitaph for Publius Caledius Rufus, a boy who pleased his teachers and 'spoke well, wrote well and painted well' and 'applied his mind to learning' before he died at 14. He was apparently also learning to write Greek shorthand (*notas Graecas*).	
C4.	*CIL* VIII, 726 = *ILTun* 591 = *CLEAfr* 2, 220 = *AE* 2014, +1487	Africa Proconsularis: Municipium Avula	3c. CE Both this epitaph and the identical [C15] are dated to the third century by Cugusi 2014 (*CLEAfr*).	Epitaph for Clarus Bonicianus, a young man who is praised for his morals and intellect (*moribus et ingenio clarus*, see [C14] and [C15] for an identical expression) and died at 21. This epitaph is	

				identical to an epitaph from Agger for Torquatus Crescens [C15]. For other inscriptions praising young men for their *ingenium*, see [C5], [C14], [C16] (2–3c. CE); [C15] (3c. CE) and [C31] (4c. CE).	
C5.	*CIL* VIII 1540 = *CIL* VIII 26671 = *ILTun* 1446 = *MAD* 1190 = *CLE* 1880	Africa Proconsularis: Thugga	3c. CE? The reference to mastery of Latin and Greek suggests a third-century date, in line with other epigraphic testimonia for *utraque lingua eruditi*, see [C9], [C26], [C27] and [C28]. See also [C20].	Epitaph for Terentius Fortunatus, who was distinguished by his 'military skills, intellect and great spirit' (*armis, ingenio, animo maximo*) and was in command of both Latin and Greek. For other inscriptions praising young men for their *ingenium*, see [C14], [C16] (2–3c. CE); [C4], [C15] (3c. CE) and [C31] (4c. CE).	
C6.	*CIL* VIII 5370 = *CIL* VIII 17497 = *ILAlg* 1, 326 = *CLE* 112	Africa Proconsularis: Calama	3c.–4c. CE The majority of references to *studia* are firmly dated to the third century or later, see [C2], [C8], [C18], [C26], [C32], [E6] (3c. CE); see also [C13], [C17] (2c.–3c. CE).	Epitaph for two young men, whose father laments financing their education (*studia*) and then losing them at a young age. The epitaph appears to have belonged to a family mausoleum, see Vössing 1997a: 214–16.	
C7.	*CIL* VIII 5530 = *CIL* VIII 18864 = *ILS* 2956 = *ILAlg* 2.2 4722 = *CLENuovo* 89 = *CLEAfr* 2, 226	Numidia: Thibilis	3c. CE The formula *DMS* dates this inscription to the second century at the earliest, see Lassère 1973: 119–26. The formula becomes progressively more common in the second half of the 2c. References to oratory are in line with numerous epitaphs that are firmly dated to the third century, see [C2], [C9], [C10], [C13], [C14], [C18], [C26], [C30]; see also [B1ab], [B2ab], [B5], [B6], [B7], [B10], [B13] and [B16].	Epitaph from a funerary statue of a young orator from an eminent family, who was skilled in forensic pleading, declamation and the composition of prose and poetry, and consorted with senators and equestrians. In my view, the reconstruction *i[n* ***agen]/do*** *orator nobilis* is preferable to *i[n dicen]/do orator nobilis* (Pflaum, *ILAlg*). *Agendo* creates a chiastic opposition between forensic and epideictic oratory (*agendo* +	*D[3]/a[3]/p[3]/p[3]/i[3]/ae [3]/ai[3]/ric[3]/pie[3]/renv [3]/[prop]inqu[orum suorum]/amator et patriae lae[sit ne]/minem clarissimorum vi[ror(um)]/ et equit(um) R(omanorum) propinqu(u)s et mir[a]/ eloquentia facundus i[n* ***agen]/do*** *orator nobilis declamat[or]/facilis*

(*continued*)

Table 19.3. Continued

	Inscription	Place	Date	Description	Emendations
				orator nobilis vs. *declamator facilis + extemporalitate*). For a similar opposition between the two genres, see Seneca the Elder on the rhetorical style of Asinius Pollio: *floridior erat aliquanto in declamando quam in agendo* (Sen. *contr.* 4 *praef.* 3).	*extemporalitate di[a]/ logorum et epistularum e[t]/ edyliorum conscriptor/quae ex[ta]nt et ob [i]ngente[m]/ [copiam ingeni]i facilis in c[om]/[ponend(is) ecl]ogis annum X[*
C8.	*CIL* VIII 7432 = *ILAlg* 2.1 1258 = *AntAfr* 1973, 135	Numidia: Cirta	late 2c.–early 3c. CE For the date, see Lassère 1973: 135. Dating criteria include the *tribus* (*t.a.q.* mid–3c., see Forni 1979) and the presence of the formula *DM.*	Epitaph for Quintus Iulius Felix, a young 'expert in all disciplines' (*peritissimus omnium studiorum*) who died at 20.	
C9.	*CIL* VIII 8500 = *ILS* 7761 = *MEFR* 1964, 141	Mauretania Caesariensis: Sitifis	229 CE The epitaph contains a consular date.	Epitaph for Marcus Damatius Urbanus, who had mastered the liberal arts, was 'perfectly proficient in both Latin and Greek' (*utriusque linguae perfecte eruditus*) and 'in possession of the utmost eloquence' (*optima facundia praeditus*). He died at 22. For other *utraque lingua eruditi* in African inscriptions, see [C5], [C26], [C27] and [C28], see also [C20].	
C10.	*CIL* VIII 9182 = *CBI* 830	Mauretania Caesariensis: area of Auzia	3c. CE The formula *memoriae* suggests a date in the third century or later, see Lassère 1973: 103–5.	Epitaph from family tomb that mentions Castus, a young forensic orator or student of rhetoric (*adulescens scolasticus*). For another third-century *scholasticus,* see [C18].	
C11.	*CIL* VIII 11433		late 2c.–3c. CE or later		

	= *ILCV* +4336	Africa proconsularis: Sufes	The presence of a *signum* dates the epitaph to the late second century at the earliest, see Kajanto 1966: 53ff.	Epitaph for Quintus Iulius Crispinus, a boy (*puer*) of 'great talent' (*optimae indolis*) who died at 13. For other references to *indoles*, see [C1], [C12], [C19], [C21], [C24] (2–3c. CE); [C23], [C25] (3c. CE); [C33] (3–4c. CE).
C12.	CIL VIII 12021	Africa proconsularis: Civitas Sivalitana	2c.–3c. CE The monumental letter-forms of this inscription suggest an Antonine or Severan date.	Inscription from the base of an honorific statue of a member of the local civic elite whom the city honors 'on account of the meritorious deeds of his ancestors and the talent (*indoles*) of his son' whose name is Pomponius Martialis Octavianus. For other references to *indoles*, see [C1], [C19], [C21], [C24] (2-3c. CE); [C11], [C23], [C25] (3c. CE); [C33] (3-4c. CE).
C13.	*CIL* VIII 12152 = *ILTun* 594	Africa Proconsularis: Agger	2c.–3c. CE The formula *DMS* dates this inscription to the second century at the earliest, see Lassère 1973: 119–26. The formula becomes progressively more common in the second half of the 2c. The majority of references to *studia* are firmly dated to the third century or later, see [C2], [C6], [C8], [C18], [C26], [C32], [E6] (3c. CE); see also [C17] (2c.–3c. CE).	Epitaph for Lucius Baebius Barbarus, who was studying at Carthage when he died at 20.
C14.	*CIL* VIII 12159 = *ILTun* 595	Africa Proconsularis: Agger	2c.–3c. CE The formula *DMS* dates this inscription to the second century at the earliest, see Lassère 1973: 119–26. The formula becomes progressively more common in the second half of the 2c. The reference to	Epitaph for Marcus Antonius Faustianus Nepos Principinus, a young man who is praised for his morals and intellect (*moribus et ingenio clarus,* see [C4] and [C15] for an identical expression) and was 'recognized by his community as an expert

(continued)

Table 19.3. Continued

	Inscription	Place	Date	Description	Emendations
			oratory is in line with numerous epitaphs that are firmly dated to the third century, see [C2], [C9], [C10], [C13], [C14], [C18], [C26], [C30]; see also [B1ab], [B2ab], [B5], [B6], [B7], [B10], [B13] and [B16].	in speaking' (*acceptus patriae dicendi peritus*) before he died at 18. For other inscriptions praising young men for their *ingenium,* see [C5], [C16] (2–3c. CE); [C4], [C15] (3c. CE) and [C31] (4c. CE).	
C15.	*CIL* VIII 12190 = *CLEAfr* 2, 221 = *AE* 2014, +1487	Africa Proconsularis: Agger	3c. CE Both this epitaph and the identical [C4] are dated to the third century by Cugusi 2014 (*CLEAfr*). The formula *DMS* supports a late second or third-century date, see Lassère 1973: 119–26.	Epitaph for Torquatus Crescens, a young man who is praised for his morals and intellect (*moribus et ingenio clarus,* see [C11] for an identical expression). This epitaph is identical to an epitaph from Avula for Clarus Bonicianus [C4]. For other inscriptions praising young men for their *ingenium,* see [C5], [C14], [C16] (2–3c. CE); [C4] (3c. CE) and [C31] (4c. CE).	
C16.	*CIL* VIII 14632 = *CLE* 1577 = *ILTun* 1255	Africa Proconsularis: Simitthus	2c.–mid-3c. CE The presence of the *tribus* dates the inscription before the mid-3c. CE, see Forni 1979.	Epitaph for Gn. Domitius Optatus, who is praised for his *ingenium* and died at 18. For other inscriptions praising young men for their *ingenium,* see [C5], [C14] (2–3c. CE); [C4], [C15] (3c. CE) and [C31] (4c. CE).	
C17.	*CIL* VIII 15987 = *CLE* 1240 = *ILTun* 1592 = *ILTun* 1596 = *CLEAfr* 60	Africa Proconsularis: Sicca Veneria	2c.–3c. CE The majority of references to *studia* are firmly dated to the third century or later, see [C2], [C6], [C8], [C18], [C26], [C32], [E6] (3c. CE); see also [C13] (2c.–3c. CE).	Epitaph for Gaius Cornelius Fortunatianus, a young man who excelled in his studies (*studiis praecellens*), was beautiful in appearance (*formaque decorus*) and died at 23.	

C18.	*CIL* VIII 20274 = *AE* 1895, 146	Mauretania Caesariensis: Satafis (35 km from Sitifis)	3c. CE A third-century date is indicated by the cursive ductus of the inscription, see Vossing 1997: 43 n.112. The majority of references to *studia* are firmly dated to the third century or later, see [C2], [C6], [C8], [C26], [C32], [E6] (3c. CE); see also [C13], [C17] (2c.–3c. CE).	Epitaph for A. Valerius Urbicus Iunior, a young student of rhetoric (*scholasticus iunior*) who died while pursuing his studies (*studens defunctus*). Alternatively, he may have been an aspiring forensic orator who died 'on the job' while pleading a case (*studens*). On *studere* with reference to forensic oratory, see the sources cited in Vössing 1997a: 43 n. 112. For another third-century *scholasticus*, see [C10].
C19.	*CIL* VIII 20767	Mauretania Caesariensis: Auzia	2c.–mid-3c. CE The presence of the *tribus* dates the inscription before the mid-3c. CE, see Forni 1979.	Epitaph for Gaius Calpurnius Maximianus, a boy (*puer*) of 'good talent' (*bonae indolis*). For other references to *indoles*, see [C1], [C12], [C21], [C24] (2-3c. CE); [C11], [C23], [C25] (3c. CE) and [C33] (3-4c. CE).
C20.	*CIL* VIII 23243	Africa Proconsularis: area of Sufetula	3c. CE Monceaux 1902 dates the mausoleum to the second or third century. A third-century date is preferred by Simon 1946. The term *eruditus*, attested in several inscriptions from the third century, likewise supports a third-century date, see [C9], [C26], [C27] and [C28].	Epitaph from the family Mausoleum of the Aurelii for Publius Aurelius Felicianus, a young man who died at 18 and is praised by his parents as *eruditus*. For other *eruditi* in African inscriptions, see [C9], [C26], [C27] and [C28].
C21.	*CIL* VIII, 25744 = *AE* 1905, 123 = *AE* 1906, +48	Africa Proconsularis: Thuburnica	2c.–3c. CE The formula *DMS* dates this inscription to the second century at the earliest, see Lassère 1973: 119–26. The formula becomes progressively more common in the second half of the 2c.	Epitaph for Q. Octavius Primus, a young man of great talent (*adulescens optime indolis*) who had been designated for the aedileship and died at 23. For other references to *indoles*, see [C1], [C12], [C19], [C24] (2-3c. CE); [C11], [C23], [C25] (3c. CE); [C33] (3–4c. CE).

(*continued*)

Table 19.3. Continued

	Inscription	Place	Date	Description	Emendations
C22.	CIL VIII 27505 = *ILTun* 1675 = *CLEAfr* 59 = *CLEAfr* 2, 236 = *AE* 2012, +1814 = *AE* 2014, +1515	Africa Proconsularis: area of Masculula (Simitthus?)	*c.*200–50 CE A reference to the *tribus Quirina* dates the inscription before the mid-third century (see Forni 1979) and suggests a link with the nearby veteran colony of Simitthus, whose citizens had this *tribus*. Liebs 1993: 21 sees the language of outspoken praise in this epitaph as favoring a third-century date.	Epitaph for Quintus Pomponius Fortunatus, a young aedile who among his many virtues (*frugalitas, innocentia, modestia, integritas, fides, gravitas*) was a *iuris peritus* (inscribed on the stone as *ruris peritus*) and died at 22.	
C23.	*Haidra* 6 add, 15 = *AE* 2013, 2046	Africa proconsularis: Ammaedara	3c. CE	Epitaph for Iulius Subitanus, a young foundling (*puer, alumnus*) of 'good talent' (*bonae indolis*) who died at 12 and is commemorated by his foster father Iulius Generosus. For other references to *indoles*, see [C1], [C12], [C19], [C21], [C24] (2–3c. CE); [C11], [C25] (3c. CE); [C33] (3–4c. CE).	
C24.	*IAM* 2.2, 457 = *ILM* 93 = *Volubilis* 84 = *AE* 1923, 18	Mauretania Tingitana: Volubilis	2c.–mid-3c. CE The mention of the *tribus* dates this inscription before the mid-third century, see Forni 1979.	Epitaph for Lucius Caecilius Fronto, who died at 25 while at Rome. His remains were conveyed back to Volubilis for a public funeral, decreed by the *ordo decurionum* on account of the merits of his parents (*ob merita*) and his own talent (*indoles*). It can be inferred that he was studying oratory and law at Rome. For other references to *indoles*, see [C1], [C12], [C19], [C21] (2-3c. CE); [C11], [C23], [C25] (3c. CE); [C33] (3-4c. CE).	

C25.	*ILAfr* 571 = *Dougga* 85 = *AE* 1914, 184	Africa proconsularis: Thugga	205–50 CE The date is determined by the civic titulature of Thugga as a *municipium Septimium Aurelium liberum.*	Inscription from the base of an honorific statue of Gaius Sedius Honoratus Africanus, who is praised for his 'extraordinary talent' (*egregia indoles*) and 'utmost indulgence' (*summum obsequium*) toward his community. A reference to his family and ancestry suggests that he was a young scion of a wealthy local family. For other references to *indoles*, see [C1], [C12], [C19], [C21], [C24] (2–3c. CE); [C11], [C23] (3c. CE); [C33] (3–4c. CE).
C26.	*ILAlg* 1, 1363 = *ILS* 7742a = *MEFR* 2007, 186 = *AE* 1903, 320 = *AE* 1904, +58 = *AE* 1904, +81	Africa Proconsularis: Thubursicu Numidarum	*c.*200–50 CE On the date, see [B20] above.	Epitaph for Lucius Vetidius Maternus Vetidianus, *eques Romanus,* son of Vetidius Iuvenalis ([B20] above), who was proficient in both Latin and Greek (*utraque lingua eruditus*) and was studying at Carthage when he died at 18. By special permission from the *proconsul,* his remains were conveyed to his hometown. For other *utraque lingua eruditi* in African inscriptions, see [C9], [C27] and [C28]; see also [C5] and [C20].
C27.	*ILAlg* 1, 1364 = *AE* 1903, 321 = *AE* 1904, +58 = *AE* 1904, +81	Africa Proconsularis: Thubursicu Numidarum	*c.*200–50 CE On the date, see [B20] above.	Epitaph for Quintus Vetidius Felix Honoratianus, *eques Romanus,* son of Vetidius Iuvenalis ([B20] above), who was proficient in both Latin and Greek (*utraque lingua eruditus*) and died at 21. For other *utraque lingua eruditi* in African inscriptions, see [C5], [C9], [C26] and [C28]; see also [C20].

(*continued*)

Table 19.3. Continued

	Inscription	Place	Date	Description	Emendations
C28.	*ILAlg* 2.2, 4694 = *AE* 1968, 643	Numidia: Thibilis	late 2c.–early 3c. CE The date is provided by the formula *equo publico,* which ceases to be attested after the early third century, as well as firmly dated epigraphic testimonia for *utraque lingua eruditi* in the Severan age, see [C9], [C26] and [C27]. See also [C5] and [C20].	Epitaph for []ianus, a young *eques equo publico* who was 'most admirable' in both Latin and Greek (*utraque lingua*). For other *utraque lingua eruditi* in African inscriptions, see [C5], [C9], [C26] and [C28]; see also [C20].	
C29.	*ILAlg* 2.3 8027 = *CLEAfr* 1, 57 = *CLEAfr* 2, 182 = *AE* 1913, 155 = *AE* 1913, +226	Numidia: Cuicul	3c. CE The villa looks onto the Severan forum and therefore postdates it, see Blanchard-Lemée 1975: 153–70.	Verse inscription on a mosaic pavement of a third-century villa (the so-called house of Castorius) honoring two brothers who were 'attending the auspicious tribunals of Libya' (*faustis Lybiae tribunalibus adsunt*) having been decorated with 'everlasting honor' (*honore perenni*). Evidently, the brothers were orators or *assessores* at the court of the governor. My reconstruction of line 6 would imply that the two sons were honoring their deceased parents, from whom they had inherited the villa.	*Haec domus est hinc orti* *iuvenes quos inclu[ta* ***Cuicul]*** *et fratres et socios magno* ***fabore [deorum]*** *miratur edidisse [si]mul et* *honore per[enni]* *ornati faustis Lybiae tribun* *[al]ibus [a]dsunt.* ***[O]*** *fortunato[s] qui sic [m]* *eruere parentes!* ***[La]ụde per ḥ[eredes genit]*** ***orum*** *nomina* ***v[ivent]***
C30.	*ILTun* 1107 = *Zarker* 137 = *CLEAfr* 45 = *CLEAfr* 2, 217 = *AE* 1925, 25 = *AE* 2014, +1515	Africa Proconsularis: Carthage	2c.–3c. CE In inscriptions from Carthage, the abbreviated formula *DMS* favors a third-century date, see Lassère 1973: 45.	Epitaph for P. Annaeus Mussius, a boy (*puer*) who was 'never irreverent to no one' in his education (*disciplina nemini num/quam inreuer(e)ns,* it is unclear whether the double negative was intentionally meant to convey the boy's irreverence). The phrase *agens bonus* appears to mean that Mussius was already practicing forensic oratory. In my view, the reconstruction ***o[mne]/*** *factum bene factum* is idiomatically preferable to *q[uod]/factum bene factum* (AE 1925, 25, Poinssot and Lantier).	*D(is) M(anibus) s(acrum)/P* *(ublius) Annaeus Mussius* *pue[r]/disciplina nemini* *num/quam inreuer(e)ns* *bonus/parent{i}um suorum* *[ama]/tor agens bonus o* ***[mne]****/factum bene factum*

C31.	*ILTun* 1520 = *Dougga* 162 = *AE* 1914, 29 = *MAD* 934	Africa Proconsularis: Thugga	4c. CE? For the date, see Vössing 1997a: 118 n. 396.	Mosaic epitaph for Q. Papirius Fortunatianus Eusebius, who died at age 6 and is praised for his *ingenium*. For other inscriptions praising young men for their *ingenium,* see [C5], [C14], [C16] (2–3c. CE); [C4], [C15] (3c. CE).
C32.	*Zarker* 37 = *CLEAfr* 2, 163 = *AE* 1931, 39	Mauretania Caesariensis: Caesarea	*c.*227 CE On Titus Licinius Hierocles (PIR^2 L 202), attested as procuratorial governor in 227 CE, see Thomasson 1996: 214–15 no. 35.	Verse epitaph for Titus Licinius Claudius Hierocles, the young son of the equestrian governor Titus Licinius Hierocles, which exhorts the boy to 'begin outstripping your father in your studies and decorate your illustrious stock with your own achievements' (*incipe parve puer studiis superare parent(em) egregiumque genus propriis virtutibus orna*).
C33.	*Zarker* 79 = *CLEAfr* 1, p.128 = *CLEAfr* 1, p.139 = *CLEAfr* 2, 147 = *AE* 1949, 77	Africa proconsularis: Hippo Regius	3–4c. CE It has been argued that the non-Christian nature of this inscription makes a third-century date more likely, see Vössing 1997a: 228.	Inscription from the base of an honorific statue of Celer, who is praised for the well-regarded name of his family and the meritorious deeds of his parents. He is also celebrated for the auspicious offices he has held (*laeta per official titulis celebratus*), which attest to his innate talent (*indoles*). For other references to *indoles*, see [C1], [C12], [C19], [C21], [C24] (2–3c. CE); [C11], [C23], [C25] (3c. CE).

Appendix D

Table 19.4. Legal practice in funerary inscriptions of individuals without an officeholding career

	Inscription	Place	Date	Description	Emendations
D1.	*AE* 1957, 00185b	Numidia: Thamugadi	late 2c.–3c. CE or later The presence of a *signum* dates the epitaph to the late second century at the earliest, see Kajanto 1966: 53ff.	Epitaph on a family tomb erected by Gaius Iulius Silvanus during his lifetime. His *signum* 'Cicero of Thabudeos' (*Ciceronis Thabudeiensis*) suggests that he was a forensic orator or teacher of rhetoric in the town of Thabudeos, see Vössing 1997a: 402 n. 1370.	
D2.	CIL VIII 2775	Numidia: Lambaesis	3c. CE?	Marcus Valerius Valerianus? See [B7]	
D3.	*CIL* VIII 3506 = *CLE* 1236 = *ILS* 7747 = *CLEAfr* 113 = *PCV* 31	Numidia: Lambaesis	2c.–3c. CE The formula *DMS* dates this inscription to the second century at the earliest, see Lassère 1973: 119–26. The formula becomes progressively more common in the second half of the 2c.	Verse epitaph for Lucius Calpurnius Flamininus, a forensic orator who 'pleaded cases happily' (*oravi causas felix*) before suddenly losing his entire family. He died at 75.	
D4.	*CIL* VIII 10490 = *CIL* VIII 11045	Africa Proconsularis: Gigthis	3c.–early 4c. CE	Iunius Urbanus? See [B12]	
D5.	*Zarker* 103 = *BCTH* 1951/52, 211 = *CLEAfr* 1 p. 76 = *CLEAfr* 2, 16 = *CLENuovo*, p 87 = *AE* 1955, 53	Africa Proconsularis: area of Bisica (El Fahs)	3c. CE? The reference to oratory is in line with numerous epitaphs that are firmly dated to the third century, see [C2], [C7], [C9], [C10], [C13], [C14], [C18], [C26], [C30]; see also [B1ab], [B2ab], [B5], [B6], [B7], [B10], [B13], [B16] and [D1], [D3], [D6].	Verse epitaph for Agmenia Secunda erected by her husband Gaius Modius Silvanus, whose *agnomen* Ciceronianus and description as *meus Cicero* suggests that he was a forensic orator or teacher of rhetoric, see Vössing 1997a: 402 n. 1370.	
D6.	*ZPE* 152: 91 = *AE* 1998, 1530	Africa Proconsularis: Ammaedara	late 3c. CE The metrical errors and *ductus* of the inscription lead the editors to date it to the second half of the third century.	Epitaph for a man who lived for 70 years 'not caring about the laws or the crowds of the forum' (*nec turbas fori nec leges curavi*).	

Appendix E

Table 19.5. The careers of *advocati fisci* from the African provinces

	Inscription	Place	Date	Description	Emendations
E1.	*BCTH* 1918, CC = *AE* 1917/18, 85	Numidia: Lambaesis	*c.*200–50 CE On the deputy-governor Lucius Titinius Clodianus, attested in office in 259–61 CE, see Thomasson 1996: 196 no.77 and Pflaum 1960–1 no. 331.	Inscription from the base of an honorific statue erected by Gaius Vibius Maximus, a Roman *eques* and officeholder at Lambaesis (*flamen perpetuus*), who honors the ducenariate procurator and deputy governor Lucius Titinius Clodianus as his *patronus*, in thanks for his nomination to the *advocatio fisci* (*candidatus eius*).	
E2.	*CIL* VIII 822 = *CIL* VIII 12345 = *CIL* VIII 23963 = *ILS* 1347 = *ILTun* 741 = *AE* 1894, +50 = *AE* 1894, +53 = Pflaum 1960–1961 no. 327	Africa Proconsularis: Municipium Aurelium C[]	after 235 CE	Inscription from the base of an honorific statue of Gaius Attius Alcimus Felicianus, a native and *patronus* of the *municipium* and *vir perfectissimus*, who had served as *advocatus fisci* in eleven provinces, then received a series of procuratorial appointments that culminated in the praetorian prefecture.	
E3.	*CIL* VIII, 1174 = *ILS* 1451 = *MEFR* 1985, 459 = Pflaum 1960–1961 no. 142	Africa Proconsularis: Avita Bibba	161–9 CE	Honorific inscription honoring Sextus Caecilius Crescens Volusianus, a native and *patronus* of the *municipium*, who had served as *advocatus fisci* at Rome, eventually progressing to the secretariate *ab epistulis*.	

(*continued*)

Table 19.5. Continued

	Inscription	Place	Date	Description	Emendations
E4.	*CIL* VIII 1439 = *CIL* VIII 15255 = *ILS* 1430 = Pflaum 1960–1961 no. 291	Africa Proconsularis: Thubursicum Bure	3c. CE	Inscription from the base of an honorific statue of Quintus Acilius Fuscus, a native and *patronus* of Thubursicum Bure, who had been an *advocatus fisci codicillaris* (i.e. by special appointment of the emperor) at Rome, then progressed to procuratorial posts in Italy and ultimately served as *procurator annonae.*	
E5.	*CIL* VIII 2757 = *ZPE* 69, 209 = *AntAfr* 1977, 149 = *AE* 1977, 863 = *AE* 1987, 1065	Numidia: Lambaesis	257–60 CE	Epitaph for Aelius Rufus, an officeholder at Lambaesis (*flamen perpetuus*) who was 'thrice promoted to the *advocatio fisci*' in three different regions of Africa and Numidia. He is commemorated by his brothers, who had both held top civic offices at Lambaesis and were engaged in the pursuit of equestrian careers (*a militiis*).	
E6.	*CIL* VIII 9249 = *AE* 2003, +65	Mauretania Caesariensis: Rusguniae	ca. 200–50 CE The *tribus* dates the inscription before the mid-3c. (see Forni 1979). The majority of references to *studia* are firmly dated to the third century or later, see [C2], [C6], [C8], [C18], [C26], [C32] (3c. CE); see also [C13], [C17] (2c.–3c. CE).	Honorific inscription for Licinius Donatus, a *decurio* of Rusguniae who 'by virtue of the studies of his youth' (*beneficio studiorum prima aetate iuventutis*) was appointed (*electus*) to defend the *fiscus* in the province of Baetica and then 'by virtue of his meritorious deeds' (*pro meritis actibus*) was promoted to the *defensio populi* in Rome.	
E7.	*CIL* VIII 11341 = *CIL* VIII 23219 = *ILP Sbeitla* 50 = *ILS* 9016 = *ILTun* 362 = *AE* 1908, +64	Africa Proconsularis: Sufetula	early 3c. CE	Inscription from the base of an honorific statue of Pomponius L[e]murianus, native of Sufetula and *vir egregius*, who was first appointed *advocatus fisci ad patrimonium Karthaginis*, then served as *advocatus fisci* of the three Hispaniae, was then appointed to the prestigious post *a commentariis* of the praetorian prefects, then returned to Africa	

	= Pflaum 1960–1961 no. 320			as ducenariate procurator of the *dioecesis* of Hadrumetum. The statue was erected by Lucius Valgius Mauricus, *vir egregius*, who had studied together with Lemurianus.
E8.	*CIL* VIII 12020 = *ILS* 01411 = *ILTun* 604 = Pflaum 1960–1961 no. 282	Africa Proconsularis: Civitas Sivalitana	3c. CE	Inscription from the base of a posthumous honorific statue of Quintus Iulius Maximus Demetrianus, native and *patronus* of the town, who had held the *advocatio fisci* of the *quadragesima Galliarum* and procuratorial posts in Italy, Belgica and the Germaniae.
E9.	*CIL* VIII 18909 = *ILAlg* 2.2 4689 = *ILS* 9017 = *AE* 1892, 33 = *AE* 1957, +255 = Pflaum 1960–1961 no. 274	Numidia: Thibilis	3c. CE	Honorific inscription for Marcus Herennius Victor, a citizen of Cirta and *vir egregius*, who had held the IIIvirate of the Cirtensian confederacy before being appointed to the *advocatio [fisci Romae]* and progressing to procuratorial posts in Italy and ultimately in his home province of Numidia.
E10.	*CIL* VIII 24064 = *ILTun* 773 = *AE* 1908, 18	Africa Proconsularis: Ziqua	3c. CE	Inscription from the base of a posthumous honorific statue erected for someone by Septimianus, *advocatus fisci ad patrimonium Karthaginis,* by decree of the *ordo decurionum.*
E11.	*CIL* VIII 26582 = *ILTun* 1424 = *Dougga* 70 = *ILS* 9018 = *AE* 1911, 76 = *AE* 1957, +255 = Pflaum 1960–1961 no. 353	Africa Proconsularis: Thugga	3c. CE	Inscription from the base of an honorific statue of Aulus Vitellius Felix Honoratus, native of Thugga, who was first appointed *advocatus fisci ad patrimonium Karthaginis*, then progressed to *advocationes fisci* in Numidia and Noricum and ultimately to an *advocatio fisci* and procuratorial posts in Italy. He had undertaken an embassy on behalf of Thugga at his own expense.

(*continued*)

Table 19.5. Continued

	Inscription	Place	Date	Description	Emendations
E12.	*ILAfr* 470 = *AfrRom* 19, 2152 = *AE* 1917/18, 89 = *AE* 2012, +1874	Africa Proconsularis: Thuburnica	3c. CE	Fragmentary epitaph for an *advocatus [fisci]* who had held the secretariate *ab epistulis.*	
E13.	*ILTun* 250 = *RHP* 90 = *ZPE* 43, 690 = *AE* 1932, 34 = *AE* 1950, +83 = Pflaum 1960–1961 no. 231	Africa Proconsularis: Pheradi Maius	early 3c. CE	Inscription from the base of honorific statues of Publius Messius Saturninus (PIR[2] M 527), a native and *patronus* of Pheradi Maius, and Publius Messius Augustinus Maecianus, *clarissimus puer,* presumably, the grandson of the former. Saturninus had served as *advocatus fisci* at the imperial court (*sacrum auditorium*) at Rome, eventually progressing to the post *a declamationibus Latinis* at the court of Septimius Severus with an impressive salary of 300,000 HS. It may be possible to identify him with the Messius who serves with Papinian on the *consilium* of the emperor Septimius Severus in Paul, *Decrees* 3 (D.49.14.50).	
E14.	Pflaum 1960–1961 no. 220, Kunkel 1967: no. 56		career: 160s CE–212 CE	Aemilius Papinianus, leading jurist at Rome under Septimius Severus, who may have been a native of Africa, see Kunkel 1967:[2] 224–229. Papinian's equestrian career included service on the *consilium* of the praetorian prefects in the reign of Marcus Aurelius (D. 22.1.3.3), the secretariate *a libellis* (D.22.5.12pr.) and ultimately an appointment to the praetorian prefecture in 205 CE. In the *Historia Augusta,* it is stated that Papinian had held the *advocatio fisci* (at Rome, it may be presumed) after Septimius Severus (*HA*	

			Caracalla 8.2–3), a testimonium doubted by Mommsen 1890 and Pflaum 1960–1961 but cautiously accepted by Kunkel 1967:[2] 224 n.441.
E15.		career: 160s CE–211 CE	Septimius Severus, Roman emperor (193–211 CE) and native of Lepcis Magna, whose senatorial career may have started with the *advocatio fisci* at Rome in the 160s CE (*HA Caracalla* 8.2–3, *HA Geta* 2.4, Aurelius Victor, *Caesares* 20.28 and Eutropius 8.8). While there is skepticism regarding the accuracy of these testimonia (see Barnes 1967: 91 and Birley 1999:[2] 218) it is not possible to rule them out, as already pointed out by Kunkel 1967:[2] 224 n.441. As Barnes himself notes, the *advocatio fisci* would explain why Severus appears to have omitted two preliminary posts normally held at the start of a senatorial career (*tribunus laticlavius, vigintivir*), see Barnes 1967: 91.
E16.	Pflaum 1960–1961: no. 248	career: 180s CE–218 CE	Opellius Macrinus, Roman emperor (217–218 CE) and native of Caesarea in Mauretania. According to the *Historia Augusta* (*HA Macrinus* 4.3–7), he was active as a forensic orator and legal advisor before being appointed to the *advocatio fisci* at Rome, followed by procuratorial appointments that culminated in the praetorian prefecture under Caracalla.

REFERENCES

Avon, M. 1972. *Les avocats du fisc dans le monde romain*. Ph.D. Dissertation, Aix-en-Provence.

Barnes, T. D. 1967. The family and career of Septimius Severus. *Historia* 16, pp. 87–107.

Barnes, T. D. 1985. Proconsuls of Africa, 337–92. *Phoenix* 39, pp. 144–53.

Beck, A. 1967. *Römisches Recht bei Tertullian und Cyprian. Eine Studie zur frühen Kirchenrechtgeschichte*, 2nd edition. Aalen.

Behrends, O. 1969. Der *assessor* zur Zeit der klassischen Rechtswissenschaft. *Zeitschrift der Savigny-Stiftung für Rechtsgeschichte. Romanistische Abteilung* 86, pp. 192–226.

Birley, A. R. 1999. *Septimius Severus. The African Emperor*. 2nd ed. London.

Blanchard-Lemée, M. 1975. *Maisons à mosaïques du quartier central de Djemila (Cuicul)*. Paris.

Bodel, J. 2010. Kangaroo courts: displaced justice in the Roman novel. In: F. De Angelis (ed.), *Spaces of Justice in the Roman World*. Leiden, pp. 311–29.

Bradley, K. 2012. *Apuleius and Antonine Rome. Historical Essays*. Toronto.

Bradley, K. 2014. Apuleius' *Apology*: Text and Context. In: B. T. Lee, E. Finkelpearl and L/Graverini (eds), *Apuleius and Africa*. London, pp. 23–34.

Brown, P. 1967. *Augustine of Hippo. A Biography*. Berkeley.

Brown, P. 1992. *Power and Persuasion in Late Antiquity. Towards a Christian Empire*. Madison.

Bund, E. 1976. Salvius Iulianus, Leben und Werk. *Aufstieg und Niedergang der Römischen Welt* II 15, pp. 408–54.

Burton, G. P. 1975. Proconsuls, assizes and the administration of justice under the empire. *Journal of Roman Studies* 65, pp. 92–106.

Burton, G. P. 2000. The resolution of territorial disputes in the provinces of the Roman Empire. *Chiron* 30, pp. 195–215.

Champlin, E. 1980. *Fronto and Antonine Rome*. Cambridge, MA.

Chaniotis, A. 1997. Tempeljustiz im kaiserzeitlichen Kleinasien: Rechtliche Aspekte der Beichtinschriften. In: G. Thür and J. Vélissaropoulos-Karakostas (eds.), *Symposion 1995*. Cologne, pp. 353–84.

Chaniotis, A. 2005. Von Ehre, Schande und kleinen Verbrechen unter Nachbarn: Konfliktbewältigung und Götterjustiz in Gemeinden des antiken Anatolien. In: F. R. Pfetsch (ed.), *Konflikt*. Berlin, pp. 233–54.

Chaouali, M. 2002–3. Les *nundinae* dans les grandes domaines en Afrique du Nord à l'époque romaine. *Antiquités africaines* 38–9, pp. 375–86.

Chastagnol, A. 1979. 'empereur Julien et les avocats de Numidie. *Antiquités africaines* 14, pp. 225–35.

Coles, R. A. 1966. *Reports of Proceedings in Papyri*. Brussels.

Courtney, E. 1980. *A Commentary on the Satires of Juvenal*. London.

Cribiore, R. 2007. *The School of Libanius in Late Antique Antioch*. Princeton.

Crook, J. A. 1954. *Consilium Principis. Imperial Councils and Counsellors from Augustus to Diocletian*. Cambridge.

Crook, J. A. 1995. *Legal Advocacy in the Roman World*. Ithaca.

Cugusi, P. 2014. *Carmina latina epigraphica Africarum provinciarum post Buechelerianam collectionem editam reperta cognita* (*CLEAfr*). Faenza.

David, J.-M. 1992. *Le patronat judiciaire au dernier siècle de la République romaine*. Rome.

Demandt, A. 1989. *Die Spätantike. Römische Geschichte von Diocletian bis Justinian*. Munich.

de Ruggiero, E. (ed.) 1895–1950. *Dizionario epigrafico di antichità romane*. Rome.

Dolganov, A. 2018a. *Empire of Law: Legal Culture and Imperial Rule in the Roman Province of Egypt*. Ph.D. Dissertation, Princeton University.

Dolganov, A. 2018b. Review of Tuori 2016. *Journal of Roman Studies* 108, pp. 222–4.
Dörner, F. K. 1952. *Bericht über eine Reise in Bithynien*. Vienna.
Drecoll, C. 1997. *Die Liturgien im Römischen Kaiserreich des 3. und 4. Jh. n. Chr. Untersuchung über Zugang, Inhalt und wirtschaftliche Bedeutung der öffentlichen Zwangsdienste in Ägypten und anderen Provinzen*. Stuttgart.
Duncan-Jones, R. P. 1962. Costs, Outlays and Summae Honorariae from Roman Africa. *Papers of the British School at Rome* 30, pp. 47–115.
Duncan-Jones, R. P. 1982. *The Economy of the Roman Empire. Quantitative Studies*. 2nd ed. Cambridge.
Duncan-Jones, R. P. 2016. *Power and Privilege in Roman Society*. Cambridge.
Eck, W. 1983. Jahres- und Provinzialfasten der senatorischen Statthalter von 69/70 bis 138/139. *Chiron* 13, 147–238.
Eingartner, J. 2005. *Templa cum Porticibus. Ausstattung und Funktion italischer Tempelbezirke in Nordafrika und ihre Bedeutung für die römische Stadt der Kaiserzeit*. Rahden.
Färber, R. 2014. *Römische Gerichtsorte. Räumliche Dynamiken von Jurisdiktion im Imperium Romanum*. Munich.
Forni, G. 1979. La più recente menzione di tribù romana. In: *Atti dell'Accademia Romanistica Costantiniana, III Convegno Internazionale*. Perugia: pp. 231–7.
Frier, B. 1985. *The Rise of the Roman Jurists*. Princeton.
Fuhrmann, C. J. 2011. *Policing the Roman Empire. Soldiers, Administration and Public Order*. Oxford.
Garnsey, P. D. A. 1978. Rome's African empire under the Principate. In: P. D. A. Garnsey and C. R. Whittaker (eds.), *Imperialism in the Ancient World*. Cambridge, pp. 223–54.
Gascou, J. 1982a. La politique municipale de Rome en Afrique du Nord, I. De la mort d'Auguste au début du IIIe siècle. *Aufstieg und Niedergang der Römischen Welt* II.10.2, pp. 136–229.
Gascou, J. 1982b. La politique municipale de Rome en Afrique du Nord, II. Après la mort de Septime-Sévère. *Aufstieg und Niedergang der Römischen Welt* II.10.2, pp. 230–320.
Gordon, R. 2013. Fixing the races: managing risks in the North African circus. In: M. Piranomonte and F. Marco Simón (eds.) *Contesti magici, Contextos mágicos*. Rome, pp. 47–71.
Grelle, F. 1986. Le categorie dell'amministrazione tardoantica. Officia, munera, honores. In: A. Giardina (ed.), *Società romana e impero tardoantico I. Istituzioni, ceti, economie*. Bari, pp. 37–56.
Grelle, F. 1999. I 'munera civilia' e le finanze cittadine. In: *Il capitolo delle entrate nelle finanze municipali in Occidente ed in Oriente. Actes de la Xe rencontre franco-italienne sur l'épigraphie du monde romain: Rome, 27–29 mai 1996*. Rome, pp. 137–53.
Guerin, V. 1862. *Voyage archéologique dans la Régence de Tunis*, 2 vols. Paris.
Haensch, R. 1995. *A commentariis* und *commentariensis*: Geschichte und Aufgaben eines Amtes im Spiegel seiner Titulaturen. In: Y. Le Bohec (ed.), *La hiérarchie (Rangordnung) de l'armée romaine sous le Haut-Empire*. Paris, pp. 267–84.
Haensch, R. 1997. Zur Konventsordnung in der Provinz Aegyptus und den übrigen Provinzen des römischen Reiches. In: B. Kramer, W. Luppe, H. Maehler and G. Poethke (eds.), *Akten des 21. Internationalen Papyrologenkongresses, Berlin, 13.–19.8.1995*. Stuttgart: Teubner, 320–91.
Heath, M. 2004. *Menander. A Rhetor in Context*. Oxford.
Honoré, A. M. 1994. *Emperors and Lawyers*. 2nd ed. Oxford.
Hopkins, M. K. 1961. Social Mobility in the Later Roman Empire: The evidence of Ausonius. *Classical Quarterly* 11, pp. 239–49.
Humfress, C. 2007. *Orthodoxy and the Courts in Late Antiquity*. Oxford.
Hunink, V. 1997. *Apuleius of Madauros: Pro Se de Magia*, 2 vols. Amsterdam.
Hunink, V. 2001. *Apuleius of Madauros: Florida*. Amsterdam.

Jacques, F. 1984. *Le privilège de liberté. Politique impériale et autonomie municipale dans les cités de l'occident romain (161–244)*. Rome.

Jarrett, M. G. 1962. The Career of L. Titinius Clodianus. *Latomus* 21, pp. 853–9.

Jones, A. H. M. 1964. *The Later Roman Empire, 284–602. A Social Economic and Administrative Survey*. Oxford.

Jones, C. P. 2007. Juristes romains dans l'Orient grec. *Comptes rendus des séances de l'Académie des Inscriptions et Belles-Lettres* 151, pp. 1331–59.

Kajanto, I. 1966. *Supernomina. A study in Latin epigraphy*. Helsinki.

Kantor, G. 2017. Qui in consilio estis: The governor and his advisers in the Early Empire. *Istoricheskij vestnik* 19, pp. 50–87.

Kaster, R. A. 1988. *Guardians of Language. The Grammarian and Society in Late Antiquity*. Berkeley.

Keulen, W. 2014. Fronto and Apuleius: two African careers in the Roman Empire. In: B. T. Lee, E. Finkelpearl and L. Graverini (eds.), *Apuleius and Africa*. London, pp. 129–53.

Kotula, T. 1969. *Utraque lingua eruditi*. Une page relative à l'histoire de l'éducation dans l'Afrique romaine. In: J. Bibauw (ed.), *Hommages à M. Renard*, vol. 2. Bruxelles, pp. 386–92.

Kunkel, W. 1967². *Herkunft und soziale Stellung der römischen Juristen*. 2nd ed. Graz.

Lassère, J.-M. 1973. Recherches sur la chronologie des épitaphes païennes de l'Africa. *Antiquités africaines* 7, pp. 7–151.

Lehne-Gstreinthaler, C. 2019. *Iurisperiti et oratores. Eine Studie zu den römischen Juristen der Republik*. Cologne.

Lepelley, C. 1979. *Les cités de l'Afrique romaine au Bas-Empire*, 2 vols. Paris.

Liebs, D. 1993. *Römische Jurisprudenz in Africa mit Studien zu den pseudopaulinischen Sentenzen*. Berlin.

Liebs, D. 1997a. L. Octavius Cornelius P. Salvius Iulianus Aemilianus. In: K. Sallmann (ed.), *Die Literatur des Umbruchs. Von der römischen zur christlichen Literatur, 117 bis 284 n. Chr.* Munich, pp. 101–5.

Liebs, D. 1997b. L. Volusius Maecianus. In: K. Sallmann (ed.), *Die Literatur des Umbruchs. Von der römischen zur christlichen Literatur, 117 bis 284 n. Chr.* Munich, pp. 130–3.

Liebs, D. 2010. *Hofjuristen der römischen Kaiser bis Justinian*. Munich.

Lopuszanski, G. 1951. La police romaine et les chrétiens. *L'Antiquité Classique* 20, pp. 5–46.

Magdelain, A. 1950. Ius respondendi. *Revue historique de droit français et étranger* 29, pp. 1–22.

Magioncalda, A. 2009. L'anonimo di CIL VI 1628 (= 41294) e il giurista Erennio Modestino. In: *Studi in onore di Remo Martini*, vol. 2. Siena, pp. 555–74.

Marrou, H.-I. 1981. *Histoire de l'éducation dans l'Antiquité, vol. 2: Le monde romain*. Paris.

Millar, F. 1977. *The Emperor in the Roman World (31 B.C.–A.D. 337)*. London.

Mommsen, T. 1890. Zu Papinians Biographie. *Zeitschrift der Savigny-Stiftung für Rechtsgeschichte. Romanistische Abteilung* 11, pp. 30–3.

Monceaux, P. 1902. Païens judaïsants. Essai d'explication d'une inscription africaine. *Revue Archéologique* 40, pp. 208–26.

Neesen, L. 1981. Die Entwicklung der Leistungen und Ämter (munera et honores) im römischen Kaiserreich des 2.–4. Jahrhunderts. *Historia* 30, pp. 203–35.

Nicols, J. 2014. *Civic Patronage in the Roman Empire*. Leiden.

Palme, B. 1999. Die *officia* der Statthalter in der Spätantike: Forschungsstand und Perspektiven. *Antiquité Tardive* 7, pp. 85–133.

Palme, B. 2014. Roman litigation—reports of court proceedings. In J. G. Keenan, J. G. Manning and U. Yiftach-Firanko (eds.), *Law and Society in Egypt from Alexander to the Arab Conquest*. Cambridge, pp. 482–502.

Panciera, S. 2006. Le virtù del governatore provinciale nelle iscrizioni latine da Augusto a Diocleziano. In: S. Demougin, X. Loriot, P. Cosme and S. Lefebvre (eds.), *H.-G. Pflaum: un historien du XXe siècle*. Genève, pp. 457–84.

Peachin, M. 2016. Lawyers in administration. In: P. J. du Plessis, C. Ando and K. Tuori (eds.), *The Oxford Handbook of Roman Law and Society*. Oxford, pp. 164–75.

Petit, P. 1957. *Les Etudiants de Libanius*. Paris.

Petzl, G. 1994. *Die Beichtinschriften Westkleinasiens*. Bonn.

Petzl, G. 1998. Neue Inschriften aus Lydien (II). Addenda und Corrigenda zu 'Die Beichtinschriften Westkleinasiens'. *Epigraphica Anatolica* 28, pp. 69–79.

Pflaum, H.-G. 1950. *Les procuratures équestres sous le Haut-Empire romain*. Paris.

Pflaum, H.-G. 1960–1. *Les carrières procuratoriennes équestres sous le Haut-Empire romain*, 3 vols. Paris.

Pikhaus, D. 1981. Les origines sociales de la poésie épigraphique latine: l'exemple des provinces nord-africaines. *L'Antiquité Classique* 50, pp. 637–54.

Rankin, D. I. 1997. Was Tertullian a Jurist? *Studia Patristica* 31, pp. 335–42.

Rébillard, E. 2017. *Greek and Latin Narratives about the Ancient Martyrs*. Oxford.

Ricci, C. 1994. Africani a Roma. Testimonianze epigrafiche di età imperiale di personaggi provenienti dal Nordafrica. *Antiquités africaines* 30, pp. 189–207.

Shaw, B. D. 1981. Rural markets in North Africa. *Antiquités africaines* 17, pp. 37–83.

Shaw, B. D. 2011. *Sacred Violence. African Christians and Sectarian Hatred in the Age of Augustine*. Cambridge.

Simon, M. 1946. Le judaisme berbère dans l'Afrique ancienne. *Revue d'histoire et de philosophie religieuses* 26, pp. 1–31, 105–45.

Sivan, H. 1993. *Ausonius of Bordeaux. Genesis of a Gallic Aristocracy*. London.

Skeat, T. C. and E. P. Wegener 1935. A trial before the prefect of Egypt Appius Sabinus, c. 250 A.D. *Journal of Egyptian Archaeology* 21, pp. 224–47.

Speidel, M. A. 2006. Militia. Zu Sprachgebrauch und Militarisierung in der kaiserzeitlichen Verwaltung. In: A. Kolb (ed.), *Herrschaftsstrukturen und Herrschaftspraxis. Konzeption, Prinzipien und Strategien der Administration im römischen Kaiserreich*. Berlin, pp. 263–8.

Stolte, B. 2003. Jurisdiction and representation of power, or, the emperor on circuit. In: L. de Blois (ed.), *The Representation and Perception of Roman Imperial Power*. Amsterdam, pp. 261–8.

Stone, D. L. 1998. Culture and Investment in the Rural Landscape: the North African *bonus Agricola*. *Antiquités africaines* 34, pp. 103–13.

Syme, R. 1980. Hadrianic proconsuls of Africa. *Zeitschrift für Papyrologie und Epigraphik* 37, pp. 1–18.

Thomasson, B. E. 1984–90. *Laterculi Praesidum*, 3 vols. Göteborg.

Thomasson, B. E. 1996. *Fasti Africani. Senatorische und ritterliche Amtsträger in den römischen Provinzen Nordafrikas von Augustus bis Diokletian*. Stockholm.

Tuori, K. 2004. The *ius respondendi* and the freedom of Roman jurisprudence. *Revue Internationale des droits de l'Antiquité* 51, pp. 295–333.

Tuori, K. 2016. *The Emperor of Law. The Emergence of Roman Imperial Adjudication*. Oxford.

van den Hout, M. P. J. 1999. *A Commentary on the Letters of M. Cornelius Fronto*. Leiden.

van Mal-Maeder, D. 2007. *La fiction des déclamations*. Leiden.

Vitton, I. 1924. *Concetti giuridici nelle opere di Tertulliano*. Roma.

Vössing, K. 1996. Africa nutricula causidicorum? Die römische Jurisprudenz in Africa. In: M. Khanoussi, P. Ruggieri and C. Vismara (eds.), *Africa romana: Atti dell'IX convegno di studio, Cartagine, 15–18 dicembre 1994*. Ozieri, pp. 127–54.

Vössing, K. 1997a. *Schule und Bildung im Nordafrika der Römischen Kaiserzeit*. Brussels.

Vössing, K. 1997b. Review of Liebs 1993. *Gnomon* 69, pp. 435–41.

Warmington, B. H. 1954. The municipal patrons of Roman North Africa. *Papers of the British School at Rome* 22, pp. 39–55.

Weiling, H. 1996. Advokaten im spätantiken Rom. *Atti dell'Accademia Romanistica Costantiniana. XI Convegno Internazionale in onore di Felix B. J. Wubbe.* Naples, pp. 419–63.

Wilkins, P. I. 1990. Roman Africa's municipal patrons. Ph.D. Dissertation, University of Tasmania.

Winterbottom, M. 1964. Quintilian and the *vir bonus. Journal of Roman Studies* 54, pp. 90–7.

Ziwsa, K. 1893. *S. Optati Milevitani libri VII. Recensuit et commentario critico indicibusque instruxit Carolus Ziwsa. Accedvnt decem monumenta vetera ad Donatistarum historiam pertinentia.* Vienna.

20

Law, Empire, and Identity between West and East

The Danubian Provinces

Benedikt Eckhardt

1. INTRODUCTION

When looking for provincial appropriations of Roman law, for creative usage, transformation and instrumentalization, we normally focus our attention on the papyrological documentation from the Near East. We think of the use of stipulations in Egypt, of Babatha getting her hands on the formula of the *actio tutelae*, or of Dionysia assembling a dossier of documents to confront her father, skillfully navigating between Roman and (supposed) local law. We are less likely to bring inscriptions from the Danubian region into the picture. Everything here seems thoroughly regulated, with little room for provincial adaptation. Municipal laws laid down a tight normative framework, and the continuous presence of soldiers and veterans ensured a strong Roman component of local societies. What is more, the Illyrian, Dalmatian, Thracian and other tribes whose territories were seized and redistributed by Roman rule are not known to have developed complex indigenous legal traditions, unlike Egyptians, Nabateans or Greeks. Where Roman law rules supreme, there seems to be little reason to even ask for the provincial perspective.

This chapter argues for a shift in perspective. While all of the above may be true, it is not the whole story. Much like their Eastern counterparts, provincials in the West are likely to have experimented with Roman law, fitting it to their own purposes while at the same time deriving a sense of identity and belonging from their integration into the Roman legal order. The problem is that we usually do not see them do so, because the documents available—usually stone inscriptions set up in public places—are so different from the documentation of private engagement with the law that we find preserved in Egypt or Arabia. Letting weather conditions shape our assessment of the uses of law in different parts of the empire is quite unsatisfactory. While we cannot study material that is not there, we can legitimately apply general insights from some provinces to others

Benedikt Eckhardt, *Law, Empire, and Identity between West and East: The Danubian Provinces* In: *Law in the Roman Provinces.* Edited by: Kimberley Czajkowski and Benedikt Eckhardt in collaboration with Meret Strothmann,
Oxford University Press (2020).
DOI: 10.1093/oso/9780198844082.003.0020

and see what happens. This means that we can take material from the Danubian provinces and think about how Roman law was experienced on the ground, how its conception was shaped by provincial needs, and how it contributed to the forging of 'imperial identities'.[1]

In light of the limits of our evidence, this approach requires a more active role of the researcher for the West than it does for the East. In some respects, we have to create the problems to be discussed ourselves, on the assumption that law as such is never as unproblematic as public inscriptions tend to suggest. This chapter offers three investigations of different legal problems: the spread of a concept resembling modern legal personality, the use of law in private transactions, and the shaping of municipal identities through recourse to Roman legislation. Each investigation involves questions about the impact of Roman administrative procedures on different levels, and about their local perceptions. They therefore contribute to another methodological question raised in this volume, namely how to conceptualize the relationship between provincial administration and provincial agency as two sides of the same coin.

A note on the geographical scope of this chapter is in order. The 'Danubian provinces' are a traditional designation for a vast area, from Noricum in the West to Northern Thracia and Moesia Inferior in the East.[2] Some places of relevance are hundreds of kilometers away from the Danube, and there was much variety particularly with regard to pre-Roman population groups. It nevertheless seems justified to group together inscriptions relating to legal matters from this artificially defined region. One reason is practicality: with the possible exception of Dacia, one single province would not furnish enough material. In addition, some general characteristics, like the use of Latin, the importance of the military for settlement patterns and the spread of a Roman municipal order in the second century CE, connect the provinces under discussion, separating them from both Achaea and Macedonia in the South and Germania in the North. Still, due to the exemplary nature of the following discussion, it will be impossible to address all the existing differences within the region. While the starting points of the three investigations—Solva in Noricum, Alburnus Maior in Dacia, and Troesmis in Moesia Inferior—allow for a geographical progression of the argument from West to East, the actual discussion has to cross provincial boundaries freely in order to uncover meaningful patterns.

2. LEGAL PERSONALITY

The starting point of our first investigation is the *municipium* Flavia Solva in Noricum (near Leibnitz in Austria). We do not know a lot about this city, but it seems certain that weaving and other forms of textile production were one of its main economic features.[3] Apart from the hundreds of loom weights found in the area, one piece of evidence supporting this is an inscription from October 205 CE,

[1] A term used in recent contributions by Ando (2010), Vanacker & Zuiderhoek (2017).

[2] Cf. the historical overview by Wilkes (2000), and the archaeological overview by Wilkes (2005).

[3] Cf. Gostenčnik (2013), 69–71. The inscriptions are collected by Wedenig (1997), 200–32.

an honorific inscription set up by a *collegium centonariorum* for its 'father' (*pater*) Marcus Secundius Secundinus.[4] *Centonarii* were people involved in textile production or trade, likely catering to military demands as well.[5] Although the inscription is technically an honorific monument for the association's leader, the inscription mainly contains a list of 93 members of the *collegium*, preceded by a letter of the emperor Septimius Severus to the provincial governor Iuventius Surus Proculus. Significant parts of the letter are not preserved, but according to one reconstruction,[6] it reads as follows:

> It is not right that the benefits which have been granted to the association[7] of textile-dealers through an order by the highest class or some other emperor should be revoked rashly. But what has been sanctioned by laws shall be observed, and those who, as you say, enjoy their wealth without burden shall be forced to take over the obligatory public duties. For the privilege of the associations shall be of use neither to those who do not practice the craft nor to those who have higher (financial) abilities from the outset. So against them, the remedy (defined in) the law[8] has to be used. The number need not be reduced because of them. In general, all others[9] may have full enjoyment of an exemption that would not with good reason be subtracted from the benefits of the association.

Some of the reconstructions are debated, but the general sense is clear. The *centonarii* were an association registered under Roman law, i.e. a legitimate *collegium*, which means that the members received certain privileges, but were also expected to contribute to the common good (*utilitas publica*).[10] In some way or other, this system of mutual recognition was in place since the Augustan legislation on *collegia*,[11] and the commentaries of several Severan jurists show

[4] First published by Cuntz (1915); for later editions see below.

[5] For full discussion, see Liu (2009).

[6] AE 1983, 731, ll. 2–8: *beneficia quae amplissimo ordine vel aliquo princi*|[*pe iubente collegiis c*] *entonar(iorum) concessa sunt temere convelli non oportet.* | [*quod autem legibus etia*]*m sanxum* (sic) *est custodiatur et ii quos dicis diviti(i)s suis sine onere* | [*assuscipienda m*]*unera compellantur. neque enim collegiorum privilegium pro*|[*sit aut iis qui artem non*] *exercent aut iis qui maiores facultates praefi(ni)to modo possident. adver*|[*sus hos igitur leg*]*is ad(h)ibendum est remedium. non propter hos minue(n)dus numerus alioquin* | [*omnes alii perfr*]*uantur vacatione quae non competit beneficiis coll(egiorum) derogari.*

[7] All reconstructions (including the one cited in the previous note) have the plural here and in l. 8. But in view of general politics towards associations, it seems more likely that Severus distinguished between the *beneficia* granted to this particular *collegium* (ll. 3 and 8), and the laws regulating *collegia* in general (l. 5); hence we should read [*collegio c*]*entonar(iorum)* in l. 3 and *coll(egii) derogari* in l. 8.

[8] The reconstruction *adver*|[*sus hos igitur leg*]*is ad(h)ibendum est remedium* goes back to Alföldy (1966), 440–1. He thinks that the *remedium* was mentioned in the *lex* of this specific *collegium*. Weber (1968), 112 accepts the reconstruction (as do all later treatments except Schulz-Falkenthal (1973), 24), but plausibly argues that *lex* refers to general legislation on *collegia*, alluded to through the preceding *collegiorum privilegium*.

[9] With Weber (1968), 112 against Alföldy (1966), 441 and Schulz-Falkenthal (1973), 24 ([*tenuiores perfr*]*uantur*).

[10] Callistratus, *On judicial inquiries* 1 (D. 50.6.6.12): . . . *et si qua eandem rationem originis habent, id est idcirco instituta sunt, ut necessariam operam publicis utilitatibus exhiberent.* Cf. I. Ephesos 215 (late second century CE) with references to the *κοινῇ συμφέρον* and the *ἀναγκαία ἐργασία* of the Ephesian bakers.

[11] Asconius, *Corn.* 75 attributes exceptions on the grounds of *utilitas civitatis* already to the senate's decree against associations in 64 BCE. For a reference to the Augustan *lex Iulia* (most likely *de collegiis*), see CIL VI 2193 = 4416.

that it was an important aspect of third-century legal discourse as well. A significant part of imperial legislation focused on preventing abuse of privileges. Marcus Aurelius had ruled that one could not be a member in more than one legitimate *collegium*, preventing people from amassing exemptions.[12] The problem pertinent here is rich people who were obligated to fulfil civic *munera* trying to get around that obligation by joining a legitimate *collegium*. What happened in Solva is exactly the problem discussed by the jurist Callistratus a few decades later:

> Nor is immunity given indiscriminately to every one enrolled in these *collegia*, but only to craftsmen. Nor can men of any age be adlected, as the deified Pius decided, in excluding men of advanced or very tender years. But it has been established in many ways that those who have increased their resources and are capable of supporting the *munera* of the communities can no more avail themselves of dispensations which were granted to poorer men who are divided among *collegia*.[13]

The provincial governor had informed Severus that people had tried to avoid *munera* by entering the *collegium centonariorum*. The emperor responds that the *beneficia* need not be withdrawn—a solution that was obviously on the table, as was the exclusion of members. Still, the 'remedy of the law' (if the reconstruction is to be trusted) shall be used against the wealthy. There is no reason to doubt that this refers to general laws on *collegia*, although the concrete solution was still debatable.[14] The association seems to have been content with this decision and honors its *pater*, presumably for acting as a mediator in the process. The majority of the civic elite should also have endorsed the decree—assuming that the number of those who disguised themselves as textile dealers was limited, these black sheep enhanced the burden for others.[15]

Textile dealers were among the most widespread *collegia* in the Western provinces, often appearing together with the *fabri* ('builders') and the *dendrophori* ('tree-carriers' involved in the cult of Magna Mater). We find all of them in the Danubian provinces, alongside other professional associations and, more often than elsewhere, ethnic groups organized as *collegia*. It is not clear that all of these groups had the same legal status. There is little evidence outside Italy for the application of recognition procedures, e.g. in the form of a reference to a senate's decree granting an association the right of assembly. Apart from an obscure text

[12] Marcian, *Institutes* 3 (D. 47.22.1.2): *Non licet autem amplius quam unum collegium licitum habere, ut est constitutum et a divis fratribus: et si quis in duobus fuerit, rescriptum est eligere eum oportere, in quo magis esse velit, accepturum ex eo collegio, a quo recedit, id quod ei competit ex ratione, quae communis fuit.*

[13] Callistratus, *On judicial inquiries* 1 (D. 50.6.6.1): *Nec omnibus promiscue, qui adsumpti sunt in his collegiis, immunitas datur, sed artificibus dumtaxat. nec ab omni aetate allegi possunt, ut divo pio placuit, qui reprobavit prolixae vel inbecillae admodum aetatis homines. sed ne quidem eos, qui augeant facultates et munera civitatium sustinere possunt, privilegiis, quae tenuioribus per collegia distributis concessa sunt, uti posse plurifariam constitutum est* (transl. Watson).

[14] Schulz-Falkenthal (1973), 24, followed by Wedenig (1997), 229, thinks that it would have been superfluous as a mere application of existing laws and posits a special case. Cuntz (1915), 104 plausibly suggested that the governor was ill-informed.

[15] Weber (1968), 113 argues for a conflict between the association and the city, restoring [*coll(egii) popu*]*lus* in l. 9 as the dedicator, against Alföldy's (1966), 443 [*ordo et popu*]*lus*. The restoration is plausible because Marcus is called *pater* (an internal title used by the *collegium*), but assuming a conflict between the association as such and the city is not necessary.

from Ulpiana (near Priština in Kosovo) that has probably been misunderstood,[16] the inscription from Solva is the only one from the Danubian provinces that directly connects associations with Roman law. However, while the Italian way of prominently displaying authorization by the senate or the emperor on stone was clearly not popular in other epigraphic cultures, the evidence we do have does not allow for the conclusion that recognition procedures were unknown outside Rome and its immediate environment.[17] It is true that many groups must have remained without formal recognition.[18] But the difference is often hard to tell, which may not be too surprising if we apply theoretical insights into the behavior of organizations in insecure environments. Sporadic application of Roman laws on *collegia* was enough to trigger the creation of a largely uniform, isomorphic associational culture that replicated the Roman order.[19] Two immigrant groups in Dacian Alburnus Maior (Roșia Montană in Romania) called themselves *κολλήγιον*, and several dedications in Thracia were made by *κολλῆγαι*.[20] These are conscious attempts to communicate within the frame of reference established by the legal regulations on *collegia*. In Thracian Philipoppolis (Plovdiv in Bulgaria), two professional associations were led by *δεκανεύοντες*, a word not otherwise attested and possibly a translation of *decuriones*.[21] Distributions of money by benefactors regularly included organized groups like hymn-singers or doctors,[22] and throughout the region, *collegia* of *fabri* are frequently attested.[23] Patterns thus emerged that were largely created by provincials, but could ultimately be controlled by the emperors, as the inscription from Solva has shown.

[16] AE 1981, 732 (third century CE), ll. 7–12: *collegius* [sic] *DEIRB* | *ex testament* | *A<l>exandriae s (upra) s(criptae)* | *quot* [sic] *suis sumpti|bus fecerat per s(enatus) c(onsultum)* | *pos(u)erunt* [sic]. Apart from the association's name (a *collegium dei*?) and the incongruent plural, the obvious question is what a senate's decree (nowhere else introduced with *per*) has to do with the erection of a funerary inscription in Ulpiana. An excellent photo has been published on Wikipedia: https://en.wikipedia.org/wiki/Ulpiana#/media/File:Ulpiana25.JPG, accessed 13 February 2018. It shows that the last line in fact reads BSERUNT, which makes *<p>(o)s(u)erunt* difficult to maintain. A slightly more satisfactory text could combine ll. 11–12 to *persc[ri]|bserunt*. Although the inscription is completely preserved, at least one letter is missing at the end of l. 4 and 5 as well; *i* could even have stood at the beginning of l. 12, the only part where the stone is significantly damaged.

[17] They are explicitly attested for Sevilla (CIL II 1167; *centonarii*), Nicomedia (Pliny, *Epistulae* 10.33–4; *fabri*), Cyzicus (CIL III 7060 = FIRA I 48; *νέοι*), Miletus (Ehrhardt & Günther (2013) = SEG 63.974; *ναύκληροι*) and (likely) Sidyma (TAM II 175; *γερουσία*). According to Pliny, *Panegyricus* 54, senators in Domitian's time were regularly consulted *de instituendo collegio fabrorum* (whereas Trajan did not bother to molest senators which such irrelevant matters).

[18] De Ligt (2001) justly connects the application procedure with privileges and advancement to a 'semi-public' status. See Eckhardt (2018) for the argument that most groups that scholars refer to as 'unregistered associations' did not have to be 'tolerated', but were simply not important enough to qualify as (banned or privileged) *collegia*.

[19] For a delineation of this approach, see Eckhardt (2016).

[20] IDR III 398 and 340 (= AE 1944, 22 and 25; second/third century CE) for *κολλήγιον*; for *κολλῆγαι*, see IGBulg III.1 1519 (Cillae near Philippopolis); IV 2039 (Serdica), 2250 (Neine); IMS I 113 (Babe in Moesia Superior).

[21] IGBulg III.1 917, 1401bis (second/third century CE). The Italian *collegia* could be grouped in *decuriae*.

[22] E.g. IGBulg I^2 15 (Dionysopolis in Thracia); IScM I 57 (Histria in Moesia Inferior).

[23] Surveys of the data on associations exist for Noricum (Alföldy (1974), 264–73) and Dacia (Ardevan (1998), 282–312).

But *collegia* did not only spread patterns of social organization, they also introduced, to many for the first time, a concept of corporate representation that resembles the modern idea of legal personality.[24] It is the basis of Gaius' definition of legitimate *collegia* that they are treated *ad exemplum rei publicae*: they were allowed 'on the pattern of the state to have common property, a common treasury, and an attorney or syndic through whom, as in a state, what should be transacted and done in common is transacted and done'.[25] Through this *actor*, contractually bound to the association, *collegia* could be legally represented when handling financial issues, receiving an inheritance, or dealing with Roman or municipal administration.[26] As the same was—as Gaius says—true for cities, the idea as such was introduced to the region through the very process of municipalization. But the spread of *collegia* added an additional dimension: it multiplied the number of corporate bodies (*corpora* or *universitates*) that could have legitimate legal interests, and because of the self-governing nature of *collegia*, the members must have had much closer exposure to this way of legal thinking than they had as inhabitants of a *municipium*.

To some degree, these observations are necessarily theoretical. Yet again, the epigraphic evidence for *actores* of *collegia* is limited to four or five inscriptions that are somewhat ambiguous.[27] But the role of *actor* could be hidden behind some other internal designation. We should also consider the possibility that *actores* could be professional legal experts who did not have to (and in fact could not) become members of an association of craftsmen, which would explain why they do not normally figure in the self-presentation of *collegia*. This is a possible background for two short inscriptions from Sarmizegetusa. Cornelius Cornelianus was 'the *defensor* of the litter-bearers', and the 'merchants of the province (Dacia) Apulensis' honored their *optimus defensor* Crassus Macrobius with a monument.[28] While there is a possibility that the term *defensor* refers more broadly to benefaction and patronage, it more likely means a person 'who represented another in a legal sense',[29] the other persons in these cases being the respective *collegia*. We may also remember Marcus Secundius Secundinus from Solva, who had perhaps acted as the *collegium*'s *actor vel syndicus* in the debate with the provincial governor.

The concept of corporate legal representation and, perhaps, legal personality spread in the Danubian provinces in the second and third centuries CE. Not everyone may have entirely grasped the implications, as may perhaps be deduced from the occasional use of plural verbs together with the singular *collegium*—but the same mistakes are found in Italy.[30] The legal separation of the group from its

[24] On this debate, which has produced a massive body of literature especially by German and Italian scholars of Roman law, see now comprehensively Groten (2015).

[25] Gaius, *On the provincial edict* 3 (D. 3.4.1.1): *Quibus autem permissum est corpus habere collegii societatis sive cuiusque alterius eorum nomine, proprium est ad exemplum rei publicae habere res communes, arcam communem et actorem sive syndicum, per quem tamquam in re publica, quod communiter agi fierique oporteat, agatur fiat* (transl. Watson).

[26] Cf. Aubert (1999).

[27] Discussed by Aubert (1999), 65–9.

[28] CIL III 1438; 1500.

[29] Frakes (2001), 20.

[30] E.g. AE 1981, 732 cited above, n. 16, or RIU V 1062 (Intercisa in Pannonia, 233 CE): *Fortun(a)e | pro sal(ute) d(omini) n(ostri) Severi [[Alexan|dri]] Aug(usti) col|legius Fort|un(a)e ex voto | posuer(unt)*. Cf. for the argument (and Italian parallels) Kurz (1960), 136–9.

members was a new and somewhat counterintuitive idea. It is all the more remarkable that the best ancient example for its application comes from the mining district Alburnus Maior in Dacia. A unique document preserved on a wax-tablet records the dissolution of the *collegium Iovis Cerneni* in 167 CE because only seventeen of the fifty-four members had remained in Alburnus Maior, one *magister* had disappeared, and no meetings had taken place for a long time due to the remaining members' unwillingness to attend.[31] As in many associations, the members, probably for the most part peregrines,[32] had paid contributions for their future burial. The remaining magistrates thus publicly dissolved the association in the presence of seven witnesses (*publice testantur*), stating that 'no-one should think that he still has a *collegium* or can demand a funeral from them'.[33] The whole procedure is legally sound. Through dissolving the *collegium*, the remaining leaders secured themselves against any demands, for as Ulpian would later write: 'a debt to a corporate body is not a debt to individuals and a debt of a corporate body is not a debt of individuals'.[34] Any claims would have to be directed against the *collegium Iovis Cerneni*, which did not exist anymore.

It is very unlikely that this rather insignificant *collegium* had ever received official recognition by the senate or by an emperor. The members nevertheless knew the legal conception of *collegia vel corpora*, and meticulously applied it to their association. How their arrangement would have played out in a Roman court is unclear, but an appropriation of Roman law was certainly better than nothing. It also fits a local pattern that is worth exploring further. For with this remarkable document, we have reached the point of departure for our second investigation.

3. LAW IN TRANSACTIONS

Dacia was integrated into the empire only in 106, but quickly developed structures known from other provinces; a process facilitated by the presence of the military and Roman interest in the Dacian gold mines. The *vicus* Alburnus Maior was a settlement that almost entirely depended on mining. From this village, twenty-four wax tablets (*tabulae ceratae*) recording legal affairs between 139 and 167 CE are known. Not all of them can be deciphered, but those that are readable offer unusual insights into legal practice in a Western province.

[31] IDR I 31 (= FIRA III 114; 9 February 167 CE).

[32] The names of the remaining 17 are not given, but the *magistri* are peregrines; Biró (1969), 3 argues for mixed membership and also points to freedmen and slaves as possible members. Of the seven witnesses listed at the end, five are Roman citizens, but Ardevan (1998), 295 justly notes that since the witnesses were likely selected by status, the list does not accurately represent the distribution of membership (except that one may guess that five of 17 were Roman citizens).

[33] Tab. 3, ll. 7–9: *ut, si quis defunctus fuerit, ne putet se colle|gium <h>abere aut ab eis aliquem petition|em funeris <h>abiturum*. On the names of the witnesses (five Roman citizens), see Noeske (1977), 388. *Collegium habere* is the standard legal expression for membership.

[34] Ulpian, *On the edict* 10 (D. 3.4.7.1): *Si quid universitati debetur, singulis non debetur: nec quod debet universitas singuli debent.*

The very form of these documents clearly shows the influence of Roman law. Most of them are triptycha, and they all follow the regulations laid out in the *Senatus Consultum Neronianum* of 61 CE, according to the *Sententiae Pauli*:

> The senate decreed that those *tabulae*, which contain the writing of either public or private *contractus*, are—once witnesses have been summoned—to be sealed in this way: the tablets, having been perforated on the top edge towards the middle, are bound around with a tripled string, and the seals of the wax placed on top of the string are impressed, so that the interior preserves the *fides* of the writing by means of the exterior. Tablets produced in another fashion have no value.[35]

But it is not only the material form that bears clear traces of Roman legal conceptions. Apart from the dissolution of the *collegium Iovis Cerneni*, most documents are contracts: credit agreements, contracts of sale, employment contracts and, in one case, an agreement between two money lenders about the foundation of a *societas*. The latter document can serve to demonstrate the extent of accuracy that could be reached in these documents. It is a contract completely in line with what we know about how *societates* should be arranged, and it ends with a proper *stipulatio*: 'That this is given, that it is done and that it is handed over Cassius Frontinus has stipulated, and Iulius Alexander has solemnly promised.'[36] According to Gaius, the verb *spopondit* could only be used by Roman citizens,[37] and this is in fact the only wax tablet that records a contract between two parties who possessed Roman citizenship. Normally, at least one of the parties was of peregrine status,[38] and they used other formulae.

A good impression is provided by one of the best-preserved contracts, of 142 CE:

> Dasius Breucus has bought and accepted through taking by hand the boy Apalaustus, or if he is (known) by any other name, of Greek origin, receipted for two ounces, for 600 Denarii from Bellicus son of Alexander, with Marcus Vibius Longus acting as guarantor. It is vouched for that this boy has been handed over healthy, not charged with theft and damage, and neither a fugitive nor a truant. And if anyone shall have claimed back from him this boy in question or a part of him, so that it is not legal for the above-mentioned buyer or the one to whom the affair will be relevant to properly possess and use him, Dasius Breucus has requested in good faith that however much it will be that will be taken away from him in this way, precisely the double amount of that money shall properly be given, and Bellicus son of Alexander has promised in good faith that it will be given. Vibius Longus has affirmed the same in good faith. And Bellicus son of Alexander states that he has received and possesses for this boy, who is named above, the price of 600 Denarii from Dasius Breucus.
>
> Done in the settlement of the Legio XIII Gemina, 17 days before the calends of June, in the consulate of Rufinus and Quadratus.

[35] *Pauli Sententiae* 5.25.6: *Amplissimus ordo decrevit eas tabulas, quae publici vel privati contractus scripturam continent, adhibitis testibus ita signari, ut in summa marginis ad mediam partem perforatae triplici lino constringantur atque impositae supra linum cerae signa imprimantur, ut exteriori scripturae fidem interior servet. Aliter tabulae prolatae nihil momenti habent.* Translation by Meyer (2004), 167.

[36] IDR I 44 (= FIRA III 157), Tab. 2r ll. 18–19: *Id d(ari) f(ieri) p(raestari)que stipulatus est | Cassius Frontin[us, spopon]dit Iul(ius) Alexander.* For detailed discussion, see Pólay (1960).

[37] Gaius, *Inst.* 3.92–3; cf. Meyer (2004), 115–16.

[38] Pólay (1971).

(Seals of) Appius Proclus, veteran of the Legio XIII Gemina. Antonius Celer. Iulius Viator. Ulpius Severinus. Lucius Firmius Primitivus. Marcus Vibius Longinus, the guarantor. Bellicus son of Alexander, the seller.[39]

In general, this is a typical contract for the sale of a slave. Other examples are known from Italy or Britain, and it is plausible to assume that the text was taken from a handbook. Two other contracts are very similar: in 139 CE, Maximus son of Bato bought the slave-girl Passia from Dasius son of Verzo, 'a Pirustian from Kavieretium', and in 160, the soldier Claudius Iulianus bought the woman Theodote from Claudius Philetus.[40] The degree to which the standard text was personalized could vary: Both Dasius Breucus and Claudius Iulianus appear once as *emptor s(upra) (scriptus)*, which presumably just copies the formula from the book, whereas Maximus' name is always given in full. But in general, all transactions followed the same pattern, to the extent that scribal errors occasionally occur when the situation required changing standard expressions, e.g. from masculine to feminine.[41]

As was commonly done in such contracts, the clauses distinguish between deficiencies which lie in the object itself (like health) and those that might result from legal uncertainties (ownership of someone else). The legal context for this is the edict of the curule aediles, which stated that 'those who sell slaves are to apprise purchasers of any disease or defect in their wares and whether a given slave is a runaway, a loiterer on errands, or still subject to noxal liability; all these matters they must proclaim in due manner when the slaves are sold'.[42] However, it has plausibly been argued that this edict did not make such warranties obligatory, but only prescribed the form of warranties if they were given.[43] The market would have regulated which warranties were necessary to find a buyer.

None of the three contracts of slave-sale shows a transaction between two Roman citizens. The stipulations thus look different from the previous example: *fide rogavit—fide promisit*. Again, we have seven witnesses, one of whom was the seller himself. Seven seals are found below all three documents, and the contracts of Dasius and Maximus also feature a guarantor (*fideiussor*). The concept of

[39] IDR I 37 (= FIRA III 88), Tab. 1 and 2r: *Dasius Breucus emit mancipioque accepit | puerum Apalaustum sive is quo alio nomine | est n(atione) Gr(a)ecum apoc(h)atum pro unci(i)s duabus | (denariis) DC de Bellico Alexandri f(ide) r(ogato) M(arco) Vibio Longo | eum puerum sanum traditum esse furtis noxaque | solutum erronem fugiti(v)um caducum non esse | pr(a)estari et si quis eum puerum q(uo) d(e) a(gitur) | partenve* [sic] *quam quis ex eo evicerit q(uo) m(inus) | emptorem s(upra) s(criptum) eunve* [sic] *ad q(uem) ea res pertinebit | uti frui habere possidereq(ue) recte liceat | tunc quantum id erit quod ita ex eo evic|tum fuerit || t(antam) p(ecuniam) duplam p(robam) r(ecte) d(ari) f(ide) r(ogavit) Dasius | Breucus d(ari) f(ide) p(romisit) | Bellicus Alexandri id[em] fide sua esse | iussit Vibius Longus | proque eo puero qui s(upra) s(criptus) e(st) pretium | eius (denarios) DC accepisse et habere se dixit | Bellicus Alexandri ab Dasio Breuco | act(um) kanab(is) leg(ionis) XIII G(eminae) XVII Kal(endas) Iunias | Rufino et Quadrato co(n)s(ulibus)*. Tab. 2, right margin: *Appi Procli vet(erani) leg(ionis) XIII g(eminae) | Antoni Celeris | Iul(i) Viatoris | Ulp(i) Severini | L(uci) Firmi Primitivi | M(arci) Vibi Longi | fideiussor(is) | Bellici Alex[a]n|dri vendit(oris).*

[40] IDR I 36 and 38 (= FIRA III 87 and 89).

[41] Noted by Ciulei (1983), 21.

[42] Ulpian, *On the edict* 1 (D. 21.1.1.1): *Aiunt aediles: 'Qui mancipia vendunt certiores faciant emptores, quid morbi vitiive cuique sit, quis fugitivus errove sit noxave solutus non sit: eademque omnia, cum ea mancipia venibunt, palam recte pronuntianto'* (transl. Watson).

[43] Cf. the overview provided by Arzt-Grabner (2010); on the purpose of the edict, see Jakab (2015), 226–8.

fideiussio is applied as could be expected from Roman legal texts. In one case, the *fideiussor* was apparently unable to write Latin, but nevertheless, clumsily and in Greek letters, signed as *secundus auctor*.[44] Ulpian later noted that the *fideiussor* could *vulgo* be called *secundus auctor*, and it has been argued that this is a case where provincial practice influenced the development of imperial law.[45] Be that as it may, someone must have felt that Alexandros son of Antipatros, who most likely lacked a proper legal understanding of the term, should identify his seal in this particular way.

The phrasing of the actual transaction—*emit mancipioque accepit*—is standardized in the sales contracts from Alburnus Maior, often followed by *apochatum pro uncis duabus*, 'receipted for two ounces'. Strictly speaking this makes little sense, as the formula combines two legal procedures of a different kind, the *emptio-venditio* (the contractual sale) and the *mancipatio* (the act of transferring property into by *manus* in a ritualized form including a ritual and a symbolic payment).[46] As the same phrasing can be found in Herculaneum and London,[47] it appears to have been a more widely known variation, brought to Dacia by merchants or legal experts. The inclusion of *mancipatio* nevertheless offers a window into the provincial experience of Roman law, the significance of which should not be underestimated.

According to Ulpian, only Roman citizens or peregrines with *ius commercii* could perform a legally valid *mancipatio*.[48] In the contracts from Alburnus Maior, the partners are usually of peregrine status. Gaius gives a list of things that can be transmitted via *mancipatio* (slaves, animals, and properties on Italian soil) and thereby provides us with a second problem, for one of the contracts records the transmission of half a house by *mancipatio*—although it was not on Italian soil and should therefore have been among the *res nec mancipi*.[49] To remedy this confusing situation, it has been proposed that the peregrines of Alburnus Maior actually possessed the *ius commercii*, and that the village as such had the *ius Italicum*.[50] However, positing the *ius commercii* for a very diverse group of people to make their transactions legitimate is a circular argument, and while Alburnus Maior as a mining district was certainly subject to imperial control, the granting of *ius Italicum* is unlikely.[51] We are left with people who should not be able to perform a valid *mancipatio*, but nevertheless mancipate even things that should not be mancipated according to Roman law.

[44] IDR I 38 (= FIRA III 89), Tab. 2, right margin, l. 8–11: *ΑΛΕΞΑΝΔΡΥΣ* | *ΑΝΤΙΤΑΤΡΙ* | *ΣΕΚΟΔ - ΑΥΚΤΩΡ* | *ΣΕΓΝΑ*VI.

[45] Ulpian, *On the edict* 32 (D. 21.2.4*pr*): . . . *an is qui mancipium vendidit debeat fideiussorem ob evictionem dare, quem vulgo auctorem secundum vocant*; cf. Pólay (1962a), 156.

[46] On the problems, see Arangio-Ruiz (1956), 182–202; Pólay (1962b), 57–65; Ciulei (1983), 18–38; Jakab (1997), 167–8. The word used in the documents is *mancipium*, on which see Thormann (1969), 58–67.

[47] TH 61 (re-edited by Camodeca (2000), 74–6); AE 2003, 1016 = AE 2006, 709.

[48] *Regulae* 19.4: *mancipatio locum habet inter cives Romanos et Latinos coloniarios Latinosque Iunianos eosque peregrinos, quibus commercium datum est.*

[49] Gaius, *Inst.* 2.18–22; IDR I 39 (= FIRA III 90).

[50] Weiß (1916); Meyer (2004), 182. Against this, see already Pólay (1962b), 63–7.

[51] Cf. on the *ius Italicum* Zack (2014), who also notes (286 n. 134) regarding Alburnus Maior that the sale of a house is not the same as the sale of the plot of land on which it stands.

Because of the presence of elements taken from *emptio-venditio*, *mancipatio* is not an essential part of these contracts, and there may even be an awareness of the contractual partners that the actual consequences of their *mancipationes* would not be legally enforceable. Otherwise, the inclusion of the *stipulatio duplae* in case of eviction (the promise to pay the double amount in case the property actually belonged to a third party) would not have been necessary, because *mancipatio* would have yielded the right to use the *actio auctoritatis* in such cases, with the same result.[52] It has in fact been argued that *mancipatio* was not actually performed anymore at that period, but had degenerated into a mere phrase without meaning.[53] However, apart from the question why it would still be found in handbooks used in a Roman province created only in 106 CE (as well as in Gaius and Ulpian), this approach relies on questionable methodological assumptions. The reason for not believing that people did what they say they did in front of witnesses is not positive evidence to the contrary, but a normative perspective that cannot see a legal rationale behind these deeds. But not only can people behave irrationally, they may also invest legal procedures with meaning beyond the restrictions envisioned by Roman jurists. A historical model for the spread of a 'legal mentality' in Roman Dacia—and other Western provinces—would have to integrate the possibility of provincial agency.

Such agency cannot be adequately assessed by reducing it to mere lack of understanding. The apodictic statement that the people of Alburnus Maior, or at least those who drafted the contracts of sale, simply lacked 'adequate knowledge or practical experience' with regard to Roman law because they 'did not receive expert advice' leaves much to be desired.[54] Some expertise must have been around. A *fideiussor* who does not know Latin, but signs as *secundus auctor* cannot be explained otherwise, and neither can the scrupulous distinction between stipulations available to everyone and those to be used only by Roman citizens. In some cases of *locatio-conductio*, the contracts were written by third persons because the employee was illiterate;[55] who were those persons? The contracts of temporary employment in the mines are unproblematic from a legal point of view. In all likelihood, the reason for this is that the gold-mines were controlled by the state. The persons responsible would thus have model contracts readily available.[56] But people were still needed who were able to write up the individual contracts, insert the wages and the additional clauses. Not all contracts were identical; one of them is even written in Greek. These people could act as distributors of legal knowledge, mediated through handbooks perhaps, and they were the ones who could be asked if someone wanted to buy a slave or half a house. When people saw their neighbors entering into Roman contracts, this must have shaped their idea of law, and inspired them to search for advice for their own dealings. They found it in the environment of the mines, but perhaps also in the military. Some of the parties to the transactions are soldiers or veterans. The fact that they are explicitly singled out shows that most others were not, but the presence of such people—with

[52] Pólay (1962a), 144–6 points to a possible legal reasoning. [53] Nowak (2011).

[54] Quotations from Wolf (2015), 66 and 67. [55] IDR I 40–2 (41–2 = FIRA III 150).

[56] The calculations by Cuvigny (1996) suggest that the contracts from Dacia offered the same wages as those from Egypt, which points to standardization. On the administration of the mines, see also Hirt (2010).

contacts to army scribes and other small-scale experts—likely contributed to the development of Dacian legal culture.

The ensuing standardization was a matter of practice. People would not find a buyer for their slave without including *mancipatio* in their contracts and agreeing to a *stipulatio duplae*. Roman law would then have to be regarded as a repository providing people with a large amount of contractual elements—but which elements were chosen was a matter neither of strict obligation nor of mere individual preferences, but determined by regionally contingent ideas of what constituted law, and specifically 'Roman law'. Against this view, one might object that 'the application of the law of commerce shows the romanization of the new province, one of whose principal means was imposing the obligation to make use of the Roman legal order'.[57] But it is far from clear that these people drafted their documents to be used in Roman courts, and the claim that they were forced to do so is a strong one that would require proof. If we see the Roman order as less obligatory and more participatory, it is not a huge problem anymore that people might end up with legal formulae that, from a Roman legal perspective, did not concern them at all. A famous point of comparison would be Babatha's possession of the formula for the *actio tutelae*.[58] Roman law was put to use as these people saw fit, and the legal culture thus created could become normative without a formal obligation imposed by Rome.

Two conditions for this development can perhaps be surmised. As a mining district, Alburnus Maior and its environs came into close contact not only with the military, but also with other elements of Roman administration. At the same time, Alburnus Maior was not a Roman *colonia* or *municipium*. The use of 'Roman' law had a symbolic dimension that may not easily be inferred from normative texts like the municipal laws from Spain. We have thus reached the intersection between provincial agency and a normative Roman order, with a possible dividing line constituted by the different status of settlements. The final investigation will therefore focus on normative texts from cities directly governed by Roman law, testing the validity of the perspective adopted here under hostile circumstances.

4. PRECEDENT AND IDENTITY

Municipia and *coloniae* received their laws from Rome. While there was room for modifications specific to a given city, basic principles and many concrete regulations were standardized.[59] It is clear that we cannot expect to find many traces of provincial agency in these documents. The shift in perspective may nevertheless contribute to an understanding of the symbolic dimension of Roman law, and its importance for the formation of 'imperial identities' in the Danubian provinces.

The most important pieces of evidence are the two bronze tablets from the *municipium* Troesmis (near Tulcea in Romania), first offered for sale on Ebay in

[57] Wolf (2015), 67.
[58] P. Yadin 28–30; see Czajkowski (2017), 93–105.
[59] See Eck and Strothmann in this volume.

2005, repatriated to Romania in 2015 and now published in two editions.[60] It was of course to be expected that municipal laws existed not only in Spain. For the Danubian provinces, fragments from Lauriacum had already pointed towards a municipal law from the time of Caracalla, and fragments of a municipal law from Ratiaria in Moesia Superior have recently been identified.[61] That *leges* could govern many areas of municipal life also emerges from other evidence like a funerary inscription from Doclea in Southern Dalmatia, where a fifteen year old boy from one of the leading families was decreed 'as many honors as he was allowed to receive by law'.[62] But the tablets from Troesmis put the whole discussion on a new footing, as they actually contain some of the regulations governing a Roman city in Moesia Inferior. In addition to its content, the material form of the *lex* as it can be deduced from the fragments provokes the question how the publication of legal texts could in itself be a symbolic gesture. The psychological effect of roughly one hundred shiny bronze tablets containing Roman law, exhibited on a fifty-meter long wall in the centre of the city, has justly been stressed.[63] The setup is likely to have reassured everyone, even those who could not read, that this was still Rome, or at least a fairly accurate copy of it.

The fragments preserve parts of chapter 11, 27 and 28 of the *lex*. There are very close similarities to the *lex Irnitana* and the *lex Malacitana*, but the order of chapters is different, and in general, the text from Troesmis is longer.[64] There is a lot of common ground, but also interesting deviations. For our purposes, the most interesting part is chapter 27, which deals with eligibility for municipal offices. The part preserved concentrates on the priesthood:

> The one who holds the assemblies shall take care that the calculation of the years is done for someone who requests the priesthood, if he is less than 35 years old, as stipulated and guaranteed by the *lex Iulia de maritandis ordinibus*, chapter 6, which is also stipulated and guaranteed by the *commentarius* on which the *lex Papia Poppaea* is based, (the *commentarius*) proposed on June 28 in the year when Cn. Cinna Magnus and Volesus Valerius Caesus were consuls, chapter 49, and confirmed by the *lex Papia Poppaea*, chapter 44. Whoever is appointed in a manner different from the one allowed by this law shall be neither annual *duumvir*, nor *quinquennalis*, nor *aedilis*, nor *quaestor*, nor priest. And whoever appoints them deliberately, in bad faith, shall be forced to pay 10,000 *sestertii* to the citizens of *municipium* M. Aur. Ant.

[60] Cîrjan (2016); Eck (2016).

[61] See Eck's article in this volume.

[62] CIL III 12693 = AE 1897, 8 (71–130 CE), ll. 1–10: *M(arco) Flavio M(arci) f(ilio) | Quir(ina) | Balb [i]no ann(orum) XV | huic defunct(o) ord(o) | mun(icipii) Docl(eatium) funus | public(um) e[t] statuam | [ped]estre[m] decr(evit) item | [primo Docl(eatium)] honores | qua[n]tos per [l]eges caper(e) | [licuit et statuam] equest(rem)*... Wilkes (2000), 592 understands the text to mean that young Balbinus had held 'all the offices permitted to him by law', an example of the 'early enthusiasm for municipal life', before the burdens connected with political offices became too heavy. But the *honores* mentioned here are clearly the 'gesetzmäßigen Ehren' as noted by Sticotti (1913), 197; cf. CIL III 8287 regarding the same person: *M(arco) Fl(avio) M(arci) f(ilio) Quir(ina) Balbino [huic defu]nc(to) ordo Docl(eatium) honores omnes et statuam | equestr(em) decr(evit)*.

[63] Eck (2016), 601. Eck (2013), 88 had initially calculated 50 tablets and 25 meters.

[64] Chapter 11 in Troesmis (on the selection of ambassadors and the financial regulations on embassies) corresponds to chapter 45 in Irni, and chapter 28 in Troesmis (on the voting procedures) to chapter 55 in Malaga. On structure and length, see Eck (2016), 596–600.

> and L. Aurel. Commod. Aug. in Troesmis. And any citizen of the *municipium* may have a right of action, claim and prosecution for and in connection to this amount, if he or she so wishes.[65]

The clause on the *actio petitio persecutio* is known, with very little variation, from both the *lex Irnitana* and the *lex Malacitana*.[66] The rest is, at the present stage of our knowledge, unique. A minimum age for priests is not known from other Roman legal texts, and the age chosen here is higher than the usual age limits for magistrates known from municipal laws. One attempt to explain this has focused on regional preferences: it seems that in Moesia and other Danubian provinces, priesthoods marked the end of a successful municipal career.[67] In any case, unless we emend the text significantly,[68] this is a locally specific modification. More intriguing is the reference to no less than three sources of law: the *lex Iulia de maritandis ordinibus* of 18 BCE, a *commentarius* published in 5 CE, and the *lex Papia Poppaea* of 9 CE, which according to our text was based on the *commentarius*. In each case, precise chapters are given. Quotation as such is not unknown from municipal laws,[69] but nowhere do we find such a complex array of sources. The parallel passage in the *lex Malacitana* may also draw on Augustan legislation, but does not cite it.[70] The *lex* from Troesmis seems to deliberately create a small network of references that makes the *ratio annorum* appear as an undisputable Roman requirement. The *commentarius* receives the most detailed treatment,

[65] B ll. 4–17 as presented by Eck (for debate, see n. 68): *E<i>u<s>* [the text reads *eum*], *qui sacerdotium petet, | quo<d> minor ann(orum) XXXV sit, rationem annorum habendam, | quae utiq(ue) legis Iuliae de maritandis ordinibus lata<e> kap(ite) VI | cauta conprehensaque <est>* [the text reads *sunt*], *quaeq(ue) utiq(ue) commentari(i), ex | quo lex P(apia) P(oppaea) lata est, propositi Cn(aeo) Cinna Magno, Vol(eso) Val(erio) | {Caeso} <Messalla> co(n)s(ulibus) IIII kal(endas) Iulias kap(ite) XLVIIII cauta conprehensaque | <est>* [the text reads *sunt*] *et confirmata legis P(apiae) P(oppaeae) k(apite) XLIIII, conservanda, qui quaeq(ue) | comitia habebit, curato. qui aliter quam hac lege licebit | creatus erit, is neque annu<u>s IIvir neque q(uin)q(uennalis) neque aedilis | neque quaestor neque sacerdos esto. quique eorum quem | scie(n)s d(olo) m(alo) creaverit, is <in> singulas res s(upra) s(criptas) X (milia) n(ummum) munici<pi>bus | municipi(i) M(arci) Aureli Antonini et L(uci) Aureli Commodi | Aug(usti) Troesm(ensium) d(are) d(amnas) esto eiusque pecuniae deque ea pecu|nia munici<pi>bus municipi(i) eius, qui volet cuique per hac | lege licebit, actio petitio persecutio esto.*

[66] Eck (2016), 594 cites the parallels. [67] Cîrjan (2015), 141–2.

[68] Platschek (2017), 158–62 offers an ingenious solution that brings the text into line with common principles of Roman law: *XXXV* should be emended to *XXV* (the common minimum requirement for passive franchise), *habendam* should be *habend<u>m* (keeping *eum* in the text instead of Eck's *e<i>u<s>*), and *rationem* is corrupt for *maiorem*. The result is a legal fiction: if an applicant is younger than 25 years old, he should be treated as if he was of age—because it is 'just' a priesthood. Platschek's text relies on very significant emendations, but so does Eck's, and Platschek is right to note several problems with Eck's version. He further argues (*ibid.*, 162) that everything from *quae utiq(ue)* onwards has nothing in particular to do with the priesthood (for in his text, *quae* cannot refer back to *rationem* anymore). He takes *quae utiq(ue)* . . . *conservanda* . . . *curato* to mean 'he shall take care that what (is prescribed in the sources cited) is always observed'. The benefit of this is that we do not have to change *sunt* to *est* (as Eck does); the downside is what seems to me a questionable position (and repetition) of *utiq(ue)*, and a meaning that it never seems to have in the *Lex Irnitana*. As for content, given that the *lex Iulia de maritandis ordinibus* seems to have specified rules for subtracting years from the minimum requirement in case of married men with children, a satisfactory meaning can be deduced from Eck's text: despite the unusual age limit, the rules on *ratio annorum* still apply. (I thank Fabio Guidetti for discussing this passage with me.)

[69] *Lex Irnitana* § 91 cites a *Lex Iulia*.

[70] *Lex Malacitana* § 56 and 57; see Eck (2016), 590–1.

excluding any possible misunderstanding as to precisely which text is meant. This emphasis seems strange, given that the *commentarius* leads to a famous *lex*, which could easily have been cited without going into the details of its history. All this is especially interesting because there is no other evidence for a *commentarius* of 5 CE which formed the basis of the *lex Poppaea*. The law from late second-century-CE Troesmis thus actually helps to elucidate the history of Augustan legislation.[71]

But why? As the *municipium* had only just been founded, this was neither a re-inscription nor a modification of a previously existing text. It was published at a time when knowledge of the details of Augustan legislation was not necessarily widespread even among legal experts.[72] And would said *commentarius* really have been available to potential readers at Troesmis? Apart from the question what the *lex Iulia de maritandis ordinibus* may have said on age limits for priests, we also should ask why this small piece of legal history was embedded into a municipal law in the first place. There may be an unspectacular answer: the text used for the *lex Troesmensium* was not a development of the tradition we find in the Flavian laws from Spain, but an earlier version much closer in time to the *lex Papia Poppaea*. The law could thus reflect debates of the Augustan period that had nothing whatsoever to do with high imperial Troesmis. While this possibility cannot technically be ruled out, it raises the question why a pre-Flavian version would be used at such a late date. Other options have been suggested: Troesmis may have been a *municipium* of Roman rather than Latin citizens (as opposed to the *municipia* in Spain)—but that is not certain, and there is also no obvious connection between citizenship and extensive referencing of legal texts.[73] A special interest of Marcus Aurelius and Commodus in the *lex Iulia et Papia* may emerge from an *oratio* prohibiting senators from certain marriages; hence a jurist of his *consilium* (Scaevola?) could have inserted these references into the municipal law(s) of the time.[74] But why would he do that, and is it a coincidence that they seem to give legitimacy to an unusual age limit?

This is the only municipal law we know in some detail that dates to a time when legal documentation and archives had become widespread. Perhaps the style of municipal laws had changed accordingly, with regionally specific issues being addressed with elaborate historical arguments. Perhaps the unusual age limit for priests was one of the issues that required such special justification, provided by a legal expert who made it look like the most Roman law imaginable.[75] We cannot know, but it seems clear that this unusual paragraph holds more in store than a piece of additional information on an Augustan law.

Invoking Augustan legal history certainly contributed to the self-understanding of the citizens of Troesmis as proud Romans in a foreign—and increasingly hostile—territory. Municipal laws were not the only medium of such recourse

[71] Cf. Eck (2016), 601–5 on how it does so.

[72] Gaius already refers to the *lex Iulia et Papia* as a whole: 1.145, 194.

[73] For the explanation, see Eck (2016), 591. But Mentxaka (2017), 488–510 tends towards seeing Troesmis as a *municipium* of Latin citizens, without deciding the issue.

[74] Mentxaka (2016), 27–9, with reference to Ulpian, *On the lex Julia et Papia* 3 (D.23.1.16).

[75] This argument would of course have to be abandoned if the emendations by Platschek (2017) are accepted (above n. 68). It is clear from the text that the Augustan legislation applies to all elections, not just to those of priests, but see n. 68 for the question where the specific reference to the laws ends.

to famous precedents. The importance of Roman analogies also emerges from the dedicatory inscription of an altar set up in Dalmatian Salona (modern Solin in Croatia), at both the Western and Southern fringe of our area of interest. In 137 CE, Gaius Domitius Valens, duumvir of *colonia Martia Iulia Salona*, dedicated the altar to Jupiter Optimus Maximus and established a law (*legem dixit*) regarding sacrifice. A sacrifice without exposure of the entrails is to be considered valid (*probe factum*). 'The other laws of this altar shall be the same as those established for the altar of Diana on the Aventine Hill.'[76] Both this reference to the cult of Diana and the exception regarding entrails appear, in almost identical words, on an altar re-inscribed in the Antonine period, but originally dedicated in 12 CE to the *numen Augusti* in *colonia Julia Paterna Narbo Martius* (Narbonne in Gaul).[77] Parts of the introductory formula can already be found on an altar dedicated in Furfo in 58 BCE, and Diana's altar on the Aventine was also invoked in the dedication of an altar for the *salus Augusti* in Ariminum.[78] We are undoubtedly dealing with standard procedure.

And yet again, this insight does little to elucidate the local understanding of this *lex*. It has plausibly been suggested that the people at Narbo or Salona did not in fact know the *leges* governing sacrifice on the Aventine, which were supposedly recorded on an ancient stele mentioned (but not cited) by Dionysius of Halicarnassus in the Augustan period.[79] The altar of Gaius Domitius Valens was dedicated much later than the two Augustan examples, where the reference to Diana on the Aventine could perhaps be explained with the particular interest of the Augustan period in religious restoration (the altar from Furfo does not yet mention her). Unlike the examples from Narbo and Ariminum, it was not dedicated to the worship of Augustus.[80] So what does it mean under these circumstances that the city's duumvir, certainly working from a rulebook, *legem dixit*—a claim not made by an individual in the other examples?[81] And how would the reference to Diana on the Aventine have been understood in Hadrianic times, when the 'Augustan restoration' was a thing of the past? Clearly the symbolic dimension—the appropriation of a formula otherwise used in slightly different contexts, the authority of the duumvir who cites such precedent, the equation of one's own religious rules with a famous example of Roman religion—is more important for understanding the text than a mere enumeration of parallels can reveal.

[76] CIL III 1933 = FIRA III 74, ll. 7–8: *ceterae leges huic arae eaedem sunto, quae arae Dianae sunt in Aventino monte dictae.*

[77] CIL XII 4333 B = FIRA III 73, ll. 20–2: *ceterae* | *leges huic arae titulisq(ue)* | *eadem sunto, quae sunt arae* | *Dianae in Aventino*; cf. ll. 13–15: *sive* | *quis hostia sacrum faxit, qui* | *magmentum nec protollat, id|circo tamen probe factum esto* with the altar from Salona, l. 6: *si quis hic hostia sacrum faxit, quod magmentum nec protollat, it circo tamen probe factum esto.*

[78] Furfo: CIL IX 3513 = FIRA III 72, l. 3: *olleis legibus illeis regionibus* with the altar from Salona, ll. 5–6: *ollis legib(us)* | *ollisque regionibus*. Ariminum: CIL XI 361, l. 5, where the abbreviation has been explained as *h(aec) a(edes) S(alutis) A(ugustae) h(abet) ll(eges) q(uas) D(ianae) R(omae) in A(ventino)*.

[79] Ando (2009), 100–1; Dion. Hal. 4.26.4–5.

[80] The altar from Narbo has been regarded as 'the prototype for all other dedications to the Numen Augusti in the western provinces' (Spickermann (2015), 418).

[81] After the introduction, the inscriptions from Narbo and Solva both continue in the first person singular, likely following an established formula. But in Narbo, no speaker is mentioned.

5. CONCLUSION

As this last example has perhaps most clearly shown, what is proposed here is not a radical revision of our approach to law in the Latin speaking provinces, but an extension. If the claim that Roman law was simply a given and not subject to any provincial agency has been debunked for the East, good reasons would be needed to hold on to it in the study of more Western provinces. The preliminary assumption in this chapter has been that the enormous gap between West and East might be grounded in the nature of the available evidence to a higher degree than has yet been acknowledged. The importance of municipal structures and the legal status of different kinds of settlements are not negligible factors, and the argument that other regions had more complex pre-Roman legal traditions is most likely correct. Nevertheless, this should not prevent us from investigating provincial perspectives, and to make the most of the limited evidence available.

This chapter has discussed three different thematic areas, all of which can on first sight only serve to illustrate the normative aspects of Roman law. But in each case, it has been possible to reconstruct varying (sometimes rather subtle) degrees of provincial agency, through asking questions inspired by the situation in the Eastern provinces. The legal spheres under investigation were rather different: imperial legislation on *collegia vel corpora* in the first example, the law of transactions in the second, the statutes of Roman cities outside Italy in the third. We have also met different actors: merchants and aspiring craftsmen, soldiers and veterans, Roman citizens and peregrines. The exposure to Roman legal conceptions can thus be traced across different strata of society, and so can the possible responses.

We have not found the traces of local law that make the material from the Eastern provinces so fascinating. It is unlikely that Babatha and Dionysia will be joined by Dasius Breucus or Bellicus son of Alexander anytime soon in introductions to law in the Roman provinces. However, the local configurations of Roman law in the Danubian provinces could be complex. They offer important insights into the role of law in the formation of imperial identities, particularly if we deduce from the nature of the available evidence that what we have seen is merely the tip of the iceberg.

REFERENCES

Alföldy, G. 1966. Zur Inschrift des *collegium centonariorum* von Solva. *Historia* 15, pp. 433–44.

Alföldy, G. 1974. *Noricum*. London.

Ando, C. 2009. Diana on the Aventine. In: H. Cancik & J. Rüpke (eds.), *Die Religion des Imperium Romanum. Koine und Konfrontationen*. Tübingen, pp. 99–113.

Ando, C. 2010. Imperial Identities. In: T. Whitmarsh (ed.), *Local Knowledge and Micro-identities in the Imperial Greek World*. Cambridge, pp. 17–45.

Arangio-Ruiz, V. 1956. *La compravendita in diritto romano. Vol. 1.* 2nd ed. Napoli.

Ardevan, R. 1998. *Viața municipală în Dacia Romană*. Timisoara.

Arzt-Grabner, Peter 2010. 'Neither a Truant nor a Fugitive': Some Remarks on the Sale of Slaves in Roman Egypt and Other Provinces. In: T. Gagos (ed.), *Proceedings of the Twenty-Fifth International Congress of Papyrology*. Ann Arbor, pp. 21–32.

Aubert, J.-J. 1999. La gestion des *collegia*: aspects juridiques, économiques et sociaux. *Cahiers du Centre Gustave Glotz* 10, pp. 49–69.

Biró, J. 1969. Das *Collegium funeraticium* in Alburno maiore. In: M. N. Andreev, J. Irmscher, E. Pólay & W. Warkallo (eds.), *Gesellschaft und Recht im griechisch-römischen Altertum*. Berlin, pp. 1–19.

Camodeca, G. 2000. Tabulae Herculanenses: riedizione delle emptiones di schiavi (TH 59–62). In: U. Manthe & C. Krampe (eds.), *Quaestiones Iuris. Festschrift für Joseph Georg Wolf zum 70. Geburtstag*. Berlin, pp. 53–76.

Cîrjan, R. 2015. La nomination des candidats aux magistratures et les sacerdoces municipaux selon *lex Troesmensium*, Ch. XXVII. *Ephemeris Napocensis* 25, pp. 135–46.

Cîrjan, R. 2016. The Municipal Law of Troesmis: Preliminary Remarks. In: A. Panaite, R. Cîrjan & C. Căpiță (eds.), *Moesica et Christiana. Studies in Honour of Professor Alexandru Barnea*. Brăila, pp. 289–300.

Ciulei, G. 1983. *Les triptyques de Transylvanie*. Zutphen.

Cuntz, O. 1915. Ein Reskript des Septimius Severus und Caracalla über die *centonarii* aus Solva. *Jahreshefte des Österreichischen Archäologischen Institutes in Wien* 18, pp. 98–114.

Cuvigny, H. 1996. The Amount of Wages Paid to the Quarry-Workers at Mons Claudianus. *Journal of Roman Studies* 86, pp. 139–45.

Czajkowski, K. 2017. *Localized Law. The Babatha and Salome Komaise Archives*. Oxford.

De Ligt, L. 2001. D. 47,22,1,pr.-1 and the Formation of Semi-Public *Collegia*. *Latomus* 60, pp. 345–58.

Eck, W. 2013. Das Leben römisch gestalten. Ein Stadtgesetz für das *municipium Troesmis* aus den Jahren 177–180 n. Chr. In: G. de Kleijn & S. Benoist (eds.), *Integration in Rome and in the Roman World*. Leiden, pp. 75–88.

Eck, W. 2016. Die *lex Troesmensium*: ein Stadtgesetz für ein *municipium civium Romanorum*. Publikation der erhaltenen Kapitel und Kommentar. *Zeitschrift für Papyrologie und Epigraphik* 200, pp. 565–606.

Eckhardt, B. 2016. Romanization and Isomorphic Change in Phrygia: the Case of Private Associations. *Journal of Roman Studies* 106, pp. 147–71.

Eckhardt, B. 2018. *Religionis causa*? Zur rechtlichen Lage der Vereine 'fremder' Götter in der römischen Kaiserzeit. In: M. Blömer & B. Eckhardt (eds.), *Transformationen paganer Religion in der römischen Kaiserzeit. Rahmenbedingungen und Konzepte*. Berlin, pp. 113–52.

Ehrhardt, N. & Günther, W. 2013. Hadrian, Milet und die Korporation der milesischen Schiffseigner. Zu einem neu gefundenen kaiserlichen Schreiben. *Chiron* 43, pp. 199–220.

Frakes, R. M. 2001. *Contra potentium iniurias: the* defensor civitatis *and Late Roman Justice*. Munich.

Gostenčnik, K. 2013. Textile Production and Trade in Roman Noricum. In: M. Gleba & J. Pásztókai-Szeöke (eds.), *Making Textiles in Pre-Roman and Roman Times. People, Places, Identities*. Oxford, pp. 60–86.

Groten, A. 2015. corpus *und* universitas. *Römisches Körperschafts- und Gesellschaftsrecht: zwischen griechischer Philosophie und römischer Politik*. Tübingen.

Hirt, A. M. 2010. *Imperial Mines and Quarries in the Roman World. Organizational Aspects 27 BC–AD 235*. Oxford.

Jakab, E. 1997. *Praedicere und cavere beim Marktkauf. Sachmängel im griechischen und römischen Recht*. Munich.

Jakab, E. 2015. Sale and Community from the Roman World. In: E. Jakab (ed.), *Sale and Community Documents from the Ancient World. Individuals' Autonomy and State Interference in the Ancient World*. Trieste, pp. 213–31.

Kurz, K. 1960. Methodische Bemerkungen zum Studium der Kollegien im Donaugebiet. *Acta Antiqua Academiae Scientiarum Hungaricae* 8, pp. 133–44.

Liu, J. 2009. Collegia Centonariorum. *The Guilds of Textile Dealers in the Roman West*. Leiden.

Mentxaka, R. 2016. Divagaciones sobre legislación municipal romana a la luz de la *lex Troesmensium*. In: I. Piro (ed.), *Scritti per Alessandro Corbino. Vol. 5.* Tricase, pp. 5–32.

Mentxaka, R. 2017. Apunte sobre el municipio de Troesmis: Cives Romani Latinive cives? In: U. Babusiaux, P. Nobel & J. Platschek (eds.), *Der Bürge einst und jetzt. Festschrift für Alfons Bürge.* Zürich, pp. 483–515.

Meyer, E. A. 2004. *Legitimacy and Law in the Roman World. Tabulae in Roman Belief and Practice.* Cambridge.

Noeske, H.-C. 1977. Studien zur Verwaltung und Bevölkerung der dakischen Goldbergwerke in römischer Zeit. *Bonner Jahrbücher* 177, pp. 271–416.

Nowak, M. 2011. Mancipatio and its Life in Late-Roman Law. *Journal of Juristic Papyrology* 41, pp. 103–22.

Platschek, J. 2017. Zur Lesung von Kap. 27 der *lex Troesmensium. Tyche* 32, pp. 151–65.

Pólay, E. 1960. Ein Gesellschaftsvertrag aus dem römischen Dakien. *Acta Antiqua Academiae Scientiarum Hungaricae* 8, pp. 417–38.

Pólay, E. 1962a. Die Obligationssicherheit in den Verträgen der siebenbürgischen Wachstafeln. *Klio* 40, pp. 142–58.

Pólay, E. 1962b. Die Zeichen der Wechselwirkungen zwischen dem römischen Reichsrecht und dem Peregrinenrecht im Urkundenmaterial der siebenbürgischen Wachstafeln. *Zeitschrift der Savigny-Stiftung für Rechtsgeschichte. Romanistische Abteilung* 79, pp. 51–85.

Pólay, E. 1971. Der *status civitatis*, der Ursprung und die Berufe der in den siebenbürgischen Wachstafeln vorkommenden Personen. *Journal of Juristic Papyrology* 16, pp. 71–83.

Schulz-Falkenthal, H. 1973. Römische Handwerkerkollegien im Dienst der städtischen Gemeinschaft und ihre Begünstigung durch staatliche Privilegien. *Wissenschaftliche Zeitschrift der Martin Luther-Universität Halle-Wittenberg. Gesellschafts- und sprachwissenschaftliche Reihe* 22/2, pp. 21–35.

Spickermann, W. 2015. Monumental Inscriptions. In: R. Raja & J. Rüpke (eds.), *A Companion to the Archaeology of Religion in the Ancient World.* Malden, pp. 412–24.

Sticotti, P. 1913. *Die römische Stadt Doclea in Montenegro.* Vienna.

Thormann, K. F. 1969. *Der doppelte Ursprung der Mancipatio. Ein Beitrag zur Erforschung des frührömischen Rechtes unter Mitberücksichtigung des nexum.* 2nd ed. Munich.

Vanacker, W. and Zuiderhoek, A. (eds.) 2017. *Imperial Identities in the Roman World.* Abingdon.

Weber, E. 1968. Zur Centonarierinschrift von Solva. *Historia* 17, pp. 106–14.

Wedenig, R. 1997. *Epigraphische Quellen zur städtischen Administration in Noricum.* Klagenfurt.

Weiß, E. 1916. Peregrinische Manzipationsakte. *Zeitschrift der Savigny-Stiftung für Rechtsgeschichte. Romanistische Abteilung* 37, pp. 136–76.

Wilkes, J. J. 2000. The Danube Provinces. In: P. Garnsey, D. Rathbone & A. K. Bowman (eds.), *The Cambridge Ancient History. Vol. 11: The High Empire, A.D. 70–192.* Cambridge, pp. 577–603.

Wilkes, J. J. 2005. The Roman Danube: an Archaeological Survey. *Journal of Roman Studies* 95, pp. 124–225.

Wolf, J. G. 2015. Documents in Roman Practice. In: D. Johnston (ed.), *The Cambridge Companion to Roman Law.* Cambridge, pp. 61–84.

Zack, A. 2014. Forschungen über die rechtlichen Grundlagen der römischen Außenbeziehungen während der Republik bis zum Beginn des Prinzipats. V. Teil: Das *Ius Italicum* und die kaiserzeitliche Befreiung des provinzialen Grundbesitzes von der Besteuerung: eine Kritik der Deutung von Carl von Savigny. *Göttinger Forum für Altertumswissenschaft* 17, pp. 247–308.

21

'Provincial Law' in Britannia

Paul du Plessis

1. INTRODUCTION

Providing a survey of 'provincial law' for any given province of the Roman Empire in any given period is not an easy task. Aside from issues of method and coverage, the very concept of 'provincial law' is fraught with complexity, especially when utilized in the sense first employed in the work of Ludwig Mitteis on the relationship between Roman law and local law in the Eastern provinces of the Roman Empire.[1] The reasons for the complexity are twofold. First, by employing the term 'provincial law', Mitteis implicitly drew a distinction between law at the centre of the Empire and law in the provinces. This distinction suggested a level of difference, the centre being the benchmark and the periphery being something less. In second place, few would now deny that Mitteis' endeavour was ideologically driven and linked to an anachronistic view, prevalent in nineteenth-century Germany, that the history of the Roman Empire and its laws could be used to solve contemporary problems.[2] Phrased differently, for Mitteis, law, and more specifically Roman law, was an instrument of 'Romanization' through which the Romans demonstrated the superiority of their civilization to the conquered masses in the provinces.[3]

Apart from issues of ideology, issues of coverage must also be mentioned. Mitteis' work focused almost exclusively on the 'Greek East' (including Egypt) where evidence of local law abounded and where the interaction between Roman law and local law could be studied through masses of papyrological evidence. Thus, in his view, the idea of 'provincial law' was rather narrowly drawn and referred to those instances where Roman law, as the law of the Empire, engaged with pre-existing local laws (in a form that the Romans could comprehend, that is, mostly written law, but also unwritten custom) where these existed. It does not take much to appreciate that in this sense, the 'Greek East' with its sophisticated, written legal culture that long predated Roman annexation, was viewed rather differently from the 'Latin West' where, to quote Humfress, the Romans encountered a different scenario:

[1] Mitteis (1891), generally; see now Czajkowski (2017) generally.

[2] See now Beiser (2015), specifically the entries on Savigny and von Ranke.

[3] Compare Ehrlich (1962) generally.

Paul du Plessis, *'Provincial Law' in Britannia* In: *Law in the Roman Provinces.* Edited by: Kimberley Czajkowski and Benedikt Eckhardt in collaboration with Meret Strothmann, Oxford University Press (2020). © Oxford University Press.
DOI: 10.1093/oso/9780198844082.003.0021

> In contrast to the Hellenized provinces of the East, the Western provinces—and especially those within the Libyan, Iberian, Celtic and Germanic linguistic zones—seem to present a relatively 'barren' pre-Roman legal landscape. Notwithstanding the highly technical nineteenth-century vocabulary and early twentieth-century debates over the concept of *Volksrecht* and the continuing scholarly discussions of the persistence of 'Germanic legal customs' or 'Germanic customary law', the prevailing sense is that the legal Romanization in the West was a simpler process than in the East: . . .[4]

If Humfress is correct in her assessment, then the treatment of law in the Western provinces of the Roman Empire by contemporary scholarship will look rather different from that in the East. For one thing, there will be no 'local law' (of the written variety) with which to engage as in the 'Eastern Provinces' and one will merely be looking for evidence of the (often rather mangled) application of Roman law.[5] One cannot deny, however, that the arrival of the Romans and their laws had an impact on the province. As De la Bédoyère observes:

> One of the most significant changes to life in Britain was the arrival of the codified legal system of Roman law, its enforcement through the Roman administrative system and the appearance of legal documents.[6]

As will be shown in this chapter, however, a narrative of the kind proposed by Humfress is perhaps too simplistic, and for two reasons. First, it presupposes a passive local population upon which Roman law was imposed from above (at the expense of their local customs) and which they were forced to use in as much as they were obliged to engage with their Roman conquerors. In second place, it does not fully take account of the interconnectedness of the Empire and the extent to which 'networks', to use a New Institutional Economics term, facilitated the spread of Roman law.[7]

As with any chapter of this kind, it would be impossible to provide a survey of the law in Roman Britain from the invasion under Julius Caesar until the withdrawing of Roman troops in the early fifth century CE. The evidence is too fragmentary and any attempt to create a narrative of continuity would conflict with the vast changes in style of government as well as in the fate of the Empire of

[4] Humfress (2012), 44. But see Eckhardt, Chapter 20 in this volume for a discussion of the Danubian provinces. See also Wibier, Chapter 22 in this volume for a discussion of legal education in a Western province.

[5] There would, of course, have been Britonic custom, since there is no evidence of written law before the arrival of the Romans, but much like with the Germanic customs described by Tacitus in his survey of Germany, it is clear that the Romans took an interest in them because they were somehow different or indicative of cultural specificity. We have no similar information regarding Britonic custom. There is, of course, one spectacular case from Roman Britain in which the Roman disregard for local custom had far-reaching consequences, namely the revolt of Boudica in 60 CE and her subsequent destruction of a number of Roman settlements. Although we cannot be sure exactly what triggered this revolt (we have to accept Tacitus' narrative as being entirely truthful), it is possible that the revolt may have been triggered in part by the Roman disregard for local custom in matters of succession. Other motivations for this revolt have been mooted as well.

[6] De la Bédoyère (2015), 66–7. One may quibble slightly about the 'codified' portion of this quotation. Roman law was not codified when it arrived in Britain and would not be codified until after the Romans had left the province for good.

[7] Kehoe, Ratzan, and Yiftach (2015).

which Britannia formed a part. To that end, the time period will be drawn rather narrowly to encompass the founding of the province during the reign of the Emperor Claudius in 43 CE to the granting of universal citizenship to most free inhabitants of the Roman Empire in 212 CE.[8] Within this period, three events are worthy of note. The first is the revolt of the Iceni under their leader, Boudica, in 60 CE, which led to near destruction of at least three important Roman cities and considerable loss of life. The second was the campaigns of the governor, Agricola, father-in-law of Tacitus, who documented his campaigns in Britain (and the expansion of the provincial territory to the west and the north). The third is the construction of two boundaries, a stone structure during the reign of the Emperor Hadrian *c.*122 CE and a turf rampart further north under his successor, Antoninus Pius in the period 139–142 CE. Our survey ends with the death of the Emperor Severus in York in 211 CE and the accession of his sons, Caracalla and Geta. Although, by this time, Severus had divided the province into two separate entities, primarily owing to the uprising under Clodius Albinus, a governor of Britain, that he had quashed in the period 192–196/7 CE, enough of the structures of a unified province remain to sustain a discussion of this kind.

The method employed in this chapter is as follows. First, an overview of the legal contours of the province will be sketched. The aim of this is to provide a broad framework within which to view the subsequent evidence. Thereafter, a survey of the references to legal issues connected to the province will be provided. Once this has been done, I will focus my attention on a number of more recent discoveries from the Walbrook excavations in London and the Vindolanda tablets to demonstrate the extent to which these augment our understanding of the existing sources. Finally, I will discuss certain themes, which have emerged from the evidence discussed thus far, and I will draw various conclusions.

2. THE LEGAL CONTOURS OF THE *PROVINCIA*

At the start of any discussion about a Roman province, it should be borne in mind that the term *provincia* did not necessarily refer always to a geographic area. Instead, the term should be seen more as representing the extent of Rome's influence that could be mapped onto a shifting geographic area.[9] Although no two *provinciae* were the same, their legal contours were broadly similar from the perspective of the Imperial government located in Rome. By collating what is known about the province of Britannia during the period under discussion, a broad and impressionistic picture may be created in which to situate further discussions. Britannia belonged to the class of 'imperial provinces', that is those group of provinces over which the Emperor (as opposed to the senate) had greater control.[10] The consequences of this were twofold, first, that the Emperor as a rule had a greater involvement in the appointment of the governors of such provinces

[8] De la Bédoyère (2015), generally, for a survey of the literary sources.
[9] Richardson (2008), especially Appendix 3 for an exposition of the legal terminology.
[10] Salway (1997), 69–70; De la Bédoyère (2006), 83–4. See also Mattingly (2006) generally.

and, secondly, that the tax revenues from said provinces were diverted into the Imperial (as opposed to senatorial) coffers. It is not known on which basis provinces were classified as 'Imperial' or 'senatorial', and the distinction was by no means static.[11] One scholarly view is that the Emperor was placed in charge of more unsettled parts of the Empire where a continued military presence was required.[12] This is certainly borne out by the circumstances in Britannia for much of the period under discussion.

The Emperor's representative in the province held the title of *legatus Augusti* (*pro praetore*) and was appointed for a period of up to five years (sometimes for longer where military campaigning required it).[13] These individuals tended to be from the upper echelons of Roman society, having already completed the *cursus honorum* and having served as senators in Rome. In the case of Britannia, where the names of these individuals are by and large known, they also seem to have had extensive prior military experience, which suggests that an expectation of military campaigning was part and parcel of the job description.[14] The governor's main task was to promote the interests of the Roman state through the maintaining of law and order. In some provinces, this mission was enshrined in a so-called *lex provinciae*, but this practice was not universal and there is no evidence of the existence of such a *lex* for Britannia.[15] The governor was served by a small staff of civil servants that was sent with him from Rome and, as military commander in the province, he also had the ability to use some of the soldiers stationed there as a security detail.[16] He could command the troops stationed in the province to quell any unrest or insurrection as the exploits of Agricola confirm.

In order to understand the main tasks of the governor, a brief excursus into the physical landscape of Roman Britannia is required. The province over which the governor was appointed was predominantly rural and the majority of inhabitants lived in the countryside rather than in towns. In fact, there is good archaeological evidence for the view that urbanization was a Roman development, mostly unknown to the Britons before the invasion.[17] As Millett has recently stated (here referring to the heyday of the province):

> ...Roman Britain was primarily a rural society. Assessing the total size of the population is very difficult, but at a rough estimate it amounted to perhaps 3.6 million people of whom about 3.4 per cent were associated with the military, 6.5 per cent were urban dwellers (using the broadest definition of towns), while the remaining 90 per cent lived in the countryside.... [18]

Unlike other provinces, there were few towns of any great size in Britannia. Legal evidence shows that towns were divided into *coloniae* and *municipia*, the former

[11] Daguet-Gagey (2004).

[12] De la Bédoyère (2006), 86.

[13] De la Bédoyère (2006), 83–4.

[14] De la Bédoyère (2006), 87 for a list of all of the names of the known governors. See Frere (1967), 223.

[15] Salway (1997), 69.

[16] Lintott (1993), 54. That the governor had to draw on local troops in the province to act as his guards, see Tab. Vindol. II, 154, the 'strength report of the first cohort of Tungrians', ll. 1–4. Scullard (1999), 86; Frere (1967), 226. For a good survey of the rights and duties of the Roman governor, see Lintott (1993), 43–69.

[17] See Pitts (2016). See also Rogers (2016).

[18] Millett (2016), 700.

being colonies of Roman citizens (often retired soldiers), the latter being smaller towns inhabited by a mixture of Roman citizens, Latins and local inhabitants.[19] As is known from the Flavian municipal charters, *coloniae* and *municipia* often had town charters setting out the rights and obligations of the inhabitants, but it is not known whether this was a universal feature across the Empire and no evidence of such town charters have been found in Britannia.[20] Indeed, given the small number of towns in Roman Britain and the problems with their legal classification, scholars such as Creighton have suggested that perhaps the legal classification alone is less useful and should be augmented by the 'lived experience'.[21] It cannot be denied, however, that the legal classification of towns does present us with a starting point for a survey of 'provincial law'.

One important legal feature of these two classes of towns and the lands associated with them was that Roman law, as a rule, applied to their inhabitants. Roman law certainly applied to all Roman citizens living in a Roman colony, while *municipia* in which a mixture of Roman citizens, Latin and other inhabitants were based, followed mainly Roman law. A third type of settlement, called *civitas*-capitals by scholars of Roman Britain, referred to centres created for Britons.[22] Not much is known of the legal structure of these or indeed of their function, though modern scholarship has suggested that they perhaps focused as nodes of trade or engagement with the local Britons.[23] Apart from these towns and the lands associated with them, one must therefore imagine the countryside filled with people and populated with local Briton communities, Roman villas, Imperial estates where natural resources were exploited by entrepreneurs, and forts with associated small settlements of traders and families of soldiers such as the one at Vindolanda.

Since the prime task of the governor was the maintaining of law and order, some remarks about the administration of civil and criminal justice is required. It must of course be remembered that for the period under discussion, Roman law did not have general territorial application in the province, but only applied to Roman citizens or inhabitants who had been granted special dispensation (*commercium*). As the third-century jurist, Ulpian, reminds us:[24]

> *Ius civile est, quod neque in totum a naturali vel gentium recedit nec per omnia ei servit: itaque cum aliquid addimus vel detrahimus iuri communi, ius proprium, id est civile efficimus.*
>
> The *ius civile* is neither wholly distinct from the *ius naturale* or the *ius gentium*, nor is it wholly subservient to it. Thus, when we add something to, or detract something from the common laws, we create the *ius proprium*, that is, the *ius civile.*

[19] For the complexities surrounding the legal status of different towns, see González Fernández and Crawford (1986); see also Frere (1967), 236–7 and Eck, Chapter 16 in this volume.

[20] Scullard (1999), 89–91; Lintott (1993), 129–53.

[21] Creighton (2008), 75–6.

[22] Frere (1967), 237. Frere (1967), 230–240 thinks that these capitals were the natural successors to the client-king system operative during the early days of the settlement of the province.

[23] Creighton (2008), 72–6 for a discussion of the problems with the concept of *civitas*-capitals. See now Millett (2016). For an earlier account, see Millett (2003), Chapters 4 and 5.

[24] Ulpian, *Institutes* 1 (D. 1.1.6 *pr*). All translations are my own unless otherwise stated.

What follows therefore only applies to these categories of people as we are totally in the dark concerning the treatment of legal disputes among Britons, for example (although see below).

First, in matters of criminal justice, the *duumviri* in charge of *coloniae* or *municipia* could deal with less serious matters at a municipal level, while more serious matters were deferred to the governor as the court of first (and in many cases also last) instance, with the exception of Roman citizens who had the right to appeal to the Emperor.[25] The same regime broadly also applied to civil matters. As is known from the Flavian municipal charters, *coloniae* and *municipia* had courts that mimicked the administration of justice in Rome. These municipal courts had limited jurisdiction (both financially and in terms of subject matter).[26]

Matters that were excluded from local jurisdiction on these grounds had to be referred to the court of the governor in which Roman law applied. It stands to reason that a visible governor, as opposed to one ensconced in a specific town, would be much more useful for the administration of justice in a province. It is for this reason that the governor's court moved around the province hearing issues brought before it from a municipal level.[27]

To this must be added an additional government official created during the reign of the Flavian emperors, the *iuridicus*, who seemed to have acted as deputy for the governor in legal matters when the latter was occupied elsewhere. Our sources present an interesting connection between the post of the *iuridicus* in Britannia and the intellectual world of the Roman jurists in Rome.[28] De la Bédoyère explains:

> Judicial legates had usually served as legionary legates first, and would go on to govern provinces. If the governor was absent, they could stand in. The late Roman Digest of Law preserves details of a case presided over by Britain's judicial legate, Lucius Iavolenus Priscus, in the 70s or 80s, concerning the estate of a helmsman in the *classis Brittanica* whose son had predeceased him.[29]

An interesting tablet has recently come to light in the context of the Walbrook excavations:[30]

> *Imper(atore) Ca[e]sare Vespasiano VII / Tit[o] V c[o](n)s(ulibus) XI K(alendas) Nov (embres) / opera in V Id(us) Novembres / inter Litugenum et / Magunum data ab / Ca [e]sare praeiudico /* [
>
> In the year of the seventh consulship of the Emperor Vespasian and the fifth consulship of Titus, on the 11th day before the Calends of November, I have given a praeiudicium, authorized by Caesar, in the legal matter between one Litugenus and one Magunus, heard on the fifth day before the Ides of November.

[25] Frere (1967), 224; Lintott (1993), 97–107.

[26] González Fernández and Crawford (1986), see chapter 84 of the *Lex*. For a number of inscriptions mention *duoviri iuridicundo* in Britain, see Ireland (2008), 207 (No. 465).

[27] Frere (1967), 224.

[28] Birley (1980), 47–8 shows that of the names of the *iuridici* which are known, one was a famous advocate in Rome, Salvius Liberalis, the other a leading Roman jurist, Lucius Iavolenus Priscus. See also Frere (1967), 225.

[29] De la Bédoyère (2006), 86. On these officials, see Scullard (1999), 87–8.

[30] WT 51, see Tomlin (2016), 170–1.

This rather frustratingly incomplete tablet, only published in 2016, is a record of some sort regarding a court case between one Litugenus and one Magunus. Both of these are non-Roman names (in fact Tomlin suggests that they are Celtic). The date of the tablet is 22 October 76 CE. This would place it round about the time of the introduction of the office of *iuridicus* in Britain, but as Tomlin has rightly point out, the evidence remains scant. Much more important, however, is the term *opera*, which suggests to Tomlin that jurisdiction to judge the case had been delegated by the Emperor to whomever wrote this tablet. The term 'praeiudico' suggests a preliminary judgement as is well known from Roman legal procedure.[31] The fact that these were non-Romans seem to suggest a more complex legal infrastructure than the one proposed by Humfress or indeed by Korporowicz, who observed:

> When the Romans created the province of Britain in 43 AD they introduced Roman law to the Celtic inhabitants of the island. But, according to the rules of Roman civil law, the Celtic subjects of the Empire were not treated as Roman citizens. Most of them held simply the status of *peregrini*, foreigners, who did not obtain any rights in Roman law.[32]

In my view, the statement by Korporowicz presents an overly binary view. We know, from elsewhere in the Empire, that locals who were not Romans could access Roman justice. There is no reason to suspect otherwise for Britannia. Before stepping away from this survey of the legal contours of the province, a few comments about its financial administration are required, since these also impacted on the former. An Imperial procurator was charged with overseeing the tribute from the province. This official and his staff operated independently from the governor and the former was directly answerable to Rome. They were responsible for exacting two forms of tribute, namely the *annona* (grain levy) and the taxes levied in coin.[33] The latter took one of two forms, namely land tax and poll tax (presumably on those individuals who did not own land).[34] Not much is known about the infrastructure supporting the activities of this official or his staff other than that he was most likely based in London. A land tax presupposes centuriation and the maintaining of accurate records of ownership, while a poll tax presupposes the holding of a regular census and the maintaining of accurate records for the purposes of taxation.[35] Sadly, our evidence for either of these is virtually non-existent and, as more recent research by authors such as Millett has shown, one cannot assume that the entirety of the area of the province was indeed subject to the same rules of law:

> ... [W]e certainly cannot assume that there was any single application of supposed Roman legal norms. Indeed, wide variations in the patterns of rural settlement witnessed in the archaeological evidence suggest that there was a range of practice. It is important to acknowledge this level of ignorance, since many past discussions of

[31] See, for example, Ulpian, *On the edict* 9 (D. 3.3.35.2).

[32] Korporowicz (2012), 134.

[33] Scullard (1999), 88–9; Lintott (1993), 70–96.

[34] De la Bédoyère (2006), 91–4.

[35] De la Bédoyère (2006), 95–100. For an earlier survey of our limited information about centuriation, see Frere (1967), 301.

villas, in particular, have been founded on very simplistic notions of landownership that are almost certainly anachronistic.[36]

3. THE LEGAL EVIDENCE (NARROWLY CONSTRUED) CONCERNING BRITANNIA

To date, two surveys of the legal evidence have been undertaken, first, by Birley[37] and since by Korporowicz.[38] While the former focused almost exclusively on information obtained from the standard Roman legal sources contained in the *Corpus Iuris Civilis*, the latter also included some of the more recent discoveries relating to Roman legal practice. Birley, the original excavator at Vindolanda, wrote during a time when few of the examples from legal practice, which have since come to light, both there and in the London excavations, were known. Korporowicz's survey is more recent, but it does not include the discoveries from the Walbrook excavations published by Tomlin. For the sake of comprehensiveness, a survey will be presented here. The aim of this survey is to show how the legal contours of the *provincia* as outlined above map onto the existing evidence.

At an Imperial level, there are two types of evidence. First, a small number of Imperial decrees are concerned with issues in Britannia.[39] They mostly fall into the category of legal matters referred to the Emperor for a ruling/classification or an Imperial fiat sent to the governor of the province. The earliest dates from the reign of Hadrian,[40] the next from the reign of Septimius Severus,[41] and the last from the reign of Constantine and Licinius.[42]

The second body of evidence contains a small number of Imperial decrees that were most likely produced in the province during an Imperial visit, but since the Emperor was effectively dealing with matters addressed to him from across the Empire, these do not reveal much that is particularly relevant to the British context.[43]

As this brief survey has demonstrated, the legal evidence (narrowly construed), is not particularly helpful in reconstructing 'provincial law' in Britannia. They reveal a top-down perspective from the Imperial government and, given the considerable time period covered, cannot be used to draw any conclusions concerning the frequency with which matters were referred to from the court of the governor to the Imperial bureaucracy or whether any legal problems endemic to the province required Imperial intervention. At best they demonstrate that

[36] Millett (2016), 701. For a similar assessment, see Lintott (1993), 154–67. For a good survey of how matters were dealt with by the governor of an Imperial province in the Greek East, see Pliny's letters to Trajan. For a discussion, see Winsbury (2014), 185–215.

[37] Birley (1953). [38] Korporowicz (2012). [39] Birley (1953), 49.

[40] Ulpian, *On Sabinus* 10 (D. 28.3.6.7). For a discussion of this text, see Korporowicz (2012), 141.

[41] Ulpian, *On Sabinus* (D. 28.6.2.4). For a discussion of this text, see Korporowicz (2012), 141; Frere (1967), 224.

[42] *CTh.* 11.7. 2 (20 November 319 CE). For a discussion of the text, see Korporowicz (2012), 141–2. It is worth mentioning that Korporowicz cites another text, *CTh.* 9.36.1, but its connection to Britannia is tenuous at best.

[43] Korporowicz (2012), 142–3.

there was a functioning Imperial bureaucracy and that issues of Roman law arose in the context of provincial matters.

4. THREE CASE STUDIES THAT INFORM THE LEGAL CONTOURS OF THE *PROVINCIA*

In order to form a more comprehensive picture of 'provincial law' in Britannia, a different body of evidence must be examined. As already noted by Korporowicz, more 'legal' information may be extracted from epigraphic sources, such as writing tablets, gravestones, public inscriptions and private graffiti, curse tablets and military diplomas.[44] It must be borne in mind, however, that these sources present a very different picture from the legal sources (narrowly construed) mentioned above. Since these were the product of those living in the province, they provide a picture of the 'lived experience' or 'living law' to use Ehrlich's term, which do not always correspond to the information provided in dogmatic sources concerning Roman law.[45]

In addition, the issue of 'lived experience' or 'living law' cannot be addressed without entering into the debates concerning 'Romanization'. Did Roman law act as a 'Romanizing' institution? Earlier scholarship certainly suggested so. As Frere wrote in the late 60s:

> Private litigation was bound to increase with the spread of civilised manners: it is no coincidence that just at this period we begin to find Roman legal terms on tablets excavated in London.[46]

The phrase 'civilised manners' is telling. In Frere's view, Roman law had a 'civilising' effect and its application contributed to the 'Romanizing' of the province. The spectre of Mitteis is still well and truly present in this quotation. It is not difficult to see why scholars arrived at this conclusion. After all, Roman law was intellectually sophisticated and would have dealt with matters in a different way from the customs of the Britons, but difference does not necessarily imply superiority and, if the subsequent history of colonialism has taught us anything it is that the law of the colonizer does not remain immune to influences arising from provincial circumstances. How this legal complexity worked in practice remains a mystery.[47] Frere again:

> The legal aspects of the governor's task were complication by the variety of codes which might have to be taken into account. Roman law was probably binding on Roman citizens and communities, but *peregrini* still lived under their local Celtic codes of law save so far as these might conflict with basic Roman principles.

This is a nice idea, but we just do not have the evidence to support it. It paints the Roman governor as a benevolent colonial judge, who scrupulously and without bias applied the correct law to the appropriate legal dispute brought before him. In my view, however, the question posed (whether Roman law acted as a

[44] Ireland (2008), 218–21 (Nos 518–24). [45] See Hope (2016).
[46] Frere (1967), 225. [47] Ando (2015).

'Romanizing' institution) is too simplistic. As recent scholarship concerning the concept of 'Romanization' has shown, the term is less than useful for explaining the impact of a Roman provincial presence upon a local population. To that end, and drawing upon more recent insights into the notion of 'hybridization' (as a more useful term than 'Romanization'), I wish to suggest that the matter be broken down into two separate questions, namely, first, the impact of a visible Roman legal presence upon Britons and whether such a presence influenced the way in which individuals dealt with legal conflict (in other words whether it led to the adoption of 'Roman ways' of dispute resolution), and, secondly, whether provincial circumstances may have had an impact on the development of Roman law.[48]

As already set out above, the fragmentary wooden writing tablet containing a prejudgement in relation to a court case between two Celts does suggest access to and use of the Roman legal order. Furthermore, it is clear that the local population not only utilized Roman secular justice, as the curse tablets from Bath and Uley show, but were also familiar with Roman divine justice.[49] For the sake of comprehensiveness, I will quote two only. The first is an undated curse tablet from Bath:

> *Pet(it)io / Rovet(a)e / Victoria Vindo/cunu(s) maritus / Cunomolius / Minervina ussor (!) / Cunitius ser(v)us / Senovara ussor(!) / Lavidendus ser(v)us / Mattonius ser(v)us / Catinius exsactoris(!) / furem / Methianu[s ---] // [---] dono [---] // [---] amicus [---] / TPIASV / GINENINVSV [-] / [-]igienunus*[50]

One cannot take much from this tablet other than that it records the names of quite a few individuals, none of whom appear to be Roman citizens. The names have a Celtic ring to them and some are explicitly noted as slaves. Other than that, we are mostly in the dark about the nature of the problem and whether these individuals were the actors or objects of the curse. The second is a curse tablet from Uley, also undated (AE 1979, 384):

> *Commonitorium deo / Mercurio a Satur/nina muliere de lintia/mine quod amisit ut il/ le qui hoc circumvenit non / ante laxetur nissi(!) quando / res ss(upra) dictas ad fanum ss(upra) dic/tum attulerit si vir si mu/lier si servus s[i] liber // deo ss(upra) dicto tertiam / partem donat ita ut / exsigat(!) ista res quae s(upra) s(crip)ta(e) sunt / ac a quae(!) perit deo Silvano / tertia pars donatur ita ut / hoc exsigat(!) si vir si femina si serv/us si liber [---]E[---]tat*

This tablet is slightly more comprehensive and details the stealing of a piece of linen. What is noteworthy about both these texts is the legalistic language employed, the first one being described as a petition, the second as a memorandum. Furthermore, the use of the phrase 'whether man or woman, slave or free' has a contractual feel. It is not my intention to provide a complete overview of the complexities surrounding these tablets and I refer the reader to the work by the Dutch scholar, Versnel.[51] For the purposes of this survey, I wish to emphasize three points. First, it is clear that these types of curses relating to theft of property form a distinct category that was used by a broad spectrum of the provincial

[48] On this debate, see now Moore (2016). An important earlier work is that of Woolf (2003).

[49] Bradley (2011) generally for an extensive survey.

[50] For the sake of consistency, I will use the text as reproduced in the Heidelberg Epigraphic Database. HD 001042 = AE 1982, 0664.

[51] Versnel (2010).

population, both Roman and Briton. In second place, the divine justice sought in these tablets dovetailed with options available according to secular justice. Under Roman law, the action for theft was notoriously difficult to bring and could result in *infamia* to the accuser if deemed by a judge to have been brought without cause. It is therefore not surprising to see other forms of justice being appeal to in the absence of a clear case of theft where the perpetrator could be identified. Finally, one cannot help but speculate about the legalistic terms used in these curses. It seems quite likely that scribes, who had some knowledge of Roman law, drafted them, thus hinting at the existence of a provincial 'legal culture'.[52]

In the remainder of this chapter, I will focus on a number of recent discoveries in the epigraphic record that, in my view, demonstrate how provincial contexts affected Roman law as the law of the Empire.

4.1. Property Law: The Case of the Wood

This incomplete waxed tablet records some legal aspects of the sale of a wood in Kent and can be dated to 118 CE:[53]

> *Imp(eratore) Traiano [Had]ri[ano] Caesare Aug(usto) II Gn(aeo) / Fusco Salinatore co (n)s(ulibus) pr(idie) Idus Martias / cum ventum esset in rem praesentem / silvam Verlucionium arepennia de/cem quinque plus minus quod est in ci/vitate Cantiacorum pago DIBVSSV[---] / [---]RABI[---]A[--]S adfinibus heredibus / et heredibus Caesenni Vitalis et via / vicinale quod se emisse diceret L(ucius) / Iulius Bellicus de T(ito) Valerio Silvino / |(denariis) quadraginta sicut emptione continetur / Lucius Bellicus testatus est se / [------*[54]
>
> In the consulship of the Emperor Trajan Hadrian Caesar Augustus for the second time, and Gnaeus Fuscus Salinator, on the day before the Ides of March [14 March 118]. Whereas, on arriving at the property in question, the wood Verlucionium, fifteen arepennia more or less, which is in the canton of the Cantiaci in Dibussu[ ] parish, [ ], neighboured by the heirs [of... | and the heirs of Caesennius Vitalis and the vicinal road, Lucius Julius Bellicus said that he had bought it from Titus Valerius Silvinus for forty denarii, as is contained in the deed of purchase. Lucius Julius Bellicus attested that he [ ]

I have discussed the tablet at length elsewhere and will merely provide a summary of my suggestions here (and they can be no more than suggestions since concrete proof is lacking).[55] The text records that someone had arrived at a wood called Verlucio of certain dimensions and located in the *civitas* of the *Cantiaci*. After providing the name of the wood and its dimensions, the author of the tablet follows the standard conventions known from the Digest in which a piece of land is described with reference to the owners of the lands that abound it. We are also informed that this wood was the object of a sale and the names of the seller and purchaser appear Roman judging by the use of the *tria nomina*.

[52] Bradley (2011), 42. [53] Translation from Tomlin (1996), 211.

[54] For the purposes of this chapter, I will use the reconstruction in the Heidelberg epigraphic database. HD051539 = AE 1994, 1093.

[55] See my contribution, du Plessis (2015), 171–80. On Kent in the Roman period more generally, see Booth (2017).

Other than this, very little concrete can be said of this tablet. First, it is unclear what its legal purpose was. It is certainly not the record of the sale, as many examples of sales of land from elsewhere in the Empire will attest. In second place, it is not clear who arrived at the land and what to do with the rather legalistic sounding '*in rem praesentem*', which has something of a whiff of a lawsuit about it. The dominant interpretation, by Tomlin, is that this is a record of a judicial inspection *in loco* where a magistrate had been summoned to the land to assess some aspect of it in the context of the preceding sale.[56] This is certainly plausible and, if correct, would make it unique since no other record of such a judicial inspection is known. One is tempted to attempt some parallel to the travelling court of the governor or the activities of the *iuridicus*, but the information is just not there.

A different interpretation, put forward by me more recently, is that this may have been the field notes of a land surveyor who was assessing the extent of the land for the purposes of land tax in the context of its recent sale.[57] Admittedly, this interpretation is not based on stronger evidence than the one proposed by Tomlin. Ultimately, either of these interpretations is possible and until more of this text is discovered or others like it which are more complete, the matter must remain unresolved.

Three aspects of this tablet are worth mentioning specifically. First, the use of the term *arepennia* to denote the size of the plot must be noted. It is not a Roman term of measurement and has been identified as a Celtic loan word. Given the location of the wood and the proximity to Gaul, this is not entirely unexpected.[58] The second issue concerns the listing of the price in *denarii* rather than *sestertii* as was the standard Roman convention.[59] It has been pointed out that this method of listing the price suggests a military context where prices are often given in *denarii*. Yet again, this should not be overstated. The final aspects relate to the nature of the legal right the parties were hoping to vest over the wood in question. As is well known, it was not technically legally possible to obtain *dominium* over land in the provinces unless these had previously been granted the *ius italicum*. Since we don't know whether this land was associated with one of the Roman *coloniae* (the territory of a Roman *colonia* was not always adjacent to it), it is impossible to speculate on the matter. In all likelihood, this is an example of the sale of centuriated provincial land over which the purchaser could establish little more than 'provincial ownership' (a form of legally protected possession) subject to the payment of land tax.

4.2. Commercial Law: Complex Transactions

In this section, I will present three different texts dealing with aspects of Roman business law. The first document is an undated letter forming part of the Vindolanda tablets. It records part of an ongoing financial discussion between to business associates concerning a shared business venture involving animal

[56] Tomlin (1996) generally. [57] See note 46 above.

[58] Tomlin (1996), 213. On the linguistic changes in Roman Britain, see Mullen (2016).

[59] See Walton and Moorhead (2016).

hides. Given the lack of information, it is impossible to date it securely or to speculate on the status of the individuals mentioned. At best one may venture a date around the turn of the first century CE. It is assumed by most scholars that the individuals mentioned in the letter were civilian traders (perhaps freedmen) who supplied the army with animal hides:[60]

> *Octavius Candido fratri suo / salutem / a Marino Nervio pondo centum / explicabo e quo tu de hac / re scripseras ne mentionem / mihi fecit aliquotiens tibi / scripseram spicas me emisse / prope m(odios) quinque milia prop/ter quod |(denarii) mihi necessari sunt / nisi mittis me aliquit(!) |(denariorum) // minime quingentos futurum / est ut quod arr(a)e dedi perdam / |(denarios) circa trecentos et erubes/cam ita rogo quam primum aliquit(!) / |(denariorum) mi mitte Coria qu(a)e scribis / esse Cataractonio scribe / dentur mi et karrum de quo / scribis et quit(!) sit cum eo karro / mi scribe iam illec(!) cepissem / nissi(!) iumenta non curavi vexsare(!) / dum viae mal(a)e sunt vide cum Tertio / de d(enariis) VIII s(emis) quos a Fatale accepit / non illos mi accepto tulit // scito mae explesse coria CLXX et bracis excussi habeo / m(odios) CXI fac |(denarios) mi mittas ut poss/im spicam habere in excusso/rio iam autem si quit(!) habui / perexcussi contuber/nalis Fronti amici hic fuerat / desiderabat coria ei ad/signarem et ita | (denarios) datur/us erat dixi ei coria in/tra K(alendas) Martias daturum Idibus // Ianuariis constituerat se ventur/um nec intervenit nec curavit / accipere cum haberet coria si / pecuniam daret dabam ei Fronti/nium Iulium audio magno lice/re pro cori (r) atione quem hic / comparavit |(denarios) quinos / saluta Spectatum Ian[ua]/rium Firmum / epistulas a Gleucone accepi / vale // Vindol(andae)*[61]
>
> (i) Octavius to his brother Candidus, greetings. The hundred pounds of sinew from Marinus—I will settle up. From the time when you wrote about this matter, he has not even mentioned it to me. I have several times written to you that I have bought about five thousand modi, of ears of grain, on account of which I need cash. Unless you send me some cash, (ii) at least five hundred denarii, the result will be that I shall lose what I have laid out as a deposit, about three hundred denarii, and I shall be embarrassed. So, I ask you, send me some cash as soon as possible. The hides which you write are at Cataractomum—write that they be given to me and the wagon about which you write. And write to me what is with that wagon. I would have already been to collect them except that I did not care to annoy the animals while the roads are bad. See with Tertius about the 8½ denarii which he received from Fatalis. He has not credited them to my account. (iii) Know that I have completed the 170 hides and I have 119 (?) modii of threshed bracis. Make sure that you send me cash so that I may have ears of grain on the threshing-floor. Moreover, I have already finished threshing all that I had. A messmate of our friend Frontius has been here. He was wanting me to allocate (?) him hides and that being so, was ready to give cash. I told him I would give him the hides by the Kalends of March. (iv) He decided that he would come on The Ides of January. He did not tum up nor did he take any trouble to obtain them since he had hides. If he had given the cash, I would have given him them. I hear that Frontinus Iulius has for sale at a high price the leather-making (things) which he bought here for five denarii apiece. Greet Spectatus and . . . and Firmus. I have received letters from Gleuco. Farewell. (Back) (Deliver) at Vindolanda.

[60] Ireland (2008), 213 (Nos 494–501) for epigraphic evidence of such traders. See also the insightful collection of chapters in Mac Mahon and Price (2005), especially Chapters 4, 8, and 9.

[61] For the sake of consistency, I have again used the reproduction of the text following the Heidelberg epigraphic database. HD017610 = AE 1990, 0671. Tab. Vindol. II, 343. Translation Bowman (1994/2003), 144–6.

I have elsewhere discussed the complexities of this letter and how it should be interpreted, so I will merely provide a survey here.[62] Since this is private correspondence, it is impossible to deduce the true legal nature of the business relationship between these two individuals. One may speculate that they were engaged in some joint partnership of sorts, but we can never know, especially also because their statuses are not clear. With that said, three aspects of the discussion between these individuals do cast additional light on legal practice in the provinces. The first two concern the transaction mentioned at the start of the letter. A contract to purchase a substantial quantity of animal hides had been made. One partner had provided a down payment and was now seeking the rest of the money from the other partner. The tone of the request is quite urgent and it seems that this was not the first request for the money. As part of this request, two pieces of information are revealed. First, there is the threat that the collapse of the transaction will lead to financial embarrassment (. . . *et erubescam* . . .). This is, as far as I know, the only example where the Roman legal principle of *bona fides* is explained in concrete terms. Much of Roman commerce was based on connections or 'networks' in which the parties trusted each other to behave in a trustworthy manner. Any breach of such behaviour would constitute bad faith and would lead to a loss of 'face'. Another interesting feature is the use of the phrase (. . . *est ut quod arr(a) e dedi perdam* . . .). The term *arrha* (or *arra*) is well known to scholars of the Roman law of consensual sale as denoting an 'earnest', in other words a token of good faith that the purchaser intends to follow through with the transaction, but as far as Roman legal doctrine is concerned, the failure of the legal transaction for whatever reason normally did not result in the loss of the 'earnest'.[63] Whether one can take this use of the 'earnest' as legally significant and as evidence of a provincial practice spreading from Gaul, for example, is difficult to ascertain given our limited information about the true legal nature of the enterprise or the status of the parties. One may also point to the discussion about credit and the fact that this points to the existence of moneylenders or bankers who are able to credit accounts held in different places. The third and final aspect that deserves mention concerns the discussion towards the end of the document concerning a failed transaction. Again, this reinforces the idea of 'networks' since the two business associates are discussing a common acquaintance of theirs who had seemingly behaved in a way that is incompatible with the good faith on which commercial transactions are seemingly based. The tenor of this discussion appears to be that no future business will be done with said individual on account of this behaviour.

Another example from legal practice is the record of a sale of a slave from Roman London:[64]

> *Vegetus Montani Imperatoris Aug(usti) ser(vi) Iucun/diani vic(arius) emit mancipioque accepit pu/ellam Fortunatam sive quo alio nomine / est natione Diablintem de Albiciano / LEG[---] |(denariis) sescentis / ea(m)que puella(m) de qua agitur sanam*

[62] Du Plessis (2014); Bowman (1994/2003), 144–6.

[63] See, for example, Ulpian, *On the edict* 32 (D. 19.1.11.6).

[64] For the sake of consistency, I have used the reconstruction from the Heidelberg Epigraphic Database. HD045507 = AE 2003, 1016. Translation Tomlin (2003), 41–51 (modified).

tradi/tam esse erronem fugitivam non esse / praestari quod si qu[i]s eam puellam de / qua agitur part[em]ve quam [quis ex] ea e[vi]/cerit, quo m[i]nu[s Vege]tum M[ontani Imp(eratoris)] / Caesaris ser(vi) [vi]c(arium) eu[mv]e [a]t que[m] ea res // [pertinebit habere possidereque recte liceat]

Vegetus, assistant slave of Montanus the slave of the August Emperor and sometime assistant slave of Iucundus, has bought and received by mancipium the girl Fortunata, or by whatever name she is known, by nationality a Diablintian, from Albicianus [. . .] for six hundred denarii. And that girl in question is transferred in good health, that she is warranted not to be liable to wander or run away, but that if anyone lays claim to the girl in question or to any share in her, as a result of which Vegetus, assistant slave of Montanus, the slave of the emperor Caesar, or he to whom the affair will be relevant will not be allowed to have and to possess her rightfully [. . .].

It is not my intention to discuss this document in full, as it has recently been the subject of debate, both in terms of content and also regarding the reconstruction.[65] For the purposes of this chapter, I wish to point out three notable legal points. First, the slave woman is from Gaul, thereby reinforcing the notion that slaves were not only exported from Britannia, but that there was two-way traffic between the southern part of the province and Gaul. In second place, the wording follows Roman law quite closely, up to and including the use of boilerplate provisions concerning latent defects in the sold slave as was required by Roman law. Much more noteworthy legally speaking, however, are the parties to this sale. The slave woman appears to have been bought by a slave, using a *mancipatio*, a legal transaction originating from the *ius civile* and normally reserved for Roman citizens. Furthermore, the slave purchaser appears to have been an under-slave of another slave. Since slaves were *res mancipi* and accordingly had to be sold using the *mancipatio* process, even if at this point it functioned mostly as the mode of conveyance pursuant to an *emptio venditio*, the use of this transaction by a slave remains noteworthy and one must therefore assume that it occurred in the context of some legal structure (perhaps *peculium* or something else) which enabled slaves to operate in this fashion.

A third example from the realm of legal practice is a strange loan document in the Vindolanda tablets:

————] / Felicioni |(centurioni) mutuo [---] / XII K(alendas) Iunias / condimentorum |(sextarii) s(emissem) |(denarii) |(quadrantem) / halicae |(sextarii) s(emissem) | (denarii) |(quadrantem) / ova n(umero) IIX |(denarii) |(quadrantem) / XII K(alendas) Iulias / [————[66]

The curious element of this text is the use of the word '*mutuo*'. The Roman jurist Gaius, in his teaching manual written during the mid-second century CE, defined the Roman contract of *mutuum*.[67] This exposition of the essential qualities of the contract, followed nearly verbatim by the compilers of Justinian's teaching manual a few centuries later, defines *mutuum* as one of the obligations created by the

[65] For a survey of the disagreement between Tomlin and Camodeca regarding the reconstruction of this text, see Korporowicz (2011).

[66] In this case I have used the reconstruction from the Clauss-Slaby Database as the text does not appear in the Heidelberg Epigraphic Database at the time of writing. Tab. Vindol. II, 193 = AE 1994, 01132.

[67] Gai. 3. 90.

delivery of an object (a *datio*), which in the case of *mutuum* involved the weighing or measuring out of so-called generic objects before the contract could come into existence. Stock examples given by Gaius include money counted out, wine, oil, corn, gold and silver quantified through weighing and measuring. As Gaius makes clear in this text, the contractual obligation created by the *datio* obliged the party who received the object to return not the exact same object, but rather an object of the same *natura* as some future point. Although not mentioned in the Gaius text, *mutuum* could be [and indeed was] essentially gratuitous. Money was not charged for the 'loan' of the objects, the theory being that such an agreement would resemble a sale rather than a loan, and would not in keeping with the economics of friendship in archaic Roman society from which this contract is thought to have originated.

Given the nature of the objects mentioned above, I will focus on the case where consumable objects have been lent out on the understanding that objects of equivalent *natura* should be returned. At the outset it should be noted that information on this manifestation of *mutuum* is somewhat sparse and is overshadowed in Roman legal sources, in classical literature and generally also in modern scholarship by the money loan. Thus, for example we find only a few references to it.[68]

This selection of texts mentioned in the preceding footnote reveals a limited range of consumables that could be the object of a *mutuum*. But this should not be taken to imply that the loan of consumables was merely a theoretical legal construct existing in the minds of the jurists or perhaps a historical relic from the earliest phases of Roman society. If this were the case, there would be no need for further elaboration of it in Roman legal sources. And yet, this is not what the texts reveal. There is evidence that the legal aspects of the loan of consumables were of interest to the Roman jurists, especially when it came to determining the extent of the obligation to return an object of the same *natura*.[69]

As these texts show, the parameters of *mutuum* involving consumable objects like wine or oil became progressively more circumscribed throughout the classical period. What starts of merely as an obligation to return an agreed upon quantity of objects of the same *natura* (in Gaius), in time becomes qualified as the same *natura* and *qualitas* (or *bonitas* with reference to the age of the commodity) and also of the same *genus* (not merely *species*). Some of these discussions of the jurists were no doubt theoretical and should be related back to juristic interest in the boundaries between different types of contractual agreements in Roman law that dominated the classical period. It is not inconceivable, however, that some of these considerations were driven by real-world examples taken from commercial practice. Indeed, nowhere is this more evident than in the short Imperial decree that introduces a workaround where oil or fruit has been lent, owing to the uncertainty of their prices, so as not to fall foul of the ban on interest in cases of *mutuum*. The observant reader will have noticed that the emperors Diocletian and Maximian

[68] Julianus, *On Minucius* 4 (D.12.1.22) (Wine); Ulpian, *On the edict* 28 (D. 14.3.5.14) (Oil); C. 4.32.11(Wheat).

[69] Pomponius, *On Sabinus* 27 (D. 12.1.3); Paul, *On the edict* 28 (D. 12.1.2); *Inst.* 3.14; C. 4.32.23 *Diocl./Maxim. AA. et CC. Iasoni.*

issued this decree in 294 CE—a time of rampant inflation culminating in the enactment of the Edict on Maximal Prices of 301 CE.

This then raises the central question in relation to the text cited above. What would the possible function (or range of functions) be of a *mutuum* of consumables in the classical period of Roman law (given the existence of so many other possible forms of contract)? To explore this question, I wish to focus on what seems to be a receipt [or perhaps just a record] of a *mutuum* of consumables in the Vindolanda Tablets. The text is incomplete and the writing is not in good shape. What we seem to have here is a record of certain consumables having been lent out using a *mutuum*, perhaps to centurion mentioned at the top of the text, with an acknowledgement in a second hand, perhaps indicating that these consumables had been returned by the debtor on a given date.

The first observation about this text is that the object of the *mutuum* is fairly insignificant: some gruel, a few ounces of spices and a couple of eggs. The impression given by the legal texts (cited in the notes) is of quantities of wine, oil and wheat, though it is not possible from these texts to deduce the size of these quantities. Nevertheless, the impression is created that what is recorded here was rather at the more insignificant end of the legal spectrum when it came to the object of a *mutuum*. This then raises two questions. First, the context in which this document was created including the purpose of this loan for consumption, secondly the use of Roman law in these circumstances.

First, matters of context. This document, as so many others from the fort at Vindolanda was found in the *praetorium* of the camp. There is evidence that a great number of these documents were dumped there, perhaps to act as floor covering, during the last phases of the occupation of the fort, or even after its evacuation, so the fact that it was found in this location should not necessarily be taken to mean that it was drawn up in connection with official camp business. It may equally well have been one of the documents produced one of the civilian traders living in the *vicus* outside the camp walls. All that can really be said is that someone kept a note of a loan for consumption and was diligent enough to record when the consumables were returned at a specific date. Let us assume that the loan of these foodstuffs was made to one Felicio a centurion. As Bowman has noted (corroborated by Kakoschke), the name of Felicio was of such generality that he cannot be identified with any degree of certainty.[70] We do come across a Felicio the centurion again in the Vindolanda tablets [e.g. number 182] where he is noted as having been given 45 pounds of bacon and 15 pounds of bacon lard, to the value of 8 *denarii* and 2 asses. A Felicio appears in one or two other documents, but most are so fragmentary that one cannot get much of them.

This then begs the question why a centurion would be engaging in such seemingly mundane borrowing of foodstuffs. To answer this question one must look at the payment practices of Roman soldiers. Although we do not have direct evidence from Vindolanda itself (there are hints of it), a papyrus from Roman Egypt, roughly contemporary with the text in question will be used as a comparator. It is widely accepted that payment strategies of Roman soldiers were fairly

[70] http://vto2.classics.ox.ac.uk/index.php/tablets/search-for-tablets?tablet=193 (last accessed 9 February 2018); Kakoschke (2011).

uniform throughout the Empire, thereby rendering this comparison valid. In this papyrus (P. Gen. Lat. 1), we find a camp account, officially compiled by the camp accountant, of the annual pay of a Roman soldier born in Damascus together with deductions made and sums deposited as a savings account in the strongbox of the camp.[71] What we can deduce from this account is that a soldier received a gross pay against which deductions were made for military equipment, etc. If a positive balance remained, this could either be paid out or returned to the strongbox as savings. Much has been written about the relative costs of the food and equipment deducted by the army. The matter is of particular interests to economic historians who have pointed out that the prices of these commodities are always somewhat inflated and that the Roman army effectively created a stable market for such goods.[72] But it is not the equipment I wish to focus on here. Rather, I wish to focus on the deductions for food. Any Roman soldier, of whatever rank, received a food ration from the army. Much is known about the size of these rations and their nature. In short, a Roman soldier received a portion of unground corn, oil, dried meat, salt and cheese per day [augmented by whatever else could be obtained from the local region]. It was not a luxury diet and nutritionists have calculated that it was just about sufficient to fulfill the nutritional need of a soldier on active service. There is ample evidence that the civilian traders living in the makeshift communities around Roman forts imported more luxury items like fish sauce and wine that could be purchased with their own money by soldiers to augment their basic diet provided by the military bureaucracy.

But if these commodities could be bought (and indeed bought on credit as Tab. Vindol. II, 182 suggests), why did Felicio the centurion enter into a loan for consumption for eggs, gruel and some spices? We cannot rule out that this document may have been drafted in the context of a personal temporary liquidity crisis. Centurions were not badly paid, in fact some sources suggest that they were considerably better off in terms of pay than the average soldier, and yet one cannot rule out that the centurion perhaps just did not have 'ready money' when he needed these commodities, either because he had spent it all, or perhaps had saved it all for future use upon discharge. To my mind, however, this does not fully account for the existence of this text. After all, the goods could have been 'sold' to him by one of the traders on credit. I would therefore like to propose that there is a little bit more to this text than meets the eye.

The Roman army, when stationed for a prolonged period in a location such as Vindolanda, was reliant on a steady supply of food. While part of their food supply could be secured from local hunting activities (as archaeological evidence from the fort at Chesters show), the bulk of it (especially the corn that formed the staple of the diet) were brought from elsewhere along state roads. Given the logistic constraints of land transport in antiquity, this was expensive and time consuming, not to mention notoriously unreliable, since so much depended on weather, condition of the roads and the coordination of a vast supply chain. Food security was a major concern for the local troops and Roman military law protected the supply chain. In his *Iuris Graeco-Romani Tomi Duo* published in 1596, the Humanist and Byzantinist Johannes Leunclavius added as an appendix a

[71] See Herz (2011), 309–10. [72] See Kehne (2011).

'code of military law of one Rufus' that he had compiled out of Greek and Roman sources.[73] Law 46 states the following 'no one can buy provisions that are sent to the army. Such a person, if he is of higher rank, will be proscribed, and if he is of humbler rank, will be killed.' An investigation into the sources of this law reveals that it is based on a reading of C.4.40.4:

> *Honor./Theodos. AA. Faustino pp. Ne frumentum, quod devotissimo exercitui mittitur, in praedam lucrumque vertatur, hac sanctione decernimus, ut, quicumque hoc fuerint forte mercati, honestiores quidem stilum proscriptionis incurrant, inferiores autem vilioresque personae capitali supplicio subiaceant.*<a. 410 *vel* 413?>
>
> Lest grain, which is sent to the devoted army, be turned to prey and gain, we direct by this ordinance, that any persons trading therein will, if of honourable station, be banished, and if of low and servile station, suffer capital punishment.[74]

There is nothing that binds this law directly to our case. Nor can we determine whether similar rules about food security existed at the end of the first century CE. Nevertheless, there is a hint of exasperation emanating from this imperial decree. It seems to suggest that individuals were interfering with the supply chain of the Roman army when it came to food and that drastic action was needed to persuade such individuals otherwise.

This then brings us back to the tablet in question. In my view, this tablet was most likely generated between a civilian trader around the fort and the centurion Felicio, not because Felicio did not have 'ready money', but because the supply chain of food to the fort was irregular. Felicio needed some foodstuffs and the trader had some. He could have sold them to Felicio outright or on credit, but in doing so, might have created the impression that he was somehow taking advantage of the misfortune of others, not a good business decision in a small community such as Vindolanda where returning customers and their business was important. To that end, in my view, this example of *mutuum* should be viewed in the context of 'relational contract theory'. Both the civilian trader and centurion had a vested interest in the contract. In a contained environment where the army was your main source of business, it would not be good business sense to charge regular customers. Of course this trader was no fool. He still had enough business sense to record the transaction.

This then brings us to the final point, the use of Roman law in this tablet. It is sometimes argued that at the edges of empire, less use would be made of Roman law and more of informal barter-style agreements (compare the comment above about the difference between Roman and provincial law). While a barter-type exchange would clearly not have worked in this case, assuming my hypothesis is correct, it also shows that even at the furthest edges of the empire, civilian traders were working under the belief that Roman law applied and could potentially be used to resolve the dispute. And it cannot be the case that the word *mutuum* was merely used by accident. In fact, we have an example of *commodatum* from one of the other texts. Thus, whoever drafted these documents had some knowledge of the law. To that end perhaps the time has also come for us to start looking more closely at legal forms and their use by traders following the army and army personnel.

[73] Included at the end of Brand (2011). [74] Blume's translation.

5. A NEW MODEL OF EXCHANGE

But should we abandon the idea of barter as a form of exchange in the provinces altogether? What form did the commercial exchanges between Romans and Britons take? Trade between Romans and Britons is a given,[75] but should we assume that they always used Roman law? Although there is no direct evidence for this type of exchange, I wish to make a case for reconsidering barter (in the sense of giving object x in return for object y) as a form of commercial exchange at local level in the Roman province of Britannia.

That the Roman jurists did not pay much attention to barter in the legal texts is a well-documented and often repeated fact.[76] Apart from a comment by Gaius in his second-century textbook (repeated in the Justinianic Institutes) and a few texts attributed to mainly Severan jurists, Roman legal sources present a rather fragmentary picture of barter and then mainly in the context of the discussion of the contract of sale.[77] In general, the lack of juristic interest and value judgements by the Roman jurists concerning the 'primitive' nature of the transactions and the peoples who employ it have been cited in modern literature as reasons for this slight treatment.[78] Be that as it may, the classical jurists had a clear notion of the origins of the contract of sale:[79]

> *Origo emendi vendendique a permutationibus coepit. olim enim non ita erat nummus neque aliud merx, aliud pretium vocabatur, sed unusquisque secundum necessitatem temporum ac rerum utilibus inutilia permutabat, quando plerumque evenit, ut quod alteri superest alteri desit. sed quia non semper nec facile concurrebat, ut, cum tu haberes quod ego desiderarem, invicem haberem quod tu accipere velles, electa materia est, cuius publica ac perpetua aestimatio difficultatibus permutationum aequalitate quantitatis subveniret. eaque materia forma publica percussa usum dominiumque non tam ex substantia praebet quam ex quantitate nec ultra merx utrumque, sed alterum pretium vocatur.*
>
> The origins of *emptio venditio* is to be found in acts of barter. Once upon a time, money was not known, and there was no term for *merx* or *pretium*, but all people, in accordance with the requirements of the time and circumstances exchanged articles which were useless to them for other things which they needed; for it often happens that what one has a superabundance of, another lacks. But, because it did not always or readily happen that when you had what I wanted, or, on the other hand that I had what you were willing to take, a substance was selected whose public and perpetual value, by its uniformity as a medium of exchange, overcame the difficulties arising from barter, and this substance, having been coined by public authority, represented use and ownership, not so much on account of the material itself as by its value, and both articles were no longer designated *merx*, but one of them was called the *pretium* of the other.

This text is noteworthy for a number of reasons. First, it is the only text in the Digest in which the origins of the contract of sale are located in barter. In second place, it provides a survey of the reasons why, according to the third-century

[75] For a good survey, see Paterson (1998). [76] Watson (2001).

[77] The main sources are Gaius, *Inst*.3.141; *Inst*.3.23.2; D.18.1.1pr–1; D.19.4.

[78] See Aubert (2014).

[79] Paul, *On the edict* 33 (D. 18.1.1. pr.); translation adapted from Scott's.

jurist, Paul, barter became insufficient as a medium of exchange and had to be replaced by sale. Much has been made surrounding the comments of Paul (both in this text and in others on the relationship between sale and barter, specifically in relation to consent about the price) and about the strength of his arguments and the coherence of his reasoning. It is also worth mentioning that Paul's comment, which articulates the 'Sabinian' view, stood in opposition to the position of those jurists who followed the 'Proculian' view, namely that barter and sale were distinct (compare D. 18.1.1.1). Setting these aside for the moment, I wish to focus on the first part of the text. For Paul, sale arose out of barter, a primordial transaction.[80]

Paul's statement on this matter is interesting for a number of reasons. First, as Aubert has shown, it should be read into the larger context of Greco-Roman historiography where comments about barter are often associated with 'primitive people'.[81] Furthermore, according to Aubert, comments of this kind often have a moral overtone in which their authors cast a negative judgement over the level of civilization of people who still employ barter. Far more interesting, however, to the historian of law is the nature of the history of sale set out by Paul and the linear nature of his understanding of legal development (from primitive to sophisticated). It is these two aspects to which I will now turn.

The first aspects concern the history of sale as stated by Paul. We can never know which information Paul had at his disposal when writing this statement and thus what it was meant to convey in the original context. One thing is clear, though. Much about the origins of the consensual contract of sale in Roman law was unclear to the Romans (and remains unclear to modern scholars) and the fact that Paul links these two transactions makes for interesting speculation. Modern literature on the topic has largely taken Paul's statement as an accurate reflection of historical reality (at least, according to the Sabinians), although how exactly barter fits into the history of sale has never been fully resolved. The point at which most scholars of Roman law begin their discussion of the history of the contract of sale is when it has already acquired a legal form (i.e. post-barter) using money as a medium of exchange. Thus, according to the main writers on the topic (summarized in Watson[82]), the earliest forms of 'sale' that existed in Roman law before the creation of the consensual contract of sale was either a simultaneous, on the spot transaction (perhaps a *mancipatio*) or a *stipulatio* for a future transaction. How this situation 'developed' into a consensual sale (recognized at the latest in the mid-second century BCE) is unclear and much of the modern literature has struggled to find the 'missing link'.[83] Modern scholars have offered a range of options though none of these are wholly convincing. Most recently, having surveyed the strengths and weakness of each of these options, Gordley has suggested that none of them adequately explain the transition and that more emphasis should be placed on its factual origins.[84]

But where does this leave us in relation to barter? The idea that barter is somehow 'primitive' not only pervaded Greco-Roman historiography; it also

[80] Incidentally, Paul employs a similar technique when discussing the origins of *dominium* in Paul, *On the edict* 54 (D. 41.2.1.1) where he argues (citing Nerva *filius*) that it arose out of some primordial act of possession.

[81] See Daube (1949). [82] Watson (2001). [83] Gordley (2010), 1440–5.

[84] Gordley (2010), 1449.

found a home in contemporary literature on ancient law. As Westbrook has shown, much of the narrative of the early history of law arose in the seventeenth and eighteenth centuries in the works of Enlightenment scholars.[85] These scholars theorized about an idealized state of nature that was in turn used to critique contemporary society and to explain the need for the social contract among other things. The works of these scholars had various flaws owing to the limited amount of information available (some comments from classical antiquity and from the Old Testament). Relying on these comments and on accounts of 'primitive peoples', Enlightenment scholars created the notion of four successive stages of societal evolution, namely 1) hunting; 2) pastoralism; 3) agriculture, and finally 4) commerce. It would be in stages 1 and 2 (and perhaps also 3), according to Enlightenment scholars, that barter arose and became the primary mode of exchange. This notion of societal evolution in stages was enthusiastically absorbed by the scientific writers of the nineteenth century such as Maine, Bachofen and Fustel de Coulange who not only perpetuated these Enlightenment ideas, but also bolstered them using further discoveries in the field of Ethnography. Their ideas have proved remarkably resilient during the course of the early twentieth century as is evident in the spate of books on 'primitive law', the most famous of which is undoubtedly by Diamond.[86] But, as Westbrook has demonstrated, there are persistent problems with this narrative, especially in relation to its shaky foundations and the use of early ethnographic literature concerning so-called 'primitive people'.

While it might seem remarkable that the third-century jurist Paul and generations of legal scholars from the Enlightenment onward arrived at the same conclusion about barter as the primordial transaction from which sale arose, it has to be remembered that certainly latterly, the narrative seems to have become self-reinforcing. Added to this is ethnographic literature from the nineteenth and early twentieth centuries about the customs of 'primitive peoples' and an almost perfect storm is created. As scholars of Roman law, however, we have been taught to remain sceptical of any 'potted history', especially statements such as those of Paul about the origins of sale in barter.

In light of these problems, the place of barter in Roman law must be revisited. But rather than focus purely on the rules of law, I wish to make a case for including principles of economic theory and anthropology (without the value judgements inherent in its precursor discipline, ethnography) in the discussion. Let us first look at economic theory.[87] According to classical economic theory, all economies progress through four stages, namely: 1) barter; 2) 'primitive money'; 3) minted coins and, finally, 4) bills of exchange. In each instance, the progression to new stage leads to a replacement of what has come before, all in the name of greater economic 'efficiency'. It does not take much to appreciate that this view of 'progression' through stages most likely also had its origins in Enlightenment scholarship (the very point at which economics came to be recognized as a distinct discipline). Also, if the stages of societal evolution were mapped onto the stages of economic development, barter would be towards the front end (hunting and pastoralism, perhaps even agriculture). In light of what we have said above

[85] Westbrook (2010). [86] Diamond (1971). [87] Pankhurst (2007), 156.

about the veracity of this narrative of progress, a healthy dose of scepticism is required. And herein lies the issue. The jurist Paul never locates the existence of barter at some early point in the history of Rome. Knowing what we now know about the history of the Roman civilization, taking 753 BCE as an accurate starting point, it would be difficult to place barter historically in the rise of Rome.[88] If we take the introduction of coined money in Rome, conventionally dated 280 BCE, as the start of economic phase 3, and we know, from early laws like the 12 Tables, that 'primitive money' (ingots) were already commonly in circulation as early as 450 BCE, it leaves an incredibly short period of time (in civilization terms) for barter to arise and to become a type of primordial transaction. Added to this, the astute observation by Aubert, that before the introduction of 'primitive money', the earliest Romans likely used Greek money.[89] All of this leads to the inescapable conclusion that Paul's potted history of the origins of sale in the contract of barter is an invented history with little factual support.

This then brings us to the anthropological angle. Apart from the 1992 book by Humphrey and Hugh-Jones,[90] more recent work on the anthropology of barter in the history of Ethiopian law[91] has provided fresh new insights into the purpose of this transaction. A number of important conclusions have been reached by these studies. First, barter is by no means confined to 'primitive peoples' or the archaic stages of an economy or of a legal system. It frequently coexists and often overlaps with other phases of economic development, even with coined money. In fact, Humphrey and Hugh-Jones has gone as far as to suggest that barter should be viewed as a form of exchange in its own right that people employ within a specific social context.

This is not an unimportant point. In his discussion of the second life of barter in the writings of scholars of the European legal tradition, Gordley demonstrated that the main attack against the distinction between barter and sale came from the Spanish scholastics.[92] Of course, their views should be seen against the backdrop of the rise of a general principle of contract in early-modern European legal scholarship, a topic too vast to engage in here. Nonetheless, Gordley makes an important point regarding the distinction between sale and barter as two types of economic exchange. Consensual sale (*emptio venditio*) is designed to deal with a very specific situation, namely where the parties wish to 'lock in' a bargain because of the uncertainty caused by price fluctuations. Thus, consent becomes a fundamental requirement to enable this to occur. As Gordley rightly surmises, however, we cannot and should not assume that the parties to a barter have the same motivations.[93] They might not have cared so much about fluctuations in price, since they were more concerned with other aspects e.g. the immediate availability of the object or the ability to bypass the use of money as a medium of exchange. All this ties in with Aubert's conclusions that barter was in no way confined to some mythical archaic point in the earliest days of Rome. In fact, there is evidence from legal practice that it continues right the way through the classical period of Roman law and beyond. In this context, one might take heed of Walton and

[88] Cornell (1995). [89] Aubert (2014). [90] Humphrey and Hugh-Jones (1992).
[91] Pankhurst (2007). [92] Gordley (2010), 1451. [93] Gordley (2010), 1452–6.

Moorhead's observation about Roman coin use in the first century CE in Britannia, commenting on the use of *denarii* in the Vindolanda tablets:

> [I]t might reflect the demands of a local population who viewed *denarii* not as one denomination in a monetary system but as convenient stores of precious metal. Tacitus implies that Roman coinage was used in much this way on the Germanic frontier, where the native population was reputed to pick out older, silver Roman coinage for use in trade (Tacitus, *Germania* 5, 3–5), and this is amply confirmed by evidence from the area outside the empire.[94]

This may also go some way to explaining the deposits of silver *denarii* as hoards in those areas beyond the frontiers (of Hadrian and Antoninus Pius).

6. CONCLUSIONS

This survey is but one possible way of writing the history of law in Britannia. Much of the epigraphic material remains tantalizingly unexplored and the glut of recent discoveries from the Walbrook excavation in London, combined with the ongoing discoveries at Vindolanda, suggest that the story about 'provincial law' in Britannia is only beginning. One thing is clear from the current narrative, however. The story of 'provincial law' in this province will have to be told in terms of 'living law'. To that end, it cannot consist of a trawl through the Digest or the Codex to find scraps of material relating to the province. Not only had this already been done, but the results have also proven to be of limited use. Thus, if the story of 'provincial law' is to be told for Britannia, it will be told from the perspective of the peoples who lived it and the larger forces, like the Roman army, which played an important role in the province. It may well be that the Roman law (or indeed the local customs) found here are incompatible with what we currently understand Roman legal doctrine to be, but then again, Roman law was a working legal order that adapted to the circumstances of it contexts. There is much left to be said on this topic and I would urge scholars to keep a close eye on the ongoing excavations. My hunch is that we will see much more law in years to come.

REFERENCES

Ando, C. 2015. 'Fact, Fiction, and Social Reality in Roman Law'. *Law and Philosophy Library* 110, pp. 295–324.

Aubert, J-J. 2014. For Swap or Sale? The Roman law of Barter. In: C. Apicella, M.-L. Haack, and F. Lerouxel, eds. *Les affaires de Monsieur Andreau: économie et société du monde romain*. Bordeaux; Paris, pp. 109–21.

Beiser, F. C. 2015. *The German Historicist Tradition*. Oxford.

Birley, A. 1980. *The People of the Roman Britain*. Berkeley.

Birley, E. 1953. *Roman Britain and the Roman Army. Collected Papers*. Kendal.

Booth, 2017. Kent: Roman Rural Settlement. In: D. Bird, ed. *Agriculture and Industry in South-Eastern Roman Britain*. Oxford; Philadelphia, pp. 55–83.

[94] Walton and Moorhead (2016), 839. See also Davies (1998).

Bowman, A. K. 2003. *Life and Letters on the Roman Frontier: Vindolanda and Its People.* Rev., Expanded and updated ed. London. [First published 1994]

Bradley, C. M. 2011. *Romano-British Curse Tablets: The Religious and Spiritual Romanization of Ancient Britain.* Lexington, Ky.

Brand, C. E. 2011. *Roman Military Law.* Austin.

Cornell, T. 1995. *The Beginnings of Rome: Italy and Rome from the Bronze Age to the Punic Wars (c.1000–264 BC).* London.

Creighton, J. 2008. *Britannia: The Creation of a Roman Province.* London.

Czajkowski, K. 2017. *Localized Law: The Babatha and Salome Komaise Archives.* Oxford.

Daguet-Gagey, A. 2004. Old provinces. Administration of the senatorial provinces in the imperial Greek provinces. *Revue Historique* 631, pp. 605–9.

Daube, D. 1949. *The Three Quotations from Homer in Digest 18.1.1.1.* London.

Davies, J. K. 1998. Ancient Economies: models and muddles. In: H. Parkins, and C. J. Smith (eds). *Trade, Traders and the Ancient City.* London; New York, pp. 221–52.

De la Bédoyère, G. 2006. *Roman Britain: A New History.* New York.

De la Bédoyère, G. 2015. *The Real Lives of Roman Britain: A History of Roman Britain through the Lives of Those Who Were There.* Yale.

Diamond, A. S. 1971. *Primitive Law, Past and Present.* London.

Du Plessis, P. 2014. A Letter from the Edge of the World. *Ars Aequi*, pp. 5–7.

Du Plessis, P. 2015. Return to the Wood in Roman Kent. In: É. Jakab (ed.), 2015. *Sale and community: Documents from the ancient world: Individuals' autonomy and State interference in the ancient world. Proceedings of a Colloquium supported by the University of Szeged. Budapest 5–8.10.2012.* Trieste, pp. 29–40.

Ehrlich, E. 1962. *Fundamental Principles of the Sociology of Law.* New York.

Frere, S. 1967. *Britannia: A History of Roman Britain.* London.

González Fernández, J. and Crawford, M. H. 1986. The *Lex Irnitana:* a New Flavian Municipal Law. *Journal of Roman Studies* 76, pp. 147–243.

Gordley, J. 2010. The Origins of Sale: Some Lessons from the Romans. *Tulane Law Review* 84: 6, pp. 1437–70.

Herz, P. 2011. Finances and Costs of the Roman Army. In: P. Erdkamp, (ed). *A Companion to the Roman Army.* Malden; Oxford; Chichester, pp. 306–22.

Hope, V. M. 2016. Inscriptions and Identity. In: M. Millett, L. Revell, and A. Moore (eds). *The Oxford Handbook of Roman Britain.* Oxford, pp. 285–302.

Humfress, C. 2012. Law and Custom under Rome. In: A. Rio (ed.), *Custom in the Middle Ages.* London, pp. 23–47.

Humphrey, C. and Hugh-Jones, S. 1992. *Barter, Exchange, and Value: An Anthropological Approach.* Cambridge; New York.

Ireland, S. 2008. *Roman Britain: A Sourcebook.* Hoboken.

Kakoschke, A. 2011. *Die Personennamen Im Römischen Britannien.* Alpha-Omega. Reihe A, Lexika, Indizes, Konkordanzen Zur Klassischen Philologie, CCLIX. Hildesheim.

Kehne, P. 2011. War- and Peacetime Logistics: Supplying Imperial Armies in East and West. In: P. Erdkamp, (ed). *A Companion to the Roman Army.* Malden; Oxford. Chichester, pp. 323–38.

Kehoe, D. P., Ratzan, D. M. and Yiftach, U. 2015. *Law and Transaction Costs in the Ancient Economy.* Ann Arbor.

Korporowicz, Ł. J. 2011. Buying a Slave in Roman Britain. The Evidence from the Tabulae. *Revue internationale des droits de l'antiquité* 58, pp. 211–24.

Korporowicz, Ł. J. 2012. Roman Law in Roman Britain: An Introductory Survey. *The Journal of Legal History* 33: 2, pp. 133–50.

Lintott, A. W. 1993. *Imperium Romanum: Politics and Administration.* London; New York.

Mac Mahon, A. and Price, J. 2005. *Roman Working Lives and Urban Living.* Oxford.

Mattingly, D. J. 2006. *An Imperial Possession: Britain in the Roman Empire, 54 BC–AD 409.* Penguin History of Britain 1. London; New York.
Millett, M. 2003. *The Romanization of Britain: An Essay in Archaeological Interpretation.* Cambridge.
Millett, M. 2016. 'By Small Things Revealed': Rural Settlement and Society. In: M. Millett, L. Revell, and A. Moore (eds). *The Oxford Handbook of Roman Britain.* Oxford, pp. 699–719.
Mitteis, L. 1891. *Reichsrecht und Volksrecht in den östlichen Provinzen des Römischen Kaiserreichs mit Beiträgen zur Kenntniss des griechischen Rechts und der spätrömischen Rechtsentwicklung.* Leipzig.
Moore, A. 2016. The Life Course. In: M. Millett, L. Revell, and A. Moore (eds). *The Oxford Handbook of Roman Britain.* Oxford, pp. 321–40.
Mullen, A. 2016. Sociolinguistics. In: M. Millett, L. Revell, and A. Moore (eds). *The Oxford Handbook of Roman Britain.* Oxford, pp. 573–98.
Pankhurst, A. 2007. The Logic of Barter in Ethiopian History and Its Resilience in Contemporary Society: Case Studies in the Exchange of Food, Clothing and Household Goods. *Journal of Ethiopian Studies* 40, pp. 155–79.
Paterson, J. 1998. Trade and traders in the Roman world: scale, structure, and organisation. In: H Parkins, and C. J. Smith (eds). *Trade, Traders and the Ancient City.* London; New York, pp. 145–64.
Pitts, M. 2016. Rural Transformation in the Urbanized Landscape. In: M, Millett, L. Revell, and A. Moore (eds). *The Oxford Handbook of Roman Britain.* Oxford, pp. 720–40.
Richardson, J. 2008. *The Language of Empire: Rome and the Idea of Empire From the Third Century BC to the Second Century AD.* Leiden.
Rogers, A. 2016. The Development of Towns. In: M. Millett, L. Revell, and A. Moore (eds). *The Oxford Handbook of Roman Britain.* Oxford, pp. 741–66.
Salway, P. 1997. *A History of Roman Britain.* Oxford; New York.
Scullard, H. H. 1999. *Roman Britain: Outpost of the Empire.* London.
Tomlin, R. 1996. A Five-Acre Wood in Roman Kent. In: J. Bird, M. W. C. Hassall, H. Sheldon (eds). *Interpreting Roman London: Papers in Memory of Hugh Chapman (Oxford 1996).* Oxford, pp. 209–16.
Tomlin, R. 2003. 'The Girl in Question': A New Text from Roman London. *Britannia* 34, pp. 41–51.
Tomlin, R. 2016. *Roman London's First Voices.* London.
Versnel, H. S. 2010. Prayers for Justice, East and West: New Finds and Publications since 1990. *World Religions in the Graeco-Roman World* 16, pp. 275–354.
Walton, P. and Moorhead, S. 2016. Coinage and the Economy. In: M. Millett, L. Revell, and A. Moore (eds). *The Oxford Handbook of Roman Britain.* Oxford, pp. 834–49.
Watson, A. 2001. *The Evolution of Western Private Law.* Baltimore.
Westbrook, R. 2010. The Early History of Law: A Theoretical Essay. *Zeitschrift Der Savigny-Stiftung Fur Rechtsgeschichte* 127, pp. 1–13+713.
Winsbury, R. 2014. *Pliny the Younger: A Life in Roman Letters.* London and New York.
Woolf, G. 2003. *Becoming Roman: The Origins of Provincial Civilization in Gaul.* Cambridge.

22

Legal Education and Legal Culture in Gaul during the Principate*

Matthijs Wibier

This chapter explores questions about law and the development of a legal culture in the Western Roman provinces, in particular Gaul, from the perspective of legal education. It has often been pointed out at a conceptual level that education is an important channel for the diffusion of cultural models, expectations, and standards. Using literary sources as well as the papyrological record, scholars have amply charted the extensive proliferation of the Greek model known as *enkyklios paideia* and its role in spreading knowledge of the Greek language and of Greek culture far beyond the traditional Greek heartland.[1] Similar developments have been traced for Roman education and Latin literacy in the provinces of the East and the West,[2] although the sources for the Western parts of the Roman Empire are considerably more indirect and substantially less comprehensive than those for the East.[3] Furthermore, studies on the evolution of provincial Roman cultures in the West, a process involving complicated interactions between local and more mainstream Roman practices,[4] have focused on many aspects of daily life, including literacy. Yet legal culture, including legal education, has largely been left unstudied for the Western provinces before the fourth century,[5] even if it must

* I would like to express my thanks to the editors of this volume for their invitation to participate. I am also very grateful to José-Domingo Rodríguez Martín and to the anonymous reviewer for their constructive feedback. Finally, I gladly acknowledge that my postdoctoral fellowship at the ERC project Redhis (Pavia) reinforced my interest in and understanding of the *Fragmenta Augustodunensia*.

[1] Most importantly Morgan (1998) and Cribiore (2001).

[2] I find still most helpful the relevant parts of Kaster (1988) (though focusing on Late Antiquity) and of Adams (2003) (though focusing on bilingualism); see also Woolf (1998).

[3] In comparison, the West suffers from a near complete loss of papyri and other perishable writing materials (except for several hoards of writing tablets, though many are hardly legible). For the mechanics of learning Latin in the East, see first and foremost Dickey (2016) and (2012). Scappaticcio (2016) provides a corpus of Latin grammatical texts on papyrus with an (unfortunately) truly minimalist attempt at embedding these works culturally (epilogue by Swiggers and Wouters).

[4] e.g. Woolf (1998); Hingley (2010); Johnston (2017).

[5] Even for the city of Rome itself, legal education has received relatively little attention recently. This is mainly due to poor and problematic evidence. For good recent treatments, see Harries (2016) and Riggsby (2015). An older relevant piece is Liebs (1976). On legal culture, including education, in Gaul in Late Antiquity, see Liebs (2002).

Matthijs Wibier, *Legal Education and Legal Culture in Gaul during the Principate* In: *Law in the Roman Provinces*. Edited by: Kimberley Czajkowski and Benedikt Eckhardt in collaboration with Meret Strothmann, Oxford University Press (2020).

DOI: 10.1093/oso/9780198844082.003.0022

have formed an important dimension of the phenomenon of 'Romanization'.[6] This volume's chapters on Britain and the Danubian provinces provide detailed and nuanced surveys of the legal culture, the law as it was used and experienced 'on the ground', in two Western areas. While including a survey of similar evidence for Gaul, this chapter has a slightly different focus by discussing how legal culture, in all its richness and nuances, was passed on and developed within the setting of provincial Gaul, by means of instruction and education.

The most important obstacle to studying legal education in early Imperial Gaul is no doubt the lack of much very direct evidence, which is symptomatic of the larger underlying problem of limited evidence for the legal culture in the early Imperial West to begin with.[7] There is, nonetheless, a set of scattered evidence that allows us to piece together a picture of legal education in Gaul during the Principate up until the year 300. In particular, the generous fragments of a paraphrase of Gaius' *Institutes* found in Autun, usually known as the *Fragmenta Augustodunensia* (*FA*), have been unduly marginalized.[8] By exploiting this text and further evidence, this chapter aims to offer a better understanding of how students in Imperial Gaul were trained in the basics of Roman law. My focus on education makes that the discussion below pays attention primarily to Roman private law and knowledge thereof in Gaul, while it largely sidesteps the epigraphical evidence pertaining to public matters such as the status of towns, municipal administration, and benefactions. This latter evidence about public life has been served relatively well in studies of the culture of the Roman provinces.[9] Furthermore, given the nature of the evidence, I focus primarily on the training of forensic lawyers. We will see below that specialists who could draw up legal documents must have been prevalent in Gaul as well. Recent scholarship, working on the basis of the rich documentary evidence found in the papyri, has highlighted the importance of legal scribes and their networks in adapting contractual forms in provincial settings, which in some cases became the new local standard.[10] The training of scribes in these localities must have played a key role in diffusing the new, adapted forms. For this reason, it is very unfortunate that the evidence on scribal training in early Imperial Gaul is extremely minimal.

At the outset, I should point out two considerations about the geographical and chronological parameters that have a direct bearing on the use of source material. Firstly, I use the term Gaul throughout in a fairly wide sense to include what is

[6] On the concept of Romanization and its problems, see for example Woolf (1998) and Hingley (2010). I use this term without inverted commas or other markers of caution throughout.

[7] On the evidence and productive approaches to it for the North West, see first and foremost the chapters of Eckhardt and Du Plessis. See also the chapters on Iberia and North Africa in this volume.

[8] The work should probably be dated to the window stretching from the mid-third to early fourth century, while standing in a text book tradition that goes back further. The (partly unobserved) evidence is discussed below. On the *FA*, see first and foremost Rodríguez Martín (1998), which includes Krüger's edition.

[9] For towns and administration, see the recent survey of Roselaar (2016) and the conceptual discussion of Galsterer (1986). For Gaul, see e.g. the general remarks at Woolf (1998), 65–7 and the detailed work on the Narbonese towns by Christol (collected papers in Christol (2010)). For the Iberian Peninsula (and its spectacular evidence in this respect), see the chapters of Strothmann and Eck in this volume.

[10] See for example Keenan, Manning, and Yiftach-Firanko (2014); Alonso (2016).

now France, Switzerland (Raetia), the Rhine area, and the Low Countries. I freely use epigraphic material from these areas. The Iberian Peninsula and Noricum feature minimally, since they have chapters of their own. I exclude the former Gallia Cisalpina altogether so as to avoid allowing in Italian material. Secondly, this chapter focuses on the period from the very early Principate to the early days of the Tetrarchy. As we will see, however, some of the most valuable evidence about education in Gaul, including legal education, dates to the Tetrarchic period. This period saw many reforms, not least in the legal sphere. But since the first attestation of a practice does not necessarily mean that it was a newly instituted practice, one of the questions lurking in the background is to what extent an early fourth-century report codifies existing practices, and to what extent it indicates that there was a real transformation of legal culture in Gaul under the Tetrarchy, not least through the stimulation of legal education.

Given the fragmentary state of the evidence, it is helpful to outline the main building blocks of this chapter briefly. I first review the evidence of legal education in the Early Empire and discuss the models that this evidence allows. Although it has often been taken for granted that rhetorical and legal education were separate affairs, pursued in institutionally different types of school, I will demonstrate that there is little evidence in support of this view beyond rhetorical commonplace polemics that Quintilian and later writers borrowed from Cicero. On the basis of the considerable legal knowledge found among rhetoricians, we are led to infer that basic legal instruction could often be obtained in the course of advanced study associated with the rhetoricians.

Secondly, I argue that higher education along the lines of the rhetorical schools could be found in Gaul as well. The *Panegyric* that the rhetoric teacher Eumenius gave in the late 290s CE, celebrating the schools of Autun, makes clear that the town was an established centre of education and learning already in the early third century, and probably even earlier. For authors such as Tacitus, Gaul enjoyed a reputation for producing excellent orators and intellectuals, and he singles out Autun as an educational hub in particular (*Ann.* 3.43). Several of the *Panegyrics* mention that their authors were employed in the imperial administration in positions for which they must have had some legal knowledge. I argue that Autun must have provided some instruction in Roman law by the third century at the latest. Similar educational centres may have provided similar legal instruction.

Thirdly, I discuss the *FA*. Although it cannot be proven that the work in its surviving form predates the Tetrarchy, it can be proven that the work goes back to a text-book tradition that had a Western circulation. This type of elementary work would seem to fit very well in the educational world of early Imperial provincial Gaul, of which I present Autun as the best attested instance.

Finally, after surveying the use of Roman law in Gallic legal practice, the last section explores what view of law in the Roman provinces the *FA* project to their audience. While the admittedly scarce record contains traces pointing to peculiarities in the way Roman law was used in Gaul, the *FA* have an extremely Romano-centric worldview. Taken together with the work's focus on private law, this indicates that the work was directed to prepare students to join the Romanized elite, to provide them with the right cultural capital, for example to serve as forensic orators or perhaps, like Eumenius, in the imperial administration.

1. SITUATING LEGAL EDUCATION IN THE ROMAN WORLD

Before turning to the evidence pertaining to Gaul, it is worth presenting a succinct orientation of where and how legal instruction took place in the Roman world. Rather than providing a full-scale survey, the major point developed here is that legal education was not confined to specialist law schools.[11]

Latin literary authors such as the Elder Seneca, Quintilian, and Suetonius provide us with considerable information about how education was organized in ancient Rome. Generally speaking, the children of those who could afford it started their school careers with the grammarians.[12] These offered education in basic linguistic skills, including reading and writing based on intensive study of especially Vergil and Cicero. The schools of the grammarians appear to have had no set number of years with distinct cohorts, nor did they award degrees of any formal sort. Most students probably finished their school careers with some training at the grammarians, but for those who wanted and had the resources, there was the possibility of continuing for more advanced education in the rhetorical schools. Cicero and Quintilian both indicate that after their rhetorical training students might seek further specialist instruction in Roman law.[13] Overall, however, the sources are not as clear about how exactly individuals acquired legal knowledge. From the scattered record, it is possible to point to at least three formats of legal instruction; the existence of none of these excludes any of the others.[14]

Firstly, Cicero mentions about his own experiences in the Late Republic that his legal training took place under the tutelage of Quintus Mucius Scaevola (first the Augur, then the Pontifex). About the Augur, we hear that he simply had young men observe his daily routine of giving legal advice to individuals.[15] Tacitus reports that this type of learning was the standard practice in the Late Republic.[16] Students would attach themselves to a well-known forensic orator and observe the dealings of the forum closely, thus acquiring by experience the skills and knowledge necessary to function well in that legal world. This apprenticeship is usually known as the *tirocinium fori*. Describing the practice in much the same way, Quintilian indicates that the rise of the rhetorical schools after the Late Republic had not obviated the need for this type of apprenticeship, since students still needed to get acquainted with the practical side of the legal business at the forum.[17] Tacitus mentions in the *Dialogus* that he himself had sought the mentorship of Marcus Aper and Iulius Secundus in order to learn about the ways of the forum.[18] In sum, then, the apprenticeship was an important way in which

[11] Cannata (1963), 245 is a classic instance of considering rhetorical schools and law schools as different planets *by assumption*.

[12] Suetonius, *De Grammaticis et Rhetoribus*, Quintilian, *Institutio oratoria* 1.4. Quintilian discusses at 1.1 the ideal training of infants before they are old enough to go the grammarians.

[13] See below, p. 466.

[14] For recent discussions, see Harries (2016) and Riggsby (2015).

[15] Cicero, *Laelius de amicitia* 1.1, Cicero, *Brutus* 89.306.

[16] Tacitus, *Dialogus de oratoribus* 34 with extensive description, which mentions knowledge of laws (*leges*, 34.6).

[17] Quintilian, *Institutio oratoria.* 12.6; also 10.5.19.

[18] Tacitus, *Dialogus de oratoribus* 34; cf. Pliny, *Epistulae.* 2.14.10 (about Quintilian).

young orators were able to obtain legal know-how that was directly relevant to a career as a forensic lawyer.[19]

Despite the emphasis on learning about forensic law by practical experience, it is important to realize that the rhetorical schools themselves were geared towards imparting forensic skills. One of the centre-pieces of this education were the *controversiae*, in which students were given (often fantastical) scenarios and fictitious legal precepts, and were then asked to argue the case on behalf of one of the parties involved. From Seneca the Elder's monumental collection of *controversiae*, it is clear that students were taught to use standardized argumentative techniques. One important strategy was to press one's case by focusing either on a law's supposedly literal meaning or, if that went against the case, to construct the opposite argument by claiming that the spirit of the law pointed in that opposite direction. Most orators, including Quintilian, place much emphasis on how to forge a strong argument. They have very little to say about Roman law as it must have featured in the actual courts. In order to train argumentative skills, the rhetorical handbooks in fact often provide completely fictitious laws to begin with. It is nonetheless conceivable in principle that some attention was paid to Roman law in the rhetorical schools. The evidence in support of this idea is very thin, but it is worth considering briefly. Most importantly, *Major Declamation* 13, one of the sample speeches for rhetorical education that has survived under the name of Quintilian, deals with the scenario that the bees of a poor man feed on the flowers in the garden of a rich man. The brief description at the opening of the speech mentions that the legal rule around which the ensuing conflict between the neighbours revolves is the *actio damni per iniuriam dati*, which clearly references the action of the *Lex Aquilia* available under Roman law.[20] What is more, the speech itself is acutely aware of the technical juristic literature that debated the controversies surrounding the exact applicability of this action, as many scholars have pointed out.[21] The author of the speech was therefore clearly knowledgeable about Roman law, and in this respect he lived up to the ideal set by Quintilian himself that an orator should have sufficient legal competence to judge legal claims that may be raised in the course of a trial (12.3). While Quintilian also mentions that much of this knowledge can be acquired simply by reading, it is entirely plausible that some sort of legal instruction took place in the type of setting in which the anonymous declaimer was active. The setup of that instruction remains less clear, and it may have taken the form of private tutoring. This last format is suggested much later by Libanius when he invites one Silanus to take up the job of law tutor at Libanius' school. By adding that he has kept the position free for Silanus, he appears to imply the tutorship was a continuing position at the school rather than a one-off job.[22] In the third century, we find a certain Marcus Aristonicus in the capacity of 'leader of the Museum, in charge of jurisprudence (?)'

[19] Although evidence is exceedingly hard to find, apprenticeships must have been the major format for training scribes specializing in legal documentation. For a useful discussion based on papyri, see Bucking (2007).

[20] Often referred to as *damnum iniuria* (with or without *datum*). See e.g. Gaius, *Inst.* 3.210–19; the excerpts at *D.* 9.2.

[21] See for example the discussion in Frier (1983). See also Mantovani (2007).

[22] Libanius, *Epistulae* F433/B162.

at Smyrna (ἡγησάμενον Μουσείου ἐπὶ τῶν νόμων ἐμπειρίᾳ, *IGR* 4.618). Given these indications, then, it is likely that at least some rhetorical schools facilitated legal instruction in one format or another.

In the third place, there is the vexed question of the existence of separate law schools, first in Rome and later also elsewhere in the empire. The most securely and extensively attested law school is that of Berytus, primarily in the letters of Libanius and in several Late Antique legal texts.[23] Libanius' works also strongly suggest that a similar institution existed in Rome, and a constitution of the emperor Theodosius from the year 425 institutes state-paid law teachers in Constantinople.[24] The school in Berytus was in existence by 239 CE.[25] Before the third century, the only evidence for specialized legal teaching comes from Pliny the Younger and virtually the jurist Pomponius. Pliny mentions the existence of a *Cassiana schola* for those with legal interests, founded by the jurist C. Cassius Longinus (*Ep.* 7.24.8). The reference is made in passing, with no more information given. In line with Suetonius' use of the word *schola* in his work *On grammarians and rhetors*, we should probably take Pliny to be describing a group of students around Cassius Longinus, probably frequenting his house;[26] but the term does not necessarily imply an institution dedicated fully to teaching. It is plausible at least that those studying with Cassius Longinus sought the type of more profound legal training associated with the jurists. Several decades later, Pomponius claims that since the Augustan Age there had been two rival law schools, the Cassian school and the Proculian school, which were antagonized over fundamental differences in principle.[27] Pomponius' claims about the Augustan pedigree must be an exaggeration, as the names of the schools indicate. In addition, there is very little evidence to support Pomponius' claims about doctrinal polarity. While his contemporary Gaius repeatedly juxtaposes his own teachers and those of another *schola*, it is not easy to see what the differences between them are based on. The (sometimes extensive) fragments of the jurists who are listed as heads of the schools do also not show the two doctrinal camps that Pomponius imposed on his school division.[28]

For the present purposes, we should take it as established that legal instruction was not exclusively the domain of the law schools. Forensic orators must have learned much of the legal know-how they needed for successfully exercising their job from apprenticeships and in the setting of the rhetorical schools. The details remain unclear, but the evidence indicates that reading books, private tutoring, and classroom instruction are all plausible scenarios. At this point, I should note that the boundaries between the categories of forensic rhetorical education and legal education were not as exclusive as they have often been assumed to be.[29]

[23] The standard study about the school of Beirut is still Collinet (1925).

[24] e.g. Libanius, *Orationes* 2.44, 48.22–9; *CTh.* 14.9.1 (this law allows private tutors to continue their business as well).

[25] Gregory Thaumaturgus, *Panegyricus ad Origenem* 5. Note also that *Fr. Vat.* 204 (Ulpian quoting Caracalla) suggests that young men came to Rome to study law in the Severan Age.

[26] e.g. Suet. *DGR* 17. [27] Pomponius, *Enchiridion* (*D.*1.2.2.47).

[28] Kübler (1914). For a more recent discussion of the problems and the scholarship, see Leesen (2010).

[29] Much the same point can be made about the exclusiveness of the categories orator and jurist (this assumption clearly underlies e.g. Champlin (1987), 204). Wibier (2016) shows that the construction of antagonistic personas of orator vs. jurist is a Ciceronian legacy that was partly, but only limitedly,

2. HIGHER EDUCATION IN ROMAN GAUL: THE CASE OF AUTUN

The previous section sketched a model of Roman higher education in which rhetorical schools play an important role in facilitating basic legal instruction to aspiring elites. Since the discussion relied on evidence mostly pertaining to the city of Rome, at this point we need to consider its validity for the provincial setting of Gaul.[30] Overall, the evidence indicates overwhelmingly that elites in Gallic towns valued advanced education and that they were eager to display their tastes and show off their learning. There is also good evidence to suggest that some form of legal instruction was available in certain places.

It is quite clear that by the end of the first century CE Gaul had been acquiring a name for its rhetorical culture.[31] One of the earliest reports is a famous passage in Strabo claiming that Marseille offered such good education that many elite Romans went there instead of to Athens (4.1.5).[32] Although no further details are given, it is likely that we are dealing with rhetorical instruction that was at least partly in Greek. Along the same lines, the Elder Seneca and Tacitus both mention that the sophist Moschus, after he was banished from Pergamum, moved to live as an exile in Marseille and began teaching there.[33] Seneca also tells us about a certain Agroitas, an accomplished declaimer in Latin and Greek hailing from Gaul.[34] Other orators who originated from Gaul and may have received training there are Votienus Montanus and Marcus Aper.[35] We are on firmer ground with the orator Favorinus of Arles, who was trained in Gaul and Rome and went on to acquire great fame as a sophist who spoke primarily in Greek.[36] In his work about Julius Agricola, Tacitus emphasizes not only that Agricola was well educated but that he had Marseille as his *magistra studiorum* (*Agr.* 4.2). We hear that he spent much of his days there reading philosophy. Whether or not this is entirely accurate, it suggests at the very least that it was conceivable to avail of books with advanced readings in Gaul, something that is confirmed by Pliny's self-proclaimed

cultivated in the rhetorical schools; Lehne-Gstreinthaler (2016) surveys the existence of many legal experts in the Late Republic who fall outside the two categories in their Ciceronian conceptions.

30 Note the relevant but hopelessly generalizing statement of the Severan jurist Modestinus about 'law teachers who teach in the provinces' (νόμων δὲ διδάσκαλοι ἐν ἐπαρχίᾳ διδάσκοντες, *De exc.* 2 (*D.* 27.1.6.12)).

31 Gleason (1995), 4 and Mullen (2013), 267–8 collect much of the evidence. For an older account, including evidence, see Haarhoff (1958) 33–8.

32 IGF 17, from Marseille, preserves an expression of thanks of a Titus Pompeius to his teacher (καθηγητής) Titus Flavius Nicomachus (late 1st/early 2nd cent.).

33 Seneca, *Controversiae* 2.5.13; Tacitus, *Annales* 4.43. The information is also found in the scholia to Horace, *Epistulae* 1.5.9.

34 Seneca, *Controversiae* 2.6.12.

35 Votienus Montanus: Seneca, *Controversiae* 7.5.12; this orator was accused of insulting Tiberius (Tacitus, *Annales* 4.42). Aper: Tacitus, *Dialogus de oratoribus* 10.2; though focusing on poets, Aper may be suggesting here that there was movement of people from the provinces to Rome to see (and study with) famous orators. By extension, we may wonder whether Agroitas, Votienus Montanus, and Aper were ever active in their hometowns at all.

36 See Gleason (1995), 3–8 for the scattered sources. Aulus Gellius 20.1 suggests that Favorinus had considerable understanding of Roman law. Whether accurate or not, the scene gives some indication of the knowledge an orator or sophist might be imagined to possess.

astonishment at hearing that book sellers in Lyon were apparently selling his own works (*Ep.* 9.11). Tacitus brings up the issue of education again when describing Agricola's initiatives to make Britain more Roman. In addition to stimulating the construction of public buildings, he offered education in the *liberales artes* to the sons of the British leaders. The *artes liberales* amounted to a general education in a variety of subjects; the specific combination of subjects on offer appears to have differed from teacher to teacher until a canonical set of liberal arts crystallized in Late Antiquity.[37] The terms *litterae* and *bonae artes* are very similar notions, although they may designate more advanced studies.[38] Tacitus compares the British students favourably to the 'studied nature of the Gauls' (*studiis Gallorum*, 21.2).[39] While dealing with education of a more elementary level, Suetonius stresses that grammarians could be found across the provinces, particularly all over Gaul.[40] Finally, relating events of the year 21 CE, Tacitus mentions that Autun (Augustodunum) was the place where 'the most noble youth of the Gauls dedicated themselves to the *liberalia studia*' (*nobilissimam Galliarum subolem, liberalibus studiis ibi operatam*, Tac. *Ann.* 3.43).[41] There is no doubt that this is a reference to the same educational institution that several of the Latin Panegyrics memorialize in the late third and early fourth century.[42]

Before turning to the panegyrics in more detail, we should briefly note another indication of the vibrant rhetorical culture of Gaul. The record suggests strongly that there was a market for sophistic performances, presumably for an audience beyond the schools. Suetonius and Juvenal mention that Lyon was home to competitions in Latin and Greek eloquence.[43] Individual orators and sophists are attested as well. Apart from Favorinus of Arles, we read that Lucian made several tours of the Gallic towns and made a fortune there, while Philostratus mentions Heliodorus' forensic career in Gaul.[44] At a less stratospheric level, the *rhetor graecus* Calidius Zoilus who found himself in Cologne may illustrate as well the wide interest in rhetorical culture, also in the Greek language, across the Gallic lands.[45]

The most extensive evidence about higher education in Gaul before the age of Constantine is provided by the Latin Panegyrics. At least four of the earlier speeches, written during the reigns of Diocletian and Constantine, were authored

[37] e.g. Cicero, *De oratore* 1.17, 3.127 with the discussion of Leeman and Pinkster (1981) 39–40. The development of the seven liberal arts, divided into the trivium and the quadrivium, is a later development.

[38] On the difference between *artes liberales* and *bonae*, see for example Quintilian, *Institutio oratoria* 1.10, 12.1.7.

[39] See the comm. of Woodman with Kraus (2014) *ad loc.* on *studium* vs. *ingenium*.

[40] *DGR* 3.6. Note IGF 21, mentioning Athenades, γραμματικὸς ῥωμαϊκός (late 2nd/early 3rd cent., Marseille).

[41] Note also Fronto's remark about Reims (*illae vestrae Athenae*, Fr. *Epist.* fr. 6 (p. 270) VdH).

[42] Furthermore, Ausonius' repeated reports about the schools in Bordeaux and Toulouse, tied up with a family history, indicates that they had been in existence for a while. See Sivan (1993).

[43] Suetonius, *Gaius* 20; Juvenal 1.44.

[44] Lucian, *Bis accusatus sive tribunalia* 27, *Apol.* 15; Philostratus, *Vitae sophistarum* 625–6.

[45] AE 2004.0976 (70–200 CE). The damaged text has been restored: *Cali[dius] Zoi[lus] rhet[or] grae-[cus]*.

by men who claim to be (or to have been) teachers at the school of Autun.[46] In the case of *Panegyrics* 9 and 8 (late 290s), it is reasonably clear that the speakers already had teaching careers before Diocletian came to power. For *Panegyrics* 6 and 5 (*c.*310–11), it is very likely that their authors were educated in the later third century before Diocletian and thus remembered those times. The scarce information in the speeches about their authors does not allow us to conclude that they were written by four distinct individuals. Yet it is likely that, given the allusions to different life stories, the two speeches from the 290s are the work of two different individuals, who were both teachers at the school.

Panegyric 9 offers a particularly rich picture of the educational institution in Autun known as *scholae Maenianae*. It was written by Eumenius in the late 290s, who tells us that he taught in the town before a career as *magister sacrae memoriae* in the imperial administration (11.2). At the moment of writing, he had recently been appointed to the headship of the school and the professorship of rhetoric by Constantius. The oration is framed as a request to the emperor (through its direct addressee, probably the governor of Lugdunensis) for permission to use his state-paid teacher salary for reconstructing Autun's delipidated school buildings.[47] Over the course of the speech, Eumenius combines a eulogy of the schools' past heydays, before the sack of Autun in 269/270,[48] with a detailed vision of restored splendor in the time ahead. Several points in the speech are worth singling out in particular. In the first place, Eumenius ties up the glorious history of the schools closely with the presence of his family in the town for the past three generations. Referring to the town as his *patria* several times, he tells us that his grandfather, an Athenian by birth who made his educational career at Rome, settled in Autun to teach well into his eighties. Even though the story of the grandfather's move to Autun serves rhetorically to enhance the importance of the school, it still testifies to the school's ability (whether through its reputation or through financial resources) to attract and keep teachers from across the empire. The presence of a Greek teacher is also in line with the interest in sophistic performances that we have seen above.[49] Secondly, while Eumenius presses constantly the importance of restoring the buildings of the school, we glean from his speech that education kept being offered in the town in different venues. Eumenius mentions for example that the *Maenianae* fell into disuse before he was born (17.3), while also mentioning that he spent much of his life teaching rhetoric at Autun. We get much the same impression from the author of the contemporary *Panegyric* 8, who taught in

[46] The speeches were delivered probably at Trier, except for *Pan.* 9 (possibly Lyon). See the introductions to each speech in Nixon and Rodgers (1994), also for the information in the rest of this paragraph.

[47] See Goffaux (2010) for a discussion of the epigraphic evidence for individuals rebuilding *scholae* in Gaul (especially Avenches), though these were mostly communal buildings for *collegia* rather than schools for literary education.

[48] As Nixon and Rodgers (1994), 167–8 remark, there are reasons to believe the school had fallen into decline already by the time of the sack. Rebourg (1998) is an archaeological survey of the town of Autun.

[49] Second-century (?) mosaics displaying an Anacreontic poem and referencing the Epicurean philosopher Metrodorus were discovered in 1965, underscoring the Greek tastes of some in Autun. See Rebourg (1998), 145 as a starting point.

the town, worked for the imperial administration, and retired to the countryside. Moreover, Eumenius mentions that his appointment to lead the school was prompted by the death of the previous head (14.3). In short, then, teaching clearly continued in Autun throughout the third century. In addition, Eumenius' speech also gives some impression of the type of education offered. The speech is packed with the vocabulary of *liberalia studia*, *optimae artes* and most of all *litterae*. We have already seen that in the Roman educational imagination these terms designated a potentially wide array of subjects beyond literature or poetry in a narrow sense.[50] The literary allusions throughout the speech may give some indication of the school's reading list.[51] An ecphrasis of the physical class room, whose walls are covered with a map of the world, leaves no doubt that the students worked on geography.[52] While other subjects are not explicitly mentioned, a good case for basic legal instruction can be made.

For starters, we have already seen that Eumenius interrupted his teaching career to act as a *magister sacrae memoriae* in the bureaucracy of Constantius, probably at Trier. While Eumenius himself says that he noted down the emperor's thoughts (6.2), other sources indicate clearly that this official was concerned importantly with drafting legal responses and paperwork.[53] For this reason, we may plausibly infer from Eumenius' selection for the position that he had skills relevant to the job, which probably included some legal expertise. The speech leaves many gaps as to filling out Eumenius' biography, but nowhere does he imply that he was educated outside Autun. We should note that Eumenius refers to Autun as a place for the *optimae artes*, while Pliny and Gellius include law without hesitation among the *bonae artes*.[54] The possibility of attaining some working knowledge of Roman law in Autun is further suggested by the author of *Panegyric* 6 (of *c*.310). Like Eumenius, this man was a teacher of rhetoric before taking up an unspecified position at the imperial court. At the end of his speech, he mentions not only that his son is now an *advocatus fisci*, but also that a great number of his students are either active in the law courts (*tutela fori*, 23.2) or have a position in the emperor's administrative apparatus (*palatii officia*).[55] Even if this last claim may be exaggerated, it is a plausible inference that one might finish one's studies in Autun with enough legal know-how for a career in the courts and the administration. This is in line with the picture emerging from the pseudo-Quintilianic declamation that we have seen above. Writing in the fourth century, Ausonius of Bordeaux gives a

[50] See La Bua (2010) for a somewhat cursory exploration of Eumenius' educational programme, assuming throughout that *litterae* refers to poetry.

[51] See the comm. of Nixon and Rodgers (1994) for several references in general. La Bua (2010) offers a good treatment of Eumenius' Ciceronian intertexts. This chapter is not the place for a discussion whether knowledge of Latin literature was based on reading originals, anthologies, or a combination of both.

[52] In addition to La Bua's (2010), 312–14 emphasis on the mnemotechnic function of the map, note the imperial dimension. For not only is the whole world said to be Roman, a single gaze cannot encompass the entire Roman expanse; rather, one needs to shift one's gaze repeatedly in order to see the entire empire.

[53] e.g. *Notit. dign.* Or. 19.

[54] Eumenius (*Pan. Lat.* 9) 3.2; Pliny, *Epistulae* 1.22; Aulus Gellius, *Noctes Atticae* 13.10.

[55] On the basis of this information, it has been suggested that this orator specialized in forensic oratory and that his position at the imperial court may have been *a libellis*, the official in charge of responding to petitions. See the introduction to this speech in Nixon and Rodgers (1994).

similar impression. He himself was clearly familiar with the writings of the Roman jurists.[56] But he also looks back on his elder uncle Aemilius Magnus Arborius, a high-profile rhetoric professor at Toulouse who reportedly went to Spain to pursue a forensic career (*Parent.* 3.14).[57] It is unfortunate that the epigraphic record has preserved vanishingly little information about individuals who received their education in Gaul and worked in the courts. There is an intriguing inscription from second/third-century Mainz in which an L. Sextius Pervvincus describes himself as *decurio civitatis Auderiensium causidicus.*[58] At the end of the day, however, it is impossible to extrapolate any educational trajectory for this individual.[59]

Even though it is very likely that legal instruction was available in a place such as Autun, we remain completely in the dark about how this exactly functioned. Given the lack of any positive evidence, it is overly speculative to postulate the existence in Autun of an institutionally separate law school similar to the one well attested in Berytus.[60] On the other hand, it is possible that, like Libanius seems to suggest for the later fourth century, the school of rhetoric employed a law tutor (rather than an official professor) to whom part of the school's funding was directed. But it also entirely plausible that individuals professing to have legal expertise acted as private tutors on the model that we find in Theodosius' constitution about Constantinople mentioned earlier. Finally, we cannot exclude that basic legal expertise was partly transmitted through a practice like the traditional *tirocinium fori* or further training on the job, although it is inherently plausible that the ultimate source of the expertise may have been formed by a basic legal textbook, thus making this model very much akin to that of the private tutor. In this light, we should note that several individuals describing themselves as legal experts survive in the epigraphic record of Gaul for the second and early third centuries. We know about two *iuris studiosi* from Nîmes, one Q. Valerius Virillio and an L. Baebius Eucles,[61] and a fairly recent inscription from Carros (near Nice) mentions a *iuris prudens* whose name has been lost.[62] Traditional readings of this evidence have emphasized that these men served as legal advisors in local politics

[56] Honoré (1987), 168, n. 194, offering good reason to believe (though no definitive proof) that Ausonius read Gaius, *Institutiones.*

[57] Sivan (1993), 63.

[58] CIL 13.07063 (spelling *sic*). The stone has disappeared. It is also unknown who the *Auderienses* were.

[59] More tantalizing is the *scholasticus* C. Rutilius Primus attested in a mid-third-century inscription from Cologne (IKöln² #438). The term *scholasticus* is used to denote teachers and students of rhetoric by Quintilian and Pliny, yet in Late Latin it often refers to an orator with particular legal expertise (first unambiguously attested at *CTh.* 8.10.2, a law of Constantius of 344); according to Augustine this is a person who can be hired to craft legal petitions to the emperor (*Tractatus in Evangelium Iohannis* 7). Could Rutilius Primus have been this last type of *scholasticus*? Gallic funerary inscriptions usually feature *scholasticus* in the sense of 'schoolboy', as indicated by their having died as teenagers. The present inscription stands somewhat apart by not preserving any such information. While the scholarship largely favours the lawyerly *scholasticus*, there are no real positive indications that confirm this view.

[60] This is the implication of Nelson (1981) 103, from the assumption that the *FA* could not have been used in a rhetorical school. See the critique at Cannata (1963) 240, contradicting himself at p. 245.

[61] CIL 12.3339 = Liebs (2002) #1 (2nd cent.); and CIL 12.5900 = Liebs (2002) #2 (early 3rd cent.).

[62] AE 2000.0847 (early 3rd cent.).

and legal affairs.[63] This is of course very much to the point. Yet given what we know about the jurists whose writings survive, we cannot exclude at all that jurists in the provinces saw training or mentoring others as part of their task.[64]

3. THE *FRAGMENTA AUGUSTODUNENSIA*: AN INSTANTIATION OF A WESTERN TEACHING MANUAL

So far, I have avoided bringing in the *FA* as evidence for legal instruction in Autun in the third century. This basic-level paraphrase of Gaius' *Institutes* would fit very well in the educational setting of Autun as I have sketched it above, and it would strongly support the case for rudimentary legal instruction in the context of rhetorical education. Discovered by Emile Chatelain in 1898 in Autun's Grand Séminaire, the surviving text is the lowest, mostly erased layer of writing of a codex containing the *Institutes* of Cassian that was created by putting together palimpsested and cut-to-different-size folios from various older codices.[65] Our work's extant, lacunose portion covers fifteen folios and consists of five more or less continuous fragments paraphrasing and elucidating Gaius' *Institutes* on status, inheritances, and the law of actions.[66]

At this point we must face two crucial problems that show that exploiting this evidence for the time frame of this chapter is in fact rather complicated. Neither of these destroys the *FA* as evidence. Firstly, while the single palimpsest manuscript was discovered in Autun, it needs little argumentation that this does not mean that the manuscript was produced or copied in Autun as well. With no further information available about where (and when) the manuscript came into the collection of the seminary, we are confined to making the most out of the handwriting. While palaeographical studies have concluded differently as to where and when exactly the *FA*'s manuscript was produced, the area of convergence is Southern France, with Lyon at the centre but not excluding Autun itself.[67] Secondly, palaeographers overwhelmingly date the manuscript to the earlier fifth century.[68] But this does not mean the text (as opposed to the manuscript) was produced in the

[63] See e.g. Liebs (2002), notes on #1 and #2. Champlin (1987), 203–6 has argued ingeniously that CIL 12.4036 = CLE 1112 from Nîmes commemorates the great jurist Cervidius Scaevola, who may have been an honorary citizen. On this basis, Liebs has speculated that he may have been Valerius Virillio's teacher, who in turn trained Baebius Eucles. While it might be correct, the first speculation strips away by assumption any local legal community (however small), reducing genealogies to known individuals in Rome.

[64] From later-third-century Spain, there is the *iuris studiosus* P. Gabinius Firmanus from Guadix/Acci (near Granada) (ILPG 77 = Liebs (2002) #3).

[65] Folios 97–8, 98b–110 of Bibliothèque Municipale S 28 (24) + Bibliothèque Nationale de France, Nouvelles acquisitions latines 1629. For a codicological discussion, see Nelson (1981) 96–9, Rodríguez Martín (1998) 13–51, Ammirati (2015) 104. Rodríguez Martín (2013) has signalled that more text has been preserved and might be readable than has been previously thought.

[66] *FA* 1–10 (~ Gaius, *Inst.* 1.93–8); *FA* 11–22 (~ 1.124–9); *FA* 23–60 (~ 2.162–71); *FA* 61–78 (~ 2.247–71); *FA* 79–114 (~ 4.39–107).

[67] *CLA* 6.726; Nelson (1981), 103 by implication; Liebs (2002), 123.

[68] *CLA* 6.726; Ammirati (2015), 104; Nelson (1981), 99 dates the ms. to the fourth century, forging a stronger link between Eumenius and the *FA*.

fifth century. What can be said about the dating of the work? Nelson has argued persuasively that the text should be dated to the later third or early fourth century. As we will see further below, the text refers to distinctions between citizens and Latins in the past tense, which indicates that it dates after the Constitutio Antoniniana of 212. At the same time, the work places considerable emphasis on discussing *cretiones* (*FA* 23–60), which fell out of use by the early fourth century. Finally, the text preserves an extensive (though garbled) treatment of the law of actions (*FA* 79–114), which was abolished at the latest in 342.[69] This leaves us with a window stretching from 212 to the early fourth century.[70] In sum, the work clearly predates the manuscript; and since it was in all likelihood copied in Southern Gaul in the early fifth century, the text must have been available in Gaul before then, quite possibly for a considerable while already.[71]

With these considerations in place, it still remains a stretch to tie the *FA* to Autun's educational scene in the third century before the Tetrarchy. All the same, it is possible to show that the *FA* stand in a textbook tradition based on Gaius' *Institutes* that is attested for the West. To put it in other words, a good case can be made for the idea that earlier versions of Gaius adaptations circulated in the Western provinces. Our starting point here is the textual material in De Churruca's brilliant study of Gaius as a source of Isidore of Seville. By triangulating the textual evidence of Gaius and several adaptations of the *Institutes*, it is possible to obtain more clarity as to how these texts relate to one another.[72] The most important case is the following, where we can compare Gaius, the *FA*, the Ulpianic *Liber singularis Regularum* (*LSR*),[73] and Isidore (and his source):

Gai. *Inst.* 2.164
extraneis heredibus solet cretio dari, id est finis deliberandi, ut intra certum tempus vel adeant hereditatem vel, si non adeant, temporis fine summoveantur.

***FA* 59**
omnis cretio certum NUMERUM dierum *habet. nam testator cum* <dat> *cretionem non simpliciter dicit 'cernito', sed dicit 'cernito in diebus tot'.*

***LSR* 22.27–8**
cretio est certorum dierum *spatium,* ***quod*** *datur* ***instituto*** *heredi ad deliberandum, utrum expediat ei adire hereditatem nec ne, velut . . .*

[69] Nelson (1985) 15, with further references to Kaser (1971), 2.525; and Kaser (1966), 412, Kaser (1971), 2.21.

[70] As Liebs (2002), 123 points out, the claim at *FA* 34 that the family *sacra* used to be important to Romans in the past (*illo tempore*) is probably merely a paraphrase of Gaius' *fuit* at 2.55. On the other hand, reading it as a contrast with the *FA*'s here and now, Nelson (1985), 15 suggested the world of its author must have been predominantly Christian, favouring as late a date in our window as possible.

[71] The work's repeated pairing of the praetor and the provincial governor (e.g. *FA* 26, 33, 100) clearly include provincial readers among its projected audience. See Nelson (1985) 4.

[72] De Churruca (1975). See also Nelson (1981), 148–63.

[73] Following Gaius closely in structure and diction, this early-third-century work is usually taken to descend from Gaius' main source. See Nelson (1981) 80–96. But the matter is very much open to debate. The text survives independently under the heading *tituli ex corpore Ulpiani* in ms. Vaticanus latinus Reginensis 1128. Cited by the *Collatio* and the Digest as Ulpian's *Liber singularis regularum*, there is little reason to believe the text is not a genuine work of Ulpian.

Isidore, *Origines / Etymologiae* 5.24.15
cretio est certus dierum *NUMERUS*, ***in quo institutus*** *heres aut adit hereditatem, aut finito tempore cretionis excluditur*

This not the place for a full-scale philological analysis of these passages.[74] The most important point for the present purpose is that the *FA*, the *LSR*, and Isidore all feature variations of the *Institutes* text that have elements (of syntax and information) in common with each other against Gaius.[75] Since it is exceedingly unlikely that they came up with these same adaptations at the same place independently from each other, we must conclude that they either depend on a common source (or source tradition), or ultimately form a chain of direct dependency on each other. Given the considerable differences between the three later works, however, and given that there is no consistent pattern of connections between the individual works for other passages we can compare, positing a common source tradition is by far the most plausible explanation.[76]

The comparison of the *FA* with the *LSR* and Isidore thus offers a glimpse into an earlier layer of this textbook tradition. The works also suggest that this textbook tradition had a Western circulation. It is my contention that the *FA* can be seen as a reasonably accurate representative of the instructional texts that were used in Western educational settings, also those from before the moment the *FA* crystallized in the form in which they have survived. To be sure, I am not suggesting that we can conclude that the *FA* were used in specifically Autun in or even before the days of the Tetrarchy. Rather, I suggest that they give a good impression of the kind of legal instruction manuals that were used in the type of educational setting that Autun exemplifies.

4. LAW AND LEGAL PRACTICE IN GAUL: USING ROMAN LAW IN A PROVINCIAL SETTING

Questions may at this point certainly be raised about law in practice in Gaul in a rather general sense. After all, the presence of legal experts in the provinces, as we have seen attested in the epigraphic record, presupposes that there was need or demand for legal knowledge in the first place. Moreover, if the argument so far about the availability of legal instruction has any merit, it only strengthens the idea that there was considerable demand for legal services. This section surveys the evidence for the use of law in Gaul in order to provide the cultural background against which to read the *FA*. In line with the aims of the volume, the discussion pays attention in particular to questions about Roman law versus local law, and about continuities and changes around the Constitutio Antoniniana. Since it is my

[74] For a full discussion, see De Churruca (1975), 125–34.

[75] I note that the *FA* and *Isidore* have an additional element in common (*numerus*), as do the *LSR* and Isidore (relative clause, perfect participle). The ramifications of these observations fall beyond the scope of this chapter.

[76] Similarly, Isidore's *Differentiae* 1.430 goes back to Gaius, *Inst.* 4.83–4 but has adaptations in common with *FA* 91–3. See De Churruca (1975), 112–13.

aim here to contextualize legal teaching as represented by the *FA*, I focus primarily on material pertaining to private law.[77]

That being said, the first thing to note is that the record has preserved very little material that is specific enough to address these questions in detail. Julius Caesar famously mentioned that the inhabitants of Gaul's three *partes* 'differ from each other in language, customs, and laws' (*lingua, institutis, legibus inter se differunt*, Caesar, *Bellum Gallicum* 1.1). But it remains unclear what those laws exactly entailed. The Celtic inscriptions from Gaul have also not been able to clarify much detail here.[78] Similarly, the Roman jurists report in general that *civitates* without Roman citizenship kept their own laws, but the few concrete examples given do not include mention of non-Roman laws from Gaul.[79]

There is better evidence for the use of Roman law in early Imperial Gaul. The most important source material comes from writing tablets that have been found individually as well as in hoards across France, Switzerland, the Rhine area, and the Netherlands.[80] These tablets appear to create a similar picture of trade and transactions at the individual level as the British and the Danubian tablets do, although the Gallic record has preserved a very low proportion of texts that are legible beyond single words and names.[81] Overall, however, the tablets point to a fairly vibrant legal life.[82] An illuminating case is a tablet from Tolsum, Frisia from the year 29 CE that records a loan given by a slave of one Iulia (?) Secunda.[83] Formerly thought to preserve the sale of an ox, the text is interesting because it hints at the manoeuvring space in economic life that Roman law allowed to slaves.[84] In addition, a bronze tablet from Nijmegen contains part of a contract (102 CE), while a wooden tablet from Hanau mentions a loan of 200 denarii received at Mainz.[85] Among the hundreds of wooden tablets from Vindonissa, a military settlement on the north-western side of the Alps, we find the remains of a loan statement that includes the language of *stipulationes* (90 CE), as well as part of a contract signed by witnesses with Roman names (94 CE). A fragmentary tablet mentioning a wine-seller points to a transregional trading network.[86]

[77] For a discussion of the municipal laws of the West, see the chapter by Eck (this volume).

[78] Collected in the series *Recueil des Inscriptions Gauloises* (4 vols.).

[79] e.g. Gaius, *Inst.* 1.92; Ulpian *LSR* 20.14. For juristic comments on Gallic varieties of Roman law, see below.

[80] I am leaving out CIL 12.4036 = CLE 1112 from Nîmes in legalese, because it appears to have a connection with the jurist Cervidius Scaevola rather than (exclusively) with local legal communities. See Champlin (1987).

[81] On the rich British and Danubian material, see the chapters of Du Plessis and Eckhardt (this volume). In terms of source material, the major point of reference for tablets with legal writing are the archives found in Pompeii and Herculaneum. Meyer (2004) provides a major general discussion of writing tablets and law.

[82] Hartmann (2015) is an extremely helpful recent inventory of (published and unpublished) wooden writing tablets from the Roman world. According to this overview, the number of (mostly extremely fragmentary) tablets from Gaul is in the order of one thousand. Of course, not all of them are legal. Essential is also Meyer (2004), 177.

[83] See Bowman, Tomlin, and Worp (2009). For a discussion of some of the legal aspects of this tablet, see Zwalve (2009), who suggests that it need not have been drawn up in Frisia but may have found its way there as part of someone's personal archive or even as a commodified promissory note or IOU.

[84] See for example Johnston (1999), 77–111.

[85] AE 2000.1015 (Nijmegen tablet); AE 1999.1169 (Hanau).

[86] See Speidel (1996) #3, #4, and #47. Speidel suggest the otherwise lost letter of a certain Comus in Trier to Micus in Vindonissa may have had to with trade as well (#48).

The Vindolanda tablets seem to indicate that this type of trade was bound to involve a considerable amount of legal documentation.[87] Perhaps the sum of money mentioned in the tablet from Oedenburg-Biesheim was part of a similar type of document.[88] Furthermore, a cache of about 200 tablets from the reigns of Claudius and the Flavians has been found in Cologne. Remaining as yet unpublished, it has been reported repeatedly that many of them are legal documents.[89] Some of the completely illegible tablets in triptych format are also likely to have been legal documents, since this was the required format for legal transactions from mid-first century.[90] Among these are tablets from Valkenburg (40–69 CE), Oberwinterthur (first century), and several of the undeciphered tablets from Saintes near Bordeaux (first century).[91]

A tablet from Arae Flaviae (modern Rottweil), a *municipium* in Germania Superior, offers a particularly fascinating glimpse of legal life in the Gallic lands. Dated to 186 CE, the tablet records part of a court proceeding over a complicated dispute involving money, perhaps an inheritance. As far as we can see, the text follows the principles of Roman law:[92]

2 [- - - - - - - - - - - - - - - - - -]*entos ex condemnatione Iuventi Caesiani*
3 [*legati felicissimi Augusti l*]*egionis\octavae/Augustae piae fide legatos Secundio Secundi*
4 [*filio?* - - - - - - - - - - - - - -] . *Prifernio Victorino denarios quingentos faeneratos*
5 [- - - - - - - - - - - - - - - - - -] *ntos sebtuaginta sex denarios reliquos*
6 [- - - - - - - - - - - - - - - - - -]. *sescentos sebtuaginta tres creditos denarios*
7 [- - - - - - - - - - - - - - - - - -] - - - - - -. . *ẹ ṇ . ụ . d i. . a r. du . . . s. . ị vindicaret*
8 [- - - - - - - - - - - - - - - - - -] . *ni traderet in quam rem pari examine*
9 [- - - - - - - - - - - - - - - - - -] *actum municipio Aris pridie Nonas Augustas*

(. . .) on the basis of a verdict by Iuventius Caesianus, the most felicitous Emperor's legate of the eighth legion 'Augustaa', faithful and loyal left (?) to Secundius the son? of Secundus (. . .) to Prifernius Victorinus five hundred denarii lent on interest (. . .) and seventy-six remaining (. . .) six hundred seventy-three denarii due (. . .) ? claimed through *vindicatio* (. . .) handed over for which thing (?) through a similar investigation (. . .) passed at the *municipium* Arae Flaviae on 4 August (*followed by consular date of 186* CE)

It is not clear from the text who exactly pronounced a decision in this dispute. The subscription indicates that the ruling was probably given in Arae Flaviae, but line 2 mentions a *condemnatio*, probably an earlier case decision,[93] by Iuventius Caesianus, legate of the eighth legion that was stationed in Argentorate

[87] Du Plessis (this volume).

[88] Hartmann (2015) #36, unpublished. No precise date is given for this tablet.

[89] Hartmann (2015) #14, with further references.

[90] Suetonius, *Nero* 17; see Meyer (2004), 27.

[91] Hartmann (2015) #57 (Valkenburg); #61 (Oberwinterhur); Vienne (1992), 215–6 (Saintes).

[92] See Wilmanns (1981), whose text I follow (= AE 1981.0691). Earlier editions diverge substantially at various points. The text quoted above is not the entire text.

[93] This interpretation is compellingly argued for by Wilmanns (1981), 46–9, who points out that the genitive should be taken as a subjective genitive on the basis of (1) parallels in juristic texts from the *Digest* and (2) the legal difficulty of getting a legate convicted in the camp.

(Strasbourg). The tablet thus shows not only that military legates could be actively involved in dispensing justice; it also indicates that they may have kept an archive with case decisions for future reference. It is hard to say anything with certainty about the source of their knowledge of Roman law when making a judgment such as this one. Perhaps they simply relied on memory (of some basic instruction in the past), perhaps on books or documentary models,[94] or perhaps an advisor. Similarly, we may wonder whether the litigating parties made any claims based on legal arguments, and whether they would rely on advisors and/or advocates in such cases. The *causidicus* L. Sextius Pervvincus attested in Mainz indicates that this latter scenario is not impossible.[95]

The remnants of two summonses that have recently been identified also point to the occurrence of legal conflict in Gaul. The one is a *vadimonium* found in Tricasses (Troyes) and dating to 60–90 CE. Nothing of the contents survives, but the index on the outside tells us that the tablet contained a *vadimonium* of a woman called Nerta, whose Celtic (single) name suggests that she was not a Roman citizen.[96] The other summons is a *litis denuntiatio* on a *terra nigra* ceramic sherd from Mainz, dating to the early 120s CE. The text is very fragmentary and preserves no information about the dispute. But since the writing was inscribed before the clay was baked, it is not unreasonable to suggest that the production facility of *terra nigra* ware was one of the parties. It is very likely that in this case we are dealing with a business dispute.[97]

The material reviewed above is thin but nonetheless gives the impression that legal transactions were carried out in many places, much like what can be seen for Britain and the Danubian provinces. Needless to say, many of the Gallic tablets were found in places where there was a presence of the Roman army, which means inevitably that we are witnessing individuals who imported habits and practices from other parts. Yet since several tablets also appear to involve primarily civilians, for example traders in the Rhine area, it would be too simplistic and monogenetic to conclude that the use of Roman law in Early Imperial Gaul is a transplant that should be located primarily in the military camps. Given economic activities and the concomitant unavoidable risk of disputes and litigation, there must have been a demand for people with some legal know-how to help draft contracts and advise in case of legal confrontations. To put it differently, the tablets in general indicate the availability of people capable of drawing up

[94] The so-called *Formula Baetica* (1st–2nd cent.), preserved on bronze, may have served as a formulaic model.

[95] Two more tentative pieces of evidence encourage us to see forensic lawyers in more Gallic towns. First, we have already met the *scholasticus* C. Rutilius Primus in IKöln² #438. For some of the problems here, see above. Second, a curse tablet from Aumagne (Western France) curses an opponent and his *advocati* in a lawsuit (*litis*) (ILA (Santons) #104). While curse tablets are not straightforward evidence for historical events, we should note that the text imagines as its occasion a lawsuit in Roman terms—which it may very well have been.

[96] Frei-Stolba, Hartmann and Roms (2016), 149–54. The dating of the tablet depends on the excavation's stratigraphy. On a peregrine being involved with Roman law, compare the evidence for Britain and Noricum in the chapters of Du Plessis and Eckhardt (this volume).

[97] On this inscription (as well as the scholarship on the history of the *litis denuntiatio*), see first and foremost the excellent discussion by Haensch (2017). The dating of the inscription depends on a prosopographical identification of a legionary commander mentioned in the text.

documents in line with Roman practices; and evidence such as the tablet from Arae Flaviae and several inscriptions suggests that there were individuals one could turn to for help in case of a dispute. This in turn raises questions about how and where these people were trained.

The presently known Gallic writing tablets are too damaged to obtain a good impression of the extent to which people in Gaul used Roman law in its 'pure' form (i.e. as known to us from the Roman jurists). The chapters on Roman Britain and the Danubian provinces show clearly that inhabitants of these regions were exposed to Roman law and that they appropriated legal instruments to suit their local and immediate circumstances. The record for these provinces provides several cases in which the 'living law', or the law as used 'on the ground', clearly drew on Roman legal forms but put them to use in ways that are unorthodox from a textbook perspective. There is no good reason to assume that the situation was very different in Gaul, yet I have found it hard to track down clear illustrations in the available epigraphical material.[98] For this reason, an attempt at charting living Roman law in Gaul will for now largely have to confine itself to the remarks made by the jurists about the peculiarities of law in the provinces.[99] For starters, the jurists are very well aware that the application of law is closely related to customary practices, and that customs differ from place to place and from one region to the next. To mention one example, Ulpian states that a guardian may owe interest payments to his ward in certain cases, clarifying that the specific cases in which such interest is due depend 'on the customary practice of the province' (*secundum morem provinciae*, Ulpian, *On the edict* 35 (*D*.26.7.7.10)). Apparently, then, different provinces have different legal regimes. But this is not all. Ulpian continues by mentioning that interest rates themselves may differ from province to province as well. More examples can be added.[100] It should be noted that the surviving works of the jurists tend to mention provincial practice in general terms. We hear very little about which customary, and ultimately legal, practices are specific to which particular area.

About the peculiarities of Roman law in Gaul, we nonetheless find two short but revealing juristic comments. Writing in the earlier third century, Ulpian mentions in the context of dowries that the goods a woman brings along to the house of her husband in addition to her dowry are called (and hence possibly considered) *peculium* in Gaul (Ulpian, *On Sabinus* 31 (*D*. 23.3.9.3)). On a more orthodox understanding of Roman law, a *peculium* was the allowance available to people in power, typically sons and slaves, while wives by this time were usually not in the power of their husbands.[101] Secondly, there is a reference to *ius Gallicum* in the work known as *Pauli Sententiae*, a legal textbook that was perhaps compiled in the Tetrarchic period and that might be a reworking of material from

[98] Note again that the *vadimonium* of Nerta may involve a peregrine woman.

[99] On notions of (Roman) law in the provinces and of provincial (Roman) law, see first and foremost the Introduction to this volume. See also the foundational discussion of Galsterer (1986).

[100] For instance, Gaius in his *Commentary on the Provincial Edict* mentions that a person who sells a farm needs to be apprehensive about *evictio* 'according to the customary practice of that region' (*ex consuetudine eius regionis*, Gaius, *On the provincial edict* 10 (*D*. 21.2.6)). The region remains unspecified in the fragment.

[101] See for example Johnston (1999), 32–6.

Ulpian's contemporary Paul.[102] The fragment briefly states that, *iure Gallico*, legitimate heirs have one hundred days to accede to an inheritance before forfeiting it.[103] Other sources indicate that the period for coming to a decision may have allowed more flexibility, although a limit was set at the behest of the praetor.[104] In sum, then, even though much remains completely opaque, these remarks[105] point to a perception, if not an awareness, by the jurists that Roman law as used in Gaul had its idiosyncrasies, and that these could be called Gallic.[106]

Together, the scant evidence from the tablets and the jurists indicate strongly that there was an active legal life in early Imperial Gaul, which must have come with a considerable demand for people with legal training.[107]

5. LAW AND LEGAL EDUCATION IN GAUL: QUESTIONS OF ROMANIZATION

With the discussion above in place, we need to consider at last what the *FA* themselves tell us about law and legal education. What sort of view of the legal world does the text project to its provincial audience?[108]

In exploring these questions, it is helpful to compare the text to Gaius' *Institutes*, since the *FA* follow Gaius closely but clearly position themselves in a world after the Constitutio Antoniniana.[109] A striking difference between the two works is that, while Gaius shows considerable interest in the customs and habits of non-Roman people, the *FA* have an extremely Romano-centric worldview. In a famous passage, Gaius explains that the Roman *tutela* of women exists in similar but far from identical ways in peregrine legal systems (apud peregrinos), which are said to put women *quasi in tutela*. He then supports this claim by citing a *lex Bithynorum* (1.193). When discussing the *patria potestas*, Gaius claims that this institution

[102] The transmission and early history of *Pauli Sententiae* are extremely complicated and controversial, and the bibliography is enormous. See Liebs (2005) for a starting point.

[103] Preserved at *ALRW* 1.7 (this text is *Appendix I* to the *Lex Romana Visigothorum*). Krüger in his edn. considers this entire excerpt a later interpolation into *PS* 4.8.19, without further arguments. Gaudemet (1965) 19 sees no problem with taking it as authentic.

[104] Gaius, *Inst.* 2.170.

[105] The examples mentioned by Jullian (1924) 278 fn. 3 do, in my view, ultimately not point to the same type of peculiarities.

[106] Note that this aggregate perspective of the jurists gives a much more monolithic idea of a provincial variety of Roman law than do the individual tablets for Britain and the Danubian lands. Thus, while highlighting trends as perceived by expert contemporaries, it nonetheless offers only a very partial view of law 'on the ground' in imperial Gaul.

[107] A further set of evidence is formed by imperial rescripts that were issued in Gaul. While the officials drafting the rescripts may simply have been passing through Gaul, the petitioners (and their advisors and scribes) presumably tended to be from the region. I have only been able to locate two rescripts predating the year 300 in Gaul with certainty: one of Diocletian to Boncius Secundus, Mainz, June 286 (*Fr. Vat.* 271) and one of Diocletian to Ulpia Rufina, Reims, February 290 (*Fr. Vat.* 315). Note, however, that rescripts from emperors before Diocletian tend not to record their place of issuing (see the *CJ*).

[108] As mentioned above, the *FA* repeatedly refer to the praetor and the provincial governor together (e.g. *FA* 26, 33, 100).

[109] Given that the *FA* contain several lemmas taken from Gaius, it is in fact very plausible that the *FA* and Gaius were used jointly in teaching sessions. However, the text of the *FA* appears in general clear enough to function on its own as well.

amounts to something uniquely Roman. No other peoples allow any such power over sons, we hear, with the possible exception of the Galatians (1.55). In the third book, readers are told that non-Roman *civitates* may have different understandings of when an obligation on the basis of an oath is binding (3.96).[110] In addition to furnishing this comparative perspective, it is remarkable that Gaius does not give his readers the impression that he finds Roman law superior to non-Roman law. While usually posing as a neutral observer, in the case of the *tutela* for women he in fact criticizes the Romans for requiring this to begin with, because 'no good reason' has ever been given for it (*fere nulla pretiosa ratio*, 1.190).

The *FA* offer no such outward looking perspective. The surviving text locates its readers in a world that is entirely Roman. The rare references to people without Roman citizenship are consistently in the imperfect tense (e.g. *FA* 6–8).[111] This includes the antiquarian digression about those who before Caracalla's citizenship law had the *ius Latii*. After setting out briefly along the lines of Gaius that peregrines were able to ask for the *ius Latii*, the work adds an aetiology that is not in Gaius but that highlights the author's complete focus on Rome:[112]

> *cum enim [ex La]tio origo civium Romanorum duceretur, ideo ius Latii [dict]um est ius civitatis Romanae.* (*FA* 6)
>
> for since the origin of the Roman citizens is derived from Latium, therefore the law of the Roman state is called the *ius Latii*.

It has been pointed out repeatedly that this claim is not accurate in light of mainstream ancient accounts of Rome's earliest history.[113] But instead of concluding that the author was incompetent, we should note that the account of how Rome in its earliest phase appropriated and became synonymous with Latium reveals at core a deeply imperial conception of Rome and its entire history. This is further underscored by the immediately following sentence, stating (more accurately) that the *populus* and the emperor could bestow the *ius Latii* on a *civitas*. The text thus rewrites the history of the *ius Latii* in a way that reflects a more or less completely Roman world. Although we have very little evidence, this may reflect a trend in the discourse about the remote Roman past as it developed over the course of the imperial period. Thus the *Origo gentis Romanae*, probably a fourth-century work incorporating older material, sketches the history of the Roman people before Romulus (*praef.*). In the process of describing the oldest inhabitants of Italy, the text quotes Vergil's *Aeneid* 8.321–3 in order to claim that Saturn gave them laws and called them Latins (3.3). While the *Origo* does not explicitly equate Latins and Romans at this point, the proximity of the preface with its emphasis on the Roman people is clearly suggestive, especially in the absence of any further articulation of how Latins and Roman relate.[114] In sum, the *FA* appear to fit in a thought world that is increasingly more Romano-centric. There is little to no

[110] Further examples at 1.197, 2.40.

[111] It is true that *FA* 4 uses a variety of tenses, but this section is framed as a question-and-answer interaction rather than direct instruction by an authoritative lecturer.

[112] Letters in brackets are supplements (not deletions) in the editions of Krüger' and FIRA.

[113] Rodríguez Martín (1998), 128–9; Liebs (1987), 144–50.

[114] Similarly, Liebs (1987), 144–50, pointing to Vergil's importance in ancient education.

consideration for any outside perspective.[115] Finally, while the work presumes to absorb its audience in this fully Roman world, the surviving text as far as we can see does not show awareness that some of its teachings may have been considered peculiar and provincial by observers such as Ulpian and (pseudo-)Paul.

Another aspect of the *FA* as evidence is their focus on private law. Like the texts of the jurists, but unlike much of the famous epigraphic evidence from the Western provinces, the *FA* provide a valuable insight in a tradition of private law (and instruction therein) in the West. The work's surviving parts go to great lengths to explain legal topics such as claiming inheritances, with potentially large consequences for people's assets and wealth. For example, the explanation about the *restitutio in integrum* for individuals under 25 and that about *cretiones* have been expanded considerably as compared to the original passage in Gaius (*FA* 26–34 ~ Gaius, *Inst.* 2.163; *FA* 35–60 ~ Gaius, *Inst.* 2.164–171).[116] This interest in private law is a salutary reminder that the use of law at the individual level was often tied to property-related matters, which in turn suggests that those involved in legal issues were people with a certain amount of property. For all we know, this is also the class of people from which the relatively well-to-do audiences of the schools for higher education came. Legal instruction on the basis of texts such as the *FA* thus in effect prepared students to guard and negotiate their own interests (and those of their allies and dependents) within this social segment. Moreover, considering the conception of the Roman world that emerges from reading the work, the *FA* not simply provide their audience with knowledge of Roman law. They importantly also offer the kind of cultural currency that prepares their audience to join the Romanized elite, for example to serve as forensic orators, like the *causidicus* of Mainz or the students of the author of *Panegyric* 6, or to secure position in the imperial administration in the way Eumenius and the sixth panegyrist and his entourage did. This Romanizing agenda is in line with what Tacitus in the *Agricola* says about Agricola's reasons for setting up schools in Britain.[117]

6. CONCLUSION

The aim of this chapter has been to explore the volume's theme about law in the Roman provinces by surveying the evidence for a legal culture in Roman Gaul and by addressing questions about the development and transmission of that culture through education. I have presented a model of legal education that pairs basic instruction in law with the training offered in the rhetorical schools of the

[115] As far as we can see, digressions in the *FA* usually elucidate Roman practices, such as the family *sacra* and noxal surrender. It has also been suggested that the poorly informed discussion of the *actiones* indicates that the author was unfamiliar with them, probably because they had fallen mostly out of use in the area where he was working (Liebs (1987), 144–50).

[116] While at least partly an accident of survival, the next more or less continuous stretch of text (*FA* 61–78) still deals with the law of succession. The final stretch (*FA* 79–114) treats the law of actions, regularly bringing up property and damage suits.

[117] cf. Eumenius (*Pan. Lat.* 9) 19.4, 8.2.

Roman empire.[118] As I hope to have shown, there is much evidence that points in the direction of the availability of legal instruction, in one form or another, in pre-Tetrarchic Gaul, although much of the material is at the end of the day indirect evidence. Rather than summarizing the entire chapter once more, I would like to finish with the following two observations.

In the first place, one of the underlying agendas of this chapter has been to explore conceptually the ways in which we can study Roman legal education without the ultimately rather limiting idea that this happened only in law schools. Given the limitations of our evidence, it will remain a crux to form a good impression of the well-attested law schools in the first place. But even if conceptual clarity (and consensus) were possible about what exactly an ancient Roman law school amounted to, I hope to have made it clear that there is good reason not to export the notion to wherever a legal text or a *magister iuris* happens to be attested.[119] The other side of the coin is that we also need to consider carefully what we mean when we use the convenient shorthand term 'rhetorical school'.

Secondly, I have primarily explored an idea, a model. As a consequence, I have mostly focused on the dimension of continuity. On the present evidence, however, it will be a challenge to trace differences from place to place or chart the evolution over time before the Late Antique period. We will have to see what new discoveries bring.

REFERENCES

Adams, J. N. 2003. *Bilingualism and the Latin Language*. Cambridge.

Alonso, J. L. 2016. Juristic Papyrology and Roman Law. In: P.J. du Plessis, C. Ando, and K. Tuori (eds.). *The Oxford Handbook of Roman Law and Society*. Oxford, pp. 56–69.

Ammirati, S. 2015. *Sul libro latino antico. Ricerche bibliologiche e paleografiche*. Pisa–Rome.

Bowman, A., R. Tomlin, and K. Worp 2009. *Emptio Bovis Frisica*: the 'Frisian Ox Sale' Reconsidered. *Journal of Roman Studies* 99, pp. 156–70.

Bucking, S. 2007. On the Training of Documentary Scribes in Roman, Byzantine, and Early Islamic Egypt: A Contextualized Assessment of the Greek Evidence. *Zeitschrift für Papyrologie und Epigraphik* 159, pp. 229–47.

Cannata, C. A. 1963. Sull'origine dei 'Fragmenta Augustodunensia'. *Studia et Documenta Historiae Iuris* 29, pp. 238–52.

Champlin, E. 1987. Miscellanea Testamentaria. *Zeitschrift für Papyrologie und Epigraphik* 69, pp. 197–206.

Christol, M. (2010). *Une histoire provinciale. La Gaule narbonnaise de la fin du IIe siècle av. J.-C. au IIIe siècle ap. J.-C. Scripta varia*. Paris.

Collinet, P. 1925. *Histoire de l'école de droit de Beyrouth*. Paris.

Cribiore, R. 2001. *Gymnastics of the Mind. Greek Education in Hellenistic and Roman Egypt*. Princeton.

De Churruca, J. 1975. *Las instituciones de Gayo en San Isidoro de Sevilla*. Bilbao.

Dickey, E. A. 2012. *The Colloquia of the Hermeneumata Pseudodositheana. Volume 1*. Cambridge.

[118] I reiterate that apprenticeships, probably also away from the rhetorical schools, may have played a major role in the training of scribes specialised in drawing up legal documentation.

[119] e.g. in CIL 8.12418 (near Tunis, 2nd–4th cent.); in CIL 3.8822 (Salona, near Split, 3rd–4th cent.).

Dickey, E. A. 2016. *Learning Latin the Ancient Way: Latin Textbooks from the Ancient World*. Cambridge.

Frei-Stolba, R., B. Hartmann, and C. Roms (2016). *Vadimonium Nertae*. Zum römischen Privatrecht in den gallischen Provinzen. *Tyche* 31, pp. 149–55.

Frier, B. W. 1983. Bees and Lawyers. *Classical Journal* 78, pp. 105–14.

Galsterer, H. 1986. Roman Law in the Provinces: Some Problems of Transmission. In: M. Crawford (ed.). *L'impero romano e le strutture economiche e sociali delle province romane*. Como, pp. 13–27.

Gaudemet, J. 1965. *Le Bréviaire d'Alaric et les Epitome*. Milan.

Gleason, M. W. 1995. *Making Men: Sophists and Self-Presentation in Ancient Rome*. Princeton.

Goffaux, B. 2010. Scholae et espace civique à Avenches. *Bulletin de l'association Pro Aventico* 52, pp. 7–26.

Haarhoff, T. J. 1958. *Schools of Gaul. A Study of Pagan and Christian Education in the Last Century of the Western Empire*. Second edition. Johannesburg.

Haensch, R. (2017). Cui bono? Die Funktion der in Mainz gefundenen Schüssel mit der Nennung des pr(a)etorium Poblici Marcelli. In: U. Babusiaux, P. Nobel, and J. Platscheck (eds.), *Der Bürge einst und jetzt. Festschrift für Alfons Bürge*. Zurich, pp. 455–66.

Harries, J. D. 2016. Legal Education and Training of Lawyers. In: C. Ando, P. du Plessis, and K. Tuori (eds.), *The Oxford Handbook of Roman Law and Society*. Oxford, pp. 151–63.

Hartmann, B. 2015. Die Hölzernen Schreibtafeln im Imperium Romanum—ein Inventar. In: M. Scholz and M. Horster (eds.). *Lesen und Schreiben in den römischen Provinzen. Schriftliche Kommunikation im Alltagsleben*. Mainz, pp. 43–58.

Hingley, R. 2010. Cultural Diversity and Unity: Empire and Rome. In: S. Hales and T. Hodos (eds.). *Material Culture and Social Identities in the Ancient World*. Cambridge–New York, pp. 54–75.

Honoré, T. 1987. Scriptor Historiae Augustae. *Journal of Roman Studies* 77, pp. 156–76.

Johnston, A. C. 2017. *The Sons of Remus. Identity in Roman Gaul and Spain*. Cambridge Mass.

Johnston, D. 1999. *Roman Law in Context*. Cambridge.

Jullian, C. 1924. *Histoire de la Gaule*. Third edition. Paris.

Kaser, M. 1966. *Das römische Zivilprozessrecht*. Munich.

Kaser, M. 1971. *Das römische Privatrecht*. Second edition. Munich.

Kaster, R. A. 1988. *Guardians of Language. The Grammarian and Society in Late Antiquity*. Berkeley.

Keenan, J. G., J. G. Manning, and U. Yiftach-Firanko (eds.) (2014). *Law and Legal Practice in Egypt from Alexander to the Arab Conquest. A Selection of Papyrological Sources in Translation, with Introductions and Commentary*. Cambridge.

Kübler, B. 1914. Rechtsschulen. *RE* I.A1, pp. 380–94.

La Bua, G. 2010. Patronage and Education in Third-Century Gaul: Eumenius' Panegyric for the Restoration of the Schools. *Journal of Late Antiquity* 3.2, pp. 300–15.

Leeman, A. D. and Pinkster, H. 1981. *Cicero. De Oratore libri III. Buch 1, 1–165*. Heidelberg.

Leesen, T. 2010. *Gaius Meets Cicero. Law and Rhetoric in the School Controversies*. Leiden.

Lehne-Gstreinthaler, C. 2016. 'Jurists in the Shadows'. The Everyday Business of the Jurists of Cicero's Time. In: P. du Plessis (ed.). *Cicero's Law. Rethinking Roman Law of the Late Republic*. Edinburgh, pp. 88–99.

Liebs, D. 1976. Rechtsschulen und Rechtunterricht im Prinzipat. *ANRW* II.15, pp. 197–286.

Liebs, D. 1987. *Die Jurisprudenz im spätantiken Italien*. Berlin.

Liebs, D. 2002. *Römische Jurisprudenz in Gallien (2. bis 8. Jahrhundert)*. Berlin.

Liebs, D. 2005. *Römische Jurisprudenz in Africa: mit Studien zu den pseudopaulinischen Sentenzen*. Second edition. Berlin.

Mantovani, D. 2007. I giuristi, il retore e le api. Ius controversum e natura nella Declamatio maior XIII. In: D. Mantovani and A. Schiavone (eds.), *Testi e problemi del giusnaturalismo romano*. Pavia, pp. 323–85.

Meyer, E. A. 2004. *Legitimacy and Law in the Roman World: Tabulae in Roman Belief and Practice*. Cambridge.

Morgan, T. 1998. *Literate Education in the Hellenistic and Roman Worlds*. Cambridge.

Mullen, A. 2013. *Southern Gaul and the Mediterranean: Multilingualism and Multiple Identities in the Iron Age and Roman Periods*. Cambridge.

Nelson, H. L. W. 1981. *Überlieferung, Aufbau und Stil von Gai Institutiones*. Leiden.

Nelson, H. L. W. 1985. Das Fragment über die cretio in der Autuner Gaiusparaphrase. *Subseciva Groningana* 2, pp. 1–20.

Nixon, C. E. V. and Saylor Rodgers, B. 1994. *In Praise of Later Roman Emperors: The Panegyrici Latini*. Berkeley.

Rebourg, A. 1998. L'urbanisme d'*Augustodunum* (Autun, Saône-et-Loire). *Gallia* 55, pp. 141–236.

Riggsby, A. 2015. Roman Legal Education. In: W.M. Bloomer (ed.), *A Companion to Ancient Education*. Chichester, pp. 444–51.

Rodríguez Martín, J.-D. 1998. *Fragmenta Augustodunensia*. Granada.

Rodríguez Martín, J.-D. 2013. Neu entdeckte Schriftspuren im Palimpsest des Gaius von Autun. *Zeitschrift der Savigny-Stiftung für Rechtsgeschichte. Romanistische Abteilung* 130, pp. 478–87.

Roselaar, S. T. 2016. Local Administration. In: C. Ando, P. du Plessis, and K. Tuori (eds.), *The Oxford Handbook of Roman Law and Society*. Oxford, pp. 124–36.

Scappaticcio, M. C. 2016. *Artes grammaticae in frammenti. I testi grammaticali latini e bilingui greco-latini su papiro*. Berlin.

Sivan, H. 1993. *Ausonius of Bordeaux: Genesis of a Gallic Aristocracy*. London–New York.

Speidel, M. A. 1996. *Die römischen Schreibtafeln von Vindonissa. Veröffentlichungen der Gesellschaft Pro Vindonissa* (12). Brugg.

Vienne, G. 1992. Les tablettes à écrire conservées au musée archéologique de Saintes. In: E. Lalou (ed.), *Les tablettes à écrire de l'antiquité à l'époque moderne*. Turnhout, pp. 211–20.

Wibier, M. H. 2016. Cicero's Reception in the Juristic Tradition of the Early Empire'. In: P. du Plessis (ed.), *Cicero's Law. Rethinking Roman Law of the Late Republic*. Edinburgh, pp. 100–22.

Wilmanns, J. C. 1981. Die Doppelurkunde von Rottweil und ihr Beitrag zum Städtewesen in Obergermanien. *Epigraphische Studien* 12, pp. 1–182.

Woodman, A. J., with Kraus, C. S. 2014. *Tacitus. Agricola*. Cambridge.

Woolf, G. 1998. *Becoming Roman. The Origins of Provincial Organization in Gaul*. Cambridge.

Zwalve, W. J. 2009. Exit Bos Frisica, The Tolsum Tablet and Roman Law. *Tijdschrift voor Rechtsgeschiedenis* 77: 3–4, pp. 355–66.

23

Perspectives*

Giovanna D. Merola

Much more could be said about the application of Roman law in the provinces. The debate about the relationship between Roman law and local laws, which has been going on for more than a century,[1] is neither concluded nor solved; it has simply changed perspective.

The overcoming of an exclusively Romano-centric view has affected all areas of classical research. It has also encouraged us to look at 'law in the Roman provinces' rather than 'Roman law in the provinces', and to focus on juridical practice rather than its theoretical elaboration. Such a line of research is undoubtedly favoured by a growing body of evidence: while the literary sources (not just the legal texts) generally give us the image of Roman law as it should have been, and inscriptions tend to reproduce what was supposed to be communicated to the populace or passed on to future generations, it is the papyri, parchments, and wax tablets that bring us closest to the local reality, to the actual application of law and even its distortions.[2]

It is certainly indicative that almost all contributions to the volume are centred on texts transmitted through epigraphical or papyrological channels. In fact, the documentary sources supply us with a wealth of information that is constantly growing, thanks to the discovery of new texts, to the publication of unpublished documents, and to new readings and new editions of those that had previously been misunderstood.[3] It is an enormous and varied documentation, extraordinarily

* This chapter is translated from the Italian by Benedikt Eckhardt.

[1] Initiated by the work of Mitteis (1891). Cf. Amelotti (1999); Mazza (2010).

[2] However, we should not underestimate the large body of legal literature transmitted through papyri and parchments, which is of fundamental importance for understanding the circulation of juristic treatises in the provinces. Since 2014, the project REDHIS 'Rediscovering the hidden structure. A new appreciation of juristic texts and patterns of thought in late antiquity', directed by Professor D. Mantovani and funded by the European Research Council, is occupied with collecting and editing the works of the classical jurists that have survived outside the manuscript tradition (http://redhis.unipv.it); cf. Ammirati (2019). Since 2015, the project PLATINUM (Papyri and LAtin Texts: INsights and Updated Methodologies. Towards a philological, literary, and historical approach to Latin papyri), directed by Professor M. C. Scappaticcio and again funded by the European Research Council (https://platinum-erc.it), continues the study and publication of Latin texts preserved on papyrus, parchment, wax tablets and ostraca, a considerable number of which are legal documents; cf. Scappaticcio (2019).

[3] See the interesting panorama offered by Migliardi Zingale (1999).

Giovanna D. Merola, *Perspectives* In: *Law in the Roman Provinces.* Edited by: Kimberley Czajkowski and Benedikt Eckhardt in collaboration with Meret Strothmann, Oxford University Press (2020). © Oxford University Press.
DOI: 10.1093/oso/9780198844082.003.0023

interesting and equally complex; a good knowledge of its historical context and geographical origins is needed to make correct, scholarly use of it.[4] For these and other reasons, it is the 'series' of documents rather than the individual text that can prove to be truly revealing.

The 'legal reality of everyday life' is the sphere in which the studies can make the most progress: it is indeed in this area that the contribution of new sources can most significantly supplement or alter our knowledge. However, the attention directed to the specifics of local realities cannot and should not imply that we abandon attempts to reconstruct a general framework of law in the provinces. It is certainly a complex enterprise, taking into account the well-known differences between East and West, between Romanized territories and those that were more recently conquered, but also the legal heterogeneity that is attested even within one and the same province. Still, alongside the peculiarity of individual contexts, some scholarly effort must also be dedicated to gathering the common elements that unite different geographical areas, to identifying common rules and prevailing tendencies, and to distinguishing between what Roman authorities imposed from above and what individuals or local communities requested from their Roman representatives. To reach a result like that, we need, as noted above, a correct historico-juridical evaluation of the documentary sources, but we also need to keep paying attention to the sources transmitted via the literary channels. As recent studies have demonstrated, even the best known and most discussed sources transmitted through manuscripts, be they of a technical or non-technical nature, can be read anew and interpreted differently—not least (but not exclusively) thanks to the contribution of epigraphical and papyrological texts. It is only when we engage with all types of testimonies, being well aware of their respective genesis, that we can assess how profoundly Roman law pervaded the provincial reality and, at the same time, what influence pre-Roman regulations exerted on the evolution of Roman law.

In this regard, the watershed that has always been upheld in historiography on the subject is the emergence of the *Constitutio Antoniniana*:[5] the grant of Roman citizenship should have created a series of new problems regarding the application of law in the provinces and, in consequence, the relationship between Roman law and local laws. Hence the enormous number of studies that aim to investigate the survival (and the legal classification) of local norms in the new imperial order after 212 CE. However, the limited echo of Caracalla's edict among contemporary (or slightly later) authors[6] leaves much room for doubting the explosive impact this provision had on daily legal practice (the level of theoretical discourse is, of course, a different matter).[7] The focus therefore has to shift backwards in time, to the

[4] We always have to keep in mind that natural circumstances or human choices have determined an altogether arbitrary selection of the documentary material that has reached us.

[5] Talamanca (1976), 102 defines it as a 'cesura sostanziale'.

[6] Except for the brief mention in Cassius Dio 77.9.5, general silence about Caracalla's edict dominates the works of the historians of this epoch. Neither did the *Constitutio* fare any better among the Justinianic compilers: it is mentioned in a single fragment in the Digest, 1.5.17 (Ulpianus 22 *ad ed.*). It is a noteworthy detail that Justinian cites the provision in *Novella* 78.5, but attributes it to Antoninus Pius. On this topic, see Spagnuolo Vigorita (1993).

[7] On the famous passage in Menander of Laodicea (Spengel 3.363 ll. 4–14; 364, ll. 10–16), interpreted by many as proof that after 212 CE, the only admissible law was Roman law, see the

moment of conquest and then to the progressive diffusion of Roman citizenship, in particular among the provincial elites. This consideration has justly inspired many of the authors who have participated in the realization of this volume.

Throughout the empire, the Roman expansion brought with it inevitable innovations in the legal sphere, but it did not, or at least not immediately, devalue pre-existing legal mechanisms. In these situations, Roman pragmatism clearly shows. It is the same pragmatism that led them to avoid a unified form of government, and instead take into account the historical, cultural and social peculiarities of the conquered territories—in all areas, including the law. Of course we are dealing with a controlled pluralism, always 'in the protective shadow of the Roman Empire'.[8] The history of the development of law in the provinces thus has to be read as one of interaction and gradual assimilation, rather than one of conflict between local laws and Roman law. Knowledge and use of Roman norms gradually found a space in provincial reality, not always and not necessarily imposed from above, but rather as a consequence of ever more intense contact with the Romans who were, in various ways, present throughout the empire. The decline of local autonomy was slow and gradual, and certainly favoured by the provincials' attraction to the 'victorious' Roman model.

These tendencies become particularly visible in the administration of justice, the most relevant occasion for encounters between the Roman governor and the provincial population.[9] Plutarch reprimands his own fellow-citizens for putting before Roman authorities any decision, great or small, thus making the Romans more powerful masters than they themselves want to be (*Praecepta gerendae rei publicae* 814e–815b). The frequent recourse to the Roman tribunals by the inhabitants of the province is not determined by the absence of a recognized local jurisdiction. They simply regarded Roman authority as more reassuring.[10]

In the same way, the Roman 'model' found a space in contractual activities that went well beyond what was legally necessary, especially in the higher strata of the provincial population. The documentary sources show that even before Roman law, the Roman legal form was spread throughout the provinces, seen by the populace as an instrument of protection, as a safeguard of local law. Sometimes indigenous legal practice was masked as Roman forms, especially when there was the prospect of a possible evidentiary use of the document: this explains the assiduous recourse to the so-called stipulatory clauses in documents from Egypt (where they are even added to unilateral legal transactions), or the formula of the *actio tutelae* attested in three copies in the archive of Babatha (P. Yadin 28–30).[11]

opposing interpretations by Talamanca (1971) and Mélèze Modrzejewski (1982). The passage is a fundamental point of reference in more recent works as well; see for example the treatment by Humfress (2011).

[8] Spagnuolo Vigorita (1993), 33. See also Spagnuolo Vigorita (1996).

[9] Cicero considers jurisdiction the most onerous of the tasks with which a governor was entrusted (*ad Quintum fratrem* 1.1.20). For a general treatment of jurisdictional activity in the provinces, see Masi (2014).

[10] Numerous examples in Spagnuolo Vigorita (1993), 23–8.

[11] On the origin of the formula, the number of copies and their use, see Czajkowski (2017), 93–105. Regarding the guardianship of under-aged children, the sources show profound differences between Roman law and the legal traditions of the oriental provinces, but also some similarities: in Rome, mothers could not be guardians of their children during the classical period, unless an authorization by

But still, and only apparently paradoxically: even when Rome and its law had become preeminent in the Roman provinces, it did not impose an absolute legal uniformity. On the contrary, Roman authority accommodated norms and institutions of provincial origin,[12] to fill gaps in Roman law or simply to support the ancient traditions of a given place.[13]

We are left with the strong impression that a neat distinction between the application of Roman law and of local laws was never actually made. Inevitably, such fluidity also left space for various forms of 'usurpation' of the central government's prerogatives by local communities. A significant example is the management of public order. It was requested from the local communities only to a limited degree; and yet, in case of an emergency, it was in fact exercised by provincials in ways that went well beyond the limits defined by Rome. When Rome considered it impossible to intervene, it tolerated and occasionally applauded local initiatives. However, such conduct could also lead to severe punishments for the provincials (the literary sources record numerous episodes).

It is even more difficult to define the distinction between jurisdiction and coercion, between delegation and usurpation in the administration of justice: a delimitation of spheres of competence between the Roman authorities (the governor) and the local courts certainly existed, based on the value of the lawsuit, the seriousness of the crime committed, or the expected punishment. But the boundary was rather fluid; even within the same province, it could change from one community to the next, and it did not always depend on the legal status of the

the *princeps* had been granted, and in the absence of legitimate or testamentary male guardians; in Egypt, on the other hand, a woman could be guardian following a clear manifestation of her husband's explicit approval (either in the testament or in the marriage contract). From 132 CE onwards, Egyptian papyri mention the ἐπακολουθήτρια, the woman who supports the guardian in the tutelary duties, who has many traits in common with the function of ἐπίσκοπος carried out by Julia Crispina (P. Yadin 20 and 25) and with the Roman 'administrative mother' that Roman jurists allow for. There are no further attestations of guardian mothers in Egypt after 212; there is only the ἐπακολουθήτρια, perhaps as a consequence of the extension of Roman citizenship to the whole of Egypt, although various different interpretations have been proposed by scholars; cf. Gagliardi (2012).

[12] In the second century CE, the *fragmentum pseudo-Dositheanum de manumissionibus* 12 refers to a case in which even the *praetor* would have to apply a *lex peregrina*; cf. Cascione (2009), 67–70. On the reception of *iura peregrina*, which was not ignored by Republican sources but 'affrontata come una questione tecnica solo a partire dagli Antonini', see D'Alessio (2016), who collects many significant occurrences.

[13] One of the best known cases is certainly the *lex Rhodia de iactu*, preserved in title 14.2 of the *Digest*, which regulated the legal consequences of throwing parts of the cargo into the sea in order to avoid shipwreck. In the past, scholars have been divided between those who admitted the Roman adoption of a Rhodian law and those who excluded any such influence. More recently, Chevreau (2005) has dealt with the topic and reached very interesting conclusions: according to her, the principle of contribution in case of communal damage was derived from Mediterranean commercial practice, but its practical realization was exclusively tied to the Roman system. I do not want to recall the whole history of scholarship on this occasion; I simply want to note that even on such a debated topic, a new contribution has been made by an epigraphic text. In particular, the fragment of Volusius Maecianus transmitted in D. 14.2.9 ('Eudaimon's shipwreck') has been subjected to new and convincing interpretations by Purpura, who demonstrated an extraordinary correspondence with a clause from a regulation from Caunus, an epigraphic text that probably dates to Hadrianic times, published in 1954 and re-edited, with new fragments, in 2006 (Marek [2006], 175–215 no. 35); cf. Purpura (1985) (= Purpura [1996], 31–89); Merola (2007).

persons involved.[14] This fluidity did not obstruct Rome's control over its empire, but rather made it possible in the first place. When internal order was threatened, the governor obviously intervened in a decisive manner, but in most cases, the Roman attitude was to let the provincial populations 'sort things out themselves', thereby conceding to them a degree of autonomy that went beyond anything stated in Roman norms. Moreover, as is well known, the slender bureaucratic apparatus of Rome, particularly evident precisely in the provincial context, made it necessary to limit interference solely to situations that could either create instability and threaten Roman power or had been brought up in a request by the provincials themselves. So are we really dealing with an usurpation of law? Not always, and not completely: it is rather a case of law adapting itself to changing situations, and in some cases, an usurpation tolerated by Rome. For these reasons, we need to avoid anachronistic judgements shaped by modern conceptions of the state to be able to really understand the legal reality under Rome.

As an example of the possibility of progress in Roman studies, and to demonstrate the fundamental contribution that can come from the documentary sources, I want to examine in a bit more detail the so-called Middle Euphrates papyri, a small corpus of papyri and parchments published relatively recently.[15] The dossier contains petitions, deeds of sale and private letters, dated between 232 and 256 CE and connected to the Appadana region in the Roman province of Coelesyria. As has justly been pointed out by Stolte, these documents are 'neither unique nor spectacular, yet extremely important', because they attest to the degree of penetration of Roman law in a peripheral area of the empire,[16] and add to the still meagre papyrological material of non-Egyptian provenance.[17] In these documents, we can note a mix of Roman and provincial law, which is particularly interesting given that the *Constitutio Antoniniana* was already in force for decades; besides Roman legal institutions,[18] we find, for example, contracts according to Hellenistic law.[19]

[14] E.g. Seleucus of Rhosus, who had obtained Roman citizenship from Octavian, was able to choose (if he was accused or summoned) between the Roman court, the court of his hometown or the court of a free city; see Raggi (2006), 153–65 (FIRA I 55). For other cases in which the *status civitatis* did not imply differences on the level of jurisdiction, see Spagnuolo Vigorita (1993), 21–8. He notes that 'l'erodersi della giurisdizione locale si compie più sul terreno politico che giuridico'.

[15] The seventeen Greek documents, on papyrus and parchment, were found in 1987 and published between 1995 and 2000: Feissel & Gascou (1995); Feissel, Gascou & Teixidor (1997); Feissel & Gascou (2000).

[16] On the '"buon uso" del diritto romano' in the Middle Euphrates papyri, see Mazza (2007), 65–8.

[17] It is particularly from examination of P. Euphr. 1 and P. Euphr. 6–7 that Stolte (2001) draws his conclusion that 'the existence of a legal culture in Syria in the middle of the third century AD is at least equal to that of Egypt' (pp. 174–5).

[18] The documents certainly show knowledge of Roman law: in P. Euphr. 1, the four petitioners request that the status quo should be kept intact and that violence should be stopped, with a provision that evokes an *interdictum uti possidetis*: Feissel & Gascou (1995), 74; Nasti (1993), 367, 371. The petitioners certainly allude to Roman norms when they maintain that the attempts of the συνκωμῆται to expel them from the land with violence constitute a violation of divine commandments (θεῖαι διατάξεις) that 'establish that those who are in possession remain so until the verdict', *leges* that—they add—the governor knows and venerates more than anything else. In P. Euphr. 2, it is quite probable that the petitioner wants the procurator to put an end to the abusive and violent occupation of a vineyard, something analogous to a restitutory interdict. Moreover, in P. Euphr. 15 a woman refers to the *ius trium liberorum* in order to be able to conclude a contract without a guardian (while also clarifying that she is a widow).

[19] Like the παρακαταθήκη contract in P. Euphr. 12, also attested in numerous Egyptian papyri.

But the area where the Euphrates papyri make the most important contribution is, in my view, the administration of justice in a provincial context.[20] The picture that emerges frequently from the literary sources (legal or otherwise) and from the inscriptions, both for the Republican period and for the Principate, is that of the governor as primary and sometimes sole referent of judicial activity in the provinces. In the Middle Euphrates papyri, various governors are indeed called upon to give judgement: from P. Euphr. 1 in particular, we learn that the four petitioners had taken upon themselves a long journey to Antioch, the capital of Coelesyria, to be able to present their request to the governor. They had to stay in the city for a long time (eight months) before they had an audience with Iulius Priscus, without even arriving at a definitive solution; in fact the governor postponed the evaluation of the question to the next *conventus*.[21]

However, the *plenissima iurisdictio* of the provincial governor[22] did not exclude a whole series of other 'bodies' that were called upon to participate in judicial activity in various ways. In fact, besides the governor, there were other representatives of Roman authority who found themselves involved in the administration of justice by delegation. There does not seem to have been a precise rule for deciding which questions were delegated: the governor was able to select freely which situations required his direct jurisdiction. Furthermore, in some cases delegation did not derive from the governor's initiative at all, but was explicitly requested by the petitioner. We have evidence for this from Egypt,[23] but also in the Middle Euphrates papyri: in P. Euphr. 1 and 2, the petitioners ask the governor for delegation by means of *subscriptio* (δι' ὑπογραφῆς), a formulation that frequently appears in third-century Egypt as well.[24] The stylistic and formal aspect, starting with the choice of words, constitutes a further commonality between the Syrian petitions and those from Egypt, with the sole but substantial difference that in the Egyptian cases, the delegate was generally the *stratēgos*, whereas in the Middle Euphrates papyri it is the procurator.

In addition, the documents from the Euphrates attest to a strong involvement of military personnel in the administration of justice. The participation of soldiers, especially centurions, in administrative and legal processes was in fact already known for Egypt; the new documents have allowed us to extend the relevant investigations to other provinces. The problem that has been debated for a long time is to what degree and, most importantly, in which capacity the soldiers were involved in jurisdiction: whether they gave judgments solely by delegation from the governor, or whether they had usurped and/or acquired a certain judicial competence, at least in specific periods and contexts. In the Euphrates papyri, the centurions are the addressees of some petitions made by the populace

[20] For more information, I allow myself to refer to my own work: Merola (2012).

[21] This demonstrates that the governor carried out judicial functions even beyond the *conventus* circuit, but probably without a precise calendar of audiences; hence the wait.

[22] Ulpian (D. 1.16.7.2) defines the jurisdiction of the governor as *plenissima iurisdictio*, by virtue of which he has authority over all the trials that at Rome are decided through ordinary and extraordinary cognition; on the interpretation of this passage see Masi Doria (2014), 383–9.

[23] On the requests to the prefect of Egypt to delegate local functionaries see Foti Talamanca (1979), 131–44.

[24] By contrast, in the Egyptian petitions of the first and second centuries, people requested to 'write' to the *strategos* in order to delegate him, i.e. they asked that the prefect should make provisions by means of an *epistula*.

(P. Euphr. 2 and 5), but their role seems to be that of police, and not of a judicial nature. The centurion thus represents an intermediary stage, a preparatory phase before involving a superior body.[25] But the interpretation changes when we consider another non-Egyptian papyrus, again published not very long ago by Gascou:[26] P. Bostra 1 (of 29 May 260 CE) comes from the Roman province of Arabia, and according to the editor shows the same diplomatic characteristics as the Syrian documents. The petition is addressed to the *beneficiarius* by a woman who reports two crimes and asks for the parties to be brought before the centurion with authority over the territory, declaring herself ready to make the accusation against them. From the Bostra papyrus, it would appear that it fell to the centurion to adjudicate on the controversy, as if it was his duty to also perform judicial tasks. Thus, centurions were required to fulfil the functions of a police force (maintaining order, investigative activity), but the petitioners also turned to them on the assumption that they could receive a solution for their case: in fact, they wanted a verdict. Evidently, it was the circumstances that turned these soldiers into a stable point of reference for the population, who in practice invested them with the role of 'judges'—an alternative, so to speak, to the judicial role of the governor. It is Roman jurisdiction 'seen from below', from the perspective of those who look for justice, not those who administer it.

In conclusion, the way to continue the study of provincial law is to understand law in the provinces as a moment of communication, of exchange, and hence not simply as a unilateral process of progressive affirmation of the Roman legal tradition. If put to good use, the documentary sources can be decisive for this type of research. An approach of this sort requires both the detailed study of specific realities and, at the same time, an integration of the peculiar developments in certain regions of the empire into the more general context of the Roman territory. In other words, it requires a dialogue among specialists of different areas and epochs[27]—an interaction that has, in my view, played out rather well in this volume.

REFERENCES

Amelotti, M. 1999. Reichsrecht, Volksrecht, Provinzialrecht. Vecchi problemi e nuovi documenti. *Studia et documenta historiae et iuris* 65, pp. 211–15.

Ammirati, S. 2019. New developments on Latin legal papyri: the ERC project REDHIS and the membra disiecta of a lost legal manuscript. In: *Proceedings of the 28th International Congress of Papyrology, Barcelona 2016*. Barcelona, pp. 628–37.

Cascione, C. 2009. Zur Anwendung von fremdem Privatrecht durch den römischen Prätor. In: M. Avenarius, R. Meyer-Pritzl & C. Möller (eds.), *Ars iuris. Festschrift für Okko Behrends zum 70. Geburtstag*. Göttingen, pp. 61–70.

Chevreau, E. 2005. La *lex Rhodia de iactu*. Un exemple de la réception d'une institution étrangère dans le droit romain. *Revue d'histoire du droit* 73, pp. 67–80.

Czajkowski, K. 2017. *Localized Law. The Babatha and Salome Komaise Archives*. Oxford.

[25] The role of the centurion as intermediary for transmitting a petition had been known for a long time from the legal sources; cf. D. 47.2.73 (Modestinus 7 *resp.*).

[26] Gascou (1999), 71–3.

[27] See also the acts of the seminar *Il diritto romano e le culture straniere. Influenze e dipendenze interculturali nell'antichità*, published by Lamberti, Gröschler & Milazzo (2015).

D'Alessio, R. 2016. Flussi normativi nel Mediterraneo romano. In: P. Buongiorno, R. D'Alessio & N. Rampazzo (eds.), *Diritti antichi. Percorsi e confronti* I. *Area mediterranea* 1. *Oriente*. Napoli, pp. 333–60.

Feissel, D. & Gascou, J. 1995. Documents d'archives romains inédits du Moyen Euphrate (IIIe s. après J.-C.) I. Les pétitions (P. Euphr. 1 à 5). *Journal des Savants*, pp. 65–119.

Feissel, D. & Gascou, J. 2000. Documents d'archives romains inédits du Moyen Euphrate (IIIe s. après J.-C.) III. Actes divers et lettres (P. Euphr. 11 à 17). *Journal des Savants*, pp. 157–208.

Feissel, D., Gascou, J. & Teixidor, J. 1997. Documents d'archives romains inédits du Moyen Euphrate (IIIe s. après J.-C.) II. Les actes de vente-achat (P. Euphr. 6 à 10). *Journal des Savants*, pp. 3–57.

Foti Talamanca, G. 1979. *Ricerche sul processo nell'Egitto greco-romano*. II.1 *L'introduzione del giudizio*. Milano.

Gagliardi, L. 2012. La madre tutrice e la madre ἐπακολουθήτρια: osservazioni sul rapporto tra diritto romano e diritti delle province orientali. *Index* 40, pp. 423–46.

Gascou, J. 1999. Unités administratives locales et fonctionnaires romains. Les données des nouveaux papyrus du Moyen Euphrate et d'Arabie. In: W. Eck (eds.), *Lokale Autonomie und römische Ordnungsmacht in den kaiserzeitlichen Provinzen vom 1. bis 3. Jahrhundert*. München, pp. 61–73.

Humfress, C. 2011. Law & Custom under Rome. In: A. Rio (ed.), *Law, Custom, and Justice in Late Antiquity and the Early Middle Ages*. London, pp. 23–47.

Lamberti, F., Gröschler, P. & Milazzo, F. 2015 (eds.). *Il diritto romano e le culture straniere. Influenze e dipendenze interculturali nell'antichità*. Lecce.

Marek, C. 2006. *Die Inschriften von Kaunos*. München.

Masi Doria, C. 2014. Tribunali e ordinamento territoriale: prospettive provinciali. *Index* 42, pp. 373–408.

Mazza, M. 2007. Processi di interazione culturale nel Medio Eufrate: considerazione sulle Papyri Euphratenses. *Mediterraneo Antico* 10, pp. 49–69.

Mazza, M. 2010. Affari privati di una signora ebrea del secondo secolo d.C. (su Volksrecht e Reichsrecht in una provincia romana dell'impero romano). *Mediterraneo Antico* 13, pp. 285–310.

Mélèze Modrzejewski, J. 1982. Ménandre de Laodicée et l'édit de Caracalla. In: *Symposion. Vorträge zur griechischen und hellenistischen Rechtsgeschichte (Chantilly, 1977)*. Köln–Wien, pp. 335–63 [= *Droit impérial et traditions locales dans l'Egypte romaine*. Aldershot 1990, nr. XII].

Merola, G. D. 2007. Una *lex collegii* marittima? A proposito di D. 14, 2, 9. In: E. Lo Cascio and G. D. Merola (eds.), *Forme di aggregazione nel mondo romano*. Bari, pp. 259–72.

Merola, G. D. 2012. *Per la storia del processo provinciale romano. I papiri del Medio Eufrate*. Napoli.

Migliardi Zingale, L. 1999. Diritto romano e diritti locali nei documenti del vicino Oriente. *Studia et documenta historiae et iuris* 65, pp. 217–31.

Mitteis, L. 1891. *Reichsrecht und Volksrecht in den östlichen Provinzen des römischen Kaiserreiches*. Leipzig.

Nasti, F. 1993. Un nuovo documento dalla Siria sulle competenze di governatori e procuratori provinciali in tema di interdetti. *Index* 21, pp. 365–80.

Purpura, G. 1985. Il regolamento doganale di Caunus e la *lex Rhodia* in D.14, 2, 9. *Annali del Seminario Giuridico dell'Università di Palermo* 38, pp. 273–331.

Purpura, G. 1996. *Studi Romanistici in Tema di Diritto Commerciale Marittimo*. Soveria Mannelli.

Raggi, A. 2006. *Seleuco di Rhosos. Cittadinanza e privilegi nell'Oriente greco in età tardo-repubblicana*. Pisa.

Scappaticcio, M. C. 2019. Papyri and LAtin Texts: INsights and Updated Methodologies. Towards a philological, literary, and historical approach to Latin papyri (PLATINUM

Project—ERC-StG 2014 no. 636983). In: *Proceedings of the 28th International Congress of Papyrology, Barcelona 2016*. Barcelona, pp. 619–27.

Spagnuolo Vigorita, T. 1993. Cittadini e sudditi tra II e III secolo, In: A. Schiavone (ed.), *Storia di Roma* 3. *L'età tardoantica* 1. *Crisi e trasformazioni*. Torino, pp. 5–50.

Spagnuolo Vigorita, T. 1996. *Città e impero*. Napoli (repr. 1999).

Stolte, B. H. 2001. The impact of Roman Law in Egypt and the near East in the third century AD: The Documentary Evidence. Some Considerations in the Margin of the Euphrates Papyri (P.Euphr.). In: L. De Blois (ed.), *Administration, Prosopography and Appointment Policies in the Roman Empire*. Amsterdam, pp. 167–79.

Talamanca, M. 1971. Su alcuni passi di Menandro di Laodicea relativi agli effetti della 'Constitutio Antoniniana'. In: *Studi in onore di Edoardo Volterra*, V. Milano, pp. 433–560.

Talamanca, M. 1976. Gli ordinamenti provinciali nella prospettiva dei giuristi tardoclassici. In: *Istituzioni giuridiche e realtà politiche nel tardo impero (III–V sec. d.C.). Atti di un incontro tra storici e giuristi (Firenze 2–4 maggio1974)*. Milano, pp. 95–246.

Index of Sources

A. Legal Writings

B. Literary Sources

C. Inscriptions

Subject Index

The manufacturer's authorised representative in the EU for product safety is Oxford University Press España S.A. of el Parque Empresarial San Fernando de Henares, Avenida de Castilla, 2 – 28830 Madrid (www.oup.es/en or product.safety@oup.com). OUP España S.A. also acts as importer into Spain of products made by the manufacturer.

www.ingramcontent.com/pod-product-compliance
Lightning Source LLC
LaVergne TN
LVHW011857200926
848484LV00002B/470

9780198844082